CompTIA
Cloud+®

Certification Study Guide, Second Edition
(Exam CV0-002)

Scott Wilson
Eric Vanderburg

New York   Chicago   San Francisco
Athens   London   Madrid   Mexico City
Milan   New Delhi   Singapore   Sydney   Toronto

$40

S0-BDO-235

Library of Congress Cataloging-in-Publication Data

Names: Wilson, Scott (Writer on information technology), author. |
  Vanderburg, Eric, author.
Title: CompTIA cloud+ certification study guide (exam CV0-002) / Scott
  Wilson, Eric Vanderburg.
Description: Second edition. | New York : McGraw-Hill Education, 2018. |
  Includes index.
Identifiers: LCCN 2018001235| ISBN 9781260116618 (set/package : alk. paper) |
  ISBN 9781260116588 (book : alk. paper) | ISBN 9781260116595 (CD) | ISBN
  1260116611 (set/package : alk. paper) | ISBN 1260116581 (book : alk.
  paper) | ISBN 126011659X (CD)
Subjects: LCSH: Cloud computing—Examinations—Study guides. | Electronic
  data processing personnel—Certification.
Classification: LCC QA76.585 .W555 2018 | DDC 004.67/82—dc23 LC record available at
  https://lccn.loc.gov/2018001235

McGraw-Hill Education books are available at special quantity discounts to use as premiums and sales promotions, or for use in corporate training programs. To contact a representative, please visit the Contact Us pages at www.mhprofessional.com.

CompTIA Cloud+® Certification Study Guide, Second Edition (Exam CV0-002)

1 2 3 4 5 6 7 8 9   LCR   21 20 19 18

ISBN: Book p/n 978-1-260-11658-8 and CD p/n 978-1-260-11659-5
of set 978-1-260-11661-8

MHID: Book p/n 1-260-11658-1 and CD p/n 1-260-11659-X
of set 1-260-11661-1

Sponsoring Editor
Amy Stonebraker

Technical Editor
Daniel Lachance

Production Supervisor
James Kussow

Editorial Supervisor
Janet Walden

Copy Editor
William McManus

Composition
Cenveo Publisher Services

Project Manager
*Radhika Jolly,
Cenveo® Publisher Services*

Proofreader
Rick Camp

Illustration
Cenveo Publisher Services

Indexer
Claire Splan

Art Director, Cover
Jeff Weeks

Acquisitions Coordinator
Claire Yee

Information has been obtained by McGraw-Hill Education from sources believed to be reliable. However, because of the possibility of human or mechanical error by our sources, McGraw-Hill Education, or others, McGraw-Hill Education does not guarantee the accuracy, adequacy, or completeness of any information and is not responsible for any errors or omissions or the results obtained from the use of such information.

To Justin Vanderburg. Your flame was bright, but brief, and yet we still feel its warmth. You are always in my heart! This book is for you.

—Eric Vanderburg

ABOUT THE AUTHORS

Scott Wilson is currently helping to revolutionize the MSP offering in the SMB space as a partner at HubWise Technology. He has 22 years of experience consulting, managing, and training IT organizations across multiple industries on how to better deliver value to their customers. He is also the owner of Courseware Experts, a technical publishing company. Scott's certifications include CompTIA Cloud+, MCT, MCSE, MCSA, MCTS, MCITP, MCP, ITIL Certified Foundations 2011, Release Control and Validation, Operational Support and Analysis, and ITIL Certified Trainer.

Eric Vanderburg is Vice President of Cybersecurity at TCDI and a well-known blogger, speaker, and thought leader. He is best known for his insight on cybersecurity, privacy, cloud, and storage. Vanderburg is also a licensed private investigator with an MBA and several undergraduate degrees. He is a continual learner and has earned over 40 technology certifications from Microsoft, Cisco, CompTIA, (ISC)², Rapid7, EMC, CWNP, and Hitachi Data Systems. Eric is passionate about sharing cybersecurity and technology news, insights, and best practices. He regularly presents on security topics and publishes insightful articles. You can find him throughout the day posting valuable and informative content on his social media channels:

Twitter: @evanderburg
LinkedIn: https://www.linkedin.com/in/evanderburg
Facebook: https://www.facebook.com/VanderburgE

About the Technical Editor

Daniel Lachance, CompTIA Cloud Essentials, CompTIA Server+, CompTIA A+, CompTIA Network+, CompTIA Security+, MCT, MCSA, MCITP, MCTS, is the owner of Lachance IT Consulting Inc., based in Halifax, Nova Scotia. Dan has delivered technical IT training for a wide variety of products for more than 20 years. He has recorded IT support videos related to security and various cloud-computing platforms. Dan has developed custom applications and planned, implemented, troubleshot, and documented various network configurations and conducted network security audits. Dan has worked as a technical editor on a number of certification titles and has authored titles including *CompTIA Cloud+ Certification Practice Exams (Exam CV0-002)*, *CompTIA Server+ Certification All-in-One Exam Guide (Exam SK0-004)*, and *CompTIA Security+ Certification Practice Exams, Second Edition (Exam SY0-401)*.

When not performing with the Halifax-based cover band Clusterfunk, Dan loves being around family and spending time outdoors.

Becoming a CompTIA Certified
IT Professional Is Easy

It's also the best way to reach greater professional opportunities and rewards.

Why Get CompTIA Certified?

Growing Demand

Labor estimates predict some technology fields will experience growth of more than 20% by the year 2020. (Source: CompTIA 9th Annual Information Security Trends study: 500 U.S. IT and Business Executives Responsible for Security.) CompTIA certification qualifies the skills required to join this workforce.

Higher Salaries

IT professionals with certifications on their resume command better jobs, earn higher salaries, and have more doors open to new multi-industry opportunities.

Verified Strengths

Ninety-one percent of hiring managers indicate CompTIA certifications are valuable in validating IT expertise, making certification the best way to demonstrate your competency and knowledge to employers. (Source: CompTIA Employer Perceptions of IT Training and Certification.)

Universal Skills

CompTIA certifications are vendor neutral—which means that certified professionals can proficiently work with an extensive variety of hardware and software found in most organizations.

Learn

Learn more about what the exam covers by reviewing the following:

- Exam objectives for key study points.

- Sample questions for a general overview of what to expect on the exam and examples of question format.

- Visit online forums, like LinkedIn, to see what other IT professionals say about CompTIA exams.

Certify

Purchase a voucher at a Pearson VUE testing center or at CompTIAstore.com.

- Register for your exam at a Pearson VUE testing center.

- Visit pearsonvue.com/CompTIA to find the closest testing center to you.

- Schedule the exam online. You will be required to enter your voucher number or provide payment information at registration.

- Take your certification exam.

Work

Congratulations on your CompTIA certification!

- Make sure to add your certification to your resume.

- Check out the CompTIA Certification Roadmap to plan your next career move.

Learn More: Certification.CompTIA.org/certifications/cloud

CompTIA Disclaimer

CONTENTS

The objective of this study guide is to prepare you for the CompTIA Cloud+ (CV0-002) exam by familiarizing you with the technology and terminology tested on the exam. Because the primary focus of the book is to help you pass the exam, we don't always cover every aspect of the related technology. Some aspects of the technology are covered only to the extent necessary to help you understand what you need to know to pass the exam, but we hope this book serves as a valuable professional resource long after the exam is over.

In This Book

This book is organized to serve as an in-depth review for the CompTIA Cloud+ exam for network administrators and cloud system engineers. Each chapter covers a major aspect of the exam, with an emphasis on the "why" as well as the "how to" of working with and implementing cloud technologies in a cloud-computing environment.

We have created a set of chapter components that call your attention to important items, reinforce key points, and provide helpful exam-taking hints. Take a look at what you will find in the chapters:

- Every chapter begins with **Certification Objectives**—what you need to know in order to pass the objective on the exam dealing with the chapter topics. The Certification Objective headings identify the objectives within the chapter.
- **Exam Watch** notes call attention to information about, and potential pitfalls in, the exam.
- **Exam at Work** sidebars provide real-world examples of cloud computing technologies in the workplace today.
- The **Certification Summary** is a succinct review of the chapter and a restatement of salient points regarding the exam.
- The **Key Terms** section highlights and defines the most important terms discussed in the chapter. A complete list of key terms and their definitions can be found in the glossary.

- ■ The **Two-Minute Drill** is a checklist of the main points of the chapter. It can be used for last-minute review.
- ■ The **Self Test** offers questions similar to those found on the exam. The answers to these questions, as well as explanations of the answers, can be found at the end of each chapter. By taking the Self Test after completing each chapter, you'll reinforce what you've learned from that chapter while becoming familiar with the structure of the exam questions.

Exam Readiness Checklist

At the end of the Introduction, you will find the Exam Readiness Checklist. This table has been constructed to allow you to cross-reference the official exam objectives with the objectives as they are presented and covered in this book. This checklist also helps you gauge your level of expertise with each objective at the outset of your studies. This will allow you to check your progress and make sure you spend the time you need on more difficult or unfamiliar sections. The exam objectives are listed exactly as CompTIA presents them, and each objective has a cross-reference to the chapter, with the corresponding section of the study guide, that covers that objective.

Some Pointers

Once you've finished reading this book, set aside some time to do a thorough review. You might want to return to the book several times and make use of all the methods it offers for reviewing the material:

1. *Reread all the Two-Minute Drills* or have someone quiz you. You also can use the drills as a way to do a quick cram before the exam. You may want to make flash cards out of 3×5 index cards with the Two-Minute Drill material.

2. *Reread all the Exam Watch notes and Exam at Work sidebars.* Remember that these notes are written by authors who have taken the exam and passed. They know what you should expect—and what you should be on the lookout for.

3. *Retake the Self Tests.* Taking the tests right after you've read the chapter is a good idea, because the questions help reinforce what you've just learned. However, it's an even better idea to go back later and answer all the questions in the book in a single sitting. Pretend that you're taking the live exam. When you go through the questions the first time, you should mark your answers on a separate piece of paper. That way, you can run through the questions as many times as you need to until you feel comfortable with the material.

ACKNOWLEDGMENTS

We would like to thank our spouses, Aimee Vanderburg and Megan Wilson, for having patience with us while we finished this project. Without their love, encouragement, and support this project would have not been possible. The support by our families throughout this project is the primary reason for its success.

In addition to his wife Aimee, Eric thanks his children, Faith and Jacob, for their understanding when Daddy had to work instead of conquering dragons, constructing skyscrapers, or sitting down to tea with some stuffed friends. He thanks his parents for the example they set of working hard to accomplish great things, for modeling excellence and integrity, and for giving him the freedom to fail enough to succeed.

No matter the size, each book is a team effort. It has been a real pleasure to work with the professional editors at McGraw-Hill, especially acquisitions editor Amy Stonebraker and executive editor Timothy Green. Thank you for your patience, flexibility, and honest feedback. Dan Lachance deserves special mention for his outstanding contributions as technical editor. His comments, clarifying notes, and perspective brought polish and refinement to this work. We also want to thank Claire Yee for her attention to detail and friendly support. It has been a blessing to work with such a skilled editorial team. We are also grateful to Mike Mercer for his software development insight and Bogdan Salamakha for his valuable comments on penetration testing. Lastly, we want to acknowledge the excellent work of McGraw-Hill's production team.

Thank you all so much! May this book be a testimony to your efforts, assistance, and guidance.

C loud computing is becoming more and more popular, and the skill sets required to support cloud computing environments are in high demand. Organizations are examining cloud computing and looking to implement cloud environments to reduce cost and increase IT capabilities.

Why Cloud Computing?

Cloud computing provides something that the IT industry has always needed: a way to increase capacity and add resources as necessary without having to invest in infrastructure. Cloud computing enables an organization to expand its business on demand as it grows.

Growing Need for Cloud Administrators

As more and more organizations adopt a cloud model, the need for cloud administrators increases. Whether the organization is implementing a private cloud, public cloud, or hybrid cloud, it is going to need someone to administer and maintain that cloud environment. Having the skills necessary to support a cloud environment will set you apart as an IT administrator.

Preparing for the CompTIA Cloud+ Exam

This book is designed to help you prepare for the CompTIA Cloud+ certification exam, CV0-002. After successfully passing this exam, you will have demonstrated that you have the knowledge required of IT practitioners working in a cloud environment and that you understand how to deliver a cloud infrastructure. Passing this exam is not an easy step on your way to being a cloud administrator; you will be required to learn new terminology and implementation concepts as they relate to a cloud computing environment.

How This Book Is Organized

This book is divided into chapters based on meeting the objectives of the CompTIA Cloud+ exam. While many individuals taking the exam have been in the IT industry for many years, the terminology used in a cloud computing environment and on the exam may be new to them. Understanding this terminology is a key step to passing the CompTIA Cloud+ exam and becoming a cloud administrator. Throughout the book, you will learn the different components that make up a cloud environment along with the best practices for implementing those components in the cloud. If you are an experienced IT administrator, some of these components will be very familiar to you, but understanding how those components work in a cloud environment could be a challenge. This book is not meant to be a complete guide to cloud computing; it is designed to cover all of the objectives of the CompTIA Cloud+ exam.

Chapter 1: Cloud Computing Concepts, Models, and Terminology   This chapter focuses on the terminology as it pertains to a cloud environment. You will learn about the various cloud service models, along with cloud deployment models, object storage, and key terms as they relate to cloud computing.

Chapter 2: Disk Storage Systems   Chapter 2 discusses how disk configurations and redundancy are implemented in the cloud. You will learn the different file types that are part of a cloud environment, along with how to use data tiering to maximize the organization's storage.

Chapter 3: Storage Networking   After becoming familiar with the disk storage systems involved in a cloud environment, the next thing to understand is how to implement and provision those disk storage systems. In this chapter, you will learn about the various storage technologies, how to implement them in the most efficient manner, and how to protect storage through high availability and replication.

Chapter 4: Network Infrastructure   Network configuration is a primary component of cloud computing. In this chapter, you will learn the different types of network configurations and how to optimize those networks. You will also be introduced to the different network ports and protocols that are part of cloud computing.

Chapter 5: Virtualization Components   Virtualization is the key component to cloud computing. This chapter explains the basic concepts of virtualization, including the virtualization host, hypervisor, and virtual machines. You will also learn about virtualized infrastructure service elements, including DNS, DHCP, certificate services, and load balancing.

Chapter 6: Virtualization and the Cloud   Chapter 6 expands on what you learned in Chapter 5 and explains the benefits of virtualization in a cloud environment. You will also learn how to migrate an organization's current environment to a virtual environment using the various tools that are available, including P2V and V2V.

Chapter 7: DevOps   DevOps teams are a combination of software development and IT operations that more effectively support applications throughout their life cycle. This chapter covers some primary areas of responsibility for DevOps including monitoring the cloud and tools for remote access and administration. The chapter then presents life cycle management, an overarching concept in DevOps for how applications are specified, developed, tested, deployed, and maintained.

Chapter 8: Performance Tuning   Optimizing performance and allocating resources is something that needs careful consideration and planning. You will learn how to configure virtualization host resources and guest resources and how to optimize those configurations.

Chapter 9: Systems Management   This chapter explores the nontechnical aspects of implementing a cloud environment. You will learn how to implement the proper policies and procedures as they pertain to a cloud environment, along with best practices for systems management and how to perform system maintenance.

Chapter 10: Security in the Cloud   This chapter explains a variety of security concepts as they pertain to a cloud environment. You will learn how to secure the network and the data that is part of the cloud environment.

Chapter 11: Security Best Practices   This chapter explains cloud security best practices. You will learn about system hardening, layered security, security governance, and vulnerability management.

Chapter 12: Business Continuity and Disaster Recovery   Disaster recovery and business continuity are still primary concerns for an organization when implementing a cloud environment. This chapter describes the different options an organization has when building both business continuity and disaster recovery plans and implementing high availability. It ends with a discussion on backup and recovery methods.

Chapter 13: Testing, Automation, and Changes   Service and maintenance availability must be considered when choosing a cloud provider. This chapter explains the testing techniques that can be used to ensure adequate performance, proper functionality, and availability. The chapter then introduces methods to automate and orchestrate activities and then discusses how to manage changes and configurations.

Chapter 14: Troubleshooting   Knowing how to solve issues effectively will set you apart from other professionals. This chapter teaches you troubleshooting tools, documentation, and analysis. The chapter then introduces CompTIA's troubleshooting methodology and explains how to troubleshoot deployment, capacity, automation, connectivity, and security issues using the CompTIA troubleshooting methodology.

Glossary   In addition, a glossary has been put together to give you a place to go to quickly find key terms that are discussed throughout the book. We hope that it can become a reference to use both during your time studying for the test and after you successfully pass the CompTIA Cloud+ exam.

Certification Summary, Two-Minute Drill, and Self Test Sections

A few of the most important tools in this study guide are the end-of-chapter Certification Summary and Two-Minute Drill sections. In these sections, you will find a high-level review of the chapter and all of the key subject matter that was discussed in the chapter as it pertains to the CompTIA Cloud+ exam.

The questions provided in the Self Test at the end of each chapter are to help you review what you have learned in that particular chapter. They serve as a guide to help you understand what was discussed and to help you determine if more studying is required on a particular subject. Answering all of the questions at the end of the chapters correctly does not guarantee that you will pass the CompTIA Cloud+ exam. Instead, they should be used as a guide to determine how comfortable you are with a given topic.

The Total Tester

Included with this book is access to practice exam software that contains even more practice questions with detailed explanations of the answers. Using this set of practice questions provided in the Total Tester exam engine is another tool to help you prepare for the CompTIA Cloud+ exam. Please see the appendix for more information about accessing the Total Tester.

Moving Forward

At this point, we hope that you are excited about cloud computing and all of the exciting new challenges that come with implementing a cloud computing environment. We wish you luck in your endeavors and want to be the first to welcome you to the field of cloud computing.

Exam CV0-002

Exam Readiness Checklist					
Domain and Objective	**Study Guide Coverage**	**Ch. #**	**Beginner**	**Intermediate**	**Expert**
1.0 Configuration and Deployment					
1.1 Given a scenario, analyze system requirements to ensure successful system deployment.					
Appropriate commands, structure, tools, and automation/orchestration as needed	Storage Types and Technologies	3			
Platforms and applications	Cloud Service Models	1			
Interaction of cloud components and services	Cloud Service Models	1			
Network components	Cloud Service Models	1			
Application components	Cloud Service Models	1			
Storage components	Cloud Service Models	1			
Compute components	Cloud Service Models	1			
Security components	Cloud Service Models	1			
Interaction of non-cloud components and services	Cloud Service Models	1			
Baselines	Resource Monitoring Techniques	7			
Target hosts	Cloud Characteristics and Terms	1			
Existing systems	Cloud Characteristics and Terms	1			
Cloud architecture	Cloud Deployment Models and Services	1			
Cloud elements/target objects	Cloud Deployment Models and Services	1			
1.2 Given a scenario, execute a provided deployment plan.					
Apply the Change Management Process	Change and Configuration Management	13			
Approvals	Change and Configuration Management	13			
Scheduling	Change and Configuration Management	13			
Refer to documentation and follow standard operating procedures	Policies and Procedures	9			

Exam Readiness Checklist

Domain and Objective	Study Guide Coverage	Ch. #	Beginner	Intermediate	Expert
Execute workflow	Policies and Procedures	9			
Configure automation and orchestration, where appropriate, for the system being deployed	Automation and Orchestration	13			
Use commands and tools as needed	Systems Maintenance	9			
Document results	Systems Management Best Practices	9			
1.3 Given a scenario, analyze system requirements to determine if a given testing plan is appropriate.					
Underlying environment considerations included in the testing plan	Testing Techniques	13			
Shared components	Testing Techniques	13			
Storage	Testing Techniques	13			
Compute	Testing Techniques	13			
Network	Testing Techniques	13			
Production vs. development vs. QA	Testing Techniques	13			
Sizing	Testing Techniques	13			
Performance	Testing Techniques	13			
High availability	Testing Techniques	13			
Connectivity	Testing Techniques	13			
Data integrity	Testing Techniques	13			
Proper function	Testing Techniques	13			
Replication	Disaster Recovery Methods	12			
Load balancing	Network Optimization	4			
Automation/orchestration	Automation and Orchestration	13			
Testing techniques	Testing Techniques	13			
Vulnerability testing	Vulnerability Management	11			
Penetration testing	Vulnerability Management	11			
Load testing	Testing Techniques	13			

Exam Readiness Checklist

Domain and Objective	Study Guide Coverage	Ch. #	Beginner	Intermediate	Expert
1.4 Given a scenario, analyze testing results to determine if the testing was successful in relation to given system requirements.					
Consider success factor indicators of the testing environment	Testing Techniques	13			
Sizing	Testing Techniques	13			
Performance	Testing Techniques	13			
Availability	Testing Techniques	13			
Connectivity	Testing Techniques	13			
Data integrity	Testing Techniques	13			
Proper functionality	Testing Techniques	13			
Document results	Documentation and Analysis	14			
Baseline comparisons	Resource Monitoring Techniques	7			
SLA comparisons	Testing Techniques	13			
Cloud performance fluctuation variables	Optimizing Performance	8			
1.5 Given a scenario, analyze sizing, subnetting, and basic routing for a provided deployment of the virtual network.					
Cloud deployment models	Cloud Deployment Models and Services	1			
Public	Cloud Deployment Models and Services	1			
Private	Cloud Deployment Models and Services	1			
Hybrid	Cloud Deployment Models and Services	1			
Community	Cloud Deployment Models and Services	1			
Network components	Systems Maintenance	9			
Applicable port and protocol considerations when extending to the cloud	Network Ports and Protocols	4			

Exam Readiness Checklist

Domain and Objective	Study Guide Coverage	Ch. #	Beginner	Intermediate	Expert
Determine configuration for the applicable platform as it applies to the network	Network Security	10			
VPN	Data Security	10			
IDS/IPS	Network Security	10			
DMZ	Network Security	10			
VXLAN	Routing and Switching	4			
Address space required	Routing and Switching	4			
Network segmentation and micro-segmentation	Routing and Switching	4			
Determine if cloud resources are consistent with the SLA and/or change management requirements	Change and Configuration Management	13			
1.6 Given a scenario, analyze CPU and memory sizing for a provided deployment.					
Available vs. proposed resources	Testing Techniques	13			
CPU	Testing Techniques	13			
RAM	Testing Techniques	13			
Memory technologies	Virtualization Host	5			
Bursting and ballooning	Virtualization Host	5			
Overcommitment ratio	Virtualization Host	5			
CPU technologies	Virtualization Host	5			
Hyperthreading	Virtualization Host	5			
VT-x	Virtualization Host	5			
Overcommitment ratio	Virtualization Host	5			
Effect to HA/DR	Virtual Resource Migrations	6			
Performance considerations	Virtual Resource Migrations	6			
Cost considerations	Benefits of Virtualization in a Cloud Environment	6			
Energy savings	Benefits of Virtualization in a Cloud Environment	6			
Dedicated compute environment vs. shared compute environment	Benefits of Virtualization in a Cloud Environment	6			

Exam Readiness Checklist

Domain and Objective	Study Guide Coverage	Ch. #	Beginner	Intermediate	Expert
1.7 Given a scenario, analyze the appropriate storage type and protection capability for a provided deployment.					
Requested IOPS and read/write throughput	Storage Provisioning	3			
Protection capabilities	Storage Provisioning	3			
High availability	Business Continuity Methods	12			
Failover zones	Business Continuity Methods	12			
Storage replication	Storage Protection	3			
Regional	Storage Protection	3			
Multiregional	Storage Protection	3			
Synchronous and asynchronous	Storage Protection	3			
Storage mirroring	Virtual Resource Migrations	6			
Cloning	Virtual Resource Migrations	6			
Redundancy level/factor	Virtual Resource Migrations	6			
Storage types	Storage Types and Technologies	3			
NAS	Storage Types and Technologies	3			
DAS	Storage Types and Technologies	3			
SAN	Storage Types and Technologies	3			
Object storage	Storage Types and Technologies	3			
Access protocols	Storage Provisioning	3			
Management differences	Storage Provisioning	3			
Provisioning model	Storage Provisioning	3			
Thick provisioned	Storage Provisioning	3			
Thin provisioned	Storage Provisioning	3			
Encryption requirements	Storage Provisioning	3			
Tokenization	Storage Provisioning	3			
Storage technologies	Storage Types and Technologies	3			
Deduplication technologies	Storage Types and Technologies	3			
Compression technologies	Storage Types and Technologies	3			

Exam Readiness Checklist

Domain and Objective	Study Guide Coverage	Ch. #	Beginner	Intermediate	Expert
Storage tiers	Storage Provisioning	3			
Overcommitting storage	Storage Provisioning	3			
Security configurations for applicable platforms	Access Control	10			
ACLs	Access Control	10			
Obfuscation	Data Security	10			
Zoning	Storage Provisioning	3			
User/host authentication and authorization	Access Control	10			
1.8 Given a scenario, analyze characteristics of the workload (storage, network, compute) to ensure a successful migration.					
Migration types	Virtual Resource Migrations	6			
P2V	Virtual Resource Migrations	6			
V2V	Virtual Resource Migrations	6			
V2P	Virtual Resource Migrations	6			
P2P	Virtual Resource Migrations	6			
Storage migrations	Virtual Resource Migrations	6			
Online vs. offline migrations	Virtual Resource Migrations	6			
Source and destination format of the workload	Virtual Resource Migrations	6			
Virtualization format	Migration Considerations	6			
Application and data portability	Migration Considerations	6			
Network connections and data transfer methodologies	Migration Considerations	6			
Standard operating procedures for the workload migration	Migration Considerations	6			
Environmental constraints	Migration Considerations	6			
Bandwidth	Migration Considerations	6			
Working hour restrictions	Migration Considerations	6			
Downtime impact	Migration Considerations	6			
Peak timeframes	Migration Considerations	6			

Exam Readiness Checklist

Domain and Objective	Study Guide Coverage	Ch. #	Beginner	Intermediate	Expert
Legal restrictions	Migration Considerations	6			
Follow-the-sun constraints/time zones	Migration Considerations	6			
1.9 Given a scenario, apply elements required to extend the infrastructure into a given cloud solution.					
Identity management elements	Access Control	10			
Identification	Access Control	10			
Authentication	Access Control	10			
Authorization	Access Control	10			
Approvals	Access Control	10			
Access policy	Access Control	10			
Federation	Access Control	10			
Single sign-on	Access Control	10			
Appropriate protocols given requirements	Access Control	10			
Element considerations to deploy infrastructure services such as:	Network Ports and Protocols	4			
DNS	Network Ports and Protocols	4			
DHCP	Network Ports and Protocols	4			
Certificate services	Virtualized Infrastructure Service Elements	5			
Local agents	Virtualized Infrastructure Service Elements	5			
Antivirus	Virtualized Infrastructure Service Elements	5			
Load balancer	Virtualized Infrastructure Service Elements	5			
Multifactor authentication	Virtualized Infrastructure Service Elements	5			
Firewall	Virtualized Infrastructure Service Elements	5			
IPS/IDS	Virtualized Infrastructure Service Elements	5			

Exam Readiness Checklist

Domain and Objective	Study Guide Coverage	Ch. #	Beginner	Intermediate	Expert
2.0 Security					
2.1 Given a scenario, apply security configurations and compliance controls to meet given cloud infrastructure requirements.					
Company security policies	Security Governance and Strategy	11			
Apply security standards for the selected platform	Security Governance and Strategy	11			
Compliance and audit requirements governing the environment	Security Governance and Strategy	11			
Laws and regulations as they apply to the data	Security Governance and Strategy	11			
Encryption technologies	Data Security	10			
IPSec	Data Security	10			
SSL/TLS	Data Security	10			
Other ciphers	Data Security	10			
Key and certificate management	Data Security	10			
PKI	Data Security	10			
Tunneling protocols	Data Security	10			
L2TP	Data Security	10			
PPTP	Data Security	10			
GRE	Data Security	10			
Implement automation and orchestration processes as applicable	Security Governance and Strategy	11			
Appropriate configuration for the applicable platform as it applies to compute	Security Governance and Strategy	11			
Disabling unneeded ports and services	Security Governance and Strategy	11			
Account management policies	Security Governance and Strategy	11			
Host-based/software firewalls	Security Governance and Strategy	11			
Antivirus/antimalware software	Security Governance and Strategy	11			
Patching	Systems Maintenance	9			
Deactivating default accounts	Security Governance and Strategy	11			

Exam Readiness Checklist

Domain and Objective	Study Guide Coverage	Ch. #	Beginner	Intermediate	Expert
2.2 Given a scenario, apply the appropriate ACL to the target objects to meet access requirements according to a security template.					
Authorization to objects in the cloud	Access Control	10			
Processes	Access Control	10			
Resources	Access Control	10			
Users	Access Control	10			
Groups	Access Control	10			
System	Access Control	10			
Compute	Access Control	10			
Networks	Access Control	10			
Storage	Access Control	10			
Services	Access Control	10			
Effect of cloud service models on security implementations	Access Control	10			
Effect of cloud deployment models on security implementations	Access Control	10			
Access control methods	Access Control	10			
Role-based administration	Access Control	10			
Mandatory access controls	Access Control	10			
Discretionary access controls	Access Control	10			
Non-discretionary access controls	Access Control	10			
Multifactor authentication	Access Control	10			
Single sign-on	Access Control	10			
2.3 Given a cloud service model, implement defined security technologies to meet given security requirements.					
Data classification	Security Governance and Strategy	11			
Concepts of segmentation and micro-segmentation	Data Security	10			
Network	Data Security	10			

Exam Readiness Checklist

Domain and Objective	Study Guide Coverage	Ch. #	Beginner	Intermediate	Expert
Storage	Data Security	10			
Compute	Data Security	10			
Use encryption as defined	Data Security	10			
Use multifactor authentication as defined	Access Control	10			
Apply defined audit/compliance requirements	Security Governance and Strategy	11			
2.4 Given a cloud service model, apply the appropriate security automation technique to the target system.					
Tools	Network Security	10			
APIs	Network Security	10			
Vendor applications	Network Security	10			
CLI	Network Security	10			
Web GUI	Network Security	10			
Cloud portal	Network Security	10			
Techniques	Automation and Orchestration	13			
Orchestration	Automation and Orchestration	13			
Scripting	Automation and Orchestration	13			
Custom programming	Automation and Orchestration	13			
Security services	Network Security	10			
Firewall	Network Security	10			
Antivirus/antimalware	Network Security	10			
IPS/IDS	Network Security	10			
HIPS	Network Security	10			
Impact of security tools to systems and services	Network Security	10			
Scope of impact	Network Security	10			
Impact of security automation techniques as they relate to the criticality of systems	Network Security	10			
Scope of impact	Network Security	10			

Exam Readiness Checklist

Domain and Objective	Study Guide Coverage	Ch. #	Beginner	Intermediate	Expert
3.0 Maintenance					
3.1 Given a cloud service model, determine the appropriate methodology to apply given patches.					
Scope of cloud elements to be patched	Systems Maintenance	9			
Hypervisors	Systems Maintenance	9			
Virtual machines	Systems Maintenance	9			
Virtual appliances	Systems Maintenance	9			
Networking components	Systems Maintenance	9			
Applications	Systems Maintenance	9			
Storage components	Systems Maintenance	9			
Clusters	Systems Maintenance	9			
Patching methodologies and standard operating procedures	Systems Maintenance	9			
Production vs. development vs. QA	Systems Maintenance	9			
Rolling update	Systems Maintenance	9			
Blue-green deployment	Systems Maintenance	9			
Failover cluster	Systems Maintenance	9			
Use order of operations as it pertains to elements that will be patched	Systems Maintenance	9			
Dependency considerations	Systems Maintenance	9			
3.2 Given a scenario, apply the appropriate automation tools to update cloud elements.					
Types of updates	Systems Maintenance	9			
Hotfix	Systems Maintenance	9			
Patch	Systems Maintenance	9			
Version update	Systems Maintenance	9			
Rollback	Systems Maintenance	9			
Automation workflow	Automation and Orchestration	13			
Runbook management	Automation and Orchestration	13			
Single node	Automation and Orchestration	13			

Exam Readiness Checklist

Domain and Objective	Study Guide Coverage	Ch. #	Beginner	Intermediate	Expert
Orchestration	Automation and Orchestration	13			
Multiple nodes	Automation and Orchestration	13			
Multiple runbooks	Automation and Orchestration	13			
Activities to be performed by automation tools	Systems Maintenance	9			
Snapshot	Systems Maintenance	9			
Cloning	Systems Maintenance	9			
Patching	Systems Maintenance	9			
Restarting	Systems Maintenance	9			
Shut down	Systems Maintenance	9			
Maintenance mode	Systems Maintenance	9			
Enable/disable alerts	Systems Maintenance	9			
3.3 Given a scenario, apply an appropriate backup or restore method.					
Backup types	Backup and Recovery	12			
Snapshot/redirect-on-write	Backup and Recovery	12			
Clone	Backup and Recovery	12			
Full	Backup and Recovery	12			
Differential	Backup and Recovery	12			
Incremental	Backup and Recovery	12			
Change block/delta tracking	Backup and Recovery	12			
Backup targets	Backup and Recovery	12			
Replicas	Backup and Recovery	12			
Local	Backup and Recovery	12			
Remote	Backup and Recovery	12			
Other considerations	Backup and Recovery	12			
SLAs	Backup and Recovery	12			
Backup schedule	Backup and Recovery	12			
Configurations	Backup and Recovery	12			
Objects	Backup and Recovery	12			

Exam Readiness Checklist

Domain and Objective	Study Guide Coverage	Ch. #	Beginner	Intermediate	Expert
Dependencies	Backup and Recovery	12			
Online/offline	Backup and Recovery	12			
3.4 Given a cloud-based scenario, apply appropriate disaster recovery methods.					
DR capabilities of a cloud service provider	Disaster Recovery Methods	12			
Other considerations	Disaster Recovery Methods	12			
SLAs for DR	Disaster Recovery Methods	12			
RPO	Disaster Recovery Methods	12			
RTO	Disaster Recovery Methods	12			
Corporate guidelines	Disaster Recovery Methods	12			
Cloud service provider guidelines	Disaster Recovery Methods	12			
Bandwidth or ISP limitations	Disaster Recovery Methods	12			
Techniques	Disaster Recovery Methods	12			
Site mirroring	Business Continuity Methods	12			
Replication	Disaster Recovery Methods	12			
File transfer	Disaster Recovery Methods	12			
Archiving	Disaster Recovery Methods	12			
Third-party sites	Disaster Recovery Methods	12			
3.5 Given a cloud-based scenario, apply the appropriate steps to ensure business continuity.					
Business continuity plan	Business Continuity Methods	12			
Alternate sites	Business Continuity Methods	12			
Continuity of operations	Business Continuity Methods	12			
Connectivity	Business Continuity Methods	12			
Edge sites	Business Continuity Methods	12			
Equipment	Business Continuity Methods	12			
Availability	Business Continuity Methods	12			
Partners/third parties	Business Continuity Methods	12			
SLAs for BCP and HA	Business Continuity Methods	12			

Exam Readiness Checklist

Domain and Objective	Study Guide Coverage	Ch. #	Beginner	Intermediate	Expert
3.6 Given a scenario, apply the appropriate maintenance automation technique to the target objects.					
Maintenance schedules	Automation and Orchestration	13			
Impact and scope of maintenance tasks	Automation and Orchestration	13			
Impact and scope of maintenance automation techniques	Automation and Orchestration	13			
Include orchestration as appropriate	Automation and Orchestration	13			
Maintenance automation tasks	Optomizing Performance	8			
Clearing logs	Optomizing Performance	8			
Archiving logs	Optomizing Performance	8			
Compressing drives	Optomizing Performance	8			
Removing inactive accounts	Optomizing Performance	8			
Removing stale DNS entries	Optomizing Performance	8			
Removing orphaned resources	Optomizing Performance	8			
Removing outdated rules from firewall	Security Governance and Strategy	11			
Removing outdated rules from security	Security Governance and Strategy	11			
Resource reclamation	Security Governance and Strategy	11			
Maintain ACLs for the target object	Security Governance and Strategy	11			
4.0 Management					
4.1 Given a scenario, analyze defined metrics to determine the presence of an abnormality and/ or forecast future needed cloud resources.					
Monitoring	Resource Monitoring Techniques	7			
Target object baselines	Resource Monitoring Techniques	7			
Target object anomalies	Resource Monitoring Techniques	7			
Common alert methods/messaging	Resource Monitoring Techniques	7			
Alerting based on deviation from baseline	Resource Monitoring Techniques	7			
Event collection	Resource Monitoring Techniques	7			

Exam Readiness Checklist

Domain and Objective	Study Guide Coverage	Ch. #	Beginner	Intermediate	Expert
Event correlation	Resource Monitoring Techniques	7			
Forecasting resource capacity	Resource Monitoring Techniques	7			
Upsize/increase	Resource Monitoring Techniques	7			
Downsize/decrease	Resource Monitoring Techniques	7			
Policies in support of event collection	Resource Monitoring Techniques	7			
Policies to communicate alerts appropriately	Resource Monitoring Techniques	7			
4.2 Given a scenario, determine the appropriate allocation of cloud resources.					
Resources needed based on cloud deployment models	Cloud Deployment Models and Services	1			
Hybrid	Cloud Deployment Models and Services	1			
Community	Cloud Deployment Models and Services	1			
Public	Cloud Deployment Models and Services	1			
Private	Cloud Deployment Models and Services	1			
Capacity/elasticity of cloud environment	Systems Management Best Practices	9			
Support agreements	Systems Management Best Practices	9			
Cloud service model maintenance responsibility	Systems Management Best Practices	9			
Configuration management tool	Change and Configuration Management	13			
Resource balancing techniques	Optimizing Performance	8			
Change management	Change and Configuration Management	13			
Advisory board	Change and Configuration Management	13			
Approval process	Change and Configuration Management	13			

Exam Readiness Checklist

Domain and Objective	Study Guide Coverage	Ch. #	Beginner	Intermediate	Expert
Document actions taken	Change and Configuration Management	13			
CMDB	Change and Configuration Management	13			
Spreadsheet	Change and Configuration Management	13			
4.3 Given a scenario, determine when to provision/deprovision cloud resources.					
Usage patterns	Migration Considerations	6			
Cloud bursting	Migration Considerations	6			
Auto-scaling technology	Migration Considerations	6			
Cloud provider migrations	Migration Considerations	6			
Extending cloud scope	Migration Considerations	6			
Application life cycle	Life Cycle Management	7			
Application deployment	Life Cycle Management	7			
Application upgrade	Life Cycle Management	7			
Application retirement	Life Cycle Management	7			
Application replacement	Life Cycle Management	7			
Application migration	Life Cycle Management	7			
Application feature use	Life Cycle Management	7			
Increase/decrease	Life Cycle Management	7			
Business need change	Life Cycle Management	7			
Mergers/acquisitions/divestitures	Life Cycle Management	7			
Cloud service requirement changes	Life Cycle Management	7			
Impact of regulation and law changes	Life Cycle Management	7			
4.4 Given a scenario, implement account provisioning techniques in a cloud environment to meet security and policy requirements.					
Identification	Access Control	10			
Authentication methods	Access Control	10			
Federation	Access Control	10			
Single sign-on	Access Control	10			

Exam Readiness Checklist

Domain and Objective	Study Guide Coverage	Ch. #	Beginner	Intermediate	Expert
Authorization methods	Access Control	10			
ACLs	Access Control	10			
Permissions	Access Control	10			
Account life cycle	Access Control	10			
Account management policy	Access Control	10			
Lockout	Access Control	10			
Password complexity rules	Access Control	10			
Automation and orchestration activities	Security Governance and Strategy	11			
User account creation	Security Governance and Strategy	11			
Permission settings	Security Governance and Strategy	11			
Resource access	Security Governance and Strategy	11			
User account removal	Security Governance and Strategy	11			
User account disablement	Security Governance and Strategy	11			
4.5 Given a scenario, analyze deployment results to confirm they meet the baseline.					
Procedures to confirm results	Testing Techniques	13			
CPU usage	Testing Techniques	13			
RAM usage	Testing Techniques	13			
Storage utilization	Testing Techniques	13			
Patch versions	Testing Techniques	13			
Network utilization	Testing Techniques	13			
Application version	Testing Techniques	13			
Auditing enable	Testing Techniques	13			
Management tool compliance	Testing Techniques	13			
4.6 Given a specific environment and related data (e.g., performance, capacity, trends), apply appropriate changes to meet expected criteria.					
Analyze performance trends	Resource Monitoring Techniques	7			
Refer to baselines	Resource Monitoring Techniques	7			
Refer to SLAs	Host and Guest Resource Allocation	8			

Exam Readiness Checklist

Domain and Objective	Study Guide Coverage	Ch. #	Beginner	Intermediate	Expert
Tuning of cloud target objects	Testing Techniques	13			
Compute	Testing Techniques	13			
Network	Testing Techniques	13			
Storage	Testing Techniques	13			
Service/application resources	Testing Techniques	13			
Recommend changes to meet expected performance/capacity	Testing Techniques	13			
Scale up/down (vertically)	Testing Techniques	13			
Scale in/out (horizontally)	Testing Techniques	13			
4.7 Given SLA requirements, determine the appropriate metrics to report.					
Chargeback/showback models	Systems Management Best Practices	9			
Reporting based on company policies	Systems Management Best Practices	9			
Reporting based on SLAs	Systems Management Best Practices	9			
Dashboard and reporting	Systems Management Best Practices	9			
Elasticity usage	Systems Management Best Practices	9			
Connectivity	Systems Management Best Practices	9			
Latency	Systems Management Best Practices	9			
Capacity	Systems Management Best Practices	9			
Overall utilization	Systems Management Best Practices	9			
Cost	Systems Management Best Practices	9			

Exam Readiness Checklist

Domain and Objective	Study Guide Coverage	Ch. #	Beginner	Intermediate	Expert
Incidents	Systems Management Best Practices	9			
Health	Systems Management Best Practices	9			
System availability	Systems Management Best Practices	9			
Uptime	Systems Management Best Practices	9			
Downtime	Systems Management Best Practices	9			
5.0 Troubleshooting					
5.1 Given a scenario, troubleshoot a deployment issue.					
Common issues in the deployments	Troubleshooting Methodology	14			
Breakdowns in the workflow	Troubleshooting Methodology	14			
Integration issues related to different cloud platforms	Troubleshooting Methodology	14			
Resource contention	Troubleshooting Methodology	14			
Connectivity issues	Troubleshooting Methodology	14			
Cloud service provider outage	Troubleshooting Methodology	14			
Licensing issues	Troubleshooting Methodology	14			
Template misconfiguration	Troubleshooting Methodology	14			
Time synchronization issues	Troubleshooting Methodology	14			
Language support	Troubleshooting Methodology	14			
Automation issues	Troubleshooting Methodology	14			
5.2 Given a scenario, troubleshoot common capacity issues.					
Exceeded cloud capacity boundaries	Troubleshooting Methodology	14			
Compute	Troubleshooting Methodology	14			
Storage	Troubleshooting Methodology	14			

Exam Readiness Checklist

Domain and Objective	Study Guide Coverage	Ch. #	Beginner	Intermediate	Expert
Networking	Troubleshooting Methodology	14			
IP address limitations	Troubleshooting Methodology	14			
Bandwidth limitations	Troubleshooting Methodology	14			
Licensing	Troubleshooting Methodology	14			
Variance in number of users	Troubleshooting Methodology	14			
API request limit	Troubleshooting Methodology	14			
Batch job scheduling issues	Troubleshooting Methodology	14			
Deviation from original baseline	Troubleshooting Methodology	14			
Unplanned expansions	Troubleshooting Methodology	14			
5.3 Given a scenario, troubleshoot automation/ orchestration issues.					
Breakdowns in the workflow	Troubleshooting Methodology	14			
Account mismatch issues	Troubleshooting Methodology	14			
Change management failure	Troubleshooting Methodology	14			
Server name changes	Troubleshooting Methodology	14			
IP address changes	Troubleshooting Methodology	14			
Location changes	Troubleshooting Methodology	14			
Version/feature mismatch	Troubleshooting Methodology	14			
Automation tool incompatibility	Troubleshooting Methodology	14			
Job validation issue	Troubleshooting Methodology	14			
5.4 Given a scenario, troubleshoot connectivity issues.					
Common networking issues	Troubleshooting Methodology	14			
Incorrect subnet	Troubleshooting Methodology	14			
Incorrect IP address	Troubleshooting Methodology	14			
Incorrect gateway	Troubleshooting Methodology	14			
Incorrect routing	Troubleshooting Methodology	14			
DNS errors	Troubleshooting Methodology	14			
QoS issues	Troubleshooting Methodology	14			

Exam Readiness Checklist

Domain and Objective	Study Guide Coverage	Ch. #	Beginner	Intermediate	Expert
Misconfigured VLAN or VXLAN	Troubleshooting Methodology	14			
Misconfigured firewall rule	Troubleshooting Methodology	14			
Insufficient bandwidth	Troubleshooting Methodology	14			
Latency	Troubleshooting Methodology	14			
Misconfigured MTU/MSS	Troubleshooting Methodology	14			
Misconfigured proxy	Troubleshooting Methodology	14			
Network tool outputs	Troubleshooting Methodology	14			
Network connectivity tools	Troubleshooting Tools	14			
ping	Troubleshooting Tools	14			
tracert/traceroute	Troubleshooting Tools	14			
telnet	Troubleshooting Tools	14			
netstat	Troubleshooting Tools	14			
nslookup/dig	Troubleshooting Tools	14			
ipconfig/ifconfig	Troubleshooting Tools	14			
route	Troubleshooting Tools	14			
arp	Troubleshooting Tools	14			
ssh	Troubleshooting Tools	14			
tcpdump	Troubleshooting Tools	14			
Remote access tools for troubleshooting	Troubleshooting Tools	14			
5.5 Given a scenario, troubleshoot security issues.					
Authentication issues	Troubleshooting Methodology	14			
Account lockout/expiration	Troubleshooting Methodology	14			
Authorization issues	Troubleshooting Methodology	14			
Federation and single sign-on issues	Troubleshooting Methodology	14			
Certificate expiration	Troubleshooting Methodology	14			
Certification misconfiguration	Troubleshooting Methodology	14			
External attacks	Troubleshooting Methodology	14			
Internal attacks	Troubleshooting Methodology	14			

Exam Readiness Checklist

Domain and Objective	Study Guide Coverage	Ch. #	Beginner	Intermediate	Expert
Privilege escalation	Troubleshooting Methodology	14			
Internal role change	Troubleshooting Methodology	14			
External role change	Troubleshooting Methodology	14			
Security device failure	Troubleshooting Methodology	14			
Incorrect hardening settings	Troubleshooting Methodology	14			
Unencrypted communication	Troubleshooting Methodology	14			
Unauthorized physical access	Troubleshooting Methodology	14			
Unencrypted data	Troubleshooting Methodology	14			
Weak or obsolete security technologies	Troubleshooting Methodology	14			
Insufficient security controls and processes	Troubleshooting Methodology	14			
Tunneling or encryption issues	Troubleshooting Methodology	14			
5.6 Given a scenario, explain the troubleshooting methodology.					
Always consider corporate policies, procedures and impacts before implementing changes	Troubleshooting Methodology	14			
1. Identify the problem	Troubleshooting Methodology	14			
Question the user and identify user changes to computer and perform backups before making changes	Troubleshooting Methodology	14			
2. Establish a theory of probable cause (question the obvious)	Troubleshooting Methodology	14			
If necessary, conduct internal or external research based on symptoms	Troubleshooting Methodology	14			
3. Test the theory to determine cause	Troubleshooting Methodology	14			
Once theory is confirmed, determine the next steps to resolve the problem	Troubleshooting Methodology	14			
If the theory is not confirmed, reestablish a new theory or escalate	Troubleshooting Methodology	14			
4. Establish a plan of action to resolve the problem and implement the solution	Troubleshooting Methodology	14			
5. Verify full system functionality and, if applicable, implement preventive measures	Troubleshooting Methodology	14			
6. Document findings, actions, and outcomes	Troubleshooting Methodology	14			

Chapter 1

Cloud Computing Concepts, Models, and Terminology

M oving an organization's entire infrastructure to the cloud provides a number of benefits to that organization, including power savings, on-demand storage, ease of administration, ability to pay for only the resources it uses, and a metered environment that can offer almost 100 percent uptime if included in the service level agreement (SLA)—a costly undertaking when provided by the organization itself. An SLA is a contract between a cloud provider and a cloud consumer that formally defines the cloud service and who is responsible for it. This chapter covers the basic concepts, models, and terminology that are the building blocks of cloud computing. It lays a foundation for the rest of the book by building scenarios for cloud deployments that the subsequent chapters can be compared to and modeled against for a better understanding of what cloud computing is, how it can be deployed, and the value it provides both to information technology (IT) organizations and the customers that they support.

Cloud Service Models

A cloud service model is a set of IT-related services offered by a cloud provider. The cloud provider is responsible for supplying cloud-based IT resources to a cloud consumer under a predefined and mutually agreed upon SLA. The cloud provider is responsible for administrative maintenance and management of the cloud infrastructure, which allows the cloud consumer to focus its administrative effort on other aspects of the business. In essence, the cloud consumer is buying or leasing its IT infrastructure from the cloud provider.

The entity that legally owns the cloud service is known as the cloud service owner. Either the cloud provider or the cloud consumer can be the cloud service owner, depending on the terms of the SLA.

It is critical to understand who is responsible for the services hosted in the cloud. Before an organization migrates any piece of its business to the cloud, it needs to understand who is "in control" of those resources. There are a variety of cloud service models that offer the cloud consumer a number of different options. To implement a successful cloud deployment, you need to understand each of the cloud service models and the service that each provides. In this section you will learn about each of the different cloud service models and when to implement each.

Infrastructure as a Service (IaaS)

Infrastructure as a Service (IaaS) is the model by which the cloud consumer outsources responsibility for its computer hardware, network, and operating systems to an external cloud provider. The cloud provider not only owns the equipment that provides the infrastructure resources but is also responsible for the ongoing operation and maintenance of those resources. In this model, the cloud consumer is charged on a "pay-as-you-use" or "pay-as-you-grow" basis. IaaS can include the server storage, the infrastructure, and the connectivity domains. For example, the cloud consumer could deploy and run its own applications and operating systems, while the IaaS provider would handle the following:

- Storage resources, including replication, backup, and archiving
- Compute resources, which are the resources traditionally provided by servers or server farms, including processor, memory, disk, and networking
- Connectivity domains, including infrastructure management and security, such as network load balancing and firewalls

FIGURE 1-1

Infrastructure as
a Service (IaaS)
provider services

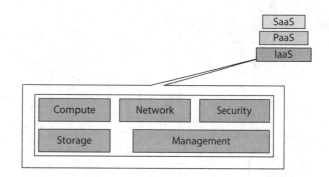

When an organization utilizes IaaS, it no longer has to buy, maintain, or upgrade server hardware, which can help it save resources, time, and money. Since IaaS allows an organization to pay only for the resources it uses, the organization no longer needs to outlay expenditures for hardware resources it either is not using or is not using to maximum capacity. IaaS allows an organization to spin up additional resources quickly and efficiently without having to purchase physical hardware. For example, the IT department might need a development environment to test a new application; with IaaS this development environment could be spun up quickly and then removed when the new application has been fully tested. IaaS allows an organization to meet hardware capacity spikes without having to add resources to its data center. Figure 1-1 shows you a graphical representation of the services that are offered by an IaaS provider.

Platform as a Service (PaaS)

Platform as a Service (PaaS) enables customers to have applications deployed without the time, cost, and human resources required to buy and manage their own back-end hardware and software. PaaS applications are either consumer-created or acquired web applications or services that are entirely accessible from the Internet. The tools and programming languages used to create PaaS applications are usually supplied by the cloud provider.

PaaS web applications enable cloud consumers to control the deployed applications via an application programming interface (API) without having to manage the complexity of all the underpinning servers, operating systems, or storage. In some circumstances, the cloud consumer is also allowed to control the application-hosting environment. PaaS offers cloud consumers a speedy time to market and an integrated way to provision services over the Web. PaaS facilitates the immediate delivery of business requirements such as application design, development, and testing at a fraction of the cost.

PaaS providers offer a variety of services and service combinations spanning the entire application deployment life cycle. Some of the service features are source code, application usage tracking, versioning, and testing tools. Figure 1-2 shows you a graphical representation of the services offered by PaaS providers.

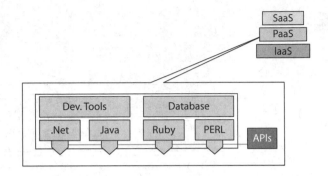

FIGURE 1-2

Platform as a
Service (PaaS)
provider services

Software as a Service (SaaS)

Software as a Service (SaaS) is a cloud service model that enables a cloud consumer to use
on-demand software applications delivered by the cloud provider via a thin client device,
typically a web browser over the Internet. The web-based application features of SaaS
have been around for quite some time before cloud became a term. Such applications
were referred to as application service provider (ASP) software. SaaS customers delegate
both the management and control of the infrastructure (such as storage, servers, network,
or operating systems) and the configuration of the application's capabilities to their
cloud provider. SaaS is a quick and efficient service model for key business applications
such as customer relationship management (CRM), enterprise resource planning (ERP),
HR, and payroll. Figure 1-3 shows you a graphical representation of the services offered
by SaaS providers.

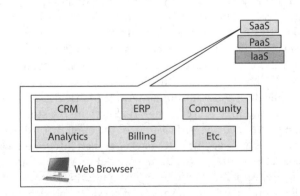

FIGURE 1-3

Software as a
Service (SaaS)
provider services

Database as a Service (DBaaS)

Database as a Service (DBaaS) is essentially a form of software specializing in the delivery of database operations. This service enables cloud providers to offer database functionality to multiple, discrete cloud consumers. DBaaS infrastructures support the following competencies:

- Self-service provisioning for the customer of database instances
- Monitoring of attributes and quality-of-service levels to ensure compliance with provider-defined service agreements
- Carefully measured usage of database services, enabling chargeback functionality for each individual cloud consumer

A DBaaS infrastructure may also support service elasticity, secure multitenancy, access using a wide range of devices, automated resource management, and capacity planning. These concepts will be discussed later in this chapter.

Communications as a Service (CaaS)

Communications as a Service (CaaS) enables customers to utilize enterprise-level voice over IP (VoIP), virtual private networks (VPNs), private branch exchange (PBX), and unified communications without the costly investment of purchasing, hosting, and managing their infrastructure. With the cloud provider being responsible for the management and operation of this infrastructure, the customer also has the advantage of not having to source and staff its own trained personnel, bringing significant relief to both operational and capital costs.

Business Process as a Service (BPaaS)

Business Process as a Service (BPaaS) is a relatively new concept. It mixes business process management (BPM) with one or more aspects of a cloud service model: SaaS, IaaS, or PaaS. Business process management is an approach that aims to make a company's workflow more effective, efficient, and agile, allowing it to respond quickly to changes driven by business requirements. This kind of workflow enables businesses to be more flexible and to decrease their spending. Traditional business process management systems (BPMSs) integrate business processes and keep track of running their corresponding instances; a BPMS coordinates the execution of a business process step by step. Each process instance is monitored by the BPMS and provides users with feedback on progress to validate successful completion or to alert on failures. In case of a failure, the BPMS shows where the process failure occurred. By monitoring, analyzing, and identifying where business processes fail, customers can act proactively and optimize the deployment of their business service. This ultimately leads to lower costs and improved customer satisfaction.

A BPaaS is any business process that is delivered as a service by utilizing a cloud solution. With BPaaS, one or more business processes are uploaded to a cloud service that performs each process step and monitors them while they execute. As with any other cloud environment, BPaaS enables customers to use cloud software in a pay-per-use model, instead of having to invest in hardware and maintenance.

Anything as a Service (XaaS)

Anything as a Service (XaaS) is the delivery of IT as a service through a combination of cloud service models; it works with one or a combination of SaaS, IaaS, PaaS, CaaS, DBaaS, or BPaaS. The X in XaaS is a variable that can be changed to represent a variety of different cloud services. XaaS is simply a term used to describe the distribution of different IT components within the cloud model.

Accountability and Responsibility by Service Model

Now that you understand all the different cloud service models, you need to become familiar with who is responsible for those services. Accountability in the cloud can be split between multiple parties, including cloud consumers, infrastructure providers, and cloud providers. Accountability in cloud computing is about creating a holistic approach to achieve security in the cloud and to address the lack of consumer trust. The very nature of cloud computing brings a new level of complexity to the issue of determining who is responsible for a service outage, and cloud providers are faced with the difficult task of achieving compliance across geographic boundaries. A service outage can be the result of a variety of issues, such as software vulnerabilities, power outages, hardware failure, network disruption, application error, or user error.

The three primary service models in cloud computing have differing security approaches for businesses. With SaaS, the cloud provider is responsible for maintaining the agreed upon service levels between the cloud provider and the cloud consumer and for security, compliance, and liability expectations. When it comes to PaaS and IaaS, the cloud consumer

TABLE 1-1	Service Model	Cloud Provider Responsibility	Cloud Consumer Responsibility
Service Level Responsibility	Software as a Service (SaaS)	X	
	Platform as a Service (PaaS)		X
	Infrastructure as a Service (IaaS)		X

is responsible for managing the same expectations, while the cloud provider takes some of the responsibility for securing the underlying infrastructure. Service outages can also be attributed to the end-user device having misconfiguration or hardware failures. Table 1-1 provides a quick reference of the party responsible for maintaining the service levels of each cloud service model.

When discussing accountability and responsibility in the cloud, it is important to classify risk according to the service model being utilized and the location of the data. For example, if a business is using a hybrid cloud, both the consumer and the cloud provider can be responsible for the same risks since part of the data is in the cloud and part is in the internal data center. It is important that the SLAs and any other agreements signed between the cloud consumer and cloud provider clearly state who is responsible for preventing and remedying outages and how those outages are classified, identified, and measured. Figure 1-4 shows who the typical cloud consumer is for each cloud model.

Another consideration is the division of responsibility of maintenance tasks in a cloud environment. Patching and maintenance contribute greatly to the overall security and performance in a cloud solution. Responsibility is broken out in such a way that the cloud provider is responsible for the patching and maintenance "of" the cloud, and the cloud consumer is responsible for patching "in" the cloud. We will explore this concept further in Chapter 9 when diving into systems management.

FIGURE 1-4	
Cloud service models and their consumers	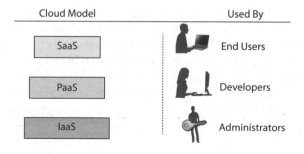

CERTIFICATION OBJECTIVE 1.02

Cloud Deployment Models and Services

You have just learned about the different service models available for implementing a cloud computing solution. To realize the value from these service models and for the customers to have access to them, a deployment model must be chosen. Implementing a cloud deployment model can vastly impact an organization. Implementation requires careful consideration and planning to be successful. If your role is the IT administrator, it is your responsibility to educate the organization on the benefits and challenges of implementing a cloud deployment model. You need to evaluate the business needs and determine what benefits a cloud deployment model would bring to your organization. Whichever cloud deployment model you choose, whether it be private, public, or hybrid (described next), it needs to map well to the business processes you are trying to achieve.

Private Cloud

In a private cloud deployment model, the cloud is owned by a single organization and enables central access to IT resources for departments and staff distributed among a variety of locations. A private cloud solution is implemented behind the corporate firewall and is maintained by the local IT department. A private cloud utilizes internal resources and is designed to offer the same benefits of a public cloud without relinquishing control, security, and recurring costs to a cloud provider. In a private cloud model, the same organization is both the cloud consumer and the cloud provider.

The decision to implement a private cloud is usually driven by the need to maintain control of the environment because of regulatory or business reasons. For example, a bank might have data security issues that prevent it from using a public cloud service, so the bank might implement a private cloud to achieve the benefits of a cloud computing model.

A private cloud is a combination of virtualization, data center automation, chargeback metering, and identity-based security. Virtualization allows for easy scalability, flexible resource management, and maximum hardware utilization. A private cloud solution also involves having the ability to auto-provision physical host computers through orchestration software, which is discussed later in this chapter. Some organizations use private clouds to share storage between internal systems or departments. This is referred to as a private cloud space (PCS).

watch A private cloud allows you to take advantage of a cloud environment without exposing your data to the entire population of the Internet.

One of the downsides to a private cloud is that an organization does not get the return on investment it does with other cloud models. This is because the organization is still responsible for running and managing the resources instead of passing that responsibility to a cloud provider.

Public Cloud

Unlike a private cloud that is owned by the organization, a public cloud is a pool of computing services delivered over the Internet via a cloud provider. A cloud provider makes resources such as applications and storage available to organizations over the Internet. Public clouds use a pay-as-you-go model, which gives organizations the benefit of paying only for the resources that they consume. Public clouds allow for easy and inexpensive setup because the hardware, application, and bandwidth costs are covered and maintained by the cloud provider and charged as part of the service agreement.

on the job You may recognize SaaS offerings such as cloud storage and online office applications (e.g., Microsoft Office 365) as public cloud offerings. What you may not know is that IaaS and PaaS offerings, including cloud-based web hosting and development environments, can be part of a public cloud as well.

Public clouds are used when an organization is less likely to need the level of infrastructure and security offered by private clouds. Organizations requiring data security can still utilize public clouds to make their operations significantly more efficient with the storage of nonsensitive content, online document collaboration, and webmail.

A public cloud offers ultimate scalability because cloud resources are available on demand from the cloud provider's vast pool of resources. Organizations do not need to purchase and implement hardware to scale the environment; they just need to obtain more resources from the cloud provider. The availability of the public cloud via an Internet connection allows the services to be used wherever the client is located, making a public cloud location independent. Some examples of public cloud providers are Microsoft Windows Azure, Google Apps, SAP HANA, Oracle Cloud, IBM Cloud Foundry, VMware vCloud, and Amazon Web Services.

Hybrid Cloud

A hybrid cloud is a cloud service that utilizes both private and public clouds to perform distinct functions within the same organization. An organization might have a need for both a local server running specific applications for security reasons and a public cloud hosting additional applications, files, and databases. These two environments would be configured for scalability and interoperability.

In a hybrid cloud model, an organization continues to provide and manage some resources internally while other resources are provided externally by a cloud provider. A hybrid cloud allows an organization to take advantage of the scalability and cost-effectiveness of a public cloud without exposing mission-critical data to a public cloud provider.

A cloud model is defined as a hybrid cloud if an organization is using a public development platform that sends data to a private cloud. Another example of a hybrid cloud model is when an organization uses multiple SaaS applications and moves that application data between a private cloud or an internal data center.

A cloud is not considered a hybrid if an organization uses SaaS applications and does not move the data to a private cloud or internal data center. A cloud environment is labeled as a hybrid cloud only if there is a combination of private and public clouds or if data is moved between the internal data center and the public cloud. You can see an example of a hybrid cloud environment in Figure 1-5.

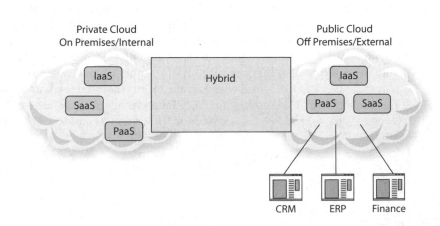

FIGURE 1-5

Components of a hybrid cloud environment

Community Cloud

A community cloud is a cloud offering where the infrastructure is shared between several organizations from a specific group with common computing needs or objectives. Community clouds are built and operated specifically for a targeted group who have common cloud requirements and whose ultimate goal is to work together to achieve a specific business objective.

Community clouds are usually implemented for organizations working on joint projects that require a central cloud for managing and executing those projects. A finance community cloud, for example, could be set up to provide specific security requirements or optimized to provide low latency to perform financial transactions. A community cloud can be either on premises or off premises and can be managed by a cloud provider or by the organizations themselves.

exam

ωatch **A community cloud provides a segregated approach to cloud computing for increased security. The key to a community cloud is that it can be scoped to a specific group.**

EXAM AT WORK

Community Cloud in the Health Care Industry

IT shops that support the healthcare industry need to design solutions that satisfy regulatory compliance with the Health Insurance Portability and Accountability Act, or HIPAA. Community clouds provide IaaS, PaaS, and SaaS options that enable those IT departments to deliver technical service offerings that both fulfill their customer needs and pass regulatory inspection. To demonstrate the value of the community cloud to the healthcare industry, let's look at an example of how it could be implemented in a real-world IT scenario.

Deeter is an application developer who builds custom applications for a series of family doctors' offices. All of these offices are tied into Midwest HealthNet, which is a community cloud solution that aggregates patient data across some healthcare providers, from hospitals to family practices, across several Midwestern states. Midwest HealthNet's primary offering is a SaaS solution called "HealthNet Online" that is accessible only to members of the Midwest HealthNet network. Deeter uses PaaS to develop applications for his customers that present the data available in HealthNet Online in a format that is easier for them to work with and is customized for each of their practices. Since all of his development takes place in the community cloud, and HealthNet Online is also in the community cloud, the data is protected and remains in compliance with HIPAA regulations.

On-Premises vs. Off-Premises Hosting

On-premises hosting is the solution that IT professionals are most familiar with. On-premises hosting is the traditional way of managing a data center. In an on-premises environment, the virtualized servers are hosted on-site at the organization's internal data center, and the organization owns and maintains that server hardware. The benefit to on-premises hosting is that the organization has complete control over the daily management and maintenance of its servers. The downside to on-premises hosting is that the organization has to pay the costs of maintaining the internal data center, including power, security, maintenance, licenses, hardware, and other costs.

Off-premises hosting is sometimes referred to as cloud computing. With off-premises hosting, the IT resources are hosted in the cloud and accessed online. Off-premises hosting can be used for server virtualization or applications to be hosted in the cloud. One of the benefits of off-premises hosting is that the cost is usually lower than on-premises hosting because the resources are hosted online instead of in the organization's data center. This allows the organization to convert IT costs to the pay-as-you-grow model, keeping IT costs down. Off-premises hosting is sometimes perceived as less secure or as having a higher security risk since the organization loses control of its data because it is hosted in the cloud.

Orchestration Platforms

Automation of day-to-day administrative tasks is becoming more and more of a requirement for IT departments. Orchestration platforms provide an automated way to manage the cloud or computing environment. They make it possible to achieve a dynamic data center by aligning business requests with applications, data, and infrastructure. A typical business model defines policies and service levels that an IT department must meet. Orchestration platforms help an IT department meet these requirements through automated workflows, provisions, and change management features. This allows for a dynamic and scalable infrastructure that is constantly changing based on the needs of the business. For example, with an orchestration platform, a developer could request the creation of a virtual machine via a service portal, and the orchestration software would automatically create that virtual machine based on a predefined template. Orchestration software can also be used for centralized management of a resource pool, including billing, software metering, and chargeback or showback for resource utilization.

Orchestration platforms provide companies with automated tools to perform tasks that would typically take a team of administrators to complete. These platforms offer an automated approach to creating hardware and software, allowing them to work together to deliver a predefined service or application. Orchestration platforms make it possible for the cloud environment to easily scale and provision new applications and services on demand through workflows.

Some examples of orchestration platforms include Cloudify, Terraform, Ansible, IBM Cloud Orchestrator, Flexiant Cloud Orchestrator, and Microsoft System Center Orchestrator. All of the orchestration platforms allow for the creation of workflows to automate day-to-day administrative tasks.

CERTIFICATION OBJECTIVE 1.03

Cloud Characteristics and Terms

When implementing a cloud computing model, an organization needs to understand the terminology of cloud computing and the characteristics of remote provisioning of a scalable and measured IT resource. The IT administrator as a cloud consumer needs to work with the cloud provider to assess these characteristics and measure the value offering of the chosen cloud platform.

Elasticity

Elasticity can be thought of as unlimited space that allows the organization to dynamically provision and deprovision processing, memory, and storage resources to meet the demands of its network. Elasticity allows an organization to shift and pool resources across dissimilar infrastructure, allowing data to be more synchronized and avoiding overprovisioning of hardware. It is one of the many benefits of cloud computing because it allows an IT department to be scalable without having to purchase and stand up hardware in its internal data center. The primary difference between elasticity and scalability is that scalability is the ability of a system to increase its workload on the current hardware resources, whereas elasticity is the ability of a system to increase its workload by adding hardware resources.

Demand-Driven Service

In an on-demand self-service environment, users have access to cloud services through an online portal. This gives them the ability to provision cloud resources on demand wherever and whenever they need to. On-demand, or "just-in-time," self-service allows cloud consumers to acquire computing resources automatically and on demand without human interaction from the cloud provider.

Pay-as-You-Grow

One of the advantages of the public cloud is the pay-as-you-grow philosophy. The pay-as-you-grow charging model allows an organization to pay for services by the hour or based on the compute resources it uses. Therefore, pay-as-you-grow does not require a large up-front investment by the organization for infrastructure resources. It is important for an organization to design and plan its cloud costs before deploying its first application in the cloud. Most cloud providers have a calculator to help organizations figure the costs they would incur by moving to the cloud. This gives organizations a better understanding of the pay-as-you-grow model when it comes to cloud pricing and using the public cloud infrastructure.

Chargeback

IT chargeback is an accounting strategy that attempts to decentralize the costs of IT services and apply them directly to the teams or divisions that utilize those services. This system enables organizations to make better decisions about how their IT dollars are spent, as it can help determine the true cost of a particular service. Without a chargeback system, all IT costs are consolidated under the IT department umbrella, and the ability to determine the true profitability of the individual business services the IT department supports is limited or impossible. Chargeback allows an organization to charge the actual department or user of the IT resource instead of putting all of the expense under the IT umbrella. Most private clouds and internal IT departments use the term "showback" instead of chargeback to describe the amount of resources being consumed by a department.

Ubiquitous Access

With ubiquitous access, a cloud provider's capabilities are available over the network and can be accessed through standard mechanisms by many different types of clients, and without the requirement for application deployment or a specific operating system configuration. This does not necessarily mean Internet access. Ubiquitous access does, however, allow a cloud service to be widely accessible via a web browser, from anywhere. A cloud consumer can get the same level of access whether at home, at work, or in a coffee shop.

Metering

Metering is the ability of a cloud platform to track the use of its IT resources and is geared primarily toward measuring usage by cloud consumers. A metering function allows the cloud provider to charge a cloud consumer only for the IT resources actually being used. Metering is closely tied to on-demand or demand-driven cloud usage.

Metering is not only used for billing purposes; it can also be used for general monitoring of IT resources and usage reporting for both the consumer and the provider. This makes metering a benefit for not only public clouds but private cloud models as well.

Multitenancy

Multitenancy is an architecture that provides a single instance of an application to serve multiple clients or tenants. Tenants are allowed to have their own view of the application and make customizations while remaining unaware of other tenants who are using the same application.

Multitenant applications ensure that tenants do not have access to change the data and configuration of the application on their own. However, tenants are allowed to change the user interface to give the application their own look and feel.

Implementing a multitenant application is, of course, more complicated than working with a single-tenant application. Multitenant applications must support the sharing of multiple resources by multiple users (e.g., databases, middleware, portals) while maintaining the security of the environment.

Cloud computing has broadened the definition of multitenancy because of the new service models that can take advantage of virtualization and remote access. A SaaS service provider can run an instance of its application on a cloud database and provide web access to multiple customers. Each tenant's data is isolated and remains invisible to other tenants.

Cloud Bursting

Cloud bursting is the concept of running an application on the organization's internal computing resources or private cloud and "bursting" that application into a public cloud on demand when the organization runs out of resources on its internal private cloud. Cloud bursting is normally recommended for high-performance, noncritical applications that have nonsensitive data. It allows a company to deploy an application in an internal data center and "burst" to a public cloud to meet peak needs.

When an organization is looking to take advantage of cloud bursting, it needs to consider security and regulatory compliance requirements. An example of when cloud bursting is a good option is in the retail world, where a company might experience a substantial increase in demand during the holiday season. The downside to this is that the retailers could be putting sensitive data into the public cloud and exposing their customers to risk. Figures 1-6 and 1-7 show an example of an application experiencing heavy use and subsequently "bursting" into the public cloud.

watch   **Cloud bursting is a short-term way to increase your available cloud resources on demand, but it does come with the security risk of moving your data into a public cloud.**

FIGURE 1-6

Operating within the organization's internal computing resources (no public cloud needed)

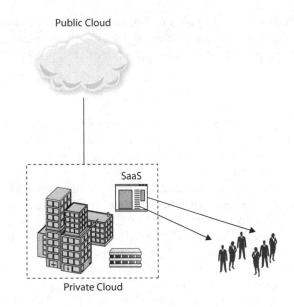

FIGURE 1-7

Operating after cloud bursting (using the public cloud)

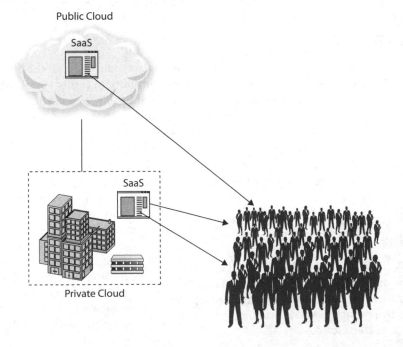

Auto-Scaling Technology

Auto-scaling is the logical next step after cloud bursting for the demand-driven cloud. Cloud consumers can capitalize on the elasticity and orchestration of a cloud provider by bursting resources to the cloud automatically when necessary. This feature takes the enablement of cloud resources to the next level by provisioning not just more compute resources as necessary for the subscribed set of virtual machines or instances but also provisioning more virtual machines and instances themselves to deliver the performance and availability that the consumer is looking to achieve. Auto-scaling technology can help consumers offset unknown or unexpected spikes in demand without adversely affecting their deliverable.

Baselines

Baselines are the starting point for all measurements to be compared against. A baseline is a recorded state or configuration against which planned changes and performance comparisons can be made. Establishing a baseline is the first step in controlling any environment.

Organizations typically take a baseline of an existing system when migrating it to the cloud. They take another baseline when the system is deployed and under normal load to compare performance metrics between the two baselines and ensure that performance meets the needs of the business and application. Baselines should be taken at different milestones in the cloud life cycle. For example, when a cloud is deployed and is being used by the workforce, conduct a baseline to understand normal activity. However, the system's usage may grow or shrink over time and new behavior will be considered normal, thus requiring a new baseline. Similar applications on the same platform should also be baselined and compared against each other to ensure that the organization takes advantage of optimizations that may be in place in one application but not another.

The importance of baselines cannot be overemphasized in cloud operations. Appropriate tools and procedures should be put in place to perform the following functions:

- Evaluate performance
- Ensure user satisfaction
- Fulfill service level agreement requirements
- Demonstrate proof of compliance

The inability to prove compliance may put a company at risk financially, as many contracts specify penalties if the company is unable to demonstrate their fulfillment of the stated requirements.

The following methodology can be used to demonstrate proof of compliance:

1. *Establish baselines.* Create a baseline measurement of the environment for each area that has defined service levels.

2. *Monitor baselines.* Establish procedures to regularly and consistently monitor and measure the baseline and to understand the pattern of varying measurements over the course of time, in a process known as trending. The cloud service administrator (CSA) also needs to be alerted to significant deviations from the baseline so that they can restore service to the previously defined baseline state.

3. *Make baselines available.* Share baselines with customers to provide evidence of SLA compliance.

4. *Maintain baseline states.* Once the baselines have been established, documented, and contractually agreed upon, it is then the goal of service operations to ensure that they consistently beat baseline performance metrics.

Source and Target Hosts

When moving workloads in a cloud environment, the compute resources that run the workload in the current position are owned by the "source" host. The host that owns the compute resources that an administrator intends to move to is referred to as the "target" host.

Existing Systems

Cloud environments are not usually developed as an entirely new solution running by itself. To provide continuity, workloads are often shared by existing systems and cloud systems. Migration plans are established, and existing systems are slated for removal over time as functionality is slowly migrated to the cloud.

Cloud Elements

The cloud is not made up only of virtual machines and virtual hosts. Services have been developed that allow consumers to leverage cloud objects such as storage, databases, and applications from disparate cloud providers. There are a wide variety of computing resources available to cloud consumers through cloud services. These resources can become pieces of a larger system or solution. When utilizing cloud services, application components are called from APIs and are referred to as "target objects."

This enables a diverse approach to cloud computing and gives consumers more choice on how they can develop the solutions they want to build. As a foundation to understanding cloud computing, it is important to understand how the terms cloud element and target object are used. Cloud elements are the pieces that make up a cloud solution. Some of those pieces could be accessed by cloud consumers and programs, while others are used in support of those resources. When cloud consumers reference cloud elements, those elements are referred to as target objects. For example, when a backup program is pointed to cloud storage to archive it onto another storage medium, the cloud storage is the target object. Table 1-2 shows a number of cloud elements and how they can be a target object. It provides an example for how it would be a target object and chapter references for where you can learn more. Since these are foundational terms, you will learn much more about them as they are used in conveying other important cloud concepts.

TABLE 1-2   Cloud Elements and Target Objects

Cloud Element	Example	Chapter and Section Reference
Hypervisor	A patch management system would reference hypervisors to apply patches to them.	Ch 5, "Hypervisor" Ch 9, "Patch Management"
Virtual resources (vCPU/Memory)	Virtual resources would be a target object for a management tool that collects resource utilization metrics, benchmarks, and thresholds.	Ch. 7, "Baselines and Thresholds"
Virtual machine	A virtual machine would be a target object for a cloud backup solution.	Ch 5, "Virtual Machine" Ch. 12, "Backup Target"
Virtual appliance	A virtual appliance such as a cloud firewall or a CASB would be a target object for cloud dashboards.	Ch. 5, "Firewall" Ch. 9, "Virtual Appliances" Ch. 10, "Firewall" and "Cloud Access Security Broker"
Applications	Application components would be target objects for systems that call their APIs.	Ch. 10, "APIs"
Storage	Clients synchronize with cloud storage in solutions like Dropbox. The cloud storage, in this case, would be the target object for the synchronization.	Ch. 3, "Storage Types and Technologies"
Logs	When a security information and event management (SIEM) system pulls logs from cloud servers, these logs would be target objects.	Ch. 10, "SIEM"
Workflow	A workflow would be the target object of orchestration.	Ch. 13, "Automation and Orchestration"
Cluster	Code updates may be deployed to cluster nodes independently by a deployment tool or orchestration tool. This tool would trigger failovers and code updates on the target objects.	Ch. 9, "Clusters" and "Code Updates"

CERTIFICATION OBJECTIVE 1.04

Object Storage Concepts

Object-based storage is a concept that was developed to help provide a solution to the ever-growing data storage needs that have accompanied the IT explosion since the late twentieth century. It acts as a counterpart to block-based storage, allowing large sets of files to be grouped and to move the processing power for those files away from server and workstation CPUs and closer to the storage itself. This processing power is utilized to assist in the implementation of such features as fine-grained security policies, space management, and data abstraction.

Object ID

Since object-based storage is not addressed in blocks, like most of the storage used in everyday workstation and server environments, the object storage device (OSD) interface requires some way to find out how to address the data it contains. Objects are the individual pieces of data that are stored in a cloud storage system. Objects are composed of parts: an object data component, which is usually a file that is designated to be stored in the cloud storage system, and an object metadata component, which is a collection of values that describe object qualities. The OSD interface uses object IDs as a unique identifier for the combination of data and metadata that comprises each of the objects.

Metadata

Along with all the files that each object contains is an associated set of metadata that can be used to describe the data component of a specific object to classify it or define relationships with other objects. This metadata is an extensible set of attributes that is either implemented by the OSD directly for some of the more common attributes or interpreted by higher-level storage systems that the OSD uses for its persistent storage.

Data BLOB

A binary large object, or BLOB, is a collected set of binary data that is stored as a single, discrete entity in a database management system. By gathering this binary data into larger collections, database administrators are able to better copy large amounts of data between databases with significantly reduced risk of error correction or data filtering.

Policies

Policies are similar to metadata in that they are attributes associated with the object. The difference is that policy tags contain information that is associated with a particular security mechanism.

Replicas

One of the primary uses of object-based storage is the practice of working with replicas. Replicas are essentially copies of one large set of data, often associated with a virtual hard drive or virtual machine. They are used to both increase availability and reduce the amount of risk associated with keeping a large amount of data in one location. Replicas are good candidates for object-based storage for several reasons:

- They are large datasets that require a copying mechanism that can run efficiently without requiring expensive error correction or filtering.
- They do not affect user performance SLAs if they are faced with I/O latency, which is often associated with object-based storage and can introduce a performance bottleneck.

CERTIFICATION SUMMARY

The definitions of cloud computing are always changing. Understanding the similarities and differences between the cloud models is key to passing the CompTIA Cloud+ exam. It is equally important to grasp how the cloud can benefit an organization. Cloud computing is a growing industry, and IT professionals are going to be required to grow with it. While the exam will not ask directly about the similarities and differences between the cloud models, that knowledge will be required to correctly answer the questions that present scenarios about choosing between them.

KEY TERMS

Use the following list to review the key terms discussed in this chapter. The definitions also can be found in the glossary.

Anything as a Service (XaaS)   Cloud model that delivers IT as a service through hybrid cloud computing and works with a combination of SaaS, IaaS, PaaS, CaaS, DBaaS, or BPaaS.

Business Process as a Service (BPaaS)   Any business process that is delivered as a service by utilizing a cloud solution.

chargeback   An accounting strategy that attempts to decentralize the costs of IT services and apply them directly to the teams or divisions that utilize those services.

cloud bursting   Running an application on the organization's internal computing resources or private cloud and extending that application or portions of the application into a public cloud on demand when the organization runs out of resources on its internal private cloud.

Communications as a Service (CaaS)   Allows a cloud consumer to utilize enterprise-level voice over IP (VoIP), virtual private networks (VPNs), private branch exchange (PBX), and unified communications using a cloud model.

community cloud   Cloud model where the infrastructure is shared between several organizations from a specific group with common computing needs and objectives.

data BLOB   Collection of binary data stored as a single, discrete entity in a database management system.

Database as a Service (DBaaS)   Cloud model that delivers database operations as a service to multiple cloud consumers over the Internet.

elasticity   Allows an organization to dynamically provision and deprovision processing, memory, and storage resources to meet the demands of the network.

hybrid cloud   Cloud model that utilizes both private and public clouds to perform distinct functions within the same organization.

Infrastructure as a Service (IaaS)   Cloud model where the cloud consumer outsources responsibility for its computer hardware, network, and operating systems to an external cloud provider, which owns the equipment such as storage, servers, and connectivity domains.

metadata   Data about data used to describe particular attributes of data including how the data is formatted.

metering   Ability of a cloud platform to track the use of its IT resources and is geared primarily toward measuring usage by cloud consumers.

multitenancy   Architecture providing a single instance of an application to serve multiple clients or tenants.

object ID (OID)   Unique identifier used to name an object.

on-demand/just-in-time self-service   Gives cloud consumers access to cloud services through an online portal allowing them to acquire computing resources automatically and on-demand without human interaction from the cloud provider.

pay-as-you-grow   Concept in cloud computing where an organization pays for cloud resources as it needs those resources.

Platform as a Service (PaaS)   Cloud model that provides the infrastructure to create applications and host them with a cloud provider.

policies   Rule sets by which users and administrators must abide.

private cloud   A cloud that is owned by a single organization and enables central access to IT resources from a variety of locations, departments, and staff.

private cloud space (PCS)   Cloud-based storage that exists within a company's own internal systems, but can be made available to other departments and units within the company.

public cloud   Pool of computing resources and services delivered over the Internet by a cloud provider to cloud consumers such as end users, IT departments, or business groups.

replica   Used to create a mirrored copy of data between two redundant hardware devices.

Software as a Service (SaaS)   Cloud model that allows a cloud consumer the ability to use on-demand software applications delivered by the cloud provider via the Internet.

ubiquitous access   Configuring a cloud service to be widely accessible via a web browser from anywhere, allowing for the same level of access either from home or work.

TWO-MINUTE DRILL

Cloud Service Models

- ❏ A cloud service model is a set of IT-related services offered by a cloud provider.
- ❏ Infrastructure as a Service (IaaS) is a cloud service model that offers server storage, infrastructure, and connectivity domains to a cloud consumer.
- ❏ Platform as a Service (PaaS) allows developers to develop and test applications without worrying about the underlying infrastructure.
- ❏ Software as a Service (SaaS) provides on-demand applications to the cloud consumer over the Internet.
- ❏ Communications as a Service (CaaS) allows a cloud consumer to outsource enterprise-level communication services such as VoIP and PBX.
- ❏ Anything as a Service (XaaS) is a generic term used to describe the distribution of different cloud components.

Cloud Deployment Models and Services

- ❏ A private cloud is a cloud deployment model that is owned and operated by a single organization, implemented behind the corporate firewall, and maintained by the internal IT department.
- ❏ A public cloud is a pool of computing services and resources delivered to a cloud consumer over the Internet by a cloud provider.
- ❏ A hybrid cloud is a combination of a public and private cloud that allows an organization to move resources between the local data center and a public cloud.
- ❏ A community cloud shares cloud resources and infrastructure between organizations for a specific group that has common computing needs or objectives.
- ❏ Orchestration software allows for an automated approach to managing cloud resources by providing for automatic deployment of virtual machines and other infrastructure.

Cloud Characteristics and Terms

- ❏ Elasticity allows an organization to dynamically provision and deprovision compute resources to meet the demands of its network.
- ❏ Demand-driven service allows a cloud consumer to provision cloud resources on demand whenever it needs to.
- ❏ Pay-as-you-grow allows a cloud consumer to pay only for the resources it is using and does not require a large up-front investment.

❑ Metering allows a cloud consumer to track who is using IT resources and charge the correct department for those resources.

❑ Cloud bursting allows a cloud consumer to "burst" an application running in a private cloud into a public cloud when demand gets too high for its internal resources.

❑ Baselines are established norms against which performance and changes can be measured.

❑ Cloud elements are disparate target objects called via an API, and can come from different providers.

❑ Auto-scaling enables customers to dynamically size their cloud computing resources without actively administering the system and allows for just-in-time resource consumption.

Object Storage Concepts

❑ Metadata uses attributes in the file to describe the data.

❑ A data BLOB is a collected set of binary data that is stored together as a single, discrete entity in a database.

❑ Replicas are copies of a large set of data used to increase availability and reduce the amount of risk associated with keeping a large amount of data in one location.

SELF TEST

The following questions will help you measure your understanding of the material presented in this chapter. As indicated, some questions may have more than one correct answer, so be sure to read all the answer choices carefully.

Cloud Service Models

1. Which of the following would be considered an example of IaaS?
    A. Providing productivity software for use over the Internet
    B. A multiuser program that is hosted by a third party
    C. Providing hardware resources over the Internet
    D. A database that is hosted in the cloud.

2. Which term is used to define the increasing number of services delivered over the Internet?
   A. XaaS
   B. CaaS
   C. MaaS
   D. C-MaaS

3. Voice over IP (VoIP) is an example of what type of cloud service?
   A. IaaS
   B. PaaS
   C. MaaS
   D. CaaS

4. Which of the following cloud solutions provides only hardware and network resources to make up a cloud environment?
   A. SaaS
   B. CaaS
   C. PaaS
   D. IaaS

5. Which of the following is usually accessed via a web browser?
   A. IaaS
   B. SaaS
   C. PaaS
   D. Virtual machines

Cloud Deployment Models and Services

6. What type of computing solution would be defined as a platform that is implemented within the corporate firewall and is under the control of the IT department?
   A. Private cloud
   B. Public cloud
   C. VLAN
   D. VPN

7. A cloud deployment has been created explicitly for the finance department. What type of cloud deployment would this be defined as?
   A. Public cloud
   B. Hybrid cloud
   C. Community cloud
   D. Private cloud

8. Which of the following statements would be used to explain a private cloud but not a public cloud?

    A. Used as a service via the Internet

    B. Dedicated to a single organization

    C. Requires users to pay a monthly fee to access services

    D. Provides incremental scalability

9. Which of the following statements is a benefit of a hybrid cloud?

    A. Data security management

    B. Requirement of a major financial investment

    C. Dependency of internal IT department

    D. Complex networking

Cloud Characteristics and Terms

10. Which of the following would be considered an advantage of cloud computing?

    A. Increased security

    B. Ability to scale to meet growing usage demands

    C. Ease of integrating equipment hosted in other data centers

    D. Increased privacy for corporate data

11. Which statement defines chargeback?

    A. The recovery of costs from consumers of cloud services

    B. The process of identifying costs and assigning them to specific cost categories

    C. A method of ensuring that cloud computing becomes a profit instead of a cost

    D. A system for confirming that billing occurs for the cloud services being used

12. When you run out of computer resources in your internal data center and expand to an external cloud on demand, this is an example of what?

    A. SaaS

    B. Hybrid cloud

    C. Cloud bursting

    D. Elasticity

Object Storage Concepts

13. A website administrator is storing a large amount of multimedia objects in binary format for the corporate website. What type of storage object is this considered to be?

    A. BLOB

    B. Replica

    C. Metadata

    D. Object ID

SELF TEST ANSWERS

Cloud Service Models

1. ☑ **C.** Providing hardware resources over the Internet is an example of IaaS. Infrastructure as a Service (IaaS) is a cloud service model that offers server storage, infrastructure, and connectivity domains to a cloud consumer.
   ☒ **A, B,** and **D** are incorrect. **A** and **B** are examples of SaaS. **D** is an example of DBaaS.

2. ☑ **A.** XaaS is a collective term that means "Anything as a Service" (or "Everything as a Service").
   ☒ **B, C,** and **D** are incorrect. Communications as a Service (CaaS), Monitoring as a Service (MaaS), and Cloud Migration as a Service (C-MaaS) are all examples of XaaS.

3. ☑ **D.** Voice over IP is an example of CaaS.
   ☒ **A, B,** and **C** are incorrect. VoIP is not an example of any of these cloud services.

4. ☑ **D.** In a cloud service model, IaaS providers offer computers and other hardware resources. Organizations would outsource the equipment needed to support their business.
   ☒ **A, B,** and **C** are incorrect. SaaS allows applications to be hosted by a service provider and made available to the organization over the Internet. CaaS provides network communication such as VoIP. PaaS offers a way to rent hardware, operating systems, storage, and network capacity over the Internet.

5. ☑ **C.** PaaS provides a platform to allow developers to build applications and services over the Internet. PaaS is hosted in the cloud and accessed with a web browser.
   ☒ **A, B,** and **D** are incorrect. In a cloud service model, IaaS providers offer computers and other hardware resources. Organizations would outsource the equipment needed to support their business. SaaS allows applications to be hosted by a service provider and made available to the organization over the Internet. Virtual machines would not be accessed via a web browser.

Cloud Deployment Models and Services

6. ☑ **A.** A private cloud is a cloud computing solution that is implemented behind a corporate firewall and is under the control of the internal IT department.
   ☒ **B, C,** and **D** are incorrect. A public cloud is a cloud computing solution that is based on a standard cloud computing model where a service provider makes the resources available over the Internet. A VLAN (virtual LAN) is a broadcast created by switches. A VPN (virtual private network) extends a private network over a public network such as the Internet.

7. ☑ **C.** A community cloud is a cloud solution that provides services to a specific or limited number of individuals who share a common computing need.
    ☒ **A, B,** and **D** are incorrect. A public cloud is a cloud computing solution that is based on a standard cloud computing model where a service provider makes the resources available over the Internet. A hybrid cloud is a cloud computing model where some of the resources are managed by the internal IT department and some are managed by an external organization. A private cloud is a cloud computing solution that is implemented behind a corporate firewall and is under control of the internal IT department.

8. ☑ **B.** A private cloud is dedicated to a single organization and is contained with the corporate firewall.
    ☒ **A, C,** and **D** are incorrect. These all describe features of a public cloud, not a private cloud. A public cloud is used as a service over the Internet, requires a monthly fee to access and use its resources, and is highly scalable.

9. ☑ **A.** A hybrid cloud offers the ability to keep the organization's mission-critical data behind a firewall and outside of the public cloud.
    ☒ **B, C,** and **D** are incorrect. These are all disadvantages of a hybrid cloud.

Cloud Characteristics and Terms

10. ☑ **B.** One of the benefits of cloud computing is the ability to easily scale and add resources to meet the growth of the organization.
    ☒ **A, C,** and **D** are incorrect. These are all disadvantages to cloud computing. The organization loses some control of its environment, has more difficulty integrating equipment hosted in multiple data centers, and deals with the uncertainty of whether other organizations have access to its data.

11. ☑ **A.** The purpose of a chargeback system is to measure the costs of IT services, hardware, or software and recover them from the business unit that used them.
    ☒ **B, C,** and **D** are incorrect. None of these options is the main focus of a chargeback system.

12. ☑ **C.** Cloud bursting allows you to add additional resources from an external cloud on an on-demand basis. The internal resource is the private cloud and the external resource is the public cloud.
    ☒ **A, B,** and **D** are incorrect. SaaS allows applications to be hosted by a service provider and made available to the organization over the Internet. A hybrid cloud is a cloud computing model where some of the resources are managed by the internal IT department and some are managed by an external organization. Elasticity provides fully automated scalability. It implies an ability to shift resources across infrastructures.

Object Storage Concepts

13.   ☑   **A.** A BLOB is a collection of binary data that is stored as a single entity. BLOBs are primarily used to store images, videos, and sound.

☒   **B, C,** and **D** are incorrect. A replica is a complete copy of the data. Metadata describes information about the set of data, including who created the data and when it was collected. It is data about the data. An object ID identifies an object in a database.

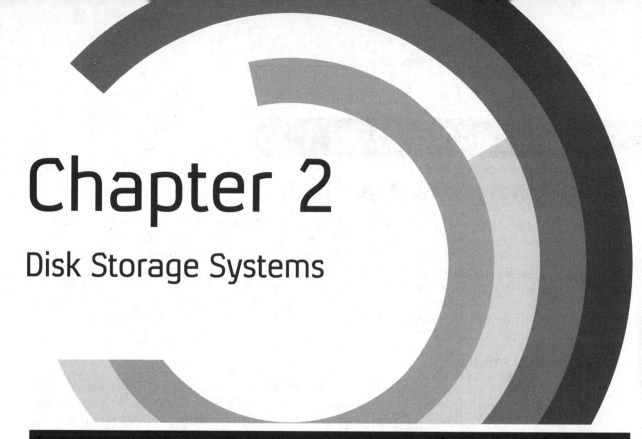

Chapter 2

Disk Storage Systems

S torage devices are the foundation of a storage network and are the building blocks of storage in a disk subsystem and stand-alone server. Disk system performance is a key factor to the overall health of the cloud environment, and you need to understand the different types of disks that are available and the benefits of each. Once an organization chooses the type of disk to use in its cloud environment, it needs to protect the data that is stored on the disk. Along with describing the different types of disks and how to connect those disks to the system, this chapter illustrates how data can be tiered to provide better utilization of disk resources and better application performance. Those who have passed the Network+ or Storage+ exam might possibly skip this chapter. Read the Certification Summary and the Two-Minute Drill sections to make sure everything covered in this chapter is familiar to you before deciding to jump to Chapter 3.

CERTIFICATION OBJECTIVE 2.01

Disk Types and Configurations

Disk drive technology has advanced at an astonishing rate over the past few years, making terabytes of storage available at a relatively low cost to consumers. Evaluating what types of disks to buy requires careful planning and evaluation of the purpose of the disk. If an organization is looking for a type of drive to support its database environment, it would be interested in a drive with high disk I/O as opposed to a drive that supports a file share on a test network (in which case the need is for disk space over disk I/O). In the following sections, we examine each of the different disk types and clarify these distinctions.

Rotational Media

Disk storage is a generic term used to describe storage mechanisms where data is digitally recorded by various electronic, magnetic, optical, or mechanical methods on a rotating disk, or media. A disk drive is a device that uses this storage mechanism with fixed or removable media. Removable media refers to an optical disc, memory card, flash media, or USB drive, and fixed or nonremovable media refers to a hard disk drive.

A hard disk drive (HDD) uses rapidly rotating disks called platters coated with a magnetic material known as ferrous oxide to store and retrieve digital information. An HDD retains the data on the drive even when the drive is powered off. The data on an HDD is read in a random-access manner. What this means is that an individual block of data can be stored or retrieved in any order rather than only being accessible sequentially, as in the case of data that might exist on a tape.

An HDD contains one or more platters with read/write heads arranged on a moving arm that floats above the ferrous oxide surface to read and write data to the drive. HDDs have been the primary storage device for computers since the 1960s. Today the most common sizes for HDDs are the 3.5 inch, which is used primarily in desktop computers, and the 2.5 inch, which is used primarily in laptop computers. The primary competitors of the HDD are the solid state drive (SSD) and flash memory cards. HDDs should remain the dominating medium for secondary storage, but SSDs are replacing rotating hard drives in portable electronic devices because of their speed and ruggedness.

e x a m

ⓦ a t c h **Hard disk drives are used when speed is less important than total storage space.**

Solid State Drive (SSD)

A solid state drive (SSD) is a high-performance storage device that contains no moving parts. It includes either dynamic random-access memory (DRAM) or flash memory boards, a memory bus board, a central processing unit (CPU), and sometimes a battery or separate power source. The majority of SSDs use "not and" (NAND)–based flash memory, which is a nonvolatile memory type, meaning the drive can retain data without power. SSDs produce the highest possible I/O rates because they contain their own CPUs to manage data storage. SSDs are less susceptible to shock or being dropped, are much quieter, and have a faster access time and lower latency than HDDs. SSDs and traditional hard disks have the same I/O interface, allowing SSDs to easily replace a traditional hard disk drive without changing the computer hardware.

While SSDs can be used in all types of scenarios, they are especially valuable in a system where I/O response time is critical, such as a database server, a server hosting a file share, or any application that has a disk I/O bottleneck. Another example of where an SSD is a good candidate is in a laptop. SSDs are shock resistant; they also use less power and provide a faster startup time than HDDs. Since an SSD has no moving parts, both sleep response time and system response time are improved. SSDs are currently more expensive than traditional hard disk drives but are less of a risk for failure and data loss. Table 2-1 shows you some of the differences between SSDs and traditional hard disk drives.

USB Drive

A universal serial bus (USB) drive is an external plug-and-play storage device that can be plugged into a computer's USB port and is recognized by the computer as a removable drive and assigned a drive letter by the computer. Unlike an HDD or SSD, a USB drive does not require a special connection cable and power cable to connect to the system, because it is powered via the USB port of the computer. Since a USB drive is portable and retains the data stored on it as it is moved between computer systems, it is a great device for transferring files quickly between computers or servers. There are many external storage devices that use USB, such as hard drives, flash drives, and DVD drives.

Tape

A tape drive is a storage device that reads and writes data to a magnetic tape. Using tape as a form of storage has been around for a long time. The role of tape has changed tremendously over the years and is still changing. Tape is now finding a niche in the market for longer-term storage and archiving of data, and it is the medium of choice for storage at an off-site location.

| TABLE 2-1 | SSD vs. HDD |

Drive Characteristic	Solid State Drive (SSD)	Hard Disk Drive (HDD)
Startup Time	Almost instantaneous. There are no moving parts to start on an SSD.	Disk spin-up can take a few seconds. If a system has multiple hard disks, it might stagger spin-up to limit power usage.
Fragmentation	Very small. Defragmenting an SSD could actually cause wear by making additional writes to the memory.	Files that are frequently written become fragmented over time. Defragmentation is required to ensure optimum performance.
Noise	Virtually none, since an SSD has no moving parts.	Noise levels vary between different models and manufacturers.
Temperature Control	Able to tolerate higher temperatures than an HDD. Special cooling usually not required.	Ambient temperatures above 95°F can shorten life. Additional cooling could be required.
Susceptibility to Failure	Extremely resistant to shock and vibrations because it has no moving parts.	Susceptible to shock and vibrations due to moving heads above rapidly rotating platters.
Reliability and Expected Lifetime	Not as likely to have a mechanical failure since it has no moving parts. Reliability varies across manufacturers.	Potential for mechanical failure from normal use due to moving parts.
Power Consumption	Flash-based on average requires half the power of an HDD. High-performance DRAM requires as much power as an HDD.	Anywhere from 0.35 watts to 20 watts, depending on size and performance.
Cost	More expensive per GB compared to HDD.	Less expensive per GB than SSD.
Installation	Not sensitive to location or orientation. No exposed circuitry.	Circuits can be exposed and should not come in contact with other metal parts. Needs to be mounted to protect against vibrations.
Data Transfer Rate	Delivers consistent read/write speed. Sleep recovery is greatly improved compared to an HDD, due to no moving parts.	Slower response time because of constant seeking to read files from various locations on the disk.

Tape drives provide sequential access to the data, whereas an HDD provides random access to the data. A tape drive has to physically wind the tape between reels to read any one particular piece of data. As a result, it has a slow seek time, having to wait for the tape to be in the correct position to access the data. Tape drives have a wide range of capacity and allow for data to be compressed to a size smaller than that of the files stored on the disk.

Interface Types

HDDs interface with a computer in a variety of ways, including ATA, SATA, Fibre Channel, SCSI, SAS, and IDE. Here we look at each of these interface technologies in greater detail. HDDs connect to a host bus interface adapter with a single data cable. Each HDD has its own power cable that is connected to the computer's power supply.

- *Advanced Technology Attachment (ATA)* is an interface standard for connecting storage devices within computers. ATA is often referred to as Parallel ATA (or PATA).
- *Integrated Drive Electronics (IDE)* is the integration of the controller and the hard drive itself, which allows the drive to connect directly to the motherboard or controller. IDE is also known as ATA.
- *Serial ATA (SATA)* is used to connect host bus adapters to mass storage devices. Designed to replace PATA, it offers several advantages over its predecessor, including reduced cable size, lower cost, native hot swapping, faster throughput, and more efficient data transfer.
- *Small Computer System Interface (SCSI)* is a set of standard electronic interfaces accredited by the American National Standards Institute (ANSI) for connecting and transferring data between computers and storage devices. SCSI is faster and more flexible than earlier transfer interfaces. It uses a bus interface type, and every device in the chain requires a unique ID.
- *Serial Attached SCSI (SAS)* is a data transfer technology that was designed to replace SCSI and to transfer data to and from storage devices. SAS is backward compatible with SATA drives.
- *Fibre Channel (FC)* is a high-speed network technology used in storage networking. Fibre Channel is well suited to connect servers to a shared storage device such as a storage area network (SAN) due to its high-speed transfer rate of up to 16 gigabits per second. Fibre Channel is often referred to as FC in the industry and on the Cloud+ exam.

Table 2-2 explains the different connection types and some of the advantages and disadvantages of each interface.

TABLE 2-2	HDD Interface Types	
Connector	**Advantages**	**Disadvantages**
Integrated Drive Electronics (IDE)	■ Lower cost ■ Large capacity	■ Only one device can read/write at a time if used in the typical master/slave configuration
Serial ATA (SATA)	■ Lower cost ■ Large capacity ■ Faster transfer rates than ATA ■ Easy configuration	■ Slower transfer rates than SCSI ■ No native support in older operating systems
Small Computer System Interface (SCSI)	■ Faster speeds ■ Greater scalability ■ Compatible with older SCSI devices ■ Reliability ■ Appropriate for large amounts of data	■ Higher cost ■ Large variety of interfaces ■ Higher RPM, causing more noise and heat ■ More difficult configuration
Serial Attached SCSI (SAS)	■ Compatibility with SATA ■ Higher transfer speeds ■ Serial communication vs. parallel ■ Increased availability	■ Higher cost ■ Use of SCSI command set

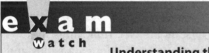

exam
watch

Understanding the differences in the interface types is key for	**the test. You need to know when to use each connector and the benefits of that connector.**

Access Speed

Just knowing the types of hard disks and the interface is not enough to calculate which drive type is best for a particular application. Understanding the speed at which a drive can access the data that is stored on that drive is critical to the performance of the application. A hard drive's speed is measured by the amount of time it takes to access the data that is stored on the drive. Access time is the response time of the drive and is a direct correlation of seek time and latency. The actuator arm and read-write head of the drive must move for data to be located. First, the actuator arm must move the head to the correct location on the platter.

TABLE 2-3	Rotational Speed (RPM)	Latency (ms)
Hard Disk Speed and Latency	3600	8.3
	4200	7.1
	5400	5.6
	7200	4.2
	10,000	3.0
	15,000	2.0

The time it takes for the arm to move to the correct location is known as seek time. At the same time, the platter must rotate to the desired sector. The time it takes for the platter to spin to the desired location is known as rotational latency, or just latency for short.

The access time of an HDD can be improved by either increasing the rotational speed of the drive or reducing the time the drive has to spend seeking the data. Seek time generally falls in the range of 3 to 15 milliseconds (ms). The faster the disk can spin, the faster it can find the data and the lower the latency for that drive will be. Table 2-3 lists the average latency based on some common hard disk speeds.

Redundant Array of Independent Disks (RAID)

So far in this chapter you have learned about the different disk types and how those disk types connect to a computer system. The next thing you need to understand is how to make the data that is stored on those disk drives as redundant as possible while maintaining a high-performance system. RAID is a storage technology that combines multiple hard disk drives into a single logical unit so that the data can be distributed across the hard disk drives for both improved performance and increased security according to their various RAID levels.

There are four primary RAID levels in use and several additional RAID levels, called nested RAID levels, that are built on top of the four primary types. RAID 0 takes two disks and stripes the data across them. It has the highest speed, but a failure of any disk results in data loss for the entire RAID set. RAID 1, also known as a mirror, stores identical copies of data on two drives for reliability. However, speeds are limited to the capabilities of a single drive and twice as much storage is required for data. RAID 5 stripes data across disks in the set and uses parity to reconstruct a drive if it fails in the set. RAID 5 requires at least three drives. It has good read performance, but the computation of parity can reduce write speeds in what is known as the write penalty. RAID 6 is like RAID 5 except it stores double parity and can recover from a loss of two drives. It has a higher write penalty.

Nested RAID consists of RAID 10 (RAID 1+0), which takes a number of mirror sets and stripes data over them. It has high read and write performance but requires double the drives for storage. RAID 50 is another type of nested RAID where two RAID5 sets are striped together. It can offer higher performance than the RAID 5 arrays could individually while still retaining the parity on the underlying RAID 5.

Table 2-4 compares the different RAID configurations to give you a better understanding of the advantages and requirements of each RAID level.

There are two different options available when implementing RAID: software RAID and hardware RAID using a RAID controller. Software RAID is implemented on a server by using software that groups multiple logical disks into a single virtual disk. Most modern operating systems have built-in software that allows for the configuration of a software-based RAID array. Hardware RAID controllers are physical cards that are added to a server to off-load the overhead of RAID and do not require any CPU resources; they allow an administrator to boot straight to the RAID controller to configure the RAID levels. Hardware RAID is the most common form of RAID due to its tighter integration with the device and better error handling.

e x a m

ⓦ a t c h **You need to understand the difference between each RAID level and when each particular level is appropriate to use.**

| TABLE 2-4 | RAID Level Benefits and Requirements |

Level	Description	Minimum Number of Disks	Fault Tolerance	Storage Efficiency
RAID 0	Blocks are striped. No mirror or parity.	2	None	100%
RAID 1	Blocks are mirrored. No striping or parity.	2	1 drive	50% or $n/2$
RAID 5	Blocks are striped. Distributed parity.	3	1 drive	Number of drives: 1
RAID 6	Blocks are striped with double distributed parity.	4	2 drives	Number of drives: 2
RAID 10	Blocks are mirrored and striped.	4	1 drive per span up to maximum of 2	50%
RAID 50	Blocks are striped across two or more RAID 5 sets.	6	1 drive per RAID 5 set	Number of drives: number of RAID 5 sets

Tiering

In the previous section, we discussed the different types of disks and the benefits of each of those disk types. Now that you understand the benefits of each disk, you know that storing data on the appropriate disk type can increase performance and decrease the cost of storing that data. Having flexibility in how and where to store an application's data is key to the success of cloud computing.

Tiered storage permits an organization to adjust where its data is being stored based on performance, availability, cost, and recovery requirements of an application. For example, data that is stored for restoration in the event of loss or corruption would be stored on the local drive so that it can be recovered quickly, whereas data that is stored for regulatory purposes would be archived to a lower-cost disk like tape storage.

Tiered storage can refer to an infrastructure that has a simple two-tier architecture, consisting of SCSI disks and a tape drive, or to a more complex scenario of three or four tiers. Tiered storage helps organizations plan their information life cycle management, reduce costs, and increase efficiency. Tiered storage requirements can also be determined by functional differences, for example, the need for replication and high-speed restoration.

With tiered storage, data can be moved from fast, expensive disks to slower, less expensive disks. Hierarchical storage management (HSM), which is discussed in the next section, allows for automatically moving data between four different tiers of storage. For example, data that is frequently used and stored on highly available, expensive disks can be automatically migrated to less expensive tape storage when it is no longer required on a day-to-day basis. One of the advantages of HSM is that the total amount of data that is stored can be higher than the capacity of the disk storage system currently in place.

Performance Levels of Each Tier

Hierarchical storage management (HSM) operates transparently to users of a system. HSM organizes data into tiers based on the performance capabilities of the devices, with tier 1 containing the devices with the highest performance and each tier after that containing storage with lower performance than the tier before it. HSM tiers can include a wide variety of local and remote media such as solid state, spinning disk, tape, and cloud storage.

HSM places data on tiers based on the level of access required and the performance and reliability needed for that particular data or based on file size and available capacity. Organizations can save time and money by implementing a tiered storage infrastructure. Each tier has its own set of benefits and usage scenarios based on a variety of factors. HSM can automatically move data between tiers based on factors such as how often data is used, but organizations can also specify policies to further control where HSM stores data and what priority it gives to migration operations between tiers.

The first step in customizing HSM policies is to understand the data that will reside on HSM storage. Organizations and IT departments need to define each type of data and determine how to classify it so that they can configure HSM policies appropriately. Ask yourself some of the following questions:

- Is the data critical to the day-to-day operation of the organization?
- Is there an archiving requirement for the data after so many months or years?
- Is there a legal or regulatory requirement to store the data for a period of time?

Once the data has been classified, the organization can create HSM policies so that data is moved to the appropriate tier and given the correct priority.

Tier 1

Tier 1 data is defined as mission-critical, recently accessed, or secure files and should be stored on expensive and highly available disks such as RAID with parity. Tier 1 storage systems have better performance, capacity, reliability, and manageability.

Tier 2

Tier 2 data is data that runs major business applications, for example, e-mail and ERP. Tier 2 is a balance between cost and performance. Tier 2 data does not require sub-second response time but still needs to be reasonably fast.

Tier 3

Tier 3 data includes financial data that needs to be kept for tax purposes but is not accessed on a daily basis and so does not need to be stored on the expensive tier 1 or tier 2 storage systems.

Tier 4

Tier 4 data is data that is used for compliance requirements for keeping e-mails or data for long periods of time. Tier 4 data can be a large amount of data but does not need to be instantly accessible.

Policies

A multitiered storage system provides an automated way to move data between more expensive and less expensive storage systems, as an organization can implement policies that define what data fits into each tier and then manage how that data migrates between the tiers. For example, when financial data is more than a year old, the policy could be to move that data to a tier 4 storage solution, much like the HSM defined earlier.

Tiered storage provides IT departments with the best solution for managing the organization's data while also saving time and money. Tiered storage helps IT departments meet their service level agreements at the lowest possible cost and the highest possible efficiency.

File System Types

After choosing a disk type and configuration, an organization needs to be able to store data on those disks. The file system is responsible for storing, retrieving, and updating a set of files on a disk. It is the software that accepts the commands from the operating system to read and write data to the disk. It is responsible for how the files are named and stored on the disk.

The file system is also responsible for managing access to the file's metadata ("the data about the data") and the data itself and for overseeing the relationships to other files and file attributes. It also manages how much available space the disk has. The file system is responsible for the reliability of the data on the disk and for organizing that data in an efficient manner. It organizes the files and directories and tracks which areas of the drive belong to a particular file and which areas are not currently being utilized.

This section explains the different file system types. Each file system has its own set of benefits and scenarios under which its use is appropriate.

Unix File System

The Unix file system (UFS) is the primary file system for Unix and Unix-based operating systems. UFS uses a hierarchical file system structure where the highest level of the directory is called the root (/, pronounced "slash") and all other directories span from that root. Under the root directory, files are organized into subdirectories and can have any name the user wishes to assign. All files on a Unix system are related to one another in a parent-child relationship, and they all share a common parental link to the top of the hierarchy.

Figure 2-1 shows an example of the UFS structure. The root directory has three subdirectories called bin, tmp, and users. The users directory has two subdirectories of its own called Nate and Scott.

Extended File System

The extended file system (EXT) is the first file system created specifically for Linux. The metadata and file structure is based on the Unix file system. EXT is the default file system for most Linux distributions. EXT is currently on version 4, or EXT4, which was introduced in

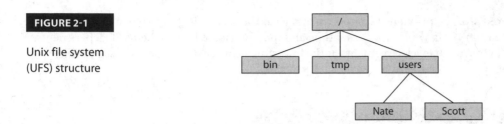

FIGURE 2-1

Unix file system
(UFS) structure

2008 and supports a larger file and file system size. EXT4 is backward compatible with EXT3 and EXT2, which allows for mounting an EXT3 and EXT2 partition as an EXT4 partition.

File Allocation Table File System

The file allocation table (FAT) file system is a legacy file system that provides good performance but does not deliver the same reliability and scalability as some of the newer file systems. The FAT file system is still supported by most operating systems for backward compatibility reasons but has mostly been replaced by NTFS (more on this in a moment) as the preferred file system for the Microsoft operating system. If a user has a drive running a FAT32 file system partition, however, they can connect it to a computer running Windows 7 and retrieve the data from that drive because. All modern versions of Windows, including 7, 8, and 10, still support the FAT32 file system.

The FAT file system is used by a variety of removable media, including solid state memory cards, flash memory cards, and portable devices. The FAT file system does not support the advanced features of NTFS like encryption, VSS, and compression.

New Technology File System

The new technology file system (NTFS) is a proprietary file system developed by Microsoft to support the Windows operating systems. It first became available with Windows NT 3.1 and has been used on all of Microsoft's operating systems since then. NTFS was Microsoft's replacement for the FAT file system. NTFS has many advantages over FAT, including improved performance and reliability, larger partition sizes, and enhanced security. NTFS uses the NT LAN Manager (NTLM) protocol for authentication.

Starting with version 1.2, NTFS added support for file compression, which is ideal for files that are written to on an infrequent basis. However, compression can lead to slower performance when accessing the compressed files; therefore, it is not recommended for .exe or .dll files, or for network shares that contain roaming profiles due to the extra processing required to load roaming profiles.

NTFS version 3.0 added support for volume shadow copy service (VSS), which keeps a historical version of files and folders on an NTFS volume. Shadow copies allow you to restore a file to a previous state without the need for backup software. The VSS creates a copy of the old file as it is writing the new file so the user has access to the previous version of that file. It is best practice to create a shadow copy volume on a separate disk to store the files.

Encrypting File System

The encrypting file system (EFS) provides an encryption method for any file or folder on an NTFS partition and is transparent to the user. EFS encrypts a file by using a file encryption key (FEK), which is associated with a public key that is tied to the user who encrypted the file. The encrypted data is stored in an alternate location from the encrypted file. To decrypt the file, EFS uses the private key of the user to decrypt the public key that is stored in the file header. If the user loses access to their key, a recovery agent can still access the files. NTFS does not support encrypting and compressing the same file.

Disk quotas allow an administrator to set disk space thresholds for users. This gives an administrator the ability to track the amount of disk space each user is consuming and limit how much disk space each user has access to. The administrator can set a warning threshold and a deny threshold and deny access to the user once they reach the deny threshold.

Resilient File System

The resilient file system (ReFS) is a proprietary file system developed by Microsoft to support the Windows operating systems. It first became available with Windows Server 2012 and is supported on Windows Server 2012 and later server operating systems as well as Windows 8.1 and later versions.

Rather than fully replacing NTFS, ReFS offers support for some new features by sacrificing some other features. ReFS's new features include the following:

- **Integrity checking and data scrubbing** These features are a form of file integrity monitoring (FIM) that checks data for errors and automatically replaces corrupt data with known good data. It also computes checksums for file data and metadata.
- **Storage virtualization** Remote mounts such as SAN storage can be formatted as local storage. Additionally, mirroring can be applied to disks in a logical volume to provide redundancy and striping to provide better performance.
- **Tiering** Multiple storage types with different capacity and performance ratings can be combined together to form tiered storage.
- **Disk pooling** A single ReFS logical volume can consist of multiple storage types. Unlike RAID, the drives do not need to be the same size and type to be in a pool.
- **Support for longer file paths than NTFS** NTFS was limited to 256-character file names and file paths, but ReFS can support file names and file paths up to 32,768 characters in length each. This allows for more descriptive names and deeper folder hierarchies.
- **Block cloning** A feature that decreases the time required for virtual machine copies and snapshots.
- **Sparse valid data length (VDL)** A feature that reduces the time required for creation of thick-provisioned virtual hard disks.

These new features, however, come at a cost. Microsoft has sacrificed some NTFS features that system administrators have become quite comfortable with including support for EFS, compression, data deduplication, and disk quotas.

Virtual Machine File System

The virtual machine file system (VMFS) is VMware's cluster file system. It is used with VMware ESXi server and vSphere and was created to store virtual machine disk images, including virtual machine snapshots. It allows for multiple servers to read and write to the file system simultaneously while keeping individual virtual machine files locked. VMFS volumes can be logically increased by spanning multiple VMFS volumes together.

Z File System

The Z file system (ZFS) is a combined file system and logical volume manager designed by Sun Microsystems. The ZFS file system protects against data corruption and support for high storage capacities. ZFS also provides volume management, snapshots, and continuous integrity checking with automatic repair.

ZFS was created with data integrity as its primary focus. It is designed to protect the user's data against corruption. ZFS is currently the only 128-bit file system. It uses a pooled storage method, which allows space to be used only as it is needed for data storage.

Table 2-5 compares a few of the different file system types, lists their maximum file and volume sizes, and describes some of the benefits of each system.

TABLE 2-5	File System Characteristics			
File System	**Maximum File Size**	**Maximum Volume Size**	**Encryption**	**Resizable Volumes**
Unix File System (UFS)	32PB	1YB	No	Offline but cannot be shrunk
New Technology File System (NTFS)	16TB	256TB	Yes	Online
File Allocation Table (FAT32)	4GB	2TB	No	Offline
Virtual Machine File System (VMFS)	2TB	64TB	No	Offline but cannot be shrunk*
Z File System (ZFS)	16EB	16EB	Yes	Online but cannot be shrunk

*Newest version of VMFS allows dynamic resizing but must be supported by the OS for it to be utilized without a reboot or additional sizing tools.

You should know the maximum volume size of each file system type for the exam. For example, if the requirement is a 3TB partition for a virtual machine drive, you would not be able to use the FAT file system; you would need to use NTFS.

CERTIFICATION SUMMARY

Understanding how different storage technologies affect the cloud is a key part of the CompTIA Cloud+ exam. This chapter discussed the various physical types of disk drives and how those drives are connected to systems and each other. It also covered the concept of tiered storage with HSM. We closed the chapter by giving an overview of the different file system types and the role proper selection of these systems plays in achieving scalability and reliability. It is critical to have a thorough understanding of all these issues as you prepare for the exam.

KEY TERMS

Use the following list to review the key terms discussed in this chapter. The definitions also can be found in the glossary.

Advanced Technology Attachment (ATA)   Disk drive implementation that integrates the drive and the controller.

encrypting file system (EFS)   A feature of the NTFS file system that provides file-level encryption.

extended file system (EXT)   First file system created specifically for Linux where the metadata and file structure is based on the Unix File System.

Fibre Channel (FC)   Technology used to transmit data between computers at data rates of up to 10 Gbps.

file allocation table (FAT)   Legacy file system used in Microsoft operating systems and is still used today by a variety of removable media.

file integrity monitoring (FIM)   A computer system process that reviews data in applications of the computer operating system and compares data values with known good values to identify if data has been altered.

hard disk drive (HDD)   Uses rapidly rotating aluminum or nonmagnetic disks, referred to as platters, that are coated with a magnetic material (ferrous oxide) that stores bits of information grouped into sectors, which in turn allows an individual block of data to be stored or retrieved in any order rather than only being accessible sequentially, as in the case of data that exists on a tape.

hierarchical storage management (HSM)   Allows for automatically moving data between four different tiers of storage.

Integrated Drive Electronics (IDE)   Integrates the controller and the hard drive, enabling the manufacturer to use proprietary communication and storage methods without any compatibility risks as it allows the drive to connect directly to the motherboard.

new technology file system (NTFS)   Proprietary file system developed by Microsoft to support the Windows operating system. NTFS was Microsoft's replacement for the FAT file system and has many advantages over FAT, including improved performance and reliability, larger partition sizes, and enhanced security.

NT LAN Manager (NTLM)   A Microsoft networking protocol that uses challenge-response for authentication in some Windows operating systems.

RAID   Storage technology that combines multiple hard disk drives into a single logical unit so that the data can be distributed across the hard disk drives for both improved performance and increased security according to their various RAID levels.

resilient file system (ReFS)   A proprietary file system developed by Microsoft to support the Windows operating systems that includes support for file integrity monitoring, data wiping, and additional disk health measurements.

Serial ATA (SATA)   Used to connect host bus adapters to mass storage devices.

Serial Attached SCSI (SAS)   Data transfer technology that was designed to replace SCSI and to transfer data to and from storage devices.

Small Computer System Interface (SCSI)   Set of standard electronic interfaces accredited by ANSI for connecting and transferring data between computers and storage devices.

solid state drive (SSD)   High-performance storage device that contains no moving parts.

tape   Can be used to save data by using digital recordings on magnetic tape to store the data.

Unix file system (UFS)   Primary file system for Unix and Unix-based operating systems that uses a hierarchical file system structure where the highest level of the directory is called the root (/, pronounced "slash") and all other directories span from that root.

USB drive   External plug-and-play storage device that is plugged into a computer's USB port and is recognized by the computer as a removable drive and assigned a drive letter.

virtual machine file system (VMFS)   VMware's cluster file system used with VMware ESXi server and vSphere to store virtual machine disk images, including virtual machine snapshots.

Z file system (ZFS)   Combined file system and logical volume manager designed by Sun Microsystems that provides protection against data corruption and support for high storage capacities.

TWO-MINUTE DRILL

Disk Types and Configurations

❑ A solid state drive (SSD) is a high-performance drive that contains no moving parts, uses less power than a traditional hard disk drive (HDD), and provides a faster startup time than an HDD.

❑ A USB drive is an external plug-and-play storage device that provides a quick and easy way to move files between computer systems.

❑ A tape drive reads and writes data to a magnetic tape and differs from an HDD because it provides sequential access rather than random access to data.

❑ HDDs connect to a computer system in a variety of ways, including ATA, SATA, FC, SCSI, SAS, and IDE.

❑ The speed at which an HDD can access data stored on it is critical to the performance of the server and the application it is hosting.

❑ RAID is a storage technology that combines multiple hard disk drives into a single logical unit to provide increased performance, security, and redundancy.

Tiering

❑ Tiered storage allows data to be migrated between storage devices based on performance, availability, cost, and recovery requirements.

❑ There are four levels of tiered storage. The tiers range from tier 1, which is mission-critical data stored on expensive disks, to tier 4, which stores data for compliance requirements on less expensive disks.

File System Types

❑ The file system is responsible for storing, retrieving, and updating files on a disk.

❑ UFS is the file system that is predominantly used in Unix-based computers.

❑ The EXT file system is the first file system created specifically for Linux.

❑ FAT is a legacy file system that provides good performance but without the scalability and reliability of newer file systems.

❑ NTFS was developed by Microsoft to replace FAT and provides improved performance and reliability, larger partition sizes, and enhanced security.

❑ VMFS is VMware's cluster file system and is used with ESXi server and vSphere.

❑ ZFS was developed by Sun Microsystems and provides protection against data corruption with larger storage capacities.

SELF TEST

The following questions will help you measure your understanding of the material presented in this chapter. As indicated, some questions may have more than one correct answer, so be sure to read all the answer choices carefully.

Disk Types and Configurations

1. A(n) _____ is a storage device that has no moving parts.
   A. HDD
   B. SSD
   C. Tape
   D. SCSI

2. Which type of storage device would be used primarily for off-site storage and archiving?
   A. HDD
   B. SSD
   C. Tape
   D. SCSI

3. You have been given a drive space requirement of 2 terabytes for a production file server. Which type of disk would you recommended for this project if cost is a primary concern?
   A. SSD
   B. Tape
   C. HDD
   D. VLAN

4. Which of the following storage device interface types is the most difficult to configure?
   A. IDE
   B. SAS
   C. SATA
   D. SCSI

5. If price is not a factor, which type of storage device interface would you recommend for connecting to a corporate SAN?
   A. IDE
   B. SCSI
   C. SATA
   D. FC

6. What RAID level would be used for a database file that requires minimum write requests to the database, a large amount of read requests to the database, and fault tolerance for the database?
   A. RAID 10
   B. RAID 1
   C. RAID 5
   D. RAID 0

7. Which of the following statements can be considered a benefit of using RAID for storage solutions?
   A. It is more expensive than other storage solutions that do not include RAID.
   B. It provides degraded performance, scalability, and reliability.
   C. It provides superior performance, improved resiliency, and lower costs.
   D. It is complex to set up and maintain.

Tiering

8. Which data tier would you recommend for a mission-critical database that needs to be highly available all the time?
   A. Tier 1
   B. Tier 2
   C. Tier 3
   D. Tier 4

9. Which term describes the ability for an organization to store data based on performance, cost, and availability?
   A. RAID
   B. Tiered storage
   C. SSD
   D. Tape drive

10. Which data tier would you recommend for data that is financial in nature, is not accessed on a daily basis, and is archived for tax purposes?
    A. Tier 1
    B. Tier 2
    C. Tier 3
    D. Tier 4

File System Types

11. Which of the following file systems is used primarily for Unix-based operating systems?
    A. NTFS
    B. FAT
    C. VMFS
    D. UFS

12. Which of the following file systems was designed to protect against data corruption and is a 128-bit file system?
    A. NTFS
    B. UFS
    C. ZFS
    D. FAT

13. The following file system was designed to replace the FAT file system:
   A. NTFS
   B. ZFS
   C. EXT
   D. UFS

14. Which of the following file systems was the first to be designed specifically for Linux?
   A. FAT
   B. NTFS
   C. UFS
   D. EXT

A SELF TEST ANSWERS

Disk Types and Configurations

1. ☑ **B.** A solid state drive is a drive that has no moving parts.
   ☒ **A, C,** and **D** are incorrect. A hard disk drive has platters that rotate. A tape drive writes data to a magnetic tape. SCSI is an interface type.

2. ☑ **C.** Tape storage is good for off-site storage and archiving because it is less expensive than other storage types.
   ☒ **A, B,** and **D** are incorrect. HDD and SSD have different advantages and would normally not be used for off-site or archiving of data. SCSI is an interface type.

3. ☑ **C.** You should recommend using an HDD because of the large size requirement. An HDD would be considerably cheaper than an SSD. Also, since it is a file share the faster boot time provided by an SSD is not a factor.
   ☒ **A, B,** and **D** are incorrect. While an SSD can work in this situation, the fact that cost is the primary concern rules it out. Although tape storage is considered cheap, it is not fast enough to support the requirements. VLAN is not a type of storage.

4. ☑ **D.** SCSI is relatively difficult to configure, as the drives must be configured with a device ID and the bus has to be terminated.
   ☒ **A, B,** and **C** are incorrect. All of these interface types are relatively easy to configure.

5. ☑ **D.** Fibre Channel delivers the fastest connectivity method, with speeds of up to 16 Gbps, but it is more expensive than the other interface types. If price is not a factor, FC should be the recommendation for connecting to a SAN.
   ☒ **A, B,** and **C** are incorrect. While IDE is the least expensive of the group, it does not deliver the speed that FC would. SCSI would be a good choice if price were a limitation. Since price is not a limiting factor in this case, FC would be the better choice. SATA is similar to SCSI, as it delivers a viable option when price is the primary concern for connecting to a SAN. Since price is not a factor, FC is the better choice.

6. ☑ **C.** RAID 5 is best suited for a database or system drive that has a lot of read requests and very few write requests.
   ☒ **A, B,** and **D** are incorrect. RAID 10 would be used for a database that requires a lot of write requests and needs high performance. RAID 1 is used when performance and reliability are more important than storage capacity and is generally used for an operating system partition. RAID 0 provides no fault tolerance and would not be recommended.

7. ☑ **C.** Using RAID can provide all these benefits over conventional hard disk storage devices.
   ☒ **A, B,** and **D** are incorrect. RAID can be a more expensive solution compared to conventional storage because of the loss of storage space to make up for redundancy. This is not a benefit of RAID. RAID does not provide degraded performance, scalability, or reliability. RAID can be more complex to configure and maintain, so this would not be a benefit of implementing RAID.

Tiering

8. ☑ **A.** Tier 1 data is defined as data that is mission-critical, highly available, and secure data.
   ☒ **B, C,** and **D** are incorrect. Tier 2 data is not mission-critical data and does not require the same response time as tier 1. Tier 3 data is data that is not accessed on a daily basis. Tier 4 data is used for archiving and is kept for compliance purposes.

9. ☑ **B.** Tiered storage refers to the process of moving data between storage devices based on performance, cost, and availability.
   ☒ **A, C,** and **D** are incorrect. RAID is the process of making data highly available and redundant. It does not allow you to move data between storage devices. SSD and tape drive are types of storage devices.

10. ☑ **C.** Tier 3 storage would be for financial data that you want to keep for tax purposes and is not needed on a day-to-day basis.
    ☒ **A, B,** and **D** are incorrect. Tier 1 storage is used for data that is mission-critical, highly available, and secure data. Tier 2 data is not mission-critical data but, like tier 1, is considerably more expensive than tier 3. Tier 4 data is used for archiving data and is kept for compliance purposes.

File System Types

11. ☑ **D.** UFS is the primary file system in a Unix-based computer.

☒ **A, B,** and **C** are incorrect. NTFS is a proprietary Microsoft file system and is used on Microsoft-based operating systems. FAT is a legacy file system used to support older operating systems. VMFS is used for VMware's cluster file system.

12. ☑ **C.** ZFS was developed by Sun Microsystems and is focused on protecting the user's data against corruption. It is currently the only 128-bit file system.

☒ **A, B,** and **D** are incorrect. The other file systems were not designed for protecting against data corruption and are not 128-bit file systems.

13. ☑ **A.** NTFS was designed by Microsoft as a replacement for FAT.

☒ **B, C,** and **D** are incorrect. The other file system types were designed for operating systems other than Microsoft Windows.

14. ☑ **D.** EXT was the first file system designed specifically for Linux.

☒ **A, B,** and **C** are incorrect. These file systems were not designed for Linux and are used primarily in other operating systems.

Chapter 3

Storage Networking

S torage is the foundation of a successful infrastructure. The traditional method of storing data is changing with the emergence of cloud storage. Storage is the instrument that is used to record and play back the bits and bytes that the compute resources process to provide their functions for delivering cloud services and applications.

Cloud storage is being leveraged for a wide range of enterprise functions from end user computing to enterprise storage and backup. Furthermore, cloud storage is a platform for explosive growth in organizational data because it is highly available and almost infinitely scalable. Understanding the advantages and disadvantages of storage types and technologies is a key concept for IT and cloud professionals because it will be your responsibility to help the organization understand the risks and the benefits of moving to cloud storage.

CERTIFICATION OBJECTIVE 3.01

Storage Types and Technologies

Just as there are many different environments in which computers are used, there are many types of storage to accommodate the needs of each of those environments. Some storage types are designed to meet primary organizational storage concerns such as cost, performance, reliability, and data security. Figure 3-1 displays a graphical comparison of the three storage types, DAS, SAN, and NAS, which we explore in more detail directly. A fourth type is object storage.

In addition to the four storage types, this section also covers two storage technologies. These technologies, deduplication and compression, improve storage efficiencies by removing unnecessarily redundant data.

FIGURE 3-1

Three major storage types: DAS, SAN, and NAS

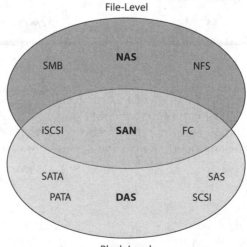

Direct Attached Storage (DAS)

Direct attached storage (DAS) is one or more drives that are connected to a machine as additional block-level storage. Some storage protocols that are used to access these storage devices are eSATA, USB, FC, SCSI, and SAS. USB and eSATA are most frequently utilized by desktops and laptops to connect to DAS, while companies typically connect DAS to servers using FC, SCSI, or SAS.

DAS is typically the least expensive storage option available for online storage (as opposed to offline storage such as a tape). As its name suggests, this type of storage is directly attached to the host computer that utilizes it and does not have to traverse a network to be accessed by that host. Direct attached storage is made available only to that local computer and cannot be used as shared storage. Shared storage, in this context, refers to storage that is made available to multiple machines at the block level. It is possible for a machine to share out storage that was provided to it by DAS.

Direct attached storage (DAS) cannot provide shared storage to multiple hosts.

Storage Area Network (SAN)

A storage area network (SAN) is a high-performance option that is employed by many data centers as a high-end storage solution with data security capabilities and a very high price tag to go along with it. A SAN is a storage device that resides on its own network and provides block-level access to computers that are attached to it.

The disks that are part of a SAN are combined into RAID groups for redundancy and higher performance. These RAID groups are then carved up into subdivisions called logical unit numbers (LUNs) that provide the block-level access to specified computers. LUNs can be interacted with just like a logical drive.

SANs are capable of very complex configurations, allowing administrators to divide storage resources and access permissions very granularly and with very high-performance capabilities. However, SAN maintenance and operations can be complicated, often requiring specialized skill sets and knowledge of proprietary technology (because each SAN solution is vendor specific). The role of SANs is mission critical, so there is little if any margin for error. Many storage administrators go to specialized training for their specific SAN solution, and they spend much of their time in the workplace giving SANs constant monitoring and attention. These administrative burdens add to the cost of deploying a SAN solution.

SANs are also able to provide shared storage or access to the same data at the same time by multiple computers. This is critical for enabling high availability (HA) in data center environments that employ virtualization solutions that require access to the same virtual machine files from multiple hosts. Shared storage allows hosts to perform migrations of virtual machines without any downtime, as discussed in more detail in Chapter 5.

Computers require a special adapter to communicate with a SAN, much like they need a network interface card (NIC) to access their data networks. The network that a SAN utilizes is referred to as a fabric and can be composed of fiber-optic cables, Ethernet adapters, or specialized SCSI cables.

A host bus adapter (HBA) is the most common device used to connect a machine to a SAN. An HBA is usually a PCI add-on card that can be inserted into a free slot in a host and then connected either to the SAN disk array directly or, as is more often the case, to a SAN switch. Virtual machines can use a virtual HBA, which emulates a physical HBA and allocates portions of the physical HBA's bandwidth to virtual machines. Storage data is transferred from the disk array over the SAN to the host via the HBA, which prepares it for processing by the host's compute resources.

There are two other adapters that may be used to connect to a storage network. A converged network adapter (CNA) can be used in lieu of an HBA. CNAs are computer expansion cards that can be used as an HBA or a NIC. NetApp has a proprietary adapter called universal target adapter (UTA). UTA has ports for one or more Ethernet or Fibre transceivers and can support Ethernet transceivers up to 10 Gbps and Fibre transceivers at native fibre channel speeds.

In addition to SANs, organizations can use a virtual SAN (VSAN), which can consolidate separate physical SAN fabrics into a single larger fabric, allowing for easier management while maintaining security. A VSAN allows identical Fibre Channel IDs to be used at the same time within different VSANs. VSANs allow for user-specified IDs that are used to identify the VSAN. VSANs can also span data centers with the use of VXLANs, discussed more in Chapter 4, or with encapsulation over routable network protocols.

HBAs usually can increase performance significantly by offloading the processing required for the host to consume the storage data without having to utilize its processor cycles. This means that an HBA enables greater efficiency for its host by allowing its processor to focus on running the functions of its operating system (OS) and applications instead of on storage I/O.

Network Attached Storage (NAS)

Network attached storage (NAS) offers an alternative to storage area networks for providing network-based shared storage options. NAS devices utilize TCP/IP networks for sending and receiving storage traffic in addition to data traffic. NAS provides file-level data storage that can be connected to and accessed from a TCP/IP network. Because NAS utilizes TCP/IP networks instead of a separate SAN fabric, many IT organizations can utilize existing infrastructure components to support both their data and storage networks. This use of common infrastructure can greatly cut costs while providing similar shared storage capabilities. Expenses are reduced for a couple of reasons:

- Data networking infrastructure costs significantly less than storage networking infrastructure.
- Shared configurations between data and storage networking infrastructure enable administrators to support both with no additional training or specialized skill sets.

NAS uses file sharing protocols to make shares available to users across a network. NAS systems typically support both the common Internet file system (CIFS)/Server Message Block (SMB) for Windows and the network file system (NFS) for Linux. NAS may also support uploading and downloading files to it via FTP or SSL/TLS-enabled FTP such as FTPS and SFTP.

One way to differentiate NAS from a SAN is that NAS appears to the client operating system as a file server, whereas a SAN appears to the client operating system as a disk (typically a LUN) that is visible in disk management utilities. This allows NAS to use Universal Naming Convention addressable storage. Network attached storage leverages protocols such as TCP/IP and iSCSI, both of which are discussed later in this chapter in more detail.

A storage area network (SAN) provides much better performance than network attached storage (NAS).

NAS also differs from SAN in that NAS natively allows for concurrent access to shares. However, there are some functions that can only be performed on block storage such as booting from SAN storage or loading applications from SAN storage. SAN connections usually offer much higher throughput to storage for high-performance needs.

Object Storage

Traditional file systems tend to become more complicated as they scale. Take, for example, a system that organizes pictures. Thousands of users may be requesting pictures from the site at the same time, and those pictures must be retrieved quickly. The system must track the location of each picture and, in order to retrieve them quickly, maintain multiple file systems and possibly multiple NAS devices for that data. As the user base grows further from the data center, latency issues can come up, so the data must be replicated to multiple sites and users directed to the location that has the lowest latency. The application now tracks the NAS where each picture resides, the location on that NAS, and which country the user is directed to, and it must keep the data synchronized between each site by tracking changes to the pictures. This application complexity makes applications harder to maintain and results in more processing to perform normal application functions. The solution is object storage.

Object storage is a storage system that abstracts the location and replication of data, allowing the application to become more simplified and efficient. Traditional file systems store data in blocks that are assembled into files, but the system does not know what each file actually contains. That is the responsibility of the application. However, object storage knows where the data is located and what the data is by utilizing metadata as a file organization method. For example, an application residing on top of object storage can ask the storage for the picture of John Doe at Middleton Beach on August 4, 2017, and the object storage will retrieve it for the application.

Object storage is often used for media files such as music, pictures, and video in cloud storage. Object storage has lower storage overhead because of the way data is organized. Objects have a unique identifier, but the application requesting the data does not need to know where it is stored. Object storage further avoids overhead by using a flat organization method rather than a hierarchical storage system. Hierarchical storage systems can only expand so far until suffering from latency in traversing directory trees, but object storage does not utilize such directory trees.

Object storage is heavily reliant upon metadata. Data and metadata are stored separately, and metadata can be expanded as needed in order to track additional details about the data. Object storage indexes metadata so that the data can be located using multiple criteria. Object stores are also application agnostic, supporting multiple applications for the same data set. In this way, the same data can be utilized for multiple applications, avoiding redundancy in storage and complexity in managing the data.

With object storage, capacity planning is done at the infrastructure level rather than the application level. This means that the application owners and the application itself do not need to monitor its capacity utilization, and it allows the system to be much more scalable.

Object storage is scalable because it uses a scale-out method that creates new object stores to handle additional data. These stores can exist at multiple sites, and redundancy can be defined per data type or per node so that the object store replicates data accordingly both to ensure that it is available if a single copy is lost and to avoid latency issues with satisfying application requests.

However, you should be aware that object storage requires changes to the application. You can move between different storage and database models usually by just changing a few parameters in the application, but moving to object storage requires the application to interface with the storage differently, so developers will need to modify their code accordingly. The change from traditional storage to object storage, therefore, is a dev change rather than an ops change.

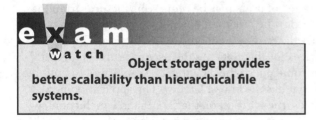

Object storage provides better scalability than hierarchical file systems.

Deduplication Technologies

Deduplication technologies remove redundant data from a storage system to free up space. There are two forms of deduplication technologies: file-level deduplication and block-level deduplication.

File-level deduplication hashes each file on a file system and stores those hashes in a table. If it encounters a file with a hash that is already in its table, it places a pointer to the existing file on the file system rather than storing the data twice. Imagine a document that is e-mailed to 100 people at an office. Because each person who stores that file would be storing a duplicate on the system, file-level deduplication would save only one copy of that data, with pointers for all the remaining ones. File-level deduplication can remove many duplicates, but it is not nearly as efficient as block-level deduplication.

Block-level deduplication hashes each block that makes up a file. This allows deduplication to take place on the pieces of a file, so deduplication does not require that a file be 100 percent identical to perform deduplication. For example, a user may store nine versions of a spreadsheet. Each version is slightly different from the others as new information was added to it. File-level deduplication would see each file hash as different, so no deduplication would be performed. However, block-level deduplication would see that many of the blocks are the same between these different versions and would store only one block for each duplicate. In this example, block-level deduplication could save up to 90 percent of the space that otherwise would be used.

Compression Technologies

Compression is another method used to reduce space. Some forms of compression result in a loss of information. These forms are known as lossy compression. Other types, known as lossless compression, do not result in a loss of information.

In most cases, you will want to employ lossless compression, but there are cases, such as in the transmission of audio or video data, where lossy compression may be utilized to transmit data at a lower quality level when sufficient bandwidth for higher quality is not available or when it would interrupt more time-sensitive data streams. Lossy compression might also be used on a website in order to increase the speed at which site objects load.

Lossless compression uses mathematical formulas to identify areas of files that can be represented in a more efficient format. For example, an image might have a large section that is all one color. Rather than storing the same color value repeatedly for that section, the lossless compression algorithm would note the range of pixels that contain that color and the color code.

CERTIFICATION OBJECTIVE 3.02

Storage Access Protocols

Now that you have learned about the various storage technologies that are available, we can turn our attention to the access protocols and applications that utilize these technologies to transmit, shape, and prioritize storage information between hosts and their storage devices.

Fibre Channel (FC)

Fibre Channel is a technology for transmitting data between computers at data rates of up to 128 Gbps. IT organizations have made Fibre Channel the technology of choice for interconnecting storage controllers and drives when architecting infrastructures that have high-performance requirements. Fibre Channel architecture is composed of many interconnected individual units, which are called nodes. Each of these nodes has multiple ports, and these ports connect the nodes in a storage unit architecture using one of three different interconnection topologies: point-to-point, arbitrated loop, and switched fabric. Fibre Channel also can transmit over long distances. When deployed using optical fiber, it can transmit between devices up to about six miles apart. While Fibre Channel is the transmission medium, it still utilizes SCSI riding on top of it for its commands.

Fibre Channel is deployed when the highest levels of performance are required.

Fibre Channel Protocol

The SCSI commands that ride atop the Fibre Channel transport are sent via the Fibre Channel Protocol (FCP). In order to increase performance, this protocol takes advantage of hardware that can utilize protocol offload engines (POEs). This assists the host by offloading processing cycles from the CPU, thereby improving system performance.

FCP uses addresses to reference nodes, ports, and other entities on the SAN. Each HBA has a unique world wide name (WWN), which is an 8-byte identifier similar to an Ethernet MAC address on a network card. There are two types of WWNs on an HBA: a world wide node name (WWNN), which can be shared by either some or all of the ports of a device, and a world wide port name (WWPN), which is unique to each port. Fibre switches also have WWPN for each switch port. Other devices can be issued a world wide unique identifier (WWUI) so that they can communicate on the SAN.

The frames in Fibre Channel Protocol consist of three components: an encapsulating header called the start-of-frame (SOF) marker, the data frame itself, and the end-of-frame (EOF) marker. This encapsulated structure enables the FC frames to be transported across other protocols, such as TCP, if desired.

Fibre Channel over Ethernet (FCoE)

Fibre Channel over Ethernet (FCoE) enables the transport of Fibre Channel traffic over Ethernet networks by encapsulating Fibre Channel frames over Ethernet networks. Fibre Channel over Ethernet can utilize Ethernet technologies up to 10 Gigabit Ethernet (10GigE) networks and higher speeds as they are developed, while still preserving the FC protocol.

Ethernet

Ethernet is an established standard for connecting computers to a local area network (LAN). Ethernet is a relatively inexpensive and reasonably fast LAN technology, with speeds ranging from 10 Mbps to 10 Gbps. Because it enables high-speed data transmission and is relatively inexpensive, Ethernet has become ubiquitous in IT organizations and the Internet.

Ethernet technology operates at the physical and data link layers of the OSI model (layers 1 and 2). Although it is capable of high speeds, it is limited by both the length and the type of cables over which it travels. The Ethernet standard divides its data traffic into groupings called frames. These frames are utilized by storage protocols to deliver their data from one point to another, such as from a NAS device to a server.

TCP/IP

Internet Protocol (IP) is a protocol that operates at the network layer of the OSI model (layer 3) and provides unique addresses and traffic-routing capabilities. Computers utilizing the IPv4 protocol are addressed using dotted decimal notation with four octets divided by dots. As the name suggests, IP is the protocol that enables the Internet. Like Ethernet networks, it is ubiquitous in IT departments and provides a proven and relatively inexpensive and well-understood technology on which to build storage networks.

Transmission Control Protocol (TCP) is a protocol that provides reliable transport of network data through error checking. TCP uses ports that are associated with certain services and other ports that can be dynamically allocated to running processes and services. TCP is most often combined with IP and it operates at the transport layer of the OSI model (layer 4).

Internet Fibre Channel Protocol

Internet Fibre Channel Protocol (iFCP) enables the transport of Fibre Channel traffic over IP networks by translating FC addresses to IP addresses and FC frames to IP packets. iFCP reduces overhead as compared with other protocols that transport FC over IP because it does not use tunneling to connect FC devices.

Internet Small Computer System Interface (iSCSI)

iSCSI is a protocol that utilizes serialized IP packets to transmit SCSI commands across IP networks and enables servers to access remote disks as if they were locally attached. iSCSI "initiator" software running on the requesting entity converts disk block-level I/O into SCSI commands that are then serialized into IP packets that traverse any IP network to their targets. At the destination storage device, the iSCSI packets are interpreted by the storage device array into the appropriate commands for the disks it contains. Figure 3-2 shows an example of how multiple servers can leverage iSCSI to connect to shared storage over an IP network.

iSCSI is limited by the transmission speeds of the Ethernet network it travels over; when administrators design iSCSI networks, they should pay close attention to the design so that the storage traffic is isolated from the data network traffic. Although its performance is not as high as that of a Fibre Channel SAN, iSCSI can be an inexpensive entry into shared storage for IT departments or a training ground using repurposed equipment for administrators who

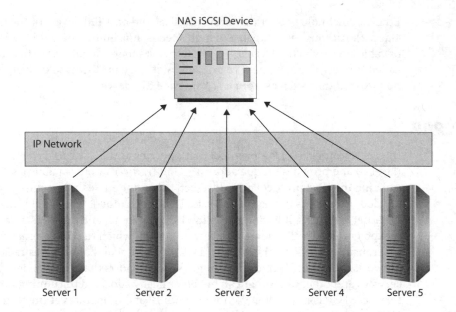

FIGURE 3-2

Using iSCSI over
an IP network

NAS iSCSI Device

IP Network

Server 1   Server 2   Server 3   Server 4   Server 5

want to get hands-on experience with storage networking. iSCSI can be implemented on a
NAS device or on a general-purpose machine. iSCSI's flexibility and implementation ease
make it a popular and versatile storage protocol.

The iSCSI address given to an initiator is known as an initiator qualified name (IQN).
Initiators reside on clients in an iSCSI network and initiators connect to targets such as
storage resources over the iSCSI network. An IQN uses the following naming convention:
iqn.yyyy-mm.naming-authority:unique name

on the job

**While working at a small IT shop that wanted to explore the use of virtualization,
our focus was to create some solutions for our customers that promised higher
availability. We needed to get some shared storage that we could use to enable
some of the automatic migration and performance tuning capabilities of our
virtualization platform. We did not, however, have much of a budget to spend on
research and development. We wound up repurposing a Gigabit Ethernet switch,
some category 6 Ethernet cable, and a couple of retired servers to set up our test
environment with very little cost. Using the built-in capabilities of the operating
system and some open-source software, we had everything we needed to build
out an entire lab and evaluate the capabilities of our proposed solutions.**

CERTIFICATION OBJECTIVE 3.03

Storage Provisioning

Now that you understand the technologies, protocols, and applications for moving storage data around networks, we will explore how that data is presented to computers. Data can be made available to computers in a number of ways, with varying degrees of availability and security.

Performance

Everyone has an expectation of performance for a system, and these expectations tend to increase as computing power increases. Storage systems also cannot stay the same. They must keep up with application and end-user demand. In order to do this, storage systems need a way to measure performance in a meaningful way. The most common method is input/output operations per second (IOPS). Storage must be provisioned to provide the required IOPS to the systems that utilize that storage. This requires having an understanding of the read and write throughput that different RAID sets and drive types can produce as well as the performance enhancements that can be gained from storage tiering.

IOPS

IOPS is a measurement of how much data is provided over a period of time. It is usually expressed in bits per second (bps), bytes per second (Bps), megabytes per second (MBps), or gigabytes per second (GBps). Drives are typically rated regarding the IOPS they can support. Hard disk drives may provide values for average latency and average seek time, or those value can be computed from their spindle speed. The formula for IOPS is as follows:

IOPS = 1 / (average latency + average seek time)

For example, if a SATA drive running has an average latency of 3.2 ms and an average seek time of 4.7 ms, we would take 1 / (.0032 + .0047), which gives us 126.58, or 127 IOPS rounded to the nearest integer.

When drives are combined together into a RAID array, the RAID technology will utilize a combination of these IOPS. For example, a RAID 5 array of six drives, each with 127 IOPS, would provide 635 IOPS. The array would have five drives for striping and one for parity, so that is five times 127 to produce the 635 read IOPS. There is a difference between read and write IOPS, as will be explained next.

Read/Write Throughput

The RAID types chosen as well as the caching settings can determine how many IOPS will be produced by a logical volume. Read and write throughput are also expressed as either sequential reads or writes or random reads or writes. Sequential reads are when data is read from contiguous portions of the disk, while random reads are when data is read from various locations on the disk. It is more efficient to be able to pull data from contiguous portions of the disk because the drives do not need to spend as much time seeking for the data.

Caching can also have an impact on read and write IOPS. Caching settings can be optimized for reading or writing or a little of both. A cache can hold files that were recently requested in case they are requested again, improving read speeds when those files are fetched from cache instead of disk. Similarly, files can be placed in cache and then written to the disk when it is most efficient to store the data so that the application does not need to wait for the data to actually be written to the disk if it exists in the write cache. The four read/write throughput values are thus as follows:

- **Random read IOPS**   The average number of read I/O operations that can be performed per second when the data is scattered around the disk
- **Random write IOPS**   The average number of write I/O operations that can be performed per second when the data must be written to scattered portions of the disk
- **Sequential read IOPS**   The average number of read I/O operations that can be performed per second when the data is located in contiguous sections of the disk
- **Sequential write IOPS**   The average number of write I/O operations that can be performed per second when the data must be written to contiguous sections of the disk

Storage Tiers

Storage tiering is an essential part of storage optimization. Not all data will be requested all the time, and so it does not have to be treated the same way. Tiering combines multiple classes of storage into a single storage pool to intelligently satisfy storage demands. Higher-speed storage is used for the data that is most often needed or that the system predicts will be needed, while data that is requested less often is moved down to lower tiers.

For example, the highest-speed storage tier could be made up of 5TB of high-speed SLC SSD storage, while the second tier would be 10TB of lower-speed MLC SSD storage, the third tier 20TB of TLC SSD storage, and the fourth tier 50TB of 15k SAS storage, drives that spin at 15,000 rotations per minute. This is shown in Figure 3-3. The application would see an 85TB pool of storage available to it that is made up of these different types of storage. The storage system intelligently moves the data around on the different tiers so that data is most often served from the highest speed storage.

FIGURE 3-3

Tiered storage
pool

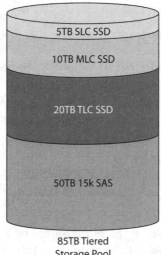

5TB SLC SSD

10TB MLC SSD

20TB TLC SSD

50TB 15k SAS

85TB Tiered
Storage Pool

exam
watch

Solid state storage was discussed in Chapter 2. There are three common types of SSDs in use today. Single-level cell (SLC) is the fastest but can store only one binary value in a cell, making it the SSD storage type with the smallest capacity. Looking at it another way, SLC has the highest cost per gigabyte. Multi-level cell (MLC) can store two binary values in each cell but is slower than SLC. Triple-level cell (TLC) is the slowest of the three, but it has the highest capacity because it can store three binary values per cell. This makes TLC the lowest cost per gigabyte in SSDs.

Logical Unit Numbers (LUNs)

Logical unit numbers, or LUNs (introduced earlier), have been around for a long time and were originally used to identify SCSI devices as part of a DAS solution for higher-end servers. Devices along the SCSI bus were assigned a number from 0 to 7, and SCSI 2 utilized 0 to 15, which designated the unique address for the computer to find that device. In storage networking, LUNs operate as unique identifiers, but now they are much more likely to represent a virtual hard disk from a block of allocated storage within a NAS device or a SAN. Devices that request I/O process are called initiators, and the devices that perform the operations requested by the initiators are called targets. Each target can hold up to eight other devices, and each of those devices is assigned a LUN.

Network Shares

Network shares are storage resources that are made available across the network and appear as if they are resources on the local machine. Traditionally, network shares are implemented using the Server Message Block (SMB) protocol when using Microsoft products and the network file system (NFS) protocol in Linux. It is also possible to share the same folder over NFS and SMB so that both Linux and Windows clients can access it. Access to these shares happens within an addressable file system as opposed to using block storage.

Zoning and LUN Masking

SANs are designed with high availability and performance in mind. In order to provide the flexibility that system administrators demand for designing solutions that utilize those capabilities, servers need to be able to mount and access any drive on the SAN. This flexible access can create several problems, including disk resource contention and data corruption. To mitigate these problems, storage devices can be isolated and protected on a SAN by utilizing zoning and LUN masking, which allow for dedicating storage on the SAN to individual servers.

Zoning controls access from one node to another. It enables isolation of a single server to a group of storage devices or a single storage device or associates a set of multiple servers with one or more storage devices. Zoning is implemented at the hardware level on Fibre Channel switches and is configured with what is referred to as "hard zoning" on a port basis or "soft zoning" using a WWN. In Figure 3-4, the Fibre Channel switch is controlling access to the red server and the blue server to connect to storage controllers 0–3. It grants access to the blue server to the LUNs on controllers 0 and 3, while the red server is granted access to all LUNs on all storage controllers.

LUN masking is executed at the storage controller level instead of at the switch level. By providing LUN-level access control at the storage controller, the controller itself enforces access policies to the devices. LUN masking provides more detailed security than zoning

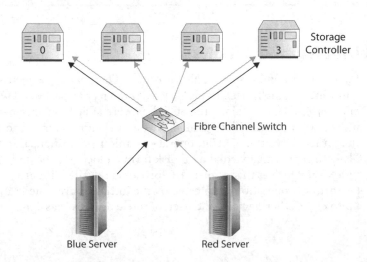

FIGURE 3-4

Zoning using a
Fibre Channel
switch

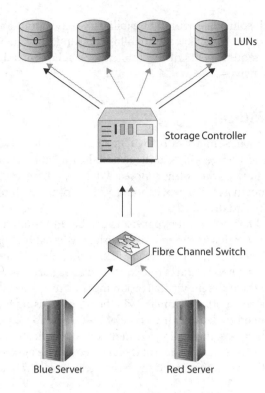

FIGURE 3-5

LUN masking
using the storage
controller

because LUNs allow for sharing storage at the port level. In Figure 3-5, LUN masking is demonstrated as the blue server is granted access from the storage controller to LUNs 0 and 3, while the red server is granted access to all LUNs.

Multipathing

Whereas zoning and LUN masking are configuration options that limit access to storage resources, multipathing is a way of making data more available or fault tolerant to the computers that need to access it. Multipathing does exactly what its name suggests, in that it creates multiple paths for the machine to reach the storage resources it is attempting to contact.

The redundant paths in multipathing are created by a combination of hardware and software resources. The hardware resources are multiple NICs, CNAs, or HBAs deployed to a single computer. These multiple adapters provide options for the software to run in multipath mode, which allows it to use either of the adapters to send traffic over in case one of them were to fail.

Setting up multipathing on the computer, however, is not enough to ensure high availability of the applications designed to run on it. The entire network infrastructure that the data traffic travels upon should be redundant so that a failure of any one component will not interrupt the storage data traffic. This means that in order to implement an effective multipath solution, redundant cabling, switches, routers, and ports on the storage devices must be considered as well. Enabling this kind of availability may be necessary to meet the business requirements of the applications being hosted, but such a configuration can be very expensive.

Provisioning Model

Cloud storage administrators will need to determine how to best provision storage depending on how the storage will be utilized and the available storage at hand. Some storage needs increase slowly, while others increase quickly. There are two options for provisioning storage. One is known as thick provisioning and the other as thin provisioning. Each has its own set of benefits and drawbacks.

Virtual hard disks on hypervisors can be provisioned as a thick disk or a thin disk. The size of a thick disk (termed a fixed disk in Microsoft Hyper-V) is specified and allocated during the creation of the virtual disk. A thin disk (termed a dynamically expanding disk in Microsoft Hyper-V) starts out small and adds space as required by the virtual machine.

While the different virtualization manufacturers use different terms to define their virtual disks, the concepts are similar. Whether you are using Hyper-V, VMware ESXi, or XenServer, you still need to decide which type of disk to use for which application. If you are concerned about disk space, then using a thin disk or dynamically expanding disk would be the best option. If size is not a concern, then you could use a fixed-size or thick disk.

Now that you understand the basics, let's look at thin and thick provisioning in more detail.

Thick Provisioning

Thick provisioning allocates the entire size of the logical drive upon creation. This means that the virtual disk is guaranteed and consumes whatever amount of disk space is specified during the creation of that virtual disk. Thin provisioning ensures that space will not be claimed by some other application and keeps the provisioned storage in contiguous space on the disk. Thick provisioning provides better performance because the drive size is not being built as the application requires more drive space. Thick provisioning is best suited for volumes that are expected to multiply in size or for those that require dedicated performance.

For example, a thick-provisioned volume of 400GB will consume 400GB of space on the storage system. This storage will be allocated entirely upon creation and made available to the system.

Thin Provisioning

Thin provisioning allocates only the space that is actually consumed by the volume. For example, a 400GB thin-provisioned volume will start off consuming zero bytes of storage. As data is written to the volume, the storage system will continue to allocate more storage out of a storage pool until the volume reaches its max of 400GB. This results in storage space that is allocated from wherever there is free space on the drive at the time it is needed, so not all space assigned to the thin-provisioned volume will be in contiguous space.

Thin provisioning does not have the same performance level as a thick disk and needs to be monitored closely to prevent running out of available disk space since storage space is by definition overcommitted.

When comparing thin and thick provisioning and considering which one works best in the organization's environment, it is important to keep a few things in mind. First, determine the performance requirements for the system, including the amount of data reads and writes you expect the system to perform. Each time new data is added to a thin-provisioned disk, space from the pool on which the thin-provisioned disk resides is allocated to the disk. This can lead to extensive fragmentation of the thin-provisioned volume if it grows frequently and rapidly. For example, an application that writes a lot of data to the drive, such as a database application, would not perform as well on a thin-provisioned disk. On the other hand, if space is a concern and a web server is not writing to the virtual disk that often, a thin-provisioned disk would be more appropriate.

Second, determine how often the data will grow. Excessive growth of thin-provisioned disks can fill up the storage pool on which the disks reside if overprovisioning, discussed next, is not properly controlled.

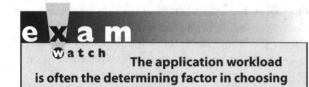

Storage Overprovisioning

Storage overprovisioning, also known as overcommitting or oversubscribing, is the process of creating multiple volumes using thin provisioning with a total maximum size that exceeds available storage. Overprovisioning is often done because some volumes will never utilize the maximum available, yet applications perform better when there is some space available for temporary data. However, storage administrators must monitor overprovisioned storage closely to ensure that it does not fill up and cause downtime to the systems that are provisioned from it.

Each of the major virtualization manufacturers have different terms when describing virtual disk configurations. For example, if you are using Microsoft Hyper-V, you would have the options of making a dynamically expanding virtual disk, a fixed virtual disk, or a differencing virtual disk. If you are creating a fixed-size disk, you would specify the size of the disk when it is created. If you are creating a dynamically expanding virtual disk, the disk starts at a small size and adds storage as needed.

Encryption Requirements

Disk encryption is quickly becoming a minimum requirement for regulated industries and for protecting the data of cloud consumers. Some customers require their volumes to be encrypted so that other tenants or the cloud provider cannot read their data.

Disk encryption takes an entire drive and converts it to a form that is unreadable unless the decryption key is provided. Disk encryption can be performed on local drives or removable media. The process is mostly transparent to the user. Users provide their decryption key when they log onto the computer and from that point on, files are encrypted when stored and decrypted when opened without additional interaction. Disk encryption is also referred to as full disk encryption (FDE). Some software-based disk encryption methods encrypt all contents but not the MBR, while hardware disk encryption methods are able to encrypt the contents and the MBR. Hardware disk encryption does not store the decryption key in memory. Drives encrypted with hardware disk encryption are also known as self-encrypting drives (SEDs). Many disk encryption systems support trusted platform module (TPM), a processor on the system mainboard that can authenticate the encrypted hard drive to the system to prevent an encrypted drive from being used on another system.

Some limitations of disk encryption include the fact that once a user is logged in, the entire disk is available to them. Malicious code or a lost password could allow access to the entire drive even if it is encrypted. Additionally, some disk encryption systems have been circumvented, including those with TPM, by stealing the keys stored in memory shortly after a cold shutdown (not a controlled shutdown) before memory data fully degrades. Still, disk encryption is overall an effective way to prevent unauthorized access to data stored on local drives and removable disks.

Tokenization

Tokenization can be used to separate sensitive data from storage media that does not have a high enough security classification. Tokens are identifiers that can be mapped to sensitive data. The token is just an identifier and cannot be used to create the data without interfacing with the tokenization system.

A system storing data on a cloud might store public data and then store a token in place of each sensitive data element, such as personally identifiable information (PII) or protected health information (PHI). The PII or PHI would be stored in the tokenization system, and the public cloud storage would retain the token for that information. When retrieving the data, the system would retrieve public data directly from the cloud storage, but would need to query the tokenization system to pull out the sensitive data, a process known as de-tokenization.

CERTIFICATION OBJECTIVE 3.04

Storage Protection

Storage protection guards against data loss, corruption, or unavailability. Users expect their data to be present when they request it, and loss of data is almost always considered unacceptable to cloud consumers. Storage protection must guard against equipment failures, site failures, user error, data corruption, malware, and other threats that could damage data integrity or availability.

High Availability

High availability (HA) refers to systems that are available almost 100 percent of the time. These systems are usually measured in terms of how many "nines" of availability they offer. For example, a system that offers 99.999 percent availability is offering five nines of availability. This equates to 5.39 minutes of downtime in a year.

HA systems achieve such availability through redundancy of components and sites. HA systems might also replicate data to multiple sites, co-locations (COLOs), or cloud services to protect against site failure or unavailability. Storage replication is discussed after failover zones.

Failover Zones

HA systems utilize clusters to divide operations across several systems. Some systems are active-active, where all systems can service application requests, whereas others are active-passive, where one or more systems services requests while one or more remain in a standby state until needed. Active-active systems must retain enough available resources to handle the remaining load if a system in the cluster becomes unavailable. This is known as N+1 redundancy because they can suffer the loss of one system.

HA systems require regular maintenance and yet, in the five-nines example, 5.39 minutes of downtime per year is hardly enough time to perform regular maintenance. HA systems accomplish this by performing upgrades to redundant equipment independently. In a cluster, the services on one cluster node are failed over to other cluster nodes. That node is upgraded, and then services are failed back to it. Maintenance or upgrades continue on the other nodes in the same fashion until all are upgraded. Throughout the process, the user does not experience any downtime. Clustering typically requires some level of shared storage where each node can access the same storage. When shared storage is not available, systems will use some form of replication to keep each system consistent with other systems. For example, when failover is performed across sites, replication is usually required in order to keep both sites consistent.

Storage Replication

Storage replication transfers data between two systems so that any changes to the data are made on each node in the replica set. A replica set consists of the systems that will all retain the same data. Multiple sites are used to protect data when a single site is unavailable and also to ensure low-latency availability by serving data from sources that are close to the end user or application.

Replication can be implemented as regional replication with redundant locations chosen in such a way that a disaster impacting one site would not impact the redundant site. Multiregional replication expands replication to many different sites in multiple regions.

Replication is performed synchronously or asynchronously. Synchronous replication writes data to the local store and then immediately replicates it to the replica set or sets.

The application is not informed that the data has been written until all replica sets have acknowledged receipt and storage of the data. Conversely, asynchronous replication stores the data locally and then reports back to the application that the data has been stored. It then sends the data to replication partners at its next opportunity.

Regional Replication

Regional replication uses replication to store data at a primary site and a secondary site. In regional replication, the secondary site is located in a different region from the primary site so that conditions impacting the primary site are less likely to impact the secondary site. Site unavailability is usually the result of a natural disaster such as a flood, fire, tornado, or hurricane. Many data centers are placed in regions where natural disasters are less common. For example, you will not find many data centers on the Florida coast. Not only is this land very expensive, but it is also prone to floods and hurricanes, which could render the site unavailable. Redundant sites are usually chosen in different regions that are far enough apart from one another that a single disaster will not impact both sites.

When implementing sites in different regions, also consider the power distribution method. Choose regions that are serviced by different power suppliers so that a disruption in the power network will not impact both sites.

Data will need to be replicated to these regions. This requires a connection between the data centers. This can be a leased line such as an MPLS network or dark fibre (fiber optic cable that is not owned and operated by a telco), or it could be a VPN tunnel over a high-speed Internet link. Ensure that the link between the sites will support the amount of replication data plus some overhead and room for spikes. Some Internet service providers will allow for a consistent data rate with bursting for the occasional large transfer. Bursting allows the connection to exceed the normal data transmission limits, but it comes at a charge from the ISP.

Multiregional Replication

Multiregional replication replicates data between many different sites in multiple regions. Replication schemes should be planned so that the entire replica set can be consistent with a minimum of effort and yet still provide redundancy in case of site link failures.

Each site typically has one or more replication partners, but they will not replicate with all sites. This is to save on bandwidth costs and latency since longer distance links will incur additional latency and cost more to operate. A hub-and-spoke model is often utilized with redundant links added in to protect against site link failure. This is depicted in Figure 3-6.

Synchronous and Asynchronous Replication

There are two forms of replication that can be used to keep replica sets consistent, synchronous and asynchronous. Synchronous replication writes data to the local store and then immediately replicates it to the replica set or sets. The application is not informed that the data has been written until all replica sets have acknowledged receipt and storage

FIGURE 3-6 Multiregional replication

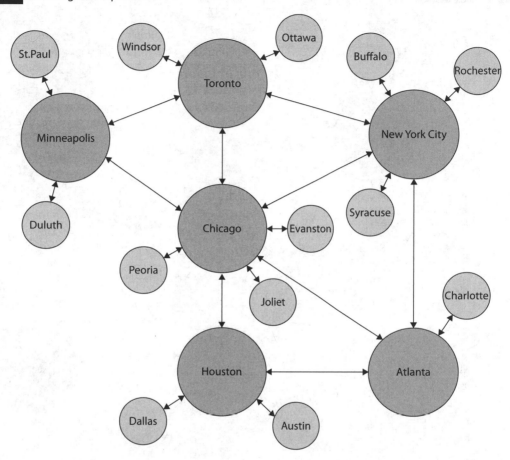

of the data. Asynchronous replication stores the data locally and then reports back to the application that the data has been stored. It then sends the data to replication partners at its next opportunity.

Synchronous replication requires high-speed, low-latency links in between sites in order to ensure adequate application performance. Synchronous replication ensures greater consistency between replication partners than asynchronous replication.

Asynchronous replication can tolerate fluctuations that are more significant in latency and bandwidth, but not all members of the replica set may be fully consistent in a timely manner if latency is high or bandwidth is low. This can lead to issues with multiple concurrent access from different sites that are dependent upon transactions being current. Figure 3-7 shows the multiregional replication scheme with a combination of asynchronous and synchronous replication. The sites that are farther away are using asynchronous replication, while the closer sites with lower latency are using synchronous replication.

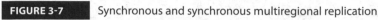

FIGURE 3-7   Synchronous and synchronous multiregional replication

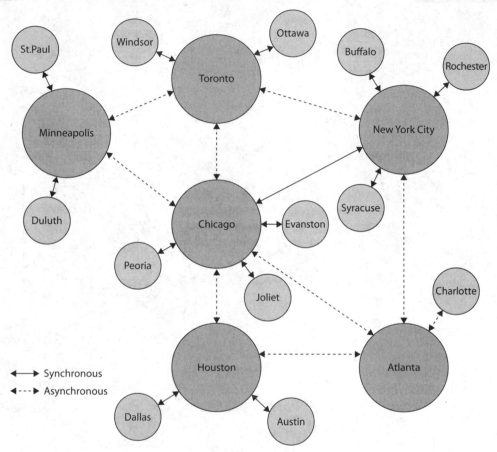

CERTIFICATION SUMMARY

Storage networking is an essential component of the CompTIA Cloud+ exam and it is the foundation of a successful cloud infrastructure. This chapter discussed storage types and technologies, how to connect storage to devices, how to provision storage and make it available to devices, and how to protect storage availability through replication and redundancy.

The chapter began with a discussion on storage types and technologies. Understanding when to use the different storage types is important for optimizing a cloud deployment. These include direct attached storage (DAS), consisting of one or more drives that are connected to a single machine to provide block-level storage; SAN storage that is made available to one or more machines at the block level; NAS shares that make data available to multiple machines at the file level; and object storage, a system that stores and retrieves data based on its metadata, not on its location within a hierarchy.

In addition to the four storage types, this section also covers two storage technologies. These technologies are deduplication and compression and they are designed to improve storage efficiency. Deduplication improves storage efficiency by removing unnecessarily redundant data while compression improves efficiency by decreasing the amount of storage required to store the data. Lossy compression results in some reduction in data quality, while lossless does not change the data when it is decompressed.

Storage needs to be connected to devices for it to be useful. The second section of this chapter provided details on storage connectivity. Connecting to storage can be simple, as in the case of DAS since it is connected to only one machine, but NAS and a SAN can involve complex networking to ensure adequate storage performance and reliability needed in today's cloud environments. This includes how devices are connected to storage networks or how NAS is connected to traditional networks as well as the benefits of each connection type. Connection types include FC, FCP, FCoE, Ethernet, IP, iFCP, and iSCSI.

The next section covered how storage is provisioned. The first step is to create storage that meets the performance requirements of the applications that will use it. SAN storage may be created from many disks and the portions that are carved out from those disks are called LUNs. Next, storage is made available only to the devices that need it through the use of zoning and LUN masking. There are some options when provisioning storage on how much space is allocated when new storage is created. Thin and thick provisioning offer two different methods to provision storage. Thick provisioning consumes all the allocated storage immediately, while thin provisioning allocates only what is actually used. Thin provisioning can help companies maximize capacity and utilization, but it can impact performance. Thick provisioning results in underutilized resources in order to offer more reliable performance.

The chapter closed with a discussion on some methods used to protect storage against data loss, corruption, or unavailability. The concept of high availability (HA) was presented first. HA systems are systems that are available almost 100 percent of the time. Next, storage replication was discussed. Storage replication transfers data between two systems so that any changes to the data are made on each node in the replica set. A replica set consists of the systems that will all retain the same data. Multiple sites are used to protect data when a single site is unavailable and also to ensure low-latency availability by serving data from sources that are close to the end user or application.

KEY TERMS

Use the following list to review the key terms discussed in this chapter. The definitions also can be found in the glossary.

asynchronous replication   The process of copying data between replica sets where applications are notified of successful writes when the data has been written to the local replica set. Other replicas are made consistent at the earliest convenience.

co-location (COLO) A facility owned and operated by a third party that houses technology assets such as servers, storage, backup systems, and networking equipment.

converged network adapter (CNA) A computer expansion card that can be used as a host bus adapter or a network interface card.

direct attached storage (DAS) Storage system that is directly attached to a server or workstation and cannot be used as shared storage at the block level because it is directly connected to a single machine.

failover Switching from one service node to another without an interruption in service.

Fibre Channel (FC) Technology used to transmit data between computers at data rates of up to 10 Gbps.

Fibre Channel over Ethernet (FCoE) Enables the transport of Fibre Channel traffic over Ethernet networks by encapsulating Fibre Channel frames over Ethernet networks.

Fibre Channel Protocol (FCP) Transport protocol that transports SCSI commands over a Fibre Channel network.

host bus adapter (HBA) A network card that allows a device to communicate directly with a storage area network (SAN) or a SAN switch.

initiator qualified name (IQN) The iSCSI address given to an initiator. Initiators reside on clients in an iSCSI network and initiators connect to targets such as storage resources over the iSCSI network. An IQN uses the following naming convention: iqn.yyyy-mm .naming-authority:unique name

input/output operations per second (IOPS) A measurement of how much data is provided over a period of time.

Internet Fibre Channel Protocol (iFCP) A communication protocol that enables the transport of Fibre Channel traffic over IP networks by translating FC addresses to IP addresses and FC frames to IP packets.

Internet Small Computer System Interface (iSCSI) The communication protocol that leverages standard IP packets to transmit typical SCSI commands across an IP network; it then translates them back to standard SCSI commands, which enables servers to access remote disks as if they were locally attached.

logical unit number (LUN)   Unique identifier used to identify a logical unit or collection of hard disks in a storage device.

LUN masking   Makes a LUN available to some hosts and unavailable to others.

multipathing   Creates multiple paths for a computer to reach a storage resource.

network attached storage (NAS)   Provides file-level data storage to a network over TCP/IP.

network shares   Storage resources that are made available across a network and appear as if they are a resource on the local machine.

overprovisioning   The process of creating multiple volumes using thin provisioning with a total maximum size that exceeds available storage.

Server Message Block (SMB)   Network protocol used to provide shared access to files and printers.

Session Control Protocol (SCP)   A protocol that manages multiple connections over TCP. SCP operates at layer 4 of the OSI model.

storage area network (SAN)   Storage device that resides on its own network and provides block-level access to computers that are attached to it.

synchronous replication   The process of copying data between replica sets where applications are notified of successful writes only when the data has been written to all synchronous replica sets.

thick provisioning   Allocates the entire size of the logical drive upon creation.

thin provisioning   Allocates only the space that is actually consumed by the volume.

tokenization   Replaces sensitive data with identifiers called tokens. De-tokenization returns the value associated with the token ID.

Transmission Control Protocol (TCP)   A protocol that provides reliable transport of network data through error checking. TCP uses ports that are associated with certain services and other ports that can be dynamically allocated to running processes and services. TCP is most often combined with IP.

trusted platform module (TPM)   A microprocessor that is dedicated to performing cryptographic functions. TPM are integrated into supporting systems and include features such as generation of cryptographic keys, random number generation, encryption, and decryption.

universal target adapter (UTA)   A proprietary network adapter from NetApp that is extremely versatile due to its use of transceivers. UTA has ports for one or more Ethernet or Fibre transceivers and can support Ethernet transceivers up to 10 Gbps and Fibre transceivers at native Fibre Channel speeds.

virtual SAN (VSAN)   Consolidating separate physical SAN fabrics into a single larger fabric, allowing for easier management while maintaining security.

world wide name (WWN)   Unique identifier used in storage technologies similar to Ethernet MAC addresses on a network card.

world wide node name (WWNN)   A unique identifier for a device on a Fibre Channel network.

world wide port name (WWPN)   A unique identifier for a port on a Fibre Channel network. A single device with a WWNN will have multiple WWPN if it has multiple Fibre Channel adapters or adapters with multiple ports.

world wide unique identifier (WWUI)   An address that is not used by other entities on a network and can represent only one entity.

zoning   Controls access from one node to another in a storage network and enables isolation of a single server to a group of storage devices or a single storage device.

 ## TWO-MINUTE DRILL

Storage Types and Technologies

❑ A direct attached storage (DAS) system is a storage system that is directly attached to a server or workstation and does not have a storage network between the two devices.

❑ A storage area network (SAN) is a storage device that resides on its own network and provides block-level access to computers that are attached to the SAN.

❑ Network attached storage (NAS) is a file-level data storage device that is connected to a computer network and provides data access to a group of clients.

❑ Object storage is a storage system that abstracts the location and replication of data, allowing the application to become more simplified and efficient. Object storage stores and retrieves data based on its metadata.

❑ Deduplication and compression storage technologies improve storage efficiencies. Deduplication does this by removing unnecessarily redundant data, while compression improves efficiency by decreasing the amount of storage required to store the data.

Storage Access Protocols

❑ Fibre Channel (FC) can be used to connect servers to shared storage devices with speeds of up to 10 Gbps.

❑ Fibre Channel frames can be encapsulated over Ethernet networks by utilizing Fibre Channel over Ethernet (FCoE) or over IP using iFCP.

❑ Ethernet is an established standard for connecting computers to a LAN. It is relatively inexpensive and can provide data speeds ranging from 10 Mbps to 10 Gbps.

❑ Internet Small Computer System Interface (iSCSI) utilizes serialized IP packets to transmit SCSI commands across IP networks and enables servers to access remote disks as if they were locally attached.

Storage Provisioning

❑ A logical unit number (LUN) is a unique identifier assigned to an individual hard disk device or collection of devices (a "logical unit") as addressed by the SCSI, iSCSI, or FC protocol.

❑ A LUN identifies a specific logical unit, which can be a portion of a hard disk drive, an entire hard disk, or several hard disks in a storage device like a SAN.

❑ A network share provides storage resources that are accessible over the network.

❑ Multipathing creates multiple paths for a computer to reach storage resources, providing a level of redundancy for accessing a storage device.

Storage Protection

❑ HA systems are systems that are available almost 100 percent of the time.

❑ HA systems utilize clusters to divide operations across several systems.

❑ Storage replication transfers data between two systems so that any changes to the data are made on each node in the replica set.

❏ Replication can be implemented as regional replication with redundant locations chosen in such a way that a disaster impacting one site would not impact the redundant site. Multiregional replication expands replication to many different sites in multiple regions.

❏ Replication is performed synchronously or asynchronously. Synchronous replication writes data to the local store and then immediately replicates it to the replica set or sets. Conversely, asynchronous replication stores the data locally and then reports back to the application that the data has been stored. It then sends the data to replication partners at its next opportunity.

SELF TEST

The following questions will help you measure your understanding of the material presented in this chapter. As indicated, some questions may have more than one correct answer, so be sure to read all the answer choices carefully.

Storage Types and Technologies

1. Which type of storage system is directly attached to a computer and does not use a storage network between the computer and the storage system?
   A. NAS
   B. SAN
   C. DAS
   D. Network share

2. Which of the following characteristics describe a network attached storage (NAS) deployment?
   A. Requires expensive equipment to support
   B. Requires specialized skill sets for administrators to support
   C. Delivers the best performance of any networked storage technologies
   D. Provides great value by utilizing existing infrastructure

3. Which statement would identify the primary difference between NAS and DAS?
   A. NAS cannot be shared and accessed by multiple computers.
   B. DAS provides fault tolerance.
   C. DAS does not connect to networked storage devices.
   D. NAS uses an HBA and DAS does not.

4. Which storage type can take advantage of Universal Naming Convention addressable storage?
    A. SAN
    B. NAS
    C. DAS
    D. SATA

5. Which storage type provides block-level storage?
    A. SAN
    B. NAS
    C. DAS
    D. SATA

6. Which of the following connects a server and a SAN and improves performance?
    A. Network interface card
    B. Host bus adapter
    C. Ethernet
    D. SCSI

Storage Access Protocols

7. Which of the following protocols allows Fibre Channel to be transmitted over Ethernet?
    A. HBA
    B. FCoE
    C. iSCSI
    D. SAN

8. Which of the following is considered a SAN protocol?
    A. FCP
    B. IDE
    C. SSD
    D. DTE

9. Which of the following allows you to connect a server to storage devices with speeds of 128 Gbps?
    A. Ethernet
    B. iSCSI
    C. Fibre Channel
    D. SAS

10. Which of the following uses IP networks that enable servers to access remote disks as if they were locally attached?
    A. SAS
    B. SATA
    C. iSCSI
    D. Fibre Channel

Storage Provisioning

11. Warren is a systems administrator working in a corporate data center, and he has been tasked with hiding storage resources from a server that does not need access to the storage device hosting the storage resources. What can Warren configure on the storage controller to accomplish this task?
    A. Zoning
    B. LUN masking
    C. Port masking
    D. VLANs

12. Which of the following would increase availability from a virtualization host to a storage device?
    A. Trunking
    B. Multipathing
    C. Link aggregation
    D. VLANs

13. Which of the following allows you to provide security to the data contained in a storage array?
    A. Trunking
    B. LUN masking
    C. LUN provisioning
    D. Multipathing

14. Which provisioning model would you use if data is added quickly and often? The solution must ensure consistent performance.
    A. Thin provisioning
    B. Thick provisioning
    C. Overprovisioning
    D. Encryption

Storage Protection

15. Which HA solution involves multiple servers that each service requests concurrently, but can assume the load of one member if that member fails.
    A. Active-passive
    B. Active-active
    C. Passive-passive
    D. Passive-active

16. Which of the following are requirements for adequate application performance when using synchronous replication? (Choose two.)
    A. Object storage
    B. Low latency
    C. Multipathing
    D. High-speed links

A SELF TEST ANSWERS

Storage Types and Technologies

1. ☑ **C.** DAS is a storage system that directly attaches to a server or workstation without a storage network in between the devices.
☒ **A, B,** and **D** are incorrect. NAS provides file-level storage that is connected to a network and supplies data access to a group of devices. A SAN is a dedicated network and provides access to block-level storage. A network share is a storage resource on a computer that can be accessed remotely from another computer.

2. ☑ **D.** Network attached storage can utilize existing Ethernet infrastructures to deliver a low-cost solution with good performance.
☒ **A, B,** and **C** are incorrect. Expensive and often proprietary hardware and software along with systems administrators with specialized skill sets are required to run storage area networks. Storage area networks, although more expensive to build and support, provide the best possible performance for storage networking.

3. ☑ **C.** DAS is a storage system that directly attaches to a server or workstation without a storage network in between the devices.
☒ **A, B,** and **D** are incorrect. NAS can be shared and accessed by multiple computers over a network. DAS would not provide fault tolerance since it is connected to a single server, and neither NAS nor DAS technologies utilize HBAs as a part of their solution.

4. ☑ **B.** NAS appears to the client operating system as a file server, which allows it to use Universal Naming Convention addressable storage.
☒ **A, C,** and **D** are incorrect. A SAN only provides storage at a block level. DAS is directly attached to a server and is accessed directly from an indexed file system. SATA is an interface technology, not a storage type.

5. ☑ **A.** A SAN is a storage device that resides on its own network and provides block-level access to computers that are attached to it.
☒ **B, C,** and **D** are incorrect. NAS provides file-level storage. DAS is not accessible over a storage network. SATA is an interface technology, not a storage type.

6. ☑ **B.** An HBA card connects a server to a storage device and improves performance by offloading the processing required for the host to consume the storage data without having to utilize its own processor cycles.
☒ **A, C,** and **D** are incorrect. A network interface card connects a computer to an Ethernet network or an iSCSI network but does not improve performance. Ethernet and SCSI would not improve performance, because they cannot offload the processing for the host computer to connect to the storage device.

Storage Access Protocols

7. ☑ **B.** Fibre Channel over Ethernet (FCoE) enables the transport of Fibre Channel traffic over Ethernet networks by encapsulating Fibre Channel frames over Ethernet networks.

☒ **A, C,** and **D** are incorrect. iSCSI is a protocol that utilizes serialized IP packets to transmit SCSI commands across IP networks and enables servers to access remote disks as if they were locally attached. A SAN is a storage technology and an HBA is an adapter used to improve the performance of a SAN. They are not protocols.

8. ☑ **A.** The Fibre Channel Protocol is a transport protocol that transports SCSI commands over a Fibre Channel network. These networks are used exclusively to transport data in FC frames between storage area networks and the HBAs attached to servers.

☒ **B, C,** and **D** are incorrect. IDE is used to connect devices to a computer. SSD is a type of hard drive. DTE stands for "data terminal equipment." A computer is an example of DTE.

9. ☑ **C.** You can use Fibre Channel (FC) to connect servers to shared storage devices with speeds of up to 128 Gbps. FC also comes in 64, 32, 16, 8, 4, and 2 Gbps versions.

☒ **A, B,** and **D** are incorrect. Ethernet and iSCSI have max transmission speeds of 10 Gbps running over 10GigE. SAS has a max speed of 12 Gbps, and 22.5 Gbps is in the works.

10. ☑ **C.** iSCSI utilizes serialized IP packets to transmit SCSI commands across IP networks and enables servers to access remote disks as if they were locally attached.

☒ **A, B,** and **D** are incorrect. SAS and SATA do not allow you to connect to remote disks as if they were locally attached to the system. Fibre Channel utilizes the Fibre Channel Protocol to transmit data packets to SANs across a fabric of fiber-optic cables, switches, and HBAs.

Storage Provisioning

11. ☑ **B.** LUN masking is executed at the storage controller level instead of at the switch level. By providing LUN-level access control at the storage controller, the controller itself enforces access policies to the devices, making it more secure. This is the reason that physical access to the same device storing the LUNs remains "untouchable" by the entity using it.

☒ **A, C,** and **D** are incorrect. LUN masking provides more detailed security than zoning because LUNs allows for sharing storage at the port level. Port masking occurs at the switch level instead of the controller, and VLANs are also not modified at the controller. VLANs are discussed in Chapter 4.

12. ☑ **B.** Multipathing creates multiple paths for the computer to reach the storage resources it is attempting to contact, improving fault tolerance and possibly speed.

☒ **A, C,** and **D** are incorrect. Trunking provides network access to multiple clients by sharing a set of network lines instead of providing them individually. Link aggregation combines multiple network connections in parallel to increase throughput. VLANs do not have any effect on increasing availability to storage resources.

13. ☑   **B.** LUN masking enforces access policies to storage resources, and these storage policies make sure that the data on those devices is protected from unauthorized access.
☒   **A, C,** and **D** are incorrect. Trunking provides network access to multiple clients by sharing a set of network lines instead of providing them individually. LUN provisioning does the opposite of LUN masking by making LUNs available for data access, and multipathing creates multiple paths for the computer to reach the storage resources that it is attempting to contact.

14. ☑   **B.** Thick provisioning would consume all the allocated space upon creation of the LUN, but performance would be consistent for a LUN that expects data to be added quickly and often because storage would not need to be continually allocated to the LUN and the storage would not be fragmented.
☒   **A, C,** and **D** are incorrect. Thin provisioning saves space but can result in lower performance when there are frequent writes. Overprovisioning is the allocation of more space than is available in the storage pool. It requires thin provisioning, so it is also incorrect. Encryption would increase security but it would come at a cost to performance and this question is asking about performance, not security.

Storage Protection

15. ☑   **B.** Active-active solutions allow for all systems to service application requests.
☒   **A, C,** and **D** are incorrect. Active-passive solutions involve one or more systems that service requests while one or more remain in a standby state until needed. Passive-passive and passive-active are not HA types.

16. ☑   **B** and **C.** Synchronous replication requires high-speed, low-latency links in between sites in order to ensure adequate application performance.
☒   **A** and **D** are incorrect. Object storage allows data to be retrieved based on its metadata, and multipathing provides more than one connection to a node. Neither of these would be required for synchronous replication.

Chapter 4

Network Infrastructure

N etwork configuration is an integral piece of cloud computing and is key to cloud computing performance. One of the factors an organization must consider is the impact of networking on cloud computing performance and the differences that exist between their current network infrastructure and what would be utilized in a cloud computing infrastructure.

This chapter introduces you to networking components that are used in cloud computing. After reading this chapter, you should understand the different types of networks and how to optimize an organization's network for cloud computing. You will also learn how network traffic is routed between the various cloud models and how to secure that traffic. And you will find out about the different network protocols used in cloud computing and when to use those protocols. It is important for you to have a thorough understanding of these topics for the exam. Those who have passed the Network+ exam might possibly skip this chapter. Read the Certification Summary and the Two-Minute Drill sections to make sure everything covered in this chapter is familiar to you before deciding to skip it.

CERTIFICATION OBJECTIVE 4.01

Network Types

A network is defined as a group of interconnected computers and peripherals that are capable of sharing resources, including software, hardware, and files. The purpose of a network is to provide users with access to information that multiple people might need to perform their day-to-day job functions.

There are numerous advantages for an organization to construct a network. It allows users to share files so that multiple users can access them from a single location. An organization can share resources such as printers, fax machines, storage devices, and even scanners, thus reducing the total number of resources they have to purchase and maintain. A network also allows for applications to be shared by multiple users as long as the application is designed for this and the appropriate software licensing is in place.

There are three types of networks: intranet, Internet, and extranet. They all rely on the same Internet protocols but have different levels of access for users inside and outside the organization. This section describes each of these network types and when to use them.

Intranet

An intranet is a private network based on the Internet Protocol (IP) that is configured and controlled by a single organization and is only accessible to users that are internal to that particular organization. An intranet can host multiple private websites and is usually the focal point for internal communication and collaboration.

An intranet allows an organization to share information and websites within the organization and is protected from external access by a firewall or a network gateway.

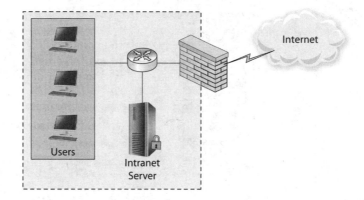

FIGURE 4-1

An intranet network configuration, where access is private

For example, an organization may want to share announcements, the employee handbook, confidential financial information, or organizational procedures with its employees but not with people outside the organization.

An intranet is very similar to the Internet except an intranet is restricted to specific users. For example, a web page that is designed for the intranet may have a similar look and feel like any other website that is on the Internet, the only difference being who is authorized to access the web page. Public web pages that are accessible over the Internet are typically available to everyone, whereas an intranet is owned and controlled by the organization and that organization decides who can access that web page. Figure 4-1 shows an example of an intranet configuration.

Internet

The Internet is a global system of interconnected computer networks that use the same Internet protocols (TCP/IP) as an intranet network uses. Unlike an intranet, which is controlled by and serves only one organization, the Internet is not controlled by a single organization and serves billions of users around the world. The Internet is a network of multiple networks relying on network devices and common protocols to transfer data from one intermediate destination (sometimes called a hop) to another until it reaches its final destination.

Aside from a few countries that impose restrictions on what people in their country can view, the Internet is largely unregulated, and anyone can post or read whatever they want on the Internet. The Internet Corporation for Assigned Names and Numbers (ICANN) is a nonprofit organization that was created to coordinate the Internet's system of unique identifiers, including domain names and IP addresses.

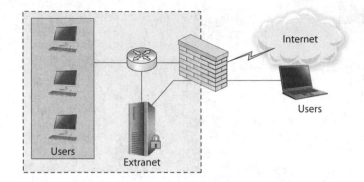

FIGURE 4-2

An extranet
network
configuration,
where outside
access is limited

Extranet

An extranet is an extension of an Intranet, with the primary difference that an extranet allows controlled access from outside the organization. An extranet permits access to outside users with the use of firewalls, access profiles, and privacy protocols. It allows an organization to share resources with other businesses securely. For example, an organization could use an extranet to sell its products and services online or to share information with business partners.

Both intranets and extranets are owned and supported by a single organization. The way to differentiate between an intranet and an extranet is by who has access to the private network and the geographical reach of that network. Figure 4-2 shows an example configuration of an extranet network.

w a t c h   **The difference between an intranet and an extranet is that an intranet does not allow access to resources from outside the organization.**

Network Optimization

Now that you know about the different types of networks, you need to understand the components of those networks and how they can be optimized. In this section, you will learn about the components that make up intranet and extranet networks and how to configure them so that they perform most efficiently.

Network optimization is the process of keeping a network operating at peak efficiency. To keep the network running at peak performance, an administrator must perform a variety of tasks, including updating the firmware and operating system on routers and switches, identifying and resolving data flow bottlenecks, and monitoring network utilization. By keeping the network optimized, a network administrator as well as cloud providers can more accurately meet the terms of the organization's SLA.

Network Scope

The scope of a network defines its boundaries. The largest network on Earth was described earlier. It is the Internet, but millions of other networks span organizational or regional boundaries. The terms LAN, MAN, and WAN are used to differentiate these networks.

LAN

A local area network (LAN) is a network topology that spans a relatively small area like an office building. A LAN is a great way for people to share files, devices, pictures, and applications and is primarily Ethernet based.

There are three different data rates of modern Ethernet networks:

- **Fast Ethernet** Transfers data at a rate of 100 Mbps (megabits per second)
- **Gigabit Ethernet** Transfers data at 1,000 Mbps
- **10 Gigabit Ethernet** Transfers data at 10,000 Mbps

MAN

A metropolitan area network (MAN) is very similar to a LAN except that a MAN spans a city or a large campus. A MAN usually connects multiple LANs and is used to build networks with high data connection speeds for cities or college campuses. MANs are efficient and fast because they use high-speed data carriers such as fiber optics.

WAN

A wide area network (WAN) is a network that covers a large geographic area and can contain multiple LANs or MANs. WANs are not restricted by geographic areas. The Internet is an example of the largest WAN. Some corporations use leased lines to create a corporate WAN that spans a large geographic area containing locations in multiple states or even countries.

on the
ϳob

Working for a large organization with regional offices all across the United States, we were tasked with setting up a WAN. The company's offices ranged from 5 to 100 or more employees. To accommodate their needs, we set up a VPN connection using leased Internet lines at each location to connect into a central data center. This allowed every employee to connect into the data center and share resources no matter where their physical location.

Network Topologies

How the different nodes, or devices, in a network are connected and how they communicate is determined by the network's topology. The network topology is the blueprint of the connections of a computer network and can be either physical or logical. Physical topology refers to the design of the network's physical components: computers, switches, cable installation, and so on. Logical topology can be thought of as a picture of how the data flows within a network.

As an IT professional, you need to understand the pros and cons of the different network topologies when you are building and designing a network. After evaluating the needs of the organization, you can then choose the most efficient topology for the intended purpose of the network. The primary physical topologies to be considered are bus, star, ring, mesh, and tree.

Bus

In a bus topology, every node is connected to a central cable, referred to as the bus or backbone. In a bus topology, only one device is allowed to transmit at any given time. Since a bus topology uses a single cable, it is easy to set up and cost-effective.

The bus topology is not recommended for large networks because of the limitations to the number of nodes that can be configured on a single cable. Troubleshooting a bus topology is much more difficult than troubleshooting a star topology because in a bus topology you have to determine where the cable was broken or removed. In a star topology, the central device offers a simple place to conduct troubleshooting. Figure 4-3 shows an example of a network configured to use a bus topology.

Star

In a star topology, each node is connected to a central hub or switch, and the nodes communicate by sending data through the central hub. In a star topology, new nodes can easily be added or removed without impacting the rest of the nodes on the network.

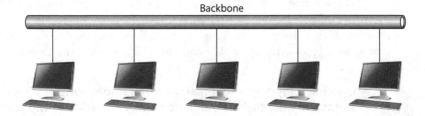

FIGURE 4-3

Network configuration using a bus topology

Backbone

FIGURE 4-4

Network
configuration
using a star
topology

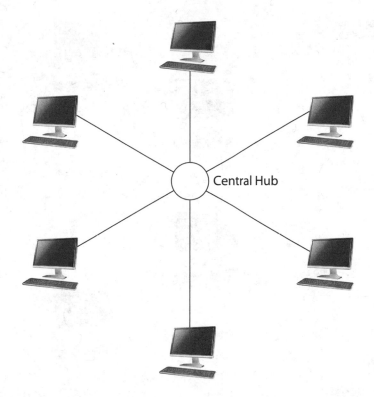

Central Hub

The star topology offers improved performance over a bus topology. The star topology is also more resilient than a bus topology because failure of one node does not affect the rest of the network. Problematic nodes can be easily isolated by unplugging that particular node; if the problem disappears, it can be concluded that it is related to that node, making troubleshooting much simpler in a star topology.

The main drawback to the star topology is that if the central hub or switch fails, all the nodes connected to it are disconnected and unable to communicate with the other nodes. Figure 4-4 shows an example of a network configured to use a star topology.

Ring

In a ring topology, each node is connected to another, forming a circle or a ring. Each packet is sent around the ring until it reaches its target destination. The ring topology is hardly used in today's enterprise environment because all network connectivity is lost if one of the links in the network path is broken. Figure 4-5 shows an example of a network configured to use a ring topology.

FIGURE 4-5

FIGURE 4-5

Network
configuration
using a ring
topology

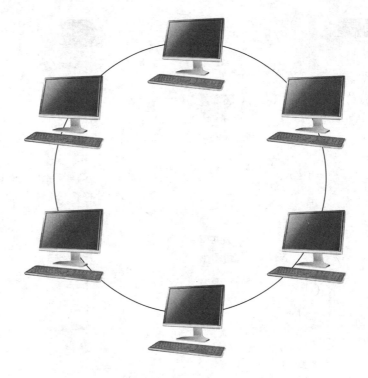

Mesh

In a true mesh topology, every node is interconnected to every other node in the network, allowing transmissions to be distributed even if one of the connections goes down. A mesh topology is, however, difficult to configure and expensive to implement and is not commonly used. It is the most fault tolerant of the physical topologies, but it requires the most amount of cable. Since cabling is expensive, the cost must be weighed against the fault tolerance achieved. Figure 4-6 shows an example of a network configured to use a mesh topology.

FIGURE 4-6

Network
configuration
using a mesh
topology

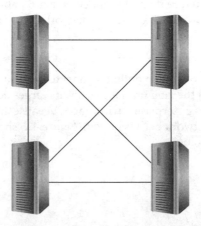

Note that most real-world implementations of a mesh network are actually a partial mesh where additional redundancy is added to the topology without incurring the expense of connecting everything to everything.

Tree

In a tree topology, multiple star networks are connected through a linear bus backbone. As you can see in Figure 4-7, if the backbone cable between the two star networks fails, those two networks would no longer be able to communicate; however, the computers on the same star network would still maintain communication with each other. The tree topology is the most commonly used configuration in today's enterprise environment.

Bandwidth and Latency

Now that you understand the different network topologies that you can configure, you need to know what other factors affect network performance. When moving to the cloud, network performance is crucial to the success of your deployment because the data is stored off-site. Two of the necessities to determining network performance are bandwidth and network latency. Bandwidth is the speed of the network. Network latency is the time delay that is encountered while data is being sent from one point to another on the network.

There are two types of latency: low latency and high latency. A low-latency network connection is a connection that experiences very small delays while sending and receiving traffic. A high-latency network has long delays while sending and receiving traffic. Network latency, when it is excessive, can create bottlenecks that prevent data from using the maximum capacity of the network bandwidth, thereby decreasing the effective bandwidth.

FIGURE 4-7

Network configuration using a tree topology

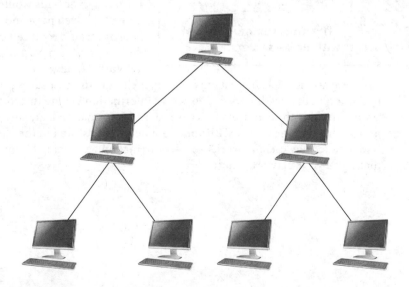

Compression

Compression is defined as the reduction in the size of data that is traveling across the network, which is achieved by converting that data into a format that requires fewer bits for the same transmission. Compression is typically used to minimize required storage space or to reduce the amount of data transmitted over the network. When using compression to reduce the size of data that is being transferred, a network engineer sees a decrease in transmission times since there is more bandwidth available for other data to use as it traverses the network. Compression can result in higher processor utilization because a packet must be compressed and decompressed as it traverses the network.

Network compression can automatically compress data before it is sent over the network to help improve performance, especially where bandwidth is limited. Maximizing the compression ratio is vital to improving application performance on networks with limited bandwidth. Compression can play a key role in cloud computing. As an organization migrates to the cloud network, compression is vital in controlling network latency and maximizing network bandwidth.

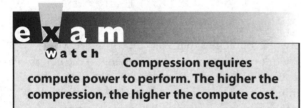

e x a m

⟳ a t c h　　**Compression requires compute power to perform. The higher the compression, the higher the compute cost.**

Caching

Caching is the process of storing frequently accessed data in a location closer to the device that is requesting the data. For example, a web cache could store web pages and web content either on the physical machine that is accessing the website or on a storage device like a proxy server. This would increase the response time of the web page and reduce the amount of network traffic required to access the website, thus improving network speed and reducing network latency.

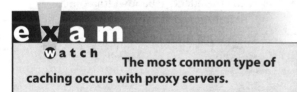

e x a m

⟳ a t c h　　**The most common type of caching occurs with proxy servers.**

There are multiple benefits to caching, including the cost savings that comes with the reduction of bandwidth needed to access information via the Internet and the improved productivity of the end users (because cached information loads significantly faster than non-cached information). With your data now being stored in the cloud, it is important to understand how caching works and how to maximize caching to improve performance and maximize your network bandwidth.

Load Balancing

Throughout this section, we have discussed the importance of optimizing network traffic and infrastructure. In order to optimize network traffic, the data must be routed as efficiently as possible. For example, if an organization's network has five routers and three of them are running at 5 percent, and the other two are running at 90 percent, the network utilization is not as efficient as it possibly could be. If each of the routers were running at 20 percent utilization, it would improve network performance and limit network latency. The same could be said for a website that is getting thousands of hits every minute; it would be more efficient if the traffic were split between multiple web servers that are part of a web farm. This would increase performance and remove the single point of failure connected with having only one server respond to the requests.

Load balancing is the process of distributing incoming HTTP or application requests evenly across multiple devices or web servers so that no single device is overwhelmed. Load balancing allows for achieving optimal resource utilization and maximizing throughput without overloading a single device. Load balancing increases reliability by creating redundancy for your application or website by using dedicated hardware or software. Figure 4-8 shows an example of how load balancing works for web servers.

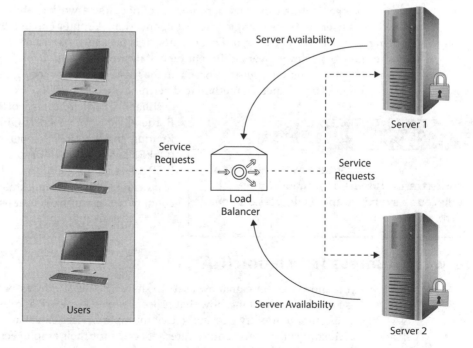

FIGURE 4-8

An illustration of load balancing

CERTIFICATION OBJECTIVE 4.03

Routing and Switching

We have discussed the different options and configurations that are available for setting up a network. Now let's explore how to route traffic to and from networks. Knowing how a network operates is the most important piece to understanding routing and switching. In the previous section, you learned that a network operates by connecting computers and devices in a variety of different physical configurations. Routers and switches are the networking devices that enable other devices on the network to connect and communicate with each other and with other networks. They are placed on the same physical network as the other devices.

While routers and switches may give the impression they are rather similar, the devices are responsible for very different operations on a network. A switch is used to connect multiple devices to the same network or LAN. For example, a switch connects computers, printers, servers, and a variety of other devices and allows those devices to share network resources with each other. This makes it possible for users to share resources, saving valuable time and money for the organization. A router, on the other hand, is used to connect multiple networks together and allows a network to communicate with the outside world. An organization would use a router to connect its network to the Internet, thus allowing its users to share a single Internet connection. A router can analyze the data that is being sent over the network and change how it is packaged so that it can be routed to another network or even over a different type of network.

A router makes routing decisions based on the routing protocol configured on it. Each routing protocol uses a specific method to determine the best path a packet can take to its destination. Some routing protocols include Border Gateway Protocol (BGP), Interior Gateway Routing Protocol (IGRP), open shortest path first (OSPF), and Routing Information Protocol (RIP). BGP uses rule sets, IGRP uses delay, load, and bandwidth, OSPF uses link state, and RIP uses hop count to make routing decisions.

w a t c h **A router has the ability to route traffic outside of your local network, whereas a switch connects devices on your internal network.**

Network Address Translation (NAT)

Now that you know a router can allow users to share a single IP address when browsing the Internet, you need to understand how that process works. Network address translation, or NAT, allows a router to modify packets so that multiple devices can share a single public IP address. Most organizations require Internet access for their employees but do not have enough valid public IP addresses to allow each individual to have his or her own public address to locate resources outside of the organization's network. The primary purpose of NAT is to limit the number of public IP addresses an organization needs.

NAT allows outbound Internet access, including for cloud-based virtual machines, but prevents inbound connections initiated from the Internet directly to inside machines or cloud-based virtual machines, which route through the NAT devices as their default gateway.

For example, most organizations use a private IP address range, which allows the devices on the network to communicate with all the other devices on the network and in turn makes it possible for users to share files, printers, and the like. But if those users need to access anything outside the network, they would require a public IP address. If Internet queries originate from various internal devices, the organization would need to have a valid public IP address for each device. NAT consolidates the addresses needed for each internal device to a single valid public IP address, allowing all of the organization's employees to access the Internet with the use of a single public IP address.

To fully understand this concept, you first need to know what makes an IP address private and what makes an IP address public. Any IP address that falls into one of the IP address ranges that are reserved for private use by the Internet Engineering Task Force (IETF) is considered to be a private IP address. Table 4-1 lists the different private IP address ranges.

A private network that adheres to the IETF published standard RFC 1918 is a network address space that is not used or allowed on the public Internet. These addresses are commonly used in a home or corporate network or LAN when a public IP address or globally routed address is not required on each device. Because these address ranges are not made available as public IP addresses, and consequently are never assigned specifically for use to any organization, they receive the designation of "private" IP addresses. IP packets that are addressed by private IP addresses cannot be transmitted onto the public Internet over the backbone.

There are two reasons for the recent surge in using RFC 1918 addresses: one is that Internet Protocol version 4 (IPv4) address space is rapidly diminishing, and the other is that a significant security enhancement is achieved by providing address translation, whether it is NAT or PAT (described shortly) or a combination of the two. A perpetrator on the Internet cannot directly access a private IP address without the administrator taking significant steps to relax the security. A NAT router is sometimes referred to as a poor man's firewall. In reality, it is not a firewall at all, but it shields the internal network (individuals using private addresses) from attacks and from what is sometimes referred to as Internet background radiation (IBR).

In order to access resources that are external to its network, an organization is required to have at least one "routable" or public IP address. This is where NAT comes into play. NAT allows a router to change the private IP address into a public IP address so that the organization can access resources that are external to it; then the NAT router tracks those IP address changes. When the external information being requested comes back to

TABLE 4-1			
Private IP Addresses	**Address Range**	**Usable IPs**	**Network Class**
	10.0.0.0–10.255.255.255	16,777,216	Class A network
	172.16.0.0–172.31.255.255	1,048,576	Class B network
	192.168.0.0–192.168.255.255	65,536	Class C network
	169.254.0.0–169.254.255.255	65,534	Class B network

the router, the router changes the IP address from a public IP address to a private IP address so that it can forward the traffic back to the requesting device. Essentially, NAT allows a single device like a router to act as an agent or a go-between for a private network and the Internet. NAT provides the benefits of saving public IP addresses, higher security, and ease of administration.

In addition to public and private IP addresses, there is also automatic private IP addressing (APIPA; sometimes called Autoconfig), which enables a Dynamic Host Configuration Protocol (DHCP) client to receive an IP address even if it cannot communicate with a DHCP server. APIPA addresses are "nonroutable" over the Internet and allocate an IP address in the private range of 169.254.0.1–169.254.255.254. APIPA uses Address Resolution Protocol (ARP) to verify that the IP address is unique in the network.

e x a m

w a t c h You need to be able to quickly identify a private IP address, so it is advantageous to memorize the first octet of the IP ranges (i.e., 10, 172, and 192).

Port Address Translation (PAT)

Similar to NAT, port address translation (PAT) allows for mapping of private IP addresses to public IP addresses as well as for mapping multiple devices on a network to a single public IP address. Its goal is the same as that of NAT: to conserve public IP addresses. PAT enables the sharing of a single public IP address between multiple clients trying to access the Internet.

A good example of PAT is a home network where multiple devices are trying to access the Internet at the same time. In this instance, your ISP would assign your home network's router a single public IP address. On this network, you could have multiple computers or devices trying to access the Internet at the same time using the same router. When device Y logs on to the Internet, it is assigned a port number that is appended to the private IP address.

This gives device Y a unique IP address. If device Z were to log on to the Internet at the same time, the router would assign the same public IP address to device Z but with a different port number. The two devices are sharing the same public IP address to browse the Internet, but the router distributes the requested content to the appropriate device based on the port number the router has assigned to that particular device.

e x a m

w a t c h Basic NAT provides a one-to-one mapping of IP addresses, whereas PAT provides a many-to-one mapping of IP addresses.

Subnetting and Supernetting

Subnetting is the practice of creating subnetworks, or subnets. A subnet is a logical subdivision of an IP network. Using subnets may be useful in large organizations where it is necessary to allocate address space efficiently. They may also be utilized to increase routing efficiency, and offer improved controls for network management when different networks require separation of administrator control for different entities in a large or multitenant environment. Inter-subnet traffic is exchanged by routers, just as it would be exchanged between physical networks.

All computers that belong to a particular subnet are addressed with the use of two separate bit groups in their IP address, with one group designating the subnet and the other group designating the particular host on that subnet. The routing prefix of the address can be expressed in either classful notation or classless inter-domain routing (CIDR) notation. CIDR has become the most popular routing notation method in recent years. This notation is written as the first address of a network, followed by a slash (/), then finishing with the bit length of the prefix. To use a typical example, 192.168.1.0/24 is the prefix of the network starting at the given address, having 24 bits allocated for the network prefix and the remaining 8 bits reserved for host addressing. An allocation of 24 bits is equal to the subnet mask for that network, which you may recognize as the familiar 255.255.255.0.

As subnetting is the practice of dividing one network into multiple networks, supernetting does the exact opposite, combining multiple networks into one larger network. Supernetting is most often utilized to combine multiple class C networks. It was created to solve the problem of routing tables growing too large for administrators to manage by aggregating networks under one routing table entry. It also provided a solution to the problem of class B network address space running out.

In much the same fashion as subnetting, supernetting takes the IP address and breaks it down into a network bit group and a host identifier bit group. It also uses CIDR notation. The way to identify supernetted networks is that the network prefix is always lower than 23, which allows for a greater number of hosts (on the larger network) to be specified in the host bit group.

Network Segmentation and Micro-Segmentation

Network segmentation and micro-segmentation are techniques to divide the network into smaller pieces to isolate or better control traffic and to apply more granular policies to those network segments. Both segmentation and micro-segmentation can be used to reduce the spread of malicious code or make attacks harder, as attackers will need to figure out how to move between network segments before they can attack nodes in another segment.

Virtual Local Area Network (VLAN)

A virtual local area network, or VLAN, is the concept of partitioning a physical network to create separate, independent broadcast domains that are part of the same physical network. VLANs are very similar to physical LANs but add the ability to break up physical networks into logical groupings of networks all within the same physical network.

VLANs were conceived out of the desire to create logical separation without the need for additional physical hardware (i.e., network cards, wiring, and routers). VLANs can even traverse physical networks, forming a logical network or VLAN even if the devices exist on separate physical networks. With the use of a virtual private network (VPN), which extends a private network over a public network such as the Internet, a VLAN can even traverse the entire Internet. For example, you could implement a VLAN to place only certain end users inside the VLAN to help control broadcast traffic.

VLAN tagging is the process of inserting a 4-byte header directly after the destination address and the source address of the Ethernet frame header. There are two types of VLAN tagging mechanisms: Inter-Switch Link (ISL), which is proprietary to Cisco equipment, and IEEE 802.1Q, which is supported by everyone including Cisco and is usually the VLAN option of choice. Utilizing the IEEE 802.1Q protocol, approximately 4,095 different VLAN IDs can be achieved on the same physical network segment (depending on what is supported by the switch and router devices).

A VLAN is usually associated with an IP subnet, so all the devices in that IP subnet belong to the same VLAN. In order to configure a VLAN, you must first create a VLAN and then bind the interface and IP address to it. VLANs must be routed, and there are various methods for assigning VLAN membership to switch ports. Switch ports can be assigned membership to a particular VLAN on a port-by-port basis manually; they can be dynamically configured from a VLAN membership policy server that tracks MAC addresses and their associated VLANs for port configuration; or they can be classified based on their IP address if the packets are untagged or priority tagged.

on the   **One of the organizations we worked for was a small college that had multiple**
ȯ ob   **training rooms and wanted to control broadcast traffic. This was a perfect**
situation for a VLAN. We set up a separate VLAN for each of the classrooms
so that none of the classrooms would cause unnecessary broadcast traffic to
the others.

Broadcasts by their very nature are processed and received by each member of the broadcast domain. VLANs can improve network performance by segmenting the network into groups that share broadcast traffic. For example, each floor of a building might have its own subnet. It might make sense to create a VLAN for that subnet to control broadcasts to other floors of the building, thus reducing the need to send broadcasts to unnecessary destinations (in this case, another floor of the building). The general rule for VLANs is to keep the resources that are needed for the VLAN and that are consumed by members of the VLAN on that same VLAN. Latency issues will occur whenever a packet must cross a VLAN, as it must be routed. This situation should be avoided if possible.

The type of port that supports a VLAN is called an access link. When a device connects using an access link, it is unaware of any VLAN membership. It behaves as if it were a component of a broadcast domain. All VLAN information is removed by switches from the frame before it gets to the device connected to the access link. No communication or interaction can take place between the access link devices and the devices outside of their designated VLAN. This communication is only made possible when the packet is routed through a router.

A trunk link, also known just as a "trunk," is a port that transports packets for any VLAN. These trunk ports are usually found in connections between switches, and require the ability to carry packets from all available VLANs because those VLANs span multiple switches. Trunk ports are typically VLAN 0 or VLAN 1, but there is nothing magical about those numbers. It is up to the manufacturer to determine which ID is designated as the trunk port. Specifications are spelled out in the 802.1Q protocol, but just like any other "blueprint," some manufacturers will make their own interpretation of how trunk ports should be implemented.

For cloud VLANs, it is important to understand another type of VLAN known as a private VLAN, or PVLAN. PVLANs contain switch ports that cannot communicate with each other but can access another network. PVLANs restrict traffic through the use of private ports so that they communicate only with a specific uplink trunk port. A good example of the utilization of a PVLAN is in a hotel setting. Each room of the hotel has a port that can access the Internet, but it is not advantageous for the rooms to communicate with each other.

Virtual Extensible LAN (VXLAN)

The virtual extensible LAN (VXLAN) is a method of encapsulating, or tunneling, frames across UDP port 4789. The data addressed to another member of a VXLAN is placed inside the UDP packet and routed to its destination, at which point it is de-encapsulated so that the receiving port, known as a VXLAN tunnel endpoint (VTEP), can receive it as if it were sent over a local network.

VXLANs are primarily used in cloud environments to segment different tenants. VXLANs were created because VLANs use a 12-bit VLAN ID that can have a maximum of 4,096 network IDs assigned at one time. This is not enough addresses for many large cloud environments. VXLANs use a 24-bit segment ID that allows for 16 million segments, which provides enough segments for many more customers. Similar to VLANs, switch ports can be members of a VXLAN. VXLAN members can be either virtual or physical switch ports.

Routing Tables

A routing table is a set of procedures, stored on a router, that the router uses to determine the destination of network packets it is responsible for routing. The routing table contains information about the network topology that is located adjacent to the router as well as information gathered from neighboring routers. This information is used by routers to determine which path to send packets down in order to efficiently deliver information to its destination.

Routers may know of multiple paths to a destination and the routing table will rank these paths in order of efficiency. The method of ordering the paths depends on the routing protocol used. If the most efficient path is unavailable, the router will select the next best path as defined by its routing table.

CERTIFICATION OBJECTIVE 4.04

Network Ports and Protocols

Now that you understand how to select the physical network configuration and segment and route network traffic, you need to learn about the different ports and protocols that are used in cloud computing. A network port is an application-specific endpoint to a logical connection. It is how a client program finds a specific service on a device. A network protocol, on the other hand, is an understood set of rules agreed upon by two or more parties that determines how network devices exchange information over a network. In this section, we discuss the different protocols used to securely connect a network to the Internet so that it can communicate with the cloud environment.

Hypertext Transfer Protocol (HTTP) and Hypertext Transfer Protocol Secure (HTTPS)

Hypertext Transfer Protocol (HTTP) is an application protocol built on TCP used to distribute Hypertext Markup Language (HTML) files, text, images, sound, videos, multimedia, and other types of information over the Internet. HTTP typically allows for communication between a web client or web browser and a web server hosting a website. HTTP defines how messages between a web browser and a web server are formatted and transmitted and which actions the web server and browser should take when they are issued specific commands. HTTP uses port 80 to communicate by default.

Hypertext Transfer Protocol Secure (HTTPS) is an extension of HTTP that provides secure communication over the Internet. HTTPS is not a separate protocol from HTTP; it layers the security capabilities of Secure Sockets Layer (SSL) or Transport Layer Security (TLS) on top of HTTP to provide security to standard HTTP, since HTTP communicates in plain text. HTTPS uses port 443 by default.

When a web client first accesses a website using HTTPS, the server sends a certificate with its embedded public key to the web client. The client generates a session key (sometimes called a symmetric key) and encrypts the session key with the server's public key. The server has the private key, which is the other half of the public–private key pair and can decrypt the session key, which allows for a covert and confidential exchange of a very fast session key. No entity other than the server has access to the private key.

During the standard process of authentication, the client then verifies that the certificate is in its trusted root store, thus trusting the certificate was signed by a trusted certificate authority. After the client can verify the certificate is coming from the correct web server, it creates a session key that is only accessible by that web client. It encrypts the session key using the public key it received from the web server in the form of a certificate with an embedded public key. The sending server is the only entity that should have a copy of the private key so that it can decrypt the sent session key. Now both entities have a copy of the very fast session key, and the server receives it securely. Once both the web client and the web server know the session key, the SSL/TLS handshake is complete, and the session is encrypted. As part of the protocol, either the client or the server can ask that the key be "rolled" at any time. Rolling the key is simply asking the browser to generate a new 40-, 128-, or 256-bit key or above, forcing a would-be attacker to shoot at a moving target.

e x a m

ⓦatch   **Some organizations may use a proxy for connecting to the Internet. Proxy automatic configuration (PAC) is a system that automatically configures devices to** **use a proxy server if one is required for a web connection. PAC is also known as proxy auto-config.**

on the
ⓙob   **A good example of using HTTPS comes from an experience working for a large retail firm. The employer needed an e-commerce web page that could receive credit card payments over the Internet, which in turn required a secure form of transmission for data as it traveled over the Internet. So the organization had to purchase a certificate from a trusted certificate authority (e.g., Verisign) and deploy it on its internal web servers. Once the certificate was purchased and deployed to the servers, customers were able to use HTTPS to communicate with the web page and thus purchase products using their credit card information in a secure manner.**

File Transfer Protocol (FTP) and FTP over SSL (FTPS)

Unlike HTTP, which is used to view web pages over the Internet, the File Transfer Protocol (FTP) is used to download and transfer files over the Internet. FTP is a standard network protocol that allows for access to and transfer of files over the Internet using either the FTP client or command-line interface. An organization hosts files on an FTP server so that people from outside the organization can download those files to their local computers. Figure 4-9 shows an example of a graphical-based FTP client.

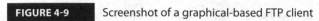

FIGURE 4-9   Screenshot of a graphical-based FTP client

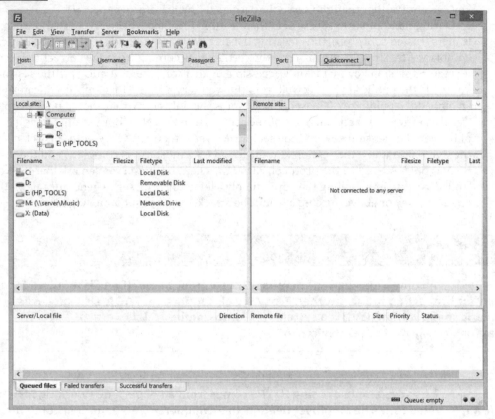

FTP is built on a client-server architecture and provides a data connection between the FTP client and the FTP server. The FTP server is the computer that stores the files and authenticates the FTP client. The FTP server listens on the network for incoming FTP connection requests from FTP clients. The clients, on the other hand, use either the command-line interface or FTP client software to connect to the FTP server.

After the FTP server has authenticated the client, the client can download files, rename files, upload files, and delete files on the FTP server based on the client's permissions. The FTP client software has an interface that allows you to explore the directory of the FTP server, just like you would use Windows Explorer to explore the content of your local hard drive on a Microsoft Windows–based computer.

Similar to how HTTPS is an extension of HTTP, FTPS is an extension of FTP that allows clients to request that their FTP session be encrypted. FTPS allows for the encrypted and secure transfer of files over FTP using SSL or TLS. There are two different methods for securing client access to the FTP server: implicit and explicit. Implicit mode gives an FTPS-aware client the ability to require a secure connection with an FTPS-aware server without affecting the FTP functionality of non-FTPS-aware clients. With explicit mode, a client must explicitly request a secure connection from the FTPS server; then the security and encryption method must be agreed upon between the FTPS server and the FTPS client. If the client does not request a secure connection, the FTPS server can either allow or refuse the client's connection to the FTPS server.

Secure Shell File Transfer Protocol (SFTP)

Secure Shell File Transfer Protocol (SFTP) is a network protocol designed to provide secure access to files, file transfers, file editing, and file management over the Internet using a Secure Shell (SSH) session. Unlike FTP, SFTP encrypts both the data and the FTP commands, preventing the information from being transmitted in clear text over the Internet. SFTP differs from FTPS in that SFTP uses SSH to secure the file transfer and FTPS uses SSL or TLS to secure the file transfer.

SFTP clients are functionally similar to FTP clients, except SFTP clients use SSH to access and transfer files over the Internet. An organization cannot use standard FTP client software to access an SFTP server, nor can it use SFTP client software to access FTP servers.

There are a few things to consider when deciding on which method should be used to secure FTP servers. SFTP is generally more secure and superior to FTPS. If the organization is going to connect to a Linux or Unix FTP server, SFTP is the better choice because it is supported by default on these operating systems. If one of the requirements for the FTP server is that it needs to be accessible from personal devices, such as tablets and smartphones, then FTPS would be the better option since most of these devices natively support FTPS but may not support SFTP.

It is important to understand that FTPS and SFTP are not the same thing. FTPS uses SSL or TLS and certificates to secure FTP communication, and SFTP uses SSH keys to secure FTP communication.

Domain Name System (DNS) and Dynamic Host Configuration Protocol (DHCP)

The Domain Name System (DNS) distributes the responsibility for both the assignment of domain names and the mapping of those names to IP addresses to the authoritative name servers within each domain. An authoritative name server is responsible for maintaining its specific domain name and can also be authoritative for subdomains of that primary domain. For example, if you want to go to a particular web page like https://www.comptia.org, all you do is type the name of the web page into your browser, and it displays the web page.

FIGURE 4-10 The steps in a DNS search

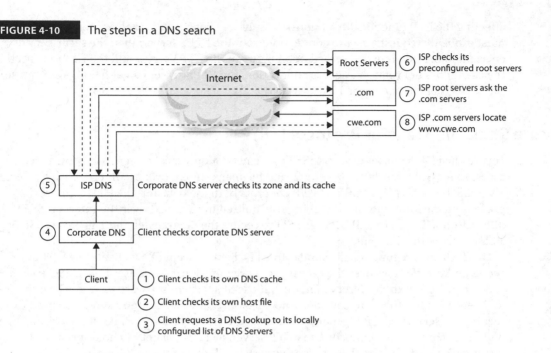

For your web browser to display that web page by name, it needs to be able to locate it by IP address. This is where DNS comes into play.

DNS translates Internet domain or host names into IP addresses. DNS would automatically convert the name https://www.comptia.org into an IP address for the web server hosting that web page. In order to store the entire name and address information for all the public hosts on the Internet, DNS uses a distributed hierarchical database. DNS databases reside in a hierarchy of database servers where no one DNS server contains all the information. Figure 4-10 shows an example of how a client performs a DNS search.

DNS consists of a tree of domain names. Each branch of the tree has a domain name and contains resource records for that domain. Resource records describe specific information about a particular object. The DNS zone at the top of the tree is called the root zone. Each zone under the root zone has a unique domain name or multiple domain names, and the owner of that domain name is considered authoritative for that DNS zone. Figure 4-11 shows the DNS hierarchy and how a URL is resolved to an IP address.

DNS servers manage DNS zones. Servers store records for resources within one or more domains that they are configured and authorized to manage. A host record or "A" record is used to store information on a domain or subdomain along with its IP address. A canonical name (CNAME) record is an alias for a host record. For example, a CNAME record testing for the comptia.org domain pointing to www would allow for users to enter the URL www.comptia.org or testing.comptia.org to go to the same site. A mail exchanger (MX) record stores information on the mail server for the domain, if one exists.

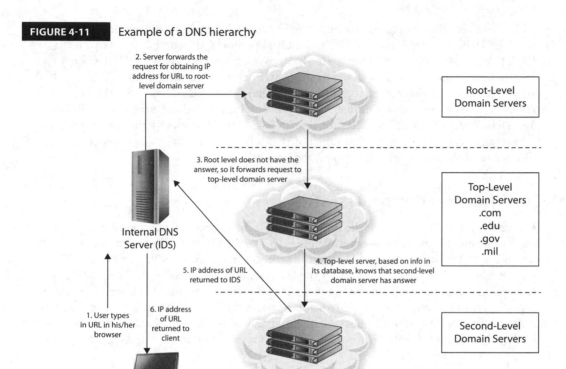

FIGURE 4-11   Example of a DNS hierarchy

Dynamic Host Configuration Protocol (DHCP) is a network protocol that allows a server to automatically assign IP addresses from a predefined range of numbers, called a scope, to computers on a network. DHCP is responsible for assigning IP addresses to computers, and DNS is responsible for resolving those IP addresses to names. A DHCP server can register and update resource records on a DNS server on behalf of a DHCP client. A DHCP server is used any time an organization does not wish to use static IP addresses (IP addresses that are manually assigned).

DHCP servers maintain a database of available IP addresses and configuration options. The DHCP server leases an IP address to a client based on the network to which that client is connected. The DHCP client is then responsible for renewing its lease or IP addresses before the lease expires. DHCP supports both IPv4 and IPv6. It can also be used to create a static IP address mapping by creating a reservation that assigns a particular IP address to a computer based on that computer's media access control (MAC) address.

If an organization's network has only one IP subnet, clients can communicate directly with the DHCP server. If the network has multiple subnets, the company can still use a DHCP server to allocate IP addresses to the network clients. To allow a DHCP client on a subnet that is not directly connected to the DHCP server to communicate with the DHCP server, the organization can configure a DHCP relay agent in the DHCP client's subnet. A DHCP relay agent is an agent that relays DHCP communication between DHCP clients and DHCP servers on different IP subnets. DNS and DHCP work together to help clients on an organization's network communicate as efficiently as possible, and allow the clients to discover and share resources located on the network.

Simple Mail Transfer Protocol (SMTP)

Documents and videos are not the only pieces of information that you might want to share and communicate over the Internet. While HTTP and FTP allow you to share files, videos, and pictures over the Internet, SMTP is the protocol that allows you to send e-mail over the Internet. SMTP uses port 25 and provides a standard set of codes that help to simplify the delivery of e-mail messages between e-mail servers. Almost all e-mail servers that send e-mail over the Internet use SMTP to send messages from one server to another. After the e-mail server has received the message, the user can view that e-mail using an e-mail client, such as Microsoft Outlook. The e-mail client also uses SMTP to send messages from the client to the e-mail server.

Well-Known Ports

Ports are used in a TCP or UDP network to specify the endpoint of a logical connection and how the client can access a specific application on a server over the network. Port binding is used to determine where and how a message is transmitted. Link aggregation can also be implemented to combine multiple network connections to increase throughput. The well-known ports are assigned by the Internet Assigned Numbers Authority (IANA) and range from 0 to 1023. The IANA is responsible for maintaining the official assignments of port numbers for a specific purpose. You do not need to know all of the well-known ports for the CompTIA Cloud+ exam, so we are going to focus only on the ports that are relevant to the exam. Table 4-2 specifies the server process and its communication port.

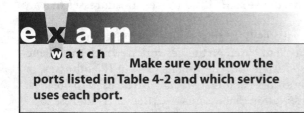

TABLE 4-2		Well-Known Server Processes and Communication Ports	

Service	Port(s)	Transport Protocol	Description
FTP	20, 21	TCP	File Transfer Protocol, used to transfer data.
SFTP	22	TCP	Secure Shell File Transfer Protocol, used for secure logins, file transfers, and port forwarding.
Telnet	23	TCP	Telnet, used to send unencrypted text messages.
SMTP	25	TCP	Simple Mail Transfer Protocol, used to route e-mails between mail servers.
DNS	53	TCP/UDP	Domain Name System.
DHCP	67, 68	UDP	Dynamic Host Configuration Protocol, used to assign IP addresses to computers.
HTTP	80	TCP	World Wide Web Hypertext Transfer Protocol.
POP	110	TCP	Post Office Protocol, used for retrieving mail from a mail server.
NTP	123	UDP	Network Time Protocol, synchronizes the system clock with a time server.
IMAP	143	TCP	Internet Message Access Protocol, another protocol used to send and receive mail. It is considered more advanced than POP, with push methods and other features.
SNMP	161	TCP/UDP	Simple Network Management Protocol, used to send network management information.
LDAP	389	TCP/UDP	Lightweight Directory Access Protocol, for exchanging directory information.
HTTPS	443	TCP	HTTP over Secure Sockets Layer (SSL).
FTPS	990	TCP	One of two secure versions of FTP. FTPS runs over SSL/TLS.

CERTIFICATION SUMMARY

A network's physical topology is a key factor in its overall performance. This chapter explained the various physical topologies and when to use each of them. It also discussed how traffic is routed across the network, which is key to understanding how to implement cloud computing. Since most information is accessed over an Internet connection, it is very important to know how to properly configure a network and how it is routed.

There are a variety of different ways to reduce network latency and improve network response time and performance, including caching, compression, load balancing, and maintaining the physical hardware. These issues are critical for ensuring that an organization meets the terms of its SLA.

KEY TERMS

Use the following list to review the key terms discussed in this chapter. The definitions also can be found in the glossary.

bandwidth   The amount of data that can be transferred from one network location to another in a specific amount of time.

Border Gateway Protocol (BGP)   A protocol used to direct packets across an internetwork. BGP makes routing decisions based on rule sets and network policies.

bus   The communication system used to transfer data between the components inside of a computer motherboard, processor, or network device. It gets its name from the concept of a bus line where the bus stops and allows people to get off and board. It is a communication system that is attached at many points along the bus line.

caching   Process of transparently storing data at a quicker response location so that any future requests for that data can be accessed faster than through the slower medium.

canonical name (CNAME)   A DNS record that specifies an alternate name for a host record.

compression   Reduction in the size of data being sent across the network.

Domain Name System (DNS)   Translates Internet domain or host names into IP addresses.

Dynamic Host Configuration Protocol (DHCP)   Network protocol that automatically assigns IP addresses from a predefined range of numbers, called a scope, to computers on a network.

extranet   Extension of an intranet, with the difference being an extranet allows access to the network from outside the organization.

File Transfer Protocol (FTP)   Network protocol that allows for access to and the transfer of files over the Internet.

FTP over SSL (FTPS)   Uses Secure Sockets Layer (SSL) or Transport Layer Security (TLS) to secure the transfer of files over FTP.

Hypertext Transfer Protocol (HTTP)   Protocol used to distribute HTML files, text, images, sound, videos, multimedia files, and other information over the Internet.

Hypertext Transfer Protocol Secure (HTTPS)   An extension of HTTP that provides secure communication over the Internet using Secure Sockets Layer (SSL) or Transport Layer Security (TLS).

Interior Gateway Routing Protocol (IGRP)   A Cisco routing protocol used to direct packets across an internetwork. IGRP can use a number of metrics to determine the ideal route including reliability, delay, load, and bandwidth.

Internet   A global system of interconnected computer networks that are not controlled by a single organization or country.

intranet   Private network that is configured and controlled by a single organization and is only accessible to users who are internal to that organization.

latency   The delay in time calculated from the time a service request is made until that request is fulfilled. Typically used to describe network and hard drive speeds.

load balancing   Distributes workloads across multiple computers to optimize resources and throughput and prevent a single device from being overwhelmed.

local area network (LAN)   Network topology that spans a relatively small area, such as an office building, and allows people within that area to share files, devices, printers, and applications.

mail exchanger (MX)   A DNS record that stores information on the mail server for the domain, if one exists.

mesh   Network topology where every node is interconnected to every other node in the network.

metropolitan area network (MAN)   Network topology connecting multiple LANs together to span a large area, such as a city or a large campus.

network address translation (NAT)   Allows a router to modify packets so that multiple devices can share a single public IP address.

open shortest path first (OSPF)   A protocol used to direct packets across an internetwork. The OSPF routing protocol uses link state routing to determine the best path to the destination.

port   Application-specific endpoint to a logical connection.

port address translation (PAT)   Mapping of both ports and IP addresses from a private system to a public system.

proxy automatic configuration (PAC)   A system that automatically configures devices to use a proxy server if one is required for a web connection. Also known as proxy auto-config.

ring   Network topology where each node is connected to another, forming a circle or a ring.

router   Device that connects multiple networks together and allows a network to communicate with the outside world.

Routing Information Protocol (RIP)   A protocol used to direct packets across an internetwork. RIP uses hop count to determine the best route to a network.

routing table   Data table stored on a router that is used by the router to determine the best path to a remote network destination of network packets it is responsible for routing.

Secure Shell (SSH)   A cryptographic protocol that creates an encrypted channel to access remote servers, configure network equipment, secure logins, transfer files, and perform port forwarding.

Secure Shell File Transfer Protocol (SFTP)   Provides secure access to files, file transfers, file editing, and file management over the Internet using Secure Shell (SSH).

Simple Mail Transfer Protocol (SMTP)   Protocol used to send e-mail over the Internet.

star   Network topology where each node is connected to a central hub or switch and the nodes communicate by sending data through the central hub.

subnetting   Creates subnetworks through the logical subdivision of IP networks.

supernetting   Combines multiple networks into one larger network.

switch   Network device that connects multiple devices together on the same network or LAN.

tree   Network topology containing multiple star networks that are connected through a linear bus backbone.

virtual extensible local area network (VXLAN)   Partitions a physical network to create separate segments for multitenant cloud environments.

virtual local area network (VLAN)   Partitions a physical network to create separate, independent broadcast domains that are part of the same physical network.

virtual routing and forwarding (VRF)   A technique where a router contains multiple routing tables at the same time, allowing for identical IP addresses to coexist without conflict.

wide area network (WAN)   Network that covers a large geographic area and can contain multiple LANs or MANs.

TWO-MINUTE DRILL

Network Types

- ❑ A network is a group of interconnected computers and peripherals capable of sharing resources.
- ❑ An intranet is a private network that is controlled by a single organization and is only accessible to users who are internal to the organization.
- ❑ The Internet is a global system of interconnected computer networks and, unlike an Intranet, is not controlled by a single organization.
- ❑ An extranet is similar to an intranet in the fact that it is controlled by a single organization, but it also allows controlled access from outside the organization.

Network Optimization

❑ A LAN is a network that connects computers to each other and allows them to communicate over a short distance. Similar to a LAN, a MAN connects computers to one another, but a MAN spans a city or a large campus.

❑ A WAN can contain multiple LANs and MANs and spans a large geographic area.

❑ A network's topology determines how computers communicate.

❑ Network latency is the time delay that is encountered while data is being transferred over a network.

❑ Compression converts data into a smaller format and works to reduce network latency.

❑ Caching stores frequently accessed information closer to the device that is requesting it.

❑ Load balancing allows for distribution of incoming HTTP requests across multiple web servers to improve network performance and response time.

Routing and Switching

❑ NAT allows a router to modify packets so that multiple devices can share a single public IP address.

❑ PAT is similar to NAT, except PAT allows for mapping multiple devices to a single public IP address by changing its port number.

❑ Subnetting allows a network to be divided into smaller networks to ease administration.

❑ A VLAN makes it possible to divide a large network into smaller networks, even if every device physically does not connect to the same switch. Up to 4,096 network IDs can be addressed at once.

❑ A VXLAN segments traffic for multitenant cloud environments. Up to 16 million segments can be addressed at once.

❑ A router has a built-in database called a routing table that stores information about the network's topology and the devices that are connected to the router.

Network Ports and Protocols

❑ HTTP allows for communication between a web client and a web server over the Internet using port 80 by default.

❑ HTTPS is an extension of HTTP that uses port 443 and secures the communication between the web client and the web server.

❑ FTP uses port 21 by default and allows you to download and transfer files over the Internet.

❑ FTP communication can be secured using FTPS or SFTP. FTPS uses SSL or TLS to encrypt FTP communication, while SFTP uses SSH keys to encrypt FTP communication.

❑ DHCP is used to automatically assign IP addresses to computers based on a predefined scope. DNS then translates those addresses into readable and easily recognized host names.

❑ E-mail is transferred over the Internet between mail servers using SMTP over port 25.

SELF TEST

The following questions will help you measure your understanding of the material presented in this chapter. As indicated, some questions may have more than one correct answer, so be sure to read all the answer choices carefully.

Network Types

1. Which network type is not accessible from outside the organization by default?
   A. Internet
   B. Extranet
   C. Intranet
   D. LAN

2. Which of the following statements describes the difference between an extranet and an intranet network configuration?
   A. An intranet does not require a firewall.
   B. An extranet requires less administration than an intranet.
   C. An intranet is owned and operated by a single organization.
   D. An extranet allows controlled access from outside the organization.

3. Which of the following is a network of multiple networks relying on network devices and common protocols to transfer data from one destination to another until it reaches its final destination and is accessible from anywhere?
   A. Intranet
   B. Extranet
   C. Internet
   D. LAN

Network Optimization

4. Which of the following terms defines the amount of data that can be sent across a network at a given time?
    A. Network latency
    B. Bandwidth
    C. Compression
    D. Network load balancing

5. Which of the following causes network performance to deteriorate and delays network response time?
    A. Network latency
    B. Caching
    C. Network bandwidth
    D. High CPU and memory usage

6. After taking a new job at the state university, you are asked to recommend a network topology that best fits the large college campus. The network needs to span the entire campus. Which network topology would you recommend?
    A. LAN
    B. WAN
    C. MAN
    D. SAN

7. You administer a website that receives thousands of hits per second. You notice the web server hosting the website is operating at close to capacity. What solution would you recommend to improve the performance of the website?
    A. Caching
    B. Network load balancing
    C. Compression
    D. Network bandwidth

Routing and Switching

8. Which process allows a router to modify packets so that multiple devices can share a single public IP address?
    A. NAT
    B. DNS
    C. VLAN
    D. Subnetting

9. Which of the following IP addresses is in a private IP range?
  A. 12.152.36.9
  B. 10.10.10.10
  C. 72.64.53.89
  D. 173.194.96.3

10. Which of the following technologies allows you to logically segment a LAN into different broadcast domains?
  A. MAN
  B. WAN
  C. VLAN
  D. SAN

Network Ports and Protocols

11. Which of the following protocols and ports is used to secure communication over the Internet?
  A. HTTP over port 80
  B. SMTP over port 25
  C. FTP over port 21
  D. HTTPS over port 443

12. SFTP uses _____ to secure FTP communication.
  A. Certificates
  B. FTPS
  C. SSH
  D. SMTP

13. In a network environment _____ is responsible for assigning IP addresses to computers and _____ is responsible for resolving those IP addresses to names.
  A. DNS, DHCP
  B. DHCP, DNS
  C. HTTP, DNS
  D. DHCP, SMTP

14. Which of these ports is the well-known port for the Telnet service?
  A. 25
  B. 22
  C. 23
  D. 443

15. This protocol is responsible for transferring e-mail messages from one mail server to another over the Internet.
    A. DNS
    B. HTTPS
    C. FTP
    D. SMTP

SELF TEST ANSWERS

Network Types

1. ☑ **C.** An intranet is a private network that is configured and controlled by a single organization and is only accessible by users that are internal to that organization.
   ☒ **A, B,** and **D** are incorrect. An extranet is similar to an intranet, but it is accessible from outside the organization. The Internet is accessible from anywhere, and a LAN is part of an intranet but is not a separate network type.

2. ☑ **D.** An extranet is an extension of an intranet with the primary difference being that an extranet allows controlled access from outside the organization.
   ☒ **A, B,** and **C** are incorrect. An extranet requires a little bit more administration due to the fact that you have to maintain access to resources outside the organization. Both an intranet and an extranet are owned by a single organization, so this is not a difference in the two network types.

3. ☑ **C.** The Internet is not controlled by a single entity and serves billions of users around the world.
   ☒ **A, B,** and **D** are incorrect. An intranet is only accessible to users within a specific organization. An extranet allows only controlled access from outside the organization. A LAN is part of an intranet.

Network Optimization

4. ☑ **B.** Bandwidth is the amount of data that can traverse a network interface over a specific amount of time.
   ☒ **A, C,** and **D** are incorrect. Network latency is a time delay that is encountered while data is being sent from one point to another on the network and impacts network bandwidth. Compression is the reduction in the size of data brought about by converting it into a format that requires fewer bits and does not define the amount of data that can be sent over the network. Network load balancing is used to increase performance and provide redundancy for websites and applications.

5. ☑ **A.** Network latency is a time delay that is encountered while data is being sent from one point to another on the network and impacts network bandwidth and performance.
☒ **B, C,** and **D** are incorrect. Caching is the process of storing frequently accessed data in a location close to the device requesting the data and helps improve network performance. Network bandwidth is the amount of data that can traverse a network interface over a specific amount of time. CPU and memory are different compute resources that need to be monitored for performance but are separate from network performance.

6. ☑ **C.** A metropolitan area network (MAN) can connect multiple LANs and is used to build networks with high data connection speeds for cities or college campuses.
☒ **A, B,** and **D** are incorrect. A local area network (LAN) is a network that connects computers to each other and allows them to communicate over a short distance and would not satisfy the requirement of spanning a large campus. A wide area network (WAN) is a network that can contain multiple LANs and/or MANs and is not restricted by geographic area. A storage area network (SAN) would not allow you to connect different LANs throughout the campus as the question requires.

7. ☑ **B.** Network load balancing is used to increase performance and provide redundancy for websites and applications.
☒ **A, C,** and **D** are incorrect. Caching is the process of storing frequently accessed data in a location close to the device requesting the data and helps improve network performance for the client, but it would not help improve the performance of the web server. Compression is defined as the reduction in the size of data, which is done by converting that data into a format that requires fewer bits and does not define the amount of data that can be sent over the network. Again, this is a technology that helps with the receiving end of the network traffic but will not alleviate performance issues on the hosting server. Network bandwidth is the amount of data that can traverse a network interface over a specific amount of time, and is a measurement but not a technique or mechanism for improving performance.

Routing and Switching

8. ☑ **A.** NAT allows your router to change your private IP address into a public IP address so that you can access resources that are external to your organization; then the router tracks those IP address changes.
☒ **B, C,** and **D** are incorrect. DNS maps host names to IP addresses but does not allow multiple hosts to operate from a single IP address. A VLAN allows you to logically segment a LAN into different broadcast domains, whereas subnetting allows you to divide one network into multiple networks.

9. ☑ **B.** 10.0.0.0–10.255.255.255 is a private class A address range.
☒ **A, C,** and **D** are incorrect. All of these are examples of public IP addresses. Only IP addresses that fall into the IP ranges listed in Table 4-1 are considered private IP addresses.

10. ☑ **C.** A VLAN allows you to configure separate broadcast domains even if the devices are plugged into the same physical switch.

   ☒ **A, B,** and **D** are incorrect. A MAN usually connects physically, not logically, separated LANs and is used to build networks with high data connection speeds for cities or college campuses. A WAN is a network that covers a large geographic area and can contain multiple physical, not logical, LANs and/or MANs. A SAN is a dedicated network used to provide access to block-level storage and not broadcast domains.

Network Ports and Protocols

11. ☑ **D.** HTTPS is an extension of HTTP that provides secure communication over the Internet and uses port 443 by default.

   ☒ **A, B,** and **C** are incorrect. HTTP uses port 80 by default and allows for communication between a web client or web browser and a web server hosting a website. SMTP uses port 25 by default to transfer e-mail messages over the Internet. FTP uses port 21 by default to download and transfer files over the Internet. None of these three protocols is a secure form of communication.

12. ☑ **C.** SFTP uses SSH keys to secure FTP communication.

   ☒ **A, B,** and **D** are incorrect. FTPS uses SSL or TLS and certificates to secure FTP communication. SMTP is used to transfer e-mail messages over the Internet.

13. ☑ **B.** DHCP is responsible for assigning IP addresses to computers and DNS is responsible for resolving those IP addresses to names.

   ☒ **A, C,** and **D** are incorrect. HTTP allows for communication between a web client or web browser and a web server hosting a website. SMTP is used to transfer e-mail messages over the Internet.

14. ☑ **C.** Telnet uses port 23 by default for its communication.

   ☒ **A, B,** and **D** are incorrect. Port 25 is used by SMTP for transferring e-mail. Port 22 is used by SSH, and port 443 is used by HTTPS to provide secure communication over the Internet.

15. ☑ **D.** SMTP is used to transfer e-mail messages from one e-mail server to another over the Internet.

   ☒ **A, B,** and **C** are incorrect. DNS translates Internet domain or host names into IP addresses. HTTPS is an extension of HTTP that provides secure communication over the Internet. FTP is a standard network protocol that allows access to and transfer of files over the Internet.

Chapter 5

Virtualization Components

Virtualization technologies have grown substantially over the years. Before that, many major software vendors would not support their applications if they were being run in a virtualized environment. Now virtualization is the standard when it comes to creating an efficient data center, and almost all application vendors support their applications running in a virtualized environment. Virtualization allows a cloud provider to deliver resources on demand to a cloud consumer as needed rather than wasting time or losing opportunities because IT could not keep up with demand. Resource flexibility and scalability are key elements of cloud computing and reasons for its rapid adoption.

The IT world has shifted from a one-to-one application-to-hardware model to a many-to-one model. Virtualization uses one physical computer to run multiple virtual servers, each with its own independent operating system and applications. Virtualization has made the IT industry more efficient and results in better utilization of existing computing assets and technology cost savings.

Virtualization plays a key role in cloud computing by empowering cloud providers to deliver lower-cost hosting environments to cloud consumers. With virtualization, an organization can do more with less physical hardware and can deliver applications to its users faster than ever.

Virtualization makes the most of physical hardware by running multiple virtual servers on one physical server. This consolidates infrastructure and reduces the total cost of ownership (TCO) by cutting data center space, power consumption, and cooling costs.

One key piece of software that has allowed the shift to virtualization is the hypervisor. Know this term for the exam. This chapter begins by looking at the various types of hypervisors and how they operate.

CERTIFICATION OBJECTIVE 5.01

Hypervisor

A hypervisor is a piece of software that creates and manages the virtual infrastructure, including virtual switch (vSwitch), virtual CPU (vCPU), virtual memory, virtual disks, and virtual machines.

The hypervisor is the entity that allows multiple operating systems to run on a single physical machine. The computer running the hypervisor is defined as the "host" computer. The virtual machines that are running on the host are called "guest" machines. The hypervisor is responsible for managing the guest operating system resources, including memory, CPU, and other resources that the guest operating system might need.

There are currently two distinct types of hypervisors: type 1 and type 2. Understanding the two types of hypervisors is critical to creating a successful virtualization environment and integrating that environment with the cloud computing models discussed in Chapter 1.

Type 1

A type 1 hypervisor is one that is created and deployed on a bare metal installation. The first thing installed on a type 1 hypervisor is the hypervisor itself; it acts as the operating system for the bare metal machine.

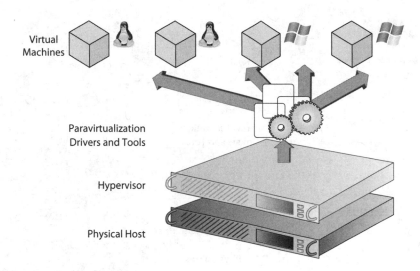

FIGURE 5-1

The layered
design of a
type 1 hypervisor

Type 1 hypervisor software communicates directly with the physical server hardware and boots before the operating system (OS). Almost all of the major virtualization distributors, including VMware, Microsoft, Citrix, Oracle, and Red Hat, currently use type 1 hypervisors. Figure 5-1 shows an example of what a type 1 hypervisor looks like. The image is meant to give you a graphical representation of the layered design, with hardware layer building on top of hardware layer.

Type 2

Unlike a type 1 hypervisor that is loaded on a bare metal server, a type 2 hypervisor is loaded on top of an already existing operating system installation. For example, a system that is running Microsoft Windows 10 might have a VMware workstation installed on top of that operating system.

Type 2 hypervisors create a layer they must traverse as they are distributed to the guest virtual machines. A type 2 hypervisor relies on the operating system and cannot boot until the operating system is loaded and operational. Since type 2 relies heavily on the underlying operating system, if the system crashes or doesn't boot, all of the guest virtual machines are affected. This makes type 2 hypervisors much less efficient than type 1 hypervisors.

Type 1 hypervisors are the best choice for high performance, scalability, and reliability since they operate directly on top of the host hardware and expose hardware resources to virtual machines. This results in less overhead and less complexity.

Type 2 hypervisors sit on top of the operating system, making the virtualized environment less scalable and more complex to manage. Figure 5-2 gives a graphical representation of a type 2 hypervisor. Notice the difference in layering as compared to the type 1 hypervisor.

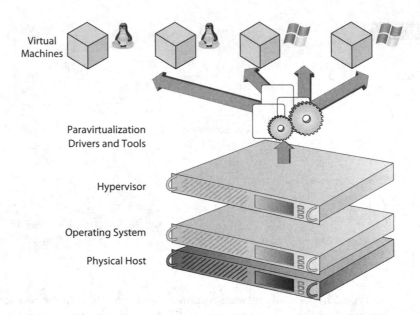

FIGURE 5-2

Image of a type 2 hypervisor

Virtual Machines

Paravirtualization Drivers and Tools

Hypervisor

Operating System

Physical Host

exam

watch

The primary difference between a type 1 hypervisor and a type 2 hypervisor is that type 1 is installed natively on the server and boots before the operating system, while type 2 is installed on top of or after the operating system.

Proprietary

When a company is choosing which type of hypervisor to use, it needs to understand the difference between a proprietary and an open-source hypervisor. A proprietary hypervisor is one that is developed and licensed under an exclusive legal right of the copyright holder. It is created and distributed under a license agreement to the customer. Hyper-V, vSphere, OVM, and FusionSphere are examples of proprietary hypervisors.

Open Source

Some say that the open-source market is growing and advancing faster than the proprietary products market. It can also be argued that the open-source hypervisors are more secure than the proprietary hypervisors because of the underlying operating system running the hypervisor.

Hypervisor	Organization	Proprietary/Open Source
FusionSphere	Huawei	Proprietary
Hyper-V	Microsoft	Proprietary
KVM	KVM Project	Open Source
OpenVZ	Virtuozzo	Open Source
OVM	Oracle	Proprietary
Red Hat Virtualization	Red Hat	Open Source
vSphere / ESXi	VMware	Proprietary
Xen XenServer	Citrix	Open Source Proprietary

An open-source hypervisor is provided at no cost and delivers the same basic functionality as a proprietary hypervisor to run multiple guest virtual machines on a single host. Some examples of open-source hypervisors are Citrix Xen, kernel-based virtual machine (KVM), and OpenVZ. However, many differences arise when evaluating advanced feature sets, migration capabilities, performance, scalability, and integration with other virtualization environments.

Choosing between proprietary and open-source hypervisors can be a difficult decision. Some of the factors that need to be considered are security, the reliability of the manufacturer, and the operating systems that are supported by the hypervisor. Some organizations also choose not to use an open source because their IT staff is not familiar with the interface. For example, an organization may choose to use Microsoft Hyper-V over Citrix Xen because its IT staff is already familiar with the Microsoft product line and will not have as big of a learning curve as it might if the organization were to choose an open-source hypervisor.

Table 5-1 shows some of the most popular hypervisors, the companies or groups behind them, and whether they are proprietary or open source. The list is arranged alphabetically.

Consumer vs. Enterprise

The difference between enterprise and consumer-level hypervisors is minute in IT today. Many of the current desktop operating systems come with a virtualization option already built in; for example, Microsoft Windows 8 and above come with Hyper-V, allowing desktop-level hardware to run a virtual environment. Similarly, KVM can be added to Linux by pulling down a few packages.

However, not all hypervisors are the same. When comparing what a consumer would use for a hypervisor to what an enterprise might use, it is important to consider the goals of the user.

The enterprise virtualization goal is to host the required virtual servers and their associated data and applications on the least amount of hardware to provide sufficient performance and redundancy. Enterprises want to run many virtual machines on each physical machine, and those virtual machines, running independent operating systems, must support many concurrent users and a variety of applications and workloads. This is the job for a type 1 hypervisor because it is built to handle this type of use case and workload effectively.

In comparison, the goal of the average consumer is to configure a virtual environment on a desktop or laptop machine that was not designed primarily for the purpose of virtualization. The machine may serve other purposes such as gaming, word processing, or Internet browsing, in addition to functioning as a hypervisor. Consumers are typically not looking to support a large number of users.

Desktop virtualization is popular for developers who want to test out applications locally without the complexity of managing a dedicated hypervisor, or IT professionals who want to test new operating systems or applications in an isolated environment that is separate from the operating system running their desktop. Linux or Mac users may use virtualization such as KVM or Parallels to run another operating system so that they can run OS-specific applications or games.

The type 2 hypervisor is more likely to fit the needs of consumers because type 2 hypervisors allow the desktop to continue to run the original operating system and its applications side by side with virtualized operating systems and applications.

CERTIFICATION OBJECTIVE 5.02

Virtualization Host

Now that you understand what a hypervisor is and how it interacts with a computer, you need to understand the virtualization host that runs the hypervisor software. The virtualization host is the system that is installed first and then hosts or contains the guest virtual machines. The host server provides all of the underlying hardware and compute resources for the guest virtual machines, including memory, CPU, hard disk, and network I/O. Since the host machine provides the resources for the guest, it must contain at least enough hardware resources to meet the minimum requirements for its guest virtual machines.

A virtualization host computer allows different operating systems to coexist on the same host computer. For example, you could have a virtual machine running Microsoft Windows Server 2016 and another virtual machine running your favorite Linux distro. The first step in configuring a virtualization host is to confirm that your system meets the requirements to be a virtualization host. Hardware requirements include BIOS configuration, sufficient memory, CPU, and at least one NIC. Figure 5-3 shows an example of a virtualization host computer.

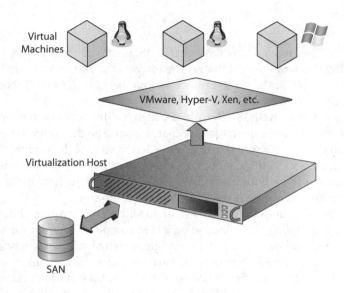

FIGURE 5-3

A graphical
representation of
a virtualization
host

Hardware-Assisted Virtualization

Hardware-assisted virtualization enables efficient full virtualization, which is used to
simulate a complete hardware environment or a virtual machine. It is basically software
that allows the hardware to provide architectural support for the host computer to support
running guest virtual machines. Hardware-assisted virtualization helps make virtualization
more efficient by utilizing the hardware capabilities built into the host computer's processor.
Both AMD and Intel support hardware-assisted virtualization.

If an organization wants to find out whether
its hardware supports hardware-assisted
virtualization, a good place to start is with the
AMD and Intel websites. Both websites have a
list of all the processors that support hardware-
assisted virtualization. It should also be noted
that all processors manufactured after 2003
have hardware-assisted virtualization built in.
Some laptops were slow to allow access to it, but
it was there.

**Hardware-assisted
virtualization enables efficient full
virtualization using the hardware
capabilities of the host computer.**

If an organization has already purchased the hardware or wants to repurpose older
hardware as a virtualization host, it can download and run free software tools that will
check to see if its hardware supports hardware-assisted virtualization. For example, if a
company is trying to use an older server as a virtualization host to run Microsoft Hyper-V,
Microsoft has a free software tool that can determine if that server supports hardware-
assisted virtualization and Microsoft Hyper-V.

BIOS

The Basic Input/Output System (BIOS) is software residing on a ROM chip or a flash memory chip that was installed from the manufacturer. The system mainboard or motherboard has a system BIOS, and some advanced components such as RAID controllers and HBAs have their own BIOS as well.

The system BIOS determines which features a computer supports without having to access any additional software that is loaded on the computer. For example, the system BIOS can contain the software that is needed to control the keyboard, the display settings, disk drives, USB settings, power options, and multiple other options. The system BIOS allows a computer to boot itself and is available even if the hard disks in the computer fail or are corrupted because it is self-contained on the chip.

So what does the BIOS have to do with virtualization? The system BIOS plays a key role when enabling virtualization on a host computer. In order for a modern computer to act as a host and have the ability to host guest virtual machines, modern operating systems rely on the system BIOS to support hardware-assisted virtualization. Some older computers do not have this feature available in the system BIOS. Other computers might need a firmware update for the system BIOS before the feature can be enabled. However, most of the newer servers from mainstream manufacturers, including the latest desktop computers, support this feature.

With the advancement in virtualization and desktop computers, it is no longer a requirement to have a host machine running server-class hardware. Much of the desktop hardware now natively supports hardware-assisted virtualization.

A BIOS has several limitations that necessitated its eventual replacement with UEFI, discussed next. A BIOS is limited to 16-bit processing and 1MB of addressable memory. The BIOS can only boot to drives that are 2.1TB or less due to limitations in the Master Boot Record (MBR).

UEFI

The Unified Extensible Firmware Interface (UEFI) is a replacement for BIOS that was introduced in 2007. UEFI is supported on Windows Vista SP1 and newer Windows operating systems as well as most Linux versions, including Ubuntu, Fedora, Red Hat Enterprise, CentOS, and openSUSE.

UEFI addresses the limitations in BIOS by allowing both 32-bit and 64-bit processing, which can significantly improve system boot times. It also allows for more than 1MB of addressable memory and drives larger than 2.1TB with support for GUID Partition Table (GPT) instead of MBR. UEFI also supports secure boot, a technology that performs OS integrity checking. This helps prevent root kits from starting up a modified version of the OS.

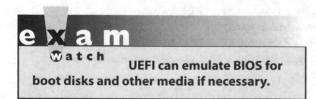

UEFI can emulate BIOS for boot disks and other media if necessary.

Firmware Configurations

Firmware is a set of instructions that is programmed for a specific hardware device. Firmware tells the hardware device how to communicate with the computer system. Firmware upgrades can be performed on a number of devices, including motherboards, network cards, and hard drives. Firmware upgrades are generally carried out so that the hardware can support new features and functionality. For example, you might do a firmware upgrade on a network card so that the card is supported in a new operating system.

In some cases, it might be necessary to do a firmware upgrade to a computer's BIOS in order for it to support hardware-assisted virtualization. This would generally be done on older hardware, as most new hardware purchased today already supports hardware-assisted virtualization. Motherboard manufacturers place firmware updates and the software needed to update the BIOS firmware on their websites for customers to download.

on the job **Recently we were brought in to help a small company set up their virtualized environment. They did not budget for new server hardware to host the virtualization environment, and they brought us in to see if the current hardware would support virtualization. We checked the manufacturer's web page and found out the hardware would support virtualization but needed a firmware upgrade before hardware-assisted virtualization could be enabled.**

CPU and Cores

Now that you understand the prerequisites to creating a host machine, you need to understand how to properly size a host machine. Host machines may be physical servers located in an organization's data center, or they could be cloud hypervisors that the organization rents from a cloud vendor. Making sure that the host machine can support at least the minimum number of guest virtual machines that the organization is trying to run is a critical step in creating a successful virtualization environment.

One of the many benefits of virtualization is the ability to provision virtual machines on the fly as the organization's demands grow, making the purchase of additional hardware unnecessary. If the host computer is not sized correctly, however, it is not possible to add virtual machines without adding compute resources to the host computer or purchasing additional resources from a cloud vendor.

The first step to sizing the host machine is purchasing the correct type and number of CPUs. Both AMD (AMD-V) and Intel (Intel VT) support virtualization, so the manufacturer is not as critical as is the number of CPU cores and the speed of the CPUs. A multicore processor is a single physical CPU with two or more independent CPUs called cores.

As a general virtualization rule, more cores is better than higher-speed processors. It is better to invest in more cores with more cache rather than faster CPU speed. For example, if a company has to choose between a system with two 6-core processors running at 2.2 GHz or a system with two 4-core processors running at 3.3 GHz, the system with two 6-core processors is the better choice. This is because with virtualization the company can spread the virtual machine load across more CPU cores, which translates into faster and more consistent virtual machine performance. Also, if you do the math, two 6-core processors is 12 cores running at 2.6 GHz, equaling 31.2 GHz of total processing power, while two 4-core processors is 8 cores running at 3.2 GHz, equaling 26.4 GHz. However, even if the math were in favor of the higher speed over cores, the best choice is still additional cores.

Once the organization has defined the processor for the host computer, it needs to evaluate how to assign those CPU resources to the guest virtual machines. Not surprisingly, virtual machines use virtual CPUs (vCPUs), which can be added to a virtual machine when it is created. The number of vCPUs that the company should add is dependent on a number of factors, but it is possible to assign multiple vCPUs to a single virtual machine.

Some products are licensed based on the number of CPUs, cores, or vCPUs. It is important to know how many CPUs you are licensed for when assigning resources so that you do not violate your license or cause a program to fail activation checks.

Hyperthreading

Hyperthreading is a technology that creates two logical CPU cores for each physical CPU core that supports hyperthreading. Hyperthreading is a proprietary technology for Intel CPUs. It was introduced in 2002 with the Xeon server and Pentium 4 desktop processors. Hyperthreading requires operating system support for symmetric multiprocessing (SMP), a feature which all current operating systems support.

Hyperthreading increases the ability of the system to run parallel processes, but whether performance increases using hyperthreading depends upon the application's ability to execute multiple steps on processors in parallel. Hyperthreading is not the same as having multiple cores in a CPU, because hyperthreading shares the CPU's pipeline, cache, and system bus interface instead of dedicating cache and interfaces to distinct cores.

Hyperthreading is very useful in virtualization, allowing for higher overcommitment ratios of vCPUs to physical CPUs, discussed later in this chapter. Hypervisors with few processor cores will see the greatest advantage from hyperthreading because they are likely running out of available processors to allocate to virtual machines.

VT-x

VT-x is a set of instructions performing virtualization functions that is built into the CPU. VT-x decreases the complexity of hypervisors that run on top of supported VT-x hardware, and it is a requirement of most modern hypervisors. VT-x also improves the speed of hypervisor functions because they can be performed in hardware rather than software.

Overcommitment Ratio

It is possible to assign more vCPUs to virtual machines than available physical CPU cores in the hypervisor in a process known as oversubscription or overcommitment. However, assigning more vCPUs than CPU cores must be done with care. Before undertaking such a move, the company should evaluate the workload of all the virtual machines on the server and whether or not that workload is processor intensive.

Virtual machines often require more CPU when starting up or when loading processes for the first time. CPU usage often then decreases significantly with occasional increases due to utilization. Overcommitment can allow the hypervisor to host more virtual machines than otherwise possible and to make better use of the available processors. The hypervisor manages CPU requests, providing each virtual machine with the CPU resources it needs up to its max.

Hypervisors can be configured to start virtual machines with a delay so that they do not all start at the same time or resume from a saved state at the same time.

However, overcommitment can result in contention for CPU resources when multiple machines attempt to utilize all their vCPUs at the same time. This results in reduced performance for the virtual machines and the applications that run on them. For this reason, it is important to understand what a reasonable overcommitment ratio is.

It is generally safe to maintain an overcommitment ratio of 3:1, with three vCPUs for each physical CPU, so a server with four physical CPU cores could assign up to 12 vCPUs. You may be able to increase this, especially for hosts that have a large number of rarely used virtual machines. Monitor resources closely when using an overcommitment ratio of 4:1 to 6:1 because it is easy to produce a situation where virtual machiness are waiting for available CPU.

Most of the time it is unsafe to assign more than six vCPUs for every CPU core on the server. However, this number may vary based on virtual machine vCPU utilization, so evaluating the environment and the goal of that environment is key.

Another important consideration is that you should not allocate more vCPUs to an individual virtual machine than you have physical cores in the hypervisor. This is because the virtual machine may try to use all assigned vCPUs, and if it tries to use more cores than are available at once, some processes that were meant to be in parallel will be serialized because there will never be enough CPUs available to satisfy the demand. This will result in less than ideal performance. For example, if a hypervisor has four CPUs with four cores each, it has 16 cores. Assign no more than 16 cores to an individual virtual machine on the host even if your overcommitment ratio is below the recommended 3:1 ratio.

It is best to allocate one vCPU to a machine and then monitor performance, adding additional vCPUs as needed. When a virtual machine attempts to use a vCPU, the hypervisor must wait for the physical CPU associated with that vCPU to become available. The virtual machine believes that vCPU to be idle and will attempt to spread the load around if the application is configured for multiprocessing, but this can have an adverse impact on virtual machine performance if the physical CPU has a large number of processes in the queue. Furthermore, even idle processors place some load on the hypervisor from host management processes, so it is best to not provision more than will be necessary.

Monitor hypervisor metrics to determine if overcommitment bottlenecks are occurring. The most important metric to watch is the CPU ready metric. CPU ready measures the amount of time a virtual machine has to wait for physical CPU to become available. It is also important to monitor CPU utilization within each virtual machine and on the host. High CPU utilization might indicate the need for additional vCPUs to spread the load, while high host CPU utilization could indicate whether virtual machines are properly balanced across hosts. If one host has high CPU utilization and others have available resources, it may be best to move one or more virtual machines to another host to relieve the burden on the overtaxed host. Host resources could also be expanded for physical hosts or requested for those provisioned in the cloud.

For example, a heavily used Microsoft SQL server is going to be a very processor-intensive virtual machine, so in that scenario, an organization would want a one-to-one CPU-to-vCPU assignment. VMware, Hyper-V, and Citrix all have calculators available to help determine exactly how to distribute vCPUs based on best practices for that particular virtualization product. Table 5-2 displays the maximum number of logical CPUs and virtual CPUs for some of the virtualization products currently available.

on the Job

A server administrator was preparing to apply patches to a large number of machines. He had experienced issues with patches crashing machines before, so he decided to take a snapshot of the machines before applying patches to them. However, he tried to create 20 snapshots at once, and the host ground to a halt. Hypervisor management functions became unavailable and then suddenly the machines became unavailable. Another administrator saw his session lock up and then he could not log in with remote administration tools, so he restarted the hypervisor, causing the machines to fail over to another cluster node. However, since a snapshot was in progress, the machines failed over in an inconsistent state. Be careful about host processes that are CPU intensive such as snapshotting. Taking a snapshot of many machines at the same time can put a strain on the host's CPU resources. Ensure that the host has been configured with a CPU reserve and a max CPU setting so that it does not utilize the resources allocated to virtual machines and vice versa.

TABLE 5-2 Virtualization Host Maximum Resources

Component	VMware ESXi 6.5	Hyper-V (Server 2016) Gen 2	XenServer 7.0
Logical CPUs per Host	576	512	288
Virtual CPUs per Host	4096	2048	2048
RAM per Host	12TB	24TB	5TB
Virtual Machines per Host	1024	1024	1000
Network Cards per Host	128	No limits imposed by Hyper-V	512

Memory Capacity and Configurations

Once the organization has decided which CPU and how many CPU cores they are going to purchase for the virtualization host, the next step is to plan the amount of random-access memory (RAM) that the host machine will need. Planning the amount of memory needed on a host machine is quite different from planning the number of CPUs. Planning for memory is critical. The more RAM and the faster the RAM speed, the better for a virtualization host.

Hypervisors have a virtual allocation table (VAT) that uses methods such as nested page tables or shadow page to map virtual memory to that of the host. Some virtualization platforms allow for adjusting virtual machine memory on the fly, essentially allowing one virtual machine to borrow memory from another virtual machine without shutting down the system. Each of the virtualization products supports virtual machine memory allocation a little bit differently, but the one thing that is consistent is that more memory on the host machine is always better. The job of the IT administrator is to maximize the cost savings of virtualization and the value it brings to the organization.

Careful planning is required to provide enough memory on the host machine to dynamically provision virtual machines as the organization's needs grow and at the same time to make the most cost-efficient choices. Table 5-2, shown earlier, includes the maximum amount of memory that is allowed on a host machine for some of the virtualization products currently available.

Memory Ballooning

Virtual machines often require more memory when starting up or when loading processes for the first time. Memory usage often then decreases significantly, with occasional increases due to utilization. However, when overcommitment ratios are high, there might not be enough memory available to start new machines.

Memory ballooning comes into play when there are not enough resources available to handle new memory requests from virtual machines. Ballooning requests memory resources from other virtual machines. These virtual machines decide which processes they can swap out to free up space, and then they loan those memory pages to the hypervisor. The hypervisor places all the memory pages loaned to it into a balloon that is temporarily allocated to a machine that urgently needs it.

The beauty of ballooning is that the hypervisor does not need to seize the memory and the virtual machine can make an intelligent decision about which memory to swap out to have the least impact on the virtual machine. The ballooning process runs as a normal Windows process. As it requests memory, Windows allocates pages to it as it would any other process, and the hypervisor then takes those pages and makes them available to others. The virtual machine believes the memory is in use by the ballooning process until the ballooning process releases it back to the virtual machine.

Memory Bursting

Virtual machines can be configured with a minimum and a maximum memory size in a technique known as dynamic memory. The machine can request up to the max amount of memory, and the hypervisor will allocate pages to the virtual machine. The burst memory is the maximum amount of memory that the virtual machine can utilize. When configuring burst values, consider how much the machine will use at peak levels and then add a buffer to that value for the burst/max memory.

Once a virtual machine bursts, it may keep the additional memory for some time even after actual utilization	**has dropped back to normal levels. It does not release the memory back immediately.**

Transparent Page Sharing

Transparent page sharing is a technology that deduplicates hypervisor memory allocated to virtual machines. Several virtual machines may load the same data into memory, especially when running the same application. In virtual desktop infrastructure (VDI), this is even more prevalent with users commonly running office productivity, web browsing, and other apps on their virtual desktops. Operating systems also load many processes into memory that may be deduplicated.

Transparent page sharing maps pages that are fixed blocks of memory. When it finds a duplicate, the memory references for the pages assigned to virtual machines are mapped to a single page on the hypervisor so that only one copy is retained.

Memory Compression

When memory is entirely consumed, operating systems are configured to dump data from memory into a page file. The page file is located on disk and is much slower to access than memory. Hypervisors can be configured to compress memory when available memory is low rather than page that memory. This consumes CPU resources to perform the compression and decompression, but it reduces memory read and write I/O since the data does not have to be read from disk.

Overcommitment Ratio

Virtual machines can be configured with a minimum and a maximum memory size. The machine can request up to the max amount of memory, and the hypervisor will allocate pages to the virtual machine. When the memory is not needed anymore, the hypervisor reclaims it for use on other virtual machines. In this way, the total maximum amount of memory configured for virtual machines can exceed the available physical memory in what is known as memory overcommitment. This works as long as the actual consumption remains lower than physical memory. Other technologies such as memory compression and transparent page sharing can further reduce memory consumption, allowing for more overcommitment.

Overcommitment can allow the hypervisor to host more virtual machines than otherwise possible and to make better use of the available memory. However, overcommitment ratios are much lower for memory than they are for CPU.

It is generally safe to maintain an overcommitment ratio of 1.25:1, with 125 percent of physical memory allocated to virtual machines, so a server with 256GB of memory could assign up to 320GB to virtual machines. You may be able to increase this comfortably to 1.5:1, in particular for hosts that have a significant number of similar virtual machines, as transparent page sharing will reduce actual memory consumption. A 1.5:1 overcommitment ratio would allow for 384GB of memory to be allocated to virtual machines in a host that has 256GB of physical memory. Monitor resources closely when using an overcommitment ratio higher than 1.25:1 because it is easy to produce a situation where virtual machines consume all available physical memory and the host is forced to page memory to disk.

Most of the time it is unsafe to operate at an overcommitment rate above 1.5:1. Be extremely careful if you operate at this level and ensure that memory metrics are configured with alerts so that administrators are aware when memory thresholds are reached. Set alerting thresholds below the level where paging will occur to avoid performance issues, and adjust virtual machine memory settings accordingly.

NIC

While choosing CPU and memory is a primary component when planning the hardware for a virtualization host, choosing the type of network cards to use is just as important. Choosing the correct network configuration and type of card is critical to the success of a virtual environment. Network latency can diminish the speed of a virtual environment, so the organization needs to carefully plan which features its network cards on the host computer need to support.

The first step when planning the NICs for the host computer is to understand the physical aspects of the network. Server-class NICs provide the best possible network performance for virtualization. It is also necessary to verify that the infrastructure between the source and destination NICs does not introduce a bottleneck. For example, if the organization is using a 10 Gbps NIC to connect to a 10 Gbps port on a switch, it must make sure that all the patch cables support 10 Gbps speeds and that the switch is configured to use 10 Gbps and is not hard coded to use 1 Gbps speeds. The network can only be as fast as the slowest link, so having a misconfigured switch or a bad cable can cause a bottleneck and result in slower performance.

There are some other key features to consider when purchasing NICs for the virtualization host computer. Table 5-3 lists those features and gives a brief description of each.

TABLE 5-3	NIC Hardware Features

Feature	Description
Checksum off-load	Off-loads the process of TCP packets to the network controller from the CPU
TCP Segmentation Off-Load (TSO)	Converts large chunks of data into smaller packets to be transmitted through the network
64-Bit Direct Memory Access (DMA) Addresses	Permits high-throughput and low-latency networking
Jumbo Frames (JF)	Extends Ethernet to 9000 bytes, allowing for less packet overhead on the server and fewer server interrupts
Large Receive Off-Load (LRO)	Increases inbound throughput by reducing CPU overhead, aggregating multiple incoming packets from a single stream into a larger buffer

CERTIFICATION OBJECTIVE 5.03

Virtual Machine

After the virtualization host computer has been carefully planned and designed, it is ready to support guest virtual machines. However, there is just as much planning, if not more, that needs to go into configuring the virtual machines. With virtualization comes the ability to maximize the physical server and no longer have "unused" resources. While this is a huge advantage and cost savings to an organization, it also requires more planning than the one-to-one way of thinking before virtualization.

Before virtualization, IT administrators were confined to the physical resources that were available on the server running a particular application. With virtualization, an IT administrator now can add compute resources to a virtual machine without having to purchase additional hardware, as long as the virtualization host computer has been designed with this in mind.

The concept of a virtual machine is sometimes difficult to grasp. Think of a virtual machine in the same way you think of a physical server hosting an application. A virtual machine emulates a physical computer, with the only difference being that its resources are managed by a hypervisor that translates resource requests to the underlying physical hardware. You can think of a virtual machine as a portable file that can be moved, copied, and reassigned to a different virtualization host with minimal administration.

Virtualization separates the physical hardware from the virtual hardware running on a virtual machine, so virtual machines can be moved to another hardware platform easily.

Physical servers are typically on a refresh cycle of several years. Every few years IT would have to build a new server and configure the applications, then migrate software. With virtualization, the underlying hardware can be upgraded while the virtual machines stay the same. This reduces the IT maintenance burden.

With full virtualization, guest operating systems are unaware that they are running in a virtual environment as opposed to paravirtualization, a virtualization method that presents a more customized virtual interface to host system hardware. Applications and software can be installed on a virtual machine as if it were a physical server. Isolation of applications is just one of the many advantages of running a virtual environment. Applications can be installed on separate virtual machines, which provides complete isolation from other applications running on the host computer or another virtual machine. This is a great way to test new applications without interfering with existing applications or to create a development environment that is completely segmented from the production environment.

Virtualization is used for both servers and desktops. Organizations will virtualize desktops so that end users can log into their desktop remotely. Desktops are maintained centrally in a cloud or data center environment where they can be more effectively managed and secured. Desktop virtualization is known as virtual desktop infrastructure (VDI).

The remainder of this section explains the compute resources that make up a virtual machine and how to manage and plan for those resources in a virtual environment.

Virtual Disks

Just like a physical server, a virtual machine needs to have a place to install an operating system and applications and to store files and folders. Simply put, a virtual disk is a file that represents a physical disk drive to the virtual machine. VMware virtual machine disks (VMDKs) have an extension of .vmdk, while Hyper-V virtual hard disks (VHD) have an extension of .vhdx.

A virtual disk file resides on the host computer and is accessed by the guest virtual machine. It contains the same properties and features of a physical drive, including disk partitions, a file system, and files and folders.

When creating a virtual disk, you need to make a few decisions, including the type of disk, the name and location of the disk, and the size of the disk. Each of the major virtualization manufacturers uses different terminology to describe virtual disk configurations. For example, if you are using Microsoft Hyper-V, you would have the options of making a dynamically expanding virtual disk, a fixed virtual disk, or a differencing virtual disk. If you are creating a fixed-size disk, you would specify the size of the disk when it is created. If you are creating a dynamically expanding virtual disk, the disk starts as a small size and adds storage as needed.

Differencing virtual disks are used in parent–child virtual disks where a parent virtual disk holds files that are inherited by its children. For example, five Windows 10 machines could all share a parent virtual disk for the operating system, while user profile directories and applications would reside on the child disks. This results in lower disk consumption and easier updating.

TABLE 5-4	Virtual Machine Limits		
Components (per Virtual Machine)	VMware ESXi 6.5	Microsoft Hyper-V (Server 2016)	Citrix XenServer 7.0
Memory	6TB	12TB	1.5TB
Virtual CPUs	128	240	32
Virtual IDE Hard Disks	4	4	255
Virtual SCSI Disks	60	256	255
Virtual NICs	10	12	7

On the other hand, if you are creating a virtual disk in VMware ESXi, you have the option of creating a thick disk or a thin disk. A thick disk is similar to a fixed disk in Microsoft Hyper-V in that the size is specified and allocated during the creation of the virtual disk. A thin disk is similar to a dynamically expanding disk in Microsoft Hyper-V in that the disk starts out small and adds space as required by the virtual machine.

While the different virtualization manufacturers use different terms to define their virtual disks, the concepts are similar. Whether you are using Hyper-V, ESXi, or XenServer, you still need to decide which type of disk to use for which application. If you are concerned about disk space, then using a thin disk or dynamically expanding disk would be the best option. If size is not a concern, then you could use a fixed-size or thick disk.

Virtual disks also use instruction sets and queueing techniques just like physical disks, and virtual disks must be created using a specific virtual disk interface such as IDE or SCSI. Some virtual machine types can only boot off a virtual IDE drive, while others, such as those requiring secure boot, require a SCSI boot drive. Table 5-4 shows the maximum number of virtual IDE and SCSI disks that are available for various types of virtual machines. Please note that XenServer does not emulate SCSI or IDE and uses a unique disk format with a maximum of 16 disks.

vNIC

Configuring and planning the virtual network interface cards is just as important as planning the virtual disk configuration. The network interface card in a computer is what allows a physical computer to interact with other virtual machines and devices on the network. Likewise, a virtual NIC (vNIC) is associated with a physical NIC and allows a virtual machine to communicate on the network. Proper configuration of the vNIC and network settings is a key component to minimizing bottlenecks in the virtual environment.

A vNIC does not have any physical components; it is a software component made up of software drivers that mimic a physical NIC. A vNIC allows an organization to change some of the properties of the vNIC, including MAC address settings, network connections, and VLAN ID. This allows for greater control over the vNIC from within the hypervisor software. Once the settings are configured, and the vNIC is installed on the virtual machine, it functions almost like a physical NIC installed on a physical server.

After attaching a vNIC to a virtual machine, you can add the vNIC to a virtual network. A virtual network is a group of network devices that are configured to access local or external network resources and consists of virtual network links. In effect, a virtual network is a network where traffic between the virtual servers is routed using virtual switches (vSwitches) and virtual routers.

A virtual router is a software-based router that allows a virtualization host to act as a hardware router over the network. This is required if you wish to enable inter-VLAN communication without a hardware router. A virtual network allows the virtual machine to interact with the rest of the LAN.

In addition to configuring a vSwitch, you may configure bridged networking, which allows the virtual machine to communicate with the outside world using the physical NIC so it can appear as a normal host to the rest of the network.

You need to consider some options when configuring a virtual machine to communicate with the rest of the LAN. Sometimes an organization may want to prevent a virtual machine from communicating with devices on the LAN, in which case you can isolate the virtual machine on a private network so that it can communicate only with other virtual machines on the same host. Virtual machine isolation with a private network is a common procedure when setting up a test lab from cloned virtual machines. The cloned machines would conflict with existing production machines if they could talk on the network, so they are isolated so that they can only talk among themselves on a private network. Also, clustered virtual machines use private networks for heartbeat connections.

In a different scenario, an organization might want to bridge the connection between its virtual machine and the LAN used by the host computer so that the virtual machine can communicate with devices that are external to the host computer. Determining how the vNIC and virtual machine use virtual networks is an important piece of virtualization. Remember, one of the many benefits of virtualization is the ability to isolate applications for testing and deployment, but that is only possible if the virtual network and vNIC are configured properly.

After the virtual machine's operating system recognizes and installs the vNIC, it can be configured just like a physical NIC. It is possible to set the IP address, the DNS, the default gateway, subnet mask, the link speed, and so on. The actual network configuration of the vNIC is identical to that of a physical network adapter. So the virtual machine connects to the network in the same manner that a physical machine would that has the same IP address and subnet mask configuration. A virtual machine can be configured to use one or more virtual Ethernet adapters, allowing each adapter to have its own MAC and IP address. Table 5-4, shown earlier, includes the maximum number of vNICs that are available on various types of virtual machines.

Virtual Switches

Once the organization has created and added a vNIC to its virtual machine, the next step in the process is to assign a vSwitch to the machine so that it can communicate with other network devices. Similar to a physical switch, a vSwitch makes it possible to connect other network devices together.

A vSwitch controls how the network traffic flows between the virtual machines and the host computer as well as how network traffic flows between the virtual machine and other network devices in the organization. Virtual switches also allow the organization to isolate network traffic to its virtual machines. A vSwitch can provide some of the same security features that a physical switch provides, including policy enforcement, isolation, traffic shaping, and simplified troubleshooting.

A vSwitch can support VLANs and is compatible with standard VLAN implementations. However, a vSwitch cannot be attached to another vSwitch; instead, more ports can be added to the existing switch.

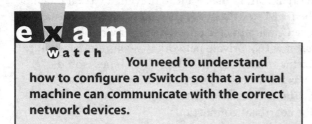

An organization can create different types of vSwitches to control network connectivity to a virtual machine. An external vSwitch allows the virtual machine to communicate with other virtual machines on the same host and with other network devices located outside the host computer. An internal vSwitch allows the virtual machines and the host to communicate with each other, but the virtual machine is unable to communicate with network devices located outside the host computer.

Planning the vSwitch configuration is extremely important to an organization's virtualization design. It is equally important for the organization to make sure the vSwitch that the virtual machine uses to communicate is configured correctly. Proper design of the vSwitch environment is critical to the virtual machine being able to communicate to the correct part of the network.

Memory

Managing memory on a virtual machine is different than managing memory on a physical server. When dealing with a physical server, an organization has to decide at the time of purchase how much memory that server needs to have. When building or deploying a virtual machine, the organization can change the memory on the fly as needed. Also, a virtual machine only consumes memory if that virtual machine is running, so memory can be freed up by shutting down less important virtual machines, if necessary.

Managing virtual machine memory is easier and allows the organization to maximize its resources for that virtual machine. It can set the initial size of the virtual machine's memory and change that setting after the virtual machine has been created and is operational. For example, the organization may have a virtual machine running file and print services and may be uncertain what the memory requirements ultimately will be. In this instance, it can configure a low amount of memory to start and then monitor the virtual machine to determine its memory utilization. If the virtual machine reaches 90 or 100 percent utilization, the organization can easily increase the amount of memory without having to purchase additional hardware.

Keep in mind, however, that increasing virtual machine memory is only possible if there is additional memory available on the virtualization host computer. The host computer must also have enough physical memory available to start the virtual machine; if there is not enough available physical memory, the virtual machine will not be allowed to start. Earlier in this chapter, you learned how to plan memory allocation on the virtualization host; now you can see why planning the host computer resources is so important.

There are three things that you should consider when provisioning a virtual machine and assigning memory to it:

■ **Operating system requirements**   Ensure that the amount of memory meets the minimum recommendations for the operating system that the virtual machine is going to be running.

■ **Application requirements**   Consider the applications the virtual machine will be running. If a particular application requires a lot of memory on a physical server, it might need a similar setup on a virtual machine.

■ **Virtual machine neighbors**   Consider what other virtual machines are running on the host computer that will be competing with this virtual machine for memory resources and whether other applications are going to be running on the host computer that might need resources as well.

Resource contention should not be a major factor on a type 1 hypervisor since best practice is not to run any additional software on the host computer. However, if there are additional applications running on the host computer besides the hypervisor, you should consider that when planning memory size on a virtual machine. On a type 2 hypervisor, other applications would be running on the host computer and would require memory, so those applications would need to be factored in when determining memory size for the virtual machine.

Memory can be assigned to a virtual machine in a couple of ways. One option is to configure a static amount of memory that is assigned to the virtual machine at all times. Static memory is a predefined amount of memory that is allocated to the virtual machine. If an organization uses this setting for all the virtual machines on a host computer, then the host computer must have at least enough physical memory to support those virtual machines.

A second option is to use dynamic memory, which allows a company to assign a minimum and maximum amount of memory to a virtual machine. With dynamic memory, a virtual machine consumes memory based on its current workload. Dynamic memory also allows for overcommitting the host computer's physical memory so that more virtual machines can be run on that host computer.

Dynamic memory can be enabled on a per-virtual-machine basis, targeting only those virtual machines that can benefit from it. One way for a company to determine if it should use static or dynamic memory is by taking into account the application the virtual machine will be running. For example, if the company has a virtual machine that is running an application that uses a fixed amount of memory, the better option is to use static memory and allocate exactly the amount of memory that virtual machine needs. Managing virtual machine memory is a key component to the performance of the virtualization environment and needs to be carefully planned and executed. Table 5-4, shown earlier, lists the maximum amount of memory that is available for various types of virtual machines.

Storage Virtualization

Planning where to store the virtual disks and configuration files for the virtual machine is something that needs careful consideration. Storage virtualization groups multiple network storage devices into a single storage unit that can be managed from a central console and used by a virtual machine or host computer.

Storage virtualization usually occurs in a storage area network (SAN) where a high-speed collection of shared storage devices can be used. Managing storage devices can be a complex and tedious task for an administrator. Storage virtualization simplifies the administration of common storage tasks, such as archiving, recovery, backups, and the configuration of storage.

A virtualized storage environment has some distinct advantages over nonvirtualized storage. In a nonvirtualized storage environment, the host computers connect directly to the storage that is internal to the host or an external array. In this scenario, the server takes complete ownership of the physical storage, with an entire disk tied to a single server.

Virtualized storage enables the use of shared storage devices and solves the issue of a single server owning the storage by allowing multiple host servers and virtual machines to simultaneously access the storage. Shared storage can present storage to a host computer, and the host computer, in turn, can present the storage to the virtual machine. Multiple host computers can access shared storage at the same time, which allows the virtual machines to migrate between host computers.Virtualization software supports all the common storage interconnects for block-based storage, including Fibre Channel, iSCSI, Fibre Channel over Ethernet (FCoE), and direct attached storage. The virtualization software provides an interface to simplify how the virtual machine accesses the storage. It also presents SCSI and IDE controllers to the virtual machines so that the operating system can recognize the storage. The virtual machine sees only a simple physical disk attached via the IDE or SCSI controller provided by the virtualization software.

Virtual storage offers the following advantages to a virtual machine:

- Ease of management
- Improved efficiency
- Support for a range of storage types that the native operating system might not support
- Flexible placement and migration

If an organization uses Fibre Channel to connect to shared storage, it is taking advantage of N_Port ID Virtualization (NPIV), a technology that allows multiple host computers to share a single physical Fibre Channel port identification, or N_Port. This allows a single host bus adapter to register multiple world wide names (WWNs) and N_Port identification numbers. By using NPIV, each host server can present a different WWN to the shared storage device, which allows each host computer to see its own storage.

In addition to storage virtualization, an organization might look to clustered storage to provide increased performance, capacity, and reliability for the storage environment that the virtual machines access. Clustered storage combines multiple storage devices together to distribute the workload between storage devices and provide access to the virtual machine files, regardless of the physical location of the files.

Guest Tools

Guest tools are software additions that are added to a virtual machine after the operating system has been installed. They enhance the performance of a virtual machine and improve the interaction between the virtual machine and the host computer. Guest tools also make it easier to manage a virtual machine by providing enhanced features, such as faster graphics performance, time synchronization between host and guest, increased network performance, and the ability to copy files between the virtual machine and the host computer. The guest tools are also responsible for integrating the drivers into the guest virtual machine operating system.

A guest virtual machine operating system can run without installing guest tools, but it loses a lot of the important functionality and ease of administration without them. Installing the guest tools is easy and straightforward on all major virtualization applications and is sometimes even built into the operating system. For example, a Windows Server 2012 virtual machine created using Microsoft Hyper-V has the virtual machine integration services already loaded. Most operating systems, including Microsoft Windows, Linux, Solaris, FreeBSD, NetWare, and MacOS, support installation of guest tools.

Virtualized Infrastructure Service Elements

Experts used to debate about which workloads were suitable for virtualization and which were not. However, today, most workloads are safe to run in a virtual machine. Virtualization is not just used for testing or development environments. Rather, enterprise-grade production systems run in highly virtualized environments. Of course, the purpose of virtual machines is to run services or applications, and this section presents some of the types of services you should be familiar with as you build out a virtualized infrastructure into a given cloud solution.

DNS

Domain Name System (DNS) is the backbone of network communication for it provides name resolution for devices on the local network, domain, or the Internet. DNS servers respond to queries for name resolution for hosts that reside within their particular space. This space is called a zone. Name resolution is the process whereby a name such as cloudplus.comptia.com is translated into its associated IP address. Each machine requires a unique IP address to communicate on a network. On the Internet, those addresses are assigned and distributed to companies, and DNS servers maintain records of which names are associated with those addresses so that users and applications can access the services on those hosts.

Computers that are configured with IP are usually configured with one or more DNS servers. These servers are typically the DNS servers closest to the computer, such as those of an organization's domain or a user's or company's Internet service provider (ISP). On a local domain network, computers can be referenced by just their name. For example, a user using a workstation on the cloudplus.com domain who wants to connect to a server called server1 can just type in the host name, server1, and their computer will query the local DNS server for the address associated with server1.cloudplus.com. However, when a computer wants to connect to a resource outside its own network, it must use a fully qualified domain name (FQDN). This includes the name of the host and the domain. For example, the FQDN of server1 in this example is server1.cloudplus.com.

DNS servers can be configured to be authoritative for a zone. Those that are authoritative are associated with the owner of the domain, and they provide the most accurate results. However, computers often receive answers to DNS queries that are nonauthoritative. That is because their local DNS server issues queries on their behalf when it does not know of other domain names. It retains a local cache of queries and can respond back from that cache until the cache expires. DNS servers inform other servers how long a DNS entry may be cached so that stale records are not provided back to users.

DHCP

Each machine on an IP network needs a unique address to communicate. These addresses can be assigned manually or automatically. Dynamic Host Configuration Protocol (DHCP) is a service that hands out IP addresses to machines upon request. This is most often used for end-user workstations or for devices that connect to an ISP. DHCP servers are configured with one or more scopes. Each scope can hand out IP addresses from a specific range. Within that range, some addresses can be reserved for a specific machine by assigning an IP address to the MAC address of the desired node in the DHCP configuration. A MAC address is a unique identifier that is placed on a network interface port from the manufacturer.

DHCP servers usually hand out other information in addition to the IP address. This information includes the DNS server, default gateway, local time server, and other options such as where server boot images can be found. (DNS servers were discussed in the previous section.) The default gateway is the device that computers will send traffic to if its destination does not reside on the local network, VLAN, or VXLAN.

Certificate Services

Certificates are cryptographic functions that can be used to encrypt data in a public key infrastructure (PKI) or verify the authenticity of devices, program code, or websites. Certificates are cryptographic in that they are a function of an encryption algorithm where a public and private key pair can be used to sign data from one another (e.g., that requires use of a public and private key pair to sign and validate data sent between the certificate holders.) Data encrypted with a public key can only be decrypted by the associated private key, and data encrypted by the private key can only be decrypted by the associated public key. Similarly, data that is signed with the private key can prove authenticity because the signature can be decrypted with the public key, proving that the signer has the private key.

As you can surmise from the names, the private key is held within the certificate and the public key is made available to anyone who wants it. In order to validate itself as authentic, a website, program code, or a device can sign data with its digital signature (private key). If the digital signature can be read with the public key, the certificate is validated because the private key is not shared.

PKI is required to manage the exchange of keys and validation of certificates. Computers obtain public keys and certificate serial numbers from a certificate server in order to validate the certificates issued by it. However, computers do not simply trust any certificate server. Computers are configured by default to trust several root certificate authorities. These authorities can issue certificates to other certificate servers, granting them the right to issue certificates for a specific domain. The certificate authority must go through a process to prove its identity before the root provides it with a subordinate certificate used to issue certificates. Externally validated certificates from trusted third parties are not free. Organizations must pay for these certificates. Most certificates are purchased for a specific use from a trusted third-party certificate authority.

Companies can issue their own certificates without being part of the trusted certificate chain leading back to a trusted certificate authority. This is often performed for authentication or encryption on a domain. Computers in the domain can be configured to trust the domain certificate authority, and that certificate authority then issues certificates to the machines on the domain so that they can authenticate each other. However, if a company tries to use certificates generated on its own domain for use over the Internet, those outside the organization will not trust the certificates assigned to the sites, and they will receive warnings or errors in displaying the page.

Local Agents

A variety of services utilize agent software to perform functions on a virtual machine. This includes backup software, licensing modules, performance monitoring, and security software, to name a few. A centralized tool coordinates tasks that run on local agents installed on individual virtual machines. The local agent can talk to the centralized tool to report back metrics, perform backup tasks, or obtain licensing information and then this information can be reviewed within the central tool. Local agents make it possible for enterprise software to manage individual devices to a greater degree than would be allowed through remote management configuration.

Cloud services offer virtual machine extensions that offer the same or similar functionality to local agents. For example, a company using Azure, Amazon Web Services, or Rackspace might purchase extensions for backup recovery, antivirus, software installation, or other features as defined by the cloud service. This makes it easy to manage cloud systems from the same centralized consoles that manage other organizational machines.

Antivirus

Antivirus software is a necessity for virtual machines. Antivirus software scans files resident on a machine and processes in memory and analyzes them for signatures or anomalous behavioral patterns. Signatures describe what a malicious process or file looks like so that antivirus software can recognize it. Behavioral patterns analyze the way a system operates to identify conditions that are outside the norm or indicative of malicious behavior, in response to which the antivirus software takes action to restrict, block, or log activity based on the software's configuration.

Some hypervisor-aware antivirus software can perform a function called hypervisor introspection where the antivirus software resides on the host rather than on individual machines. Since the host has access to the virtual memory for each virtual machine and the virtual hard disks, the hypervisor-aware antivirus software can monitor all memory for viruses and block any it recognizes as malicious without requiring a separate agent on each machine.

Load Balancing

Some services can be configured to run on multiple machines so that the work of processing requests and servicing end users can be divided among multiple servers. This process is known as load balancing.

With load balancing, a standard virtual machine can be configured to support a set number of users. When demand reaches a specific threshold, another virtual machine can be created from the standard template and joined into the cluster to balance the load.

Load balancing is also valuable when performing system maintenance, as systems can be added or removed from the load-balancing cluster at will. However, load balancing is different from failover clustering in that machines cannot be failed over immediately without a loss of connection with end users. Instead, load-balanced machines are drain stopped. This tells the coordinating process not to send new connections to the node. The node finishes servicing all the user requests and then can be taken offline without impacting the overall availability of the system.

Multifactor Authentication

Usernames and passwords are not always sufficient for authenticating to sensitive servers and services. Multifactor authentication is a method whereby several authenticating values are used instead of just one. The possible combinations include something you know, something you are, something you have, something you do, and somewhere you are.

The username/password is something you know. Something you are is a biometric value such as a fingerprint, iris scan, or facial scan. Something you have can be a token authenticator, a small device that generates a number string at regular intervals. A companion device on the server also keeps track of the same numbers. Users provide the token value along with their username and password to authenticate. Other forms of multifactor authentication include the use of proximity cards, which activate when brought close to an authenticator, account cards such as an ATM card that is used in conjunction with a pin, or software that runs on a mobile phone or a secondary device. Such software is configured to receive a pin or code that can be entered on another device. Users must have the device with the software on it in order to authenticate.

Evaluate the servers in your environment based on the security risk they represent and determine which ones should require multifactor authentication to access. Virtualization hosts are commonly selected for multifactor authentication by companies because access to the host can provide the ability to disrupt operations for the virtual machines on the host or possibly to access the data on the virtual machines.

Firewall

Firewalls are software or hardware designed to screen traffic traversing a network link. Some firewalls sit between the Internet and a location or between more and less secure network segments. Virtual machines and physical computers can also run firewall software that blocks access to the computer when that access does not meet specific criteria. These firewalls are called host-based firewalls.

IDS/IPS

An intrusion detection system (IDS) or an intrusion prevention system (IPS) is a system designed to evaluate data on a device or network link for signs of malicious behavior. The IDS or IPS operates like antivirus for network data by using signatures of known attack patterns, and heuristics that can detect behavior that appears malicious. Both IDSs and IPSs notify administrators if they detect attacks, but IPSs can also block the traffic or perform other actions as configured to prevent intrusion.

An IDS or IPS that exists on a network device is called a network-based IDS (NIDS) or network-based IPS (NIPS), while an IDS or IPS that exists on a virtual machine, workstation, or other node is called a host-based IDS (HIDS) or host-based IPS (HIPS).

CERTIFICATION SUMMARY

Knowing how to plan a virtualization environment is of great importance to any organization wishing to adopt a cloud computing infrastructure. A virtualization host computer uses software called a hypervisor that allows a single physical computer to host multiple guests called virtual machines, which can run different operating systems and have different amounts of compute resources assigned to each guest. Understanding how a host computer and a guest virtual machine interact and share resources is a key concept not only to the CompTIA Cloud+ exam but to a successful cloud computing implementation.

KEY TERMS

Use the following list to review the key terms discussed in this chapter. The definitions also can be found in the glossary.

antivirus software   A piece of software that scans files resident on a machine and processes in memory and analyzes them for signatures or anomalous behavioral patterns. If malicious code or behavior is detected, antivirus software takes action to restrict, block, or log activity based on the software's configuration.

Basic Input/Output System (BIOS)   Built-in software that allows the computer to boot without an operating system and controls the code required to manage the keyboard, display, disk drives, and some other functions.

central processing unit (CPU)   Hardware device responsible for executing all of the instructions from the operating system and software.

certificate services   The infrastructure required to manage the exchange of keys and validation of certificates.

Domain Name System (DNS)   A service that provides name resolution for devices by converting a name to its associated IP address.

Dynamic Host Configuration Protocol (DHCP)   A service that hands out IP addresses to machines upon request.

firewall   A piece of software or hardware that screens traffic traversing a network link. When the firewall screens traffic for the local links in a host, it is known as a host-based firewall.

firmware   Set of instructions that is programmed into a specific hardware device that instructs the hardware device how to communicate with the computer system.

guest tools   Software additions that are added to a virtual machine after the operating system has been installed to improve the interaction between the virtual machine and the virtualization host.

hardware-assisted virtualization   Enables efficient full virtualization used to simulate a complete hardware environment or a virtual machine.

hyperthreading   A technology that creates two logical CPU cores for each physical CPU core that supports hyperthreading.

hypervisor   A piece of software that creates and manages the virtual infrastructure, including virtual switch (vSwitch), virtual CPU (vCPU), virtual memory, virtual disks, and virtual machines.

intrusion detection system (IDS)   A piece of software or hardware that evaluates data on a device or network link for signs of malicious behavior and alerts or logs such activity.

intrusion prevention system (IPS)   A piece of software or hardware that evaluates data on a device or network link for signs of malicious behavior and blocks, restricts, alerts, or logs such activity.

load balancing   Running services on multiple machines to share the burden of processing requests and servicing end users.

memory ballooning   A process whereby virtual machines give up some of their memory for another virtual machine on the host.

memory burst   The maximum amount of memory a virtual machine can allocate from the host.

N_Port ID Virtualization (NPIV)   Allows multiple host computers to share a single physical Fibre Channel port identification or N_Port.

network interface card (NIC)   Computer component that is used to connect a computer to a computer network.

open-source hypervisor   Hypervisor software provided at no cost and delivers the same ability to run multiple guest virtual machines on a single host.

overcommitment   Assigning more resources to virtual machines than are available to the physical host.

overcommitment ratio   The number of vCPUs allocated for each physical CPU expressed as a ratio such as 3:1, meaning three vCPUs for one physical CPU.

proprietary   Software that is developed and licensed under an exclusive legal right of the copyright holder.

storage virtualization   Groups multiple network storage devices into a single storage unit that can be managed from a central console and presented to a virtual machine or host computer as a single storage unit.

thick provisioning   Allocates the amount of disk space required when the virtual disk is created.

thin provisioning   Allows a virtual disk to allocate and commit storage space on demand and use only the space it currently requires.

transparent page sharing   A technology that deduplicates hypervisor memory allocated to virtual machines.

type 1 hypervisor   Hypervisor that is created and deployed on a bare metal installation.

type 2 hypervisor   Hypervisor loaded on top of an already existing operating system installation.

virtual allocation table (VAT)   Methods such as nested page tables or shadow page tables for mapping virtual machine memory to that of the host.

virtual CPU (vCPU)   Used on a guest virtual machine and is similar to a physical CPU.

virtual desktop infrastructure (VDI)   A method of virtualizing workstation operating systems in a centralized location whereby end users connect to their virtual desktops remotely.

virtual disk   Emulates a physical disk drive to a virtual machine.

virtual hard disk (VHD)   A virtual disk format used by Microsoft hypervisors.

virtual machine/guest   Emulates a physical computer where the virtualization host translates requests for compute resources to the underlying physical hardware.

virtual machine disk (VMDK)   A virtual hard disk format used by VMware hypervisors.

virtual NIC (vNIC)   Similar to a physical NIC and can connect to a vSwitch and be assigned an IP address, default gateway, and subnet mask.

virtual switch (vSwitch)   Similar to a physical switch, allows network devices to be connected and is used to control how the network traffic flows between the virtual machines and the virtualization host.

virtualization host   System that hosts or contains guest virtual machines.

VT-x   A set of instructions performing virtualization functions that is built into the CPU.

TWO-MINUTE DRILL

Hypervisor

- ❑ A hypervisor is software that allows a computer system to run multiple operating systems on a single piece of hardware.
- ❑ A computer that runs the hypervisor and hosts multiple operating systems is called the host computer.
- ❑ A type 1 hypervisor is deployed on a bare metal system and communicates directly with the physical server hardware.
- ❑ A type 2 hypervisor is loaded on top of a system that is already running an operating system. It relies on that operating system to load a guest virtual machine.
- ❑ An open-source hypervisor is provided at no cost, whereas a proprietary hypervisor is purchased by the customer under a licensing agreement.
- ❑ A consumer is more likely to use a type 2 hypervisor, and an enterprise is more likely to use a type 1 hypervisor to host multiple guest virtual machines.

Virtualization Host

- ❑ In order for a computer to be configured as a host computer, the BIOS must support and have hardware-assisted virtualization enabled, which might require a firmware upgrade.
- ❑ Newer systems use the Unified Extensible Firmware Interface (UEFI), a system that replaces BIOS. UEFI addresses limitations in BIOS by allowing both 32-bit and 64-bit processing, more than 1MB of addressable memory, and drives larger than 2.1TB.
- ❑ Planning the resources a virtualization host requires to support the virtual environment is a key step to having a successful virtualization implementation.
- ❑ When planning how many CPUs to have in a host computer, the number of CPU cores is more important than the speed of the CPU.
- ❑ When purchasing NICs for a host computer, it is important that they support some of the advanced features, like TCP Segmentation Off-Load (TSO), Jumbo Frames (JF), checksum off-load, and Large Receive Off-Load (LRO).

Virtual Machine

- ❑ A virtual machine is very similar to a physical computer, with the primary difference being a virtual machine's compute resources are managed by a hypervisor.

❑ A virtual environment allows you to isolate a virtual machine from the rest of the network for testing and development of new applications and operating systems.

❑ A virtual disk emulates a physical disk and is managed by the virtual machine in the same manner a physical disk would be.

❑ A virtual disk can be either thick or thin. A thin-provisioned disk starts out small and grows as data is written to it, whereas a thick disk size is defined when the disk is created.

❑ A virtual NIC (vNIC) is similar to a physical NIC and can be assigned an IP address, default gateway, and subnet mask.

❑ A vNIC is connected to a vSwitch, and the vSwitch dictates how the vNIC and virtual machine communicate on the network.

❑ A virtual machine can use dynamic memory, which allows the virtual machine to start with a smaller amount of memory and increase it based on the load on the virtual machine.

❑ Storage virtualization groups multiple network storage devices into a single storage unit that can be managed from a central console and presented to a virtual machine or host computer as a single storage unit.

❑ Guest tools are software additions that provide features and enhancements to a virtual machine, along with improving the interaction between a virtual machine and a host computer.

Virtualized Infrastructure Service Elements

❑ DNS provides name resolution, translating domain names to IP addresses.

❑ Each machine on an IP network needs a unique address to communicate. These addresses can be assigned manually or automatically. DHCP is a service that hands out IP addresses to machines upon request.

❑ Certificates are used to encrypt data in a public key infrastructure (PKI) or verify the authenticity of devices, program code, or websites.

❑ Backup software, licensing modules, performance monitoring, and security software may employ agents to perform functions on machines. Agents communicate back with a server service to operate on other servers or workstations.

❑ Antivirus software scans files resident on a machine and processes in memory and analyzes them for signatures or anomalous behavioral patterns.

❑ Some services can be configured to run on multiple machines so that the work of processing requests and servicing end users can be divided among multiple servers. This process is known as load balancing.

Q SELF TEST

The following questions will help you measure your understanding of the material presented in this chapter. As indicated, some questions may have more than one correct answer, so be sure to read all the answer choices carefully.

Hypervisor

1. Which of the following hypervisors would provide the best performance for a host machine?
   A. Type 1
   B. Type 2
   C. Open source
   D. Proprietary

2. You are investigating which technology is best suited for virtualizing a server operating system for personal use on a desktop computer. Which of the following technologies would you recommend?
   A. Type 1
   B. Type 2
   C. SAN
   D. RAID 6

3. Which of the following hypervisors runs on a bare metal system?
   A. Open source
   B. Proprietary
   C. Type 1
   D. Type 2

4. What type of hypervisor is provided to an enterprise to use without cost?
   A. Proprietary
   B. Open source
   C. Type 1
   D. Type 2

5. An administrator is testing a variety of operating systems while performing other functions like surfing the Internet and word processing. What type of hypervisor is the admin most likely using?
    A. Type 1
    B. Enterprise hypervisor
    C. Type 2
    D. Open source

Virtualization Host

6. You are deploying two virtual servers. One of the virtual servers is a heavily used database server and the other is a lightly used print server. What virtual CPU configuration would you recommend?
    A. One virtual CPU for the database server and two virtual CPUs for the print server
    B. Two virtual CPUs for the database server and two virtual CPUs for the print server
    C. Two virtual CPUs for the database server and one virtual CPU for the print server
    D. Three virtual CPUs for the print server and two virtual CPUs for the database server

7. An administrator is trying to enable hardware-assisted virtualization in the BIOS of a computer and notices it is not an option. He checks the specification on the manufacturer's website and finds that the system should support hardware-assisted virtualization. What is most likely the reason why he can't enable it?
    A. The BIOS needs a firmware update.
    B. The BIOS is corrupt.
    C. Hardware-assisted virtualization is enabled in the operating system, not the BIOS.
    D. The firmware is corrupt.

8. You have been tasked with planning the purchase of a new virtualization host computer. When it comes time to recommend the processor type, which processor capability is more important?
    A. CPUs are more important than CPU cores and cache.
    B. CPU cores and cache are more important than CPUs.
    C. CPU speed is more important than CPU cores and cache.
    D. CPU cores and cache are more important than CPU speed.

9. Which of the following would be a requirement when planning the compute resources for a host computer?
    A. The host computer does not need to have enough compute resources to support the virtual machine workload.
    B. The host computer must have enough compute resources to support the virtual machine workload.
    C. The host computer must be running a support operating system.
    D. The number of virtual machines running Microsoft Windows must be known.

Virtual Machine

10. In a virtual machine, which component appears as an Ethernet adapter?
    A. Virtual HBA
    B. Virtual NIC
    C. Virtual switch
    D. Virtual router

11. An administrator deploys a new virtual machine. After logging on to the virtual machine, she notices that it has a different time setting than the host. What is most likely the cause of this issue?
    A. The virtual machine cannot communicate with the network.
    B. The guest tools are not installed.
    C. The vNIC is not configured correctly.
    D. The VLAN tag is incorrect.

12. Which of the following groups multiple network storage devices into a single storage unit that can be managed from a central console and used by a virtual machine or host computer?
    A. Virtual switch
    B. Virtual HBA
    C. Virtual NIC
    D. Storage virtualization

13. Which type of memory allows a virtual machine to start with a smaller amount of memory and increase it based on the workload of the virtual machine?
    A. Startup RAM
    B. Static memory
    C. Virtual memory
    D. Dynamic memory

14. Which component controls how the network traffic flows between the virtual machines and the host computer and also how network traffic flows between the virtual machine and other network devices in the organization?
    A. Virtual NIC
    B. Virtual storage
    C. Virtual HBA
    D. Virtual switch

Virtualized Infrastructure Service Elements

15. Which piece of information is required to create a DHCP reservation?
    A. MAC address
    B. Default gateway
    C. Server name
    D. Host record

16. Which of the following could not be used as one part of a multifactor authentication solution?
    A. Fingerprint
    B. Token
    C. Reference
    D. Proximity card

A SELF TEST ANSWERS

Hypervisor

1. ☑ **A.** A type 1 hypervisor is one that is created and deployed on a bare metal installation. The hypervisor communicates directly with the physical server hardware and boots before the operating system. Due to the way the hypervisor interacts with the host computer, a type 1 hypervisor will provide improved performance versus the other answer choices.
   ☒ **B, C,** and **D** are incorrect. A type 2 hypervisor is loaded on top of an already existing operating system installation, and the underlying operating system is what impacts performance. While it could be argued that an open-source hypervisor might perform better than a proprietary hypervisor, the open-source hypervisor would still be considered a type 1 hypervisor.

2. ☑ **B.** A type 2 hypervisor is more suited for personal use because it can be installed directly on top of an existing operating system. Most desktop manufacturers support hardware virtualization on their desktops, which would allow you to run a type 2 hypervisor on your existing operating system.
   ☒ **A, C,** and **D** are incorrect. A type 1 hypervisor is more suited for an enterprise environment where the host computer is designed and configured to do nothing but virtualization. A SAN and RAID 6 would not be a required consideration when running a personal virtualization solution.

3. ☑ **C.** A type 1 hypervisor is one that is created and deployed on a bare metal installation.
☒ **A, B,** and **D** are incorrect. A type 2 hypervisor is loaded on top of an already existing operating system installation. Type 1 or type 2 hypervisors can be either open-source or proprietary hypervisors.

4. ☑ **B.** An open-source hypervisor is provided at no cost and delivers the same ability as a proprietary hypervisor to run multiple guest virtual machines on a single host.
☒ **A, C,** and **D** are incorrect. A proprietary hypervisor is one that is developed and licensed under an exclusive legal right of the copyright holder and must be purchased by the customer. Type 1 or type 2 hypervisors can be either open-source or proprietary hypervisors.

5. ☑ **C.** A type 2 hypervisor allows an administrator to run virtual machines on top of an existing operating system while surfing the Internet and running word processing on the host computer.
☒ **A, B,** and **D** are incorrect. A type 1 hypervisor could be used to run virtual machines and at the same time surf the Internet and do word processing, but it would not be best practice. It is not advised to run additional applications on the host computer other than the type 1 hypervisor software due to security risks and resource utilization. An enterprise hypervisor is not a valid hypervisor. An open-source hypervisor can be either a type 1 or type 2 hypervisor.

Virtualization Host

6. ☑ **C.** When assigning virtual CPUs, you want to assign as many as possible to the heavily used application. If an application is not going to be heavily utilized, you should assign the minimum amount of virtual CPUs. In this case the database server is heavily utilized so it should get more CPUs than the lightly used print server.
☒ **A, B,** and **D** are incorrect. You would not need to assign the print server more than one virtual CPU, and you would want to assign the database server more virtual CPUs than the print server.

7. ☑ **A.** If the manufacturer states that the hardware should support hardware-assisted virtualization and the option is unavailable in the BIOS, the most likely cause is that the BIOS needs a firmware update to add the additional feature.
☒ **B, C,** and **D** are incorrect. While there could be additional reasons that the feature is not available in the BIOS, the first thing to consider would be to update the BIOS firmware.

8. ☑ **D.** You are better off spending money on more cores with more cache rather than on faster CPU speed. When it comes to virtualization, you want as many CPU cores as possible to assign to the virtual machine.
☒ **A, B,** and **C** are incorrect. While CPU speed is important, CPU cores and cache are more important. When determining where to spend the extra budget, you want to spend it on cores and cache over speed.

9. ☑ **B.** When you are planning for and determining the compute resources for a host computer, you need to make sure there are enough resources to handle the virtual machine workload that the host computer is expected to support.
☒ **A, C,** and **D** are incorrect. The most important thing for planning compute resources on a host computer is to have enough resources to cover the virtual machine load.

Virtual Machine

10. ☑ **B.** A virtual network interface card does not have any physical components; it is a software component made up of software drivers that mimics a physical NIC and appears as an Ethernet adapter on a virtual machine.

☒ **A, C,** and **D** are incorrect. None of these options would be shown as an Ethernet adapter on a virtual machine when they are added to a virtual machine.

11. ☑ **B.** Guest tools are software additions that are added to a virtual machine after the operating system has been installed. Among other things, the guest tools allow a virtual machine to synchronize its time with a host computer.

☒ **A, C,** and **D** are incorrect. The guest tools allow the virtual machine to use the host computer as a time source. Without the guest tools, the virtual machine might not have the correct time.

12. ☑ **D.** Storage virtualization consolidates multiple storage devices into a single unit and simplifies the administration of common storage tasks.

☒ **A, B,** and **C** are incorrect. A virtual switch, virtual HBA, and vNIC can all be used to access shared storage over the network, but they would not be used to create shared storage.

13. ☑ **D.** Dynamic memory allows you to assign a minimum and maximum amount of memory to a virtual machine. This allows a virtual machine to consume memory dynamically based on its current workload.

☒ **A, B,** and **C** are incorrect. The other memory options in the question do not allow the virtual machine to increase its memory as needed since they are statically assigned.

14. ☑ **D.** The vSwitch is responsible for how the network traffic flows between virtual machines and the host and between virtual machines and other network devices.

☒ **A, B,** and **C** are incorrect. A vNIC allows you to connect to a vSwitch. A virtual HBA would allow you to connect to a storage device. Virtual storage does not allow you to control how the virtual machine connects with the network.

Virtualized Infrastructure Service Elements

15. ☑ **A.** DHCP reservations use the system's MAC address to set aside an IP address for that machine.

☒ **B, C,** and **D** are incorrect. The default gateway is a configuration option for the DHCP server but is not used to configure DHCP reservations. The server name is not unique enough to use for DHCP reservations because a server may have multiple network interface cards. A host record is a DNS mapping of name to IP address and is not used for DHCP reservations.

16. ☑ **C.** References are used in the real world to validate a person. However, computers do not accept references as a method of authentication. The other items are all forms of multifactor authentication.

☒ **A, B,** and **D** are incorrect. Each of these is a form of multifactor authentication. A fingerprint is something you are, and the token and proximity card are both things you have. The third main type of multifactor authentication is something you know, which is usually the username and password.

Chapter 6

Virtualization and the Cloud

Virtualization is the key building block to cloud computing and it is used by cloud providers to offer services to cloud consumers. Virtualization is the component that makes it possible for cloud services to provide a scalable, elastic, and on-demand environment. For example, cloud services may have thousands of hypervisors. When a cloud consumer requests a new server, the cloud provider provisions a new virtual machine from a hypervisor. No new physical hardware needs to be put in place to service the request.

Virtualization allows an organization to easily scale its computing environment both up and down to meet its needs. When combined with cloud computing, virtualization takes advantage of the unlimited computing resources provided externally by a cloud provider to provide flexible and scalable virtualization solutions.

Virtualization will continue to play a big role in cloud computing, as it is the technology that allows a cloud provider to deliver low-cost hosting environments to organizations no matter the size of the enterprise.

CERTIFICATION OBJECTIVE 6.01

Benefits of Virtualization in a Cloud Environment

Cloud computing and virtualization go hand in hand. Virtualization makes cloud computing more efficient and easier to manage. Virtualization consolidates many physical servers into virtual machines running on fewer physical servers functioning as hosts. Through virtualization, a single host can run many guest operating systems and multiple applications instead of a single application on each server. Virtualization reduces the number of servers needed to host IT services, in turn lessening rack space, power consumption, and administration.

Virtualization transforms compute resources into a centralized, sharable pool of resources that an organization can allocate to its business units on demand while still maintaining control of resources and applications.

Shared Resources

Cloud computing can provide compute resources as a centralized resource through shared resources. Shared resources are distributed on an as-needed basis to the cloud consumer. Thus, sharing resources improves efficiency and reduces costs for an organization.

Virtualization helps to simplify the process of sharing compute resources. As we discussed in Chapter 5, virtualization also increases the efficiency of hardware utilization. The cloud, on the other hand, adds a layer of management that allows a virtual machine to be created quickly and scaled to meet the demands of the organization.

Figure 6-1 shows an example of how shared resources are configured.

Elasticity

Elastic computing allows compute resources to vary dynamically to meet a variable workload. A primary reason organizations implement a cloud computing model is the ability to dynamically increase or decrease the compute resources of their virtual environment.

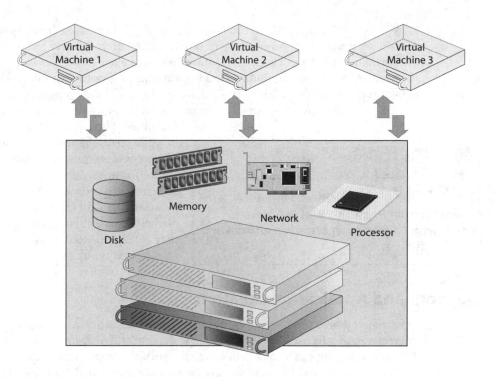

FIGURE 6-1

An illustration of shared resources in a cloud environment

A cloud provider can support elasticity by using resource pooling. Resource pooling allows compute resources to be pooled to serve multiple consumers by using a multitenant model. Resource pooling can provide a unique set of resources to cloud consumers so that physical and virtual resources can be dynamically assigned and reassigned based on cloud consumer demands.

With cloud computing and elasticity, the time to add or remove cloud resources and the time it takes to implement an application can both be drastically reduced. When an organization implements cloud computing and virtualization, it can quickly provision a new server to host an application and then provision that application, which in turn reduces the time it takes to implement new applications and services.

Elasticity allows an organization to scale resources up and down as an application or service requires. In this scenario the organization becomes a cloud consumer and the resources in the cloud appear to the consumer to be infinite, allowing the organization to consume as much or as few resources as it requires. With this new scalable and elastic computing model, an organization can respond to compute resource demands in a quick and efficient manner, saving it time and money. Not only can a cloud consumer dynamically scale the resources it needs, but it can also migrate its applications and data between cloud providers, making the applications portable. With the cloud, an organization can deploy applications to any cloud provider, making its applications portable and scalable.

While virtualization alone could provide many of these same benefits of elasticity and scalability, it would rely on compute resources being purchased and owned by the organization rather than leased from a seemingly infinite resource like a cloud provider.

Another benefit of combining cloud computing and virtualization is the ability to self-provision virtual systems. An IT department in a cloud computing model can grant permissions that give users in other departments the ability to self-provision virtual machines. The IT department still controls how the virtual machine is created and what resources are provided to that virtual machine without actually having to create it. The IT department even can charge or keep track of the users who are creating the virtual machine, making the users accountable for whether they actually need the machine and the resources it requires.

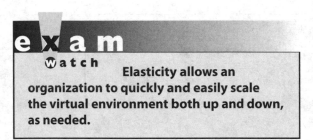

e x a m

ⓦ a t c h   **Elasticity allows an organization to quickly and easily scale the virtual environment both up and down, as needed.**

Network and Application Isolation

As discussed previously, cloud computing and virtualization can enhance network security, increase application agility, and improve scalability and availability of the environment. Cloud computing can also help to create network and application isolation.

Without network isolation, it might be possible for a cloud consumer to intentionally or unintentionally consume a significant share of the network fabric or see another tenant's data in a multitenant environment. Proper configuration of the network to include resource control and security using network isolation helps to ensure these issues are mitigated.

There are also circumstances where certain network traffic needs to be isolated to its own network to provide an initial layer of security, to afford higher bandwidth for specific applications, to enforce chargeback policies, or for use in tiered networks.

Virtualization and cloud computing now provide a means to isolate an application without having to deploy a single application to a single physical server. By combining virtualization and network isolation, it is possible to isolate an application just by correctly configuring a virtual network. Multiple applications can be installed on one physical server and then a given application can be isolated so that it can communicate only with network devices on the same isolated segment.

For example, you can install an application on a virtual machine that is the same version or a newer version of an existing application yet have that install be completely isolated to its own network for testing. The ability for an organization to isolate an application without having to purchase additional hardware is a key factor in the decision to move to virtualization and cloud computing.

Infrastructure Consolidation

Virtualization allows an organization to consolidate its servers and infrastructure by allowing multiple virtual machines to run on a single host computer and even providing a way to isolate a given application from other applications that are installed on other virtual machines on the same host computer. Cloud computing can take it a step further by allowing an organization not only to benefit from virtualization but also to purchase compute resources from a cloud provider. If an organization purchases its compute resources from a cloud provider, it requires fewer hardware resources internally.

Cost Considerations

Consolidating an organization's infrastructure using virtualization and cloud compute resources results in lower costs to the organization since it no longer needs to provide the same power, cooling, administration, and hardware that would be required without virtualization and cloud computing. The organization can realize additional cost savings in reduced time spent on maintaining the network environment since consolidated infrastructure is often easier to manage and maintain.

Energy Savings

Consolidating an organization's infrastructure using virtualization and cloud compute resources results in lower energy consumption to the organization since it no longer needs to provide the same power to equipment that was virtualized or replaced by cloud compute resources. Less hardware also results in reduced cooling needs and less square footage used in an office space.

Dedicated vs. Shared Compute Environment

A dedicated compute environment offers consistent performance because the organization does not need to contend with other tenants for compute resources. However, a dedicated compute environment is more expensive to lease than a shared compute environment because the cloud provider cannot distribute the costs for the compute resources over as many tenants.

Dedicated resources may be a requirement for some regulated industries or for companies with specific data handling or isolation contractual requirements.

Virtual Data Center Creation

Another option an organization has regarding infrastructure consolidation is a virtual data center. A virtual data center offers data center infrastructure as a service and is the same concept as a physical data center with the advantages of cloud computing mixed in.

A virtual data center offers compute resources, network infrastructure, external storage, backups, and security just like a physical data center. A virtual data center also offers virtualization, pay-as-you-grow billing, elasticity, and scalability. An administrator can control the virtual resources by using quotas and security profiles.

A cloud user of a virtual data center can create virtual servers and host applications on those virtual servers based on the security permissions assigned to their user account. It is also possible to create multiple virtual data centers based on either geographic or application isolation requirements.

CERTIFICATION OBJECTIVE 6.02

Virtual Resource Migrations

Now that you understand how cloud computing benefits from virtualization, you need to know how to migrate an organization's current resources into either a virtual environment or a cloud environment.

Migrating servers to a virtual or cloud environment is one of the first steps in adopting a cloud computing model. Organizations do not want to start from scratch when building a virtual or cloud environment; they want the ability to migrate what is in their current data center to a cloud environment.

With the advancements in virtualization and consolidated infrastructures, organizations now see IT resources as a pool of resources that can be managed centrally, not as a single resource. IT administrators now can easily move resources across the network from server to server, from data center to data center, or into a private, public, or hybrid cloud, giving them the ability to balance resource and compute loads more efficiently across multiple, even global, environments.

This section explains the different options for migrating an organization's current infrastructure to a virtual or cloud environment.

Virtual Machine Templates

When an organization is migrating its environment to the cloud, it needs to have a standardized installation policy or profile for its virtual servers. The virtual machines need to have a very similar base installation of the operating system so that all the machines have the same security patches, service packs, and base applications installed.

Virtual machine templates provide a streamlined approach to deploying a fully configured base server image or even a fully configured application server. Virtual machine templates help decrease the installation and configuration costs when deploying virtual machines and lower ongoing maintenance costs, allowing for faster deploy times and lower operational costs.

e x a m

ⓦ a t c h **Virtual machine templates create a standardized set of virtual machine configuration settings that allow for quick deployment of one or multiple virtual machines.**

A virtual machine template can be exported from one virtualization host, and then imported on another virtualization host and be used as a master virtual machine template for all virtualization hosts.

Virtual machine templates provide a standardized group of hardware and software settings that can repeatedly be reused to create new virtual machines that are configured with those specified settings. For example, a virtual machine template can be defined to create a virtual machine with 1024MB of memory, one vCPU, and three virtual hard disks. Alternatively, a virtual machine template can be set up based on an existing, fully configured virtual machine.

In essence, a virtual machine template acts as a master image that an organization can use to quickly and efficiently deploy similar virtual machine instances in its environment. The organization can then maintain the virtual machine templates by applying operating system updates and application patches so that any new virtual machine instances that are created with the template are up to date and ready to use instantly. Figure 6-2 displays a graphical representation of how virtual machine templates work.

Physical to Virtual (P2V)

Along with creating new virtual machines and provisioning those virtual machines quickly and efficiently using virtual machine templates, there will be occasions when an organization needs to convert a physical server to a virtual server. The process of creating a virtual machine from a physical server is called physical to virtual (P2V). Figure 6-3 illustrates how a P2V migration works.

FIGURE 6-2

Representation
of a virtual
machine
template

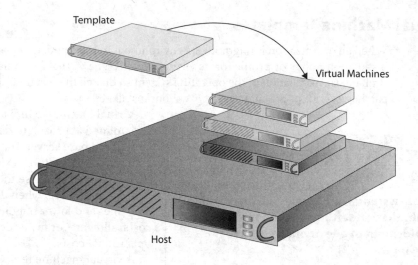

FIGURE 6-3

A graphical
representation
of physical-to-
virtual (P2V)
migration

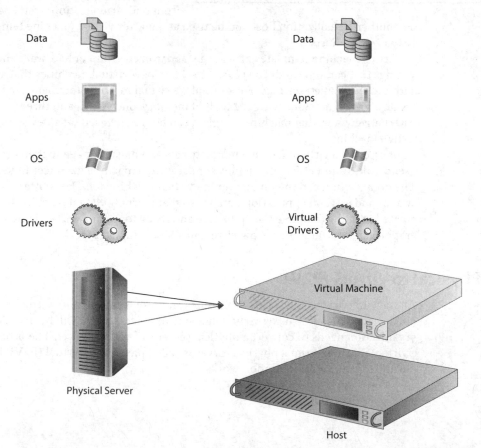

P2V enables the migration of a physical server's operating system, applications, and data to a newly created guest virtual machine on a host computer. There are a three different ways to convert a physical server to a virtual server:

- **Manual** You can manually create a new virtual machine on a host computer and copy all the files from the OS, applications, and data from the source physical server. The manual process is time-consuming and not very effective.

- **Semi-automated** A semi-automated P2V approach uses a software tool to assist in the migration from a physical server to a virtual server. This simplifies the process and gives the administrator some guidance when migrating the physical server. There are also free software tools that help migrate a physical server from a virtual server.

- **Fully automated** The fully automated version uses a software utility that can migrate a physical server over the network without any assistance from an administrator.

EXAM AT WORK

Migrating a Physical Environment to a Virtual Environment

A while back we were brought into an organization to explain the benefits of virtualization and the cloud and why this particular organization should look at virtualizing its data center. After many discussions and planning sessions, the organization decided that virtualization was the right step for it. We as the consultants were responsible for building and configuring the host computer along with the network and storage solution. After all of that was set up and configured, the next task was to migrate the organization's systems from their current physical environment to a virtual environment. We presented the options of using a manual approach or automating the P2V conversion process. We ended up using a combination of manual and automated. Some physical servers were easier to migrate manually or were not supported for migration using the fully automated piece.

We helped the organization migrate its physical server to the virtual server using P2V on the noncritical servers first; then we worked toward the more critical application servers. The automated process is driven by a wizard and was run from the physical server. We loaded the P2V software on the physical server; stopped any services that might cause an issue during the migration; and answered the prompts of the wizard, telling it what host computer to migrate the server to, the name of the virtual machine, virtual hard disk, and so on. After successfully completing that process, the next step was to shut down the physical server and start the virtual server. Once the virtual server loaded, we had to install the guest tools and configure a few minor settings, with the final step to test the application that the server was running. After all the tests ran smoothly, our conversion of the physical server to a virtual server was complete.

Migrating a virtual machine from a physical server can be done either online or offline. With an online migration, the physical computer or source computer remains running and operational during the migration. One of the advantages of the online option is that the source computer is still available during the migration process. This may not be a big advantage, however, depending on the application that is running on the source computer.

When doing an offline P2V conversion, the source computer is taken offline during the migration process. An offline migration provides for a more reliable transition since the source computer is not being utilized. For example, if you are doing a migration of a database server or a domain controller, it would be better to do the migration offline since the system is constantly being utilized.

Before migrating a physical machine to a virtual machine, it is always advisable to check with the application vendor to make sure it supports the hardware and application in a virtual environment.

Virtual to Virtual (V2V)

Similar to P2V, virtual to virtual (V2V) is the process of migrating an operating system, applications, and data, but instead of migrating them from a physical server, they are migrated from a virtual server.

Just like for P2V, software tools are available to fully automate a V2V migration. V2V can be used to copy or restore files and programs from one virtual machine to another. It can also be used to convert a VMware virtual machine to a Hyper-V-supported virtual machine or vice versa.

If the conversion is from VMware to Hyper-V, the process creates a .vhdx file and copies the contents of the .vmdk file to the new .vhdx file so that the virtual machine can be supported in Hyper-V.

The Open Virtualization Format (OVF) is a platform-independent extensible open packaging and distribution format for virtual machines. OVF allows for efficient and flexible allocation of applications, making virtual machines mobile between vendors because the application is vendor and platform neutral. An OVF virtual machine can be deployed on any virtualization platform. Similarly, an Open Virtual Appliance (OVA) is an open standard for a virtual appliance that can be used in a variety of hypervisors from different vendors.

on the job

Recently we were brought into an organization to help it convert its entire virtual environment from VMware to Hyper-V. After building the new Hyper-V host computers and configuring all the settings necessary to support a highly available Hyper-V environment, we used the Microsoft System Center Virtual Machine Manager (SCVMM) to do a V2V migration of all the VMware virtual machines to Hyper-V, again starting with the server running the least critical application and working toward the most critical.

Virtual to Physical (V2P)

The virtual-to-physical (V2P) migration process is not as simple as a P2V. A variety of tools are needed to convert a virtual machine back to a physical machine. Here is a three-step process for doing a V2P conversion:

1. *Generalize the virtual machine security identifiers.* Install and run Microsoft Sysprep on the virtual machine to prepare the image for transfer and allow for hardware configuration changes.
2. *Gather drivers.* Prepare all the drivers for the target physical server before doing the migration.
3. *Convert using a third-party tool.* Use a software tool such as Symantec Ghost or Acronis Universal Restore to facilitate the virtual-to-physical conversion and load the necessary hardware drivers onto the physical machine.

While a V2P conversion is not something that is often done, sometimes it is required, for a couple of different reasons. One of the reasons is to test how the application performs on physical hardware. Some applications may perform better on physical hardware than on virtual hardware. This is not a common circumstance, however, and it is fairly easy to increase the compute resources for a virtual machine to improve the performance of an application that is hosted there.

The more common reason to perform a V2P is that some application vendors do not support their product running a virtual environment. Today almost all vendors do support their application in a virtual environment, but there are still a few who do not. This fact and the complexities of V2P over P2V make V2P a less common scenario. Unlike the P2V process, which requires only the software tool to do the migration, the V2P process involves more planning and utilities and is much more complex.

on the **job** We were called into an organization to help troubleshoot a specific application that was not functioning correctly following a P2V conversion. We determined that an application error was causing the issue. We called the vendor to get support, and they told us they do not support their application in a virtual environment. We were required to do a V2P before the vendor would support it because they wanted to rule out that the virtualization layer was causing the application issue.

Virtual Machine Cloning

Whether an organization creates a virtual machine from scratch or uses one of the migration methods we just discussed, at some point it might want to make a copy of that virtual machine, called a clone.

Installing a guest operating system and all of the applications is a time-consuming process, so virtual machine cloning makes it possible to create one or multiple copies of a virtual machine or a virtual machine template. Clones can also be used to create virtual machine templates from existing machines.

When a company creates a virtual machine clone, it is creating an exact copy of an existing virtual machine. The existing virtual machine then becomes the parent virtual machine of the virtual machine clone. After the clone is created, it is a separate virtual machine that can share virtual disks with the parent virtual machine or create its own separate virtual disks.

Once the virtual machine clone is created, any changes made to the clone do not impact the parent virtual machine and vice versa. A virtual machine clone's MAC address and universally unique identifier (UUID) are different from those of the parent virtual machine.

Virtual machine cloning allows for deploying multiple identical virtual machines to a group. This is useful in a variety of situations. For example, the IT department might create a clone of a virtual machine for each employee, and that clone would contain a group of preconfigured applications. Or the IT department might want to use virtual machine cloning to create a development environment. A virtual machine could be configured with a complete development environment and cloned multiple times to create a baseline configuration for testing new software and applications.

Virtual Machine Snapshots

A virtual machine snapshot captures the state of a virtual machine at the specific time that the snapshot is taken. A virtual machine snapshot can be used to preserve the state and data of a virtual machine at a specific point in time. Reverting to a snapshot is extremely quick compared to restoring from a backup.

It is common for snapshots to be taken before a major software installation or other maintenance. If the work fails or causes issues, the virtual machine can be restored to the state it was in when the snapshot was taken in a very short amount of time.

A snapshot includes the state the virtual machine is in when the snapshot is created. So if a virtual machine is powered off when the snapshot is created, the snapshot will be of a powered off machine. However, if the virtual machine is powered on, the snapshot will contain the RAM and current state so that restoring the snapshot will result in a running virtual machine at the point in time of the snapshot. The snapshot includes all the data and files that make up the virtual machine, including hard disks, memory, and virtual network interface cards.

Multiple snapshots can be taken of a virtual machine. A series of snapshots is organized into a snapshot chain. A snapshot keeps a delta file of all the changes after the snapshot was taken. The delta file records the differences between the current state of the virtual disk and the state the virtual machine was in when the snapshot was taken.

Clones vs. Snapshots

Clones and snapshots have distinct uses and it is important not to confuse their use cases. Virtual machine cloning is used when you want to make a separate copy of a virtual machine for either testing, separate use, or for archival purposes.

However, if you are looking to save the current state of a virtual machine so that you can revert to that state in case of a software installation failure or an administrative mistake, you should create a virtual machine snapshot, not a virtual machine clone.

Storage Migration

Storage migration is the process of transferring data between storage devices. Storage migration can be automated or done manually. Storage migration makes it possible to migrate a virtual machine's storage or disks to a new location and across storage arrays while maintaining continuous availability and service to the virtual machine. It also allows for migrating a virtual machine to a different storage array without any downtime to the virtual machine. Figure 6-4 displays how storage is migrated between storage devices.

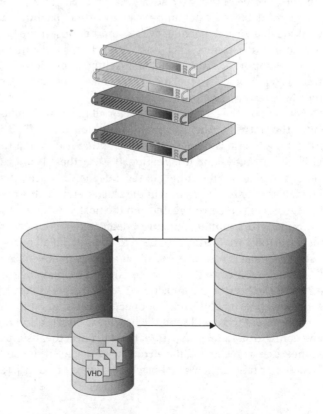

FIGURE 6-4

Using storage migration in a virtual environment

Storage migration eliminates service disruptions to a virtual machine and provides a live and automated way to migrate the virtual machine's disk files from the existing storage location to a new storage destination. Migrating virtual machine storage to different classes of storage is a cost-effective way to manage virtual machine disks based on usage, priority, and need. It also provides a way to take advantage of tiered storage, which we discussed in Chapter 2.

Storage migration allows a virtual machine to be moved from SAN-based storage to NAS, DAS, or cloud-based storage according to the current needs of the virtual machine. Storage migration helps an organization prioritize its storage and the virtual machines that access and utilize that storage.

Host Clustering and HA/DR

High availability (HA) and disaster recovery (DR) functions of a hypervisor enable automatic failover with load balancing. In order to use HA, a cluster consisting of multiple hypervisors, typically utilizing shared storage, must be configured. Some systems require management tools such as VMware's vSphere or Microsoft System Center Virtual Machine Manager to take advantage of some of the more advanced HA capabilities, profiles, and customization.

A high availability cluster auto-balances virtual machines across the available hypervisors. It can also fail a virtual machine over to another host if the host experiences issues or suffers from resource constraints. Each host in the cluster must maintain a reserve of resources so that it can support additional virtual machine migrations in the case of a host failure. HA clusters also periodically rebalance virtual machines across the cluster hosts to ensure that a comfortable resource ceiling is maintained.

Depending on the cluster size, some or all hosts in the cluster will be configured to monitor the status of other hosts and virtual machines. This is accomplished through heartbeat connections that essentially tell other nodes that the hypervisor or virtual machine is still active and functioning. If a heartbeat is not received from a host for a predetermined amount of time (15 seconds for VMware), the virtual machines on that host will be failed over to other hosts in the cluster and the host will be marked as inactive until a heartbeat signal is received again from the host.

Administrators should configure a dedicated network segment or VLAN for heartbeat traffic. Heartbeat traffic does not need to be routed if all hosts are in the same LAN. However, if hosts are spread across sites such as in multisite failover scenarios, the heartbeat network will need to be routed to the other site as well. In cloud environments, a VXLAN is a perfect solution for the heartbeat connection. VXLANs were covered in Chapter 4.

A dedicated virtual NIC does not need to be assigned to virtual machines on a cluster. The hypervisor client tools will send the heartbeat information to the hypervisor. Hypervisors can be configured to take specific actions if a heartbeat signal is not received from a virtual machine, such as restarting the virtual machine, notifying an administrator, reverting to a saved state, or failing the virtual machine over to another host.

on the Job **Virtual machine client tools provide many features to the virtual machine. In addition to the heartbeat connections just mentioned, client tools offer the ability to take snapshots, synchronize the virtual machine clock with the host, direct data transfers from host to virtual machine, and send a remote shutdown or restart command to the virtual machine from the hypervisor without connecting to the virtual machine directly. Client tools need to be installed on the virtual machine in order for these features to work. If you move to a newer hypervisor version, you may be required to upgrade the client tools to a newer version.**

CPU Effect on HA/DR

The hypervisor only has so much information when it chooses the placement of a virtual machine. Some virtual machines might not have many processors configured, but they are still processor intensive. If you find that your HA cluster frequently rebalances the machines in a suboptimal way, there are some actions you can take to remedy the situation.

HA resource determinations are based on a number of factors, including the following:

- Defined quotas and limits
- Which resource is requested by which virtual machine
- The business logic that may be applied by a management system for either a virtual machine or a pool of virtual machines
- The resources that are available at the time of the request

It is possible for the processing power required to make these decisions to outweigh the benefit of the resource allocations, and in those situations administrators can configure their systems to allocate specific resources or blocks of resources to specific hosts to shortcut that logic and designate which resources to use for a specific virtual machine or pool on all requests.

CPU affinity is one such application, in which processes or threads from a specific virtual machine are tied to a specific processor or core, and all subsequent requests from those processes or threads are executed by that same processor or core. Organizations can utilize reservations for virtual machines to guarantee an amount of compute resources for that virtual machine.

Cloud Provider Migrations

It may become necessary to migrate virtual machines or entire services from one cloud provider to another. There is a high level of standardization with cloud platforms, but the migration process still requires a high level of integration between cloud providers for seamless migration.

It is important, when evaluating cloud providers, to ensure that they offer integration and migration options. One cloud provider may not meet your scalability or security requirements, necessitating a move to another cloud provider. Additionally, you may wish to diversify cloud resources across several providers to protect against data loss or service downtime from a single provider's downtime.

In worst-case scenarios, you may need to export the virtual machines into a compatible format and then manually import them or import them with a script into the new cloud provider's environment.

Extending Cloud Scope

A major advantage of cloud systems is that cloud consumers can extend existing workloads into the cloud or extend existing cloud systems, making the cloud a powerful and flexible system for companies to rely upon for changing business needs.

CERTIFICATION OBJECTIVE 6.03

Migration Considerations

Before an organization can migrate a virtual machine using one of the migration methods discussed in the previous section, it needs to consider a few things. Among the most important of those considerations are the compute resources: the CPU, memory, disk I/O, and storage requirements. Migrating a physical server to a virtual machine takes careful planning for it to be successful. Planning the migration of physical servers to the virtual environment is the job of IT administrators, and it is critical that they perform their due diligence and discover all the necessary information about both the server and the application that the server is hosting.

Requirements Gathering

It is important to gather as much information as possible when preparing to migrate physical servers to a virtual environment. This information will help in determining which servers are good candidates for migration and which of those servers to migrate first.

When evaluating a physical server to determine if it is a good candidate for a virtual server, it is important to monitor that server over a period of time. The monitoring period helps to produce an accurate profile of the physical server and its workload.

A monitoring tool such as Windows Performance Monitor or a comparable tool in the Linux environment can be used to get an accurate assessment of the resource usage for that particular server. The longer the trends of the physical server are monitored, the more accurate the evaluation of resource usage will be.

The time spent monitoring the system also varies depending on the applications the physical server is hosting. For example, it would make sense to monitor a database server for a longer period than a print server. In the end, the organization needs to have an accurate picture of memory and CPU usage under various conditions so that it can use that information to plan the resources the physical server might need after it is converted to a virtual machine.

Another consideration to make when determining if a physical server is a good candidate for virtualization is the status of the file system. When converting a physical server to a virtual server, all the data from the physical server is copied to the virtual server as part of the P2V process. Files and data that are not required are sometimes kept on a server, and those files do not need to be migrated as part of the P2V process, nor should they be. It is important, then, to examine the hard drive of the physical server before performing a migration and to remove all files and data that are not required for the server to function and provide the application it is hosting. Examples of these files might be drivers or hardware application such as Wi-Fi tools, firmware update utilities, or other files meant to be used only by a physical machine.

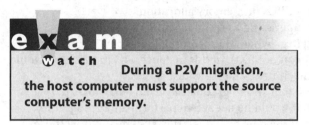

During a P2V migration, the host computer must support the source computer's memory.

Migration Scheduling

After gathering the proper information to perform a successful physical-to-virtual migration, you need to plan when the project should be completed. Migrations will not result in downtime for systems that meet online migration requirements of your specific P2V migration tool such as the VMware vCenter converter or the Microsoft virtual machine converter. However, systems under migration will likely experience slower performance while the migration is underway. It may be advisable to schedule migrations during a downtime or a period where activity is typically at its lowest, such as in the late evening or overnight.

Expect some downtime as part of the migration of a physical server to a virtual server if it does not meet the requirements of your P2V conversion tool. At a minimum, the downtime will consist of the time to start the new virtual machine and shut down the old physical server. DNS changes may also need to be made and replicated to support the new virtual instance of the physical server.

Maintenance schedules should also be implemented or taken into consideration when planning the migration of a physical server to a virtual server. Most organizations have some maintenance schedule set up for routine maintenance on their server infrastructure, and these existing scheduled blocks of time might be suitable for P2V conversions.

Provide the business case for some downtime of the systems to the change management team before embarking on the P2V migration process. Part of that downtime goes back to the resource provisioning discussion earlier in this chapter. It is a balance between under-provisioning the new virtual servers from the beginning or over-provisioning resources. Under-provisioning causes additional and unnecessary downtime of the virtual server and the application the virtual server is hosting. On the other hand, over-provisioning reserves too many resources to the virtual machine and consumes precious host resources where they are not required. This can sometimes even have a detrimental effect on performance.

Upgrading

In addition to P2V, V2P, and V2V, an organization also may upgrade an existing virtual machine to the latest virtual hardware or latest host operating system. Virtual machine hardware corresponds to the physical hardware available on the host computer where the virtual machine is created.

It may be necessary to upgrade the virtual machine hardware or guest tools on a virtual machine to take advantage of some of the features that the host provides. The host file system or hypervisor may also need to be updated to support these improvements. Virtual machine hardware features might include BIOS enhancements, virtual PCI slots, and dynamically configuring the number of vCPUs or memory allocation.

Another scenario that might require upgrading a virtual machine is when a new version of the host operating system is released (e.g., when Microsoft releases a new version of Hyper-V or VMware releases a new version of ESXi). In this instance, an organization would need to upgrade or migrate its virtual machines to the new host server.

Upgrading to a new host operating system and migrating the virtual machines to that new host requires the same planning that would be needed to perform a P2V migration. Make sure you understand the benefits of the new host operating system and how those benefits will impact the virtual machines and, specifically, their compute resources. Once again, careful planning is key before the upgrading process starts.

Workload Source and Destination Formats

The simplest migrations are performed when source and destination formats are the same, but life is not always simple and there will be times when an upgrade includes transitioning from one format to another.

Migrations or upgrades may include transitioning P2V, V2P, or V2V and from one platform such as Microsoft Hyper-V to VMware or Citrix XenServer. Migrations may also involve more advanced features such as virtual disk encryption or multifactor authentication that must be supported and configured on the destination server.

Virtualization Format   P2V migrations can be performed manually by setting up a new operating system and then installing applications, migrating settings, and copying data. However, this is time-consuming and often error-prone. It is more efficient to use software tools to fully or partially automate the P2V conversion process. Tools are specific to the destination virtualization platform and such tools gather the required information from the physical machine and then create a virtual machine on the destination virtualization platform such as Hyper-V or VMware.

V2P migrations can be performed by running Microsoft Sysprep on the virtual machine to prepare the image for transfer and allow for hardware configuration changes. Next, all the drivers for the target physical server would need to be prepared before doing the migration, and then a software tool would be used to facilitate the virtual-to-physical migration and load the necessary hardware drivers onto the physical machine. Alternatively, V2P migrations can be performed manually by setting up a new operating system and then installing applications, migrating settings, and copying data.

V2V migration can be performed by exporting the virtual machines from the previous version and importing them into the new version of the host operating system software. Additionally, some software such as VMware VMotion or Microsoft SCVMM can perform migrations from one hypervisor version to another. However, this is often a one-way move because moving from a newer version to an older version is not usually supported.

Application and Data Portability   Migrations also may move from an encrypted format to a nonencrypted format or vice versa. Migrating encrypted virtual machines does require the encryption keys, so you must ensure that these are available prior to migration and ensure that the destination system supports the same encryption standards. Certificates or other prerequisites may need to be in place first to support this or other features of the virtual machine.

Standard Operating Procedures for Workload Migrations

It is likely that you will perform migrations many times. The first time you perform a migration, create a standard process for future migrations. You may find along the way that you can improve the process here or there. Feel free to add more details to the standard process as you discover enhancements.

A standard process ensures that others who perform the same task will do so with the same level of professionalism that you do. Standard operating procedures also ensure consistent implementation, including the amount of time it takes to perform the task and the resources required.

Standard operating procedures can also be used to automate processes. Once a process has been performed several times and is sufficiently well documented, there may be methods of automating the process so that it is even more streamlined. The documentation will ensure that you do not miss a critical step in the automation and it can help in troubleshooting automation later on.

Environmental Constraints

Upgrades are also dependent upon various environmental constraints such as bandwidth, working hour restrictions, downtime impact, peak timeframes, and legal restrictions. We also operate in a global economy, so it is important to understand where all users are operating and the time zone restrictions for performing upgrades.

Bandwidth   Migrations can take a lot of bandwidth depending on the size of the virtual machine hard drives. When migrating over a 1 Gbps or 10 Gbps Ethernet network, this is not as much of a concern, but bandwidth can be a huge constraint when transferring machines over a low-speed WAN link such as a 5 Mbps MPLS connection.

Evaluate machines that are to be migrated and their data sizes and then estimate how much time it will take to migrate the machines over the bandwidth available. Be sure to factor in other traffic as well. You do not want the migration to impact normal business operations in the process. Also, be sure that others are not migrating machines at the same time.

Working Hour Restrictions   Working hours can be a restriction on when upgrades or migrations are performed. Working hour restrictions may require that some work be performed outside of normal business hours, such as before 9:00 A.M. or after 5:00 P.M. Working hours may differ in your company. For example, they may be 7:00 A.M. till 7:00 P.M. in places where 12-hour shifts are common.

Working hour restrictions also impact how work is assigned to people who work in shifts. For example, if an upgrade is to take three hours by one person, then it must be scheduled at least three hours prior to the end of that person's shift or the task will need to be transitioned to another team member while still incomplete. It generally takes more time to transition a task from one team member to another, so it is best to try to keep this to a minimum. Sometimes more than one person works on a task, but those people leave and a new group takes over at some point so that a single person or group does not get burned out trying to complete a major task.

It is also important to factor in some buffer time for issues that could crop up. In the example, if the task is expected to take three hours and you schedule it exactly three hours before the employee's shift ends, that provides no time for troubleshooting or error. If problems do arise, the task would be transitioned to another team member who would need to do troubleshooting that might require input from the first team member in order to avoid rework since the second employee may not know everything that was done in the first place. For this reason, it is important to keep a detailed log of what changes were made and which troubleshooting steps were performed, even if you do not anticipate transitioning the task to another person. This can also be helpful when working with technical support.

on the **job**

We were troubleshooting a particularly difficult problem with a three-tiered web application and needed to consult with the database vendor. The database vendor asked which troubleshooting steps had been performed and we were able to provide a detailed list of each step because we had been documenting the steps all along. We have worked with others who did not document their troubleshooting steps, and they often forget some of the steps or state them incorrectly. This makes it much more difficult for others to assist in troubleshooting.

Downtime Impact   Not all migrations and upgrades require downtime, but it is very important to understand which ones do. Upgrades or migrations that require the system to be unavailable must be performed during a downtime. Stakeholders, including end users, application owners, and other administrative teams, need to be consulted prior to scheduling a downtime so that business operations are not impacted. The stakeholders need to be informed how long the downtime is anticipated to take, what value the change brings to them, and the precautions that the IT team is taking to protect against risks.

For systems that are cloud-consumer facing, if the cloud provider can't avoid downtime to conduct a migration or upgrade, it needs to schedule the downtime well in advance and give cloud consumers plenty of notice so that the company does not lose cloud-consumer confidence by taking a site, application, or service down unexpectedly.

Peak Timeframes   Upgrades that do not require downtime could still impact the performance of the virtual machine and the applications that run on top of it. For this reason, it is best to plan upgrades or migrations for times when the load on the system is minimal.

For example, it would be a bad idea to perform a migration on a DHCP server at the beginning of the day when users are logging into systems, because that is when the DHCP server has the greatest load. Users would likely see service interruptions if a migration or an upgrade were to take place during such a peak time.

Legal Restrictions   Migrating a virtual machine from one location to another can present data sovereignty issues. Different countries have different laws, especially when it comes to privacy, and you will need to understand the type of data that resides on virtual machines and any limitations to where those virtual machines can reside.

Upgrades can also run into legal constraints when new features violate laws in the host country. For example, an upgrade may increase the encryption capabilities of software to a degree that it violates local laws requiring no more than a specific encryption bit length or set of algorithms.

Legal constraints can come up when upgrades violate laws for users of the system even if the application resides in a different country from the users. For example, the European Union's General Data Protection Regulation (GDPR) affects companies that do business with Europeans even if those businesses are not located in Europe. Consult with legal and compliance teams to ensure that you adhere with local laws and regulations.

Time Zone Constraints   Virtualized and cloud systems may have users spread across the globe. Additionally, it may be necessary to coordinate resources with cloud vendors or with support personnel in different global regions. In such cases, time zones can be a large constraint for performing upgrades. It can be difficult to coordinate a time that works for distributed user bases and maintenance teams.

For this reason, consider specifying in vendor contracts and SLAs an upgrade schedule so that you do not get gridlocked by too many time zone constraints and are unable to perform an upgrade.

Follow the Sun (FTS)   Follow the sun (FTS) is a method where multiple shifts work on a system according to their time zone to provide 24/7 service. FTS is commonly used in software development and customer support. For example, customer support calls might be answered in India during India's normal working hours, after which calls are transitioned to the Philippines, and so on, so that each group works its normal business hours. Similarly, a cloud upgrade could be staged so that teams in the United States perform a portion of the upgrade and then as soon as they finish, a team in the UK starts on the next batch. When the UK team completes their work, a team in China begins, and then back to the United States the following morning.

Testing

The process of P2V, or V2V for that matter, generally leaves the system in complete working and functional order and the entire system is migrated and left intact. With that said, any system that is being migrated should be tested both before and after the migration process. The IT administrator needs to define a series of checks that should be performed after the migration and before the virtual server takes over for the physical server. Some of the tests that should be completed on the virtual server after migration are as follows:

- Remove all unnecessary hardware from the virtual machine. (If you are migrating from a physical server to a virtual server, you might have some hardware devices that were migrated as part of the P2V process.)
- When first booting the virtual machine, disconnect it from the network. This allows the boot to occur without having to worry about duplicate IP addresses or DNS names on the network.
- Reboot the virtual machine several times to clear the logs and verify that it is functioning as expected during the startup phase.
- Verify network configurations on the virtual server while it is disconnected from the network. Make sure the IP address configuration is correct so that the virtual machine does not have any issues connecting to the network once network connectivity is restored.

Performing these post-migration tests will help to ensure a successful migration process and to minimize any errors that might arise after the migration is complete. As with anything, there could still be issues once the virtual machine is booted on the network, but performing these post-conversion tests will lessen the likelihood of problems.

CERTIFICATION SUMMARY

There are many benefits to adopting a virtualized environment, including shared resources, elasticity, and network isolation for testing applications. Migrating to a virtual environment takes careful planning and consideration to define proper compute resources for the newly created virtual machine. Understanding how to correctly perform a physical-to-virtual (P2V) migration is a key concept for the test and the real world, as you will be required to migrate physical servers to a virtual environment if you are working with virtualization or the cloud.

KEY TERMS

Use the following list to review the key terms discussed in this chapter. The definitions also can be found in the glossary.

dedicated compute environment Environment where a single tenant owns or leases equipment.

downtime Any time when the system is unavailable. Downtime can be reduced through various levels of redundancy.

elasticity Allows an organization to dynamically provision and deprovision processing, memory, and storage resources to meet the demands of the network.

follow the sun (FTS) A method where multiple shifts work on a system according to their time zone to provide 24/7 service.

network isolation Allows for a section of the network to be isolated from another section so that multiple identical copies of the environment are executed at the same time.

offline migration Migrates a physical server to a virtual machine by taking the source computer offline so that it is not available during the migration process.

online migration Migrates a physical server to a virtual machine while the source computer remains available during the migration process.

Open Virtual Appliance (OVA) An open standard for a virtual appliance that can be used in a variety of hypervisors from different vendors.

Open Virtualization Format (OVF) An open standard for a virtual hard disk that can be used in a variety of hypervisors from different vendors.

physical to physical (P2P) A transfer of the data and applications from one physical server to another physical server.

physical to virtual (P2V) Process of migrating a physical server's operating system, applications, and data from the physical server to a newly created guest virtual machine on a virtualization host.

resource pooling   Allows compute resources to be pooled to serve multiple consumers by using a multitenant model.

shared compute environment   Environment where multiple tenants share resources from a cloud vendor or hosting provider.

shared resources   Allows a cloud provider to provide compute resources as a centralized resource and distribute those resources on an as-needed basis to the cloud consumer.

storage migration   Process of transferring data between storage devices, allowing data from a virtual machine to be migrated to a new location and across storage arrays while maintaining continuous availability and service to the virtual machine.

virtual data center   Provides compute resources, network infrastructure, external storage, backups, and security similar to a physical data center.

virtual machine cloning   Allows a virtual machine to be copied either once or multiple times for testing.

virtual machine snapshotting   A method of capturing the state of a virtual machine at a specific point in time.

virtual machine template   Provides a standardized group of hardware and software settings that can be reused multiple times to create a new virtual machine that is configured with those specified settings.

virtual to physical (V2P)   Migrates a virtual machine to a physical computer.

virtual to virtual (V2V)   Migrates an operating system, applications, and data from one virtual machine to another virtual machine.

 # TWO-MINUTE DRILL

Benefits of Virtualization in a Cloud Environment

❑ Virtualization consolidates many physical servers into virtual machines running on fewer physical servers functioning as hosts. Through virtualization, a single host can run many guest operating systems and multiple applications instead of a single application on each server.

❏ Cloud computing can provide compute resources as a centralized resource through shared resources. Shared resources are distributed on an as-needed basis to the cloud consumer. Shared resources, thus, improve efficiency and reduce costs for an organization. Elastic computing allows compute resources to vary dynamically to meet a variable workload and to scale up and down as an application requires.

❏ Virtualization allows for segmenting an application's network access and isolating that virtual machine to a specific network segment.

❏ Virtualization allows an organization to consolidate its servers and infrastructure by having multiple virtual machines run on a single host computer.

❏ Virtual data centers offer data center infrastructure as a service; they have the same capabilities as a physical data center but with the advantages of cloud computing.

Virtual Resource Migrations

❏ A virtual machine template provides a standardized group of hardware and software settings that can be deployed quickly and efficiently to multiple virtual machines.

❏ The process of migrating a physical server to a virtual server is called physical to virtual (P2V).

❏ P2V allows you to convert a physical server's operating system, applications, and data to a virtual server.

❏ Virtual-to-virtual (V2V) migrations allow you to migrate a virtual machine to another virtual machine by copying the files, operating system, and applications from one virtual machine to another.

❏ An online migration of a physical server to a virtual server leaves the physical server running and operational during the migration process.

❏ If an application does not support installation on a virtual server, virtual-to-physical (V2P) migration can be used to copy the virtual machine to a physical server.

❏ Virtual machine cloning creates an exact copy of a virtual machine for use in a development or test environment.

❏ Virtual machine snapshots capture the state of a virtual machine at a specific point in time. Snapshots can return the machine to that state easily and efficiently if so desired.

❏ A virtual machine's virtual hard disk can be migrated from one storage device to another using storage migration. This allows you to take advantage of tiered storage.

❏ High availability (HA) and disaster recovery (DR) functions of a hypervisor enable automatic failover with load balancing.

❏ It may become necessary to migrate virtual machines or entire services from one cloud provider to another. A high level of integration is needed between cloud providers for a seamless migration.

Migration Considerations

- ❑ Migrating a physical server to a virtual server takes careful planning to be successful.
- ❑ It is very important for an organization to gather all the hardware and application requirements of a physical server before migrating it to a virtual server.
- ❑ It is advisable to migrate a physical server to a virtual server during scheduled and planned maintenance hours.
- ❑ Proper testing of a virtual machine after the P2V migration process is required to verify that the virtual server is operating at peak performance.

SELF TEST

The following questions will help you measure your understanding of the material presented in this chapter. As indicated, some questions may have more than one correct answer, so be sure to read all the answer choices carefully.

Benefits of Virtualization in a Cloud Environment

1. Which of the following allows you to scale resources up and down dynamically as required for a given application?
    A. Subnetting
    B. Resource pooling
    C. Elasticity
    D. VLAN

2. Which of the following data centers offers the same concepts as a physical data center with the benefits of cloud computing?
    A. Private data center
    B. Public data center
    C. Hybrid data center
    D. Virtual data center

3. How does virtualization help to consolidate an organization's infrastructure?
   A. It allows a single application to be run on a single computer.
   B. It allows multiple applications to run on a single computer.
   C. It requires more operating system licenses.
   D. It does not allow for infrastructure consolidation and actually requires more compute resources.

4. Which of the following gives a cloud provider the ability to distribute resources on an as-needed basis to the cloud consumer and in turn helps to improve efficiency and reduce costs?
   A. Elasticity
   B. Shared resources
   C. Infrastructure consolidation
   D. Network isolation

Virtual Resource Migrations

5. Your organization is planning on migrating its data center, and you as the administrator have been tasked with reducing the footprint of the new data center by virtualizing as many servers as possible. A physical server running a legacy application has been identified as a candidate for virtualization. Which of the following methods would you use to migrate the server to the new data center?
   A. V2V
   B. V2P
   C. P2P
   D. P2V

6. You have been tasked with migrating a virtual machine to a new host computer. Which migration process would be required?
   A. V2V
   B. V2P
   C. P2P
   D. P2V

7. An application was installed on a virtual machine and is now having issues. The application provider has asked you to install the application on a physical server. Which migration process would you use to test the application on a physical server?
   A. V2V
   B. V2P
   C. P2P
   D. P2V

8. You have been tasked with deploying a group of virtual machines quickly and efficiently with the same standard configurations. What process would you use?

    A. V2P

    B. P2V

    C. Virtual machine templates

    D. Virtual machine cloning

9. Which of the following allows you to migrate a virtual machine's storage to a different storage device while the virtual machine remains operational?

    A. Network isolation

    B. P2V

    C. V2V

    D. Storage migration

10. You need to create an exact copy of a virtual machine to deploy in a development environment. Which of the following processes is the best option?

    A. Storage migration

    B. Virtual machine templates

    C. Virtual machine cloning

    D. P2V

11. You are migrating a physical server to a virtual server. The server needs to remain available during the migration process. What type of migration would you use?

    A. Offline

    B. Online

    C. Hybrid

    D. V2P

Migration Considerations

12. You notice that one of your virtual machines will not successfully complete an online migration to a hypervisor host. Which of the following is most likely preventing the migration process from completing?

    A. The virtual machine needs more memory than the host has available.

    B. The virtual machine has exceeded the allowed CPU count.

    C. The virtual machine does not have the proper network configuration.

    D. The virtual machine license has expired.

13. After a successful P2V migration, which of the following tests, if any, should be completed on the new virtual machine?
    A. Testing is not required.
    B. Remove all unnecessary software.
    C. Verify the IP address, DNS, and other network configurations.
    D. Run a monitoring program to verify compute resources.

14. You are planning your migration to a virtual environment. Which of the following physical servers should be migrated first? (Choose two.)
    A. A development server
    B. A server that is running a non-mission-critical application and is not heavily utilized day to day
    C. A highly utilized database server
    D. A server running a mission-critical application

SELF TEST ANSWERS

Benefits of Virtualization in a Cloud Environment

1. ☑ **C.** Elasticity allows an organization to scale resources up and down as an application or service requires.
   ☒ **A, B,** and **D** are incorrect. Subnetting is the practice of creating subnetworks, or subnets, which are logical subdivisions of an IP network. Resource pooling allows compute resources to be pooled to serve multiple consumers by using a multitenant model. A virtual local area network (VLAN) is the concept of partitioning a physical network to create separate independent broadcast domains that are part of the same physical network.

2. ☑ **D.** A virtual data center offers compute resources, network infrastructure, external storage, backups, and security, just like a physical data center. A virtual data center also offers virtualization, pay-as-you-grow billing, elasticity, and scalability.
   ☒ **A, B,** and **C** are incorrect. The other options are definitions of cloud deployment and service models.

3. ☑ **B.** Virtualization allows an organization to consolidate its servers and infrastructure by allowing multiple virtual machines to run on a single host computer.
   ☒ **A, C,** and **D** are incorrect. These options would not help to consolidate an organization's infrastructure.

4. ☑ **B.** Shared resources give a cloud provider the ability to distribute resources on an as-needed basis to the cloud consumer, which helps to improve efficiency and reduce costs for an organization. Virtualization helps to simplify the process of sharing compute resources.
    ☒ **A, C,** and **D** are incorrect. Elasticity allows an organization to scale resources up and down as an application or service requires but does not give the cloud provider the ability to distribute resources as needed. Infrastructure consolidation allows an organization to consolidate its physical servers into a smaller virtualized data center but is not used to distribute resources automatically. Network isolation allows you to isolate the network the virtual machine is connected to but has nothing to do with distributing resources.

Virtual Resource Migrations

5. ☑ **D.** P2V would allow you to migrate the physical server running the legacy application to a new virtual machine in the new virtualized data center.
    ☒ **A, B,** and **C** are incorrect. These options do not allow you to migrate the physical server running the legacy application to a new virtual server.

6. ☑ **A.** V2V would allow you to migrate the virtual machine to a new virtual machine on the new host computer.
    ☒ **B, C,** and **D** are incorrect. These options would not be the most efficient way to migrate a virtual machine to a new host computer.

7. ☑ **B.** One of the primary reasons for using the V2P process is to migrate a virtual machine to a physical machine to test an application on a physical server if requested by the application manufacturer.
    ☒ **A, C,** and **D** are incorrect. These options do not allow you to migrate a virtual machine to a physical server.

8. ☑ **C.** Virtual machine templates would allow you to deploy multiple virtual machines and those virtual machines would have identical configurations, which streamlines the process.
    ☒ **A, B,** and **D** are incorrect. When you create a virtual machine clone, you are creating an exact copy of an existing virtual machine. P2V and V2P do not allow you to deploy multiple standardized virtual machines.

9. ☑ **D.** Storage migration is the process of transferring data between storage devices and can be automated or done manually and allows the storage to be migrated while the virtual machine continues to be accessible.
    ☒ **A, B,** and **C** are incorrect. Network isolation allows you to isolate the network the virtual machine is connected to. P2V and V2V migrate the entire virtual machine or physical server, not just the virtual machine's storage.

10. ☑ **C.** When you create a virtual machine clone, you are creating an exact copy of an existing virtual machine.

    ☒ **A, B,** and **D** are incorrect. Virtual machine templates provide a streamlined approach to deploying a fully configured base server image or even a fully configured application server but do not create an exact copy of a virtual machine. Storage migration migrates the virtual machine's storage to another storage device; it does not create an exact copy of the virtual machine. P2V would allow you to create a copy of a physical machine as a virtual machine, not an exact copy of a virtual machine.

11. ☑ **B.** With an online migration the physical computer or source computer remains running and operational during the migration.

    ☒ **A, C,** and **D** are incorrect. An offline migration requires the server to be shut down before the migration process can take place.

Migration Considerations

12. ☑ **A.** During a P2V migration the host computer must support the source computer's memory. More than likely the host does not have enough available memory to support the import of the virtual machine in a migration scenario.

    ☒ **B, C,** and **D** are incorrect. These settings would need to be planned and thought out, but they would not prevent a virtual machine from being migrated to a host computer.

13. ☑ **C.** After a successful migration, the network settings should be checked and verified before bringing the virtual machine online.

    ☒ **A, B,** and **D** are incorrect. Testing the virtual machine after a successful migration is something that should always be done. Testing the performance of the virtual machine should be done after the network settings have been configured and verified.

14. ☑ **A** and **B.** When planning a migration from a physical data center to a virtual data center, the first servers that should be migrated are noncritical servers that are not heavily utilized. A development server would be a good candidate since it is most likely not a mission-critical server.

    ☒ **C** and **D** are incorrect. You would not want to migrate mission-critical or highly utilized servers before migrating noncritical servers. This helps to prevent downtime of critical applications and provides a means of testing the migration process and the virtual environment before migrating critical servers to the virtual environment.

Chapter 7

DevOps

Many companies have combined the distinct functions of development (programming) and IT (operations) into a single group called DevOps. Instead of one team writing software and another deploying and supporting it, a single team is responsible for the entire life cycle. This has led to improved agility and a better responsiveness of DevOps teams to the issues faced by end users because the team works directly with them rather than one department removed. This chapter covers some DevOps functions including resource monitoring, remote access, and life cycle management.

Monitoring the cloud environment is a fundamental component of successful cloud computing environment management. Proper monitoring helps uncover problems early on, and it aids in detecting network outages quickly and efficiently, which leads to increased availability of servers, services, and applications. Valuable data obtained in monitoring metrics can be used to plan for future resource utilization and to become more proactive instead of reactive.

An organization needs to be able to monitor and manage the cloud environment quickly and efficiently. Remotely administering cloud virtualization is a flexible way to administer the environment and respond to issues or alerts that might arise. There are a variety of options for managing and monitoring the cloud environment securely and remotely, which are covered in this chapter.

Lastly, organizations need to be able to manage the applications that they put in place. Life cycle management includes everything from the requirements stage to retirement. Each stage has inputs and outputs that connect the stages to one another. The application life cycle enables an organization to manage each of its service offerings as efficiently and effectively as possible and ensure that each of those services continues to provide value throughout its life cycle.

CERTIFICATION OBJECTIVE 7.01

Resource Monitoring Techniques

Effective monitoring techniques provide an efficient means of monitoring all aspects of a cloud infrastructure without placing a significant performance burden on the systems and network. Monitoring techniques track the performance of enterprise systems and provide detailed information on the current usage of the cloud environment that can be consolidated and displayed on dashboards or reports.

Cloud computing provides an efficient way of load balancing, task scheduling, and allocating compute resources. Monitoring compute resources is an important part of maintaining a cloud environment and ensuring that systems have adequate resources to perform their tasks. Some key benefits of resource monitoring include providing input for chargebacks and showbacks, more intelligent resource provisioning and proactive resource expansion or contraction, more effective capacity planning, and improved technology agility in response to an ever-changing environment.

One of the goals of monitoring the environment is to ensure the overall health of key systems and applications. System health information can be published to a corporate intranet site, allowing the entire organization or select decision makers access to the health data. For example, an administrator might publish a dashboard on the company intranet site that shows the current service level agreements (SLAs) of the organization and whether or not the IT department has met those SLAs.

Another place to use monitoring is in a chargeback situation. An IT department can monitor the environment and get a report on who consumed which compute resources and for how long, allowing the organization to charge departments for their use of compute resources.

The first part of understanding resource monitoring is to understand the protocols and methods used for resource monitoring, as discussed next. Then, this section discusses configuring baselines and thresholds and forecasting resource capacity. Finally, automation can be used to send alerts for specific events and thresholds, so this section concludes with a discussion on how that can be accomplished.

Protocols and Methods

When defining a monitoring solution, it is important to understand the different protocols that are available for monitoring and the alerting options to problems that might arise in the cloud environment. Monitoring is enabled through a series of protocols and alerting methods that, in conjunction, can provide a robust system of threshold monitoring and alerting.

The following protocols and methods are presented in this section:

- Simple Network Management Protocol (SNMP)
- Windows Management Instrumentation (WMI) and Web-Based Enterprise Management (WBEM)
- Out-of-band management and Intelligent Platform Management Interface (IPMI)
- Syslog

SNMP

One of the common protocols used to manage and monitor an environment is Simple Network Management Protocol (SNMP). SNMP is commonly supported on devices such as routers, switches, printers, and servers and is used to monitor these devices for issues or conditions that might arise on the devices that would require administrative attention.

A monitoring solution that uses SNMP has an administrative computer, commonly referred to as a manager, that monitors or manages a group of network devices. Each managed device runs an agent, which reports information, using SNMP, back to the manager. For example, an SNMP agent on a router can provide information about the router's network configuration and operations (such as network interface configurations and routing tables) and transmit that information back to the manager.

There are a variety of vendors that use SNMP to monitor devices on the network; they use the information from SNMP to give an administrator a means of monitoring and managing network performance or reporting on and troubleshooting network issues. This knowledge enables administrators to better understand and prepare for network growth.

In addition to monitoring and managing an environment, SNMP allows for alerts to be generated. An administrator can use SNMP to modify and apply new configurations to network devices and be alerted when certain conditions are present on monitored network devices. SNMP uses notifications, known as SNMP traps, to alert on important information. SNMP traps are network packets that contain data relating to a particular component of the network device running the SNMP agent; they can notify the management stations, by way of an unsolicited SNMP message, that a particular event has occurred. SNMP traps are triggered when particular preprogrammed conditions are present on the monitored device.

WMI

Another option for monitoring an environment is Windows Management Instrumentation (WMI), Microsoft's version of Web-Based Enterprise Management (WBEM). WBEM is an industry initiative to develop a standardized way of accessing management information in an enterprise environment.

WMI allows you to write scripts to automate certain administrative tasks and run those scripts against remote computers. WMI can query and set information on a workstation, server, application, or supported network device.

WMI provides a way to gather hardware information from multiple physical servers or virtual servers. WMI information can be placed into a centralized database, allowing for collection and reporting on a variety of information, including CPU, memory, operating system, and hard drive space.

w a t c h   **WMI can be used to gather information about the installed software and the operating system version on a computer, along with hardware information.**

WMI information can assist in determining if a system is close to maximizing compute resources, which may necessitate an upgrade to meet demands. For example, Microsoft System Center Configuration Manager (SCCM) uses WMI to gather hardware information from its clients and allows an administrator to manage and report on those systems based on the information gathered from the WMI queries.

Out-of-Band Management and IPMI

Out-of-band management allows an administrator to remotely manage and monitor a device using a separate network segment from normal production traffic. Out-of-band

w a t c h   **Out-of-band management allows for remotely monitoring BIOS settings.**

monitoring can be implemented with the Intelligent Platform Management Interface (IPMI) protocol, which has the capability of monitoring a device that is not powered on. IPMI operates independently of the operating system, which allows BIOS settings to be remotely monitored or configured.

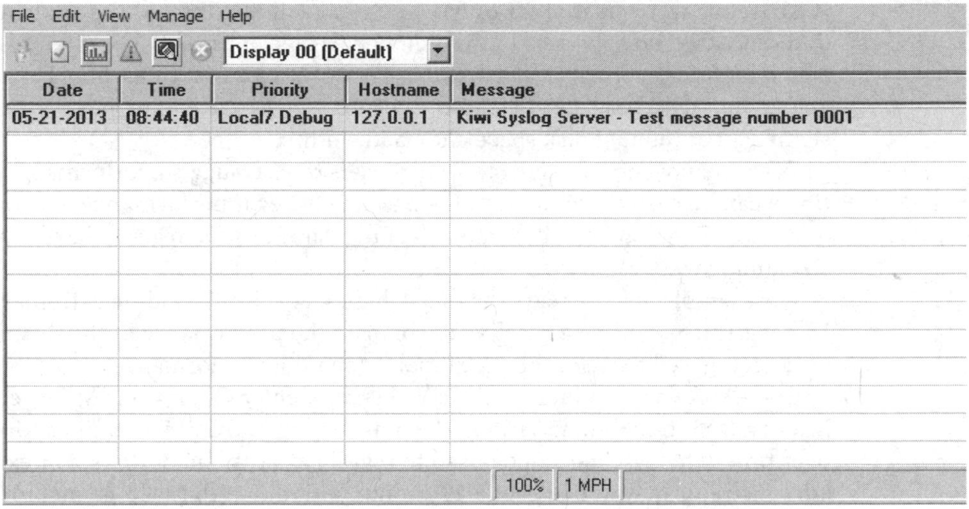

FIGURE 7-1

A sample
syslog entry

File	Edit	View	Manage	Help			

Display 00 (Default)

Date	Time	Priority	Hostname	Message
05-21-2013	08:44:40	Local7.Debug	127.0.0.1	Kiwi Syslog Server - Test message number 0001

100% 1 MPH

Syslog

One of the most common ways to gather event messages is with the use of syslog. Syslog is a logging standard that provides a mechanism for a network device to send event messages to a logging server or syslog server over UDP port 514 or TCP 514.

One of the benefits of a syslog server is that the syslog protocol is supported by a wide range of devices and can log different types of events. Syslog cannot poll devices to gather information as SNMP does; it simply gathers messages sent by various devices to a central syslog server when a specific event has triggered. Each device is configured with the location of the syslog collector and sends its logs to that server for collection. Syslog can be used to consolidate logs from multiple devices into a single location for review, analysis, or archival purposes. Figure 7-1 shows an example of a standard syslog server entry.

After an organization chooses and configures its monitoring and alerting solution, its next step is to develop a baseline.

Baselines and Thresholds

The purpose of establishing a baseline is to create a sample of resources that are being consumed by the cloud services, servers, or virtual machines over a set time period and to provide the organization with a point-in-time performance chart of its environment. Establish a baseline by selecting a sampling interval and the objects to monitor and then collecting performance data during that interval.

A good baseline must include an accurate sampling of normal activities. If the activity is roughly the same from week to week, then a baseline of one week might be sufficient. However, if activity fluctuates from week to week, the baseline would need to be longer.

If a baseline were created for only a week and activity differed the next week, those differences would appear as outliers and be flagged as potential problems when they are actually just normal activity that was not captured in the baseline. However, do not go overboard on baseline collection, because a lengthy sampling interval can consume a significant amount of disk space and bandwidth.

Performance metrics collected when users report sluggish performance or slow response times can be easily compared to the baseline to see if performance is within normal tolerance. Continue to collect metrics at regular intervals to get a chart of how systems are consuming resources.

For example, if a user says that a database server is responding extremely slowly, the IT department can use a baseline to compare the performance of the server when it was performing well to when the user reported the slow performance.

Some software products such as VMware vCenter Operations Manager (VCOP) and Microsoft System Center Virtual Machine Manager (SCVMM) build an internal baseline over time. The baseline can be used to reveal patterns and outliers. For example, a cloud administrator may notice over a 12-month period that the average memory usage has increased 10 percent, which helps in planning additional resources for the server in the near future.

In addition to establishing a baseline, an organization also needs to configure thresholds. When it comes to monitoring a cloud environment, thresholds are a key piece of the process. Thresholds can be set so that if a virtualization host consumes more than 95 percent of its CPU for more than 10 minutes, it sends an alert via either SMTP or SMS to the appropriate party (as described later in the chapter).

Setting a threshold allows for a more robust alerting system. Thresholds can also be used to automatically and dynamically create and orchestrate resources in the cloud computing environment. ("Orchestration" refers to automated tasks that could be scripted to happen based on particular conditions and triggers.)

Cloud computing allows a cloud consumer to define a threshold policy to check and manage resources when workload demands require. This allows the cloud provider to create instances of resources depending on how much the workload exceeds the threshold level. For example, a defined threshold could state that if CPU utilization for a particular virtual machine reaches 95 percent for 5 minutes, utilizing orchestration APIs, an additional processor should be added dynamically.

Target Object Baselines

Baselines should be collected not only for entire systems but also for objects within the system, such as CPU utilization, memory pages per second, CPU queue depth, memory utilization, data reads per second, data writes per second, and so forth. These values can be very useful in determining how to improve performance over time, optimize resources for utilization, and upgrade components so that they provide maximum value to the organization.

Target Anomalies

Baselines can be used to detect anomalies. Anomalies are events that are outside the norm. The baseline shows the norm, and the anomaly can indicate a short-term increase in utilization or a problem in the works. A pattern can be inferred from baseline data, and this pattern can be used to identify anomalous data collected thereafter.

Forecasting Resource Capacity

Baselining is useful in forecasting resource capacity and future utilization. Look at baseline values over time to perform a trend analysis. Some trends are based on the annual cycle, so it can be helpful to look at baselines over a 12-month period.

It is also useful to compare year-to-date numbers and compare corresponding months across years. Start tracking this data now and you will see how useful it will be later. Unfortunately, many companies wait to start collecting resource metrics until they urgently need answers. If you are not collecting data now, you will not have it available for analysis later when you need it so put such systems in place right away.

Upsize/Increase   Trends may show an increase or upsize over time. For example, if storage consumption was 100GB in January, 105GB in February, 109GB in March, 117GB in April, and 121GB in June, we can conclude that storage will need to increase a minimum of 5GB per month and that some months will increase more than that.

Downsize/Decrease   Conversely, trends may show a decrease over time. This could be due to efficiencies in the system or decreasing use of the application or system. For example, if memory consumption was 28GB in January, 24GB in February, 26GB in March, 22GB in April, and 23GB in June, we can conclude that storage will decrease about 2GB per month with a standard deviation of 4GB per month.

Automated Event Responses

While monitoring and alerting are great ways to minimize problems in the cloud environment, there are some issues that arise with using these features. When an organization is monitoring and alerting on all its devices, the number of alerts that might arise could be staggering. If an administrator gets too many alerts, he may not have enough time to respond to those alerts and some issues may go unnoticed or may not be given the attention they deserve.

This is where automated event responses can help. For example, let's say an administrator gets an alert that a hard drive is at 99 percent capacity. Instead of having to manually log into the server and delete files or run a disk cleanup program, the entire process can be scripted and executed by a trigger on the threshold. Once the threshold is hit, that triggers the script to run that performs the task. Automating minor tasks can save administrators considerable time and allow them to focus on more pressing issues. It also ensures that the tasks are carried out correctly and in a timely manner.

on the job   **Recently we were brought in to help an organization manage its monitoring environment. We recommended the organization buy monitoring software that allows for automated responses. We configured thresholds and alerts based on the organization's needs. We then configured the most common alerts with an automated response that would run a script to fix the issue and resolve the alert in the monitoring software.**

Common Alert Methods/Messaging

An organization needs a way to be alerted when certain events occur. For example, if the organization is monitoring a server and that server loses network connectivity, IT administrators need to be notified of that occurrence so they can fix the issue that is causing the problem.

Many vendors offer network monitoring and alerting solutions both for on-premises and cloud-based deployments. Most vendors provide a website or some form of web service to monitor an organization's cloud environment centrally, whether the cloud is private or public. The web service provides a dashboard that gives the administrator a quick and easy view of the entire cloud environment.

SMTP   One of the most common alerting methods used is the Simple Mail Transfer Protocol (SMTP), discussed in Chapter 4. When configured on a device, SMTP sends an e-mail when a monitored event occurs. The alert can be configured to send an e-mail to a single user or to a group of users so that more than one person receives the alert. SMTP is a quick and easy way of sending alerts from the monitoring software when certain events occur on the network.

SMS   Another option for receiving alerts is the Short Message Service (SMS), a text messaging service that allows an alert to be sent to a mobile device. The use of SMS is a great way to notify an on-call technician when an alert has been generated after hours. Monitoring an environment is normally a 24-hour job because the network needs to be available 24 hours a day.

Alerting Based on Deviation from Baseline

It is important to save baseline data. You can use simple spreadsheets, but a database is the best way to save such data because it allows you to write queries to analyze the data in different ways. As you gather the data, configure alerts to let administrators know of significant deviations from the baseline. Resources may need to be adjusted to handle short-term spikes in demand, or this could indicate the start of a new trend. Either way, it is important to be aware of these changes as soon as possible.

Alerts can be configured such that when metrics are a certain percentage above the baseline, an alert is sent to a specific individual or a distribution group. For example, you may want to send out an alert if CPU utilization is 40 percent more than average for a sustained duration of at least ten minutes. You can also configure alerts to go out when certain static thresholds are met. For example, you may plan to expand a LUN when it reaches 100GB, so you set an alert that notifies you when the LUN reaches that point.

Policies to Communicate Events Properly

Metrics are not the only thing that should prompt alerting. Some events require immediate attention. These events cannot wait until an administrator reviews the logs. For such cases, policies should be created defining which events require notification and how administrators should respond to such alerts. For example, the policy may state that a critical event requires immediate notification to the on-call administrators and that administrators must respond to the event within five minutes and resolve the event within one hour.

Once the policy is defined, technical controls can be implemented to carry out the policy. Triggers can be created to alert on such events to a person or group right away, and systems can be put in place to track resolution time and who is on call.

Event Collection and Event Collection Policies

A server can consume a lot of space with event logs. All too often companies configure small log sizes with rollover so that new events automatically replace old ones. However, these same companies often find out too late that the events they need to see have already been overwritten.

Establish policies to ensure that events are retained for a sufficiently long period of time. Your data retention policy is a good place to start. A good retention rate for logs is 18 months. This can consume a lot of space on the local machine, so it is a best practice to archive logs off to lower-cost secondary storage or to a log review platform. A log review platform can also centralize log review, log analysis, and alerting functions, simplifying the entire event management process.

Event Correlation

Events can reveal a lot of data in and of themselves, but they are immensely more valuable when correlated with events from other network devices. Networked machines do not operate in a vacuum, so log review should also take into consideration other devices when investigating issues or detecting threats.

Event correlation can combine authentication requests from domain controllers, incoming packets from perimeter devices, and data requests from application servers to gain a more complete picture of what is going on. Software exists to automate much of the process. Such software, called security information and event management (SIEM), archives logs and reviews the logs in real time against correlation rules to identify possible threats or problems. Additionally, baselines and heuristics can identify issues that crop up before they turn into bigger issues. For example, a number of informational events, when analyzed together, may present a bigger issue that can be resolved before it creates problems for end users. Without such a system, administrators likely would not notice the events until errors or warnings appeared in the log, which would probably be the same time that users of the system also experience issues.

It is much easier to fix an issue when end users are not complaining about the issue. IT administrators tend to think more clearly and logically when not under pressure. SIEM can change the way IT administrators investigate issues, eventually causing them to focus more on proactive indicators of an issue rather than reactively fighting fires.

CERTIFICATION OBJECTIVE 7.02

Remote-Access Tools

The computing environment is often is a different location from the working environment because of the environmental needs servers have and the economies of scale that can be achieved by housing thousands of servers in the same place. For cloud servers, the cloud customer might not even know where the server is being hosted. Both scenarios depend upon remote access to manage, service, and maintain systems.

Remotely accessing a server does not always have to mean accessing the server from an offsite location. There are times when simply connecting to a host computer or virtual machine from a workstation is more convenient than physically walking over to the server and logging in. When a quick fix or change needs to be made to a virtual machine or host computer, being able to access that server from a local workstation saves time and prevents the need to walk or drive to the data center and physically sit at the machine that requires the change.

Being able to remotely access and troubleshoot a virtualization host or virtual machine requires less time and makes fixing and maintaining the environment easier to accomplish. Some remote-access tools include remote hypervisor access and Remote Desktop Protocol (RDP).

Remote Hypervisor Access

There are a variety of ways to remotely connect to a hypervisor. Most vendors allow a console to be installed on a workstation or server that is not the hypervisor. This allows a user to manage the hypervisor from their workstation. The machine with the remote management tools on it is often referred to as a jump or step machine. Multiple hypervisors can be managed from a single console on a workstation, giving a single-pane-of-glass approach to hypervisor management.

Remote hypervisor tools enable administrators to perform most of the tasks for the hypervisor as if they were connecting directly to the actual hypervisor host. The client console gives them the ability to create or modify virtual machines or virtual hard disks, configure virtual machine settings, and so on. This allows them to do all the administrative tasks that are required on a day-to-day basis from a single workstation.

Users of remote hypervisor tools need to have the correct administrative permissions on the hypervisor to modify the settings for the host computer or the virtual machines. Using a console from a workstation is an excellent way to connect to a hypervisor host because it looks and acts just as it would if the user were locally logged into the hypervisor host.

RDP

Remote Desktop Protocol (RDP) differs from installing the hypervisor console on a workstation in that RDP allows for remotely connecting and logging into the desktop of the hypervisor host. RDP provides remote display and input capabilities over the network. RDP connections are made through software that supports RDP over TCP port 3389. RDP is built into Windows machines and can be executed by typing mstsc from the command prompt or run command. Figure 7-2 shows an example of RDP client software that is used to connect to a hypervisor host remotely. RDP is a multichannel protocol that provides separate virtual channels for transmitting device communication and presentation data from the server.

FIGURE 7-2

Remote Desktop
Connection:
An example of
RDP software

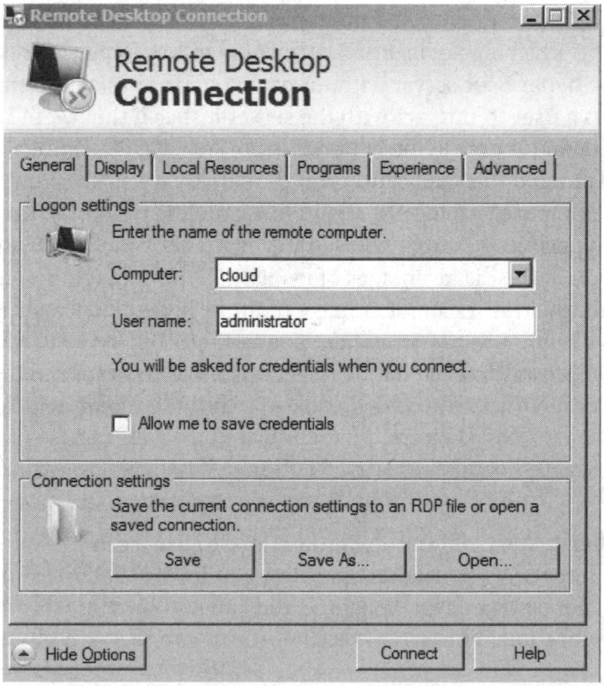

The advantage of using RDP to connect to a hypervisor is that the user has direct access to the hypervisor server without having to be physically sitting at the hypervisor host. RDP allows a user to interact with the server just as if they were sitting in front of it. So instead of just having access to the hypervisor console, RDP enables access to the entire server. The user can launch other applications on the server as well as change system settings on the hypervisor host computer itself. RDP allows for complete control of the server operating system, not just the hypervisor settings, without having to be at the hypervisor host computer physically.

One of the disadvantages of using RDP for managing a virtualization environment is that an administrator cannot manage multiple hypervisor hosts in a single RDP session like she can with a remote hypervisor client console. The option to use RDP is currently only available for the Microsoft hypervisor. Connections made to other modern hypervisors such as VMware, Citrix, and Oracle require the use of a software client installed on a jump machine.

Console Port

A console port allows an administrator to use a cable to connect directly to a hypervisor host computer or a virtual machine. The administrator can use a parallel or serial port to connect peripherals to a virtual machine and can add serial ports and change the logical COM port configuration. The virtual serial port can connect to a physical serial port or to a file on the host computer. Using a console port allows for managing a virtualization host computer directly from another computer connected to the host computer with a console cable.

SSH

The Secure Shell (SSH) protocol provides a secure way to manage network devices, including hypervisor hosts, remotely. SSH uses public key cryptography to exchange a symmetric key covertly between the SSH client and the SSH server, creating a fast and secure channel and then using that channel to authenticate a remote computer and user if required.

SSH can use a manually generated public–private key pair to perform authentication. The symmetric key is used to encrypt the connection. SSH can be used to log into a remote computer and execute certain command strings against a hypervisor host machine.

SSH provides strong authentication if using the latest version and secure communication over an insecure channel. It was designed to replace remote shell (RSH) and Telnet because RSH and Telnet send unencrypted traffic over the network, making them insecure communication methods.

When designing a virtualization environment, it is not recommended to have the hypervisor host directly exposed to the Internet. Normally the hypervisor host is installed behind a firewall or some other form of protection, which makes it difficult to access the hypervisor host off-site. SSH allows for the creation of a secure management tunnel to the hypervisor host computer or virtual machine and provides a secure way to manage those devices since all the traffic is sent through an encrypted tunnel.

exam
ⓦatch   SSH provides a way to access a hypervisor host or virtual machine from an off-site location securely.

HTTP

Another option for remotely accessing a hypervisor host machine is through a web console that is using HTTP or HTTPS. Hypertext Transfer Protocol (HTTP) is an application protocol built on TCP used to distribute Hypertext Markup Language (HTML) files, text, images, sound, videos, multimedia, and other types of information over the Internet. HTTP typically allows for communication between a web client or web browser and a web server hosting a website. Most hypervisor vendors have a web console that allows an administrator to access a hypervisor host from virtually anywhere as long as the DNS name of the hypervisor can be resolved, and HTTPS access is allowed through perimeter devices.

Administrators may have to install an additional component when doing the initial hypervisor host installation in order to provide web access to a host computer. The hypervisor host web service should be configured to use HTTPS to ensure a secure way to connect to it. Some hypervisors (like Microsoft IIS) may require additional software on the host computer as well. Connecting to a hypervisor host computer using a web console is a quick and easy way to perform simple configuration on a virtual machine.

CERTIFICATION OBJECTIVE 7.03

Life Cycle Management

Life cycle management is the process or processes put in place by an organization to assist in the management, coordination, control, delivery, and support of its configuration items from the requirements stage to retirement. The core of this is the application life cycle, or software development life cycle (SDLC). Additionally, ITIL has established a framework for implementing life cycle management, and Microsoft has a framework that is based on ITIL.

In addition to these frameworks, DevOps professionals should understand the functions involved in application replacement, retirement, migration, and changes in feature use. Business needs may also change, requiring changes to the application or retirement of the application.

Application Life Cycle

Just as creatures are born and eventually die, applications are created and eventually retired. This process is called the application life cycle. The application life cycle consists of five phases: specifications, development, testing, deployment, and maintenance. Figure 7-3 shows the application life cycle.

e x a m

⍵ a t c h　　　**No official version of the SDLC exists. There are several versions, some of which have six, seven, or even ten phases. However, each version still covers the same** | **things, just more or less granularly. It is important to understand the things that are taking place in the process, no matter how many phases are described.**

FIGURE 7-3

Application
life cycle

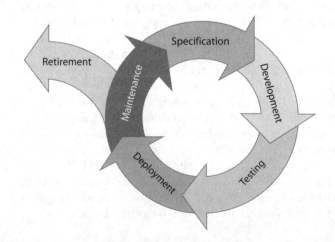

Phase 1: Specifications

The first phase of the application life cycle is the specifications phase. In this phase, the application's reason for being is documented. Users and stakeholders explain what they would like the application to do and what problem it will solve for them.

Phase 2: Development

In the development phase, project managers turn specifications into a model for a working program. They map out the requirements for different discrete tasks with the idea of creating the smallest discrete code that can be tested and validated. In this way, when bugs or flaws are identified, it is easy to pinpoint where they came from. Those tasks are assigned to developers who write that segment.

Developers write code for the current section of the program that has been designed. Only small parts of the code are written at a time to keep everything as simple to manage as possible. The more complex the code, the greater the chance that bugs will pop up.

Software code is made up of modules that contain functions and procedures. Within these functions and procedures, the elements of code are written. These include variables that store a value; classes that define program concepts containing properties and attributes; Boolean operations such as AND, OR, and NOR; looping functions that repeat sections of code; and sorting and searching functions.

Developers write code in an integrated development environment (IDE) that can check syntax of code similar to how spell checking works in a word processing application. Code is written in a selected language and each of the developers will use the same language when writing a program together.

Each time a change is made to the code, the developers publish the new code to a code repository, a program that tracks code changes. This phase continues until all the elements required in the specifications have been created in the program. Developers do some initial testing on the functions they create to ensure that they perform as they were designed to do. Once enough programming elements are gathered together to create a release, they are passed on to the testing phase.

Phase 3: Testing

In this phase, the code developed in the development phase is subjected to testing to ensure that it performs according to specifications, without errors, bugs, or security issues. Development code should never be ported directly to the production environment because developers may not be aware of bugs or other problems with the code that the testing phase can reveal. Testers may be other developers or their full job may be in testing code. Either way, they are members of the DevOps team and an overall part of delivering the program.

Code is typically deployed to a development environment where the developed application is subjected to automated testing and individual testing by users and groups. This occurs for each distinct element that is coded so that errors can be identified and isolated. Most integrated development environments (IDEs) have built-in syntax checking, variable validation, and autocomplete to help keep the majority of typos from causing problems.

Some development environments exist locally on the developer's machine. This streamlines the process for deploying code changes, and code can be executed in the development environment with breakpoints and other objects to find errors and monitor the details of program execution.

Once code is stable in the development environment, it is moved to a staging or quality assurance (QA) environment. This is when quality assurance kicks in: testers go to staging servers and verify that the code works as intended.

The staging environment needs to be provisioned, or the existing environment needs to be made current. This includes making the patch level consistent with the production environment and installing add-ons or configuration changes that have been made in production since the last release. Testers use information from the change management database on recent production changes to obtain a list of changes to be made in the QA environment.

The testing phase should include people involved in the specifications phase to ensure that the specifications were correctly translated into an application. When bugs or issues are identified with the application, developers fix those issues until the application is ready to be deployed into production.

Lastly, procedures should be documented for how the system will be deployed and used. Deployment documentation will be used in phase 4 and user documentation will be used to train users on how to use the program and its new features properly. Documentation should also include a brief list of updates that can be distributed to users for reference.

Phase 4: Deployment

In the deployment phase, the application developed and tested in previous phases is installed and configured in production for stakeholders to use. The first step is to ensure that the resources required for the application deployment are available, including compute, memory, and storage resources, as well as personnel. Teams may need to provision or deprovision cloud resources. Only then, can the remainder of the deployment be scheduled.

It can be tempting to automate this process. However, deployment needs to be performed by a human, and at a time when others are available to troubleshoot if necessary. Automatic deployments can lead to issues, particularly if someone accidentally triggers an automatic deployment to production.

Developers should do a final check of their code in this phase to remove testing elements such as debugger breakpoints and performance hogs such as verbose logging. Then, project managers work with stakeholders and customers to identify an ideal time to do the deployment. They need to select a time that is convenient for the DevOps team and one that does not fall in peak times of when customers have urgent need of the application. DevOps teams may be deploying application releases every other week so they may need to have a regularly scheduled downtime for this. Other options include blue-green deployments where the site is deployed and tested and then a switch is quickly made to make that site live with minimal disruption to the user base. See Chapter 9 for more information on deployment methodologies.

It is critical to take a backup or snapshots of the application servers before rolling out the new version. Despite all the testing in the previous phase, problems still can arise, and you will want to have a good clean version to go back to if a problem arises.

Sometimes issues are encountered when deploying to production, despite the testing that occurred in previous phases of the application life cycle. In such cases, DevOps teams may need to roll back to the snapshot if they cannot fix the deployment issues in a timely manner.

Once the application is deployed, users need to be trained on the new features or changes of the release. This could be as simple as sending out release notes or including links to video tutorials and bundling tool tips into the application, or it could be more involved such as requiring one-on-one training.

Phase 5: Maintenance

Along the way after deployment, various patches will be required to keep the application, or the resources it relies upon, functioning properly. This phase is called the maintenance phase. Here the DevOps team will fix small user-reported bugs or configuration issues, field tickets from users, and measure and tweak performance to keep the application running smoothly.

There is an element of maintenance that involves a micro version of the entire application life cycle, because small issues will result in specifications, which will lead to development and testing, and ultimately deployment into the production environment. Some of the tasks listed previously fall into this category. Suffice to say, this element is somewhat recursive.

Before adding new code, changing code, or performing other maintenance tasks that might impact application availability, the DevOps team works with stakeholders and customers to identify an ideal time to perform the activity. Some deployments may be urgent, such as fixes to address a critical vulnerability that was just discovered or a serious issue that users or customers are experiencing. In these cases, these limitations may be waived due to the criticality of the update.

It is important to note the difference between patches and releases here. Releases offer new features while patches fix bugs or security problems.

ITIL

Information Technology Infrastructure Library (ITIL) provides a framework for implementing life cycle management. ITIL's model for life cycle management is a continuum consisting of the following five phases:

1. Service strategy
2. Service design
3. Service transition
4. Service operation
5. Continual service improvement

Each phase has inputs and outputs that connect the stages to one another, and continual improvement is recognized via multiple trips through the life cycle. Each time through, improvements are documented and then implemented based on feedback from each of the life cycle phases. These improvements enable the organization to execute each of its service offerings as efficiently and effectively as possible and ensure that each of those services provides as much value to its users as possible.

Microsoft Operations Framework

Microsoft Operations Framework (MOF) is based on ITIL. MOF has shortened the life cycle to four phases:

1. Plan
2. Deliver
3. Operate
4. Manage

These phases are usually depicted graphically in a continuum, as we see in Figure 7-4. This continuum represents the cyclical nature of process improvement, with a structured system of inputs and outputs that leads to continual improvement.

Application Replacement

Eventually, the application reaches a point where significant changes are required to make it useful. This could be due to shifts in the environment, in other business processes, or in the underlying technology that the application was built upon. At this point, specifications are drafted for a replacement application or a newer version of the application, and the cycle begins anew.

FIGURE 7-4

A representation
of the MOF life
cycle continuum

Application Retirement

All applications eventually reach a point where they no longer provide value to the organization. At this point, the application should be retired. Program code and processes are documented and the resources the application uses are released for some other purpose.

Application Migration

Applications may need to be migrated to different hardware as their usage increases or decreases. The application may need to be migrated as the underlying technology environment changes. For example, the organization may move to more powerful hardware or from one cloud provider to another or from one virtualization platform to a competing platform.

Application Feature Use (Increase/Decrease)

Use of an application will change over time. Application use will be relatively limited as it is introduced because it takes a while for users to adopt a new solution. However, as the value of the program is demonstrated and more people tell others about it, the use will gradually increase. Eventually, application use will plateau and stay at a relatively consistent level for some time before it finally diminishes when other applications or newer processes supplant the application or as business conditions change.

A major thing touted in new releases is what new features the release adds.

Business Needs Change

Business needs change, sometimes quite rapidly. Business change can be frustrating for application developers who have spent much time putting an application together, hoping that it will have a long shelf life. However, businesses must adapt to their environment and meet continually changing customer needs and wants. Adaptation necessitates changes to applications, tools, systems, and personnel to adjust the technology environment to these new requirements.

Cloud technologies make such changes much easier. Cloud services can be expanded, contracted, or terminated simply by contacting the cloud vendor and requesting the change. Some services may have a contract period, with a penalty for breaking the contact, but many services are flexible.

It is also important to note that personnel changes are not as dramatic when using cloud services. If a company decides to stop using one cloud service and adopt two others, this might result in no changes to personnel. By contrast, if these were on-premises applications, one person might need to go through training to be familiar with the new application and another person may need to be hired to support the new one.

Some business changes that impact cloud professionals include

- Mergers, acquisitions, and divestitures
- Cloud service requirement changes
- Regulatory and legal changes

Mergers, Acquisitions, and Divestitures

When two companies decide to combine their businesses, this is known as a merger. One company can also choose to purchase another in an acquisition. Some companies decide to change direction and sell off a portion of their business through a divestiture.

Every company has a unique technology infrastructure that supports its business, and any company that goes through a merger, acquisition, or divestiture has to adapt its infrastructure to meet the requirements of the new corporate form. Physical hardware must be moved from one site to another, possibly rebranded, and adapted to meet the policies, standards, and compliance requirements of the new company.

Cloud services streamline this operation. Cloud accounts can be moved from one company to another and still reside with the same provider. Cloud integrations can be migrated from one system to another if necessary. Cloud migrations are easiest if cloud service integrations were performed using standard APIs.

Cloud Service Requirement Changes

Cloud service providers are continually upgrading their systems to take advantage of new technologies and improvements in processes. Unlike on-premises solutions where new software versions must be deployed by IT staff, cloud updates are deployed by the cloud provider on the organization's behalf. It is important to stay on top of what changes are made by the cloud provider in case changes are needed on the organizational side as well.

Companies may also request changes to their cloud services. In some cases, a cloud provider might offer a buffet of services, and customers can add or remove these services at will. Other solutions may be highly customized for the customer, in which case negotiation with the provider and adequate lead time are necessary for changes to be made to the environment to meet the customer requirements.

Regulatory and Legal Changes

The regulatory and legal environment is also an area that sees frequent change. When a country promulgates a new regulation or law (or changes an existing one) that affects business practices, companies that do business in that country must adhere to the new or changed law or regulation. Global organizations often have entire teams of people who monitor changes in the global regulatory environment and then work with organizational departments to implement appropriate changes.

Corporate legal teams often work with vendor management or IT to coordinate with cloud providers to ensure that legal and regulatory requirements are met. One way to validate that a cloud provider supports new regulatory requirements is through a vendor risk assessment. This involves sending a document listing each of the requirements to the cloud provider and asking the cloud provider to verify that it has the appropriate controls and measures in place to meet the compliance requirements.

Vendor risk assessments take time to administer and time to complete. It is important to give vendors plenty of time to work through the details. Some vendors will need to implement additional procedures or controls to meet the requirements, and others may decide that they do not want to make changes, forcing your organization to move its business from one cloud provider to another to remain compliant.

CERTIFICATION SUMMARY

Monitoring the network is a key component of DevOps and cloud computing. Monitoring allows an organization to plan for future resource utilization and respond to issues that arise in the cloud environment. Combining monitoring and alerting gives an administrator a way to be proactive instead of reactive when it comes to the cloud environment.

Remotely managing the virtualization environment provides flexibility and ease of administration. Being able to control multiple virtualization host computers from a single console saves time and makes managing the cloud environment an easier task.

Life cycle management is the process or processes put in place by an organization to assist in the management, coordination, control, delivery, and support of its configuration items from the requirements stage to retirement. The core of this is the application life cycle, or software development life cycle (SDLC). Additionally, ITIL has established a framework for implementing life cycle management, and Microsoft has a framework (MOF) that is based on ITIL.

KEY TERMS

Use the following list to review the key terms discussed in this chapter. The definitions also can be found in the glossary.

application life cycle   A process whereby applications are specified, developed, tested, deployed, and maintained.

console port   Allows an administrator to use a cable to connect to a hypervisor host computer or virtual machine directly.

Hypertext Transfer Protocol (HTTP)   Protocol used to distribute HTML files, text, images, sound, videos, multimedia files, and other information over the Internet.

Hypertext Transfer Protocol Secure (HTTPS)   An extension of HTTP that provides secure communication over the Internet using Secure Sockets Layer (SSL) or Transport Layer Security (TLS).

Intelligent Platform Management Interface (IPMI)   Used for out-of-band management of a computer, allowing an administrator to manage a system remotely without an operating system.

Information Technology Infrastructure Library (ITIL)   A framework for implementing life cycle management.

life cycle management   The process or processes put in place by an organization to assist in the management, coordination, control, delivery, and support of its configuration items from the requirements stage to retirement.

Microsoft Operations Framework (MOF)   A Microsoft framework for implementing life cycle management that is based on ITIL.

out-of-band management   Allows for remote management and monitoring of a computer system without the need for an operating system.

performance baseline   Performance metrics from elements of a system taken during a period of relatively normal activity.

Remote Desktop Protocol (RDP)   Provides remote display and input capabilities over a computer network.

remote hypervisor access   The ability to manage a hypervisor from another computer across a network.

remote shell (RSH)   Command-line program that executes shell commands across a network in an unsecured manner.

Secure Shell (SSH)   A cryptographic protocol that creates an encrypted channel to access remote servers, configure network equipment, secure logins, transfer files, and perform port forwarding.

Short Message Service (SMS)   Text messaging service that allows an alert to be sent to a mobile device.

Simple Mail Transfer Protocol (SMTP)   Protocol used to send e-mail over the Internet.

Simple Network Management Protocol (SNMP)   Commonly supported protocol on devices such as routers, switches, printers, and servers and can be used to monitor those devices for issues.

syslog   Provides a mechanism for a network device to send event messages to a logging server or a syslog server.

syslog server   Computer used as a centralized repository for syslog messages.

systems life cycle management   The process or processes put in place by an organization to assist in the management, coordination, control, delivery, and support of its systems from the requirements stage to retirement.

threshold   Used to set the amount of resources that can be consumed before an alert is generated.

Web-Based Enterprise Management (WBEM)   Standardized way of accessing management information in an enterprise environment.

Windows Management Instrumentation (WMI)   Protocol used to gather information about the installed hardware, software, and operating system of a computer.

 # TWO-MINUTE DRILL

Resource Monitoring Techniques

❑ Monitoring a cloud environment can ensure the overall health of the environment and gives an IT department the ability to measure the cloud service against its SLAs.

❑ Simple Network Management Protocol (SNMP) gives an administrator the ability to monitor and manage network performance, report and troubleshoot network issues, and understand and plan for network growth.

❑ Windows Management Instrumentation (WMI) allows an administrator to create scripts that can be run against a remote computer to perform administrative tasks. WMI also allows an administrator to gather information about installed software and the operating system version of a computer.

❑ Intelligent Platform Management Interface (IPMI) enables an administrator to perform out-of-band management to remotely manage and monitor a device even if the device is powered off.

❑ Syslog provides a mechanism for a network device to send event messages to a central logging server or syslog server over UDP port 514 or TCP 514 and is supported by a wide range of devices.

❑ Creating a baseline for a server can help an administrator troubleshoot performance issues for that server and plan for additional resources simply by looking for an increase in resource utilization compared to the baseline.

❑ Setting thresholds allows an administrator to be alerted when system resources are being overutilized and to respond to that alert.

Remote-Access Tools

❑ The ability to remotely manage a hypervisor host saves administration time.

❑ Multiple hypervisor hosts can be managed from a single console installed on a local workstation.

❑ Remote Desktop Protocol (RDP) allows for remotely connecting directly to a hypervisor host or virtual machine by providing remote display and input capabilities over the network.

❑ Secure Shell (SSH) provides a secure way to manage network devices remotely.

❑ A web console can be used over HTTP or HTTPS to connect to a hypervisor host computer or management device that controls that host.

Life Cycle Management

❑ Life cycle management is the process or processes put in place by an organization to assist in the management, coordination, control, delivery, and support of its configuration items from the requirements phase to retirement.

❑ The application life cycle consists of five phases: specifications, development, testing, deployment, and maintenance.

❑ In phase 1, specifications, the application's reason for being is documented. Users and stakeholders explain what they would like the application to do and what problem it will solve for them.

❑ In phase 2, development, project managers turn specifications into a model for a working program.

❑ In phase 3, testing, the code developed in the development phase is subjected to testing to ensure that it performs according to specifications, without errors, bugs, or security issues.

❑ In phase 4, deployment, the application developed and tested in previous phases is installed and configured in production for stakeholders to use.

❑ In phase 5, maintenance, small user-reported bugs or configuration issues are fixed, field tickets from users are addressed, and teams measure and tweak performance to keep the application running smoothly.

SELF TEST

The following questions will help you measure your understanding of the material presented in this chapter. As indicated, some questions may have more than one correct answer, so be sure to read all the answer choices carefully.

Resource Monitoring Techniques

1. Which of the following can be used to identify which operating system version is installed on a virtual machine?
   A. WMI
   B. SMTP
   C. SMS
   D. IMAP

2. Which of these can be used by both a cloud consumer and a cloud provider to give a visual picture of performance metrics?
   A. API
   B. SNMP
   C. Dashboard
   D. SMTP

3. Which of the following utilizes UDP port 514 when collecting events?
   A. SNMP
   B. Syslog
   C. WMI
   D. Web services

4. Which of the following can be used to create scripts that can be run against target computers to perform simple administrative tasks?
   A. WMI
   B. SMTP
   C. SMS
   D. IMAP

5. Which of the following constantly executes a software component called an agent, which reports information using the protocol back to a manager?
    A. WMI
    B. SMTP
    C. SMS
    D. SNMP

6. Which of the following alerting methods allows a technician to receive an alert on a mobile device such as a cell phone?
    A. SMTP
    B. SMS
    C. SNMP
    D. Syslog

7. Which of the following alerting methods can be configured to send an e-mail when a certain alert is triggered?
    A. SMTP
    B. SMS
    C. SNMP
    D. Syslog

8. Which of the following allows for out-of-band management of a computer?
    A. WMI
    B. SMS
    C. SNMP
    D. IPMI

Remote-Access Tools

9. You receive an alert that a virtual machine is down. The server does not respond to a ping. What tool should you use to troubleshoot the server if you are off-site?
    A. Console port
    B. SSH
    C. Hypervisor console
    D. SMTP

10. Which of the following would you use to remotely access a virtualization host in a secure fashion?
    A. Telnet
    B. Ping
    C. HTTPS
    D. Console port

11. You have been tasked with gathering a list of software installed on all the computers in your environment. You want to gather this information remotely. Which of the following would you use to gather this information?
    A. WMI
    B. SNMP
    C. HTTP
    D. Syslog

12. Which of the following would be used to directly connect to a hypervisor host remotely to modify operating system settings on the hypervisor host?
    A. RDP
    B. Console port
    C. SMTP
    D. HTTPS

13. Which of the following is a benefit of remote hypervisor administration?
    A. Only being able to modify one hypervisor host at a time
    B. Being able to remotely manage multiple hypervisor hosts from a single console
    C. Not having access to a hypervisor host
    D. Remotely accessing a hypervisor host has no benefit

Life Cycle Management

14. Which of the following terms best describes life cycle management?
    A. Baseline
    B. Finite
    C. Linear
    D. Continuum

15. What is the desired end result of ITIL?
    A. CAB
    B. Continual service improvement
    C. Service strategy
    D. Service operation

SELF TEST ANSWERS

Resource Monitoring Techniques

1. ☑ **A.** Windows Management Instrumentation (WMI) provides an administrator a way to gather hardware information from multiple physical servers or virtual servers and put that information into a centralized database.

   ☒ **B, C,** and **D** are incorrect. Simple Mail Transfer Protocol (SMTP) can send an e-mail when a certain monitored event occurs. Short Message Service (SMS) is a text messaging service that allows an alert to be sent to a mobile device. Internet Message Access Protocol (IMAP) allows an e-mail client to access e-mail on a remote mail server.

2. ☑ **C.** A dashboard is a great way for both the cloud consumer and cloud provider to access key metrics when it comes to monitoring cloud resources. A dashboard can give a summary of the current usage of the cloud resources in an easy-to-view format of charts and graphs.

   ☒ **A, B,** and **D** are incorrect. An application programming interface (API) is a protocol that can be used as an interface into a software component. Simple Network Management Protocol (SNMP) is commonly supported on devices such as routers, switches, printers, and servers and is used to monitor these devices for issues or conditions that might arise, but it does not provide performance metrics. Nor does SMTP, which is used to send e-mail alerts when certain monitored events occur.

3. ☑ **B.** Syslog provides a mechanism for a network device to send event messages to a logging server or syslog server using UDP port 514 or TCP 514.

   ☒ **A, C,** and **D** are incorrect. SNMP is one of the common protocols used to manage and monitor an environment, but it does not utilize UDP port 514. WMI allows an administrator to query and set information on a workstation, server, or application, but it does not use UDP port 514. Web services provide a centralized console to view events but again would not use UDP port 514.

4. ☑ **A.** Windows Management Instrumentation (WMI) allows you to write scripts to automate certain administrative tasks and run those scripts against remote computers.

   ☒ **B, C,** and **D** are incorrect. None of these options allow you to create scripts to automate specific administrative tasks.

5. ☑ **D.** A monitoring solution that uses SNMP has an administrative computer, commonly referred to as a manager, that monitors or manages a group of network devices. Each managed device constantly executes a software component, called an agent, that reports back to the manager.

   ☒ **A, B,** and **C** are incorrect. WMI allows you to write scripts to automate certain administrative tasks and run the scripts against remote computers. SMTP sends an e-mail alert when a certain monitored event occurs. SMS allows you to send short text messages to alert about issues and does not report back to a manager.

6. ☑ **B.** Short Message Service (SMS) is a text messaging service that allows an alert to be sent to a mobile device.

   ☒ **A, C,** and **D** are incorrect. SMTP can send an e-mail when a certain monitored event occurs, but it cannot transmit to a cell phone or other mobile device. SNMP is one of the common protocols used to manage and monitor an environment. Syslog provides a mechanism for a network device to send event messages to a logging server or syslog server using UDP port 514.

7. ☑ **A.** Simple Mail Transfer Protocol (SMTP) can be configured to send an e-mail alert when a certain monitored event occurs.

   ☒ **B, C,** and **D** are incorrect. SMS is a text messaging service that allows an alert to be sent to a mobile device. Syslog provides a mechanism for a network device to send event messages to a logging server or syslog server using UDP port 514. SNMP does not allow an administrator to receive messages on a cell phone.

8. ☑ **D.** The Intelligent Platform Management Interface (IPMI) operates independently of the operating system. It provides out-of-band management and monitoring of a system before the operating system is loaded, which allows BIOS settings to be remotely monitored or configured.

   ☒ **A, B,** and **C** are incorrect. WMI, SMS, and SNMP do not allow you to perform out-of-band management of a device.

Remote-Access Tools

9. ☑ **B.** Secure Shell (SSH) provides a secure way to remotely manage network devices, including hypervisor hosts.

   ☒ **A, C,** and **D** are incorrect. A console port would not allow management of the hypervisor host from an off-site location. SMTP sends e-mail alerts in response to monitored events; it does not remotely manage network devices. A hypervisor console would not be available since you are accessing the hypervisor host from an off-site location.

10. ☑ **C.** HTTPS gives you a way to access a virtualization host remotely in a secure fashion.

   ☒ **A, B,** and **D** are incorrect. Telnet and Ping do not allow you to access a virtualization host remotely in a secure fashion. A console port doesn't allow you to access the host remotely.

11. ☑ **A.** With Windows Management Instrumentation (WMI), it is possible to query workstations remotely and gather a list of all the software installed on those workstations.

   ☒ **B, C,** and **D** are incorrect. SNMP collects event messages from SNMP-enabled devices but does not query for installed software. HTTP does not allow you to remotely gather all the software installed on a computer. Syslog provides a mechanism for a network device to send event messages to a logging server or syslog server using UDP port 514 but will not allow you to query for installed software.

12. ☑ **A.** The Remote Desktop Protocol (RDP) lets you establish a remote connection directly to a hypervisor host. It allows you to change system settings on the hypervisor host computer itself.

   ☒ **B, C,** and **D** are incorrect. The console port gives you direct access to a hypervisor host but not remotely. SMTP does not allow you to remotely connect to the hypervisor host to modify settings. HTTPS gives you a web console that could access some management features of the hypervisor software but not the hypervisor host machine.

13. ☑ **B.** The ability to remotely manage multiple hypervisor hosts from a single console from your workstation allows for a quick and easy way to make changes to multiple hosts and is an important benefit of remote hypervisor administration.

☒ **A, C,** and **D** are incorrect. Modifying a single host remotely is not as big of an advantage as modifying multiple hosts remotely, as it would require more administration to connect to each individual host computer remotely to modify the same settings.

Life Cycle Management

14. ☑ **D.** Life cycle management is a continuum with feedback loops going back into itself to enable better management and continual improvement.

☒ **A, B,** and **C** are incorrect. Baselines are utilized for measurement but are not cyclical. By definition the word "finite" implies that there is an ending, and life cycle management has no end since it is continually improving. Linear does not fit because life cycle management has many feedback loops and it doesn't always progress forward; rather, it frequently circles back.

15. ☑ **B.** The end result of each cycle within ITIL is to identify opportunities for improvement that can be incorporated into the service to make it more efficient, effective, and profitable.

☒ **A, C,** and **D** are incorrect. Change advisory boards (CABs) are utilized for the evaluation of a proposed change (discussed in Chapter 13). Service strategy and service operation are both phases in the life cycle.

Chapter 8

Performance Tuning

Appropriately distributing compute resources is one of the most important aspects of a virtualized cloud environment. Planning for future growth and the ability to adjust compute resources on demand is one of the many benefits of a virtualized environment. This chapter explains how to configure compute resources on a host computer and a guest virtual machine and how to optimize the performance of a virtualized environment.

CERTIFICATION OBJECTIVE 8.01

Host and Guest Resource Allocation

It is important to allocate the correct resources for hosts and the guest virtual machines that reside on them. This section covers host resource allocation first since a host is needed to operate guests. This is followed by guest virtual machine resource allocation.

Host Resource Allocation

Building a virtualization host requires careful consideration and planning. First, you must identify which resources the host requires and plan how to distribute those resources to a virtual machine. Next, you must plan the configuration of the guest virtual machine that the host computer will serve.

You must attend to the configuration of resources and the licensing of the host in the process of moving to a virtualized environment or virtual cloud environment. This consists of the following:

- Compute resources
- Quotas and limits
- Licensing
- Reservations
- Resource pools

Compute Resources

Adequate compute resources are key to the successful operation of a virtualization host. Proper planning of the compute resources for the host computer ensures that the host can deliver the performance needed to support the virtualization environment.

Compute resources can best be defined as the resources that are required for the delivery of virtual machines. They are the disk, processor, memory, and networking resources that are shared across pools of virtual machines and underpin their ability to deliver the value of the cloud models, as covered in Chapter 1.

As a host is a physical entity, the compute resources that the host utilizes are naturally physical, too. However, cloud providers may allocate a subset of their available physical resources to cloud consumers to allocate to their own virtual machines. Compute resources are displayed in Figure 8-1.

For disk resources, physical rotational disks and solid state hard drives are utilized, as well as their controller cards, disk arrays, host bus adapters, and networked storage

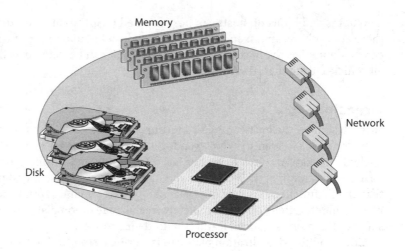

FIGURE 8-1

Host compute resources: processor, disk, memory, and network

transmission media. For network resources, network interface cards (NICs) and physical transmission media such as Ethernet cables are employed. Central processing units (CPUs) are employed for the processor, and physical banks of RAM are used to supply memory.

Quotas and Limits

Because compute resources are limited, cloud providers must protect them and make certain that their customers only have access to the amount that the cloud providers are contracted to provide. Two methods used to deliver no more than the contracted amount of resources are quotas and limits.

Limits are a defined floor or ceiling on the amount of resources that can be used, and quotas are limits that are defined for a system on the total amount of resources that can be utilized. When defining limits on host resources, cloud providers have the option of setting a soft or hard limit. A soft limit will allow the user to save a file even if the drive reaches 100GB, but will still log an alert and notify the user. A hard limit, on the other hand, is the maximum amount of resources that can be utilized. For example, a hard limit of 100GB for a storage partition will not allow anything to be added to that partition once it reaches 100GB, and the system will log an event to note the occurrence and notify the user.

The quotas that are typically defined for host systems have to do with allocation of the host compute resources to the host's guest machines. These quotas are established according to service level agreements (SLAs) that are created between the cloud provider and cloud consumers to indicate a specific level of capacity.

Capacity management is essentially the practice of allocating the correct amount of resources in order to deliver a business service. The resources that these quotas enforce limits upon may be physical disks, disk arrays, host bus adapters, RAM chips, physical processors, and network adapters. They are allocated from the total pool of resources available to individual guests based on their SLA.

Quotas and limits on hosts can be compared to speed limits on the highway; very often there are both minimum and maximum speeds defined for all traffic on the roads. A quota can be defined as the maximum speed and a limit can be defined as the minimum speed for all vehicles using that road's resources.

Licensing

After designing the host computer's resources and storage limits, an organization or cloud provider needs to identify which vendor it is going to use for its virtualization software. Each virtualization software vendor has its own way of licensing products. Some of them have a free version of their product and only require a license for advanced feature sets that enable functionality, like high availability, performance optimization, and systems management. Others offer a completely free virtualization platform but might not offer some of the more advanced features with their product.

Choosing the virtualization platform is a critical step, and licensing is a factor in that decision. Before deploying a virtualization host and choosing a virtualization vendor, the organization must be sure to read the license agreements and determine exactly which features it needs and how those features are licensed. In addition to licensing the virtualization host, the guest requires a software license as well.

Reservations

Reservations work similarly to quotas. Whereas quotas are designed to ensure the correct capacity gets delivered to customers by defining an upper limit for resource usage, reservations are designed to operate at the other end of the capacity spectrum by ensuring that a lower limit is enforced for the amount of resources guaranteed to a cloud consumer for their guest virtual machine or machines.

The importance of a reservation for host resources is that it ensures certain virtual machines always have a defined baseline level of resources available to them regardless of the demands placed on them by other virtual machines. The reason these guest reservations are so important is that they enable cloud service providers to deliver against their SLAs.

Resource Pools

Resource pools are slices or portions of overall compute resources on the host or those allocated from the cloud provider to consumers. These pools include CPU, memory, and storage and they can be provided from a single host or a cluster of hosts. Resources can be partitioned off in resource pools to provide different levels of resources to specific groups or organizations, and they can be nested within a hierarchy for organizational alignment.

Resource pools provide a flexible mechanism with which to organize the sum total of the compute resources in a virtual environment and link them back to their underlying physical resources.

Guest Resource Allocation

Before creating a guest virtual machine, an organization needs to consider several factors. A guest virtual machine should be configured based on the intended application or task that the guest is going to support. For example, a guest running a database server may require special performance considerations, such as more CPUs or memory based on the designated role of the machine and the system load. In addition to CPUs and memory, a guest may require higher-priority access to certain storage or disk types.

An organization must consider not only the role of the virtual machine, the load of the machine, and the number of clients it is intended to support but also the performance of ongoing monitoring and assessment based on these factors. The amount of disk space the guest is using should be monitored and considered when deploying and maintaining storage.

The allocation of resources to virtual machines must be attended to in the process of moving to a virtualized environment or virtual cloud environment because the organization will either be allocating these resources from its available host resources or paying for them from a cloud provider. Organizations should evaluate each of the following resources:

- Compute resources
- Quotas and limits
- Licensing
- Physical resource redirection
- Resource pools
- Dynamic resource allocation

Compute Resources

The compute resources for virtual machines enable service delivery in the same way that compute resources for hosts do. However, the resources themselves are different in that they are virtualized components instead of physical components that can be held in your hand or plugged into a motherboard.

Guest compute resources are still made up of disk, network, processor, and memory components, but these components are made available to virtual machines not as physical resources, but as abstractions of physical components presented by a hypervisor that emulates those physical resources for the virtual machine.

Physical hosts have a Basic Input/Output System (BIOS) that presents physical compute resources to a host so they can be utilized to provide computing services, such as running an operating system and its component software applications. With virtual machines, the BIOS is emulated by the hypervisor to provide the same functions. When the BIOS is emulated and these physical resources are abstracted, administrators have the ability to divide the virtual compute resources from their physical providers and distribute those subdivided resources across multiple virtual machines. This ability to subdivide physical resources is one of the key elements that make cloud computing and virtualization so powerful.

When splitting resources among multiple virtual machines, there are vendor-specific algorithms that help the hypervisor make decisions about which resources are available for each request from its specific virtual machine. There are requirements of the host resources for performing these activities, including small amounts of processor, memory, and disk. These resources are utilized by the hypervisor for carrying out the algorithmic calculations to determine which resources will be granted to which virtual machines.

Quotas and Limits

As with host resources, virtual machines utilize quotas and limits to constrain the ability of users to consume compute resources and thereby prevent users from either monopolizing or completely depleting those resources. Quotas can be defined either as hard or soft. Hard quotas set limits that users and applications are barred from exceeding. If an attempt to use resources beyond the set limit is registered, the request is rejected, and an alert is logged that can be acted upon by a user, administrator, or management system. The difference with a soft quota is that the request is granted instead of rejected, and the resources are made available to service the request. The same alert, however, is still logged so that action can be taken to either address the issue with the requester for noncompliance with the quota or charge the appropriate party for the extra usage of the materials.

Licensing

Managing hardware resources can be less of a challenge than managing license agreements. Successfully managing software license agreements in a virtual environment is a tricky proposition. The software application must support licensing a virtual instance of the application.

Some software vendors still require the use of a dongle or a hardware key when licensing their software. Others have adopted their licensing agreements to coexist with a virtual environment. A guest requires a license to operate just as a physical server does. Some vendors have moved to a per-CPU-core type of license agreement to adapt to virtualization. No matter if the application is installed on a physical server or a virtual server, it still requires a license.

Organizations have invested heavily in software licenses. Moving to the cloud does not always mean that those licenses are lost. Bring Your Own License (BYOL), for example, is a feature for Azure migrations that allows existing supported licenses to be migrated to Azure so that companies do not need to pay for the licenses twice. Software assurance with license mobility allows for licenses to be brought into other cloud platforms such as Amazon Web Service (AWS) or VMware vCloud.

EXAM AT WORK

Soft Quota Cell Phone Pain

A painful example that most people can relate to regarding soft quotas is cell phone minutes usage. With most carriers, if a customer goes over the limit of their allotted cell phone minutes on their plan, they are charged an additional nominal amount per minute over. They will receive a warning when they go over the limit if their account is configured for such alerts, or they will receive an alert in the form of their bill that lets them know just how many minutes over quota they have gone and what they owe because of their overage. They are not, however, restricted from using more minutes once they have gone over their quota. If their cell phone minutes were configured as a hard quota, customers would be cut off in the middle of a phone call as soon as they eclipsed their quota. This usage of soft quotas is a great example of engineering cellular phone service by the phone companies, and it can be utilized across many other cloud services by their providers.

Physical Resource Redirection

There are so many things that virtual machines can do that sometimes we forget that they even exist on physical hardware. However, there are occasions when you will need a guest to interface with physical hardware components. Some physical hardware components that are often mapped to virtual machines include USB drives, parallel ports, serial ports, and USB ports.

In some cases, you may want to utilize USB storage exclusively for a virtual machine. You can add a USB drive to a virtual machine by first adding a USB controller. When a USB drive is attached to a host computer, the host will typically mount that drive automatically. However, only one device can access the drive at a single time without corrupting the data, so the host must release access to the drive before it can be mapped to a virtual machine. Unmount the drive from the host and then you will be ready to assign the drive to the virtual machine.

Parallel and serial ports are interfaces that allow for the connection of peripherals to computers. There are times when it is useful to have a virtual machine connect its virtual serial port to a physical serial port on the host computer. For example, a user might want to install an external modem or another form of a handheld device on the virtual machine, and this would require the guest to use a physical serial port on the host computer. It might also be useful to connect a virtual serial port to a file on a host computer and then have the guest virtual machine send output to a file on the host computer. An example of this would be to send data that was captured from a program running on the guest via the virtual serial port and transfer the information from the guest to the host computer.

In addition to using a virtual serial port, it is also helpful in certain instances to connect to a virtual parallel port. Parallel ports are used for a variety of devices, including printers, scanners, and dongles. Much like the virtual serial port, a virtual parallel port allows for connecting the guest to a physical parallel port on the host computer.

In addition to supporting serial and parallel port emulation for virtual machines, some virtualization vendors support USB device pass-through from a host computer to a virtual machine. USB pass-through allows a USB device plugged directly into a host computer to be passed through to a virtual machine. USB pass-through allows for multiple USB devices such as security tokens, software dongles, temperature sensors, or webcams that are physically attached to a host computer to be added to a virtual machine.

The process of adding a USB device to the virtual machine usually consists of adding a USB controller to the virtual machine, removing the device from the host configuration, and then assigning the USB device to the virtual machine. When a USB device is attached to a host computer, that device is available only to the virtual machines that are running on that host computer and only to one virtual machine at a time.

Resource Pools

A resource pool is a hierarchical abstraction of compute resources that can give relative importance, or weight, to a defined set of virtualized resources. Pools at the higher level in the hierarchy are called parent pools; these parents can contain either child pools or individual virtual machines. Each pool can have a defined weight assigned to it based on either the business rules of the organization or the SLAs of a customer.

Resource pools also allow administrators to define a flexible hierarchy that can be adapted at each pool level as required by the business. This hierarchical structure makes it possible to maintain access control and delegation of the administration of each pool and its resources; to ensure isolation between the pools, as well as sharing within the pools; and finally to separate the compute resources from discrete host hardware. This last feature frees administrators from the typical constraints of managing the available resources from the host they originated from. Those resources are bubbled up to a higher level for management and administration when utilizing pools.

Dynamic Resource Allocation

Just because administrators can manage their compute resources at a higher level with resource pools, it does not mean they want to spend their precious time doing it. Enter dynamic resource allocation. Instead of relying on administrators to evaluate resource utilization and apply changes to the environment that result in the best performance, availability, and capacity arrangements, a computer can do it for them based on business logic that has been predefined by either the management software's default values or the administrator's modification to those values.

Management platforms can manage compute resources not only for performance, availability, and capacity reasons but also to realize more cost-effective implementation of those resources in a data center, employing only the hosts required at the given time and shutting down any resources that are not needed. By employing dynamic resource allocation, providers can both reduce power costs and go greener by shrinking their power footprint and waste.

CERTIFICATION OBJECTIVE 8.02

Optimizing Performance

Utilization of the allocation mechanisms we have talked about thus far in this chapter allows administrators to achieve the configuration states that they seek within their environment. The next step is to begin optimizing that performance. Optimization including the following:

- Configuration best practices
- Common issues
- Scalability
- Performance concepts
- Performance automation

Configuration Best Practices

There are some best practices for the configuration of each of the compute resources within a cloud environment. The best practices for these configurations are the focus for the remainder of this section. These best practices center on those allocation mechanisms that allow for the greatest value to be realized by service providers. To best understand their use cases and potential impact, we investigate common configuration options for memory, processor, and disk.

Memory

Memory may be the most critical of all computer resources, as it is usually the limiting factor on the number of guests that can run on a given host, and performance issues appear when too many guests are fighting for enough memory to perform their functions. Two configuration options available for addressing shared memory concerns are memory ballooning and swap disk space.

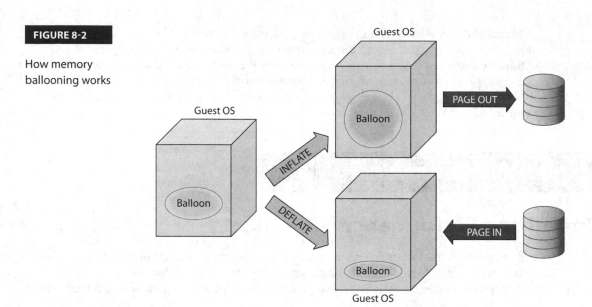

FIGURE 8-2

How memory
ballooning works

Memory Ballooning Hypervisors have device drivers that they build into the host virtualization layer from within the guest operating system. Part of this installed tool set is a balloon driver, which can be observed inside the guest. The balloon driver communicates to the hypervisor to reclaim memory inside the guest when it is no longer valuable to the operating system. If the host begins to run low on memory, it will grow the balloon driver to reclaim memory from the guest. This reduces the chance that the physical host will start to utilize virtualized memory from a defined paging file on its available disk resource, which causes performance degradation. An illustration of the way this ballooning works can be found in Figure 8-2.

Swap Disk Space Swap space is disk space that is allocated to service memory requests when the physical memory capacity limit has been reached. When virtualizing and overcommitting memory resources to virtual machines, administrators must make certain to reserve enough swap space for the host to balloon memory in addition to reserving disk space within the guest operating system for it to perform its swap operations.

Virtual machines and the applications that run on them will take a significant performance hit when memory is swapped out to disk. However, you do not need that large of a disk for swap space, so it is a good practice to keep a solid state drive in the host that can be used for swap space if necessary. This will ensure that those pages moved to swap space are transferred to high-speed storage, and it will lessen the impact of memory paging operations.

Processor

CPU time is the amount of time a process or thread spends executing on a processor core. For multiple threads, the CPU time of the threads is additive. The application CPU time is the sum of the CPU time of all the threads that run the application. Wait time is the amount of time that a given thread waits to be processed; it could be processed but must wait on other factors such as synchronization waits and I/O waits.

High CPU wait times signal that there are too many requests for a given queue on a core to handle, and performance degradation will occur. While high CPU wait time can be alleviated in some situations by adding processors, these additions sometimes hurt performance as well. Caution must be exercised when adding processors as there is a potential for causing even further performance degradation if the applications using them are not designed to be run on multiple CPUs. Another solution for alleviating CPU wait times is to scale out instead of scaling up, two concepts that we explore in more detail later in this chapter.

CPU Affinity   It is also important to properly configure CPU affinity, also known as processor affinity. CPU affinity is where threads from a specific virtual machine are tied to a specific processor or core, and all subsequent requests from that process or thread are executed by that same processor or core. CPU affinity overrides the built-in processor scheduling mechanisms so that threads are bound to specific processor cores.

- ■ **Benefits**   The primary benefit of CPU affinity is to optimize cache performance. Processor cache is local to that processor, so if operations are executed on another processor, they are unable to take advantage of the cache on the first processor. Furthermore, the same data cannot be kept in more than one processor cache, so when the second processor caches new content, it must first invalidate the cache from the first processor. This can happen when a performance-heavy threat moves from one processor to another, and it can be prevented by assigning the virtual machine thread to a processor so that its cache never moves. This also ensures that the cache that has been created for that processor is utilized more often for that virtual machine thread.

- ■ **Caveats**   Assigning CPU affinity can cause many problems and should be used sparingly. In many cases, the best configuration will be not to configure CPU affinity and to let the hypervisor choose the best processor for the task at hand. This is primarily because CPU affinity does not prevent other virtual machines from using the processor core, but it restricts the configured virtual machine from using other cores; thus, the preferred CPU could be overburdened with other work. Also, where the host would normally assign the virtual machine's thread to another available CPU, CPU affinity would require the virtual machine to wait until the CPU became available before its thread would be processed.

Test CPU affinity before implementing it in production. You may need to create CPU affinity rules for all other virtual machines to ensure that they do not contend for CPU cores. Document affinity settings so that other administrators will be aware of them when migrating virtual machines or performing other changes to the environment.

Disk

Poor disk performance, or poorly designed disk solutions, can have performance ramifications in traditional infrastructures, slowing users down as they wait to read or write data for the server they are accessing. In a cloud model, however, disk performance issues can limit access to all organization resources because multiple virtualized servers in a networked storage environment might be competing for the same storage resources, thereby crippling their entire deployment of virtualized servers or desktops. The following sections describe some typical configurations and measurements that assist in designing a high-performance storage solution. These consist of the following:

- Disk performance
- Disk tuning
- Disk latency
- I/O throttling
- I/O tuning

Disk Performance   Disk performance can be configured with several different configuration options. Media type can affect performance, and administrators can choose between the most standard types of traditional rotational media or chip-based solid state drives. Solid state drives are much faster than their rotational counterparts as they are not limited by the physical seek arm speed that reads the rotational platters. Solid state drives, while becoming more economical in the last few years, are still much more expensive than rotational media and are not utilized except where only the highest performance standards are required.

The next consideration for disk performance is the speed of the rotational media, should that be the media of choice. Server-class disks start at 7,200 rpm and go up to 15,000 rpm, with seek times for the physical arm reading the platters being considerably lower on the high-end drives. In enterprise configurations, price point per gigabyte is primarily driven by the rotation speed and only marginally by storage space per gigabyte. When considering enterprise storage, the adage is that you pay for performance, not space.

Once the media type and speed have been determined, the next consideration is the type of RAID array that the disks are placed in to meet the service needs. Different levels of RAID can be employed based on the deployment purpose. These RAID levels should be evaluated and configured based on the type of I/O and on the need to read, write, or a combination of both.

Disk Tuning   Disk tuning is the activity of analyzing what type of I/O traffic is taking place across the defined disk resources and moving it to the most appropriate set of resources.

Virtualization management platforms enable the movement of storage, without interrupting current operations, to other disk resources within their control.

Virtualization management platforms allow either administrators or dynamic resource allocation programs to move applications, storage, databases, and even entire virtual machines among disk arrays with no downtime to make sure that those virtualized entities get the performance they require based on either business rules or SLAs.

Disk Latency   Disk latency is a counter that provides administrators with the best indicator of when a resource is experiencing degradation due to a disk bottleneck and needs to have action taken against it. If high latency counters are experienced, a move to either another disk array with quicker response times or a different configuration, such as higher rotational speeds or a different array configuration, is warranted. Another option is to configure I/O throttling.

I/O Throttling   I/O throttling does not eliminate disk I/O as a bottleneck for performance, but it can alleviate performance problems for specific virtual machines based on a priority assigned by the administrator. I/O throttling defines limits that can be utilized specifically for disk resources allocated to virtual machines to ensure that they are not performance or availability constrained when working in an environment that has more demand than the availability of disk resources.

I/O throttling may be a valuable option when an environment contains both development and production resources. The production I/O can be given a higher priority than the development resources, allowing the production environment to perform better for end users.

Prioritization does not eliminate the bottleneck. Rather, prioritizing production machines just passes the bottleneck on to the development environment, which becomes even further degraded in performance as it waits for all production I/O requests when the disk is overallocated. Administrators can then assign a priority or pecking order for the essential components that need higher priority.

I/O Tuning   When designing systems, administrators need to analyze I/O needs from the top down, determining which resources are necessary to achieve the required performance levels. In order to perform this top-down evaluation, administrators first need to evaluate the application I/O requirements to understand how many reads and writes are required by each transaction and how many transactions take place each second. Once those application requirements are understood, they can build the disk configuration (specifically, which types of media, what array configuration, the number of disks, and the access methods) to support that number.

Common Issues

There are some failures that can occur within a cloud environment, and the system must be configured to be tolerant of those failures and provide availability in accordance with the organization's SLA or other contractual agreements.

Mechanical components in an environment will experience failure at some point. It is just a matter of time. Higher-quality equipment may last longer than cheaper equipment, but it will still break down someday. This is something you should be prepared for.

Failures occur mainly on each of the four primary compute resources: disk, memory, network, and processor. This section examines each of these resources in turn.

Common Disk Issues

Disk-related issues can happen for a variety of reasons, but disks fail more frequently than the other compute resources because they are the only compute resource that has a mechanical component. Due to the moving parts, failure rates are typically quite high. Some common disk failures include

- Physical hard disk failures
- Controller card failures
- Disk corruption
- HBA failures
- Fabric and network failures

Physical Hard Disk Failures   Physical hard disks frequently fail because they are mechanical, moving devices. In enterprise configurations, they are deployed as components of drive arrays, and single failures do not affect array availability.

Controller Card Failures   Controller cards are the elements that control arrays and their configurations. Like all components, they fail from time to time. Redundant controllers are costly to run in parallel as they require double the amount of drives to become operational, and that capacity is lost because it is never in use until failure. Therefore, an organization should do a return-on-investment analysis to determine the feasibility of making such devices redundant.

Disk Corruption   Disk corruption occurs when the structured data on the disk is no longer accessible. This can happen as a result of malicious acts or programs, skewing of the mechanics of the drive, or even a lack of proper maintenance. Disk corruption is hard to repair, as the full contents of the disks often need to be reindexed or restored from backups. Backups can also be unreliable for these failures if the corruption began before its identification, as the available backup sets may also be corrupted.

Host Bus Adapter Failures   HBA failures, while not as common as physical disk failures, need to be expected and storage solutions need to be designed with them in mind. HBAs have the option of being multipathed, which prevents a loss of availability in the event of a failure.

Fabric and Network Failures   Similar to controller card failure, fabric or network failures can be relatively expensive to design around, as they happen when a storage networking switch or switch port fails. The design principles to protect against such a failure are similar to those for HBAs, as multipathing needs to be in place to make certain all hosts that depend on the fabric or network have access to their disk resources through another channel.

Common Memory Issues

Memory-related issues, while not as common as disk failures, can be just as disruptive. Good system design in cloud environments will take RAM failure into account as a risk and ensure that there is always some RAM available to run mission-critical systems in case of memory failure on one of their hosts. The following are some types of memory failures:

- Memory chip failures
- Motherboard failures
- Swap files that run out of space

Memory Chip Failures   Memory chip failures happen less frequently than physical device failures since memory chips have no moving parts and mechanical wear does not play a part. They will, however, break from time to time and need to be replaced.

Motherboard Failures   Similar to memory chips, motherboards have no moving parts, and because of this, they fail less frequently than mechanical devices. When they do fail, however, virtual machines are unable to operate, as they have no processor, memory, or networking resources that they can access. In this situation, they must be moved immediately to another host or go offline.

Swap Files Out of Space   Swap space failures often occur in conjunction with a disk failure, when disks run out of available space to allocate to swap files for memory overallocation. They do, however, result in out-of-memory errors for virtual machines and hosts alike.

Network Issues

Similar to memory components, network components are relatively reliable because they do not have moving parts. Unlike memory, network resources are highly configurable and prone to errors based on human mistakes during implementation. Some common types of network failures include

- Physical NIC failures
- Speed or duplex mismatches
- Switch failures
- Physical transmission media failures

Physical NIC Failures   Network interface cards can fail in a similar fashion to other printed circuit board components like motherboards, controller cards, and memory chips. Because they fail from time to time, redundancy needs to be built into the host through multiple physical NICs and into the virtualization through designing multiple network paths using virtual NICs for the virtual machines.

Speed or Duplex Mismatches   Mismatch failures happen only on physical NICs and switches, as virtual networks negotiate these automatically. Speed and duplex mismatches result in dropped packets between the two connected devices and can be identified through getting many cyclical redundancy check (CRC) errors on the devices.

Switch Failures   Similar to fabric and network failures, network switch failures are expensive to plan for as they require duplicate hardware and cabling. Switches fail wholesale only a small percentage of the time, but more frequently have individual ports fail. When these individual ports do fail, the resources that are connected to them need to have another path available or their service will be interrupted.

Physical Transmission Media Failures   Cables break from time to time when their wires inside are crimped or cut. This can happen either when they are moved, when they are stretched too far, or when they become old, and the connector breaks loose from its associated wires. As with other types of network failures, multiple paths to the resource using that cable is the way to prevent a failure from interrupting operations.

Physical Processor Issues

Processors fail for one of three main reasons: they get broken while getting installed, they are damaged by voltage spikes, or they are damaged due to overheating from failed or ineffective fans. Damaged processors either take hosts completely off-line or degrade performance based on the damage and the availability of a standby or alternative processor in some models.

Scalability

Most applications will see increases in workloads in their life cycles. For this reason, the systems supporting those applications must be able to scale to meet increased demand. Scalability is the ability of a system or network to manage a growing workload in a proficient manner or its ability to be expanded to accommodate the workload growth. All cloud environments need to be scalable, as one of the chief tenets of cloud computing is elasticity, or the ability to adapt to growing workload quickly.

Scalability can be handled either vertically or horizontally, more commonly referred to as "scaling up" or "scaling out," respectively.

Vertical Scaling (Scaling Up)

To scale vertically means to add resources to a single node, thereby making that node capable of handling more of a load within itself. This type of scaling is most often seen in virtualization environments where individual hosts add more processors or more memory with the objective of adding more virtual machines to each host.

Horizontal Scaling (Scaling Out)

To scale horizontally, more nodes are added to a configuration instead of increasing the resources for any one node. Horizontal scaling is often used in application farms, where more web servers are added to a farm to handle distributed application delivery better. The third type of scaling, diagonal scaling, is a combination of both, increasing resources for individual nodes and adding more of those nodes to the system. Diagonal scaling allows for the best configuration to be achieved for a quickly growing, elastic solution.

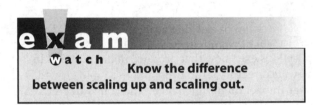

Know the difference between scaling up and scaling out.

Performance Concepts

There are some performance concepts that underlie each of the failure types and the allocation mechanisms discussed in this chapter. As we did with the failure mechanisms, let's look at each of these according to their associated compute resources.

Disk

The configuration of disk resources is an important part of a well-designed cloud system. Based on the user and application requirements and usage patterns, there are numerous design choices that need to be made to implement a storage system that cost-effectively meets an organization's needs. Some of the considerations for disk performance include

- IOPS
- Read and write operations
- File system performance
- Metadata performance
- Caching

IOPS   IOPS, or input/output operations per second, are the standard measurement for disk performance. They are usually gathered as read IOPS, write IOPS, and total IOPS to distinguish between the types of requests that are being received.

Read and Write Operations   As just mentioned, there are two types of operations that can take place: reading and writing. As their names suggest, reads occur when a resource requests data from a disk resource, and writes occur when a resource requests new data be recorded on a disk resource. Based on which type of operation takes place, different configuration options exist both for troubleshooting and performance tuning.

File System Performance   File system performance is debated as a selling point among different technology providers. File systems can be formatted and cataloged differently based on the proprietary technologies of their associated vendors. There is little to do in the configuration of file system performance outside of evaluating the properties of each planned operation in the environment.

Metadata Performance   Metadata performance refers to how quickly files and directories can be created, removed, or checked. Applications exist now that produce millions of files in a single directory and create very deep and wide directory structures, and this rapid growth of items within a file system can have a huge impact on performance. The ability to create, remove, and check their status efficiently grows in direct proportion to the number of items in use on any file system.

Caching   To improve performance, hard drives are architected with a mechanism called a disk cache that reduces both read and write times. On a physical hard drive, the disk cache is usually a RAM chip that is built in and holds data that is likely to be accessed again soon. On virtual hard drives, the same caching mechanism can be employed by using a specified portion of a memory resource.

Network

Similar to disk resources, the configuration of network resources is critical. Based on the user and application requirements and usage patterns, numerous design choices need to be made to implement a network that cost-effectively meets an organization's needs. Some of the considerations for network performance include

- Bandwidth
- Throughput
- Jumbo Frames
- Network latency
- Hop counts
- Quality of service (QoS)
- Multipathing
- Load balancing

Bandwidth   Bandwidth is the measurement of available or consumed data communication resources on a network. Performance of all networks is dependent on having available bandwidth.

Throughput   Throughput is the amount of data that can be realized between two network resources. Throughput can be substantially increased through the use of bonding or teaming of network adapters, which allows resources to see multiple interfaces as one single interface with aggregated resources.

Jumbo Frames   Jumbo Frames are Ethernet frames with more than 1,500 bytes of payload. These frames can carry up to 9,000 bytes of payload, but depending on the vendor and the environment they are deployed in, there may be some deviation. Jumbo Frames are utilized because they are much less processor intensive to consume than a large number of smaller frames, therefore freeing up expensive processor cycles for more business-related functions.

Network Latency   Network latency refers to any performance delays experienced during the processing of any network data. A low-latency network connection is one that experiences small delay times, such as a dedicated T-1, while a high-latency connection frequently suffers from long delays, like DSL or a cable modem.

Hop Counts   A hop count represents the total number of devices a packet passes through to reach its intended network target. The more hops data must pass through to reach its destination, the greater the delay is for the transmission. Network utilities like ping can be used to determine the hop count to an intended destination. Ping generates packets that include a field reserved for the hop count (typically referred to as a TTL, or time-to-live), and each time a capable device (usually a router) along the path to the target receives one of these packets, that device modifies the packet, decrementing the TTL by one. Each packet is sent out with a particular time-to-live value, ranging from 1 to 254; for every router (hop) that it traverses, that TTL count is decremented. Also, for every second that the packet resides in the memory of the router, it is also decremented by one. The device then compares the hop count against a predetermined limit and discards the packet if its hop count is too high. If the TTL is decremented to zero at any point during its transmission, an ICMP port unreachable message is generated, with the IP of the source router or device included, and sent back to the originator. The finite TTL is used as it counts down to zero to prevent packets from endlessly bouncing around the network due to routing errors.

Quality of Service (QoS)   QoS is a set of technologies that can identify the type of data in data packets and divide those packets into specific traffic classes that can be prioritized according to defined service levels. QoS technologies enable administrators to meet their service requirements for a workload or an application by measuring network bandwidth, detecting changing network conditions, and prioritizing the network traffic accordingly.

QoS can be targeted at a network interface, toward a given server's or router's performance, or regarding specific applications. A network monitoring system is typically deployed as part of a QoS solution to ensure that networks are performing at the desired level.

Multipathing   Multipathing is the practice of defining and controlling redundant physical paths to I/O devices so that when an active path to a device becomes unavailable, the multipathing configuration can automatically switch to an alternate path to maintain service availability. The capability of performing this operation without intervention from an administrator is known as automatic failover.

A prerequisite for taking advantage of multipathing capabilities is to design and configure the multipathed resource with redundant hardware, such as redundant network interfaces or host bus adapters.

Load Balancing   A load balancer is a networking solution that distributes incoming traffic among multiple servers hosting the same application content. Load balancers improve overall application availability and performance by preventing any application server from becoming a single point of failure.

If deployed alone, however, the load balancer becomes a single point of failure by itself. Therefore, it is always recommended to deploy multiple load balancers in parallel. In addition to improving availability and performance, load balancers add to the security profile of a configuration by the typical usage of network address translation, which obfuscates the IP address of the back-end application servers.

Performance Automation

Various tasks can be performed to improve performance on machines. It is typical for these tasks to be performed at regular intervals to maintain consistent performance levels. However, it can be quite a job to maintain a large number of systems, and organizational IT departments are supporting more devices per person than ever before. They accomplish this through automation. Automation uses scripting, scheduled tasks, and automation tools to do the routine tasks so that IT staff can spend more time solving the real problems and proactively looking for ways to make things better and even more efficient.

PowerShell commands are provided in many examples because these commands can be used with the AWS Command Line Interface (CLI) or the Microsoft Azure Cloud Shell. PowerShell was chosen for its versatility. However, other scripting languages can also be used depending on the platform. Scripts can be combined into tasks using AWS Systems Manager or Microsoft Azure runbooks.

This section discusses different performance-enhancing activities that can be automated to save time and standardize. They include the following:

- Archiving logs
- Clearing logs
- Compressing drives
- Scavenging stale DNS entries
- Purging orphaned resources
- Reclaiming resources

Archiving Logs

Logs can take up a lot of space on servers, but you will want to keep logs around for a long time in case they are needed to investigate a problem or a security issue. For this reason, you might want to archive logs to a logging server and then clear the log from the server.

A wide variety of cloud logging and archiving services are available that can be leveraged instead of setting up a dedicated logging server. Some services include Logentries, OpenStack, Sumo Logic, Syslog, Amazon S3, Amazon CloudWatch, and Papertrail. Cloud backup services can also be used to archive logs. Services such as AWS Glacier can be configured to pull log directories and store them safely on another system so they are not lost. These systems can consolidate logs, then correlate and deduplicate them to save space and gain network intelligence.

Clearing Logs

There is very little reason to clear logs unless you have first archived them to another service or server. The previous section outlined how to archive logs to a local logging server or to cloud services. Ensure that these are configured and that they have been fully tested before clearing logs that could contain valuable data. Logs are there for a reason. They show the activity that took place on a device, and they can be very valuable in retracing the steps of an attacker or in troubleshooting errors. You do not want to be the person who is asked, "How long has this been going on?" and you have to answer, "I don't know because we cleared the logs last night."

Here is a PowerShell function to clear the logs from computers 1 through 4 called ClearComputer1-4Logs. You first provide the function with a list of computers. It then puts together a list of all logs, goes through each, and clears the log.

```
function ClearComputer1-4Logs ($ComputerName="Computer1", "Computer2", "Computer3", "Computer4")
{
    $Logs = Get-EventLog -ComputerName $ComputerName -List | ForEach {$_.Log}
    $Logs | ForEach {Clear-EventLog -Comp $ComputerName -Log $_ }
    Get-EventLog -ComputerName $ComputerName -List
}
```

Compressing Drives

Compressing drives can reduce the amount of space consumed. However, accessing files on the drives will require a bit more CPU power to decompress before the file can be opened. Here is the command you can use to compress an entire drive. You can place this in a Windows group policy to encrypt the data drives (D:\) of various machines depending on how you apply the group policy. The following command specifies that the D:\ directory and everything below it should be compressed. The —recurse command is what causes the compression to take place on all subfolders.

```
Enable-NtfsCompression -Path D:\ -Recurse
```

Scavenging Stale DNS Entries

As mentioned in Chapter 4, DNS distributes the responsibility for both the assignment of domain names and the mapping of those names to IP addresses to the authoritative name servers within each domain. DNS servers register IP address assignments as host records in their database. Sometimes a record is created, and then that host is removed, or it is assigned a new address. The DNS server would retain a bogus record in the former case and redundant addresses in the latter case.

Scavenging is the process of removing DNS entries for hosts that no longer respond on that address. You can configure automatic scavenging on DNS servers. All you have to do is enable the scavenging feature and set the age for when DNS records will be removed. If a host cannot be reached for the specified number of days, its host record in DNS will automatically be deleted.

Purging Orphaned Resources

Applications, hypervisors included, do not always clean up after themselves. Sometimes child objects or resources from deleted or moved objects still remain on systems. These are known as orphaned resources.

In Microsoft System Center Virtual Machine Manager (SCVMM), you can view orphaned resources by opening the Library workspace and clicking Orphaned Resources. You can right-click the object to delete it, but we want to automate the task. A script to remove all orphaned resources from SCVMM would take many pages of this book, so we will point you to a resource where you can obtain an up-to-date script for free:

https://www.altaro.com/hyper-v/free-script-find-orphaned-hyper-v-vm-files/

Orphaned resources show up in the VMware vSphere web client with "(Orphaned)" after their name. You can remove them with this script after logging into the command line on the host:

```
$VMSet=Get-VM
foreach ($vm in $VMSet)
{
 if ($vm.ExtensionData.Runtime.ConnectionState -eq "orphaned") {$vm | Remove-VM}
}
```

Reclaiming Resources

Many companies have inactive virtual machines that continue to consume valuable resources while providing no business value. Metrics can identify machines that might not be used, at which point, a standard message can be sent to the owner of the machine notifying them that their machine has been flagged for reclamation unless they confirm that it is still providing business value. Alternatively, you can give the owner the option of keeping or reclaiming the resources themselves rather than automatically doing it. However, if the owner of the virtual machine does not respond in a timely manner, the organization may decide to have the machine reclaimed automatically.

If reclamation is chosen, the machine can be archived and removed from the system and the resources can be freed up for other machines. The automation can be initiated whenever metrics indicate an inactive machine. VMware vRealize has this capability built in for vCenter, and similar automation can be created for other tools. In Microsoft Azure, the Resource Manager can be configured to reclaim resources.

CERTIFICATION SUMMARY

When building a virtualization host, special consideration needs to be given to adequately planning the resources to ensure that the host is capable of supporting the virtualized environment. Creating a virtual machine requires thorough planning regarding the role the virtual machine will play in the environment and the resources needed for the virtual machine to accomplish that role. Planning carefully for the virtual machine and the primary resources of memory, processor, disk, and network can help prevent common failures.

KEY TERMS

Use the following list to review the key terms discussed in this chapter. The definitions also can be found in the glossary.

bandwidth   A measurement of available or consumed data communication resources on a network.

caching   A mechanism for improving the time it takes to read from or write to a disk resource.

compute resources   The resources that are required for the delivery of virtual machines: disk, processor, memory, and networking.

CPU wait time   The delay that results when the CPU cannot perform computations because it is waiting for I/O operations.

hop count   The total number of devices a packet passes through to reach its intended network target.

horizontal scaling   A scalability methodology whereby more nodes are added to a configuration instead of increasing the resources for any one node. Horizontal scaling is also known as scaling out.

I/O throttling   Defined limits utilized specifically for disk resources assigned to virtual machines to ensure they are not performance or availability constrained when working in an environment that has more demand than availability of disk resources.

input/output operations per second (IOPS)   A common disk performance measurement of how much data is provided over a period of time.

Jumbo Frames   Large frames that are used for large data transfers to lessen the burden on processors.

limit   A floor or ceiling on the amount of resources that can be utilized for a given entity.

load balancing   Networking solution that distributes incoming traffic among multiple resources.

memory ballooning   A device driver loaded inside a guest operating system that identifies underutilized memory and allows the host to reclaim memory for redistribution.

metadata performance   A measure of how quickly files and directories can be created, removed, or checked on a disk resource.

multipathing   The practice of defining and controlling redundant physical paths to I/O devices.

network latency   Any delays typically incurred during the processing of any network data.

orphaned resource   A child object or resource from deleted or moved objects that remains on a system.

quality of service (QoS)   A set of technologies that provides the ability to manage network traffic and prioritize workloads to accommodate defined service levels as part of a cost-effective solution.

quota   The total amount of resources that can be utilized for a system.

read operation   Operation in which a resource requests data from a disk resource.

reservation   A mechanism that ensures a lower limit is enforced for the amount of resources guaranteed to an entity.

resource pool   Partition of compute resources from a single host or a cluster of hosts.

scalability   Ability of a system or network to manage a growing workload in a proficient manner or its ability to be expanded to accommodate the workload growth.

scavenging   The process of removing DNS entries for hosts that no longer respond on that address.

throughput   The amount of data that can be realized between two network resources.

vertical scaling   A scalability methodology whereby resources such as additional memory, vCPUs, or faster disks are added to a single node, thereby making that node capable of handling more of a load within itself. Vertical scaling is also known as scaling up.

write operation   Operation in which a resource requests that new data be recorded on a disk resource.

✓ TWO-MINUTE DRILL

Host and Guest Resource Allocation

❑ Proper planning of the compute resources for a host computer ensures that the host can deliver the performance needed to support its virtualized environment.

❑ Quotas and limits allow cloud providers to control the amount of resources a cloud consumer can access.

❑ A reservation helps to ensure that a host computer receives a guaranteed amount of resources to support its virtual machine.

❑ Resource pools allow an organization to organize the total compute resources in the virtual environment and link them back to their underlying physical resources.

❑ Guest virtual machines utilize quotas and limits to constrain the ability of users to consume compute resources and can prevent users from either completely depleting or monopolizing those resources.

❑ Software applications and operating systems must support the ability to be licensed in a virtual environment, and the licensing needs to be taken into consideration before a physical server becomes a virtual server.

❑ A guest virtual machine can support the emulation of a parallel and serial port; some can support the emulation of a USB port.

❑ Dynamic resource allocation can be used to automatically assign compute resources to a guest virtual machine based on utilization.

Optimizing Performance

❑ There are a number of best practices for configuration of compute resources within a cloud environment. Cloud administrators must be able to optimize memory, disk, and processor resources as discussed in this chapter.

❑ There are multiple failures that can occur within a cloud environment, including hard disk failure, controller card failures, disk corruption, HBA failure, network failure, RAM failure, motherboard failure, network switch failure, and processor failure.

❑ Node capacity can be increased to vertically scale (scale up) or additional nodes can be added to horizontally scale (scale out).

❑ Log archiving and clearing, drive compression, DNS scavenging, purging orphaned resources, and reclaiming resources can be automated to improve performance on machines.

SELF TEST

The following questions will help you measure your understanding of the material presented in this chapter. As indicated, some questions may have more than one correct answer, so be sure to read all the answer choices carefully.

Host and Guest Resource Allocation

1. Which of the following would be considered a host compute resource?
    A. Cores
    B. Power supply
    C. Processor
    D. Bandwidth

2. Quotas are a mechanism for enforcing what?
    A. Limits
    B. Rules
    C. Access restrictions
    D. Virtualization

3. How are quotas defined?
    A. By management systems
    B. According to service level agreements that are defined between providers and their customers
    C. Through trend analysis and its results
    D. With spreadsheets and reports

4. When would a reservation be used?
    A. When a maximum amount of resources needs to be allocated to a specific resource
    B. When a minimum amount of capacity needs to be available at all times to a specific resource
    C. When capacity needs to be measured and controlled
    D. When planning a dinner date

5. How does the hypervisor enable access for virtual machines to the physical hardware resources on a host?
    A. Over Ethernet cables
    B. By using USB 3.0
    C. Through the system bus
    D. By emulating a BIOS that abstracts the hardware

6. What mechanism allows one core to handle all requests from a specific thread on a specific processor core?
   A. V2V
   B. CPU affinity
   C. V2P
   D. P2V

7. In a scenario where an entity exceeds its defined quota but is granted access to the resources anyway, what must be in place?
   A. Penalty
   B. Hard quota
   C. Soft quota
   D. Alerts

8. Which of the following must be licensed when running a virtualized infrastructure?
   A. Hosts
   B. Virtual machines
   C. Both
   D. Neither

9. What do you need to employ if you have a serial device that needs to be utilized by a virtual machine?
   A. Network isolation
   B. Physical resource redirection
   C. V2V
   D. Storage migration

10. You need to divide your virtualized environment into groups that can be managed by separate groups of administrators. Which of these tools can you use?
    A. Quotas
    B. CPU affinity
    C. Resource pools
    D. Licensing

Optimizing Performance

11. Which tool allows guest operating systems to share noncritical memory pages with the host?
    A. CPU affinity
    B. Memory ballooning
    C. Swap file configuration
    D. Network attached storage

12. Which of these options is not a valid mechanism for improving disk performance?
   A. Replacing rotational media with solid state media
   B. Replacing rotational media with higher-speed rotational media
   C. Decreasing disk quotas
   D. Employing a different configuration for the RAID array

SELF TEST ANSWERS

Host and Guest Resource Allocation

1. ☑ **C.** The four compute resources used in virtualization are disk, memory, processor, and network. On a host, these are available as the physical entities of hard disks, memory chips, processors, and network interface cards (NICs).
☒ **A, B,** and **D** are incorrect. Cores are a virtual compute resource. Power supplies, while utilized by hosts, are not compute resources, because they do not contribute resources toward the creation of virtual machines. Bandwidth is a measurement of network throughput capability, not a resource itself.

2. ☑ **A.** Quotas are limits on the resources that can be utilized for a specific entity on a system. For example, a user could be limited to storing up to 10GB of data on a server or a virtual machine limited to 500GB of bandwidth each month.
☒ **B, C,** and **D** are incorrect. Quotas cannot be used to enforce rules or setup virtualization. Access restrictions are security entities, not quantities that can be limited, and virtualization is the abstraction of hardware resources, which has nothing to do with quotas.

3. ☑ **B.** Quotas are defined according to service level agreements that are negotiated between a provider and its customers.
☒ **A, C,** and **D** are incorrect. Management systems and trend analysis provide measurement of levels of capacity, and those levels are reported using spreadsheets and reports, but these are all practices and tools that are used once the quotas have already been negotiated.

4. ☑ **B.** A reservation should be used when there is a minimum amount of resources that needs to have guaranteed capacity.
☒ **A, C,** and **D** are incorrect. Dealing with maximum capacity instead of minimums is the opposite of a reservation. Capacity should always be measured and controlled, but not all measurement and control of capacity deals with reservations. Obviously, if you are planning for a dinner date you will want to make reservations, but that has nothing to do with cloud computing.

5. ☑ **D.** The host computer BIOS is emulated by the hypervisor to provide compute resources for a virtual machine.
☒ **A, B,** and **C** are incorrect. These options do not allow a host computer to emulate compute resources and distribute them among virtual machines.

6. ☑ **B.** CPU affinity allows all requests from a specific thread or process to be handled by the same processor core.
☒ **A, C,** and **D** are incorrect. You can use a V2V to copy or restore files and program from one guest virtual machine to another. V2P allows you to migrate a guest virtual machine to a physical server. P2V allows you to migrate a physical server's operating system, applications, and data from the physical server to a newly created guest guest virtual machine on a host computer.

7. ☑ **C.** Soft quotas enforce limits on resources, but do not restrict access to the requested resources when the quota has been exceeded.
☒ **A, B,** and **D** are incorrect. Penalties may be incurred if soft quotas are exceeded, but the quota must first be in place. A hard quota denies access to resources after it has been exceeded. Alerts should be configured, regardless of the quota type, to be triggered when the quota has been breached.

8. ☑ **C.** Both hosts and guests must be licensed in a virtual environment.
☒ **A, B,** and **D** are incorrect. Both hosts and guests must be licensed in a virtual environment.

9. ☑ **B.** Physical resource redirection enables virtual machines to utilize physical hardware as if they were physical hosts that could connect to the hardware directly.
☒ **A, C,** and **D** are incorrect. These options do not allow you to redirect a guest virtual machine to a physical port on a host computer.

10. ☑ **C.** Resource pools allow the creation of a hierarchy of guest virtual machine groups that can have different administrative privileges assigned to them.
☒ **A, B,** and **D** are incorrect. Quotas are employed to limit the capacity of a resource, CPU affinity is used to isolate specific threads or processes to one processor core, and licensing has to do with the acceptable use of software or hardware resources.

Optimizing Performance

11. ☑ **B.** Memory ballooning allows guest operating systems to share noncritical memory pages with the host.
☒ **A, C,** and **D** are incorrect. CPU affinity is used to isolate specific threads or processes to one processor core. Swap file configuration is the configuration of a specific file to emulate memory pages as an overflow for physical RAM. Network attached storage is a disk resource that is accessed across a network.

12. ☑ **C.** Decreasing disk quotas helps with capacity issues, but not with performance.
☒ **A, B,** and **D** are incorrect. Changing from rotational to solid state media increases performance since it eliminates the dependency on the mechanical seek arm to read or write. Upgrading rotational media to higher rotational speed also speeds up both read and write operations. Changing the configuration of the array to a different RAID level can also have a dramatic effect on performance.

Chapter 9

Systems Management

Up until this point, this book has primarily focused on the technologies required to deliver cloud services. This chapter explores the nontechnical aspects of cloud service delivery in policies, procedures, and best practices. These components are critical to the efficient and effective execution of cloud solutions.

The chapter begins with the documents that define the rule sets by which users and administrators must abide, called policies, and the prescribed documented actions that will carry out the expectations of the policies, known as procedures.

Next, the chapter goes through system maintenance activities that must be performed to keep cloud systems operating at expected performance levels and to avoid unexpected downtime.

CERTIFICATION OBJECTIVE 9.01

Policies and Procedures

Policies and procedures are the backbone of any IT organization. While the hardware, software, and their associated configurations are the products that enable the functionality businesses desire from their IT services, it is a cloud service provider's or cloud consumer's policies and procedures that allow IT service implementation, maintenance, and ongoing support.

Policies define the rule sets by which users and cloud service administrators (CSAs) must abide, and procedures are the prescribed methodologies by which activities are carried out in the IT environment according to those defined policies.

While most IT professionals focus on the technical aspects of IT, a growing percentage of all IT organizations are emphasizing policy and procedure development to ensure that they get the most out of their technology investment. Policies can be used to enforce IT best practices to significantly affect not only the operational efficiency and effectiveness of the businesses they serve but to also protect the organization from risk by defining compliance expectations and ensuring adherence to industry regulation.

This section provides information on some key business processes that aid in managing the technology environment, making it more efficient, and planning for the future. These processes include

- Creating standard operating procedures
- Workflow
- Capacity management

Standard Operating Procedures

Standard operating procedures (SOPs) are a form of knowledge management. The experience gained from one individual can be documented so that others do not need to go through the same experience, possibly involving failure, to learn from it.

SOPs help ensure that tasks are performed consistently. It is likely that you will perform routine tasks many times. The first time you perform such a task, it is best to create a SOP for future migrations. You may find along the way that you can improve the SOP here or there. Feel free to add more details to the SOP as you discover enhancements.

A SOP will ensure that others who perform the same task do so with the same level of professionalism that you do. SOPs also ensure consistent implementation, including the amount of time it takes to perform the task and the resources required.

Workflow

Workflows are business processes that are organized in sets of discrete tasks from the beginning to the end of the processes. Workflow task details include the dependencies and requirements such as the personnel, technology, tools, and environment required to complete the task.

Workflow modeling can help visualize a workflow by placing each task on a timeline, with dependencies shown as prerequisite tasks and parallel tasks shown about one another. Relationships are depicted using paths. Each path is a set of tasks that can be performed independently of other tasks. Some paths may diverge and then join back together to express group dependencies and then a period where tasks can be carried out at the same time. Some paths may take longer to complete than others. A project management technique known as *critical path analysis* identifies paths where there is no extra time available. When resources are scarce, tasks on the critical path should be given a higher priority.

Workflow can be helpful in managing standard processes, but it can be even more effective when those processes are automated. The SOPs an organization creates in the course of doing business can now be used in establishing workflow automation. Once a process has been performed several times, and it is sufficiently well documented, there may be methods of automating the process so that it is even more streamlined. The documentation will ensure that you do not miss a critical step in the workflow, and it can help in troubleshooting workflows later on. Workflow automation with runbooks is discussed in more detail in Chapter 13.

Capacity Management

Capacity management is the process of ensuring that both the current and future capacity and performance demands of an IT organization's customers regarding service provision are delivered according to justifiable costs. Capacity management has overall responsibility for ensuring that there is adequate IT capacity (as the name suggests) to meet required service levels, that the appropriate stakeholders are correctly advised on how to match capacity and demand, and that existing capacity is optimized.

Successful capacity management requires considerable attention to be paid to the design of the system. The design phase must ensure that all service levels are understood and that the capacity to fulfill them is incorporated into the design's configuration. Once the configuration has been adequately designed and documented, operations can establish a baseline, as discussed in Chapter 7. This baseline is a measuring stick against which capacity can be monitored to understand both the current demand and trend for future needs.

The capacity management process includes producing and maintaining an appropriate capacity plan that reflects the current and future requirements of its customers. The plan is designed to accomplish the following objectives:

- Provide advice and guidance to all other areas of the business and IT on all capacity- and performance-related issues.
- Ensure that service performance achievements meet or exceed all of their agreed-upon performance targets by managing the performance and capacity of both services and resources.
- Ensure the current and future capacity and performance demands of the customer regarding IT service provision are delivered within justifiable costs.
- Assist with the diagnosis and resolution of both performance- and capacity-related incidents and problems.
- Assess the impact of any changes to the capacity plan and the performance and capacity of all IT services and resources.
- Ensure that proactive measures to improve the performance of services are implemented.

When building this capacity plan, its architects must factor in all IT resources, including both human and technical resources. Keep in mind that people are resources as well.

**on the
job**

There was a systems administrator who was in charge of a major corporate website back in the 1990s whose story serves as an excellent object lesson both for capacity and change management. His company had recently hired him to work on the ramp-up for a new website, and he worked closely with the marketing group to make sure his team designed the site for all the functionality to be captured in the capacity requirements. Subsequently, the marketing team decided to run an advertisement during the Super Bowl that was intended to drive users to their redesigned website. However, they failed to involve IT in the discussion. Since the expected capacity requirements had changed and IT had not been informed, the site, which had been designed for a far smaller load, crashed within seconds of the ad running. The IT department had not staffed administrators for support and monitoring during the costly advertisement, so they were unable to recover quickly. Because of this capacity planning failure, what had started out as a great marketing idea turned into a colossal marketing nightmare.

Systems Management Best Practices

The processes and procedures that IT organizations implement to achieve results more effectively and efficiently are the results of careful design, standardized environments, and thorough documentation.

With a view to building sustainable technology solutions that consistently deliver their intended value, system maintenance must be performed at every step of the application life cycle. Documentation of the business requirements for any proposed IT service additions or changes should be the first phase of the life cycle, followed by documentation for the proposed technical design, continuing into implementation planning documents and support documentation, and coming full circle in the life cycle through documented service improvement plans.

Documentation

Documentation is an important part of systems management. Information Technology Infrastructure Library (ITIL) is a collection of best practices for IT service management. It was put together initially by the British government but was spun off under a private best practices body called AXELOS in 2013. ITIL is one of the most widely used IT service management best practices in the world and it is very helpful in understanding best practice in IT documentation. ITIL is divided into five publications called volumes that cover the following categories:

- Service strategy
- Service design
- Service transition
- Service operation
- Continual service improvement

ITIL provides a framework for documentation for each of the five sections and this section will discuss documentation in that context.

During the service strategy phase of ITIL, business requirements are documented as the entry point for all IT services. The key piece of documentation in this stage is the service portfolio. The service portfolio is a full list of quantified services that will enable the business to achieve a positive return on its investment in the service.

During the service design phase, technical solutions, support processes, and service level agreements (SLAs) are documented in the service design package (SDP). The SDP includes the technical solutions, such as routers, switches, servers, and storage, support processes for maintaining the service, and SLAs with the customer as to the mutually agreed-upon levels of capacity, availability, and performance.

The service transition phase is focused on delivering the SDP and all of its detail into a living, breathing operational environment. This documentation stage consists of change and configuration documentation. See Chapter 13 for more details on change and configuration management.

Lastly, a service improvement register documents opportunities for improving IT services as follows:

- Opportunities are categorized as short-term, medium-term, or long-term options.
- Opportunities are assessed as part of the service strategy phase once the life cycle restarts.
- Opportunities are assigned a business value that can be weighed against implementation cost.
- Opportunity time frames, value, and costs are evaluated to determine which services to add or modify to provide the greatest value to customers.

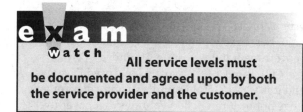

All service levels must be documented and agreed upon by both the service provider and the customer.

Documentation is one vehicle that drives effective systems administration, as it allows CSAs to expand their ability to comprehend very complex environments without having to keep all the information in their heads. Another very effective way to accomplish this goal is through standardization.

Standardization

Standardization reduces the complexities of system administration because CSAs only need to learn the standard way of doing things, since that method and configuration is applicable across many systems.

Standardization focuses on two areas: procedures and configurations. Standard procedures were discussed earlier in the "Standard Operating Procedures" section. Now we will focus on standardizing configuration. Some of the advantages of standardization include

- Systems management is performed consistently.
- System access is better controlled.
- System communication protocols are the same across applications and services.
- Uniform system logging and auditing settings are employed.
- Systems are deployed in the same manner each time.

Standardization allows for systems to be managed consistently in the same way. Organizations can specify which management protocols to use and whether centralized management utilities will be put in place. When new systems are evaluated, the selection group then ensures that new software or cloud services meet the standard requirements so that they can be managed in the same way. Consistent management reduces the amount of time spent managing devices and makes employees more efficient as they get more comfortable with the process. Consistent management means that administrators need to be familiar with fewer tools, so training administrators is easier and the company spends less on licensing because fewer tools need to be licensed.

Standardization mandates who has access by default. Some devices come with default configurations that may not be secure or in the company's best interests. Standards define which users have administrative access and which users should have functional access to newly deployed systems. This ensure that end users do not have access to systems until the systems have been fully provisioned and tested for use.

Standardization is used to enforce how systems communicate with one another. Using standard communication models allows the organization to specify fewer traffic rules on intermediary devices. This decreases the complexity of management and decreases the attack surface of systems and networks since only a small set of authorized communication protocols is allowed through. Communication standardization also makes it easier to detect unauthorized communication attempts if such attempts utilize a nonstandard communication method.

Standardization ensures consistent system logging and auditing settings are applied to servers, computers, and network devices so that accurate data is retained. Some logging settings such as file access logging or the logging of both successes and failures may not be configured everywhere, but having such information can be very useful when there are questions about what happened on a device. Standard logging methods ensure that each device will have the information the organization needs to make decisions or to remediate an incident. Furthermore, the organization will have a more complete picture because each device will be recording the same types of information.

Lastly, standardization can help confirm that systems are deployed the same way each time. This is especially important as continuous improvement and continuous delivery models produce more frequent software deployments. Each deployment should go through the same standard steps so that it is deployed correctly and efficiently.

Organizations often specify their own standards for how systems must be configured, but these standards may be based on industry standards such as the following:

- International Organization for Standardization/International Electrotechnical Commission (ISO/IEC) 27000 series
- The National Institute of Standards and Technology (NIST) standards
- The Information Systems Audit and Control Association's (ISACA) Control Objectives for Information and Related Technologies (COBIT)
- The Cloud Security Alliance (CSA) Cloud Controls Matrix (CCM)
- The Organization for the Advancement of Structured Information Standards (OASIS) Cloud Application Management for Platforms (CAMP) standard

Metrics

Metrics are an excellent way to track company performance. Metrics can be defined for all sorts of indicators. Another name for metrics is key performance indicators (KPIs). Metrics should be defined for items that are essential for organizational success. Some companies establish parameters because someone else is using them, but unless the metric contributes to the company's goals and mission, it is more likely a waste of time.

Metrics fall under the role of operations, and cloud operations (or "ops") teams often identify and track cloud-based metrics. As you can tell from the name, ops teams are part of DevOps, introduced in Chapter 7.

Cloud environments can be quite complex, with many different cloud solutions integrated into a hybrid multi-cloud. Metrics can help the cloud operations team and management track how systems are performing and the efficiency of processes.

Metrics are essential in evaluating whether service level agreements are being met and in demonstrating to customers how the provider is achieving service level agreements. Metrics also help in identifying problems.

Chargeback/Showback Models

IT is often seen as purely an organizational cost to be reduced. IT often has to defend its actions and budget. Showbacks track usage of IT services so that management can see the value of IT services in relation to their costs. This makes budgeting much easier. Also, when cutbacks are needed, management will have the data necessary to reduce services that have the least organizational impact.

IT can also push the costs of technology services onto the company departments that use those services through chargebacks. Chargebacks track usage of systems by departments or individuals and then bill the department for the utilization of the service. Chargebacks are popular in consulting organizations, law firms, accounting firms, and others that bill services to clients, because costs such as printing, faxing, and cloud service usage can be charged back to their clients as a cost of providing the service.

Reporting Based on Company Policies   Company policies specify the expectations the company has for employee behavior and how systems should operate. These items are of obvious importance to the organization because leaders took the time to write these expectations out in policy and made employees aware of the policy requirements. For this reason, policy elements can be a good guide for identifying metrics to track. As an example, if the company policy says that high vulnerabilities must be remediated within seven days, it would make sense to establish a vulnerability remediation metric to track how long it takes to remediate vulnerabilities, including high vulnerabilities.

ⓦ a t c h   **Similar to SLAs are operational level agreements (OLAs), which are documents that describe the expectations of internal units so that SLAs can be met.**

Reporting Based on SLAs   A service level agreement (SLA) is a contract that specifies the level of uptime that will be supported by the service provider. SLAs include provisions for how the service provider will compensate customers if SLAs are not met, so it is in the organization's best interest to ensure that SLAs are met.

Metrics can be defined to measure SLA performance. For example, if the SLA states that an application must be available 99.999 percent of the time, an important metric to track would be site availability.

Dashboards and Reporting

Gathering metrics is important, but they become useful when they are made available for decision-making and performance monitoring. Dashboards and reporting are two methods commonly used to make metrics available to those who need them. Dashboard panels, often consisting of a web portal or a linked spreadsheet, contain a series of metrics on specific areas. Web portals can be viewed anywhere, so they are available when needed. Spreadsheets are similarly shared, if not quite as easy to use as a web dashboard. One downside with spreadsheets is that they will not update if the resources from which they obtain their data are inaccessible, making the spreadsheet data stale. Stale spreadsheets can happen if the spreadsheet is created by someone who is authorized to collect the data and then later shared with another who is not. For this reason, web portals are far superior to spreadsheets for tracking metrics.

Metrics can also be tracked with reports that are set out at periodic intervals. This is typically an automated procedure, but upper-management reports are often consolidated from other reports and prepared by hand to give them additional polish. Applications can be configured to e-mail out reports with selected metrics on performance at certain intervals. Of course, this requires that data regarding these metrics is available to the application.

System Availability   System availability metrics are a core metric of any service provider, including cloud service providers (CSPs). Customers are purchasing an IT service, and it is important for them to know when and how often that service is unavailable through such metrics as system uptime, bandwidth, or error rate. Some services can ping websites and send out notifications if a site becomes unavailable. These sites also track availability percentages and provide dashboards for viewing all checks.

It is also possible to collect availability metrics on the underlying components that make up a system, such as web services, database services, file systems, critical service dependencies, and so forth. Notifications can be similarly configured for such systems, with dashboards for viewing the status of all essential functions in one place.

- ■ **Uptime**   Uptime can be a differentiating factor for service providers if uptime numbers are particularly high. Uptime is often measured as a percentage and described in terms of how many consecutive "nines" are in the percent. For example, a system that provides 99.999 percent availability is offering five nines of availability while a system that provides 99.999999 percent availability is offering eight nines. A service provider can conduct a competitive analysis to reveal what competing service providers are offering for uptime availability metrics so that it can be sure to meet or exceed those numbers.

- ■ **Downtime**   Periods of unavailability are called downtime, and most cloud service providers want to minimize this because disruptions for customers mean that they are finding less value in the service offering. The number of nines was used to demonstrate uptime, but downtime is represented either as the inverse percentage or as a specific amount of time the systems were unavailable. For example, the downtime number for five nines would be 0.001 percent and the number for eight nines would be 0.000001 percent. If we were to measure these in the actual amount of time the systems were unavailable, five nines would equate to 5.39 minutes of downtime in a year while eight nines would be less than 1 second of downtime.

Connectivity   Connectivity metrics measure things like bandwidth consumption, congestion, and packet loss. Connectivity metrics are essential for ensuring responsive services and applications and in avoiding performance or availability problems.

Track connectivity metrics to ensure that communication mediums do not get congested. By tracking connectivity metrics, a service provider can expand bandwidth or implement throttling to control available resources. Cloud dashboards can quickly show if, for example, a select group of virtual desktop users are utilizing more bandwidth than others. The cloud administrator may decide to implement throttling on those users if the cloud account as a whole is approaching a bandwidth limit or they may decide to upgrade to a plan that includes more bandwidth if the bandwidth consuming activity is for legitimate business purposes. Connectivity metrics are also useful to conducting trending on connectivity metrics to determine when upgrades will be necessary.

Connectivity dashboards can show connectivity parameters for links within the network and across sites. Some system tools for collecting network connectivity data include PRTG Network Monitor and SolarWinds NetFlow Traffic Analyzer. You can use SNMP and RMON to collect device statistics. Some companies perform protocol analysis as well to gain additional insight into connectivity.

Latency   Latency metrics measure site, service, or link response time. Latency metrics are essential for ensuring responsive services and applications and in avoiding performance or availability problems.

Track latency metrics to ensure that services are meeting established SLAs and that end users are receiving data from devices with the lowest latency. Implement changes or add local services when regions are not well served. It is important to monitor latency metrics in replication, especially synchronous replication, to avoid performance issues.

Capacity   Capacity metrics measure how much storage is allocated, used, and free. Capacity metrics are useful in ensuring that enough storage is available to users and applications. Track capacity metrics to ensure that volumes do not get full, and expand volumes or add storage as needed. You should also consider conducting trending on capacity metrics to determine when upgrades will be necessary.

Storage vendors produce dashboards and tools for viewing capacity metrics. These can sometimes be integrated into other reporting suites with Web-Based Enterprise Management (WBEM) or through custom vendor integration tools or APIs.

Overall Utilization   Detailed metrics are great for solving problems and for reporting, but it helps to have an overall picture of usage across the board. Overall utilization metrics can be obtained by consolidating individual metrics to give decision makers and operations teams valuable insight on current usage and trends and can enable forecasting of future needs and opportunities.

Cost   Cost is a fundamental metric in any scenario. IT costs can be a significant portion of a company's budget, so it is important for those managing IT to know where money is being spent and how those costs are contributing to business operations. In a cloud-based environment, billing is often based on consumption, so IT needs to be able to show with metrics how that consumption is contributing to IT costs.

Cost metrics will also need to be calculated for chargebacks and showbacks to show which clients or departments are to be billed for IT services as part of a chargeback initiative or just to track consumption for showbacks.

Incidents   Incidents can and will happen in your organization. It is important to have an incident response plan and to specify metrics on how long certain tasks will take. Notification periods for investigations are very strict, and there will be a lot of pressure during the incident to meet those deadlines. Be familiar with these metrics before the incident. Some metrics include investigation time, detection time, number of records affected, number of users affected, remediation cost, remediation hours, and investigation hours.

Health   Health metrics are valuable to gauge when equipment replacement is likely. Some CSAs may choose to replace equipment proactively in particularly critical environments.

Health metrics also provide information useful for determining which spare equipment should be purchased for expected substitutes. Some important hardware health metrics include

- Mean time between failures (MTBF)
- Mean time to repair (MTTR)
- Self-monitoring, analysis, and reporting technology (SMART)

MTBF is the average time a device will function before it fails. MTBF can be used to determine approximately how long a hard drive will last in a server.

MTTR, on the other hand, is the average time that it takes to repair a failed hardware component. MTTR is often part of the maintenance contract for virtualization hosts. An MTTR of 24 hours or less would be appropriate for a higher-priority server, whereas a lower-priority server might have an MTTR of seven days.

Lastly, SMART is a set of hard disk metrics that are used to predict failures by monitoring over 100 metrics such as read error rate, spin-up time, start and stop count, reallocated sectors count, and seek error rate. SMART has predefined thresholds for each metric, and those thresholds are used to determine if a drive is in an OK, warning, or error status.

Elasticity   Elasticity is a measurement of how sensitive one variable is to changes in another. Elasticity is important in tracking metrics because some metrics may be dependent upon one another or may have an impact on one another. Elasticity can track how changes in one metric affect other metrics.

Elasticity cause and effect, in turn, can be used to focus better efforts to improve performance. For example, a company may find that several key performance metrics improve when training time is increased. From a more technical perspective, backup time metrics may improve if bandwidth utilization is reduced.

Planning

Once the baseline states are documented, agreed upon in writing, and put in place, what happens when maintenance needs to occur, or system upgrades take place? Such events almost certainly disrupt a baseline. These events must be planned for under controlled circumstances by the systems administrator, and cannot happen at random times without the consent of the customer. Maintenance windows need to be established as part of any IT environment for all of its configuration items. These windows should be scheduled at periods of least potential disruption to the customer, and the customer should be involved in the maintenance-scheduling process. After all, the customer knows their patterns of business activity better than the systems administrators ever could.

All technology upgrades and patches should utilize these maintenance windows whenever possible, and the timing of their implementation should always be reviewed as part of the standard change management process by the change advisory board (CAB). Change management is discussed in Chapter 13.

Systems Maintenance

IT systems require regular maintenance to help them remain free from errors and bugs, and to keep up with the latest technologies and processes. Maintenance and development updates can consume a great deal of IT personnel time, and yet their functions are core to the business. Additionally, there are some functions that overlap and others that benefit from increased integration, so a blended group of software developers and IT operations has evolved called DevOps to handle both objectives. DevOps was introduced back in Chapter 7 and system maintenance is also a function of the DevOps team. This section covers the following important systems maintenance activities:

- Code updates
- Patch management
- Maintenance automation

Code Updates

There is usually a queue of code updates, including requests, bugs, and features, that DevOps teams try to tackle. Teams may be working on different branches of code. Each branch is a portion of the program that is duplicated so that teams can work in parallel.

Two concepts that are often discussed within DevOps are continuous integration (CI) and continuous delivery (CD). Continuous integration involves automating the elements of the coding and testing processes. CI automates testing routines so that each time a new piece of code is committed, it is subjected to testing to ensure that it meets quality standards. Other testing still needs to be performed but this function helps to catch the most routine issues early on in the development cycle with less effort.

Continuous delivery is a process that creates a pipeline of tasks leading toward deployment of regular software releases. In CD, DevOps teams make regular iterative changes to the code rather than working on a large portion of the program for a long period of time. This decreases the time from the introduction of new code to the deployment of that code in production. CD also allows for users of software to have more current versions and for stable releases to be produced in a short time frame. CD is also known as continuous development.

Some DevOps teams operate on short-term release schedules called *sprints* to accomplish some shared objective. Sprints allow developers to work as a team and celebrate the small successes rather than working on a huge project and only seeing the reward at the end.

Code Repository

Keeping track of changes in the code is essential. As the complexity of code increases, changes may cause unintended behavior that may not be caught until testing. For this reason, DevOps teams will keep a code repository. Code repositories can organize code branches to keep code consistent even when multiple teams are working on the same areas in parallel.

Developers publish code changes, or *commits*, to the repository, where a record is kept of the code that has been updated since the previous submission. Developers tag commits with a short statement on what the change accomplished. Developers can synchronize their local development environments with the code repository to receive new updates to the code or select or create branches of the code to work from. Furthermore, through the code repository, developers can easily revert to previous versions of code that they or others worked on.

Version Updates

Updating versions on end-user machines can be a big job. Three methods are used to complete version updates:

- **Manual version updates**   Manual version updates require the most time from the DevOps team. Companies that use this method send teams out to update end-user machines.

  Distributed environments may not be connected enough for end-user updating or package managers, so updates are sent to local staff at branch or regional offices who update applications for the users in their location. Some companies use this method to customize the application for certain regions or languages. For example, an accounting firm may deploy different versions of its application to offices in different states or countries so that those users receive an interface that is most compatible with their tax codes and processes.

- **End-user updating**   In the end-user updating method, new versions are pushed to an update server. The team then notifies end users that a new update is available. Notifications can be sent through email or by posting to a company message board or intranet. Users are expected to keep their applications updated to the latest version, and in some cases, the program may not work if it is not running the latest version.

- **Package manager**   The third option is to use a package manager to deploy updates. The package manager resides on each end-user machine. New versions are released to a server and the package manager checks for an update on the server when the user loads the program. If a new version exists, the package manager automatically pulls down any new code to bring the application to the current version.

   Package managers can also check for the local language settings on the operating system and region so that the appropriate software modules are loaded into their application.

Rollback

Developers used to save copies of an entire program or of specific modules, functions, or subroutines each time a milestone was reached. If the next set of changes broke the program and the solution was not apparent, it was easiest to replace the existing code with the last backup rather than try to find all the changes and remove them.

Code repositories make rollback much simpler. In fact, are now standard practice. If developers detect an error in testing and cannot find the cause, the code can be rolled back to a previous version by selecting the commit from the repository and deploying it back to the development environment. The code repository only stores the changes, so it takes much less space to store and less time to roll back.

Deployment Methodologies

Recall from the discussion of the application life cycle in Chapter 7 that deployment is the fourth phase of the application life cycle. For review, the phases are specifications, development, testing, deployment, and maintenance. In the deployment phase, the application is installed and configured for use and procedures are documented for how the system should be employed. Users are then trained on how to use the system, and the application starts performing the job it was designed for.

DevOps will need to provision the resources required for the application, such as compute, memory, and storage resources. Deployments do not happen in a day, but methodologies such as the ones mentioned in the following sections aim to keep deployments moving along on a regular schedule of releases. Some deployment methods include the following:

- **Deployment landscapes**   Releases go through development, QA, and production landscapes as they make their way from code sections to a functional release.
- **Rolling updates**   A methodology that can be used to keep an application at a stable release, with another one always in the queue to be deployed shortly thereafter.
- **Blue-green deployment**   These deployments always have an active system and one that is used for testing. When testing is complete, the testing system becomes active and the former production system is available for testing. One system is labeled "blue" and the other "green."

- **Rapid deployment** Virtualization and containerization technologies are used to create new application environments faster than ever before.

- **Failover clusters** Deployment can be performed to more than one server that work together to provide the service. Failover cluster deployments may use some of the same techniques as other deployments but they are given their own section because the implementation of that deployment methodology may differ for a clustered environment.

Landscapes Deployments are typically rolled out in three landscapes: development, quality assurance (QA), and production. The landscapes can be available to different teams that are responsible for specialized areas of development. As code is more refined, it moves to a different landscape and undergoes additional testing.

Landscapes are efficient because the simplest and most automated testing is performed to small code segments first. Since this testing is routine, it can be automated. Furthermore, the findings from those tests can be quickly resolved because the developer is very familiar with the code he or she just wrote. Later efforts can then focus on more complex testing. Second, landscapes provide higher levels of assurance as the testing environment moves closer to that of production. Landscapes also provide some isolation and separation of duties so that the people testing the product are not influenced by those writing the code.

- **Development** The first landscape is a development environment where developers can test small changes to make sure that their code changes are providing the correct results for any new features. This provides an environment where new features and changes can be previewed without committing. Testing at this phase is largely automated.

- **Quality assurance (QA)** Once a group of small changes reaches the point where it can be packaged together into a functioning element of the specifications, it is ready to move to the QA landscape, also known as the staging landscape. The QA landscape is where software testers evaluate both the added code and the impact those changes could have on other parts of the application.

   The application is tested as a whole in the QA landscape to ensure potential unintended actions, memory leaks, or security vulnerabilities do not occur. QA testing evaluates the edge cases to make sure that the application will not process data that is not within the bounds of the program. Testers will work from multiple defined use cases of the program and seek to break it by performing actions the developers might not have anticipated.

   In addition to regular QA testers, the QA landscape sometimes includes select individuals from the specifications phase (the first phase of the application life cycle) to ensure that the specifications were correctly translated into an application. The product must be thoroughly tested in the QA landscape before heading to the next landscape. The lead QA tester will usually sign off on code in QA before it is moved.

■ **Production**   In the production landscape, code is placed into production where it is available for end users. Companies will usually implement a segregation of duties in this landscape so that the same person who can deploy to the QA landscape cannot deploy to the production landscape and vice versa. These are usually separate individuals from those doing the testing as well.

The production landscape is where the maintenance and support start. Any updates have to go through the other two landscapes first to make sure that the best quality product is delivered. If there are any changes to the production environment in the future, then the end users must be contacted and notified of any potential downtime that may occur.

Rolling Updates   Traditionally, software development is done in individual release versions. However, implementing continuous integration (CI) and continuous development (CD) is quickly becoming the norm as DevOps teams work through queues of requests, bugs, and features.

Legacy release schedules have too much overhead associated with them to meet such expectations without increasing costs exponentially. Instead of having release versions that take a long time to deploy and test, developers work off increasingly smaller code segments so that issues are identified sooner, and testing is simpler.

DevOps teams do not write code from different versions. Instead, they work with a single codebase using branching to differentiate project elements and development work product from one another. Updates to the software are rolled out as releases, which are normally very small and happen frequently. A single codebase ensures that only one version of the software needs to be supported at a time.

With rolling updates, the program is never really finished. The application is always at a stable release, but DevOps teams have another one in the queue with regular deployment dates.

Blue-Green Deployment   Blue-green deployment is an excellent method for DevOps teams to test changes to systems when releases are made rapidly or as part of a continuous delivery model. However, blue-green deployment is not limited to such either. Blue-green deployment uses two environments, one called blue and the other called green. One of the environments faces the customer while the other is used for testing.

When QA teams complete testing for a new release, the two environments are swapped. For example, the blue environment is operating for production and the green for test. A new release is deployed to green and tested. When testing is complete, the DevOps team makes green production and blue becomes the new test environment.

Blue-green deployment is faster than deploying from test to production since the testing environment becomes production. Swapping rather than redeploying eliminates one step in the deployment process. Additionally, blue-green environments allow for a rapid rollback if necessary.

Blue-green switches are performed to make one environment online and available to customers and the other available to test. Blue-green switches can be implemented on cloud virtualization in a number of ways. Two ways outlined here involve virtual network swapping and resource group swapping.

For example, a CSP may host several virtual machines. These virtual machines are part of either the blue or green network depending on which virtual network they are assigned to. One set of systems may have its virtual network interface cards (NICs) on the blue virtual switch while the other set has its virtual NIC configured for the green virtual switch, where blue is production and green is test. CSAs swap the virtual switch to physical switch mapping on the hypervisor when they want to switch from blue to green or vice versa. Depending on the cloud platform, the actual switch may need to be performed by the CSP based on a request from the cloud consumer.

Another option is to use resource group swapping. In Microsoft Azure, resources can be deployed into groups, one for the green environment and one for the blue environment. The cloud servers in the resource group are all given private IP addresses, and an application gateway is configured with the outside IP address. The application gateway is then used to direct traffic to whichever environment is the current production. The CSP can redirect the application gateway to the other environment when it's time to swap.

Rapid Deployment   Rapid deployment is a way for DevOps teams to provision and release solutions with minimal management effort or service provider interaction. Rapid deployment is enabled by enhanced virtualization and container technologies such as virtual machine clones, parent-child relationships, application containerization, virtual machine templates, self-service portals, and orchestration tools that allow IT organizations to roll out systems faster than ever before.

Failover Clusters   A failover cluster is multiple systems configured to operate together to offer a set of services. If one system in the cluster fails, the others are configured to pick up the load of the failed server without a loss of availability to the application.

To deploy a failover cluster, first provision several machines. You will need at least two to form a cluster. Next, provision shared storage to all servers. Shared storage is storage from a storage array over a storage area network (SAN) such as iSCSI, Fibre Channel, or InfiniBand. Configure storage adapters in the machines such as host bus adapters (HBAs), converged network adapters (CNAs), or NICs. If using NICs for iSCSI, it is best to use ones that have TCP offload to reduce the processing burden on the CPU for storage traffic. Put the WWNs for each of the cluster members (or IP addresses of the iSCSI adapters if using iSCSI) into a host group on the storage array and then enable the storage group for concurrent access. Lastly, assign LUNs to the storage group. The storage should now be visible on each device. However, do not configure the storage yet.

Install the clustering features on each node in the cluster. The installation will set up some basic cluster resources off the bat, such as a quorum, the service that monitors if enough devices are connected to the cluster to be able to offer services. Configure each of the LUNs as a resource in the cluster and give the storage resources a name that makes sense. For example, database components like to have dedicated storage resources for different types of I/O. Typically, databases will have drives for the following types of data: tables, log files, indexes, full-text catalogs, temporary data, and backups. The storage requirements for each of these is different based on the reads and writes expected of the storage resource.

Next, install application services on the nodes and add services to the cluster. Set dependencies on the services so that the cluster will know in what order to start the services. Assign credentials to run the services and test the credentials on each node.

Lastly, start the application and ensure that it runs. Then test failing over elements from one node to another. Ensure that each one can be successfully failed over to each node in the cluster.

Patch Management

Software vendors regularly release patches for their software. Patches are software packages that modify existing software. Patches are created to fix software bugs or discovered vulnerabilities, or to add new features.

Patches must be deployed to organizational systems to protect against new vulnerabilities in the software that could be exploited by attackers or to fix bugs in the software that could cause problems for users. The strategy employed to deploy patches is known as patch management.

Some software vendors release patches on a set schedule. For example, Microsoft releases patches on the second and fourth Tuesdays of every month. Other vendors release patches as needed.

Companies issue patch rollups to address the issue of updating a new installation of a software application that has been around for a while. Rollups combine multiple patches in the same category, such as security, or a specific product component, into a single package that can be deployed more easily. Without rollups, customers would need to deploy a long list of updates in sequence.

Another type of rollup that combines even more patches is called a service pack. Companies package all patches from the last main software release or patches from the last service pack into a single update package called a service pack.

Hotfixes

Hotfixes or quick fix engineering (QFE) updates are small patches that address a specific issue. Many vendors use hotfixes to address urgent issues such as a critical vulnerability or a bug that the company cannot wait to address in its normal patching schedule.

Some hotfixes released by Microsoft address an issue that only some customers may face. Microsoft issues a knowledge base article to describe the issue and then customers can request the hotfix if they encounter the problem. Other customers need not apply the hotfix. This approach is usually taken when the hotfix has the potential of disrupting other systems, so it is only applied when the need to resolve the issue outweighs the potential drawbacks. Be aware of the drawbacks by reading the knowledge base associated with the hotfix carefully before applying the hotfix.

Patching Order of Operations

Patches are designed to be applied cumulatively, and they usually come with a version number and sometimes a build ID or other identifier that can show which patch level you are at. If you go to the About section in your software application, you can see which version you are running to identify if you need patches. Figure 9-1 shows the About screen from LibreOffice 5. As you can see, this system is running version 5.3.4.2, and the build ID is provided for querying for updates.

Service packs are usually numbered so that customers know which service pack to apply first. For example, a customer purchases an application that has been on the market for several years. After installing the software, the customer checks for updates and find 3 service packs and 22 patches. The service packs would be named service pack 1, service pack 2, and service pack 3 and the customer would install them in that order.

Newly released patches are designed to be deployed to applications running the latest service pack, so a customer would need to install service packs first and then the most recent patches. In the example, the customer would install service packs 1, 2, and 3 and then install the 22 patches in sequence.

Dependency Considerations

Patches have dependencies. Cumulative updates, of course, are dependent upon previous patches. Other patch dependencies include specific software modules or features that may or may not have been installed when the program was deployed to the machine. Attempting to deploy a patch to a system where the dependencies are not present will result in an error.

FIGURE 9-1

About screen for LibreOffice 5 showing the version number

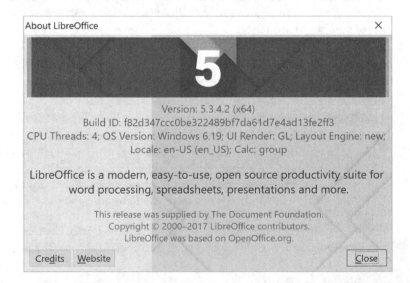

If you receive an error, double-check to ensure that you have the required dependencies. You may find that you do not need to install the patch, because you do not have the component addressed in the update.

Component Updates

There are some differences in updating different system components such as virtual machines, virtual appliances, hypervisors, networking equipment, storage, and clusters. A well-rounded IT professional needs to understand how to update each of these components.

Cloud services allow for some or many of the components to be managed by the CSP. This can reduce the time organizations spend on normal maintenance. For example, Amazon Web Service Relational Database Service (AWS RDS) hosts a database for use with applications or websites. The cloud consumer does not need to maintain the underlying server, operating system, database software, and networking. Instead, they can focus their efforts on the database housed within AWS RDS.

In an another example, hosted options running software such as cPanel allow cloud consumers to deploy databases to a MySQL instance and then access them from cloud servers or websites. Some basic maintenance tasks, such as resetting the database administrator password or changing backup schedules and restores, can be performed by the cloud consumer, but the remaining maintenance is performed by the CSP.

Virtual Machines   Virtual machines can be updated independently using the same tools as a physical machine, but you also have some additional options. Some hypervisors can deploy updates to virtual machines. For example, vSphere Update Manager can deploy updates to virtual machines that reside on hypervisors managed by vSphere.

Here is the high-level procedure for automating the update process for the virtual machines:

1. Configure repositories for where Update Manager can find updates. Repositories are indexed sources for updates.
2. Create a baseline consisting of patches, service packs, upgrades, and hotfixes.
3. Schedule synchronization with repositories so that Update Manager is aware of new patches, hotfixes, upgrades, and service packs.
4. Assign virtual machines to a baseline.
5. Scan virtual machines against the baseline to determine which patches need to be applied.
6. Stage the patches by having Update Manager download the updates to vSphere for deployment.
7. Deploy patches to the virtual machines.

Virtual Appliances   Appliances are fully built and functional virtual machines that are purchased or downloaded from a vendor to perform a specific task. Prior to the age of virtualization, appliances would be rebranded servers or small rack-mount equipment that would be purchased from a vendor to perform a task. Some vendors still offer physical equipment, but this is largely a thing of the past.

The advantage of using an appliance versus installing and configuring the software on a server is that the appliance is set up and mostly configured by the vendor. The company is provided with a ready-to-deploy virtual machine, which saves the organization valuable deployment time.

Some virtual appliances are available for free from open source groups. Vendors may offer stripped-down appliances at no cost, or they may provide a fully functional unit to educational or nonprofit groups. If you purchase a virtual appliance or get it for free, you can download it from the vendor site as a virtual hard drive. Simply copy the virtual hard drive to your hypervisor, assign it resources, and start it up.

Virtual appliances will walk you through a configuration wizard to get the product up and running. When it comes time to update the virtual appliance, the vendor will package underlying updates together with its own software updates so that you can receive all updates in one vendor package. You can configure the appliance to download updates from the vendor and deploy them on a scheduled basis. Updates from the vendor have already been tested on the virtual machine, so there is a high likelihood that they will be deployed without issue.

Public CSPs, and in some cases private clouds, often have a marketplace where virtual machine templates and appliances can be selected to deploy new virtual machines in the cloud rapidly. These systems have already been confirmed to be compatible with the underlying cloud infrastructure and they can be offered cost effectively because of the CSP's economies of scale. Research options for your CSP because some offer many different solutions while others, usually small providers, may only offer one or two solutions. The options available to you may not be the ones ideal for your workload.

Firewall, intrusion detection system (IDS), and intrusion prevention system (IPS) virtual appliances are covered in the "Network Security" section of Chapter 10.

Hypervisors   Patching hypervisors will likely result in downtime to the virtual machines that reside on it unless the hypervisor is part of a cluster. You update a hypervisor in much the same way as you would a normal computer, but any updates that require a restart or updates to hypervisor services will make the virtual machines go into a saved state or shut down.

Networking Components   Devices such as firewalls, routers, switches, and Internet of things (IoT) equipment have updates called firmware that can be downloaded from the manufacturer. Firmware updates are usually installed manually, but some vendors such as Cisco release tools that can update a multitude of systems simultaneously or in sequence. Check with the vendor of your equipment to find out which deployment options you have. It also helps to subscribe to the vendor's mailing list for firmware updates so that you can be notified as soon as they are released.

Applications   It can be difficult to keep track of all the application updates to keep your application protected. Many applications will include an agent that keeps track of your software version and then notifies you when a new software version is available. Some agents will download the new software and then prompt for installation. Unfortunately, for the average computer running many applications, this can result in applications requesting to update all the time.

The solution is to turn off the agents and use a single third-party tool to manage the updates. Third-party solutions can scan the entire server or workstation to identify the software on it. The third-party vendor keeps track of the latest versions of all software and pushes the updates down to the computer through its tool.

Storage Components   Storage systems are one of the more complex items to update. An update to a storage system, also called storage array firmware or microcode, could impact other items in the data path such as SAN switches or HBAs. Before applying a storage system update, ensure that devices on the data path (everything from the SAN to the initiator) support the upgrade. Devices on the data path often include the switch and HBA versions, but could include other devices as well.

If all firmware versions for the devices in the data path meet the acceptable level for the storage upgrade, go ahead and install it. However, if a device is not supported at its current firmware level, you will need to upgrade it to a supported level first. Ensure that when you upgrade it, the updated version is supported on the current SAN version.

Clusters   Updates for cluster nodes can be done typically with no downtime to the end user. This is great for the end user, but the upgrade process is a bit more complicated for IT administrators. You will need to fail over services to free up a node so that it is not actively hosting any of the cluster resources and then update that node. You can then fail back services to that node and fail over the services on another node. Complete this process on all nodes until each node is running the same software versions.

Maintenance Automation

It can be quite a job to maintain a large number of systems, and organizational IT departments are supporting more devices per person than ever before. They accomplish this through automation. Automation uses scripting, scheduled tasks, and automation tools to do the routine tasks so that IT staff can spend more time solving the real problems and proactively looking for ways to make things better and even more efficient.

PowerShell commands are provided in many examples because these commands can be used with the Amazon Web Services (AWS) CLI or the Microsoft Azure Cloud Shell. Scripts can be combined into tasks using AWS Systems Manager or Microsoft Azure runbooks.

This section discusses different activities that can be automated to save time and standardize. They include the following:

- Patch management
- Shutdown and restart
- Entering maintenance mode
- Enabling or disabling monitoring checks

Server Upgrades and Patches

Server upgrades and patches provide enhancements to the software running on servers that can either provide fixes for known errors or add functionality. However, deploying them can be time-consuming, if performed manually. Fortunately, there are a variety of tools available to automate the patch management process. These tools identify the installed software version number and then query the vendor's patch list to identify which patches need to be installed and in which order. Some tools are specific to a vendor, some are built in, and some are available from third parties. For example, Microsoft has packaged an update system into Microsoft Windows. The user can set their system to download and install updates automatically on a set schedule or as soon as they are released. Other third-party solutions can query the system to identify all applications and then identify the patches available for those systems.

Patch management systems can be configured to install available updates automatically or to install only approved updates. In approval mode, an administrator reviews updates, potentially applying them to a series of test systems, and if the patches appear stable, the administrator approves the patches for deployment across the enterprise.

If systems are configured to download patches automatically, those patches might trigger a restart of the system. Ensure that patch installation occurs during a period where the workstation or server can be taken offline.

Restarting

Systems run better when they are restarted regularly. However, regular restarts is not an option for all environments, but for those that can, a scheduled restart can help keep systems fresh and functional. Scheduled restarts are useful in other scenarios such as when you are performing maintenance on a host or some other system that requires many machines to be restarted.

Here is a PowerShell command that restarts four computers named computer1, computer2, computer3, and computer4. You can schedule this script to run as a scheduled task from a management machine that has rights on each of the other servers.

```
Restart-Computer -ComputerName "Computer1", "Computer2", "Computer3",
"Computer4"
```

Shutting Down

Scheduled shutdown events are useful in maintenance or triage scenarios, such as when you are turning off all nonessential systems to save on resources.

Here is a PowerShell command that shuts down four computers named computer1, computer2, computer3, and computer4. You can schedule this script to run as a scheduled task from a management machine that has rights on each of the other servers.

```
Stop-Computer -ComputerName "Computer1", "Computer2", "Computer3",
"Computer4"
```

Entering Maintenance Mode

Whenever you do work on a host, it is important to put that host in maintenance mode. In fact, many maintenance tasks cannot be performed unless the host is first in maintenance mode. Some maintenance activities include restarting the host, applying firmware updates, or applying patches to the host.

Maintenance mode will migrate all the virtual machines to another host in a cluster and prepare the host for maintenance. Exiting maintenance mode will allow for virtual machines to be rebalanced across hosts in the cluster.

Many maintenance tasks can be scripted, and the transition to maintenance mode can also be placed in the maintenance script to automate the entire process. The following command can be scripted in to enter into maintenance mode. Here we will assume our username is ESXAdmin and our password is 77}N50&a9fr-Q=i.

```
esxcli —username ESXAdmin --password 77}N50&a9fr-Q=i system
maintenanceMode set --enable true
```

You can then script the transition out of maintenance mode in the script when the maintenance is complete. The following command can be placed at the end of the script to exit maintenance mode (assuming the same username and password):

```
esxcli —username ESXAdmin --password 77}N50&a9fr-Q=i system
maintenanceMode set --enable false
```

Enabling or Disabling Monitoring Alerts

It can be very annoying to receive hundreds or thousands of e-mail notifications because someone forgot to disable monitoring alerts when doing a downtime. Everyone who has gone through this knows what this means, because it simply destroys a mailbox. The good news is that if you forget, your coworkers are likely to remind you and not let you forget again.

Disabling alerts greatly depends on which tool is being used to send out the alerts, but there is usually a master pause function that can be enabled for the downtime. If you have regularly occurring downtimes such as patch downtimes, you can likely script this action.

CERTIFICATION SUMMARY

Successful delivery of a cloud solution is driven not just by the technical components that make up that solution but by clear policies and standard operating procedures. The successful design, documentation, and methodical implementation and support of those technical resources result in an effective solution that is profitable for the IT provider and valuable to its customers.

Processes and procedures allow for control of the environment through life cycle metrics, dashboards and reporting, standardization, and planning. These control mechanisms make certain that the environments are designed to meet business requirements and are deployed and supported according to that design.

IT systems require regular maintenance to keep them free from vulnerabilities and bugs, and to keep up with the latest technologies and processes. Maintenance and development updates can consume a great deal of IT personnel time. Maintenance and development are core to the business. This includes making code updates, documenting those updates in code repositories, ensuring that patches are applied to systems in a timely manner, and automating common maintenance tasks to do more with limited IT resources.

KEY TERMS

Use the following list to review the key terms discussed in this chapter. The definitions also can be found in the glossary.

capacity management   A process to ensure that the capacity of IT services and the IT infrastructure can meet agreed size and performance-related requirements in a cost-effective and timely manner.

chargeback   IT pushes the costs of technology services onto the company departments that use those services.

cloud service provider (CSP)   A company that provides cloud services to users or companies on a subscription basis.

cloud systems administrator (CSA)   The person responsible for cloud services from the cloud consumer side of the equation. CSAs provision user accounts, add or remove services, configure integration between cloud providers, and perform other administration- and management-related tasks.

code repository A system that organizes code branches to keep code consistent even when multiple teams are working on the same areas in parallel. Developers can publish code changes to the repository, can synchronize their local copy of the code with the repository, or can revert to previously published versions.

continuous development (CD) A process that creates a pipeline of tasks leading toward deployment of regular software releases. DevOps teams make regular iterative changes to the code rather than working on a large portion of the program for a long period of time. This decreases the time from the introduction of new code to the deployment of that code in production. Continuous development is also known as continuous delivery.

continuous integration (CI) A software development process where elements of the coding and testing processes are automated and developers make regular iterative changes to the code.

dashboard A panel, typically web-based, consisting of a series of metrics on specific areas.

documentation Written copy of a procedure, policy, or configuration.

downtime Periods of unavailability.

failover cluster Multiple systems configured to operate together as one to offer a set of services.

hotfix A small patch that addresses a specific issue.

key performance indicator (KPI) A measurement of some activity. KPIs can be established for human processes or for computer functions. A KPI is also known as a metric.

maintenance mode A process on a clustered virtualization host that will migrate all the virtual machines to another host in a cluster and prepare the host for maintenance. Many maintenance tasks cannot be performed unless the host is first in maintenance mode.

maintenance window An agreed-upon, predefined period during which service interruptions are least impactful to the business. This could fall at any time and depends on the patterns of business activity for that particular entity.

metric   A measurement of some activity. Metrics can be established for human processes or for computer functions. A metric is also known as a KPI.

operational level agreement (OLA)   A document that describes the expectations of internal units so that service level agreements can be met.

patch   A software package that modifies existing software.

patch management   The strategy employed to deploy patches.

policies   Rule sets by which users and administrators must abide.

procedures   Prescribed methodologies by which activities are carried out in the IT environment according to defined policies.

server upgrades and patches   Updates to the software running on servers that can either provide fixes for known errors or add functionality.

service level agreement (SLA)   A contract or agreement between a client and a service provider such as a cloud provider on the level of availability that will be maintained and damages awarded if the SLA is violated.

showback   IT tracks usage of IT services so that management can see the value of IT services in relation to their costs.

trending   The pattern of measurements over the course of multiple time periods.

uptime   A metric showing the availability of a system or service such as a cloud application or a virtual server. Uptime is usually represented as a percentage of how much the system or service has been available versus unavailable to users, sometimes represented as the number of "nines" in the percent.

virtual appliance   Fully built and functional virtual machine that is purchased or downloaded from a vendor to perform a specific task.

workflow   A business process that is organized in a set of discrete tasks from the beginning to the end of the process.

TWO-MINUTE DRILL

Policies and Procedures

❑ Policies define the rule sets by which users and administrators must abide.

❑ Procedures are the prescribed methodologies by which activities are carried out in the IT environment according to defined policies.

❑ Capacity management is the process of ensuring that both the current and future capacity and performance demands of an IT organization's customers regarding service provision are delivered according to justifiable costs.

Systems Management Best Practices

❑ To build supportable technical solutions that consistently deliver their intended value, documentation must be maintained at every step of the life cycle.

❑ Standardization of configurations allows systems administrators to learn one set of complexities and have that same set be applicable across many systems.

❑ Maintenance windows need to be established as part of any IT environment for all of its configuration items. These windows should be scheduled at periods of least potential disruption to the customer, and the customer should be involved in the maintenance-scheduling process.

Systems Maintenance

❑ IT systems require regular maintenance to keep them free from vulnerabilities and bugs, and to keep up with the latest technologies and processes.

❑ There is usually a queue of code updates, including requests, bugs, and features, that DevOps teams try to tackle.

❑ Code repositories help developers keep track of changes to code and they can organize code branches to keep code consistent even when multiple teams are working on the same areas in parallel.

❑ As code updates are released, they can be deployed in three different ways:

    ❑ Updates can be performed manually.

    ❑ End users can update the application themselves.

    ❑ A package manager can check for new software versions upon startup.

❏ Developers roll back code when problems are encountered that are too difficult to resolve. A backup of the code is required to roll back. Code repositories can be used to revert to previous versions of the application easily. If a code repository is not in use, developers may make copies of the code when milestones are reached and then overwrite the existing code with a backup to rollback.

❏ Patch management is the strategy employed to deploy patches. Patches are software packages that modify existing software. Patches are created to fix software bugs or discovered vulnerabilities, or to add new features. Patches must be deployed to organizational systems to protect against new vulnerabilities in the software that could be exploited by attackers or to fix bugs in the software that could cause problems for users.

❏ Automate tasks when you can, because IT resources are limited. Create scripts to perform routine tasks and maintenance such as server upgrades and patching, restarting, shutting down, entering maintenance mode, and enabling or disabling alerts.

SELF TEST

The following questions will help you measure your understanding of the material presented in this chapter. As indicated, some questions may have more than one correct answer, so be sure to read all the answer choices carefully.

Policies and Procedures

1. Which of the following defines the rule sets by which users and administrators must abide?
   A. Procedures
   B. Change management
   C. Policies
   D. Trending

2. Capacity management has responsibility for ensuring that the capacity of the IT service is optimally matched to what?
   A. Demand
   B. Future trends

    C. Procedures

    D. Availability

3. Carlos works in the IT department at Sample Bank. He uses a cloud-based e-mail system and has been asked by his manager to establish metrics on mailbox usage per department so that department budgets can be billed for the expense of hosting department e-mail. What is this practice known as?

    A. Chargeback

    B. Billback

    C. Pass-through charge

    D. Showback

Systems Management Best Practices

4. When should maintenance windows be scheduled?

    A. In the morning

    B. In the evening

    C. On weekends

    D. When they will least impact customers

5. Which of the following is not a benefit of standardization?

    A. Consistent management

    B. Better control of system access

    C. Uniform logging across systems

    D. Flexible deployment scenarios

Systems Maintenance

6. Donna has been developing software for her company. She makes a copy of the directory where her code is stored each time she makes a significant change. However, the project she started years ago is now much larger and there are two other developers who also work on the program with her. She would like a way to better manage the code so that she can revert to previous states if necessary and track changes made by each person. Which technology would you suggest?

    A. Continuous integration application

    B. Code repository

    C. Workflow automation

    D. Chargebacks for each developer

7. Which of the following is not a method for deploying application updates?

    A. Manual version updating

    B. End-user updating

    C. Using DevOps ticketing

    D. Using a package manager

8. Which landscape is used for testing small changes made to code immediately after development?
   A. Development
   B. Quality assurance
   C. Testing
   D. Production

SELF TEST ANSWERS

Policies and Procedures

1. ☑ **C.** Policies are defined as rule sets by which users and administrators must abide.
   ☒ **A, B,** and **D** are incorrect. Procedures are prescribed methodologies by which activities are carried out in the IT environment according to defined policies; change management is the process of making changes to the IT environment from its design phase to its operations phase in the least impactful way; and trending is the pattern of measurements over the course of multiple time periods.

2. ☑ **A.** Capacity management's primary objective is to ensure that the capacity of an IT service is optimally matched with its demand. Capacity should be planned to meet agreed-upon levels, no higher and no lower. Because controlling costs is a component of capacity management, designs that incorporate too much capacity are just as bad as designs that incorporate too little capacity.
   ☒ **B, C,** and **D** are incorrect. Future trends are extrapolations made from trending data captured in operations. They provide inputs into capacity and availability planning but are not a good description for the entire life cycle. Procedures are predefined sets of activities that resources utilize to carry out defined policies. Availability is the ability of a configuration item to perform its defined functions when required.

3. ☑ **A.** Chargebacks can be used to establish metrics on mailbox usage per department so that department budgets can be billed for the expense of hosting department e-mail.
   ☒ **B, C,** and **D** are incorrect. The correct term for this is chargeback. Billback and pass-through charge are not industry terms. Showbacks are similar to chargebacks, but they are not used for billing back based on usage. Instead, they are simply used to track utilization.

Systems Management Best Practices

4. ☑ **D.** A maintenance window is an agreed-upon, predefined time period during which service interruptions are least impactful to the customer. This could fall at any time, and depends on the patterns of business activity for that particular customer.

    ☒ **A, B,** and **C** are incorrect. An IT organization should not define mornings, evenings, or weekends as maintenance windows without first validating that time frame with its customers and making certain that it falls during a period when business activity would least be affected by a service outage.

5. ☑ **D.** Flexible deployment scenarios is not a benefit of standardization because standardization establishes consistent deployment scenarios and does not allow for each one to be deployed however the user or administrator wishes.

    ☒ **A, B,** and **C** are incorrect. Each of these is a benefit of standardization. Consistent management reduces the amount of time spent managing devices, makes employees more efficient as they get more comfortable with the process, and requires administrators to be familiar with fewer tools, so it is easier to train administrators. Better control of system access results in better security. Uniform logging across systems ensures that organizationally required information is logged and maintained.

Systems Maintenance

6. ☑ **B.** A code repository organizes code branches to keep code consistent even when multiple teams are working on the same areas in parallel. Developers can publish code changes to the repository, can synchronize their local copy of the code with the repository, or can revert to previously published versions.

    ☒ **A, C,** and **D** are incorrect. Continuous integration is a method for automating elements of the code process, but there is not an application called a continuous integration application. Workflow automation is useful to take standard processes and have them performed by a machine. Donna could take her existing process and automate it, but that would still result in difficulties managing the code of three developers. Chargebacks are used to bill for usage of IT services and would not help in this situation except to bill for how much programming the developers do.

7. ☑ **C.** DevOps ticketing is not a method for deploying application updates. The methods are manual version updating, end-user updating, and using a package manager.

    ☒ **A, B,** and **D** are incorrect. Manual version updating, end-user updating, and using a package manager are all methods for deploying application updates.

8. ☑ **A.** Small changes made to code are tested immediately in the development landscape before being passed to other landscapes.

    ☒ **B, C,** and **D** are incorrect. The quality assurance landscape is used for testing code that has already been tested in the development environment. Testing is not one of the landscapes. The production landscape is used for code that has been fully tested.

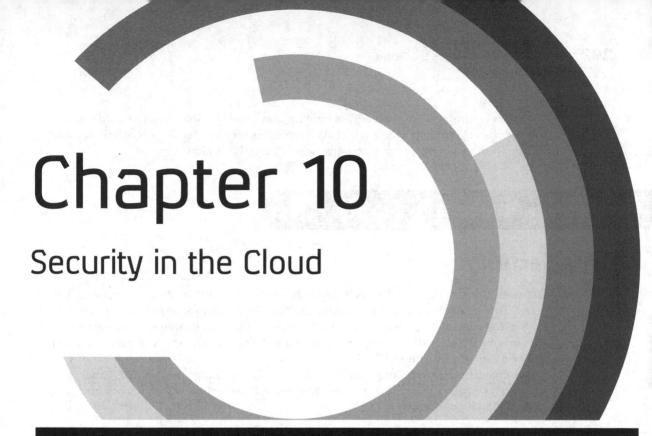

Chapter 10

Security in the Cloud

This chapter covers the concepts of security in the cloud as they apply to data both in motion across networks and at rest in storage, as well as the controlled access to data in both states. Our security coverage begins with some high-level best practices and then delves into the details of the mechanisms and technologies required to deliver against those practices. Some of these technologies include encryption (data confidentiality) and digital signatures (data integrity) and their supporting systems.

Access control is the process of determining who should be able to view, modify, or delete information. Controlling access to network resources such as files, folders, databases, and web applications is reliant upon effective access control techniques.

CERTIFICATION OBJECTIVE 10.01

Data Security

Data security encompasses data as it traverses a network as well as stored data, or data at rest. Data security is concerned with data confidentiality (encryption), ensuring that only authorized parties can access data, and data integrity (digital signatures) ensuring that data is tamper-free and comes from a trusted party. These can be implemented alongside a public key infrastructure (PKI). Encryption is also used to create secure connections between locations in a technique called tunneling. These control mechanisms can be used separately or together for the utmost in security, and this section will explore them in detail in the following sections:

■ Public key infrastructure
■ Encryption protocols
■ Tunneling protocols
■ Ciphers
■ Storage security
■ Protected backups

Public Key Infrastructure

A public key infrastructure (PKI) is a hierarchy of trusted security certificates, as seen in Figure 10-1. These security certificates (also called X.509 certificates, or PKI certificates) are issued to users, applications, or computing devices. PKI certificates are used to encrypt and decrypt data, as well as to digitally sign and verify the integrity of data. Each certificate contains a unique, mathematically related public and private key pair. When the certificate is issued, it has an expiration date; certificates must be renewed before the expiration date. Otherwise, they are not usable.

The certificate authority (CA) exists at the top of the PKI hierarchy, and it can issue, revoke, and renew all security certificates. Under it reside either user, application, and device certificates or subordinate certificate authorities.

Subordinate CAs can also issue, revoke, and renew certificates for the scope of operations provided in their mandate from the root CA. A large enterprise, for example, Acme, might have a CA named Acme-CA. For each of its three U.S. regions, Acme might create subordinate CAs

FIGURE 10-1

Illustration of
a public key
infrastructure
hierarchy

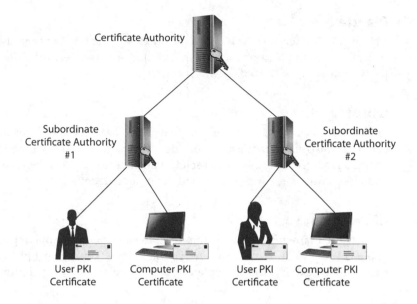

Certificate Authority

Subordinate
Certificate Authority
#1

Subordinate
Certificate Authority
#2

User PKI
Certificate

Computer PKI
Certificate

User PKI
Certificate

Computer PKI
Certificate

named West, East, and Central. These regions could be further divided into sections by creating subordinate CAs from each of those, one for production and one for development. Such a subordinate CA configuration would allow the cloud operations and development personnel in each of the three regions to control their own user and device PKI certificates without having control over resources from other regions or departments.

Certificates have a defined expiration date, but some need to be deactivated before their expiration. In such cases, administrators can revoke the certificate. Revoking a certificate places the certificate on the certificate revocation list (CRL). Computers check the CRL to verify that a certificate is not on the list when they validate a certificate.

To help you better understand encryption and PKI, this section is divided into the following topics:

- Plaintext
- Obfuscation
- Ciphertext
- Cryptographic key
- Symmetric encryption
- Asymmetric encryption
- Digital signatures

on the
Job   **Instead of creating its own PKI, an organization may want to consider acquiring PKI certificates from a trusted third party such as Symantec or Entrust. Modern operating systems have a list of trusted CAs, and if an organization uses its own PKI, it has to ensure that all of its devices trust their CA.**

Plaintext

Before data is encrypted, it is called plaintext. When an unencrypted e-mail message (i.e., an e-mail in plaintext form) is transmitted across a network, it is possible for a third party to intercept that message in its entirety.

Obfuscation

Obfuscation is a practice of using some defined pattern to mask sensitive data. This pattern can be a substitution pattern, a shuffling of characters, or a patterned removal of selected characters. Obfuscation is more secure than plaintext but can be reverse engineered if a malicious entity were willing to spend the time to decode it.

Ciphertext

Ciphers are mathematical algorithms used to encrypt data. Applying an encryption algorithm (cipher) and a value to make the encryption unique (key) against plaintext results in what is called ciphertext; it is the encrypted version of the originating plaintext.

Cryptographic Key

Many people can own the same model of lock while each has their own unique key that opens that specific lock. The same is true for cryptography. Multiple people can each use the same cryptographic algorithm, but they will each use a unique cryptographic key, or key for short, so that one person cannot decrypt the data of another.

Let's continue with the lock example. Some locks have more tumblers than others and this makes them harder to pick. Similarly, some keys are longer than others. Longer keys result in more unique ciphertext and this makes the resulting ciphertext harder to break.

Keys are used for data at rest (stored data) and data in motion (transmission data). Keys are generated and distributed as part of the encryption process or they are configured before encryption begins.

Keys that are generated as part of the encryption process are said to be created in-band. Keys are generated and exchanged during the negotiation phase of communication. Similarly, systems that encrypt stored data will need to generate a key when encrypting the data if one has not been provided to it prior to encryption.

The other approach is to provide keys before engaging in encrypted communication or encryption. For transmission partners, keys are generated out-of-band, meaning that they are created in a separate process and distributed to transmission partners before communication starts. Such a key is known as a pre-shared key (PSK). Software or tools that encrypt stored data may be provided with a key upon installation or configuration and then this key will be used in the encryption process. Some systems use a PSK to encrypt unique keys that are generated for each file, backup job, or volume. This allows a different key to be used for discrete portions of data but these keys do not all have to be provided beforehand. Without such a process, new jobs or drives would require more administrative involvement before they could be encrypted.

Distributed Key Generation   Multiple devices can work together to create a key in a process known as distributed key generation. Distributed key generation makes it harder for the system to be corrupted because there is not a single device responsible for the key. An attacker would need to compromise several systems. This is the method blockchain uses to create keys for Bitcoin and the many other services that depend on blockchain.

Key Management System   However they are provided, each key must be documented and protected so that data can be decrypted when needed. Organizations can deploy a key management system (KMS) to manage issuing, validating, distributing, and revoking cryptographic keys so that keys are stored and managed in a single place. Cloud KMSs include such systems as AWS KMS, Microsoft Azure Key Vault, and Oracle Key Manager.

Elliptic Curve Cryptography   Elliptic curve cryptography (ECC) is a cryptographic function that allows for smaller keys to be used through the use of finite field algebraic structure of elliptic curves. The math behind it is a bit complex, but the simple description is that ECC uses a curve rather than large prime number factors to provide the same security as those with larger keys. Also, a key using ECC of the same length as one using prime number factors would be considered a stronger key.

Symmetric Encryption

As just discussed, encrypting data requires a passphrase or key. Symmetric encryption, also called private key encryption, uses a single key that encrypts and decrypts data. Think of it as locking and unlocking a door using the same key. The key must be kept safe since anybody with it in their possession can unlock the door. Symmetric encryption is used to encrypt files, to secure some VPN solutions, and to encrypt Wi-Fi networks, just to name a few examples.

To see symmetric encryption in action, let's consider a situation where a user, Stacey, encrypts a file on a hard disk:

1. Stacey flags the file to be encrypted.
2. The file encryption software uses a configured symmetric key (or passphrase) to encrypt the file contents. The key might be stored in a file or on a smartcard, or the user might be prompted for the passphrase at the time.
3. This same symmetric key (or passphrase) is used when the file is decrypted.

Encrypting files on a single computer is easy with symmetric encryption, but when other parties that need the symmetric key are involved (e.g., when connecting to a VPN using symmetric encryption), it becomes problematic: How do we securely get the symmetric key to all parties? We could transmit the key to the other parties via e-mail or text message, but we would already have to have a way to encrypt this transmission in the first place. For this reason, symmetric encryption does not scale well.

Asymmetric Encryption

Asymmetric encryption uses two different keys to secure data: a public key and a private key. This key pair is stored in a PKI certificate (which itself can be stored as a file), in a user account database, or on a smartcard. Using two mathematically related keys is what PKI is all about: a hierarchy of trusted certificates each with their own unique public and private key pairs.

The public key can be freely shared, but the private key must be accessible only by the certificate owner. Both the public and private keys can be exported to a certificate file or just the public key by itself. Keys are exported to exchange with others for secure communications or to use as a backup. If the private key is stored in a certificate file, the file must be password protected.

The recipient's public key is required to encrypt transmissions to them. Bear in mind that the recipient could be a user, an application, or a computer. The recipient then uses their mathematically related private key to decrypt the message.

Consider an example, shown in Figure 10-2, where user Roman sends user Trinity an encrypted e-mail message using a PKI, or asymmetric encryption:

1. Roman flags an e-mail message for encryption. His e-mail software needs Trinity's public key. PKI encryption uses the recipient's public key to encrypt. If Roman cannot get Trinity's public key, he cannot encrypt a message to her.

2. Roman's e-mail software encrypts and sends the message. Anybody intercepting the e-mail message will be unable to decipher the message content.

3. Trinity opens the e-mail message using her e-mail program. Because the message is encrypted with her public key, only her mathematically related private key can decrypt the message.

Unlike symmetric encryption, PKI scales well. There is no need to find a safe way to distribute secret keys because only the public keys need be accessible by others, and public keys do not have to be kept secret.

Cloud providers use asymmetric encryption for communication between virtual machines. For example, AWS generates key pairs for authentication to Windows cloud-based virtual machines. AWS stores the public key, and you must download and safeguard the private key.

FIGURE 10-2

Sending an encrypted e-mail message

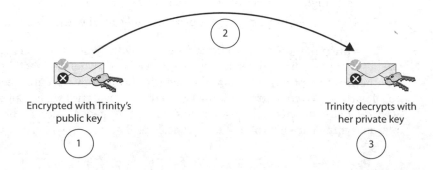

Encrypted with Trinity's public key

Trinity decrypts with her private key

Digital Signatures

A PKI allows us to trust the integrity of data by way of digital signatures. When data is digitally signed, a mathematical hashing function is applied to the data in the message, which results in what is called a message digest, or hash. The PKI private key of the signer is then used to encrypt the hash: this is the digital signature.

Notice that the message content has not been secured; for that encryption is required. Other parties needing to trust the digitally signed data use the mathematically related public key of the signer to validate the hash. Remember that public keys can be freely distributed to anyone without compromising security.

As an example of the digital signature at work, consider user Ana, who is sending user Zoey a high-priority e-mail message that Zoey must trust really did come from Ana:

1. Ana creates the e-mail message and flags it to be digitally signed.
2. Ana's e-mail program uses her PKI private key to encrypt the generated message hash.
3. The e-mail message is sent to Zoey, but it is not encrypted in this example, only signed.
4. Zoey's e-mail program verifies Ana's digital signature by using Ana's mathematically related public key; if Zoey does not have Ana's public key, she cannot verify Ana's digital signature.

Using a public key to verify a digital signature is valid because only the related private key could have created that unique signature, so the message had to have come from that party. This is referred to as nonrepudiation. If the message is tampered with along the way, the signature is invalidated. Again, unlike symmetric encryption, there is no need to safely transmit secret keys; public keys are designed to be publicly available.

For the utmost in security, data can be encrypted and digitally signed, whether it is transmitted data or data at rest (stored).

e x a m
ⓦ a t c h   **Data confidentiality is achieved with encryption. Data authentication and integrity are achieved with digital signatures.**

Encryption Protocols

There are many methods that can be used to secure and verify the authenticity of data. These methods are called encryption protocols, and each is designed for specific purposes, such as encryption for confidentiality and digital signatures for data authenticity and verification (also known as nonrepudiation).

IPSec

Internet Protocol Security (IPSec) secures IP traffic using encryption and digital signatures. PKI certificates, symmetric keys, and other methods can be used to implement this type of security. IPSec is flexible because it is not application specific, so if IPSec secures the communication between hosts, it can encrypt and sign network traffic regardless of the application generating the traffic. IPSec can be used as both an encryption protocol as well as a tunneling protocol, discussed in the next section.

SSL/TLS

Unlike IPSec, Secure Sockets Layer (SSL) or Transport Layer Security (TLS) is used to secure the communication of specially configured applications. Like IPSec, encryption and authentication (signatures) are used to accomplish this level of security. TLS is SSL's successor, although the improvements are minor.

Most computer people associate SSL/TLS with secure web servers, but SSL/TLS can be applied to any network software that supports it, such as Simple Mail Transfer Protocol (SMTP) e-mail servers and Lightweight Directory Access Protocol (LDAP) directory servers. SSL and TLS rely on PKI certificates to obtain the keys required for encryption, decryption, and authentication. Take note that some secured communication, such as connecting to a secured website using Hypertext Transfer Protocol Secure (HTTPS), uses public and private key pairs (asymmetric) to encrypt a session-specific key (symmetric). Most public cloud services are accessed over HTTPS.

Tunneling Protocols

Tunneling is the use of encapsulation and encryption to create a secure connection between devices so that intermediary devices cannot read the traffic and so that devices communicating over the tunnel are connected as if on a local network. Tunneling creates a secure way for devices to communicate with one another over less secure networks such as the Internet. This is a great way to extend an on-premises network into the public cloud.

Encapsulation is the packaging of data within another piece of data. Encapsulation is a normal function of network devices as data moves through the TCP/IP layers. For example, layer 3 IP packets are encapsulated inside layer 2 Ethernet frames. Tunneling encapsulates one IP packet destined for the recipient into another IP packet, treating the encapsulated packet simply as data to be transmitted. The reverse process of encapsulation is de-encapsulation, where the original IP packet is reassembled from the data received by a tunnel endpoint.

The nodes that form encapsulation, de-encapsulation, encryption, and decryption of data in the tunnel are called tunnel endpoints. Tunnel endpoints transmit the first packets of encapsulated data that will traverse the intermediary network.

Not all tunneling protocols encrypt the data that is transmitted through them, but all do encapsulate. If connectivity that seems local is all you are looking for, then a protocol that does not encrypt could work because it will operate faster without having to perform encryption on the data. However, for most uses of tunneling, encryption is a necessity because traffic is routed over an unsecured network. Without encryption, any node along the route could reassemble the data contained in the packets.

Tunneling consumes more network bandwidth and can result in lower speeds for connections over the tunnel because, rather than transmitting the packets themselves, network devices must take the entire packet, including header information, and package that into multiple packets that traverse from node to node until they reach their destination and are reassembled into the original packets that were sent.

Tunneling protocols are network protocols that enable tunneling between devices or sites. They consist of GRE, IPSec, PPTP, and L2TP. Table 10-1 compares each of these tunneling protocols.

GRE

Generic Routing Encapsulation (GRE) is a lightweight, flexible tunneling protocol. GRE works with multiple protocols over IP version 4 and 6. GRE is not considered a secure tunneling protocol because it does not use encryption. GRE has an optional key field that can be used for authentication using checksum authentication or keyword authentication.

IPSec

Internet Protocol Security (IPSec) is a tunneling and encryption protocol. Its encryption features were mentioned previously in this chapter. IPSec tunneling secures IP traffic using Encapsulating Security Protocol (ESP) to encrypt the data that is tunneled over it using PKI certificates or asymmetric keys. Keys are exchanged using the Internet Security Agreement/ Key Management Protocol (ISAKMP) and Oakley protocol and a security association (SA) so that endpoints can negotiate security settings and exchange encryption keys.

IPSec also offers authentication through the Authentication Header (AH) protocol. The main disadvantage of IPSec is that it encrypts the data of the original IP packet, but replicates the original packet's IP header information, so intermediary devices know the final

TABLE 10-1   Tunneling Protocols Compared

Protocol Name	Considered Secure as of 2017	Authentication	Encryption
Generic Routing Encapsulation (GRE)	No	Yes, checksum or keyword	No
Internet Protocol Security (IPSec)	Yes	Yes, AH	Yes, ESP
Point-to-Point Tunneling Protocol (PPTP)	No	Yes, PAP, CHAP, MS-CHAP version 1 or version 2, EAP-TLS, PEAP	Yes, MPPE
Layer 2 Tunneling Protocol (L2TP)	Yes (only in L2TP/IPSec mode)	Yes, AH (only in L2TP/IPSec mode)	Yes, ESP (only in L2TP/IPSec mode)

destination within the tunnel instead of just knowing the tunnel endpoint. IPSec functions in this way because it offers end-to-end encryption, meaning that the data is encrypted not from endpoint to endpoint but from the original source to the final destination.

PPTP

Point-to-Point Tunneling Protocol (PPTP) is a tunneling protocol that uses GRE and Point-to-Point Protocol (PPP) to transport data. PPTP has a very flexible configuration for authentication and encryption, so different implementations can utilize a variety of authentication and encryption protocols. PPP or GRE frames can be encrypted, compressed, or both. The primary benefit of PPTP is its speed and its native support in Microsoft Windows.

The most widely used variation of PPTP is used in Microsoft VPN connections. These connections use PAP, CHAP, MS-CHAP version 1, or MS-CHAP version 2 for authentication. At the time of this publication, weaknesses have been found in most of these protocols. The only secure implementation currently available for PPTP is Extensible Authentication Protocol Transport Layer Security (EAP-TLS) or Protected Extensible Authentication Protocol (PEAP).

PPTP data is encrypted using the Microsoft Point-to-Point Encryption (MPPE) protocol. MPPE uses RC4 key lengths of 128 bits, 56 bits, and 40 bits. Negotiation of keys is performed using the Compression Control Protocol (CCP). At the time of this publication, weaknesses in the RC4 protocol make PPTP implementations insecure because data can be decrypted using current toolsets.

L2TP

Layer 2 Tunneling Protocol (L2TP) offers improvements over PPTP. L2TP does not offer encryption built-in but can be combined with IPSec to provide encryption and authentication using Encapsulating Security Protocol (ESP) and Authentication Header (AH). However, L2TP is CPU intensive when encryption is used because data must be encapsulated twice, once with L2TP and another time with IPSec.

L2TP is a flexible tunneling protocol, allowing a variety of protocols to be encrypted through it. L2TP has been used to encrypt and tunnel IP, Asynchronous Transfer Mode (ATM), and Frame Relay data.

Ciphers

Recall that plaintext fed to an encryption algorithm results in ciphertext. "Cipher" is synonymous with "encryption algorithm," whether the algorithm is symmetric (same key) or asymmetric (different paired keys). There are two categories of ciphers: block ciphers and stream ciphers. Table 10-2 lists some of the more common ciphers.

| TABLE 10-2 | Common Block and Stream Ciphers |

Cipher Name	Creation Date	Encryption Type	Cipher Type	Cipher Strength	Usage
Advanced Encryption Standard (AES)	1998	Symmetric	Block	256 bits	Replaced DES in 2001 as the U.S. federal standard
Digital Encryption Standard (DES)	1975	Symmetric	Block	56 bits	U.S. federal standard until 2001
3DES or "triple-DES"	1998	Symmetric	Block	168 bits	An improvement on DES that performed DES operations three times
Digital Signature Algorithm (DSA)	1991	Asymmetric	Block	2048 bits	U.S. federal standard for digital signatures
Rivest Cipher (RC4)	1987	Symmetric	Stream	128 bits	Byte-oriented stream operation
Rivest Cipher (RC5)	1994	Symmetric	Block	2048 bits	A simple and fast algorithm
Rivest, Shamir, Adleman (RSA)	1977	Asymmetric	Stream	4096 bits	Some hardware and software may not support up to 4096 bits

Block Ciphers

Designed to encrypt chunks or blocks of data, block ciphers convert plaintext to ciphertext in bulk as opposed to one data bit at a time, either using a fixed secret key or by generating keys from each encrypted block. A 128-bit block cipher produces a 128-bit block of ciphertext. This type of cipher is best applied to fixed-length segments of data, such as fixed-length network packets or files stored on a disk.

Some block ciphers include DES, AES, RC5, DSA, and 3DES. Each of these ciphers is shown in Table 10-2.

DES Data Encryption Standard (DES) is a symmetric block cipher that uses block sizes of 64 bits and 16 rounds of encryption. 3DES or "triple-DES" encrypts data with DES three times using three keys. It is marginally better than DES and managed to extend the life of DES for a short time. DES and 3DES are now outdated protocols. They were succeeded by AES in 2001 as the new standard for government encryption.

AES Advanced Encryption Standard (AES) is a symmetric block cipher that uses a 128-bit block and variable key sizes of 128, 192, and 256 bits. It performs 10 to 14 rounds of encryption depending on the key size used. AES replaces DES as the new standard for government encryption.

RC5   Rivest Cipher 5 (RC5) is a symmetric block cipher used to encrypt and decrypt data. It is named for its creator, Ron Rivest. RC5 is a block cipher that uses symmetric keys for encryption. RC5 replaces RC4 and supports a cipher strength of up to 2048 bits. RC5 uses 1–255 rounds of encryption.

DSA   The digital signature algorithm (DSA) is an asymmetric block cipher used for message or data signing and verification. DSA creates keys of variable lengths and can create per-user keys. DSA is accepted as a federal information processing standard in FIPS 186. DSA has a maximum cipher strength of 2048 bits and was created in 1991.

Stream Ciphers

Unlike block ciphers that work on a chunk of data at a time, stream ciphers convert plaintext into ciphertext one binary bit at a time. Stream ciphers are considerably faster than block ciphers. Stream ciphers are best suited where there is an unknown or variable amount of data to be encrypted, such as variable-length network transmissions. Some stream ciphers include RC4 and RSA shown in Table 10-2.

RC4   Rivest Cipher 4 (RC4) is a symmetric stream cipher used to encrypt and decrypt data. RC4 uses symmetric keys up to 128 bits in length for encryption. It is named for its creator, Ron Rivest.

TKIP   Temporal Key Integrity Protocol (TKIP) is a protocol specified in IEEE 802.11i that enhances the WEP/RC4 encryption in wireless networks. It was created in 2002. TKIP takes a PSK called the secret root key and combines it with a unique random or pseudorandom value called an initialization vector. TKIP also tracks the order of pieces of encrypted data using a sequence counter. This helps protect against an attack where previous ciphertext is provided to a system to try to perform a transaction twice in what is known as a replay attack. Lastly, TKIP uses an integrity checking function called the message integrity code (MIC) to verify ciphertext in the communication stream.

RSA   Rivest, Shamir, Adleman (RSA) is an asymmetric stream cipher used to encrypt and decrypt data. It is named after its three creators, Ron Rivest, Adi Shamir, and Leonard Adleman, and was created in 1977. RSA uses asymmetric key pairs up to 4096 bits in length for encryption.

Stream ciphers are faster than block ciphers.

Storage Security

Storage security is concerned with the security of data at rest or when it is stored on a cloud system. There are a large number of cloud services specifically dedicated to storage of data, such as Dropbox, Google Drive, Amazon Drive, Microsoft OneDrive, and SpiderOak. For these services, storage is the business. For other cloud services, storage is one of the core building blocks on which the cloud service is architected and it is important to implement effective security at this level.

From the cloud consumer perspective, storage security is built into the product offering, so cloud consumers do not need to implement these controls. It is, however, still important to understand cloud security controls in order to ensure that the cloud service meets organizational security and technology stipulations, contractual agreements, and regulatory requirements. Storage security is vital when setting up a private cloud or when providing cloud services to others since storage is the underlying component behind cloud systems.

Granular Storage Resource Controls

Based on the storage technology utilized in the cloud system, security mechanisms can be put in place to limit access to resources over the network. This is important when setting up a private cloud or if you are working for a cloud provider since storage is the underlying component behind cloud systems. When using a storage area network (SAN), two techniques for limiting resource access are LUN masking and zoning. See Chapter 3 if you need a review on SANs and LUNs.

- **LUN masking**   LUN masking allows access to resources, namely storage logical unit numbers (LUNs), to be limited by the utilization of an LUN mask either at the host bus adapter or the switch level.
- **Zoning**   SANs can also utilize zoning, which is a practice of limiting access to LUNs that are attached to the storage controller.

LUN masking and zoning can be used in combination. Storage security is best implemented in layers, with data having to pass multiple checks before arriving at its intended target. All the possible security mechanisms, from software to operating system to storage system, should be implemented and configured to architect the most secure storage solution possible.

Securing Storage Resources

Data is the most valuable component of any cloud system. It is the reason that companies invest in these large, expensive infrastructures or services: to make certain that their users have access to the data they need to drive their business.

Storage is such a critical resource to the users of cloud models that special care must be taken with its security to make sure resources are available and accurate, and accessible for users who have been authorized for access.

Digital and Information Rights Management

Digital rights management (DRM) is a set of technologies that enforces specific usage limitations on data, such as preventing a document from being printed or e-mailed, or photos from being downloaded from a phone app. DRM is typically associated with consumer applications.

Similarly, information rights management (IRM) is a set of technologies that enforces specific usage limitations on data throughout enterprise systems, including cloud and distributed systems.

Protected Backups

Backups are copies of live data that are maintained in case something happens that makes the live dataset inaccessible. Because it is a copy of valuable data, it needs to have the same protections afforded it that the live data employs. It should be encrypted, password protected, and kept physically locked away from unauthorized access. See Chapter 12 for more information on backups and backup strategies.

CERTIFICATION OBJECTIVE 10.02

Network Security

Network security is the practice of protecting the usability, reliability, integrity, and safety of a network infrastructure and also the data traveling along it. As it does in many other areas, security in cloud computing has similarities to traditional computing models. If deployed without evaluating security, cloud systems may be able to deliver against its functional requirements, but they will likely have many gaps that could lead to a compromised system.

Security Systems

IT administrators and security teams have many tools at their disposal. There are systems they can deploy to implement security or vendor applications, and all these systems must be compatible with existing systems and services.

Security systems are designed to protect the network against certain types of threats. One solution alone will not fully protect the company, because attackers have multiple avenues for exploitation. Security systems should be used in conjunction with one another to protect against these avenues and to provide layers of security. If an attacker passes by one layer, he will not be able to exploit the network without bypassing another layer, and so forth. Security systems will only overlap in some places, so having 20 security systems does not mean that the organization has 20 layers.

The security systems mentioned here, and many others, can exist either as networking/ security hardware that is installed in a data center or as virtual appliances that are placed in hypervisors in much the same way as servers. Cloud environments can deploy virtual appliances to their networks easily with this method. Virtual appliances were covered in the "Systems Maintenance" section of Chapter 9. The following sections cover three important security systems, firewalls, intrusion prevention/detection systems, and SIEM systems.

Firewall

A firewall is used to control traffic. Firewalls operate at OSI layer 3 or above, meaning that, at a minimum, they can analyze packets and implement filtering on packets based on the information contained in the packet header, such as source and destination IP addresses, lengths, and sizes. However, most firewalls operate at a much higher level.

Firewalls in a cloud environment are typically virtual appliances or software services offered to cloud consumers. Common public cloud providers offer layer 4 firewalls such as the Azure Network Security Group (NSG) and AWS EC2 Security Group. These are implemented simply by configuring them on an administrative dashboard.

Such cloud firewalls perform filtering, to a large extent, with access control lists (ACLs). ACLs are made up of a series of access control entries (ACEs). Each ACE specifies the access rights of an individual principal or entity. One or more ACEs are comprised in an ACL.

The firewall processes the ACL in order from the first ACE to the last ACE. For example, the first ACE would say allow traffic over HTTP to the web server. The second ACE would say allow SMTP traffic to the e-mail server, and the third ACE would say deny all traffic. If the firewall receives DNS traffic, it will go through the rules in order. ACE 1 is not matched because this is not HTTP traffic. ACE 2 is not matched because this is not SMTP traffic. ACE 3 is matched because it is anything else, so the firewall drops the packet. In the real world, ACLs are much more complex. Some firewall capabilities include the following:

- **NAT/PAT**   Network address translation (NAT) consolidates the addresses needed for each internal device to a single valid public IP address, allowing all of the organization's employees to access the Internet with the use of a single public IP address.

   Firewalls can be configured with multiple IP addresses, and NAT can be used to translate external IP addresses with internal IP addresses so that the actual IP address of the host is hidden from the outside world.

   Port address translation (PAT) allows for mapping of private IP addresses to public IP addresses as well as for mapping multiple devices on a network to a single public IP address. PAT enables the sharing of a single public IP address between multiple clients trying to access the Internet. Each external-facing service has a port associated with it, and the PAT service knows which ones map to which internal servers. It repackages the data received, on the outside network to the inside network, addressing it to the destination server, and it makes this determination based on the port the data was sent to.

- **Port/service** The firewall can be configured to filter out traffic that is not addressed to an open port. For example, the firewall may be configured to allow traffic to HTTPS, port 443, and SMTP, port 25. If it receives data for HTTP on port 80, it will drop the packet.

- **DMZ** A demilitarized zone is a network segment that has specific security rules on it. DMZs are created to segment traffic. A typical scenario is to place public-facing web servers in a DMZ. ACLs are then defined to allow web traffic to the web servers but not anywhere else. The web servers may need to connect back to the database server on an internal cloud segment, so ACLs allow the web servers in the DMZ to talk to the database server in the internal cloud segment, but connections from the outside would not be able to talk to the database server directly.

- **Stateful packet inspection** Stateful packet inspection evaluates whether a session has been created for a packet before it will accept it. This is similar to the way an accounts receivable department looks to see if they issued a purchase order before paying an invoice. If there is no purchase order, no check is sent.

- **IP spoofing detection** Spoofing is the modification of the sending IP address to obscure the origin of a data transmission. Attackers will sometimes try to send data to a device to make it seem like the data came from another device on the local network. They spoof the sending IP address and give it some local address. Spoofing is the modification of the source IP address to obfuscate the original source. However, the firewall knows which addresses it has internally, because they are contained in its routing table, so it if sees data with a sender address from outside the network, it knows that data is spoofed.

  Spoofing is not limited to local addresses. Spoofing is often used in e-mail phishing to make e-mails appear as if they originated from a company's servers when they actually came from an attacker. Spoofing is also used in man-in-the-middle attacks so that data is routed through a middleman.

Firewalls often exist on the perimeter of the network, where they can screen the data that is going to and coming from the Internet. There is also a type of firewall called the host-based firewall that resides on an endpoint to screen the data that is received by the endpoint. If a device is not running as a web server, there is no reason for it to process web traffic. Web traffic sent to it is either malicious or sent by mistake, so it is either a waste of time to look at it or, more likely, a threat. The host-based firewall drops this traffic before it can do harm to the device.

Host-based firewalls can be configured based on policy so that many machines can use the same configuration. Chapter 9 covered how to automate configuring firewalls with scripting. You can also use Windows group policies to configure the Windows Defender firewall that comes with Windows. Many antivirus vendors bundle a host-based firewall with their products, and these can be managed with a central management application or cloud portal if the licensing for that application or portal has been purchased.

WAF   One specialized type of firewall is called a web application firewall (WAF). A WAF is a device that screens traffic intended for web applications. WAFs understand common web application attacks such as cross-site scripting (XSS) and SQL injection and can inspect traffic at the application layer of the OSI model.

Cloud Access Security Broker   Organizations may choose to have a third party screen traffic for cloud or on-premises systems. A cloud access security broker (CASB) is a cloud service that operates as the gateway between external users and other cloud systems. The CASB screens incoming traffic for malicious content and anomalous behavior and prevents that traffic from being delivered to the cloud systems it services.

Distributed Denial of Service (DDoS)   A distributed denial of service (DDoS) is an attack that targets a single system simultaneously from multiple compromised systems to make that system unavailable. The attack is distributed because it uses thousands or millions of machines that could be spread across the globe. The attack denies services or disrupts availability by overwhelming the system so that it cannot respond to legitimate connection requests. Cloud firewalls or CASB can often prevent DDoS traffic from reaching organizational cloud servers because the cloud vendor or CASB has the necessary bandwidth to withstand a DDoS attack. However, there have been some DDoS attacks such as the ones performed by the Mirai botnet that overwhelmed some of even the largest networks.

IDS/IPS

An intrusion detection system (IDS) or an intrusion prevention system (IPS) looks at traffic to identify malicious traffic. IDSs and IPSs do this through two methods, signatures and heuristics. IDSs or IPSs in a cloud environment are typically virtual appliances or software services offered to cloud consumers. Such services include Azure Network Security Groups and AWS EC2 Security Groups, which are built into the cloud provider environment as software configurations. They can also include third-party cloud solutions that are supported by the cloud provider.

Signatures are descriptions of what malicious data looks like. IDSs and IPSs review the data that passes through them and take action if they find data that matches a signature. The second screening method used is heuristics, which looks for patterns that appear malicious, such as a large number of failed authentication attempts. Heuristics operates off an understanding of what constitutes normal on the network. A baseline is configured and periodically updated, so the IDS or IPS understands what to expect from the network traffic. Anything else is an anomaly, and the device will take action.

So far, we have only said that these devices take action. IDSs and IPSs differ in how they react to the things they find. An IDS sends alerts and logs suspicious traffic but does not block the traffic. An IPS can send alerts and log, but it can also block, queue, or quarantine the traffic. IPS can be generically referred to as intrusion detection and prevention (IDP). This term is used in the same way that IPS is used.

IDSs and IPSs need to be in a position to collect network data. There are two configurations, network-based and host-based. A network-based IDS (NIDS) or IPS (NIPS) is placed next to a firewall, or built into a perimeter firewall. A firewall is an ideal place because it processes all traffic going between the inside network and the outside. If the NIPS is a separate device, it will need to have the traffic forwarded to it and then relay back instructions, or it will need to be the first device to screen the information.

The second type of IDS or IPS is the host-based IDS (HIDS) or IPS (HIPS). These devices reside on endpoints such as cloud servers or cloud virtual desktop infrastructure (VDI). A NIDS or NIPS can collect a lot of data, but it does not see everything because not all data passes through the perimeter. Consider malware that has infected a machine. It may reach out to other computers on the network without touching the perimeter device. A HIDS or HIPS would be able to identify this traffic when a NIDS or NIPS would not.

You can choose to implement both host-based and network-based IDS or IPS. They will still operate independently but also send data to a collection point so that the data between the devices can be correlated to produce better intelligence on what is normal and abnormal.

In the cloud, firewalls and IDS/IPS functionality can be achieved with cloud-specific configuration settings or by deploying a virtual appliance from the cloud provider marketplace.

SIEM

A security information and event management (SIEM) system archives logs and reviews the logs in real time against correlation rules to identify possible threats or problems. Additionally, a SIEM system monitors baselines and heuristics to identify issues that crop up before they turn into bigger issues. For example, a number of informational events, when analyzed together, may present a bigger issue that can be resolved before it creates problems for end users. Without such a system, administrators would likely not notice the events until errors or warnings appeared in the log, which would probably be the same time that users of the system also experience issues.

It is much easier to fix issues before end users discover them and begin complaining. IT administrators tend to think more clearly and logically when not under pressure. SIEM can change the way IT administrators investigate issues, eventually causing them to focus more on proactive indicators of an issue rather than fighting fires.

Security Applications

Vendors have created a vast number of applications to solve many security challenges, and many security applications are available as cloud services. Here are some vendor applications or application components you should be familiar with:

- The application programming interface (API)
- Antivirus and antimalware software
- The command-line interface (CLI)

- The web graphical user interface (GUI)
- Cloud portals

APIs

Application programming interfaces (APIs) are used to expose functions of an application or cloud service to other programs and services. APIs allow for expansion of the original application's scope, and they are used to integrate multiple applications together as part of an organization's cloud or security operations.

A vendor will create an API for its application and then release documentation so that developers and integrators know how to utilize that API. For example, Office 365, a cloud-based productivity suite that includes an e-mail application, has an API for importing and exporting contacts. Salesforce, a cloud-based customer relationship management (CRM) application, could integrate with Office 365 through that API so that contacts could be updated based on interactions in the CRM tool.

Antivirus/Antimalware

Antivirus or antimalware looks at actions on a system to identify malicious activity. Antivirus or antimalware does this through the same two methods used by an IDS/IPS, signatures and heuristics. The terms antivirus and antimalware are used interchangeably. Both antivirus and antimalware software detect viruses, trojans, bots, worms, and malicious cookies. Some antivirus or antimalware software also identify adware, spyware, and potentially unwanted applications.

Signatures are descriptions of what malicious actions looks like. Antivirus and antimalware review the data in memory and scan data on the disk or disks that are plugged into them and take action if they find data that matches a signature.

The second screening method used is heuristics, which looks for patterns that appear malicious, such as a user mode process trying to access kernel mode memory addresses. Just as with the IDS and IPS, antivirus or antimalware heuristics operates off an understanding of what constitutes normal on the device. A baseline is configured and periodically updated, so the antivirus or antimalware understands what to expect from the network traffic. Anything else is an anomaly, and the device will take action.

Many antivirus and antimalware vendors have a central management application or cloud portal option that can be purchased. These tools or portals are very valuable for ease of administration. Each antivirus or antimalware client reports in to the portal, and administrators can view all machines in a set of dashboards. Dashboards show things like machines with outdated signatures, number of viruses detected, virus detection rates, virus types, items in quarantine, number of files scanned, and much more. These administration tools usually allow administrators to deploy antivirus or antimalware software to endpoints without walking to each machine.

Some antivirus and antimalware tools come with other services bundled in. These include host-based firewalls, data loss prevention, password vaults, e-mail scanners, web scanners, and other features.

CLI

Applications can have different interfaces, and there are pros and cons to the interface depending on how the application is going to be used. The command-line interface (CLI) is an interface that is text-based. The user must type instructions to the program using predefined syntax in order to interact with the program. For example, Microsoft Azure and Amazon Web Services each have their own CLI.

CLI tools can seem cumbersome to those used to graphical user interfaces (GUIs), but their power comes with the ability to script them. A task that could take 30 minutes of clicking in a GUI to accomplish could be achieved in a few minutes with a script because all the functions are preprogrammed with a series of commands. CLI tools are usually more lightweight, so they are easier to deploy and have less of a burden on systems.

Web GUI

Graphical user interfaces are very easy to work with. Simply point and click on something to take an action. Users can get to work on an application very quickly if it has a GUI. Web GUIs offer that functionality from a web browser. The advantage of a web GUI is that tools can be administered from any machine that can connect to the web server and has the authorization to administer the tool.

Cloud Portal

A cloud portal is an interface that is accessed over the Internet to manage cloud tools or integrate with other tools. The portal displays useful dashboards and information for decision-making and ease of administration.

Cloud portals are like web GUIs, but they can be accessed from almost anywhere. Cloud portals are great for administering cloud tools and for integrating with a variety of legacy tools that would have required logging into many different web GUIs, launching traditional applications, or sending SSH commands to a CLI.

Impact of Security Tools to Systems and Services

Security tools can affect the systems they are installed on. Antivirus software could flag some legitimate applications as malicious or require additional steps to log on to tools. Security tools can take up a large amount of CPU or memory resources. Logging tools utilize a large amount of storage. Since cloud resource utilization often determines how much the cloud consumer is charged, resource utilization directly impacts the bottom line.

Some security tools do not play well together. For example, it is never a good idea to install multiple antivirus tools on the same machine. Each tool will interpret the other tool as malicious because they each are scanning large numbers of files and trying to read memory.

Some security tools may accidentally flag other security tools as malicious and cause problems running those tools. If this happens, whitelist the application in the security tool that blocks it. Some security tools can cause issues with backup jobs because the tools create locks when scanning files and folders that the backup job must wait for or try to snapshot.

CERTIFICATION OBJECTIVE 10.03

Access Control

Access control is the process of determining who or what should be able to view, modify, or delete information. Controlling access to network resources such as files, folders, databases, and web applications is reliant upon effective access control techniques. Access control is accomplished by authenticating and authorizing both users and hosts.

Authentication means that an entity can prove that it is who or what it claims to be, and authorization means that an entity has access to all of the resources it is supposed to have access to, and no access to the resources it is not supposed to have access to.

Authorization is the set of processes that determine who a claimant is and what they are allowed to do. These processes also log activity for later auditing and are sometimes referred to as AAA, which stands for authentication, authorization, and accounting.

This section includes coverage of the following access control concepts:

- Identification
- Authentication
- Authorization
- Access control methodologies
- Multifactor authentication
- Single sign-on (SSO)
- Federation

Identification

Identification is the process of claiming an identity. In the medieval days, a guard would ask, "Who goes there?" if a pair of strangers approached the gate, in response to which the strangers would reply, "Scott Wilson and Eric Vanderburg." Of course, the guard would not just take the strangers word for it, and neither should a computer when a user or service tries to connect to it or log on. The next step is authentication.

Authentication

Authentication is the process of determining who or what is requesting access to a resource. When you log on to a computer, you present credentials that validate your identity to the computer, much like a driver's license or passport identifies your identity to a police officer or customs officer. And just as the police officer or customs officer compares the photo on the ID to your face, the computer will compare the credentials you offer with the information on hand to determine if you are whom you claim to be. However, the computer may trust that you are who you say you are, but that doesn't necessarily mean that you are allowed to be there. The next step is to determine if the user identity is allowed access to the resource.

Authorization

Authorization determines if the authenticated individual should have the requested access to the resource. For example, after this book is published, if we authors go to a club to celebrate, bypass the line, and present our credentials to the bouncer, he or she will compare our names to a list of authorized individuals. If the owner of the club is a huge fan of this book, she might have put our names on the list, in which case, we are granted access to the club. If not, the bouncer will tell us to get lost. Computer systems compare the identity to the resource ACL to determine if the user can access the resource.

ACLs define the level of access, such as read-only (RO), modify (M), or full control (FC). Read-only access allows a user to view the data but not make changes to it. Modify allows the user to read the data and change it. Full control allows the user to read data, change it, delete it, or change the permissions on it.

Organizations should implement approval procedures and access policies along with authorization techniques. Approval and access policy are discussed next.

Devices may exchange authorization data using the Security Assertion Markup Language (SAML).

Approval

Approval is an audit of the authorization function. In the bouncer example, imagine that the bouncer is a fan of this book, not the owner. A supervisor who is watching over a group of club staff members, including the bouncer, sees the bouncer letting us into the club and decides to check the list to verify that Scott Wilson and Eric Vanderburg are on it. If the supervisor finds that we are not on the list or sees our names written in with the bouncer's handwriting, sanctions are soon to follow, and we might not be welcome there anymore.

Approval, when implemented in the computer setting, would see a connection from a new user who is on the ACL. Since the user has not logged in before, a second authentication would take place, such as sending a text to the user's phone or an e-mail to their inbox. The user would enter the code from the text or e-mail to prove that they know the password from the first authentication and that they have access to the phone or email as well. In future attempts, the approval step would not be needed since the user has logged in before. The concept of approval operates on a level of trust, and this can be changed depending on organizational preferences. One company could decide that approval will take place not just for new connections but the lesser of every fifth time someone logs in or every two weeks. Implementations are quite flexible.

Access Policy

Access policy is the governing activities that establish authorization levels. Access policy determines who should have access to what. Access policy requires at least three roles. The first is the authorizer. This is the person or group that can define who has access. The second is the implementer. This is the person or group that assigns access based on an authorization. The third role is the auditor. This person or group reviews existing access to verify that each access granted is authorized.

Here is how access policy plays out on the job: The organization typically defines access based on a job role. In this example, human resources (HR) is the authorizer, IT is the implementer, and audit is the auditor. When a new person is hired for a job in marketing, HR would notify IT of the new hire, their name, start date, and that they are in marketing. IT would then grant them access to the systems that others in marketing have access to. This is typically accomplished by creating the user account and then adding that account to an appropriate group.

Auditors would routinely review group memberships to determine if they match what has been defined by HR. Any inconsistencies would be brought to the attention of management. Access policies have a lifetime. Access is not provided forever and at some point, access rights are revoked. In this example, HR would notify IT to revoke access and IT would disable or remove the account when employees are terminated. On the next audit cycle, the auditor would verify that the account had been disabled.

Federation

Federation uses SSO to authorize access for users or devices to potentially many very different protected network resources, such as file servers, websites, and database applications. The protected resources could exist within a single organization or between multiple organizations.

For business-to-business (B2B) relationships, such as between a cloud customer and a cloud provider, a federation allows the cloud customer to retain their own on-premises user accounts and passwords that can be used to access cloud services from the provider. This way the user does not have to remember a username and password for the cloud services as well as for the local network. Federation also allows cloud providers to rent, on demand, computing resources from other cloud providers to service their clients' needs.

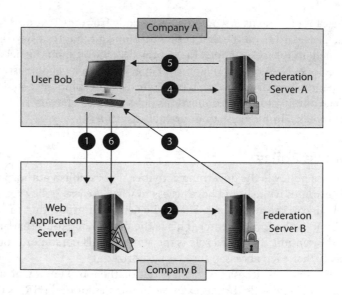

FIGURE 10-3

An example of a
B2B federation
at work

Here is a typical B2B federation scenario (see Figure 10-3):

1. User Bob in company A attempts to access an application on web application server 1 in company B.
2. If Bob is not already authenticated, the web application server in company B redirects Bob to the federation server in company B for authentication.
3. Since Bob's user account does not exist in company B, the federation server in company B sends an authentication redirect to Bob.
4. Bob is redirected to the company A federation server and gets authenticated since this is where his user account exists.
5. The company A federation server returns a digitally signed authentication token to Bob.
6. Bob presents the authentication token to the application on web application server 1 and is authorized to use the application.

Access Control Methodologies

Several methodologies can be used to assign permissions to users so that they can use network resources. These methods include mandatory access control (MAC), discretionary access control (DAC), and non-discretionary access control (NDAC). NDAC consists of role-based access control (RBAC) and task-based access control (TBAC). RBAC, MAC, and DAC are compared in Table 10-3.

Additionally, as systems become more complex and distributed, the policies, procedures, and technologies required to control access privileges, roles, and rights of users across a heterogeneous enterprise can be centralized in an identity and access management (IAM) system.

| TABLE 10-3 | Comparison of Access Control Methods |

| | Mandatory Access Control (MAC) | Discretionary Access Control (DAC) | Non-Discretionary Access Control (NDAC) | |
			Role-Based Access Control (RBAC)	Task-Based Access Control (TBAC)
Permissions	System or application determines who has access	Permissions are granted to users	Permissions are granted to groups or roles	Permissions are granted based on task
Additional Requirements	Resources must be labeled for granular control	None	None	Discrete tasks must be identified along with required access
Scope	Suited for larger organizations	Suited for smaller organizations	Suited for larger organizations	Suited for smaller organizations
Resource Access	User attributes can determine resource access	Uses the identity of a subject to determine resource access	Users are added to groups or roles to gain access to resources	Permissions are granted to tasks
Advantages	Requires need to know in addition to clearance	Easy to implement	Flexible and scales well	Useful when the person needing access changes frequently but the task remains the same
Disadvantages	Complicated to implement and manage	Considered less secure than MAC and RBAC	May not fit unique access needs of an individual	Access to tasks may require a separate authentication

Mandatory Access Control

The word *mandatory* is used to describe this access control model because permissions to resources are controlled, or mandated, by the operating system (OS) or application, which looks at the requesting party and their attributes to determine whether or not access should be granted. These decisions are based on configured policies that are enforced by the OS or application.

With mandatory access control (MAC), data is labeled, or classified, in such a way that only those parties with certain attributes can access it. For example, perhaps only full-time employees can access a specific portion of an intranet web portal. Alternatively, perhaps only human resources employees can access files classified as confidential.

Discretionary Access Control

With the discretionary access control (DAC) methodology, the power to grant or deny user permissions to resources lies not with the OS or an application but rather with the data owner. Protected resources might be files on a file server or items in a specific web application.

 Most network environments use both DAC and RBAC; the data owner can give permissions to the resource by adding a group to the ACL.

There are no security labels or classifications with DAC; instead, each protected resource has an ACL that determines access. For example, we might add user RayLee with read and write permissions to the ACL of a specific folder on a file server so that she can access that data.

Non-Discretionary Access Control

With the non-discretionary access control (NDAC) methodology, access control decisions are based on organizational rules and cannot be modified by (at the discretion) of non-privileged users. NDAC scales well because access control rules are not resource specific and can be applied across the board to new resources such as servers, computers, cloud services, and storage as those systems are provisioned.

NDAC has been implemented in the role-based access control (RBAC) and task-based access control (TBAC) methodologies. RBAC is by far the most popular, but both are discussed in this section. RBAC relies on group or role memberships to determine access while TBAC relies on the task that is being performed to make access decisions.

Role-Based Access Control
For many years, IT administrators, and now cloud administrators, have found it easier to manage permissions to resources by using groups, or roles. This is the premise of RBAC. A group or role has one or more members, and that group or role is assigned permissions to a resource.

Permissions are granted either implicitly or explicitly. Any user placed into that group or role inherits its permissions; this is known as implicit inheritance. Granting permissions to individual users is considered explicit permission assignment, and it does not scale as well in larger organizations as RBAC does. RBAC is implemented in different ways depending on where it is being performed. Solutions such as IAM can manage identity across an enterprise, including on-premises and cloud systems. However, these systems tie into locally defined groups in order to assign generalized IAM groups to the local groups. IAM can greatly improve the time it takes to provision or remove users or to change their roles across an enterprise.

Sometimes the groups or roles in RBAC are defined by cloud vendors through an IAM solution such as AWS IAM. RBAC can also be applied at the operating system level, as in the case of a Microsoft Windows Active Directory group. RBAC can be applied at the application level, as in the case of Microsoft SharePoint Server roles. In the cloud, roles may be defined by the cloud provider if cloud consumers are not using provider IAM solutions.

To illustrate how cloud-based RBAC would be implemented using an IAM solution, consider the following commands. AWS IAM can be managed through the web GUI or via the CLI. These commands can be used in the AWS IAM CLI. This first command creates a group called managers:

```
aws iam create-group --group-name Managers
```

The following command assigns the administrator policy to the managers group. AWS IAM has policies that package together a set of permissions to perform tasks. The administrator policy provides full access to AWS.

```
aws iam attach-group-policy --group-name Managers --policy-arn
arn:aws:iam::aws:policy/AdministratorAccess
```

We can then create a user named EricVanderburg with the following command:

```
aws iam create-user --user-name EricVanderburg
```

Last, we add the user EricVanderburg to the managers group with this command:

```
aws iam add-user-to-group --user-name EricVanderburg --group-name
Managers
```

Task-Based Access Control   The TBAC methodology is a dynamic method of providing access to resources. It differs greatly from the other NDAC methodology, RBAC, in that it is not based on subjects and objects (users and resources). TBAC was created around the concept of least privilege. In other models, a user might have the ability to access a reporting system, but they use that system only once a month. For the majority of each month, the user has more access than they require. In TBAC, users have no access to resources by default and are only provided access when they perform a task requiring it, and access is not retained after the task is complete.

TBAC systems provide access just as it is needed and are usually associated with workflows or transactions. TBAC can also be efficient because tasks and their required access can be defined when new processes are defined and they are independent of who performs them or how many times they are performed.

Multifactor Authentication

Authentication means proving who (or what) you are. Authentication can be done with the standard username and password combination or with a variety of other methods.

Some environments use a combination of the three authentication mechanisms; this is known as multifactor authentication (MFA). Possessing a debit card, along with knowledge of the PIN, comprises multifactor authentication. Combining these authentication methods is considered much more secure than single-factor authentication.

EXAM AT WORK

A Real-World Look at Cloud RBAC

We were asked to help a company where a disgruntled employee had defaced the company website. The employee was terminated, but the company owner wanted to make sure that it would not happen again.

The company had started small, and the owner had always used cloud services to help the company grow quickly. The owner had set up cloud services on AWS, and the AWS username and password were stored on the company intranet for people to use when they needed to access AWS for different purposes. We conducted an assessment to identify the tasks that were performed on AWS and the people who performed those tasks.

Originally, the owner had done it all, but now there was a administrator to perform backups, several programmers to create software, a QA team to test the software, and helpdesk personnel to reset passwords and make front-end changes for trouble tickets.

There were also some administrative users who managed payments for the account and a manager who approved new features.

As you can see, there were quite a few different roles, but everyone was using the same account. We provisioned accounts for each person who needed access to AWS. Accounts utilized the user's name as part of the naming convention and users were instructed not to share their passwords with others. The password for the main AWS account was changed, and the owner stored that password in a safe at the company offices. The owner was also issued a named account.

We then created roles for backup operations, development, testing, helpdesk, management, and billing and assigned the necessary AWS policies to each group so that they could do their required tasks. Lastly, we placed the appropriate users into each role.

These are the three categories of authentication that can be combined in multifactor authentication scenarios:

- **Something you know** Knowing your username and password is by far the most common. Knowing your first pet's name, or the PIN for your credit card, or your mother's maiden name all fall into this category.

- **Something you have** Most of us have used a debit or credit card to make a purchase. We must physically have the card in our possession. For VPN authentication, a user would be given a hardware token with a changing numeric code synced with the VPN server. For cloud authentication, users could employ a mobile device authenticator app with a changing numeric code in addition to their username and password.

■ **Something you do**   This measures the particular way that an individual performs a routine task to validate their identity. Handwriting analysis can determine if the user writes their name the same way or the user could be asked to count to 10 and the computer would determine if this is the way they normally count to ten with the appropriate pauses and inflection points.

■ **Someplace you are**   Geolocation is often used as an authentication method along with other methods. The organization may allow employees to access certain systems when they are in the workplace facility, but not from home. Traveling employees might be able to access some resources in the country, but not when traveling internationally.

■ **Something you are**   This is where biometric authentication kicks in. Your fingerprints, your voice, your facial structure, the capillary pattern in your retinas—these are unique to you. Of course, voice impersonators could reproduce your voice, so some methods are more secure than others.

w a t c h   **Knowing both a username and password is not considered multifactor authentication, because they are both "something you know."**

Single Sign-On

As individuals, we have all had to remember multiple usernames and passwords for various software at work, or even at home for multiple websites. Wouldn't it be great if we logged in only once and had access to everything without being prompted to log in again? This is what single sign-on (SSO) is all about!

SSO can take the operating system, VPN, or web browser authentication credentials and present them to the relying party transparently, so the user does not even know it is happening. Modern Windows operating systems use the credential locker as a password vault to store varying types of credentials to facilitate SSO. Enterprise SSO solutions such as the open-source Shibboleth tool or Microsoft Active Directory Federation Services (ADFS) let cloud personnel implement SSO on a large scale. Cloud providers normally offer identity federation services to cloud customers.

The problem with SSO is that different software and websites may use different authentication mechanisms. This makes implementing SSO in a large environment difficult.

CERTIFICATION SUMMARY

This chapter focused on data security, network security, and access control, all of which are of interest to cloud personnel.

As a CompTIA Cloud+ candidate, you must understand the importance of applying best practices to your network. Assessing the network is only effective when comparing your results with an established baseline of normal configuration and activity. Auditing a network is best done by a third party, and you may be required to use only accredited auditors that conform to industry standards such as PCI or SOX. All computing equipment must be patched and hardened to minimize the potential for compromise.

An understanding of data security measures and access control methods is also important for the exam. Data security must be in place both for data as it traverses a network and for stored data. Encrypting data prevents unauthorized access to the data, while digital signatures verify the authenticity of the data. Various encryption protocols are used to accomplish these objectives. The various access control models discussed in this chapter include role-based access control, mandatory access control, and discretionary access control.

KEY TERMS

Use the following list to review the key terms discussed in this chapter. The definitions also can be found in the glossary.

access control entry (ACE)   Specifies the access rights of an individual principal or entity. One or more ACEs are comprised in an ACL.

access control list (ACL)   A list that tracks permitted actions. An ACL for a server might contain the access rights of entities such as users, services, computers, or administrative accounts and whether those rights are permitted or denied, whereas an ACL for a firewall might contain the source address, port, and destination address for authorized communication and deny permissions for all others. ACLs are composed of a set of ACEs.

Advanced Encryption Standard (AES)   An algorithm used to encrypt and decrypt data. Principally, AES uses a 128-bit block and variable key sizes of 128, 192, and 256 bits. It performs 10 to 14 rounds of encryption depending on the key size used.

antimalware software   A piece of software that looks at actions on a system to identify malicious activity.

antivirus software   A piece of software that detects and removes malicious code such as viruses, trojans, worms, and bots.

application programming interface (API)   A structure that exposes functions of an application to other programs.

asymmetric encryption   Encryption mechanism that uses two different keys to encrypt and decrypt data.

authentication, authorization, and accounting (AAA)   The set of processes that determines who a claimant is and what they are allowed to do. These processes also log activity for later auditing.

block cipher   A method of converting plaintext to ciphertext in bulk as opposed to one data bit at a time, either using a fixed secret key or by generating keys from each encrypted block.

certificate authority (CA)   Entity that issues digital certificates and makes its public keys available to the intended audience to provide proof of its authenticity.

certificate revocation list (CRL)   A list managed by a certificate authority (CA) and often published to a public source that describes each certificate that the CA has removed from service so that users and computers know if they should no longer trust a certificate.

ciphertext   Data that has been encrypted using a mathematical algorithm.

command-line interface (CLI)   An interface that is text-based.

data classification   Practice of sorting data into discrete categories that help define the access levels and type of protection required for that set of data.

data encryption   Algorithmic scheme that secures data by scrambling it into a code that is not readable by unauthorized resources.

Data Encryption Standard (DES)   An algorithm used to encrypt and decrypt data. Principally, DES is a symmetric key algorithm that uses block sizes of 64 bits and 16 rounds of encryption.

demilitarized zone (DMZ)   A network segment that has specific security rules on it to segment traffic.

digital signature   Mathematical hash of a dataset that is encrypted by the private key and used to validate that dataset.

discretionary access control (DAC)   Security mechanism in which the power to grant or deny permissions to resources lies with the data owner.

distributed denial of service (DDoS)   An attack that targets a single system simultaneously from multiple compromised systems.

elliptic curve cryptography (ECC) A cryptographic function that allows for smaller keys to be used to provide the same security as those with larger keys through the use of finite field algebraic structure of elliptic curves.

Encapsulating Security Protocol (ESP) A cryptographic function used by IPSec to encrypt tunneled data using PKI certificates or asymmetric keys.

federation Use of single sign-on (SSO) to authorize users or devices to many different protected network resources, such as file servers, websites, and database applications.

Generic Routing Encapsulation (GRE) A lightweight, flexible tunneling protocol that works over IP but does not encrypt data.

host-based intrusion detection system (HIDS) A system that analyzes activity on a host where a HIDS agent is installed for behavior patterns and notifies if patterns match those associated with malicious activity such as hacking or malware.

host-based intrusion prevention system (HIPS) A system that analyzes activity on a host where a HIPS agent is installed for behavior patterns and takes action if patterns match those associated with malicious activity such as hacking or malware.

identity and access management (IAM) The policies, procedures, and technologies required to control access privileges, roles, and rights of users across a heterogeneous enterprise.

Internet Protocol Security (IPSec) A tunneling protocol that secures IP traffic using Encapsulating Security Protocol (ESP) to encrypt the data that is tunneled over it using PKI certificates or asymmetric keys and offers authentication through the Authentication Header (AH) protocol.

intrusion detection and prevention (IDP) A system that analyzes activity for behavior patterns and notifies or takes action if patterns match those associated with malicious activity such as hacking or malware.

key management system (KMS) A system that can issue, validate, distribute, and revoke cryptographic keys. Cloud KMS include such systems as AWS KMS, Microsoft Azure Key Vault, and Oracle Key Manager.

Layer 2 Tunneling Protocol (L2TP) A tunneling protocol that does not offer encryption on its own, but when combined with IPSec offers a high level of encryption at the cost of additional CPU overhead to encapsulate data twice.

mandatory access control (MAC)   Security mechanism in which access is mandated by the operating system or application and not by data owners.

multifactor authentication (MFA)   Authentication of resources using proof from more than one of the five authentication categories: something you know, something you have, something you do, somewhere you are, and something you are.

network address translation (NAT)   A service that consolidates the addresses needed for each internal device to a single valid public IP address, allowing all of the organization's employees to access the Internet with the use of a single public IP address.

network-based intrusion detection system (NIDS)   A system that analyzes activity on a network egress point such as a firewall for behavior patterns and notifies if patterns match those associated with malicious activity such as hacking or malware.

network-based intrusion prevention system (NIPS)   A system that analyzes activity on a network egress point such as a firewall for behavior patterns and takes action if patterns match those associated with malicious activity such as hacking or malware.

plaintext   Unencrypted data.

Point-to-Point Tunneling Protocol (PPTP)   A tunneling protocol that uses GRE and Point-to-Point Protocol (PPP) to transport data using a variety of now outdated protocols. Primarily used with older Microsoft Windows VPN connections.

port address translation (PAT)   A service that maps private IP addresses to public IP addresses to translate multiple devices on a network to a single public IP address using port to IP mappings.

pre-shared key (PSK)   A piece of data that only communication partners know that is used along with a cryptographic algorithm to encrypt communications.

private key   One of two keys used for asymmetric encryption, available only to the intended data user and is used for data decryption and creating digital signatures.

public key   One of two keys used for asymmetric encryption, available to anyone and is used for data encryption and digital signature validation.

public key infrastructure (PKI)   Hierarchy of trusted security certificates issued to users or computing devices.

Rivest Cipher 4 (RC4)   An algorithm used to encrypt and decrypt data. Principally, RC4 is a block cipher that uses symmetric keys up to 128 bits in length for encryption.

Rivest Cipher 5 (RC5)   An algorithm used to encrypt and decrypt data. Principally, RC5 is a block cipher that uses symmetric keys for encryption. RC5 replaces RC4 and supports a cipher strength of up to 2048 bits.

role-based access control (RBAC)   Security mechanism in which all access is granted through predefined collections of permissions, called roles, instead of implicitly assigning access to users or resources individually.

Secure Sockets Layer (SSL)   A cryptographic algorithm that allows for secure communications such as web browsing, FTP, VPN, instant messaging, and VoIP. *See also* Transport Layer Security (TLS).

security information and event management (SIEM)   A system that collects, correlates, and analyzes event logs. SIEM is also known as security incident event manager.

single sign-on (SSO)   Authentication process in which the resource requesting access can enter one set of credentials and use those credentials to access multiple applications or datasets, even if they have separate authorization mechanisms.

spoofing   The modification of the source IP address to obfuscate the original source.

stream cipher   A method of converting plaintext to ciphertext one bit at a time.

symmetric encryption   Encryption mechanism that uses a single key to both encrypt and decrypt data.

task-based access control (TBAC)   Security mechanism in which users have no access to resources by default and are only provided access when they perform a task requiring it. Access is not retained after the task is complete.

Temporal Key Integrity Protocol (TKIP)   A protocol specified in IEEE 802.11i that enhances the WEP/RC4 encryption in wireless networks.

Transport Layer Security (TLS)   A cryptographic algorithm that allows for secure communications such as web browsing, FTP, VPN, instant messaging, and VoIP. TLS replaces the SSL protocol. *See also* Secure Sockets Layer (SSL).

tunnel endpoint   Node that forms encapsulation, de-encapsulation, encryption, and decryption of data in the tunnel. Tunnel endpoints transmit the first packets of encapsulated data that will traverse the intermediary network.

tunneling   The use of encapsulation and encryption to create a secure connection between devices so that intermediary devices cannot read the traffic and so that devices communicating over the tunnel are connected as if on a local network.

tunneling protocol   A network protocol that enables tunneling between devices or sites.

web graphical user interface (GUI)   An interface that is point and click and accessible over the Web.

TWO-MINUTE DRILL

Data Security

- ❑ A public key infrastructure (PKI) is a hierarchy of trusted security certificates that each contain unique public and private key pairs; used for data encryption and verification of data integrity.
- ❑ Ciphertext is the result of feeding plaintext into an encryption algorithm; this is the encrypted data. Block ciphers encrypt chunks of data at a time, whereas the faster stream ciphers encrypt data a binary bit at a time. Stream ciphers are best applied where there is an unknown variable amount of data to be encrypted.
- ❑ Symmetric encryption uses the same secret key for encryption and decryption. The challenge lies in safely distributing the key to all involved parties.
- ❑ Asymmetric encryption uses two mathematically related keys (public and private) to encrypt and decrypt. This implies a PKI. The public and private key pairs contained within a PKI certificate are unique to that subject. Normally, data is encrypted with the recipient's public key, and the recipient decrypts that data with the related private key. It is safe to distribute public keys using any mechanism to the involved parties.
- ❑ A digital signature is a unique value created from the signer's private key and the data to which the signature is attached. The recipient validates the signature using the signer's public key. This assures the recipient that data came from whom it says it came from and that the data has not been tampered with.

Network Security

- ❑ Network security is the practice of protecting the usability, reliability, integrity, and safety of a network infrastructure and also the data traveling along it.
- ❑ Security systems are designed to protect the network against certain types of threats.
- ❑ A firewall is used to control traffic. It performs functions such as NAT/PAT, port and service filtering, DMZ management, stateful packet inspection, and IP spoofing detection.
- ❑ An intrusion detection system (IDS) or an intrusion prevention system (IPS) looks at traffic to identify malicious traffic. IDSs and IPSs differ in how they react to the things they find. An IDS sends alerts and logs suspicious traffic but does not block the traffic. An IPS can send alerts and log, but it can also block, queue, or quarantine the traffic.
- ❑ Application programming interfaces (APIs) are used to expose functions of an application or cloud service to other programs and services.

Access Control

- ❑ Mandatory access control (MAC) is a method of authorization whereby a computer system, based on configured policies, checks user or computer attributes along with data labels to grant access. Data labels might be applied to files or websites to determine who can access that data. The data owner cannot control resource permissions.
- ❑ Discretionary access control (DAC) allows the owner of the data to grant permissions, at their discretion, to users. This is what is normally done in smaller networks where there is a small user base. A larger user base necessitates the use of groups or roles to assign permissions.
- ❑ Non-discretionary access control (NDAC) consists of both role-based access control (RBAC) and task-based access control (TBAC). RBAC is a method of using groups and roles to assign permissions to network resources. This scales well because once groups or roles are given the appropriate permissions to resources, users can simply be made members of the group or role to inherit those permissions. TBAC was created around the concept of least privilege. In TBAC users have no access to resources by default and are only provided access when they perform a task requiring it and access is not retained after the task is complete. TBAC systems provide access just as it is needed and are usually associated with workflows or transactions.
- ❑ Multifactor authentication is any combination of two or more authentication methods stemming from what you know, what you have, what you do, where you are, and what you are. For example, you might have a smartcard and also know the PIN to use it. This is two-factor authentication.

❑ Single sign-on (SSO) requires users to authenticate only once. They are then authorized to use multiple cloud systems without having to log in each time.

❑ Federation allows SSO across multiple cloud systems using a single identity (username and password, for example), even across organizational boundaries.

SELF TEST

The following questions will help you measure your understanding of the material presented in this chapter. As indicated, some questions may have more than one correct answer, so be sure to read all the answer choices carefully.

Data Security

1. You are invited to join an IT meeting where the merits and pitfalls of cloud computing are being debated. Your manager conveys her concerns of data confidentiality for cloud storage. What can be done to secure data stored in the cloud?
   A. Encrypt the data.
   B. Digitally sign the data.
   C. Use a stream cipher.
   D. Change default passwords.

2. Which of the following works best to encrypt variable-length data?
   A. Block cipher
   B. Symmetric cipher
   C. Asymmetric cipher
   D. Stream cipher

3. With PKI, which key is used to validate a digital signature?
   A. Private key
   B. Public key
   C. Secret key
   D. Signing key

4. Which of the following is related to nonrepudiation?
   A. Block cipher
   B. PKI
   C. Symmetric encryption
   D. Stream cipher

Network Security

5. Which service does a firewall use to segment traffic into different zones?
   A. DMZ
   B. ACL
   C. Port/service
   D. NAT/PAT

6. Which device would be used in front of a cloud application to prevent web application attacks such as cross-site scripting (XSS) and SQL injection?
   A. IAM
   B. DLP
   C. WAF
   D. IDS/IPS

7. Which device would be used to identify potentially malicious activity on a network?
   A. IAM
   B. DLP
   C. WAF
   D. IDS/IPS

Access Control

8. Sean configures a web application to allow content managers to upload files to the website. What type of access control model is Sean using?
   A. DAC
   B. MAC
   C. RBAC
   D. GBAC

9. You are the administrator of a Windows network. When creating a new user account, you specify a security clearance level of top secret so that the user can access classified files. What type of access control method is being used?
    A. DAC
    B. MAC
    C. RBAC
    D. GBAC

10. John is architecting access control for a custom application. He would like to implement a non-discretionary access control method that does not rely upon roles. Which method would meet John's criteria?
    A. RBAC
    B. MAC
    C. TBAC
    D. DAC

SELF TEST ANSWERS

Data Security

1. ☑ **A.** Encrypting data at rest protects the data from those not in possession of a decryption key.
    ☒ **B, C,** and **D** are incorrect. Digital signatures verify data authenticity, but they don't deal with the question of confidentiality. Stream ciphers are best used for unpredictable variable-length network transmissions; a block cipher would be better suited for file encryption. While changing default passwords is always relevant, it does nothing to address the concern about data confidentiality.

2. ☑ **D.** Stream ciphers encrypt data, usually a bit at a time, so this works well for data that is not a fixed length.
    ☒ **A, B,** and **C** are incorrect. Symmetric and asymmetric ciphers do not apply in this context. Block ciphers are generally better suited for data blocks of fixed length.

3. ☑ **B.** The public key of the signer is used to validate a digital signature.
    ☒ **A, C,** and **D** are incorrect. Private keys create, and don't validate, digital signatures. A secret key is synonymous with an asymmetric key; PKI is implied when discussing signatures. Signing keys, as they are sometimes called, digitally sign data.

4.   ☑ **B.** PKI is related to nonrepudiation, which means that a verified digital signature proves the message came from the listed party. This is true because only the private key of the signing party could have created the validated signature.
☒ **A, C,** and **D** are incorrect. Block ciphers and stream ciphers are not related to nonrepudiation; they are types of encryption methods. Symmetric encryption excludes the possibility of a PKI, and PKI relates to nonrepudiation.

Network Security

5.   ☑ **A.** A demilitarized zone (DMZ) is a segment that has specific security rules on it. DMZs are created to segment traffic.
☒ **B, C,** and **D** are incorrect. An ACL defines allowed and denied access. Ports and services are used to define filtering rules. NAT/PAT consolidate the addresses needed for each internal device to a single valid public IP address.

6.   ☑ **C.** A web application firewall (WAF) is a specialized type of firewall that screens traffic intended for web applications. WAFs understand common web application attacks such as cross-site scripting (XSS) and SQL injection and can inspect traffic at the application layer of the OSI model.
☒ **A, B,** and **D** are incorrect. Identity and access management (IAM) systems manage entities across an enterprise. Data loss prevention (DLP) is used to restrict the flow of data to authorized parties and devices. IDS/IPS technologies look at traffic to identify malicious traffic.

7.   ☑ **D.** IDS/IPS technologies look at traffic to identify malicious traffic.
☒ **A, B,** and **C** are incorrect. A web application firewall (WAF) is a specialized type of firewall that screens traffic intended for web applications. Identity and access management (IAM) systems manage entities across an enterprise. Data loss prevention (DLP) is used to restrict the flow of data to authorized parties and devices.

Access Control

8.   ☑ **C.** Sean is using a role (content managers) to control who can upload files to the website. This is role-based access control (RBAC).
☒ **A, B,** and **D** are incorrect. DAC allows data owners to grant permissions to users. MAC uses data classification and other attributes so that computer systems can determine who should have access to what. GBAC is not an access control method.

9.   ☑ **B.** Mandatory access control (MAC) uses attributes or labels (such as "top secret") that enable computer systems to determine who should have access to what.
☒ **A, C,** and **D** are incorrect. DAC allows data owners to grant permissions to users. RBAC uses groups and roles so that their members inherit permissions to resources. GBAC is not an access control method.

10.   ☑ **C.** Task-based access control uses tasks instead of roles to determine the level and extent of access.
☒ **A, B,** and **D** are incorrect. RBAC relies on roles to access control decisions and John does not want to rely on roles. MAC and DAC are not non-discretionary access control methods.

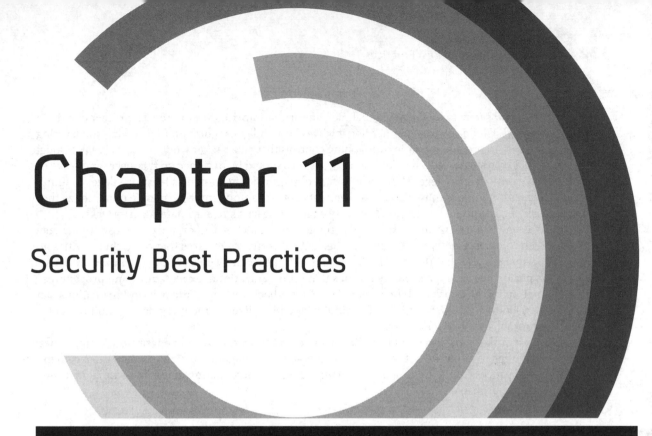

Chapter 11

Security Best Practices

C loud services make it easier for companies to adopt software, systems, and services. However, it can be easy to implement a cloud system that functions well but secures very little. There are some practical steps that can be taken to better secure systems and data in the cloud.

Cloud security engineering includes important information on how to protect cloud systems. Cloud security engineering involves host and guest computer hardening and layering security to provide multiple overlapping controls that an attacker would need to break through to get to systems and data. Additionally, systems should be designed so that users and services have only the privileges they need to function, in what is known as least privilege. Cloud security engineers must also divide elements of tasks among multiple people to minimize the risk of corruption. Lastly, cloud security engineering seeks to automate security tasks.

Security governance is the set of activities and guidelines an organization uses to manage technologies, assets, and employees. Security governance ensures that the right activities are performed and that those activities accomplish the security goals of the organization. This is performed through security policies that set organizational expectations and procedures that define how tasks will be performed. Established industry standards and regulations can be used to craft the right mix of technologies and policies to meet regulatory requirements or established best practices.

Organizations also need to perform vulnerability scanning and penetration testing. These functions together form the basis for vulnerability management. Vulnerability management is the process of identifying possible vulnerabilities and enacting controls to mitigate those that are probable.

CERTIFICATION OBJECTIVE 11.01

Cloud Security Engineering

Cloud security engineering is the practice of protecting the usability, reliability, integrity, and safety of a cloud data and infrastructure and also the users utilizing cloud systems. As it does in many other areas, security in cloud computing has similarities to traditional computing models. If deployed without evaluating security, cloud systems may be able to deliver against its functional requirements, but they will likely have many gaps that could lead to a compromised system.

As part of any cloud deployment, attention needs to be paid to specific security requirements so that the resources that are supposed to have access to data and software in the cloud system are the only resources that can read, write, or change it. This section provides coverage of the following practices and principles employed in cloud security engineering:

- Host and guest computer hardening
- Implementing layered security
- Protecting against availability attacks
- Least privilege
- Separation of duties
- Security automation

Host and Guest Computer Hardening

The hardening of computer systems and networks, whether they are on premises or in the cloud, involves ensuring that the host and guest computers are configured in such a way that reduces the risk of attack from either internal or external sources. While the specific configuration steps for hardening vary from one system to another, the basic concepts involved are largely similar regardless of the technologies that are being hardened. Some of these central hardening concepts are as follows:

- **Remove all software and services that are not needed on the system** Most operating systems and all preloaded systems run applications and services that are not needed by all configurations as part of their default. Systems deployed from standard cloud templates may contain services that are not required for your specific use case. These additional services and applications add to the attack surface of any given system and thus should be removed.

- **Maintain firmware and patch levels** Security holes are continually discovered in both software and firmware, and vendors release patches as quickly as they can to respond to those discoveries. Enterprises as well as cloud providers need to apply these patches to be protected from the patched vulnerabilities.

- **Control account access** Unused accounts should be either disabled or removed entirely from systems. The remaining accounts should be audited to make sure they are necessary and that they have only access to the resources they require. Default accounts should be disabled or renamed, because if hackers are looking to gain unauthorized access to a system and they can guess the username, then they already have half of the necessary information to log into that system.

  For the same reason, all default passwords associated with any system or cloud service should be changed as well. In addition to security threats from malicious users who are attempting to access unauthorized systems or data, security administrators must also beware of the threat from a well-meaning employee who unknowingly accesses resources that shouldn't be made available to them or, worse yet, deletes data that he or she did not intend to remove.

- **Implement the principle of least privilege (POLP)** POLP dictates that users are given only the amount of access they need to carry out their duties and no additional privileges above that for anything else. Protecting against potential insider threats and protecting cloud consumers in a multitenant environment requires that privileged user management be implemented and that security policies follow the POLP.

- **Disable unnecessary network ports** As with software and service hardening, only the required network ports should be enabled to and from servers and cloud services to reduce the attack surface.

■ **Deploy antivirus or antimalware software**   Antivirus or antimalware software should be deployed to all systems that support it. The most secure approach to virus defense is one in which any malicious traffic must pass through multiple layers of detection before reaching its potential target, such as filtering at the perimeter, through e-mail gateways, and then on endpoints such as cloud servers or end-user machines.

■ **Configure logging**   Logging should be enabled on all systems so that if an intrusion is attempted, it can be identified and mitigated or, at the very least, investigated. Cloud logging options can be leveraged to archive logs automatically, conserving space on servers and ensuring that data is available if needed. See Chapter 8 for more information on log automation.

■ **Limit physical access**   If a malicious user has physical access to a network resource, they may have more options for gaining access to that resource. Because of this, limitations that can be applied to physical access should be utilized. Some examples of physical access deterrents are locks on server room doors, network cabinets, and the network devices themselves. Additionally, servers need to be secured at the BIOS level with a password so that malicious users cannot boot to secondary drives and bypass operating system security.

■ **Scan for vulnerabilities**   Once the security configuration steps have been defined and implemented for a system, a vulnerability assessment should be performed using a third-party tool or service provider to make certain no security gaps were missed. Penetration testing can validate whether vulnerabilities are exploitable and whether other security controls are mitigating the vulnerability. Vulnerability scanning and penetration testing are discussed later in this chapter.

■ **Deploy a host-based firewall**   Software firewalls should be deployed to the hosts and guests that will support them. These software firewalls can be configured with access control lists (ACLs), as discussed in Chapter 10, and protection tools in the same fashion as hardware firewalls.

■ **Deactivate default accounts**   Many systems come provisioned with accounts that can be used to set up the software or device initially. The usernames and passwords of such accounts are well known to attackers, so it is best to deactivate these default accounts. Deactivation is better than just changing the password because attackers still know the default username, which gives them one piece of the puzzle even if the password is changed.

Implementing Layered Security

To protect network resources from threats, secure network design employs multiple overlapping controls to prevent unwanted access to protected cloud resources. Some layered security components include demilitarized zones, ACLs, and intrusion detection and prevention systems.

A demilitarized zone (DMZ) is a separate network that is layered in between an internal network and an external network to house resources that need to be accessed by both while preventing direct access from the outside network to the inside network. ACLs define the traffic that is allowed to traverse a network segment. Lastly, intrusion detection systems can detect anomalous network behavior and send alerts to system administrators to take action, while intrusion prevention systems can detect anomalies and take specific actions to remediate threats.

The real strength of demilitarized zones, ACLs, and intrusion detection and prevention systems (covered in Chapter 10) is that they can all be used together, creating a layered security system for the greatest possible security.

Consider an attacker trying to get to a cloud database. The attacker would need to first get through the firewall. A DMZ, along with appropriately configured ACLs, between networks would make the attacker have to compromise a machine in the DMZ and then pivot from that machine to another machine in the internal network. However, networks with IDS/IPS might detect this activity and notify administrators and block the attacker from making the connection. In this way, these technologies work together to provide a layered solution to protect the cloud database.

Protecting Against Availability Attacks

Attacks on availability are those designed to take a system down so that users, such as customers or employees, cannot use it. Some availability attacks are used to cause a system to restart so that weaknesses in the startup routines of the system can be exploited to inject code, start in a maintenance mode and reset passwords, or take other malicious actions.

Distributed Denial of Service (DDoS)

A DDoS attack targets a single system simultaneously from multiple compromised systems. DDoS was introduced back in Chapter 10 under the discussion on firewalls and cloud access security brokers (CASBs), but there are other protections against DDoS.

DDoS attacks are distributed because they use thousands or millions of machines that could be spread across the globe. Such an attack denies services or disrupts availability by overwhelming the system so that it cannot respond to legitimate connection requests. The distributed nature of these attacks makes it difficult for administrators to block malicious traffic based on its origination point and to distinguish approved traffic from attacking traffic. DDoS can quickly overwhelm network resources. However, large cloud systems can offer protection to cloud consumers.

Cloud DDoS protection solutions, such as those from Amazon, Microsoft, Verisign, or Cloudflare, not only protect cloud consumers from attack and loss of availability of resources but also protect against excessive usage charges since many cloud providers charge for how much data is sent and received. Cloud providers offering services such as CASB, introduced in Chapter 10, can screen out some traffic, and they also have the bandwidth to soak up most DDoS traffic without becoming overwhelmed. There have been some high-profile DDoS attacks that caused disruption, such as those committed with Internet of things (IoT) devices that took down large clouds, but most DDoS attacks cannot commit resources at that scale.

Ping of Death (PoD)

PoD attacks send malformed ICMP packets with the intent of crashing systems that cannot process them and consequently shut down. Most modern cloud firewall packages, such as AWS Shield, DigitalOcean, and Zscaler, can actively detect these packets and discard them before they cause damage.

Ping Flood Attacks

Ping flood attacks are similar to DDoS attacks in that they attempt to overwhelm a system with more traffic than it can handle. In this variety, the attack is usually attempted by a single system, which makes the attack easier to identify and block. Defense strategies for ping floods are the same as those for DDoS, including cloud DDoS protection.

Least Privilege

Another important security control is the principle of least privilege. Employees should be granted only the minimum permissions necessary to do their job. No more, no less. Incorporating the principle of least privilege limits potential misuse and risk of accidental mishandling or viewing of sensitive information by unauthorized people.

EXAM AT WORK

Least Privilege in the G Suite

We were asked to help a company determine if they had significant cybersecurity gaps. The company was using Google Docs in the G Suite enterprise for storing departmental data. They used this method instead of an internal department share structure because the workforce was distributed and often collaborated on work remotely.

Our auditors reviewed the configuration and found that all employees had access to the G Suite and all documents contained within. In discussions with the business owner, we explained the concept of least privilege and how easy it is to set up access permissions in the G Suite. However, we were told that they trusted each employee and were not concerned about it.

We then audited the users who had accessed files and found that some employees in design had been accessing information on customers. We also found that an employee in marketing had accessed HR data. We presented this to the business owner and she agreed that it was best not to tempt her employees with access to more information than they needed.

We worked out a data map for the information on the G Suite and outlined permissions for each role. We then showed administrators how to implement the permissions.

In the scenario described in the "Exam at Work" sidebar, least privilege would prevent employees from accidentally viewing salary data on other employees, which could cause morale problems and conflict. Least privilege also prevents employees from stealing that information and prevents malware from corrupting or encrypting the information using the user's credentials.

Separation of Duties

Separation of duties, also known as segregation of duties, divides the responsibilities required to perform a sensitive task among two or more people so that one person, acting alone, cannot compromise the system. Separation of duties needs to be carefully planned and implemented. If implemented correctly, it can act as an internal control to help reduce potential damage caused by the actions of a single administrator.

By limiting permissions and influence over key parts of the cloud environment, no one individual can knowingly or unknowingly exercise full power over the system. For example, in an e-commerce organization with multiple layers of security comprised in a series of cloud solutions, separation of duties would ensure that a single person would not be responsible for every layer of that security, such as provisioning accounts, implementing ACLs, and configuring logging and alerting for the various cloud services and their integrations. Therefore, if that person were to become disgruntled, they would not have the ability to compromise the entire system or the data it contains; they would only have the ability to access their layer of the security model.

Security Automation

The last part of cloud security engineering is to automate security tasks. Security tasks must be performed at regular intervals, and it is important that they be performed each time correctly. Additionally, it can be quite a job to secure a large number of systems, and organizational security departments are supporting more systems and cloud services than ever before.

Security automation helps in both these areas. Automation ensures that tasks are performed the same way every time and that they are performed precisely on schedule. Furthermore, automation frees up valuable security resources so that they can focus on other tasks. Automation uses scripting, scheduled tasks, and automation tools to perform routine tasks so that IT staff can spend more time solving the real problems and proactively looking for ways to make things better and even more efficient.

This section discusses different security activities that can be automated to save time and standardize. They include the following:

- Disabling inactive accounts
- Eliminating outdated firewall rules
- Cleaning up outdated security settings
- Maintaining ACLs for target objects

Disabling Inactive Accounts

You can automate the disabling of inactive accounts. Use this quite sparingly because disabling an account will mean that the user cannot log in anymore. Choose to disable rather than remove an account, because once you remove an account, creating it again is somewhat difficult. If you create another account with the same name, it will still have a different security identifier and will not really be the same account. That is why it is best to disable accounts first, and then at some later point, you can remove the account. Disabling is also important in case you need to take action on that account in the future, such as decrypting EFS encrypted files, viewing profile settings, or logging onto that person's e-mail. These are things that might need to be done for a terminated employee if that employee is under investigation; if the account were deleted, they would still be possible but a bit more difficult.

The following PowerShell script disables all accounts that have not been logged into for over 30 days. Of course, if you were in Europe, some people take a holiday for longer than 30 days, but you can always enable the account when the person returns.

```
Search-ADAccount -AccountInactive -TimeSpan ([timespan]30d)
-UsersOnly | Set-ADUser -Enabled $false -WhatIf
```

Eliminating Outdated Firewall Rules

It is possible through the course of adding and removing programs or changing server roles that the Windows Firewall rules for a virtual machine could become out of date. It can be difficult to automate the analysis of the rules and removal of outdated rules, so the best course of action is to remove all rules and reassign rules based on the current roles.

As mentioned many times in this book, it is imperative to document. Document the firewall rules that you put in place for virtual machines and organize the rules by role. For example, you would have one set of standard rules for database servers, web servers, file servers, domain controllers, certificate servers, VPN servers, FTP servers, DHCP servers, and a separate role for each type of application server.

Each of the firewall rules for a defined role can be scripted. Here is an example configuration for a virtual machine with the database role running Microsoft SQL Server 2016 with Analysis Services. This script allows remote management and communication over SQL Server ports. The last commands turn the firewall on, just in case it is not already on.

```
New-NetFirewallRule -DisplayName "SQL Database Management" -Direction Inbound -
Protocol UDP -LocalPort 1434 -Action allow
New-NetFirewallRule -DisplayName "SQL Server" -Direction Inbound -Protocol TCP -
LocalPort 1433 -Action allow
New-NetFirewallRule -DisplayName "SQL Service Broker" -Direction Inbound -
Protocol TCP -LocalPort 4022 -Action allow
New-NetFirewallRule -DisplayName "SQL Debugger/RPC" -Direction Inbound -Protocol
TCP -LocalPort 135 -Action allow
New-NetFirewallRule -DisplayName "SQL Analysis Services" -Direction Inbound -
Protocol TCP -LocalPort 2383 -Action allow
New-NetFirewallRule -DisplayName "SQL Browser" -Direction Inbound -Protocol TCP
-LocalPort 2382 -Action allow
New-NetFirewallRule -DisplayName "SQL Admin Connection" -Direction Inbound -
Protocol TCP -LocalPort 1434 -Action allow
New-NetFirewallRule -DisplayName "SQL Server Browse Button Service" -Direction
Inbound -Protocol UDP -LocalPort 1433 -Action allow
Set-NetFirewallProfile -DefaultInboundAction Block -DefaultOutboundAction Allow
-NotifyOnListen True -AllowUnicastResponseToMulticast True
```

Now, with the role descriptions and the scripts in hand, you can clear the configurations from a set of servers whose rules you believe are outdated and then you can reapply the company standard firewall rules for that role. Here is the command to clear the rules from the server. Essentially, this command resets the Windows Firewall to its default out-of-the-box settings.

```
netsh advfirewall reset
```

Please note that the firewall configuration formerly used just the netsh command but this command was deprecated. The new command is netsh advfirewall.

Firewalls are covered in more detail in the "Network Security" section of Chapter 10.

Cleaning Up Outdated Security Settings

VMware vSphere can be made much more secure by turning off some features for virtual machines. The first feature to disable is host guest file system (HGFS) file transfers. HGFS transfers files into the operating system of the virtual machine directly from the host, and a hacker or malware could potentially misuse this feature to download malware onto a guest or to exfiltrate data from the guest. Script these commands for each virtual machine:

```
keyword = isolation.tools.hgfsServerSet.disable
keyval = TRUE
```

The next feature to disable is the ability to copy and paste data between the remote console and the virtual machine. This is disabled by default, but in case someone turned it on, you can disable it again. Enabling copy and paste can allow for sensitive content to accidentally be placed on another machine. Script these commands for each virtual machine:

```
keyword = isolation.tools.copy.disable
keyval = TRUE
keyword = isolation.tools.paste.disable
keyval = TRUE
keyword = isolation.tools.setGUIOptions.enable
keyval = FALSE
Limiting Exposure of Sensitive Data Copied to the Clipboard
keyword = isolation.tool.copy.disable
keyval = TRUE
keyword = isolation.tool.paste.disable
keyval = TRUE
```

The third item to disable is the ability for a user to disconnect VMware devices from the virtual machine. When this is turned on, administrative users on the virtual machine can run commands to disconnect devices such as network adapters, hard disk drives, and optical drives. Script these commands for each virtual machine:

```
keyword = isolation.device.connectable.disable
keyval = TRUE
keyword = isolation.device.edit.disable
keyval = TRUE
```

The fourth item to disable is the ability of processes running in the virtual machine to send configuration messages to the hypervisor. Processes on the virtual machine that modify configuration settings can potentially damage the virtual machine or cause it to be unstable. Script these commands for each virtual machine:

```
keyword = isolation.tools.setinfo.disable
keyval = TRUE
```

Maintaining ACLs for Target Objects

You can script setting access control lists for objects by using the cacls command. ACL scripting can be very useful if you want to change permissions for a large number of files and folders. Here is the command to give a group called DevOps full control to the D:\ drive and all subfolders:

```
CACLS D:\ /E /T /C /G "DevOps":F
```

Security Governance and Strategy

Attackers keep coming up with new attacks, so the line for security best practices continues to move. There are a variety of government agencies and standards bodies that publish security best practices and standards such as the ISO/IEC 27001 or NIST SP 800-53. These can give an organization some guidance on security governance practices and valuable security strategies, but each organization needs to determine for itself what is appropriate for its security based on its specific operations.

Implementing a practice just because it is listed in a standard might improve security, but it might not improve it as much as something else. Budgets are tight, so it is crucial to choose the security controls that will give your organization the best protection for your budget. This section covers best practices for governance and strategy. This text has organized these best practices into the following sections:

- Developing company security policies
- Account management policies
- Documenting security procedures
- Assessment and auditing
- Leveraging established industry standards and regulations
- Applying platform-specific security standards
- Data classification
- Keeping employees and tools up to date
- Roles and responsibilities

Developing Company Security Policies

Security policies set the organizational expectations for certain functional security areas. Policies should be defined based on what the organization is committed to doing, not on what it might do, because once a policy is put in place, others will expect the company to adhere to it. Policies usually come with sanctions for those who do not follow the policy, such as oral or written warnings, coaching, suspensions from work, or termination.

Security policies often use the terms personally identifiable information (PII) and personal health information (PHI). PII is information that represents the identity of a person, such as name, phone number, address, e-mail address, Social Security number, and date of birth. PHI is similar to PII in the context of patient identity but is used in HIPAA compliance and other similar areas. The term PII is common in security polices of many types of organization, whereas PHI is common is security policies of healthcare organizations. Both terms are used in security policies to designate information that must not be disclosed to anyone who is not authorized to access it.

Some common security policies include the following:

- **Acceptable use policy**   States how organizational assets are to be used. This policy covers use of organizational equipment such as computers, laptops, phones, and office equipment. More importantly, it covers which cloud and other Internet services employees can use, acceptable norms for e-mail, and use of social networking.

- **Audit policy**   Specifies how often audits are to occur, the differences between internal and external audits, who should handle audits, how they are reported on, and the level of access granted to auditors. Both internal and external audits would cover internal systems and cloud systems used by the company. The audit policy also covers how audit findings and exceptions are to be handled.

- **Backup policy**   Covers how the organization will back up the data that it has. This includes both data on premise and in the cloud. The backup policy usually includes who is responsible for backing up data, how often backups will take place, the data types that will be backed up, and the recovery time objective (RTO) and recovery point objective (RPO) for each data type.

- **BYOD policy**   Specifies how employee-owned devices are to be used within the company and how they can be used if they access company cloud services and data.

- **Cloud services policy**   Defines which cloud services are acceptable for organizational use, how cloud services are evaluated, who is authorized to purchase cloud services, and how employees suggest or recommend cloud services to the review committee.

- **Data destruction policy**   Outlines how the organization will handle disposal of equipment that houses data, such as computers, servers, and hard drives. It should specify how that data will be wiped or destroyed, what evidence will be retained on the disposal or destruction, and who is authorized to dispose of assets. This includes not only digital data, but physical documents as well so these documents must be shredded when the policy requires it.

- **Data retention policy**   Specifies how long data of different types will be kept on organizational systems or cloud systems the organization utilizes. For example, the data retention policy may specify that e-mail on Office 365 will be retained for two years, financial documents on SAP S/4HANA will be retained for seven years, and other data will be retained for one year.

- **Encryption policy**   Specifies what should be encrypted in the organization and in cloud systems used by the organization, how encryption systems are evaluated, which cryptographic algorithms are acceptable, how cryptographic keys are managed, and how keys are disposed of.

- **Incident response policy**   Specifies the expectations for how long it will take to respond to an incident, recovery times, investigation times, who the members are of the incident response team, how employees are to notify the team of incident indicators, what are the indicators of an incident, and how the team will vet incidents.

Data may need to be retrieved from multiple cloud vendors so the incident response policy will specify how that will take place and the expectations of the cloud provider and the cloud consumer in an incident.

---

e x a m

w a t c h　　The incident response plan must factor in the communication and coordination activities with each cloud provider. This can add significant time to an incident response timeline.

- **Mobile device policy**　Specifies which types of mobile devices can be used for organizational purposes, who authorizes mobile devices, how those devices are to be protected, where they can be used, which cloud services can be accessed by mobile devices, how they are encrypted, and how organizational data will be removed from mobile devices when they are retired or when employees leave.
- **Privacy policy**　Includes what information the organization considers private, how the organization will handle that information, the purposes and uses of that information, and how that information will be collected, destroyed, or returned.
- **Remote access policy**　Specifies which types of remote access are acceptable, how remote access will take place, how employees are authorized for remote access, auditing of remote access, and how remote access is revoked.

There are hundreds of other policies that can be defined for more granular things. However, best practice is to keep the number of policies to the minimum necessary so that employees can easily find the organization's expectations regarding a particular subject.

Some organizations choose to bundle policies together into a handbook or a comprehensive security policy. Compliance requirements may specify which policies an organization needs to have and the minimum requirements for those policies. Be aware of which compliance requirements your organization falls under so that you can make sure your policies are in accordance with those requirements.

Account Management Policies

Account management policies establish expectations on how accounts and their associated credentials will be managed. Some simpler policies will be called a password policy. These policies deal only with the password elements of the account management policy and are often used when granularity on password requirements is needed.

---

e x a m

w a t c h　　Account management policies and password policies should apply to organizational systems and cloud systems that house organizational data.

Account management policies stipulate how long passwords need to be and how often they should be changed. They also specify who should be issued an account and how accounts are issued to users. This includes which approvals are necessary for provisioning an account. There may be rare cases where a password can be shared and account management policies will specify these circumstances, if any. These policies also establish requirements for how and when temporary passwords are issued, and the process for how and when passwords can be reset.

Two other sections in the account management policy require a bit more attention. They include the lockout policy and password complexity rules. These are covered next in their own sections.

Lockout Policy

A lockout is the automatic disabling of an account due to some potentially malicious action. The most common reason for a lockout is too many incorrect password attempts. Lockout policy can be specified on a per-resource basis or a per-domain basis. When single sign-on (SSO) is used, a single lockout policy also applies.

When a user's password is entered incorrectly too many times, either by the user or by an unauthorized person, the system will disable the user's account for a predefined period. In some cases, the account is disabled until an administrator unlocks it. Another system can be configured to lock out the account for a set amount of time that increases each time the account is subsequently locked out, until a point when an administrator is required to unlock the account again.

You may wish to notify on account lockouts. For example, if you have a cloud-based application, you may want to send users an e-mail when they enter their password incorrectly too many times. This way, if someone else tries to log on as the user, the authorized user will become aware of the attempt and can report that it was not authorized. Systems can be configured to automatically notify users when their account is locked out. Otherwise, users will find out their account is locked out when they are unable to log in.

Password Complexity Rules

Stealing or cracking passwords is one of the most common ways that attackers infiltrate a network and break into systems. People generally choose weak passwords because passwords are hard to remember. Most people try to create a password using information that is easy for them to remember, and the easiest thing to remember is something you already know, such as your address, phone number, children's names, or workplace. But this is also information that can be learned about you easily, so it is a bad choice for a password.

Password complexity has to do with how hard a password would be to break with brute force techniques, where the attacker tries all possible combinations of a password until they get the right one. If you look at just numbers, there are four combinations in a two-character password, while there are eight combinations in a three-character password.

Numbers alone are the easiest to break because there are only ten combinations for each digit (0–9). When you add letters into the mix, this creates more possibilities for the brute force attack to factor in. Special characters such as @#$%^&*&(() expand that scope even further. The best passwords are ones that you can remember, but that are unrelated to anything someone would be able to figure out about you and unrelated to any security questions you may have answered. They should also contain numbers, uppercase and lowercase letters, and special characters.

For those with multiple-language keyboards and application support, a password that combines multiple character systems such as Chinese or Russian can make it even harder to crack.

Security practitioners have for decades tried to find a balance between password complexity and usability. On the one hand, stronger passwords are harder to guess and more difficult to brute force crack. However, these more complex passwords are harder to remember. This can lead users to circumvent best practices by writing passwords down.

Similarly, frequent change intervals can cause users to construct passwords that follow specific patterns such as Fire$ale4Dec in December, Fire$ale4Jan in January, and so forth. Since users have so many passwords to remember, some use the same password in many places and change them all at the same time. However, when a data breach occurs in one location, the usernames and passwords are often put in a database that attackers use to determine other likely passwords. In this example, the attacker might breach the database at the end of December but then the user changes their passwords. An attacker reviewing the database in April would likely try Fire$ale4Apr and gain access to the system if the user continued with their pattern.

NIST has recognized these weaknesses in their special publication 800-63B. Here are some of the new guidelines. First, increase the maximum password length to at least 64 characters. Along with this, NIST recommends that password fields allow spaces and other printable characters in passwords. These two changes allow users to create longer, but more natural, passwords.

NIST has also relaxed some of the complexity rules and recommends that companies require just one uppercase, number, or symbol, not all three, and that passwords be kept longer with less frequent change intervals.

NIST also adds some requirements. They recommend that two-factor authentication be used and they exclude SMS as a valid two-factor authentication method because of the ability for others to potentially obtain the unencrypted SMS authentication data. They also require that passwords be measured for how common and easy to guess they are. Authentication systems should restrict users from creating passwords that contain simple dictionary words, common phrases, or easily guessed information.

Documenting Security Procedures

Security policies specify the company's expectations and provide general guidance for what to do, but they do not get into the specifics. This is where security procedures step in. Documenting procedures was covered in more detail in Chapter 9 so please review that section if this is unfamiliar to you. Security procedures outline the individual steps required to complete a task. Furthermore, security procedures ensure that those who follow the procedures will do the following:

- Perform the task consistently.
- Take a predictable amount of time to perform the task.
- Require the same resources each time the task is performed.

Assessment and Auditing

A network assessment is an objective review of an organization's network infrastructure regarding current functionality and security capabilities. The environment is evaluated holistically against industry best practices and its ability to meet the organization's requirements. Once all the assessment information has been documented, it is stored as a baseline for future audits to be performed against.

Complete audits must be scheduled on a regular basis to make certain that the configurations of all network resources are not changed in such a way that increases the risk to the environment or the organization.

Internal Audits

Internal audit teams validate that security controls are implemented correctly and that security systems are functioning as expected. Companies operate today in an environment of rapid change and this increased frequency of change can result in an increase in mistakes leading to security issues. Internal audits can help catch these issues before they are exploited.

Take, for example, the technologies that enable administrators to move virtual machines between hosts with no downtime and minimal administrative effort. Because of this, some cloud environments have become extremely volatile. A side effect of that volatility is that the security posture of a guest on one cloud may not be retained when it has been migrated to a different, yet compatible, cloud. The audit team would have a specification of what the security posture should look like and they would use that to determine if the machine met the requirements after being moved to the new cloud.

A change management system can help identify changes in an environment, but initial baseline assessments and subsequent periodic audits are critical. Such evaluations make it possible for administrators to correlate performance logs on affected systems with change logs, so they can identify configuration errors that may be causing problems. Change management will be covered in more detail in Chapter 13.

Utilizing Third-Party Audits

When assessing or auditing a network, it is best practice to use a third-party product or service provider. Using external resources is preferable to using internal resources, as the latter often have both preconceived biases and preexisting knowledge about the network and security configuration.

Familiarity with the environment can produce unsuccessful audits because the internal resources already have an assumption about the systems they are evaluating, and those assumptions result in either incomplete or incorrect information. A set of eyes from an outside source not only eliminates the familiar as a potential hurdle but also allows for a different (and in many cases, greater) set of skills to be utilized in the evaluation.

The results of an unbiased third-party audit are more likely to hold up under scrutiny. Many regulations and standards stipulate third-party audits.

Leveraging Established Industry Standards and Regulations

As cloud computing has become ubiquitous, various standards for best practice deployments of cloud computing infrastructures have been developed. Standards have been established to improve the quality of IT organizations. Some examples of standards include the Information Technology Infrastructure Library (ITIL) and the Microsoft Operations Framework (MOF).

Regulations specify security requirements for business systems and clouds. Non-compliance with regulations can lead to fines or the inability to do business in that industry or in the currency capacity. Some regulations include the Payment Card Industry Data Security Standard (PCI DSS), the Sarbanes–Oxley Act (SOX), and the Health Insurance Portability and Accountability Act (HIPAA). Regulatory compliance is more expensive for IT organizations than adhering to a set of standards or best practices. Regulatory compliance requires not only for the organization to build solutions according to the regulatory requirements, but also to demonstrate compliance to auditors. The tools and labor required to generate the necessary proof can be costly.

In addition to adopting published best practices, organizations can implement one of the many tools available that can raise alerts when a deviation from these compliance frameworks is identified.

Applying Platform-Specific Security Standards

Many vendors have released their own security standards or device configuration guides. It is a good idea to follow the recommendations from these vendors. After all, Cisco created Cisco switches, so who better to recommend how to configure them? Seek out the configuration guides for the equipment you have and audit your device against those security guidelines.

Some vendors release multiple guidelines that are customized for different needs. For example, you may want to harden web application servers, so you look to your web hosting provider for guidance. However, they might offer different guidelines on how to configure the server for HIPAA, PCI DSS, NIST, or their general security best practice or hardening guide. Which one you choose depends on which compliance areas you need to adhere to.

Data Classification

Data classification is the practice of sorting data into discrete categories that help define the access levels and type of protection required for that set of data. These categories are then used to determine the disaster recovery mechanisms, cloud technologies required to store the data, and the placement of that data onto physically or logically separated storage resources.

The process for data classification can be divided into four steps that can be performed by teams within an organization. The first step is to identify the present data within the organization. Next, the data should be grouped into areas with similar sensitivity and availability needs. The third step is to define classifications for each unique sensitivity and availability requirement. The last step is to determine how the data will be handled in each classification.

Here are some of the different types of data that an organization would classify into categories such as public, trade secret, work product, financial data, customer data, strategic information, and employee data:

- Account ledgers
- Application development code
- Bank statements
- Change control documentation
- Client or customer deliverables
- Company brochures
- Contracts and SLAs
- Customer data
- HR records
- Network schematics
- Payroll
- Press releases
- Process documentation
- Project plans
- Templates
- Website content

Keeping Employees and Tools Up to Date

The rapidly evolving landscape of cloud technologies and virtualization presents dangers for cloud security departments that do not stay abreast of changes to both their toolsets and their training. Companies can use new virtualization technologies and tools to more rapidly deploy new software, leading to an acceleration of software development activities in fast-forward-type deployments, known as rapid deployment. See Chapter 9 for more details.

One hazard of rapid deployment is the propensity to either ignore security or proceed with the idea that the organization will enable functionality for the system immediately, then circle back and improve the security once it is in place. Typically, however, the requests for new functionality continue to take precedence and security is rarely or inadequately revisited.

Many networks were initially designed to utilize traditional network security devices that monitor traffic and devices on a physical network. If the intra-virtual-machine traffic that those tools are watching for never routes through a physical network, it cannot be monitored by that traditional toolset. The problem with limiting network traffic to guests within the host is that if the tools are not virtualization or cloud aware, they will not provide the proper information to make a diagnosis or even to suggest changes to the infrastructure. Therefore, it is critical that monitoring and management toolsets (including cloud-based CLIs) are updated as frequently as the technology that they are designed to control.

Roles and Responsibilities

Security is a complex discipline and involves securing a variety of components, including applications, storage, network connectivity, and server configuration. There are many different security functions, security controls, and security technologies, so it is unlikely that a single person will able to handle all of the company's security needs. It is also important to evaluate methods for implementing separation of duties, introduced earlier in this chapter, by splitting the responsibilities of those managing security procedures among various people.

There are some benefits to having a different person in charge of each facet of the cloud security environment. Having different people running different configuration tests creates a system of checks and balances since not just one person has ultimate control. For example, a programmer would be responsible for verifying all of the code within their application and for making sure there are no security risks in the code itself, but the programmer would not be responsible for the web server or database server that is hosting or supporting the application. The person testing code security should be different from the person who wrote the code. Likewise, the person testing cloud service integration security should not be the person who configured it.

CERTIFICATION OBJECTIVE 11.03

Vulnerability Management

In addition to comprehensive testing of all areas affecting service and performance, it is incumbent on an organization to test for vulnerabilities as well. Security testing in the cloud is a critical part of having an optimal cloud environment. It is very similar to security testing in a traditional environment in that testing involves components like login security and the security layer in general.

Before doing any security tests, testers should always clearly define the scope, present it to the system owner, and get written permission to proceed. The contract that is in place with the cloud provider should then be reviewed to determine testing notification requirements. Inform the cloud provider of any planned security penetration testing prior to actually performing it unless the contract specifies otherwise.

Another thing for an organization to consider is that with a public cloud model, the organization does not own the infrastructure; therefore, the environment the resources are hosted in may not be all that familiar. For example, if you have an application that is hosted in a public cloud environment, that application might make some application programming interface (API) calls back into your data center via a firewall, or the application might be entirely hosted outside of your firewall.

Another primary security concern when using a cloud model is who has access to the organization's data in the cloud and what are the concerns and consequences if that data is lost or stolen. Being able to monitor and test access to that data is a primary responsibility of the cloud administrator and should be taken seriously, as a hosted account may not have all the proper security implemented. For example, a hosted resource might be running an older version of system software that has known security issues, so keeping up with the security for the hosted resource and the products that are running on those resources is vital.

Security testing should be performed on a regular basis to ensure consistent and timely cloud and network vulnerability management. Periodic security testing will reveal newly discovered vulnerabilities and recent configuration issues, enabling administrators to remediate them before (hopefully) attackers have an opportunity to exploit them.

Common testing scenarios include quarterly penetration testing with monthly vulnerability scanning or annual penetration testing with quarterly or monthly vulnerability scanning. It is absolutely necessary to run tests at intervals specified by compliance requirements. Testing should also be conducted whenever the organization undergoes significant changes.

Cloud vendors typically require notification before penetration testing is conducted on their networks. Microsoft Azure recently announced that it no longer requires such notification. Check with your cloud vendor before conducting vulnerability scanning or penetration testing to be sure you have permission.

In this section, you will learn about the following vulnerability management concepts:

- Black-box, gray-box, and white-box testing
- Vulnerability scanning
- Penetration testing
- Vulnerability management roles and responsibilities

Testing Methods

The three basic types of security testing in a cloud environment are known as black-box, gray-box, and white-box testing. They differ based on the amount of information the tester has about the targets before starting the test. When performing a black-box test, the tester knows as little as possible about the system, similar to a real-world hacker. Black-box testing is a good method, as it simulates a real-world attack and uncovers vulnerabilities that are discoverable even by someone who has no prior knowledge of the environment. However, it may not be right for all scenarios, because of the additional expense required for research and reconnaissance. Two other options are available: gray-box and white-box testing.

When performing gray-box testing, the test team begins with some information on the targets, usually what attackers would reasonably be assumed to find out through research, such as the list of target IP addresses, public DNS records, and public-facing URLs. Roles and configurations are not provided to the testing team in a gray-box test. Gray-box testing can be a cost-effective solution if one can reasonably assume that information such as the list of target IP addresses, public DNS records, and public-facing URLs would be obtained by an attacker. Gray-box testing is faster and cheaper than black-box testing because some research and reconnaissance work is reduced, but it is somewhat more expensive than white-box testing.

White-box testing is done with an insider's view and can be much faster than black-box or gray-box testing. White-box testing makes it possible to focus on specific security concerns the organization may have because the tester spends less time figuring out which systems are accessible, their configurations, and other parameters.

Since testing is typically done at regular intervals, companies often perform black-box testing the first time and then perform gray- or white-box testing after that, assuming the testing team already knows the information gained from the first black-box test.

Vulnerability Scanning

Vulnerability scanning is the process of discovering flaws or weaknesses in systems and applications. These weaknesses can range anywhere from host and service misconfiguration to insecure application design. Vulnerability scanning can be performed manually, but it is common to use a vulnerability scanning application to perform automated testing.

Automated vulnerability scanning utilizes software to probe a target system. The vulnerability scanning software will send connection requests to a computer and then monitor the responses it receives. It may insert different data types into web forms and analyze the results. This allows the software to identify potential weaknesses in the system.

Vulnerability scanning includes basic reconnaissance tools such as port scanning, a process that queries each TCP/UDP port on a system to see if it is capable of receiving data; footprinting, the process of enumerating the computers or network devices on a target network; and fingerprinting, a process that determines the operating system and software running on a device.

Management may review the vulnerabilities and make determinations as to which ones they want to remediate and who will be responsible for remediation. The vulnerability remediation request (VRR) is a formal request to make a change to an application or system to remediate a known vulnerability.

Vulnerabilities are ranked with industry standards such as the Common Vulnerability Scoring System (CVSS) numbers for vulnerability scoring. These rankings have a risk score associated with them, and the CVSS numbers can be used to find additional threat and remediation information on the vulnerability in the national vulnerability database (NVD).

This remainder of this section discusses the phases, tools, and scope options for vulnerability scanning.

Phases

The vulnerability scanning process is organized into three phases: intelligence gathering, vulnerability assessment, and vulnerability validation. The phases are shown in Figure 11-1.

Intelligence Gathering   A vulnerability scanning project begins by gathering information about the targets. Intelligence gathering is a phase of information gathering that consists of passive and active reconnaissance. Depending on your level of knowledge of the targets, this step may not be necessary.

Vulnerability Assessment   The second phase is vulnerability assessment. Vulnerability scanning tools are used at this stage to scan targets for common weaknesses such as outdated or unpatched software, published vulnerabilities, and weak configurations. The vulnerability assessment then measures the potential impact of discovered vulnerabilities. Identified vulnerabilities are classified according to CVSS numbers for vulnerability scoring.

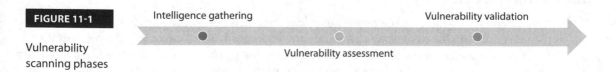

FIGURE 11-1

Vulnerability
scanning phases

Intelligence gathering

Vulnerability assessment

Vulnerability validation

Vulnerability Validation   Automated scans alone do not represent a complete picture of the vulnerabilities present on the target machines. Automated scans are designed to be nondisruptive, so they tend to err on the side of caution when identifying the presence of security weaknesses. As a result, conditions which outwardly appear to be security flaws—but which in fact are not exploitable—are sometimes identified as being vulnerabilities. It takes experience in interpreting a tool's reports, as well as knowledge of the system, to identify vulnerabilities that are likely exploitable.

Some vulnerability validation can be performed with automated tools. Such automation reduces the manual testing burden, but there will still be cases where manual validation is required to ensure a quality deliverable. Tools are discussed in the next section.

Tools

A wide variety of tools can be used to perform intelligence gathering and vulnerability assessment. Testers will likely use most of the intelligence gathering tools to gather information about their targets. Snmpwalk uses SNMP messages to obtain information on targets through their MIB data. See Chapter 7 for more information on SNMP. Fierce is used to find internal and external IP addresses for a target DNS name.

Sam Spade is a tool that combines a number of command-line functions together. These functions include Whois, a command that identifies the owner of a domain name; ping, a tool that tests to determine if a host is responding to ICMP packets; IPBlock, a tool that performs whois operations on a block of IP addresses; dig, a command that obtains resource records for a domain (see Chapter 14); traceroute, a command that identifies each hop from source to destination (see Chapter 14); and finger, a tool that obtains information on the user logged into a target machine. Please note that finger has been disabled on most machines for years now, so this tool is unlikely to work on targets today, but it remains in the Sam Spade suite of tools.

Nmap, Zenmap, and Unicornscan are each used to map a network by identifying the hosts that are online, the operating system they are running, installed applications, and security configuration such as host-based firewalls.

Some of the vulnerability assessment tools are specific for certain cloud applications. For example, the Amazon Inspector would be used for AWS servers, while the Microsoft Azure Security Center would be used for servers in an Azure environment. Nessus, Nexpose, OpenVAS, and Security Center can scan cloud systems or on-premise systems. Of the four, OpenVAS is open source and available for free. OpenVAS is an excellent tool to use to get familiar with the process.

Table 11-1 lists some of the tools along with their uses. A wide variety of the tools listed are open source. Some Linux distributions come with a large number of security tools preinstalled. The most popular security distribution is Kali, but others such as DEFT, Caine, Pentoo, Samurai Web Testing Framework, and Parrot Security offer similarly valuable tool sets, albeit with a somewhat different interface. These Linux security distributions can be

TABLE 11-1	Vulnerability Scanning Tools	

Tool	Purpose	Phase
snmpwalk	SNMP enumeration	Intelligence gathering
fierce	DNS discovery	Intelligence gathering
Sam Spade	Network reconnaissance	Intelligence gathering
Nmap	Network mapping	Intelligence gathering
Zenmap	Network mapping	Intelligence gathering
Unicornscan	Network mapping	Intelligence gathering
Microsoft Azure Security Center	Vulnerability scanning	Vulnerability assessment
OpenVAS	Vulnerability scanning	Vulnerability assessment
Nikto	Application vulnerability scanning	Vulnerability assessment
Amazon Inspector	Vulnerability scanning	Vulnerability assessment
WPScan	WordPress vulnerability scanning	Vulnerability assessment
Nessus	Vulnerability scanning	Vulnerability assessment
Nexpose	Vulnerability scanning	Vulnerability assessment
Google Cloud Security Scanner	Vulnerability scanning	Vulnerability assessment
Tenable SecurityCenter	Vulnerability scanning	Vulnerability assessment

used as a bootable DVD or can be installed on a system for permanent use. Linux security distributions contain hundreds of security tools, including many for penetration testing, vulnerability scanning, network analysis, and computer forensics.

Scope

A vulnerability scan can cover different scopes such as external scanning, internal scanning, web application scanning, or a combination of them. External scanning is conducted from outside the company's internal network, on nodes that are web-facing such as web servers, e-mail servers, FTP servers, and VPN servers.

Internal vulnerability scanning, on the other hand, is conducted from within the company network, targeting servers, workstations, and other devices on the corporate network. In both internal and external testing, web applications need close attention, as there can be significant variations in how each application works depending on its purpose and role. For example, an enterprise resource planning (ERP) system functions much differently than an asset tracking system. The ERP system has many more interconnections and is functionally more complex than the asset tracking system, just to name some of the differences.

Scans can also be performed through services offered by the cloud provider such as Microsoft Azure Security Center, Google Cloud Security Scanner, or Amazon Inspector. Some of these tools are built to scan the types of systems that reside on the cloud vendor's systems, while others are more flexible. For example, Google Cloud Security Scanner scans Google App Engine apps for vulnerabilities, while Amazon Inspector can analyze any applications running within Amazon Web Services (AWS).

Penetration Testing

Penetration testing evaluates system security at a point in time by attacking target systems as an outside attacker would and then documenting which attacks were successful, how the systems were exploited, and which vulnerabilities were utilized. Penetration testing provides realistic, accurate, and precise data on system security.

A penetration test is a proactive and approved plan to measure the protection of a cloud infrastructure by using system vulnerabilities, together with operating system or software application bugs, insecure settings, and potentially dangerous or naïve end-user behavior to obtain access to systems. Such assessments also are helpful in confirming the effectiveness of defensive mechanisms, and assessing end users' adherence to security policies.

Tests are usually performed using manual or automatic technologies to compromise servers, endpoints, applications, wireless networks, network devices, mobile devices, and alternative potential points of exposure. Once vulnerabilities are exploited on a particular system, pen testers might commit to using the compromised system to launch later exploits at other internal resources, in a technique known as pivoting. Pivoting is performed to incrementally reach higher levels of security clearance and deeper access to electronic assets and data via privilege increase.

The remainder of this section discusses the phases, tools, scope options, and testing limitations for penetration testing. The section concludes with a discussion on roles and responsibilities. Security testing requires specialized skill sets and should be performed by a team that is independent from DevOps.

Phases

The penetration testing process is organized into seven phases: intelligence gathering, vulnerability assessment, vulnerability validation, attack planning and simulation, exploitation, post-exploitation, and reporting. The phases are shown in Figure 11-2.

As you can see, penetration testing begins with the three phases of vulnerability scanning, covered in the previous section, so they will not be covered again. We will start with phase 4, attack planning and simulation.

Attack Planning and Simulation   Once the vulnerabilities have been enumerated and validated, the next step is to determine how the vulnerabilities can best be used together to exploit systems. Some of this comes with experience as penetration testers learn to see the subtle relationships between hosts that automated tools and complex scripts cannot detect. An initial plan of attack is built from this data.

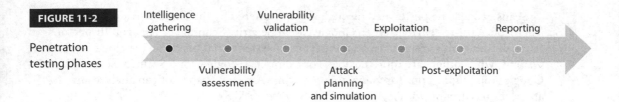

FIGURE 11-2

Penetration testing phases

This phase also involves attack plan simulations. Simulations of the exploits outlined in the attack plan are performed in a test environment or automatically in penetration testing tools to eliminate lingering false-positive results and refine the attack plan through the simulations. A full attack strategy can then be put together to be employed in the exploitation phase.

Exploitation   In the exploitation phase, penetration testers establish access to a system or resource by employing exploit packages that take advantage of discovered vulnerabilities. Penetration testing activities are performed for the approved scope following the attack strategy.

Post-exploitation   In this stage, evidence of exploitation of the vulnerabilities is collected, and remnants from the exploits are removed. As part of this, penetration testers clean up accounts and resident files that were put in place to perform the exploits.

Reporting   The last phase of penetration testing is to put all the details of the tests, including what worked and what didn't, into the report. Information on the security vulnerabilities that were successfully exploited through penetration testing is collected and documented on the report. The report is provided to a risk manager or someone in charge of security in the organization. This person will then coordinate with other teams to remediate the vulnerabilities, track remediation, and possibly schedule validation tests to ensure that the vulnerabilities identified have been successfully remediated.

Reports rank findings by risk rating and provide recommendations on how to remediate the items.

Tools

A wide variety of tools can be used to perform penetration testing. Table 11-2 lists several popular penetration testing tools. Some tools are large suites with various components, while others perform a particular task. Many tools are command-line driven, requiring familiarity with the command structure and usage.

TABLE 11-2	Penetration Testing Tools	
Tool	**Purpose**	**Phase**
Core Impact	Penetration testing suite	Exploitation
Metasploit Pro	OS- and application-level vulnerability exploitation	Exploitation
Kali	Collection of tools on a single bootable disk; can also be installed as an operating system	Exploitation
Social-Engineer Toolkit (SET)	Toolkit for performing social engineering	Exploitation

Penetration testers may try to crack passwords in order to test the strength of passwords users have created. Brute force attempts are usually made on a password database that has been downloaded from a system. Testers first obtain access to the password database and download it. However, most password databases cannot be read because the passwords in them are hashed. Penetration testers use a computer with powerful CPU or GPU or a network of distributed systems to try all possible combinations until they get in. The number of possible combinations increases exponentially as the number of characters in the password increases.

Scope

A penetration test can cover any of the following different scopes, or a combination of them:

- **External penetration testing**   External penetration testing is conducted from the Web, from outside the company's internal network, with the targets being the company's web-facing hosts. This may sometimes include web servers, e-mail servers, FTP servers, and VPN servers.

- **Internal penetration testing**   Internal penetration testing is conducted from within the company network. Targets may include servers, workstations, network devices such as firewalls or routers, and Internet of things (IoT) devices such as webcams, IP lighting, or smart TVs.

- **Web application penetration testing**   Web application penetration testing is concerned with evaluating the security of web-based applications by issuing attacks against the site and its supporting infrastructures such as database servers, file servers, or authentication devices.

- **Wireless penetration testing**   Wireless penetration testing evaluates wireless access points and common weaknesses in a company's wireless network. This includes attempting to crack wireless passwords, capture traffic on the wireless network, capture authentication information, and obtain unauthorized access to the network through a wireless connection. Wireless penetration testing also scans for rogue access points and peer-to-peer wireless connections.

- **Physical penetration testing** Physical penetration testing evaluates the ability of an outsider to obtain direct access to company facilities and areas containing sensitive data.

- **Social engineering penetration testing** Social engineering penetration testing can involve a person directly interacting with individuals, but it is more common to use remote social engineering tactics since these are most often employed by attackers.

  Remote social engineering evaluates employee response to targeted phishing attacks. The penetration tester requests a listing of e-mail addresses to be tested. A custom phishing e-mail is crafted and sent employing a spoofed source e-mail address or an external one that appears legitimate to every employee. The e-mail message will encourage the user to perform a range of nonsecure activities like clicking a link, visiting an unauthorized website, downloading a file, or revealing their username and password.

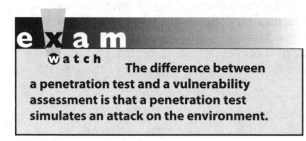

e x a m
ⓦ a t c h　　**The difference between a penetration test and a vulnerability assessment is that a penetration test simulates an attack on the environment.**

Testing Limitations

Testing limitations affect the scope of penetration testing by defining types of testing that are not allowed. Typical testing restrictions exclude from the scope memory corruption tests and similar tests that are likely to cause instability, and such testing is an assumed limitation when testing production environments. Denial of service attacks are also often excluded from the scope of testing.

Roles and Responsibilities

Security testing can be a complicated procedure and involves testing a variety of components, including applications, storage, network connectivity, and server configuration. Security testing requires specialized skill sets and should be performed by a team that is independent from DevOps.

Vulnerability scanning is an easier task to perform than penetration testing and penetration testing requires vulnerability scanning, so this is an obvious place to define roles. Vulnerability analysts detect and validate vulnerabilities and then pass that information to penetration testers who might be more familiar with certain areas such as operating systems, storage, software development, web services, communications protocols, and so forth. These penetration testers are also familiar with how such services can be exploited, and they stay up to date on new vulnerabilities, exploits, and tools.

The social engineering penetration tester may also be a different role since this requires a knowledge of human behavior and what will most effectively entice victims to read phishing e-mails and follow the instructions given.

The most important detail is that the security testing team should be distinct and independent from the DevOps team. Such a separation of duties ensures that the test accurately represents what an attacker could do. Furthermore, it provides a level of objectivity and reduces the likelihood of bias from internal knowledge or a conflict of interest that could arise if security testing team members have a personal stake, for example, in an application being launched on time.

CERTIFICATION SUMMARY

This chapter covered the concepts of cloud security engineering, security governance and strategy, and vulnerability management. Cloud security engineering is the practice of protecting the usability, reliability, integrity, and safety of information systems, including network and cloud infrastructures, and the data traversing and stored on such systems.

One method of engineering secure cloud systems is to harden them. Hardening involves ensuring that the host or guest is configured in such a way that reduces the risk of attack from either internal or external sources. Another method is to layer security technologies on top of one another so that systems are protected even if one security system fails because others are there to guard against intrusion. Next, incorporate the principle of least privilege by granting employees only the minimum permissions necessary to do their job. Along with least privilege is a concept called separation of duties, a process that divides the responsibilities required to perform a sensitive task among two or more people so that one person, acting alone, cannot compromise the system.

Security governance and strategy begins with the creation of company security policies. Security policies set the organizational expectations for certain functional security areas.

Data classification can help companies apply the correct protection mechanisms to the data they house and maintain. Data classification is the practice of sorting data into discrete categories that help define the access levels and type of protection required for that set of data. An organization establishes security policies to set their expectations for certain functional security areas. Some of these expectations may come out of standards, best practices, or compliance requirements.

Companies perform assessments and audits to identify areas where they are not meeting organizational expectations, contractual agreements, best practices, or regulatory requirements. Regulations such as HIPAA, SOX, and PCI DSS specify requirements for security controls, procedures, and policies that some organizations must comply with.

Cloud security professionals have limited time and much to do. Consider how existing security management processes can be automated. Some examples include removing inactive accounts, eliminating outdated firewall rules, cleaning up outdated security settings, and maintaining ACLs for target objects.

Lastly, it is important to test systems for vulnerabilities and to remediate those vulnerabilities so that systems will be protected against attacks targeting those vulnerabilities. Vulnerability management consists of vulnerability scanning and penetration testing to identify weaknesses in organizational systems and the corresponding methods and techniques to remediate those weaknesses. Vulnerability scanning consists of intelligence gathering, vulnerability assessment, and vulnerability validation. Penetration testing includes the steps in vulnerability scanning as well as attack planning and simulation, exploitation, post-exploitation, and reporting.

KEY TERMS

Use the following list to review the key terms discussed in this chapter. The definitions also can be found in the glossary.

data classification   Practice of sorting data into discrete categories that help define the access levels and type of protection required for that set of data.

demilitarized zone (DMZ)   A separate network that is layered in between an internal network and an external network to house resources that need to be accessed by both while preventing direct access from the outside network to the inside network.

distributed denial of service (DDoS)   An attack that targets a single system simultaneously from multiple compromised systems.

fingerprinting   A process that determines the operating system and software running on a device.

footprinting   The process of enumerating the computers or network devices on a target network.

hardening   Ensuring that a host, guest, or network is configured in such a way that reduces the risk of attack from either internal or external sources.

least privilege   Principle that states employees should be granted only the minimum permissions necessary to do their job.

network assessment   Objective review of an organization's network infrastructure regarding functionality and security capabilities used to establish a baseline for future audits.

network audit   Objective periodic review of an organization's network infrastructure against an established baseline.

penetration testing   Process of evaluating network security with a simulated attack on the network from both external and internal attackers.

personal health information (PHI)   Data that represents the identity of a patient, such as name, phone number, address, e-mail address, Social Security number, and date of birth. The PHI term is mostly used in the context of HIPAA compliance.

personally identifiable information (PII)   Data that represents the identity of a person, such as name, phone number, address, e-mail address, Social Security number, and date of birth. The PII term is mostly used in the context of privacy compliance.

ping flood   An attack that sends a massive number of ICMP packets to overwhelm a system with more traffic than it can handle.

Ping of Death (PoD)   An attack that sends malformed ICMP packets with the intent of crashing systems that cannot process them and consequently shut down.

separation of duties   A process that divides the responsibilities required to perform a sensitive task among two or more people so that one person, acting alone, cannot compromise the system.

spoofing   The modification of the source IP address to obfuscate the original source.

vulnerability assessment   Process used to identify and quantify any vulnerabilities in a network environment.

vulnerability remediation request (VRR)   A formal request to make a change to an application or system to remediate a known vulnerability.

vulnerability scanning   The process of discovering flaws or weaknesses in systems and applications.

 # TWO-MINUTE DRILL

Cloud Security Engineering

❑ To protect network resources from threats, secure network design employs multiple overlapping controls to prevent unwanted access to protected cloud resources. Some layered security components include demilitarized zones, ACLs, and intrusion detection and prevention systems.

❑ Hardening is the process of ensuring that a host or guest is not vulnerable to compromise. Logging must be enabled to track potential intrusions. Only the required software components should be installed on the system, software patches should regularly be applied, firewall and antimalware software should be functional and up to date, and any unused user accounts should be disabled or removed.

❑ Separation of duties, also known as segregation of duties, divides the responsibilities required to perform a sensitive task among two or more people so that one person, acting alone, cannot compromise the system.

❑ Incorporating the principle of least privilege limits potential misuse and risk of accidental mishandling or viewing of sensitive information by unauthorized people. Employees should be granted only the minimum permissions necessary to do their job. No more, no less. Security automation ensures that routine security procedures are performed consistently and it frees up valuable security resources to perform other duties. Some automation discussed here included disabling inactive accounts, eliminating outdated firewall rules, cleaning up outdated security settings, and maintaining ACLs.

Security Governance and Strategy

❑ Security policies set the organizational expectations for certain functional security areas.

❑ Complete audits must be scheduled on a regular basis to make certain that the configurations of all network resources are not changed in such a way that increases the risk to the environment or the organization.

❑ The rapidly evolving landscape of cloud technologies and virtualization presents dangers for cloud security departments that do not stay abreast of changes to both their toolsets and their training.

❑ Security is a complex discipline and involves securing a variety of components, including applications, storage, network connectivity, and server configuration. There are many different security functions, security controls, and security technologies, so it is unlikely that a single person will able to handle all of the company's security needs. Roles and responsibilities define who is supposed to do what in security.

Vulnerability Management

❑ Security testing helps a company stay aware of security gaps in its technology infrastructure and cloud environments.

❑ Testing can be black-box, where no information about targets is provided, gray-box, where some information is provided, or white-box, where significant information is provided about the targets to test.

❑ Vulnerability scanning is the process of discovering flaws or weaknesses in systems and applications.

❑ The vulnerability scanning process is organized into three phases: intelligence gathering, vulnerability assessment, and vulnerability validation.

❑ Penetration testing is an extension of vulnerability scanning that evaluates system security at a point in time by attacking target systems as an outside attacker would and then documenting which attacks were successful, how the systems were exploited, and which vulnerabilities were utilized.

❑ The penetration testing process is organized into seven phases: intelligence gathering, vulnerability assessment, vulnerability validation, attack planning and simulation, exploitation, post-exploitation, and reporting.

❑ A penetration test tests network and host security by simulating malicious attacks and then analyzing the results (not to be confused with a vulnerability assessment, which only identifies weaknesses that can be determined without running a penetration test).

❑ Security testing requires specialized skill sets and should be performed by a team that is independent from DevOps.

SELF TEST

The following questions will help you measure your understanding of the material presented in this chapter. As indicated, some questions may have more than one correct answer, so be sure to read all the answer choices carefully.

Cloud Security Engineering

1. You have been asked to harden a crucial network router. What should you do? (Choose two.)
   A. Disable the routing of IPv6 packets.
   B. Change the default administrative password.
   C. Apply firmware patches.
   D. Configure the router for SSO.

2. Which best practice configures host computers so that they are not vulnerable to attack?
   A. Vulnerability assessment
   B. Penetration test
   C. Hardening
   D. PKI

3. You are responsible for cloud security at your organization. The Chief Compliance Officer has mandated that the organization utilize layered security for all cloud systems. Which of the following would satisfy the requirement?
   A. Implementing ACLs and packet filtering on firewalls
   B. Configuring a DMZ with unique ACLs between networks and an IDS/IPS
   C. Specifying separation of duties for cloud administration and training additional personnel on security processes
   D. Defining a privacy policy, placing the privacy policy on the website, and emailing the policy to all current clients

Security Governance and Strategy

4. Which policy would be used to specify how all employee owned devices may be used to access organizational resources?
   A. Privacy policy
   B. Mobile device policy
   C. Remote access policy
   D. BYOD policy

5. Which policy or set of rules temporarily disables an account when a threshold of incorrect passwords is attempted?
   A. Account lockout policy
   B. Threshold policy
   C. Disabling policy
   D. Password complexity enforcement rules

Vulnerability Management

6. Which type of test simulates a network attack?
   A. Vulnerability assessment
   B. Establishing an attack baseline
   C. Hardening
   D. Penetration test

7. Which of the following phases are unique to penetration testing? (Choose all that apply.)
   A. Intelligence gathering
   B. Vulnerability validation
   C. Attack planning and simulation
   D. Exploitation

8. Which of the following describes a brute force attack?
   A. Attacking a site with exploit code until the password database is cracked
   B. Trying all possible password combinations until the correct one is found
   C. Performing a denial of service (DoS) attack on the server authenticator
   D. Using rainbow tables and password hashes to crack the password

A SELF TEST ANSWERS

Cloud Security Engineering

1. ☑ **B, C.** Changing the default passwords and applying patches are important steps in hardening a device.
☒ **A and D** are incorrect. Without more information, disabling IPv6 packet routing does not harden a router, nor does configuring it for SSO.

2. ☑ **C.** Hardening configures systems such that they are protected from compromise.
☒ **A, B,** and **D** are incorrect. While vulnerability assessments identify security problems, they do not correct them. Penetration tests simulate an attack, but do not configure machines to be protected from such attacks. PKI (public key infrastructure) is a hierarchy of trusted security certificates; it does not address configuration issues.

3. ☑ **B.** Layered security requires multiple overlapping controls that are used together to protect systems. Configuring a DMZ with ACLs along with an IDS/IPS provides multiple layers because an attacker would have to compromise a machine in the DMZ and then pivot from that machine to another machine in the internal network. However, IDS/IPS systems might detect this activity and notify administrators and block the attacker from making the connection.
☒ **A, C,** and **D** are incorrect. **A** is incorrect because implementing ACLs and packet filtering is just one component, not a set of layers. **C** is incorrect because separation of duties and cross-training address fraud and resiliency. Only the fraud element would be a layer, but since no other controls are specified, this answer does not work. **D** is incorrect because each of these elements is only concerned with the privacy policy, which does not enhance the security of the system. Rather, it ensures that customers know how the company will protect their data and what data will be collected.

Security Governance and Strategy

4. ☑ **D.** The BYOD policy is the correct answer here. Bring your own device (BYOD) is a device that is employee owned, not owned by the company; this policy governs how those devices may be used to access organizational resources.

   ☒ **A, B,** and **C** are incorrect. The privacy policy specifies the information that the organization will store and how it is handled, not how employee devices may be used. The mobile device policy could address some employee devices, but it may not address all employee owned devices because some of those devices may not be mobile, such as a home desktop computer. Lastly, the remote access policy specifies how employees can access systems remotely, but it would not address how BYOD devices are used locally to access resources.

5. ☑ **A.** An account lockout policy temporarily disables an account after a certain number of failed logons. For example, if the policy were set to 3, then a user's account would be temporarily disabled (locked out) after three failed tries until an administrator unlocks it.

   ☒ **B, C,** and **D** are incorrect. Threshold and disabling policies are not password policies. Password complexity enforcement rules ensure that users create complex passwords and that new passwords meet complexity requirements, but they do not impact users who enter their credentials incorrectly.

Vulnerability Management

6. ☑ **D.** Penetration tests simulate a network attack.

   ☒ **A, B,** and **C** are incorrect. Vulnerability assessments identify weaknesses but do not perform simulated network attacks. While establishing a usage baseline is valid, establishing an attack baseline is not. Hardening is the process of configuring a system to make it less vulnerable to attack; it does not simulate such attacks.

7. ☑ **C** and **D.** Penetration testing includes all the steps from vulnerability scanning. The two steps that are unique to penetration testing here are attack planning and simulation and exploitation.

   ☒ **A,** and **B** are incorrect. Intelligence gathering and vulnerability validation are steps that are performed both in vulnerability scanning and in penetration testing, so they are not unique to penetration testing.

8. ☑ **B.** A brute force attack tries all possible combinations of a password. A brute force attack relies on the ability to try thousands or millions of passwords per second. For example, at the time of this writing, the password cracking system that is used at TCDI for penetration testing can try 17 million passwords per minute in a brute force attack.

   ☒ **A, C,** and **D** are incorrect. Attacking a site with exploit code is the exploitation phase of penetration testing. Simply trying all possible exploits is called kitchen sink exploiting and it usually results in problems. Performing a DoS attack on the authenticator would not be a brute force attack, but it could make it impossible for users to log into the system until the authenticator comes online again. Rainbow tables and password hashes might crack the password, but using them would not constitute a brute force attack.

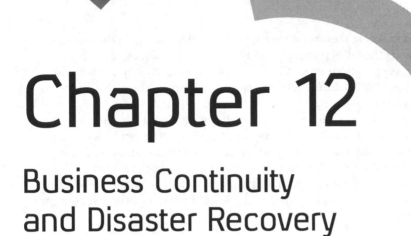

Chapter 12

Business Continuity and Disaster Recovery

A n organization's data must be backed up, and key processes like payroll and billing need to be continually available even if the organization's data center is lost due to a disaster. Choosing a disaster recovery method is an important step in a reliable cloud implementation. A cloud computing model can be seen as an alternative to traditional disaster recovery. Cloud computing offers a more rapid recovery time and helps to reduce the costs of a disaster recovery model.

Protecting organizational data requires different methods depending on the situation. Business continuity (BC) is the set of plans, procedures, and technologies necessary to ensure continued business operations or minimal disruption when incidents, technology failures, or mistakes happen. BC is different from disaster recovery (DR) in that BC is a holistic way of keeping things running, while disaster recovery (DR) addresses major events that have the potential to take down a company if the right controls are not in place. Organizations typically have a disaster recovery plan (DRP) that can be followed for specific major events. Backup and recovery are integral to both BC and DR. These functions are also useful for events that do not strain the business, such as when a user accidentally overwrites a non-urgent file and needs it recovered. Backup and recovery is used for the significant and major events as well as those not impacting business continuity and disaster recovery scenarios.

CERTIFICATION OBJECTIVE 12.01

Business Continuity Methods

Business continuity (BC) encompasses the activities that enable an organization to continue functioning, including offering services, delivering products, and conducting other activities deemed integral to running the business, during and following a disruptive incident such as data corruption, employee mistakes, a malware breach, a malicious insider attack, a system hack, or a major component failure.

Business continuity is also concerned with recovering data or systems if and when they are harmed.

Business Continuity Plan

An organization makes its guidelines known through a business continuity plan (BCP), and it enacts its guidelines through business continuity management (BCM). BCM is the process the organization goes through to create procedures to deal with threats to data integrity, data exfiltration, data confidentiality, data availability, employee safety, asset integrity, brand image, and customer relationships. The process defines the threats to those organizational resources and outlines the safeguards and practices designed to protect them from harm.

BCM is concerned with protecting organizational resources from harm and relies on contingency and resiliency.

Contingency

A major portion of the BCP is concerned with contingency. Contingency planning involves establishing alternate practices, sites, and resources that can be used in an emergency or to establish high availability (discussed later in this section).

In the contingency section of the BCP, the organization establishes a generalized capability and readiness to cope effectively with potential disasters. Contingency preparations constitute a last-resort response if resilience and recovery arrangements should prove inadequate in practice. Still, if the BCP is to be complete, it must have documented, planned for, and mapped-out contingencies.

Alternatives

In the contingency component of the BCP, the organization establishes a generalized capability and readiness to cope effectively with whatever incidents compromise business operations, including those that were not, and perhaps could not have been, foreseen.

Alternative preparations constitute a last-resort response if resilience and recovery arrangements should prove inadequate in practice. Still, if a BCP is to be complete, it must have documented, planned for, and mapped out how it will handle alternatives when primary resources are unavailable.

Alternate Sites

Alternate sites are an essential part of business continuity. For example, hot and warm sites require replication to keep data consistent. Hot sites would require continuous replication, while a warm site would require scheduled replication at certain points throughout the day, week, or month.

Using a remote site helps provide a more advanced business continuity solution since the entire site is protected in case of a disaster. Multisite configurations rely on a backup site where a company can quickly relocate its computer equipment if a disaster occurs at its primary location and data center. The backup site needs to be either another location that the company owns and has available to implement additional equipment or a space that it rents from another provider for an annual or monthly fee.

There are three types of backup sites an organization can use: a cold site, a hot site, and a warm site. The difference between each site is determined by the administrative effort to implement and maintain them and the costs involved with each type.

Cold Site   Of the three backup site options, the least expensive is the cold site. A cold site does not include any backup copies of data from the organization's original data center. When an organization implements a cold site, it does not have readily available hardware at the site; it has only the physical space and network connectivity for recovery operations, and is responsible for providing the hardware. Because there is no hardware at the backup site, the cost for a cold site is lower; however, not having readily available hardware at the cold site is also one of its downfalls. Since there is no hardware set up and ready to use at the backup site, it takes the organization longer to get up and operating after a disaster, which could end up costing it more than the extra expense of a warm or hot site, depending on the type of organization.

Hot Site   A hot site, on the other hand, is a duplicate of the original site of the organization and has readily available hardware and a near-complete backup of the organization's data. A hot site can have real-time synchronization between the original site and the backup site and can be used to mirror the original data center completely. If the original site is impacted by a disaster, the hot site is available for the organization to quickly relocate to, with minimal impact on the normal operations of the organization. This is the most expensive type of backup site and is popular with organizations that need this level of disaster recovery, including financial institutions and e-commerce providers.

e x a m

w a t c h   **A hot site is the most expensive multisite configuration but provides the quickest recovery time in the event of a disaster.**

Warm Site   A warm site is somewhere on the continuum between a cold site and a hot site. It has readily available hardware but on a much smaller scale than the original site or a hot site. Warm sites will also have backups at the location, but they may not be complete backups, or they might be a few days old.

Determining an acceptable RTO for an organization helps a cloud administrator choose between the three types of backup sites. A hot site might have an RTO of a few hours, whereas a cold site might have an RTO of a day or more. It is important that the organization and the cloud administrator completely understand the RTO of an application or service and the cost required to operate at that RTO. A hot site provides faster recovery time but also has a much higher cost than a warm site. While a cold site is the least expensive to set up, it also takes the longest to implement in the event of a disaster. Understanding the benefits and costs of each of the three types of backup sites will help an organization determine which backup type best fits its needs and which backup strategy it should implement.

Site Mirroring

A mirror site is either a hosted website or set of files that is an exact copy of the original site and resides on one or more separate computers from the original. This mirror copy ensures that the website or files are accessible from multiple locations to increase availability and reduce network traffic on the original site. It is updated on a regular basis to reflect any changes in content from the original site.

A set of distributed mirrored servers can be set up to reflect geographic discrepancies, making it faster to download from various places throughout the world in what is known as a content delivery network (CDN). For example, a site that is heavily used in the United States might have multiple mirror sites throughout the country, or even a mirror site in Germany, so that end users who are trying to download the files can access a site that is in closer proximity to their location.

Sites that offer a large array of software downloads and have a large amount of network traffic can use mirror sites to meet the demand for the downloads and improve response time for the end user. For example, Microsoft often has multiple mirror sites available for users to download its software, and Download.com (http://download.cnet.com) often has mirror sites so that end users can retrieve files from a location that is closer to them.

Resiliency

The BCP should define how the organization will implement resiliency. Resiliency requires designing systems that can still service the company when problems arise. It accomplishes this primarily through redundancy. Cloud service providers achieve resiliency by architecting cloud and information systems that can withstand assault or faults. Security controls protect against assault (see Chapter 10) and redundancy protects against component failure or failure of integrated or dependent third-party systems such as the power grid, hosting provider, or key toolset.

Redundant components protect the system from a failure and can include power supplies, switches, network interface cards, and hard disks. An example of a redundant system is RAID, which employs methods to guard against the failure of one or more drives depending on the RAID level. Review Chapter 2 if this seems unfamiliar. Another example is NIC teaming, where two or more NICs are combined into one logical NIC. If the cable, NIC, or switch link for one fails, the others will still remain to service the server.

A redundant component means you have more of that component than you need. For example, a virtualization host computer might have two power supplies to make it redundant, but it can function with a single power supply. A data center may have four connections to four different ISPs, but it can function with any one of them, except that it would incur bursting charges for additional bandwidth used.

Redundant does not mean that there is not an impact to performance or a cost if a component fails; it means that service can be restored to working condition (although the condition may be in a degraded state), without the need for external components. Redundancy differs from fault tolerance in that fault tolerance allows the system to tolerate a fault and continue running in spite of it. Fault tolerance is discussed in more detail later in the chapter.

Once an organization has established the BCP and created redundant systems, it can implement failover. Failover uses a constant communication mechanism between two systems called a heartbeat. As long as this heartbeat continues uninterrupted, failover to the redundant system will not initiate. If the heartbeat between the systems fails, the redundant system will take over processing for the primary system. If the primary system becomes operational again, the organization can initiate a failback. Failback is the process of restoring the processing back to the original state before the failure of the primary system.

High Availability

High availability (HA) is a system design approach that ensures a system or component is continuously available for a predefined length of time. Organizations need to have their applications and services available to end users at all times. If end users cannot access a service or application, it is considered to be unavailable, and the period during which it is unavailable is commonly referred to as downtime.

Downtime comes in two different forms: scheduled downtime and unscheduled downtime. Scheduled downtime is downtime that has been predefined in a service contract that allows an administrator to perform routine maintenance on a system, like installing critical updates, firmware, or service packs.

Unscheduled downtime usually involves an interruption to a service or application due to a physical event, such as a power outage, hardware failure, or security breach. Most organizations exclude scheduled downtime from their availability calculation for an application or service as long as the scheduled maintenance does not impact the end users.

Having an infrastructure that is redundant and highly available helps an organization provide a consistent environment and a more productive workforce. Determining which systems require the investment to be highly available is up to each organization. There will be some systems or applications that do not need to be highly available and do not warrant the cost involved to make them so.

One of the benefits of a public cloud model is that the cost of making the systems highly available falls on the cloud provider and allows the cloud consumer to take advantage of that highly available system.

If a system is not highly available, it means that the system will fail if a single component fails. For example, if a system that is not highly available has a single power supply and that power supply fails, the entire system will be unavailable until the power supply can be replaced.

Determining which systems and which applications require redundancy can help reduce costs and administrative overhead. A policy should be created to determine the expected availability for each application. This will govern whether HA features are required on the systems housing the application.

An organization might use a scale of 0 to 4 to rate the availability requirements of an application. In that scenario, an application that has a rating of 0 would need to be available 99.99 percent of the time, whereas an application with a rating of 4 might only have to be available 98 percent of the time. Creating a scale allows an organization to prioritize its applications and appropriately distribute costs so that it can maximize its compute resources.

on the job **Recently we worked with an organization to help define its business continuity plan (BCP). The organization had never done a BCP and had not envisioned how to start creating a highly available environment. To get the organization's team started, we had them define the importance of all the applications they were currently using. After putting a priority on each of the applications, the organization was able to clearly identify the level of redundancy and availability required for each system to function efficiently and cost-effectively.**

Fault Tolerance

Fault tolerance allows a computer system to function as normal in the event of a failure in one or more of the system's components. Fault-tolerant systems are designed for high availability and reliability by installing redundant hardware components. For example, a virtualization host computer would have multiple CPUs, power supplies, and hard disks in the same physical computer. If one of the components were to fail, the spare component would take over without bringing the system down. However, having a system that is truly fault-tolerant does result in greater expense because the system requires additional components to achieve fault-tolerant status.

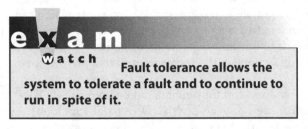

e x a m

ⓦatch **Fault tolerance allows the system to tolerate a fault and to continue to run in spite of it.**

Clustering Connecting multiple computers to provide parallel processing and redundancy is known as clustering. Clustering allows for two or more computers to be connected to act as a single computer. The computers are connected over a fast local area network (LAN), and each node (i.e., each computer used as a server) constituting the cluster runs its own operating system. Clusters can thereby improve performance and availability as compared to using a single computer, and clusters are used often in the cloud for Big Data analysis.

Geo-clustering Geo-clustering allows for the connection of multiple redundant computers while those computers are located in different geographical locations. So instead of having the nodes connected over a LAN, the nodes are connected over a wide area network (WAN) but still appear as a single highly available system. Geo-clustering allows an organization to support enterprise-level continuity by providing a system that is location independent.

Multipathing

Having a fault-tolerant system is a great start to achieving high availability, but it is not the only requirement. When planning for high availability, all aspects of the network must be considered. If the connection between the fault-tolerant systems is a single point of failure, then it is limiting the high availability of the system. Implementing multipathing allows for the configuration of multiple paths for connectivity to a storage device, providing redundancy for the system to connect to the storage device.

Load Balancing

Another component of high availability is load balancing. Load balancing allows you to distribute a workload across multiple computers, networks, and disk drives. Load balancing helps to optimize workloads and resources, allowing for maximum throughput and helps minimize response times for the end user. Load balancing can also help to create reliability with the use of multiple computers instead of a single computer and is delivered either with dedicated software or hardware.

Load balancing uses the resources of multiple systems to provide a single, specific Internet service. It can be used with a website or a File Transfer Protocol (FTP) site to distribute the load of web or file requests between two or more servers. Load balancing can distribute incoming HTTP requests across multiple web servers in a server farm, which can help distribute the load across multiple servers to prevent overloading any single server. If one of the servers in the server farm starts to become overwhelmed, load balancing begins to distribute HTTP requests to another node in the server farm so that no one node becomes overloaded.

Load balancers are supplied with an IP address and fully qualified domain name (FQDN) that is typically mapped through NAT and a firewall to an external DNS name for cloud resources. This IP address and FQDN represent the load balancer, but client connections are handled by one of the members of the load-balanced system. Internally the load balancer tracks the individual IP addresses of its members.

on the job **Recently we were tasked with creating a solution for a website that was being overwhelmed with incoming requests. The solution was to deploy a hardware load balancer and to add two additional web servers to a server farm. By adding load balancing, we were able to distribute the incoming requests across three servers, thus improving performance and reliability for the organization and the website.**

Service Level Agreements for BCP and HA

A service level agreement (SLA) is a contract that specifies the level of uptime that will be supported by the service provider. SLAs are used with Internet service providers, cloud solutions, and a variety of other technology solutions.

Review the SLA damage clauses when purchasing a complete HA solution. SLAs include provisions for how the service provider will compensate customers if SLAs are not met. At a minimum, these include some monetary compensation for the time the system was down that may be credited toward future invoices. Sometimes the provider must pay fines or damages for lost revenue or lost customer satisfaction. Ensure that the SLA specifies the expected amount of uptime and that damages for SLA violations are sufficient to cover losses due to unexpected downtime.

Similarly, when providing a solution to customers, ensure that you construct SLAs that are consistent with the HA capabilities of your systems. For example, you would not want to create an SLA that states five nines of availability if the underlying systems are only able to provide four nines.

Disaster Recovery Methods

When an organization is choosing a disaster recovery method, it has to measure the level of service required. This means understanding how critical the application or server is and then determining the proper disaster recovery method for it. When implementing disaster recovery, it is important to form disaster recovery plans (DRPs) that will describe how the organization is going to deal with potential disasters such as fires, floods, earthquakes, entire site failure, or blackouts.

It is first necessary to focus on those applications or servers that are mission critical in the DRP. A mission-critical system is any system whose failure would result in the failure of business operations. These systems need to be identified and backed by a proper disaster recovery method to ensure there is no lost revenue for the organization.

Location is also important. The company will need to determine where to place the disaster recovery center. Geographic diversity should be taken into account when planning for a disaster that may impact a particular geographic region. Disasters come in many forms, including natural disasters, so placing the disaster recovery center in a location that is 1000 miles away might prevent the same natural disaster from destroying both the primary data center and the disaster recovery center.

Corporate Guidelines

Corporate guidelines should be established so that employees understand the company's expectations for how a disaster will be handled and their own responsibilities if a disaster were to occur. Corporate guidelines are expressed through a set of plans and policies that have been approved by company leadership such as a CEO, CSO, or an executive group such as an information security steering committee. The first of these documents is the disaster recovery plan (DRP). An organization makes its DR guidelines known through the DRP and it is likely the most comprehensive DR document. Other documents are usually created by departments in support of DR initiatives, such as employee rosters, emergency checklists, emergency contact numbers, system documentation, system dependency sheets, triage lists, and so forth. This section will focus mainly on the DRP, but it is good to be aware of some of the documents just mentioned.

After a discussion on the DRP, this section introduces metrics that the organization can use to determine when components might fail or cause problems. These metrics are good to know because they will likely appear in some of the documents mentioned previously. Lastly, DR defines parameters for what losses are acceptable during recovery in terms of how much data can be lost and how much time can be spent recovering. These are defined as the recovery time objective (RTO) and the recovery point objective (RPO). Both concepts are explained in their own subsection at the end of this section.

Disaster Recovery Plan

An organization makes its guidelines for how a disaster will be handled in a disaster recovery plan (DRP). The DRP outlines the procedures to deal with threats to data, systems, and employees, such as fires, floods, hurricanes, tornados, critical infrastructure failure, pandemics, or active shooter situations. The DRP defines the threats to those organizational resources and outlines the safeguards and practices designed to allow the company to operate in a different location, using different resources while primary resources are being restored.

The DRP establishes a generalized capability and readiness to cope effectively with potential disasters. Disaster preparations constitute a last-resort response if resilience and recovery (elements of the BCP) should prove inadequate in practice. Still, if the DRP is to be complete, it must have documented, planned for, and mapped-out contingencies.

DR Metrics

Another factor to consider when planning for DR is hardware health metrics. Some important hardware health metrics include

- Mean time between failures (MTBF)
- Mean time to repair (MTTR)
- Self-monitoring, analysis, and reporting technology (SMART)

MTBF is the average length of time a device will function before it fails. MTBF can be used to determine approximately how long a hard drive will last in a server. It can also be used to plan how long it might take for a particular hardware component to fail, and thereby help with the creation of a DRP.

MTTR, on the other hand, is the average length of time that it takes to repair a failed hardware component. MTTR needs to be a factor in the DRP, as it is often part of the maintenance contract for the virtualization host computers. An MTTR of 24 hours or less would be appropriate for a higher-priority server, whereas a lower-priority server might have an MTTR of seven days.

Lastly, SMART is a set of hard disk metrics that are used to predict failures by monitoring over 100 metrics such as read error rate, spin-up time, start and stop count, reallocated sectors count, and seek error rate. SMART has predefined thresholds for each metric, and those thresholds are used to determine if a drive is in an OK, warning, or error status. All of these factors need to be considered in the DRP for the organization to have a successful disaster recovery environment.

RTO

The recovery time objective (RTO) is the maximum tolerable amount of time between an outage and the restoration of the service before an organization suffers unacceptable losses.

RTO will involve many tasks. The following is the general sequence of tasks that must be performed:

1. Notify IT or cloud backup operations of the need for a restore.
2. Locate restoration archive or media that contains the required data, such as cloud storage, local storage, a remote data center, or tape. If tape, identify if the tape is on-site or off-site. If the tape is off-site, pick it up and bring it to the location where the restore will take place.
3. Conduct the restore.
4. Validate the restore to confirm that the data is accessible, free from error, and ready for use. If errors are encountered, try restoring again. If errors continue, attempt the restore from another backup.

Figure 12-1 shows a flowchart of all the activities that could be required depending on where the data is located and how they contribute to RTO.

FIGURE 12-1 Restoration activities contributing to RTO

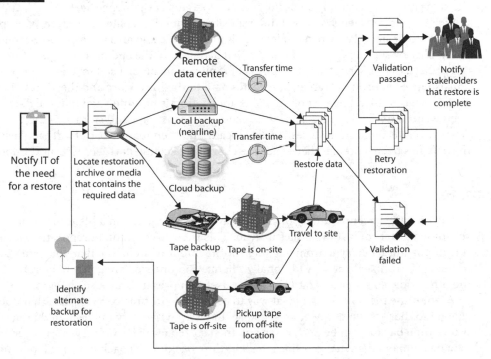

RPO

The recovery point objective (RPO) is the maximum amount of time in which data can be lost for a service due to a major incident. The RPO determines how often backups should take place. For example, if the RPO is 24 hours, then backups would occur daily.

The organization should not treat all data the same. Some data might need to have a different RPO because it has different availability needs. For example, a database of customer orders might have a RPO of 1 minute, whereas web file RPO might be 24 hours because updates are made no more than once per day, and web files are also located in web developer repositories.

One of the things that should be considered and that can help meet expected RTO and RPO is redundancy. A redundant system can be used to provide a backup to a primary system in the case of failure.

Replication

Replication transfers data between two or more systems so that any changes to the data are made on each node in the replica set. A replica set consists of the systems that will all retain the same data. Replication can occur between systems at the same site, termed intrasite replication, or between systems at different sites, termed intersite replication. Multiple sites are used to protect data when a single site is unavailable and also to ensure low-latency availability by serving data from sources that are close to the end user or application.

As discussed in Chapter 3, two forms of replication can be used to keep replica sets consistent. Synchronous replication writes data to the local store and then immediately replicates it to the replica set or sets. The application is not informed that the data has been written until all replica sets have acknowledged receipt and storage of the data. Asynchronous replication stores the data locally and then reports back to the application that the data has been stored. It then sends the data to replication partners at its next opportunity.

File Transfer

In lieu of some backups, an organization may choose to perform a file transfer or a scheduled synchronization of files instead. This is quite common in replication scenarios. It is important when synchronizing files for the intent of archiving that you configure them to not synchronize deletes. Additionally, changes on one side are going to be reflected on the other side, so synchronizations are not useful in preserving those changes.

A one-time file transfer is a great way to get a point-in-time copy for data that does not change so that you do not need to keep backing it up with every full backup that occurs. A one-time backup can be performed and then stored away for whenever it is needed. If data has remained unchanged since the one-time backup, the backup will still be consistent even though it has not been updated.

One-time backups can reduce space on backup drives and reduce the length of time required to perform backups. Ensure that if you do a one-time file transfer that you lock the files so that they cannot be changed in production. Otherwise, you might find at some later date that people have been changing the files but there is no active backup for the data.

Service Level Agreements for DR

As mentioned earlier in this chapter, a service level agreement (SLA) is a contract that specifies the level of uptime that will be supported by the service provider. SLAs should be obtained for each of the systems that will be relied upon for the DR solution. It would be a shame to failover to a DR site, only to find that the site did not meet availability expectations. Customers who have recently suffered a downtime do not want to experience other downtimes shortly thereafter so you want to ensure that your DR site will provide the required service level.

CERTIFICATION OBJECTIVE 12.03

Backup and Recovery

A backup set is a secondary copy of the organization's data and is used to replace the original data in the event of a loss. The backup process needs to be monitored just like any other process that is running in the environment. Proper monitoring of the backup system helps to ensure that the data is available if there is a disaster.

Remember, a backup is only as good as the restore strategy that is in place. Testing the restoration process of all the backups in an organization should be done on a scheduled and routine basis. Backups can be fully automated and scheduled so that they can run without interaction from an administrator.

A proper disaster recovery and data retention plan should be established to ensure that data loss is consistent with the RPO if a disaster occurs. The backup plan should include how the data is to be stored and, if the data is going to be stored off-site, how long it is kept off-site and how many copies are kept at the off-site facility. The backup plan should also specify how the data will be recovered.

Selecting the appropriate backup solution is a critical piece of a properly configured disaster recovery implementation. Creating a backup is simply the process of copying and archiving data so that the data is available to be restored to either the original location or an alternate location should the original data be lost, modified, or corrupted.

Creating backups of data serves two primary purposes. The first purpose of a backup is to restore data that is lost because either it was deleted or it became corrupt. The second purpose of a backup is to enable recovery of data from an earlier time frame.

An organization should have a data retention policy that specifies how long data needs to be kept. For example, if an organization has a data retention policy that specifies all data must be kept for two weeks, an end user who needs to have a document restored from ten days ago could do so.

When selecting a backup policy, several things need to be taken into consideration. First, the organization must determine how the backups will be stored, whether on tape, optical media, NAS, external disk, or a cloud-based storage system. Cloud storage can emulate a virtual tape library (VTL) so that existing on-premises backup solutions can see it.

If data is stored on removable media such as tapes, optical media, or external disks, first determine if the backups should be stored at an off-site location. Storing backups at an off-site location allows for recovery of the data in the event of a site disaster. After choosing a media type, the next step is to choose the style of backup.

Cloud backups exist in the cloud provider's data center so they are already outside of the organization and, thus "off-site." Cloud backups are an effective way to perform off-site backups without a large infrastructure. Files from cloud backups are easier to manage and often faster to retrieve than off-site tapes or removable media.

The available backup types are discussed next. Each backup type has its own set of advantages and disadvantages.

Backup Types

An organization can structure backups in multiple ways to strike a balance between the length of time it takes to conduct a backup and the length of time it takes to perform a restore operation. Backup types also offer different levels of recoverability, some requiring the presence of another backup to be functional. The available backup types include the following:

- Full backup
- Differential backup
- Incremental backup
- Snapshot
- Bit-for-bit backup
- Imaging

Backups utilize features such as change or delta tracking and can be stored online or offline. We will discuss those topics before covering the various backup types.

Change/Delta Tracking

Some backup types archive information depending on whether it has been backed up recently or if it has changed since the last backup. File change status is tracked using a flag on files called the archive bit. When a full backup is performed, the archive bit is set to 0. If that file changes, the archive bit is set to 1.

Online and Offline Backups

Online backups are those that are available to restore immediately, while offline backups must be brought online before they are available to restore. Some offline backups include tape backups and removable hard drives. A backup tape is offline because it must be retrieved and inserted into a tape drive before it is available to restore. Similarly, a backup hard drive stored in a safe deposit box is offline.

Online backups include nearline and cloud backups. Nearline backups are written to media that is on the network such as a NAS, a local backup server, or shared storage on a server. These backups are online because they can be retrieved without having to insert media. Cloud backups are also online backups because they are always available. Both of these online options can be restored at any time.

Full Backup

A full system backup backs up the entire system, including everything on the hard drive. It makes a copy of all the data and files on the drive in a single process. A full backup takes up the most space on storage media because it does a full drive copy every time the backup is executed. Performing a full backup every day requires the same amount of space on the backup media as the drive being backed up.

The benefit to a full backup is that an organization can take any of the backups from any day they were executed and restore data from a single backup media. The full backup resets the archive bit on all files on the computer to 0. Figure 12-2 shows an example of how a full system backup would look after four backups.

Differential Backup

The differential backup backs up only those changes that were made since the last full backup was executed. To perform a differential backup, a full backup must have been performed on the dataset previously.

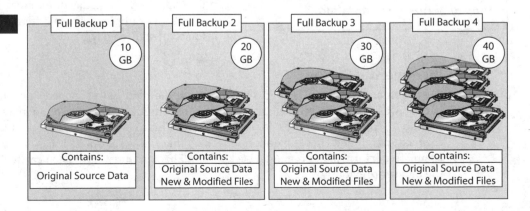

FIGURE 12-2

Illustration of a full system backup

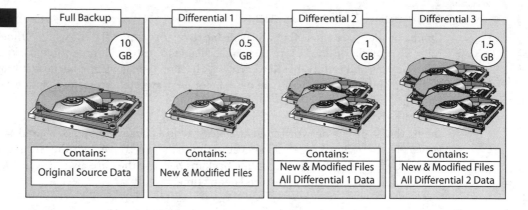

FIGURE 12-3

Illustration of a differential backup

After the full backup is executed, every differential backup executed thereafter will contain only the changes made since the last full backup. The differential backup knows which data has been changed because of the archive bit. Each changed file results in a file with an archive bit set to 1. The differential backup does not change the archive bit when it backs up the files, so each successive differential backup includes the files that changed since the last full backup because full backups do reset the archive bit.

One of the disadvantages to differential backups is that the time it takes to complete the backup will increase as files change between the last full backup. Another disadvantage is that if the organization wants to restore an entire system to a particular point in time, it must first locate the last full backup taken prior to the point of failure and the last differential backup since the last full backup.

For example, if full backups are taken every Friday night and differentials are taken each night in between, to restore a system on Wednesday to the Tuesday backup would require the full backup and the Tuesday differential. Figure 12-3 shows an example of how a differential backup looks after three days.

e x a m

ⓦ **a t c h** **Differential backups require more space to store the backup and take more time to complete, but take less time to perform a restoration.**

Incremental Backup

An incremental backup also backs up only those files that have changed since the last backup was executed, but the last backup can be either a full backup or an incremental backup. Incremental backups do reset the archive bit to 0 when they back up files, so the next incremental backup does not back up that file again unless it has changed again. To perform an incremental backup, a full backup must have been carried out on the dataset previously.

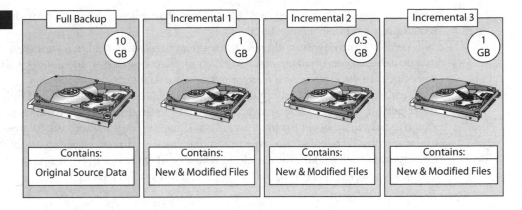

FIGURE 12-4

Illustration of an incremental backup

Backing up only files that have changed since the last backup makes incremental backups faster and requires less space. However, the time it takes to perform a restoration is longer because many backup files could need to be processed. Restores require the last full backup and all the incremental backups since the last full.

watch   **Incremental backups require less space to store the backup and complete much more quickly but require more time to perform a restoration.**

For example, if full backups are taken every Friday night and incrementals are taken each night in between, to restore a system on Wednesday to the Tuesday backup would require the full backup, the Saturday incremental, Sunday incremental, Monday incremental, and Tuesday incremental. Figure 12-4 shows an example of how an incremental backup would look after three backups.

Snapshot

A snapshot captures the state of a virtual machine or volume at the specific time when the snapshot was taken. While similar to a backup, a snapshot should not be considered a replacement for traditional backups. A virtual machine snapshot can be used to preserve the state and data of a virtual machine at a specific point in time. A snapshot can be taken before a major software installation, and if the installation fails or causes issues, the virtual machine can be restored to the state it was in when the snapshot was taken.

Other cloud data such as websites hosted in the cloud or cloud data stores perform storage snapshots that operate similarly to a virtual machine snapshot except that they are only concerned with the data stored in the snapped location.

Multiple snapshots can be taken. A series of snapshots is organized into a snapshot chain. A snapshot keeps a delta file of all the changes after the snapshot was taken. The delta file records the differences between the current state of the disk and the state the disk was in when the snapshot was taken. A marker in the chain allows the cloud provider to know which points represent snapshots.

Snapshots and snapshot chains can be created and managed in a variety of different ways. It is possible to create snapshots, revert to any snapshot in the chain, mount snapshots as data stores to view individual files, or even delete snapshots.

Since snapshots are not a replacement for regular backups, they should only be kept for a short period, preferably a few days. A snapshot continues to record from its point of origin, so if the snapshot is kept for long periods of time, the file will continue to grow larger and might eventually become too large to remove or cause disk storage constraints. This can cause performance issues for the cloud resource. If there is a need to keep a snapshot longer than a few days, it is recommended to create a full system backup.

We were asked to deploy a new application to a development server. The new application was being deployed to the development environment because it had never been tested. Instead of taking a backup of the development server before installing the application, we simply created a snapshot of the virtual machine before the install in case the new application caused a failure of the server.

Bit-for-Bit Backups

Another type of backup is the bit-for-bit backup, which captures the entire hard drive bit by bit. Because the whole hard drive was captured, the image can be used to restore an entire server in the event of a disaster, allowing the image to be restored on new hardware.

Creating an image of a server differs from the file-based backups discussed earlier in that the file-based backups only allow you to restore what was configured to be backed up, whereas an image allows for the entire restoration of the server, including files, folders, and operating system. Even if a file backup contains all the data on a drive, it cannot restore partition tables and data to the exact places and states they were in when the backup was taken, and this can cause problems if you try to do a file-level restore on a server's operating system drive or on transactional data such as data in Microsoft Exchange, IBM Notes and Domino, or an Oracle database.

Bit-for-bit backups can be scheduled much like other backup jobs and can be an excellent method for returning a system to a previous state. Bit-for-bit backups are typically used for physical machines in much the same way as a snapshot is used for virtual machines.

Imaging

Images are like bit-for-bit backups in that they are a bit-for-bit copy of the hard drive. However, images are usually taken as a one-time operation rather than a normal scheduled task. Images are taken of machines prior to deploying them to end users. Administrators may restore from the image if the user has issues with the machine at a later date.

Some administrators may choose to restore rather than troubleshoot an issue if the issue appears complex. Applying an image can quickly and easily bring a system back to the organizationally approved operating system build and set of software. Images can also be used for bringing systems back to a standard approved state.

Images can also be taken of machines that are prepped for deployments. Suppose the IT department receives 900 workstations that are all the same. They would configure the first one with all the software, configure it for use, update the system with the latest patches, and then harden the system. They would then image system and deploy the image to the other 899 machines.

Images can also be used for remote deployments. Similar to the situation described, the IT department would configure the first machine with the software, configuration, and updates and then create an image. That image would be deployed to the network, and computers could PXE boot to the image repository and the image would be deployed to them.

on the **Job**

One of this book's authors used to manage student computer labs for a university. Each lab had identical machines in it. A single image was hosted on a server for each of the labs. Some labs had custom software for certain disciplines, so they were configured with a different image. At startup, each computer would compare the blocks on their machine with the blocks on the image and replace any different ones on the local machine with the ones from the image. If a student had trouble with a machine, they would move to another and let IT know. IT would restart the machine and it would replace changed blocks with the standard ones from the image. In a few minutes, the machine would be back to its normal functional state. The only thing that would require taking the device out of service was actual failed hardware, and the university had a room full of spares. Furthermore, when patches needed to be deployed to the machines, IT would deploy to one machine and then take an image of the machine and place it on the server for deployment. They then ran a script to restart all the machines in the lab to receive the changed blocks from the image.

Backup Target

A backup target is a destination for a backup job. A backup target could be a local folder on another drive, a folder on the network, a cloud drive, a remote site, or a tape, for example. Choose a target that will offer low enough latency to be able to complete backup jobs in the required amount of time and fast enough to meet the RTO.

Backup targets are sometimes confused with replicas. The two differ in that backup targets are the destination for a backup, whereas replicas are used to create a mirrored copy of the data between the initial target and a replica target.

Local

Local targets are those that are on the same network as the source data. These are also called nearline backups. Local targets include backups to another drive on the same machine, backups to a NAS on the local network, or backups to a file server on the local network. This could also include a local cloud appliance that has local storage which is then replicated to the cloud.

Remote

To help reduce downtime in case of a disaster, an organization can set up and configure backups or replication to another site or a cloud service that is off premises. It is less likely that an event affecting the source data will also impact a remote target. For example, a forklift that knocks over a server rack in the data center would not impact the cloud backup. Remote targets include cloud backups, remote data centers, and tapes that are taken off-site.

Replicas

The closer the target is to the source, the faster the backup will run. It will also be faster to restore the data when the target is closer to the source. However, closer targets are riskier because an event that could disrupt services or corrupt the source data might also do the same to the local backup. You do not want to be in a situation where both production systems and backups are unavailable.

Typically, companies will perform a backup to a local data store in the same data center so that the backup job completes quickly and so the data is available close to the source if necessary. However, this data will then be replicated to a replica such as a cloud service, remote site, or tape.

Replicas help to improve reliability and fault tolerance. When replicating data, the data is stored on multiple storage devices at different locations so that if one location suffers a disaster, the other location is available with the exact same data. Remote sites are costly to own and operate, so cloud backups have become very popular as a replica.

Other Backup Considerations

Now that you understand the types of backups and where backups are stored, the next steps are to choose the right backup type for your organization and its RTO, configure the backups to store the right objects, and schedule backups to run at ideal times. Be aware that restoring data may require some dependencies such as backup software, catalogs, decryption keys, and licensing.

It is also important to ensure that connectivity from source to target is sufficient to back up the data in the required time frame and with minimal impact on other services that may be operating concurrently. Some companies may find that latency is preventing them from meeting backup windows, in which case they can employ edge sites to reduce the latency.

Next, procure the necessary equipment to conduct backups and restores. If you find that the cost of the equipment is prohibitive for your organization, look to contract with a third party or cloud provider to conduct backups. You will also want to be aware of the availability cost of performing backups or restores and make others aware of activities that could cause performance degradation. The availability cost is the performance impact incurred when backup or restore operations produce contention for available resources. Backup and restore operations could potentially prevent users from performing tasks or they could make systems less desirable to use.

Backup Schedules

Backup jobs must run on a schedule to be effective. A one-time backup can be useful, but it does little to protect company information that changes rapidly. Scheduled jobs allow for backups to operate at regular intervals to back up the files that have changed since the last backup or to back up all files. The determination as to what is backed up in the job is based on the backup type, discussed earlier, such as a full backup, incremental backup, differential backup, snapshot, or bit-for-bit backup.

Backup schedules should be structured such that they do not impact production activities. Backups can consume a lot of disk and network I/O. Compressed and encrypted backups consume CPU as well. Compression and decompression can place a heavy burden on the server and cause disruptions or poor performance for users if backups run during peak times.

Most backups will not require downtime, but they could still impact the performance of the virtual machine and the applications that run on top of it. For this reason, it is best to plan backups for times when the load on the system is minimal.

For example, it would be a bad idea to back up a domain controller at the beginning of the day when users are logging into systems, because that is when the domain controller must authenticate each request. Users would likely see service interruptions if a backup were to take place during such a peak time.

Virtualized and cloud systems may have users spread across the globe. Additionally, it may be necessary to coordinate resources with cloud vendors or with support personnel in different global regions. In such cases, time zones can be a large constraint for performing backups. It can be difficult to coordinate a time that works for distributed user bases and maintenance teams. In those cases, you might need to provision enough resources on machines so that backups can run concurrently with a full traffic load.

Configurations

As you choose a schedule for the backup jobs, you will also need to configure the appropriate backup type to minimize the impact on production systems and applications, yet meet backup frequency requirements, RTO, and RPO.

Some common scenarios include performing a full backup weekly and incrementals or differentials daily. Others might choose to do a full backup nightly with hourly incrementals or differentials. Bandwidth and system resources may determine which options are available to you. Of course, if company policy specifies a specific configuration, you may need to upgrade equipment to meet the requirements.

Objects

One of the most important decisions when designing backups is determining what to back up. Each item selected for backup is an object. Should you back up the company intranet? What about local machines if the policy states that data should only be stored on the network? The selection of backup objects is one that should be approved by data and application owners. Ensure that senior management sees the list as well to ensure that all data and application owners are represented. You may receive sign-off from the intranet application owner and the end-user support manager to back up local machines and the intranet, but if you forgot to include the e-mail application owner, you might be in trouble when the e-mail server goes down. We cannot stress how important it is to choose the right backup objects.

We were called in to help a company see if they could restore data from a failed RAID array. The array had failed the night before, and that morning IT informed the CEO that the payroll database was not included in the backups. This was a shock to the CEO because the payroll database had a lot of important information in it. The CEO was looking at possibly having to re-create the data in the payroll database from hard copies if the data could not be recovered. We were brought in to attempt that, but the situation could have been avoided if the right backup objects were selected.

Dependencies

Just having a backup is not always enough. You also need to have the dependencies necessary to restore that backup in an emergency. Dependencies include backup software, catalogs, decryption keys, and licensing.

Backup software is the first dependency. Each vendor stores its backup data in a different format. Usually, one vendor's backup software cannot read the backup software of another vendor, so you will need to have the backup software that originally created the backup or a newer version of the software to perform the restore.

Catalogs are also necessary. Catalogs are indexes of the data on backup media or backup files. When you want to restore data, you may not know which file contains the data you are looking for, so you query the backup system, and it uses a catalog to find the file or media, and then you can load that media or select that file to do the restore. The good news is that you can catalog media or files if the catalog does not exist. However, if you have 1000 backup files that were pulled from an old backup drive, the backup software will need to catalog all of them for you to know what is on each one.

A colleague needed to restore data from a backup at another site. The backup server there had crashed and local IT was currently rebuilding the server. The local IT sent over the backup files that were on the server, but the backup server at his site had never interacted with those files before, so he had to catalog all the files before he could find the data that needed to be restored. This added a bit of time to the restoration process.

Encryption is an important factor when storing backups. There may be many controls in place to protect data on production systems, but if backups are not encrypted, that data could be lost simply by exploiting the backup connection, backup media, or backup systems. For this reason, many companies encrypt their backups. To do the restore, you will need to provide the decryption keys, so keep these safe.

Licensing is also important. If you back up to a cloud service and then let the contract lapse, you will not be able to do a restore until you renew that license. Also, there is no guarantee that your backups will still be available if you let the contract lapse.

Connectivity

Backups, especially full ones, can take a lot of bandwidth depending on the size and type of the backup object. When migrating over a 1 Gbps or 10 Gbps Ethernet network, this is not as much of a concern, but bandwidth can be a huge constraint when performing backups over a low-speed WAN link such as a 5 Mbps MPLS connection.

Evaluate backup objects and their data sizes and then estimate how much time it will take to back them up over the bandwidth available. Be sure to factor in other traffic as well. You do not want the backup to impact normal business operations in the process.

Edge Sites

As information systems become more critical, companies are backing them up more often, even continuously. Latency can be an issue in ensuring timely backup completion when backing up to the cloud. The solution to latency with cloud backups is to select a vendor with edge sites close in proximity to the data that is being backed up. Edge sites are data centers closer to the customer.

Edge sites sometimes service requests and then synchronize back to the primary data center at a later time. Edge sites can also keep data close to the customer in their country of operation to meet data sovereignty requirements.

Equipment

You will need appropriate hardware to do the restore. If the data is on tape media, you will need a compatible tape device to do the restore. LTO drives can typically read two versions behind their stated version, and they can write to the stated version and one level down, so an LTO7 drive can read LTO 5, 6, and 7 and it can write to LTO 6 and 7.

You will also need enough storage space to do a restore. If you archived data to free up space but then later need it, you might need to purchase and install more storage first. You will also need enough bandwidth to copy down data from cloud backups.

Availability

It is very important to understand if the chosen backup requires downtime. Images of machines can sometimes fail when they are in use, so some image jobs are performed from boot disks when a server is offline.

Backups that require the system to be unavailable must be performed during a downtime. A downtime needs to be scheduled with stakeholders, such as end users and customers, and the stakeholders need to understand how long the downtime is anticipated to take.

If you anticipate performance degradation due to backups or restores, let stakeholders know. Some can adapt if they are aware of the issues, while some cannot, but they will at least know what is going on. A restore will likely be a higher priority than normal operations, but the helpdesk and other operations teams will need to be aware of the cause of the performance degradation.

Partners or Third Parties

You may use a third party or partner to perform backup services. The most common scenario is to use a cloud provider as the third-party backup service. It is important to understand your contact with the cloud vendor or other third party. Understand what their responsibilities are to you in the case of an emergency and how quickly data can be transferred from their site to yours.

If contracted IT performs backups for you, establish whether they will be available overnight or on weekends to perform emergency work if necessary. We know of one company that made the mistake of hiring a well-priced IT firm to manage its backups. The firm had two very knowledgeable people, but when the company needed a weekend restore, it learned that both IT people at the firm were out of town and unavailable.

Block-Level Backups and Transfers

Block-level backups reduce the time it takes to transfer data to the cloud. They are especially useful when dealing with large files. A block-level backup understands each of the individual blocks that make up the files in a backup set. When a file changes, the only data that is replicated to the cloud are the individual blocks that changed, rather than the entire file. A large 60GB file might be divided into many small 512KB blocks. A small change to the file would result in some of those blocks changing, and those alone would be replicated to the cloud.

Archiving

Archiving is another important function to reduce the costs of storage and backup operations. Organizations keep a lot of data, and some data is kept in the off chance that it is ever needed. This data does not need to reside on primary storage and can be moved to the cloud or to archival media instead, such as a hard drive, tape, optical media, or a flash drive. Cloud archiving options offer inexpensive ways to archive data to a data store that is available whenever users have an Internet connection. Cloud archiving options are best for portable machines such as laptops or mobile devices because they do not need to be connected to the corporate network to be archived. This preserves valuable organizational data for users on the go.

Local storage administrators should ensure that the media chosen is adequately protected against harm and that it is logged and cataloged so that it can be found if and when needed. Cloud backups should be verified periodically to ensure that data can be effectively retrieved in an acceptable amount of time.

CERTIFICATION SUMMARY

This chapter covered methods for protecting data and systems against issues that may come up such as mistakes, component failures, malicious activity, and disasters. Business continuity (BC) encompasses the activities that enable an organization to continue functioning, including offering services, delivering products, and conducting other activities deemed integral to running the business, during and following a disruptive incident.

Achieving a highly available computing environment is something that takes careful planning and consideration. There are multiple devices that need to be considered and multiple components in each device that need to be redundant and fault tolerant to achieve a highly available environment. High availability helps to prevent unplanned downtime and maintain service level agreements. An organization can set up a multisite configuration to have a hot site, warm site, or cold site so that in the event something happens to the primary data center the organization can migrate to a secondary data center and continue to operate.

Disaster recovery (DR) is the activities that are performed when a highly disruptive event occurs such as an outage for a complete site, fires, floods, or hurricanes. These events cause damage to information resources, facilities, and possibly personnel. A proper disaster recovery plan (DRP) can help an organization plan for and respond to a disaster through replication and restoration at alternate sites. Metrics such as the recovery time objective (RTO) and the recovery point objective (RPO) help organizations specify how much data can be lost and how long it should take to restore data and bring systems back to a functioning state. These decisions should be made based on the potential impact to the business so that impact is limited to acceptable levels.

This chapter wrapped up by discussing backup and recovery. A backup set is a secondary copy of the organization's data and is used to replace the original data in the event of a loss in a process known as restoration.

KEY TERMS

Use the following list to review the key terms discussed in this chapter. The definitions also can be found in the glossary.

alternate site　A facility in which an application can run if the primary site is unavailable. Alternate sites vary in how much effort and expense is required to make them functional for the application. *See also* cold site, hot site, *and* warm site.

asynchronous replication　A form of replication that stores the data locally and then reports back to the application that the data has been stored. It then sends the data to replication partners at its next opportunity.

backup target　The destination for a backup job.

bit-for-bit backup　A backup that captures the entire hard drive bit by bit.

block-level backup　A backup that captures only changed blocks of data, as opposed to the entire file.

business continuity plan (BCP)　Documented set of procedures and information about the organization that is collected and maintained so that the organization can continue operations in the event of a disaster.

cold site　An alternative site that includes only network connectivity. It is the least expensive alternative site option but takes the longest to ramp up. *See also* alternate site, hot site, *and* warm site.

contingency planning　Establishing alternate practices, sites, and resources that can be used in an emergency.

differential backup　A backup system that backs up all files that have changed since the last full backup and requires the last differential and the last full backup to perform a restore.

disaster recovery plan (DRP)　Documented set of procedures that defines how an organization can recover and protect specific IT systems in the event of a disaster.

edge sites　Data centers closer to the customer.

failback　The process of restoring operations to the primary system after a failover.

failover   The process of switching to a redundant system upon failure of the primary system.

fault tolerance   A feature of computer system design that increases reliability by adding redundant hardware components so that the system can continue to function in the event of a single component failure.

full backup   A backup that contains a complete copy of all files selected in the backup job. A full backup does not require any other backups for a restore operation.

hot site   An alternative site that is a duplicate of the original site, with complete hardware and backups. It is the most expensive alternative site option but takes the least amount of time to become fully operational. *See also* alternate site, cold site, *and* warm site.

incremental backup   A backup system that backs up the files that have changed since the last full or incremental backup and requires all incremental backups to perform a restore.

intersite replication   Replication that occurs between systems at the different sites.

intrasite replication   Replication that occurs between systems at the same site.

load balancing   A means of distributing workloads across multiple computers to optimize resources and throughput and to prevent a single device from being overwhelmed.

mean time between failures (MTBF)   The average length of time a hardware component will function before failing, usually measured in hours.

mean time to repair (MTTR)   The average length of time it takes to repair a hardware component.

mirror site   A duplicate hosted website or set of files used to provide improved performance and to reduce network traffic.

recovery point objective (RPO)   The maximum amount of data might be lost due to a disaster. Restore operations essentially bring files back to a point in time. The point in time is when the last backup was taken, if that backup is available. Any data written after that backup or "point" would be lost so the RPO defines how much data can be lost.

recovery time objective (RTO)   The maximum amount of time a system can be down after a failure or disaster. The RTO is concerned with how much time will elapse while backups are identified, loaded, restored, and verified. Data to be restored will not be available until these steps have been completed.

redundant system   A system that is used as a backup to the primary system in case of failure.

replica   A mirrored copy of data created between two redundant hardware devices.

resilience   The capability of a system to continue servicing the organization during a disruption. It is accomplished primarily through redundancy.

snapshot   A method of capturing the state of a virtual machine at a specific point in time.

synchronous replication   A form of replication that writes data to the local store and then immediately replicates it to the replica set or sets. The application is not informed that the data has been written until all replica sets have acknowledged receipt and storage of the data.

warm site   An alternative site that is somewhere on the continuum between a cold site and a hot site; it includes some hardware and some backups, although the backups could be a few days old. *See also* alternate site, cold site, *and* hot site.

TWO-MINUTE DRILL

Business Continuity Methods

❏   Business continuity (BC) encompasses the activities that enable an organization to continue functioning, including offering services, delivering products, and conducting other activities deemed integral to running the business, during and following a disruptive incident such as data corruption, a malware breach, a malicious insider attack, a system hack, or a major component failure.

❏   Contingency planning involves establishing alternate practices, sites, and resources that can be used in an emergency or to establish high availability.

❏   A mirror site can be used to create an exact copy of the original site to offset connection requests and improve performance for end users.

❏   A cold site does not include any backups or hardware. It is a physical location that has network connectivity where an organization can move its equipment in case of a failure.

❏   A hot site is a duplicate of the original site and has readily available hardware and a near-complete backup of the organization's data.

❑ A warm site is somewhere on the continuum between a hot and cold site and has readily available hardware but at a much smaller scale than a hot site.

❑ High availability is a system design approach that ensures a system or component is continuously available for a predefined amount of time. A system that is not highly available will fail if a single component fails.

❑ Fault tolerance allows a computer system to function as normal in the event of a failure in one or more of the system's components.

❑ Geo-clustering allows an organization to support enterprise-level continuity by providing a system that is location independent.

❑ Multipathing allows the configuration of multiple paths of connectivity to a storage device, providing redundancy for the connection to the storage device.

❑ Load balancing is achieved either through software or a dedicated hardware device and distributes incoming network application requests across multiple servers in a server farm to provide redundancy and maximize throughput.

❑ Resilience is achieved by architecting cloud and information systems that can withstand assault or faults.

❑ A service level agreement (SLA) is a contract that specifies the level of uptime that will be supported by the service provider.

Disaster Recovery Methods

❑ Organizations should build a disaster recovery plan (DRP) to ensure that they have implemented the proper disaster recovery strategy for their organization.

❑ A redundant system can be used to provide a backup to the primary system in case the primary system fails.

❑ Failover allows a system to automatically switch to a redundant system in the event the primary system fails.

❑ Organizations can implement a multisite configuration to create a backup site at an alternate location that allows the environment to be quickly relocated.

❑ Mean time between failures (MTBF) is the average length of time a device will function before it fails.

❑ Mean time to repair (MTTR) defines the average length of time that it takes to repair a failed component.

❑ DR defines parameters for what losses are acceptable in recovery in terms of how much data can be lost and how much time can be spent recovering. These are defined as the recovery time objective (RTO), which is the amount of time between an outage and the restoration of the service, and the recovery point objective (RPO), which is the maximum amount of data that can be lost, measured in the maximum number of hours or days of work that could be lost.

Backup and Recovery

- ❑ A backup is a process of copying and archiving data so that it is available to be restored in case the original data is lost or corrupted.
- ❑ Full system backups back up the entire system, including everything on the hard drive.
- ❑ Incremental backups back up only the files that have changed since the last backup and require the last full backup plus all the incremental backups to perform a restore.
- ❑ Differential backups only back up the changes since the last full backup and require the last full backup and the last differential to perform a restore.
- ❑ Backups are different from replication in that backups are created to store unchanged data for a predetermined amount of time and replicas are used to create a mirrored copy of data between two redundant hardware devices.
- ❑ Snapshots are used to preserve the state of virtual machine disk volumes at a specific point in time. While similar to a backup, snapshots should not be considered a replacement for traditional backups.
- ❑ Block-level backups understand each of the individual blocks that make up the files in a backup set. When a file changes, the only data that is replicated up to the cloud are the individual blocks that changed, rather than the entire file.

SELF TEST

The following questions will help you measure your understanding of the material presented in this chapter. As indicated, some questions may have more than one correct answer, so be sure to read all the answer choices carefully.

Business Continuity Methods

1. Which of the following would be considered a cold site?
   A. A site with no heating system
   B. A site that has a replication enabled
   C. A site that is fully functional and staffed
   D. A site that provides only network connectivity and a physical location

2. You are designing a disaster recovery plan that includes a multisite configuration. The backup site must include all necessary hardware and current backups of the original site. Which type of site do you need to design?

    A. Cold site

    B. Warm site

    C. Hot site

    D. Virtual site

3. Which of the following is a documented set of procedures that defines how an organization recovers and protects its IT infrastructure in the event of a disaster?

    A. MTBF

    B. MTTR

    C. RPO

    D. DRP

4. An organization recently had a disaster and the data center failed over to the backup site. The original data center has been restored and the administrator needs to migrate the organization back to the primary data center. What process is the administrator performing?

    A. Failover

    B. Failback

    C. DRP

    D. RTO

5. You have been tasked with distributing incoming HTTP requests to multiple servers in a server farm. Which of the following is the easiest way to achieve that goal?

    A. Mirror site

    B. Fault tolerance

    C. Redundancy

    D. Load balancing

6. When replicating data in a multisite configuration from the primary site to a backup site, which form of synchronization requires the system to wait before proceeding with the next data write?

    A. Asynchronous replication

    B. Synchronous replication

    C. Failover

    D. Mirror site

7. Which of the following terms can be used to describe a system that is location independent and provides failover?

    A. Clustering

    B. Load balancing

    C. Geo-clustering

    D. Failover

Disaster Recovery Methods

8. Which term is used to describe the target amount of time that a system can be down after a failure or a disaster occurs?

A. RPO

B. RTO

C. BCP

D. MTBF

9. Which of the following processes allows a system to automatically switch to a redundant system in the event of a disaster at the primary site?

A. Failback

B. DRP

C. Failover

D. Redundancy

Backup and Recovery

10. Which of the following backup processes needs the last backup and all additional backups since that backup to perform a restore?

A. Incremental

B. Differential

C. Full

D. Image

11. Which of the following backups could be restored without any additional backups?

A. Incremental

B. Differential

C. Full

D. Image

12. What is the easiest method for an administrator to capture the state of a virtual machine at a specific point in time?

A. Backup

B. Snapshot

C. Image

D. Clone

A SELF TEST ANSWERS

Business Continuity Methods

1. ☑ **D.** A cold site does not include any backup copies of data from the organization's original data center. When an organization implements a cold site, it does not have readily available hardware at the site; the site only includes the physical space and network connectivity for recovery operations, and it is the organization's responsibility to provide the hardware.
   ☒ **A, B,** and **C** are incorrect. A site that has replication enabled would not be considered a cold site. Also, a cold site would not be fully functional and staffed.

2. ☑ **C.** A hot site is a duplicate of the original site of the organization and has readily available hardware and a near-complete backup of the organization's data. A hot site can contain a real-time synchronization between the original site and the backup site and can be used to completely mirror the organization's original data center.
   ☒ **A, B,** and **D** are incorrect. A cold site does not include any backup copies of data from the organization's original data center. A warm site is somewhere on the continuum between a cold site and a hot site and would not include a current backup of the original site. Virtual sites are not a valid site type in disaster recovery.

3. ☑ **D.** A DRP (disaster recovery plan) describes how an organization is going to deal with recovery in the event of a disaster.
   ☒ **A, B,** and **C** are incorrect. MTBF (mean time between failures) is the average time a hardware component will function before failing, usually measured in hours. MTTR (mean time to repair) is the average time it takes to repair a hardware component. RPO (recovery point objective) is the maximum acceptable amount of time that data might be lost due to a disaster.

4. ☑ **B.** Failback is the process of switching back to the primary site after the environment has been shifted to the backup site.
   ☒ **A, C,** and **D** are incorrect. Failover is the process of switching to a redundant system upon failure of the primary system. A DRP is a documented set of procedures that defines how an organization can recover and protect its IT infrastructure in the event of a disaster. RTO is the maximum amount of time a system can be down after a failure or disaster.

5. ☑ **D.** Load balancing distributes workloads across multiple computers to optimize resources and throughput and to prevent a single device from being overwhelmed.
   ☒ **A, B,** and **C** are incorrect. A mirror site is a duplicate hosted website or set of files used to provide improved performance and reduce network traffic. Fault tolerance involves adding redundant hardware components to the system so it can continue to function in the event of a single component failure. Redundancy is used to protect a primary system from failure by performing the operations of a backup system. None of these options deals with balanced distribution of workloads.

6. ☑ **B.** Synchronous replication writes data to the local store and then immediately replicates it to the replica set or sets. The application is not informed that the data has been written until all replica sets have acknowledged receipt and storage of the data.
    ☒ **A, C,** and **D** are incorrect. Asynchronous replication stores the data locally and then reports back to the application that the data has been stored. It then sends the data to replication partners at its next opportunity. Failover is the process of switching to a redundant system upon failure of the primary system. A mirror site is a duplicate hosted website or set of files used to provide improved performance and reduce network traffic.

7. ☑ **C.** Geo-clustering uses multiple redundant systems that are located in different geographical locations to provide failover and yet appear as a single highly available system.
    ☒ **A, B,** and **D** are incorrect. Clustering connects computers together over a LAN, whereas geo-clustering enables connections over a WAN. Load balancing distributes workloads across multiple computers to optimize resources and throughput and to prevent a single device from being overwhelmed. Failover is the process of switching to a redundant system upon failure of the primary system.

Disaster Recovery Methods

8. ☑ **B.** RTO (recovery time objective) is the target amount of time a system can be down after a failure or disaster.
    ☒ **A, C,** and **D** are incorrect. RPO (recovery point objective) is the maximum acceptable amount of time that data might be lost due to a disaster. A BCP (business continuity plan) is a documented set of procedures and information about the organization that is collected and maintained so that the organization can continue operations in the event of a disaster. MTBF (mean time between failures) is the average length of time a hardware component will function before failing, usually measured in hours.

9. ☑ **C.** Failover is the process of switching to a redundant system upon failure of the primary system.
    ☒ **A, B,** and **D** are incorrect. Failback is the process of switching back to the primary site after the environment has been shifted to the backup site. A DRP (disaster recovery plan) is a documented set of procedures that defines how an organization can recover and protect its IT infrastructure in the event of a disaster. Redundancy is used to protect a primary system from failure by performing the operations of a backup system.

Backup and Recovery

10. ☑ **A.** An incremental backup backs up the files that have changed since the last full or incremental backup and requires all incremental backups to perform a restore.
    ☒ **B, C,** and **D** are incorrect. A differential backup backs up all files that have changed since the last full backup and requires the latest differential and the last full backup to perform a restore. A full backup contains a complete copy of all files selected in the backup job. An image is an exact copy of a system at the time the image was taken.

11. ☑ **C.** A full backup backs up the entire system, including everything on the hard drive. It does not require any additional backups to perform a restore.

☒ **A, B,** and **D** are incorrect. An incremental backup backs up the files that have changed since the last full or incremental backup and requires all incremental backups to perform a restore. A differential backup backs up all files that have changed since the last full backup and requires the last differential and the last full backup to perform a restore. An image is just an exact copy of a system at the time the image was taken.

12. ☑ **B.** Snapshots can be used capture the state of a virtual machine at a specific point in time. They can contain a copy of current disk state as well as memory state.

☒ **A, C,** and **D** are incorrect. A backup could be used to capture the state of a virtual machine if the administrator used a full backup, but the process takes considerably more time to complete than a snapshot and would not be the easiest method. An image is an exact copy of a system at the time the image was taken and would take a considerable amount of time. A clone would copy the entire contents of a disk to another disk but again would take a considerable amount of time, whereas a snapshot takes only a few seconds or minutes to complete.

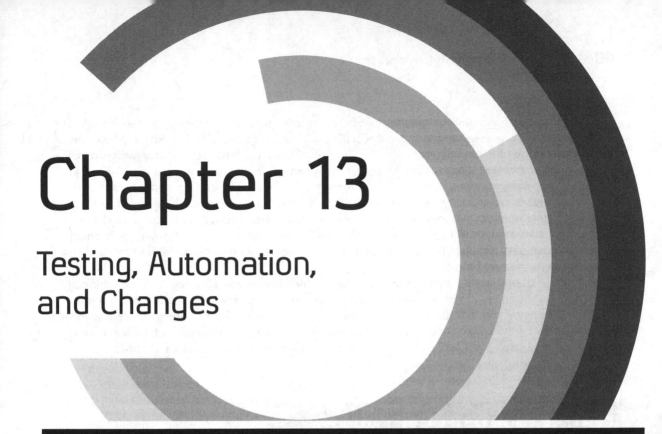

Chapter 13

Testing, Automation, and Changes

CERTIFICATION OBJECTIVES

O ne of the challenges of a cloud environment is service and maintenance availability. When organizations adopt a cloud model instead of hosting their own infrastructure, it is important for them to know that the services and data they need to access are available whenever and wherever they need them, without experiencing undue delays. Therefore, organizations need procedures for testing the cloud environment. Testing is a proactive measure to ensure consistent performance and operations of information systems.

Because maintenance tasks associated with on-premises technology are assumed by the cloud provider, operational and specific business rules need to be employed to best leverage the cloud technology to solving business problems. Standard maintenance tasks can take a significant amount of time, time that many companies just do not have. IT resources are typically stretched thin. This is where automation and orchestration step in. Automation and orchestration are two ways to reduce time spent on tasks, increase the speed of technological development, and improve efficiencies. Automation uses scripting, scheduled tasks, and automation tools to programmatically execute workflows that were formerly performed manually. Orchestration manages automation workflows to optimize efficiencies and ensure effective execution.

Improper documentation can make troubleshooting and auditing extremely difficult. Additionally, cloud systems can become extremely complex as they integrate with more systems, so a change in one place can impact systems across the enterprise if not managed correctly. Change and configuration management address these issues by tracking change requests, establishing a process for approval that considers the risks and impacts, and tracking the changes that are actually made.

CERTIFICATION OBJECTIVE 13.01

Testing Techniques

Availability does not just mean whether services are up or down. Rather, availability is also concerned with whether services are operating at expected performance levels. Cloud consumers have many options, and it is relatively easy for them to switch to another model, so it is important for cloud providers to provide consistently the level of service users expect.

Ensuring consistent performance and operation requires vigilant testing of services such as cloud systems or servers, virtual appliances, virtual networking, bandwidth, and a host of more granular metrics. Together, this data can paint a picture of where constraints may lie and how performance changes when conditions change. In this section, you will learn about the following testing techniques:

- Baseline comparisons
- Performance testing
- Configuration testing
- Testing in the cloud landscape
- Validating proper functionality
- SLA comparisons

- Testing sizing changes
- Testing high availability
- Testing connectivity
- Verifying data integrity
- Evaluating replication
- Testing load balancing

Baseline Comparisons

A baseline can be compared with actual performance metrics at any point following collection of the baseline to determine if activity represents the norm. The purpose of establishing a baseline is to create a sample of resources that are being consumed by the cloud services, servers, or virtual machines over a set time period and to provide the organization with a point-in-time performance chart of its environment.

Establish a baseline by selecting a sampling interval and the objects to monitor and then collecting performance data during that interval. Continue to collect metrics at regular intervals to get a chart of how systems are consuming resources.

The cloud providers offer the ability for each cloud virtual machine to send performance metrics to a central monitoring location in the cloud, such as with AWS CloudWatch. This also provides aggregated metrics for apps that consist of multiple virtual machines.

Procedures to Confirm Results

It is important to establish procedures to evaluate performance metrics in a baseline both in testing and production to confirm the accuracy of testing baselines. Load testing, stress testing, and simulated user behavior utilize workload patterns that are automated and standard, but these workloads may not be the same as actual user activity. Therefore, baseline comparisons from load testing, stress testing, or simulations could differ significantly from production baselines. Understand how baselines were obtained so that you do not use these baselines in the wrong context.

Decision makers use baselines to determine initial and max resource allocations, to gauge scalability, and to establish an application or service cost basis, so baseline numbers need to be accurate. Evaluate metrics for critical resources, including CPU, memory, storage, and network utilization.

CPU Utilization   CPU utilization may change as systems are moved from test to production and over time as overall utilization changes. Collect CPU metrics once systems have been moved to production and track the metrics according to system load so that numbers can be compared to testing baselines. The following list includes some of the metrics to monitor.

- **CPU time** Shows the amount of time a process or thread spends executing on a processor core. For multiple threads, the CPU time of the threads is additive. The application CPU time is the sum of the CPU time of all the threads that run the application. If an application runs multiple processes, there will be a CPU time associated with each process and these will need to be added together to get the full value.

- **Wait time** Shows the amount of time that a given thread waits to be processed.

Memory Utilization Memory utilization is also subject to changes in test versus production. Collect memory metrics once systems have been moved to production and track the metrics according to system load so that numbers can be compared to testing baselines. Some metrics to monitor include

- **Paged pool** Shows the amount of data that has been paged to disk. Paging from disk is performed when there is insufficient memory available, and it results in lower performance for each page fault.

- **Page faults** Shows the total number of times data was fetched from disk rather than memory since process launch. A high number of page faults could indicate that memory needs to be increased.

- **Peak memory usage** Shows the memory used by a process since it was launched.

Storage Utilization After evaluating CPU and memory performance compared to proposed resources, an organization must also test the performance of the storage system. Identifying how well the storage system is performing is critical in planning for growth and proper storage management. Collect storage utilization data in production. The performance metrics can be compared to baselines if load values can be associated with each metric for common comparison. Some metrics to monitor include

- **Application read IOPS** Shows how much storage read I/O was performed by the application process per second. Storage read I/O is when data is pulled from disk for the application. If an application runs multiple processes, there will be a read IOPS value associated with each process and these values will need to be added together to get the full value.

- **Application write IOPS** Shows how much storage write I/O was performed by the application process per second. Storage write I/O is when the application saves data to disk. Similar to read IOPS, if an application runs multiple processes, there will be a write IOPS value associated with each process.

- **Read IOPS** Shows how much storage read I/O was performed by the system per second.

- **Write IOPS** Shows how much storage write I/O was performed by the system per second.

Network Utilization   The fourth item to consider is network utilization. This also can change from test to production and as systems mature. Collect network metrics once systems have been moved to production. You can use network collection tools or collect statistics from network devices or the virtual machines themselves. Sometimes it is useful to collect network metrics at different points and then compare the results according to system load so that numbers can be compared to testing baselines. Some metrics to monitor include

- **Physical NIC average bytes sent/received**   Tracks the average amount of data in bytes that was sent and received over the physical network adapter per second.
- **Physical NIC peak bytes sent/received**   Tracks the largest values for the average amount of data in bytes that were sent and received over the physical network adapter. Peak values can show whether the adapter is getting saturated.
- **Virtual switch average bytes sent/received**   Tracks the average amount of data in bytes that were sent and received over the virtual switch per second. Track this for each virtual switch you want to monitor.
- **Virtual switch peak bytes sent/received**   Tracks the largest values for the average amount of data in bytes that were sent and received by the virtual switch. Track this for each virtual switch you want to monitor. Peak values can show whether the virtual switch is getting saturated.
- **Virtual NIC average bytes sent/received**   Tracks the average amount of data in bytes that were sent and received over the virtual NIC per second. Track this for each virtual NIC in the virtual machines you want to monitor.

Patch Version   Performance baselines can change following patch deployment. Patches can change the way the system processes data or the dependencies involved in operations. Security patches, in particular, can add overhead to common system activities, necessitating an update of the baseline on the machine.

Application Version   Performance baselines can change following application updates. Application vendors introduce new versions and patches when they want to address vulnerabilities, fix bugs, or add features. Each of these could result in performance changes to the application as the code changes. Applications may process data in a different way or require more processing to implement more secure encryption algorithms, more storage to track additional metadata, or more memory to load additional functions or feature elements into RAM.

Auditing Enabled   Enabling auditing functions can significantly impact performance baselines. Auditing logs when certain actions are taken such as failed logins, privilege use, error debug data, and other information useful for evaluating security or operational issues. However, tracking and storing this data increases the overhead of running processes and applications on the server and can have a big impact on the baseline.

If auditing is temporary, schedule auditing and baselining activities to occur on different dates if possible. If not, make operations aware that baseline values will be impacted due to auditing.

Management Tool Compliance   Management tools improve the process of collecting and analyzing data on performance metrics from testing, production, and other metrics and baselines collected as time progresses by putting all the data in one place where it can be easily queried, analyzed, and reported on.

Management tools can provide a dashboard of metrics that can be tweaked for operations teams to see changes, trends, and potential resource problems easily. Management tools may need to interface with cloud APIs or have an agent running on hypervisors to collect the data.

Performance Testing

A common item that is tested is how well the program or system performs. Cloud adoption is a combination of new systems and migrations of existing physical or virtual systems into the cloud. New systems will need to have new benchmarks defined for adequate performance. However, you can start with some generic role-based performance benchmarks until the applications have been tested under full load and actual performance data has been captured.

Existing systems should have performance metrics associated with ideal operational speed already, so implementers will be looking to meet or exceed those metrics in cloud implementations.

Performance metrics on systems without a load can show what the minimum resource requirements will be for the application, since the resources in use without activity on the machine represent the bare operational state. However, to get a realistic picture of how the system will perform in production and when under stress, systems will need to go through load testing and stress testing.

Load Testing

Load testing evaluates a system when the system is artificially forced to execute operations consistent with user activities at different levels of utilization. Load testing emulates expected system use and can be performed manually or automatically. Manual load testing consists of individuals logging into the system and performing normal user tasks on the test system, while automated testing uses workflow automation and runtimes to execute normal user functions on the system.

Stress Testing

Stress testing is a form of load testing that evaluates a system under peak loads to determine its max data or user handling capabilities. Stress testing is used to determine how the application will scale. Stress testing can also be used to determine how many standard virtual machine configurations of different types can exist on a single hypervisor. This can help in planning for ideal resource allocation and host load balancing.

Systems can be tested as a whole, or they can be tested in isolation. For example, testing of the web server in a test system may have allowed testers to identify the max load the web server can handle. However, in production, the operations team will deploy web servers in a load-balanced cluster. The data so far tells how many servers would be needed in the cluster for the expected workload, but the testing team needs to determine how many database servers would be required for the workload as well. Rather than spin up more web servers, the team can run a trace that captures all queries issued to the database server in the web server testing. They can then automate issuing those same queries multiple times over to see how many database servers would be required for the number of web servers.

Continuing the example, let's assume that testing revealed that the web server could host up to 150 connections concurrently. The traffic from those 150 connections was captured and then replayed to the database server in multiples until the database server reached max load. The testing team might try doubling the traffic, then tripling it, and so forth until they reach the max load the database server can handle; for this example, we will say that it is five times the load, or the load of 750 end-user connections. The testing team would typically build in a buffer since it is not good to run systems at 100 percent capacity, and then they would document system scalability requirements. In this example, assuming ideal load is 80 percent, or 120 connections instead of 150, the team would document that one web server should be allocated for each 120 concurrent user connections and that one database server should be allocated for every 600 concurrent user connections.

Taking this just a little bit further, the organization could configure rules to spin up a new virtual machine from a template based on concurrent connections so that the system as a whole auto-scales.

Remote Transactional Monitoring

After systems are deployed, operations teams will want to know how different functions within the application are performing. End users do not typically provide the best information on what is actually causing a performance problem, but remote transactional monitoring can simulate user activity and identify how long it takes to perform each task. Cloud-based options can be deployed at different locations around the world to simulate the user experience in that region.

Remote transactional monitoring, deployed in this fashion, can be used by operations teams to isolate tasks that exceed established thresholds and determine whether thresholds differ around the globe. They can then isolate the individual system processes that are contributing to the performance issue and determine whether the performance issue is localized to the edge.

Available vs. Proposed Resources

The elasticity associated with virtualization and cloud computing can result in different resources being available to a virtual machine than were proposed in requirements. Elastic computing allows computing resources to vary dynamically to meet a variable workload. (See Chapter 6 for more details.) Operations teams typically deploy machines with fewer resources than were proposed, but with a ceiling for growth.

Compute   It is best to allocate one vCPU to a virtual machine and then monitor performance, adding additional vCPUs as needed. When a virtual machine attempts to use a vCPU, the hypervisor must wait for the physical CPU associated with that vCPU to become available. The virtual machine believes that vCPU to be idle and will attempt to spread the load around if the application is configured for multiprocessing, but this can have an adverse impact on virtual machine performance if the physical CPU has a large number of processes in the queue. Furthermore, even idle processors place some load on the hypervisor from host management processes, so it is best not to provision more than will be necessary.

Where possible, monitor hypervisor metrics to determine if overcommitment bottlenecks are occurring. The most important metric to watch is the CPU ready metric. CPU ready measures the amount of time a virtual machine has to wait for physical CPU to become available. It is also important to monitor CPU utilization within each virtual machine and on the host. High CPU utilization might indicate the need for additional vCPUs to spread the load, while high host CPU utilization could indicate whether virtual machines are properly balanced across hosts. If one host has high CPU utilization and others have available resources, it may be best to migrate some of the virtual machines to another host to relieve the burden on the overtaxed host.

Memory   When configuring dynamic memory on virtual machines, ensure that you set both a minimum and a maximum. Default configurations typically allow a virtual machine to grow to the maximum amount of memory in the host unless a maximum is set. There are hypervisor costs to memory allocation that you should be aware of. Based on the memory assigned, hypervisors will reserve some amount of overhead for the virtual machine kernel and the virtual machine. VMware has documented overhead for virtual machines in its "VM Right-Sizing Best Practice Guide." According to VMware's guide, one vCPU and 1GB of memory allocated to a virtual machine produces 25.90MB of overhead for the host.

There is also the burden of maintaining overly large shadow page tables. Shadow page tables are the way hypervisors map host memory to virtual machines and how the virtual machine perceives the state of memory pages. This is necessary because virtual machines cannot access memory directly or they could potentially access the memory of other virtual machines.

These constraints can put unnecessary strain on a hypervisor if resources are overallocated. For this reason, keep resources to a minimum until they are actually required.

Configuration Testing

Configuration testing allows an administrator to test and verify that the cloud environment is running at optimal performance levels. Configuration testing needs to be done on a regular basis and should be part of a weekly or monthly routine. When testing a cloud environment, a variety of aspects need to be verified.

Data Access Testing

The ability to access data that is stored in the cloud and hosted with a cloud provider is an essential function of a cloud environment. Accessing that data needs to be tested for efficiency and compliance so that an organization has confidence in the cloud computing model.

Network Testing

Testing network latency measures the amount of time between a networked device's request for data and the network's response from the requester. This helps an administrator determine when a network is not performing at an optimal level.

In addition to testing network latency, it is also important to test the network's bandwidth or speed. Standard practice for measuring bandwidth is to transfer a large file from one system to another and measure the amount of time it takes to complete the transfer or to copy the file. The throughput, or the average rate of a successful message delivery over the network, is then determined by dividing the file size by the time it takes to transfer the file and is measured in megabits or kilobits per second. However, this test does not provide a maximum throughput and can be misleading because of overhead factors.

When determining bandwidth and throughput, it is important to understand that overhead needs to be accounted for, like network latency and system limitations. Dedicated software can be used to measure the throughput (e.g., NetCPS and iPerf) to get a more accurate measure of maximum bandwidth. Testing the bandwidth and latency of a network that is supporting a cloud environment is important since the applications and data that are stored in the cloud would not be accessible without the proper network configurations.

Application Testing

After moving an application to the cloud or virtualizing an application server in the cloud, testing of that application or server will need to be performed at regular intervals to ensure consistent operation and performance. There are a variety of different ways to test an application: some can be done manually, and some are automated.

Containerization is extremely effective at this point. Application containers are portable runtime environments that contain an application along with its dependencies such as frameworks, libraries, configuration files, and binaries. These are all bundled into the container, which can run on any system with compatible container software. This allows application testing teams to deploy multiple isolated containers to the cloud for simultaneous testing.

Performance counters are used to establish an application baseline and verify that the application and the application server are performing at expected levels. Monitor performance metrics and set alerting thresholds to know when applications are nearing limits. Baselines and thresholds are discussed in more detail in the "Resource Monitoring Techniques" section of Chapter 7. Batch files or scripts can easily automate checking the availability of an application or server or collecting performance metrics.

Applications need to be delivered seamlessly so that the end user is unaware the application is being hosted in a cloud environment. Tracking this information can help determine just how seamless that delivery process is.

A variety of diagnostic tools can be used to collect information about how an application is performing. To test application performance, an organization needs to collect information about the application, including requests and number of connections. The organization also needs to track how often the application is being utilized as well as overall resource utilization (memory and CPU).

Performance monitoring tools are valuable in evaluating application performance. Such tools can create reports on how quickly an application loads or spins up and analyze performance data on each aspect of the application as it is being delivered to the end user.

Follow this simple process in assessing application performance:

- Evaluate which piece of an application or service is taking the most time to process.
- Measure how long it takes each part of the program to execute and how the program is allocating its memory.
- Test the underlying network performance, storage performance, or performance of cloud virtual infrastructure components if using IaaS or PaaS.

In addition to testing the I/O performance of its storage system, a company can use a variety of tools for conducting a load test to simulate what happens to the storage system as the load is increased. Testing the storage system allows the organization to be more proactive than reactive with its storage and helps it plan for when additional storage might be required.

Testing in the Cloud Landscape

Cloud resources can be used as a "sandbox" of sorts to test new applications or new versions of applications without affecting the performance or even the security of the production landscape. Extensive application and application server testing can be performed on applications migrated to the cloud landscape before making cloud-based applications available to the organization's users. Testing application and application server performance in the cloud is a critical step to ensuring a successful user experience.

Testing the application from the server hosting the application to the end user's device using the application, and everything in between, is a critical success factor in testing the cloud environment.

Validating Proper Functionality

Systems are created to solve some business problem or to enhance a key business process. It is important, therefore, to test the execution of those activities to ensure that they function as expected. Functionality can be tested with the steps shown in Figure 13-1. These steps include identifying actions the program should perform, defining test input, defining expected output, running through each test case, and comparing the actual output against the expected output.

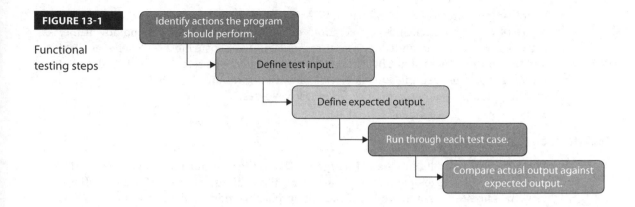

FIGURE 13-1

Functional
testing steps

Identify actions the program should perform.

Define test input.

Define expected output.

Run through each test case.

Compare actual output against expected output.

Quality assurance (QA) teams create a list of test cases, each with an establish input that should produce a specific output. For example, if we create a user, a report of all users should display the user. If we instruct the application to display the top ten customer accounts with the largest outstanding balances, we should be able to verify that the ones displayed actually have the highest balances.

SLA Comparisons

A service level agreement (SLA) is a contract that specifies the level of uptime that will be supported by the service provider as well as expected performance metrics. SLAs include provisions for how the service provider will compensate cloud consumers if SLAs are not met. At a minimum, these include some monetary compensation for the time the system was down that may be credited towards future invoices. Sometimes the provider must pay fines or damages for lost revenue or lost customer satisfaction.

SLAs are specific to a cloud service, meaning that the SLA for cloud storage might differ from the SLA for cloud databases, cloud virtual machines, and so on.

A multilevel SLA is used when different types of cloud consumers use the same services. These are a bit more complicated to read, and cloud consumers must understand which type they are to understand their expectations for availability. Multilevel SLAs are useful for cloud providers that provide a similar solution to different customer types because the same SLA can be provided to each customer. For example, a web hosting company may have different levels of service that are specified based on the customer type.

A service-based SLA describes a single service that is provided for all customers. There is no differentiation between customer expectations in a service-based SLA, unlike a multilevel SLA. For example, an Internet service provider (ISP) has specified the same SLA terms for each non-business customer.

In comparison, a customer-based SLA is an agreement that is unique between the customer and service provider. Since business terms can vary greatly, the ISP in this example may use customer-based SLAs for business customers and the service-based SLA for home users.

It is important to understand which SLAs are in place. As a customer, you should be aware of what your availability expectations are so that you can work around downtime. As a provider, you need to understand your responsibility for ensuring a set level of availability and the consequences of not living up to that agreement. The establishment of SLAs is an important part of ensuring adequate availability of key resources so that the company can continue doing business and not suffer excessive losses.

Testing Sizing Changes

Sizing is performed for hosts and their guests. First, the host must be provisioned with sufficient resources to operate the planned virtual machines with a comfortable buffer for growth. This step is not necessary if you are purchasing individual machines from a cloud vendor, because it is the cloud vendor's responsibility to size the hosts that run the machines it provides to you. However, this is an important step if you rent the hypervisor itself (this is called "dedicated hosting") in the cloud, as many companies do in order to give them flexibility and control in provisioning.

One of the many benefits of virtualization is the ability to provision virtual machines on the fly as the organization's demands grow, making the purchase of additional hardware unnecessary. If the host computer is not sized correctly, however, it is not possible to add virtual machines without adding compute resources to the host computer or purchasing additional resources from the cloud vendor.

It is a best practice to allocate fewer resources to virtual machines and then analyze performance to scale as necessary. It would seem that overallocating resources would not be a problem if the resources are available, and many administrators have fallen for this misconception. Overallocating resources results in additional overhead to the hypervisor and sometimes an inefficient use of resources.

For example, overallocating vCPUs to a virtual machine could result in the virtual machine dividing work among multiple vCPUs only to have the hypervisor queue them up because not enough physical cores are available. Similarly, overallocating memory can result in excessive page files consuming space on storage and hypervisor memory overhead associated with memory page tracking.

Test each resource independently so that you can trace the performance impact or improvement to the resource change. For example, make a change to vCPU and then test before changing memory.

Testing High Availability

High availability (HA) was introduced in Chapter 12. As HA systems are deployed, they should also be tested to ensure that they meet availability and reliability expectations. Test the failure of redundant components such as CPU, power supplies, Ethernet connections, server nodes, storage connections, and so forth. The HA system should continue to function when you simulate failure of a redundant component. It is also important to measure the performance of a system when components fail. When a drive fails in parity-based RAID (RAID 5, RAID 6, RAID 50), the RAID set must rebuild. This can have a significant performance impact on the system as a whole. Similarly, when one node in an active/active cluster fails, all applications will run on the remaining node or nodes. This can also affect performance. Ensure that scenarios such as these are tested to confirm that performance is still acceptable under the expected load when components fail.

You can test the drive rebuild for a RAID set by removing one drive from the set and then adding another drive in. Ensure that the drive you add is the same as the one removed. You can simulate the failure of one node in a cluster by powering that node down or by pausing it in the cluster.

Testing Connectivity

In addition to this end-to-end testing, an organization needs to be able to test the connectivity to the cloud service. Without connectivity to the cloud that services the organization, the organization could experience downtime and costly interruptions to its data. It is the cloud administrator's job to test the network for things such as network latency and replication and to make sure that an application hosted in the cloud can be delivered to the users inside the organization.

Verifying Data Integrity

Data integrity is the assurance that data is accurate and that the same data that is stored in the cloud is the data that is later retrieved. The data remains unchanged by unauthorized processes. Application data is valuable and must be protected against corruption or incorrect alteration that could damage its integrity. Data integrity testing can be combined with other testing elements to ensure that data does not change unless specified. For example, functional testing reviews each test case along with the specified input and output. Data integrity testing would detect data integrity issues with the direct test case, but automated integrity checks could also be built-in to verify that all other data has not changed in the process.

Similarly, when performing load testing, ensure that data does not change as the system reaches its max capacity. Performance constraints can sometimes result in a cascade failure, and you want to ensure that data is adequately protected in such a case.

Evaluating Replication

Some situations require an organization to replicate or sync data between its internal data center and a cloud provider. Replication is typically performed for fault tolerance or load balancing reasons. After testing network latency and bandwidth, it is important to check and verify that the data is replicating correctly between the internal data center and the cloud provider or between multiple cloud services.

Test by making a change on one replication partner and then confirm that the change has taken place on the other replication partners. Measure how long it takes to complete replication by creating replication metrics. Combine replication testing with load testing to ensure that replication can stay consistent even under heavy loads and to determine at what point replication performance decreases.

Testing Load Balancing

Some services can be configured to run on multiple machines so that the work of processing requests and servicing end users can be divided among multiple servers. This process is known as load balancing.

With load balancing, a standard virtual machine can be configured to support a set number of users. When demand reaches a specific threshold, another virtual machine can be created from the standard template and joined into the cluster to balance the load.

Load balancing is also valuable when performing system maintenance as systems can be added or removed from the load balancing cluster at will. However, load balancing is different from failover clustering in that machines cannot be failed over immediately without a loss of connection with end users. Instead, load-balanced machines are drain stopped. Drain stopping a node tells the coordinating process not to send new connections to the node. The node finishes servicing all the user requests and then can be taken offline without impacting the overall availability of the system.

When hosting an application in the cloud, there may be times where an organization uses the cloud as a load balancer. As discussed in Chapter 4, load balancing with dedicated software or hardware allows for the distribution of workloads across multiple computers. Using multiple components can help to improve reliability through redundancy, with multiple devices servicing the workload. If a company uses load balancing to improve availability or responsiveness of cloud-based applications, it needs to test the effectiveness of a variety of characteristics, including TCP connections per second, HTTP/HTTPS connections per second, and traffic loads simulated to validate performance under high-traffic scenarios. Testing all aspects of load balancing helps to ensure that the computers can handle the workload and that they can respond in the event of a single server outage.

CERTIFICATION OBJECTIVE 13.02

Automation and Orchestration

Organizations are adopting numerous cloud technologies that offer a myriad of services to them and often involve exchanging data through them. While the cloud provider is responsible for standard maintenance tasks associated with its on-premises technology, each organization is responsible for managing the cloud services it consumes, which includes implementing operational rules and specific business rules to best leverage the cloud technology to fulfill its operational needs. Automation and orchestration are two ways for an organization's IT staff to reduce the time spent on tasks, increase the speed of technological development, and improve efficiencies. The two concepts of automation and orchestration work well together, but they are not the same thing.

Automation uses scripting, scheduled tasks, and automation tools to programmatically execute workflows that were formerly performed manually. Orchestration manages automation workflows to optimize efficiencies and ensure effective execution.

Orchestration integrates organizational systems to provide more value to the organization. In orchestration, workflow automations are called runbooks, and each discrete step in a runbook is called an activity.

As an example of orchestration integration, an IT person working on a customer trouble ticket could generate change requests from within the ticketing system by selecting the type of change and providing relevant details. This would prompt a set of activities to get the change approved. Once approved, the runbook could be automatically executed, if one exists for the task, with the input provided by the IT person in the ticket. The output from the runbook could then be placed into the change management system and documented on employee time sheets while metrics are gathered for departmental meetings. This is the power of orchestration!

Orchestration requires integration with a variety of toolsets and a catalog of sufficiently developed runbooks to complete tasks. Orchestration often involves a cloud portal or other administrative center to provide access to the catalog of workflows along with data and metrics on workflow processes, status, errors, and operational efficiency. The orchestration portal displays useful dashboards and information for decision-making and ease of administration.

In this scenario, orchestration ensures that tickets are handled promptly, tasks are performed according to SOPs, associated tasks such as seeking change approval and entering time are not forgotten, and the necessary metrics for analytics and reporting are collected and made available to managers.

Interrelationships are mapped between systems and runbooks along with requirements, variables, and dependencies for linked workflows. This facilitates the management of cloud tools and integration of tools and processes with a variety of legacy tools. Management options are improved with each new workflow that automates management that once would have required logging into many different web GUIs, workstations, servers, or traditional applications, or sending SSH commands to a CLI to accomplish.

This section is organized into the following subsections:

- Event orchestration
- Scripting
- Custom programming
- Runbook management for single nodes
- Orchestration for multiple nodes and runbooks
- Automation activities

Event Orchestration

Event logs used to be reviewed by IT analysts who understood the servers and applications in their organization and had experience solving a variety of problems. These individuals commonly used knowledge bases of their own making or those created by communities to identify whether an event required action to be taken and what the best action was for the particular event.

The rapid expansion of the cloud and IT environments, as well as increasing complexity of technology and integrations, has made manual event log analysis a thing of the past. However, the function of event log analysis and the corresponding response to actionable events is still something companies need to perform. They accomplish this through event orchestration.

Event orchestration collects events from servers and devices such as firewalls and virtual appliances in real time. It then parses events, synchronizes time, and executes correlation rules to identify commonalities and events that, together, could form a risk. It ranks risk items, and if they exceed specific thresholds, it creates alerts on the events to notify administrators. Some events may result in runbook execution. For example, excessive logon attempts from an IP address to an FTPS server could result in runbook execution to add the offending IP address to IP block lists. Similarly, malware indicators could quarantine the machine by initiating one runbook to disable the switch port connected to the offending machine and another runbook to alert local incident response team members of the device and the need for an investigation.

Scripting

There are a wide variety of scripting languages, and some may be more applicable to certain uses. Most orchestration tools support a large number of scripting languages, so feel free to use the tools that are most effective for the task or those that you are most familiar with. The advantage of scripting languages is that they are relatively simple to learn, they can run with a small footprint, they are easy to update, and they are widely supported. Some of the most popular scripting languages include Microsoft PowerShell, JavaScript, AppleScript, Ruby, Python, SQL, Shell, Perl, PHP, Go, and R.

Custom Programming

Full-fledged programming languages can be used to create runbooks as well as hook into cloud-based APIs. Programming languages offer more capabilities than scripting languages, and there are powerful development environments that can allow for more extensive testing.

Programming languages are also good to use when runbook programs are increasingly complex because programs can be organized into flexible modules. Some of the most popular languages include C++, C#, Java, Python, Scala, and PHP.

Runbook Management for Single Nodes

As previously stated, runbooks are workflows organized into a series of tasks called activities. Runbooks begin with an initiation activity and end with some activity to disconnect and clean up. In-between activities may include processing data, analyzing data, debugging systems, exchanging data, monitoring processes, collecting metrics, and applying configurations. Runbook tools such as Microsoft System Center Orchestrator include plug-in integration packs for Azure and AWS cloud management.

Single-node runbooks are those that perform all activities on a single server or device. For example, this runbook would perform a series of maintenance activities on a database server:

1. Connect to the default database instance on the server.
2. Enumerate all user databases.
3. Analyze indexes for fragmentation and page count.
4. Identify indexes to optimize.
5. Rebuild indexes.
6. Reorganize indexes.
7. Update index statistics.
8. Perform database integrity checks.
9. Archive and remove output logs older than 30 days.
10. Remove rows from the commandlog table older than 30 days.
11. Disconnect from the default database instance on the server.

Orchestration for Multiple Nodes and Runbooks

Multiple-node runbooks are those that interface with multiple devices or servers. For example, this runbook would patch all virtual machines on all hosts in the customer cloud:

1. Enumerate virtual machines on each host.
2. Create a snapshot of virtual machines.
3. Add virtual machines to the update collection.
4. Scan for updates.
5. Apply updates to each machine, restarting load-balanced servers and domain controllers one at a time.

6. Validate service states.

7. Validate URLs.

8. Remove snapshot after 24 hours of successful runtime.

Automation Activities

A wonderful thing about runbooks is that there is a great deal of community support for them. You can create your own runbooks—and you definitely will have to do that—but you also can take advantage of the many runbooks that others have created and made available in runbook communities. Some of these can be used as templates for new runbooks to save valuable development time. Consider contributing your own runbooks to the community to help others out as well. Microsoft maintains a gallery of runbooks that can be downloaded for implementation on the Microsoft Azure cloud computing platform. Other vendors have set up community runbook repositories as well.

Here are some common runbook activities:

- **Snapshots** Activities can be created to take snapshots of virtual machines or remove existing snapshots or snapshot chains from virtual machines. Runbooks might use this activity when making changes to a virtual machine. The snapshot could be taken first, and then the maintenance would be performed. If things ran smoothly, the snapshot could be removed. Otherwise, the runbook could execute the activity to apply the snapshot taken at the beginning of the runbook. See Chapter 6 for more information on snapshots.

- **Cloning** Activities can be created to make a clone of a virtual machine. A runbook using this activity might combine it with an activity to create a template from the clone or an activity to archive the clone to secondary storage or an activity to send the clone to a remote replication site and create a virtual machine from it. See Chapter 6 for more information on cloning.

- **User account creation** Activities can be created to create a user account based on form input. For example, the activity could create the account in Windows Active Directory and on several cloud services and then add the user account to groups based on the role provided on the form input.

- **Permission setting** Activities can be created to apply permissions to a group of files, folders, and subfolders.

- **Resource access** Activities can be created to assign resources to a device such as storage LUNs, virtual NICs, or other resources. This can be useful for runbooks that provision virtual machines or provision storage.

- **User account management** Activities can be created to reset user account passwords, disable accounts, unlock accounts, or activate accounts.

CERTIFICATION OBJECTIVE 13.03

Change and Configuration Management

The process of making changes to the cloud environment from its design phase to its operations phase in the least impactful way possible is known as change management. Configuration management ensures that the assets required to deliver services are adequately controlled, and that accurate and reliable information about those assets is available when and where it is needed.

Change management and configuration management support overall technology governance processes to ensure that cloud systems are managed appropriately. All change requests and configuration items need to be documented to make certain that the requirements documented as part of the strategy phase are fulfilled by its corresponding design phase.

Change Management

Change management is a collection of policies and procedures that are designed to mitigate risk by evaluating change, ensuring thorough testing, providing proper communication, and training both administrators and end users.

A change is defined as the addition, modification, or removal of anything that could affect cloud services. This includes modifying system configurations, adding or removing users, resetting accounts, changing permissions, and a host of other activities that are part of the ordinary course of cloud operations, and also includes conducting project tasks associated with upgrades and new initiatives. It is important to note that this definition is not restricted to cloud components; it should also be applied to documentation, people, procedures, and other nontechnical items that are critical to a well-run cloud environment. The definition is also important because it debunks the notion that only "big" changes should follow a change management process. However, it is often the little things that cause big problems, and thus change management needs to be applied equally to both big and small changes.

Change management maximizes business value through modification of the cloud environment while reducing disruption to the business and unnecessary cloud expense due to rework. Change management helps to ensure that all proposed changes are both evaluated before their implementation and recorded for posterity. Change management allows companies to prioritize, plan, test, implement, document, and review all changes in a controlled fashion according to defined policies and procedures.

Change management optimizes overall business risk. It does this by building a process of evaluating both the risks and the benefits of a proposed change in the change procedure and organizational culture. Identified risks contribute to the decision to either approve or reject the change.

Lastly, change management acts as a control mechanism for the configuration management process by ensuring that all changes to configuration item baselines in the cloud environment are updated in the configuration management system (CMS).

A change management process can be broken down into several constituent concepts that work together to meet these objectives. These concepts are as follows:

- Change requests
- Change proposals
- Change approval or rejection
- Change scheduling
- Change documentation
- Change management integration

Change Requests

A request for change (RFC) is a formal request to make a modification that can be submitted by anyone who is involved with or has a stake in that particular item or service. IT leadership may submit changes focused on increasing the profitability of a cloud service; a systems administrator may file a change to improve system stability; and an end user may submit a change that requests additional functionality for their job role. All are valid requests for change.

Change Request Types   Change request types are used to categorize both the amount of risk and the amount of urgency each request carries. There are three types of changes: normal changes, standard changes, and emergency changes.

Normal changes are changes that are evaluated by the defined change management process to understand the benefits and risks of any given request. Standard changes request a type of change that has been evaluated previously and now poses little risk to the health of the cloud services. Because it is well understood, poses a low risk, and the organization does not stand to benefit from another review, a standard change is preauthorized. For example, resetting a user's password is a standard task. It still requires approval to ensure it is tracked and not abused, but it does not require the deliberation other changes might.

Emergency changes, as the name suggests, are used in case of an emergency and designate a higher level of urgency to move into operation. Even if the change is urgent, all steps of the process for implementing the change must be followed. However, the process can be streamlined. The review and approval of emergency changes, however, is usually executed by a smaller group of people than is used for a normal change, to facilitate moving the requested change into operation.

Change Proposals

Change proposals are similar to RFCs but are reserved for changes that have the potential for major organizational impact or severe financial implications. The reason for a separate designation for RFCs and change proposals is to make sure that the decision-making for very strategic changes is handled by the right level of leadership within the organization.

Change proposals are managed by the CIO or higher position in an organization. They are a high-level description of the change requiring the approval of those responsible for the strategic direction associated with the change. Change proposals help IT organizations stay efficient by not wasting resources on the intensive process required by an RFC to analyze and plan the proposed change if it is not in the strategic best interest of the organization to begin with.

Change Approval or Rejection

The change manager is the individual who is directly responsible for all the activities within the change management process. The change manager is ultimately responsible for the approval or rejection of each RFC and for making sure that all RFCs follow the defined policies and procedures as a part of their submission. The change manager will evaluate the change and decide to approve the change or reject it.

Change managers cannot be expected to know everything, nor to have full knowledge of the scope and impact of the change, despite the documentation provided in the change request because systems are highly integrated and complex. One small change to one system could have a big impact on another system. For this reason, the change manager assembles the right collection of stakeholders to help advise on the risks and benefits of a given change and to provide the input that will allow the change manager to make the right decision when he or she is unable to decide autonomously.

Change Advisory Board (CAB)   The body of stakeholders that provides input to the change manager about RFCs is known as the change advisory board (CAB). This group of stakeholders should be composed of members from all representative areas of the business as well as customers who might be affected by the change (see Figure 13-2). As part of their evaluation process for each request, the board needs to consider the following:

- The reason for the change
- The benefit of implementing the change
- The risks associated with implementing the change
- The risks associated with not implementing the change
- The resources required to implement the change
- The scheduling of the implementation
- The impact of the projected service outage concerning established SLAs
- The planned backout strategy in case of a failed change

FIGURE 13-2

The entities
represented by a
change advisory
board (CAB)

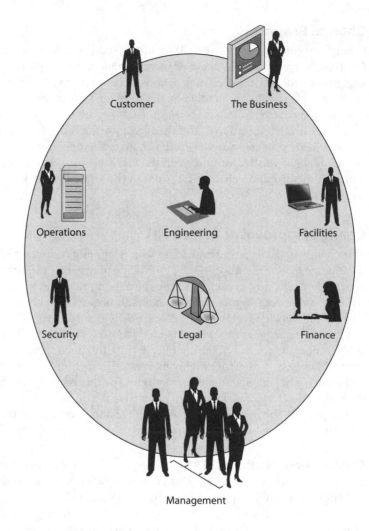

While this may seem like a lot of people involved in and much time spent on the consideration of each change to the environment, these policies and procedures pay off in the long run. They do so by limiting the impact of unknown or unstable configurations going into a production environment.

Emergency Change Advisory Board (ECAB) A CAB takes a good deal of planning to get all the stakeholders together. In the case of an emergency change, there may not be time to assemble the full CAB. For such situations, an emergency change advisory board (ECAB)

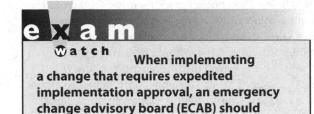

When implementing a change that requires expedited implementation approval, an emergency change advisory board (ECAB) should be convened.

should be formed. This emergency CAB should follow the same procedures as the standard CAB; it is just a subset of the stakeholders who would usually convene for the review. Often the ECAB is defined as a certain percentage of a standard CAB that would be required by the change manager to make sure they have all the input necessary to make an informed decision about the request.

Change Scheduling

Approved changes must be scheduled. There are some changes that can take place right away, but many must be planned for a specific time and date when appropriate team members are available and when stakeholders have been notified of the change.

Not all changes require downtime, but it is imperative to understand which ones do. Changes that require the system to be unavailable need to be performed during a downtime. Stakeholders, including end users, application owners, and other administrative teams, need to be consulted prior to scheduling a downtime so that business operations are not adversely impacted. They need to understand how long the downtime is anticipated to take, what value the change brings to them, and the precautions that are being taken to protect against risks For customer-facing systems, downtimes need to be scheduled or avoided so that the company does not lose customer confidence by taking a site, application, or service down unexpectedly.

Upgrades may not require downtime, but they could still affect the performance of the virtual machine and the applications that run on top of it. For this reason, it is best to plan changes for times when the load on the system is minimal.

Enterprise systems may have a global user base. Additionally, it may be necessary to coordinate resources with cloud vendors, other third parties, or with support personnel in different global regions. In such cases, time zones can be a large constraint for performing upgrades. It can be difficult to coordinate a time that works for distributed user bases and maintenance teams. For this reason, consider specifying in vendor contracts and SLAs an upgrade schedule so that you are not gridlocked by too many time zone constraints and are unable to perform an upgrade.

Working hours should also be factored in when scheduling change implementation. For example, if a change is to take three hours of one person's time, then it must be scheduled at least three hours prior to the end of that person's shift or the task will need to be transitioned to another team member while still incomplete. It generally takes more time to transition a task from one team member to another, so it is best to try to keep this to a minimum.

It is also important to factor in some buffer time for issues that could crop up. In this example, if the change is expected to take three hours and you schedule it exactly three hours before the employee's shift ends, that provides no time for troubleshooting or error.

If problems do arise, the task would be transitioned to another team member who would need to do troubleshooting that might require input from the first team member to avoid rework since the second employee may not know everything that was done in the first place.

If those implementing the change run into difficulties, they should document which troubleshooting steps they performed as well. This is especially important if others will be assisting the individual in troubleshooting the issue. This can also be helpful when working with technical support. This leads us to the next step in the change management process, documentation.

Change Documentation

It is important to keep a detailed log of what changes were made. Sometimes the impact of a change is not seen right away. Issues could crop up sometime down the road, and it helps to be able to query a system or database to view all the changes related to current issues.

After every change has been completed, it must go through a defined procedure for both change review and closure. This review process is intended to evaluate whether the objectives of the change were accomplished, whether the users and customers were satisfied, and whether any new side effects were produced. The review and closure process is also intended to evaluate the resources expended in the implementation of the change, the time it took to implement, and the overall cost so that the organization can continue to improve efficiency and effectiveness of the cloud IT service management processes.

Change documentation could be as simple as logging the data in a spreadsheet, but spreadsheets offer limited investigative and analytical options. It is best to invest in a configuration management database (CMDB) to retain documentation on requests, approvals or denials, and change implementation. The CMDB is discussed in the upcoming "Configuration Management" section.

Change Management Integration

The change process may sound very bureaucratic and cumbersome, but it does not have to be. Integrate change management into your organization in a way that fits with your organizational culture. Here are some ideas.

Users could submit change requests through a web-based portal, which would send an e-mail to the change approvers. Change approvers could post requests to the change approval board on Slack or some other medium to solicit feedback, and then use that feedback to approve or reject the change in the system. Communication on the issue could include a hashtag (a feature of Slack) with the change ID so that it could be easily tracked. Another channel could be used to communicate with stakeholders to schedule the time and resources for the change.

Some workflow can be built into the system to help automate scheduling. You can also use tools to help capture details of changes, such as scripts that dump firewall configurations to the configuration management database when they are made and archival tools to export the

CAB discussions to the database. When changes are complete, they can be updated in the same system so that everything is tracked.

Essentially, the entire process can be streamlined and still offer robust checks and balances. Don't be afraid of change management. Look for ways to integrate it into your company.

Configuration Management

Change management offers value to both information technology organizations and their customers. One problem when implementing change management, however, lies in how the objects that are being modified are classified and controlled. To this end, we introduce configuration management, which deals with cloud assets and their relationships to one another.

The purpose of the configuration management process is to ensure that the assets and configuration items (CIs) required to deliver services are adequately controlled, and that accurate and reliable information about those assets and CIs is available when and where it is needed. CIs are defined as any asset or document that falls within the scope of the configuration management system. Configuration management information includes details of how the assets have been configured and the relationships between assets.

The objectives of configuration management are as follows:

- Identifying CIs
- Controlling CIs
- Protecting the integrity of CIs
- Maintaining an accurate and complete configuration management system (CMS)
- Maintaining information about the state of all CIs
- Providing accurate configuration information

The implementation of a configuration management process results in improved overall service performance. It is also important for optimization of both the costs and risks that can be caused by poorly managed assets, such as extended service outages, fines, incorrect license fees, and failed compliance audits. Some of the specific benefits to be achieved through its implementation are the following:

- A better understanding on the part of cloud professionals of the configurations of the resources they support and the relationships they have with other resources, resulting in the ability to pinpoint issues and resolve incidents and problems much faster
- A much richer set of detailed information for change management from which to make decisions about the implementation of planned changes
- Greater success in the planning and delivery of scheduled releases
- Improved compliance with legal, financial, and regulatory obligations with less administration required to report on those obligations

- Better visibility to the true, fully loaded cost of delivering a specific service
- Ability to track both baselined configuration deviation and deviation from requirements
- Reduced cost and time to discover configuration information when required

Although configuration management may appear to be a straightforward process of just tracking assets and defining the relationships among them, you will find that it has the potential to become very tricky as we explore each of the activities associated with it.

At the very start of the process implementation, configuration management is responsible for defining and documenting which assets of the organization's cloud environments should be managed as configuration items. This is a highly important decision, and careful selection at this stage of the implementation is a critical factor in its success or failure. Once the items that will be tracked as CIs have been defined, the configuration management process has many CI-associated activities that must be executed. For each CI, it must be possible to do the following:

- Identify the instance of that CI in the environment. A CI should have a consistent naming convention and a unique identifier associated with it to distinguish it from other CIs.
- Control changes to that CI through the use of a change management process.
- Report on, periodically audit, and verify the attributes, statuses, and relationships of any and all CIs at any requested time.

If even one of these activities is not achievable, the entire process fails for all CIs. Much of the value derived from configuration management comes from a trust that the configuration information presented by the CMS is accurate and does not need to be investigated. Any activity that undermines that trust and requires a stakeholder to investigate CI attributes, statuses, or relationships eliminates the value the service is intended to provide.

on the **Job**

An enterprise IT organization at a large manufacturing company recognized the need to implement an improved configuration management process and invested large amounts of time and money into the effort. With the assistance of a well-respected professional services company leading the way and investment in best-of-breed tools, they believed they were positioned for success. After the pilot phase of the implementation, when they believed they had a good system in place to manage a subset of the IT environment, one failure in the ability to audit their CIs led to outdated data. That outdated data was used to decide on a planned implementation by the CAB. When the change failed because the expected configuration was different than the configuration running in their production environment, all support for configuration management eroded and stakeholders began demanding configuration reviews before any change planning, thus crippling the value of configuration management in that environment.

Configuration Management Database (CMDB)   A CMDB is a database used to store configuration records throughout their life cycle. The configuration management system maintains one or more CMDBs, and each database stores attributes of configuration items (CIs) and relationships with other configuration items.

Record all the attributes of the CI in a CMDB. A CMDB is an authority for tracking all attributes of a CI. An environment may have multiple CMDBs that are maintained under disparate authorities, and all CMDBs should be tied together as part of a larger CMS. One of the key attributes that all CIs must contain is ownership. By defining an owner for each CI, organizations can achieve asset accountability. This accountability imposes responsibility for keeping all attributes current, inventorying, financial reporting, safeguarding, and other controls necessary for optimal maintenance, use, and disposal of the CI. The defined owner for each asset should be a key stakeholder in any CAB that deals with a change that affects the configuration of that CI, thus providing the owner configuration control.

CERTIFICATION SUMMARY

The first part of this chapter covered testing techniques. The ability to test the availability of a cloud deployment model allows an organization to be proactive with the services and data that it stores in the cloud.

Automation and orchestration are two ways to reduce time spent on tasks, increase the speed of technological development, and improve efficiencies. Automation uses scripting, scheduled tasks, and automation tools to programmatically execute workflows that were formerly performed manually. Orchestration manages automation workflows to optimize efficiencies and ensure effective execution. Orchestration integrates organizational systems to provide more value to the organization. In orchestration, workflow automations are called runbooks, and each discrete step in a runbook is called an activity.

The chapter ended with a discussion on change and configuration management. A change is defined as the addition, modification, or removal of anything that could affect cloud services. Configuration management, on the other hand, is concerned with controlling cloud assets and their relationships to one another through configuration items (CI).

KEY TERMS

Use the following list to review the key terms discussed in this chapter. The definitions also can be found in the glossary.

approval process   The set of activities that present all relevant information to stakeholders and allows an informed decision to be made about a request for change.

asset accountability The documented assignment of a configuration item to a human resource.

automation The programmatic execution of a workflow that was formerly performed manually.

backout plan An action plan that allows a change to be reverted to its previous baseline state.

baseline A set of metrics collected over time to understand normal data and network behavior patterns.

change advisory board (CAB) The body of stakeholders that provides input to the change manager about requests for change.

change management The process of making changes to the cloud environment from its design phase to its operations phase in the least impactful way possible.

change monitoring Process of watching the production environment for any unplanned configuration changes.

configuration control The ability to maintain updated, accurate documentation of all CIs.

configuration item (CI) An asset or document that falls within the scope of the configuration management system.

configuration management (CM) The process that ensures all assets and configuration items (CIs) required to deliver services are adequately controlled, and that accurate and reliable information about them is available when and where it is needed, including details of how the assets have been configured and the relationships between assets.

configuration management database (CMDB) The database used to store configuration records throughout their life cycle. The configuration management system maintains one or more CMDBs, and each database stores attributes of configuration items and relationships with other configuration items.

configuration standardization Documented baseline configuration for similar configuration items (CIs).

data integrity   Assurance that data is accurate and that the same data remains unchanged in between storage and retrieval.

emergency change advisory board (ECAB)   The body of stakeholders that provides input to the change manager about requests for change in the case of an emergency when there may not be time to assemble the full CAB.

high availability (HA)   Systems that are available almost 100 percent of the time.

load balancing   Running services on multiple machines to share the burden of processing requests and servicing end users.

load testing   Testing that evaluates a system when the system is artificially forced to execute operations consistent with user activities at different levels of utilization.

orchestration   The management and optimization of automation workflows.

remote transactional monitoring   A system that simulates user activity to identify how long it takes to perform each task.

replication   Copying data between two systems so that any changes to the data are made on each node in the replica set.

request for change (RFC)   A formal request to make a modification that can be submitted by anyone who is involved with or has a stake in that particular item or service.

runbook   A workflow automation that can be used in orchestration tools.

stress testing   A form of load testing that evaluates a system under peak loads to determine its max data or user handling capabilities.

system logs   Files that store a variety of information about system events, including device changes, device drivers, and system changes.

testing   A proactive measure to ensure consistent performance and operations of information systems.

TWO-MINUTE DRILL

Testing Techniques

❑ A baseline can be compared with actual performance metrics at any point following collection of the baseline to determine if activity represents the norm.

❑ Performance testing evaluates the ability of a system to service requests in a timely manner. It uses performance metrics to track utilization of resources based on demand. Demand is simulated in load testing, stress testing, and remote transactional monitoring.

❑ Configuration testing allows an administrator to test and verify that the cloud environment is running at optimal performance levels.

❑ Testing in the cloud landscape utilizes cloud resources as a sandbox to test new applications or new versions of applications without affecting the performance or even the security of the production landscape. Testing should also confirm that the application or system can effectively perform the functions it was designed for.

❑ Testing should also confirm that SLA objectives can be met; that HA is implemented correctly; that sizing, replication, and load balancing have been correctly implemented; and that data integrity is not harmed by the application.

Automation and Orchestration

❑ Automation and orchestration are two ways to reduce time spent on tasks, increase the speed of technological development, and improve efficiencies.

❑ Automation uses scripting, scheduled tasks, and automation tools to programmatically execute workflows that were formerly performed manually.

❑ Orchestration manages automation workflows to optimize efficiencies and ensure effective execution. In orchestration, workflow automations are called runbooks, and each discrete step in a runbook is called an activity.

Change and Configuration Management

❑ Change management is the process of making changes to the cloud environment from its design phase to its operations phase in the least impactful way. Change management tracks changes to make auditing and future troubleshooting easier. It also ensure that change decisions follow due diligence and that all required tasks such as risk analysis and stakeholder notification are completed.

❑ Configuration management ensures that the assets and configuration items (CIs) required to deliver services are adequately controlled, and that accurate and reliable information about those assets and CIs is available when and where it is needed.

SELF TEST

The following questions will help you measure your understanding of the material presented in this chapter. As indicated, some questions may have more than one correct answer, so be sure to read all the answer choices carefully.

Testing Techniques

1. Which configuration test measures the amount of time between a networked device's request for data and the network's response?
    A. Network bandwidth
    B. Network latency
    C. Application availability
    D. Load balancing

2. Which of the following items is not included in a baseline?
    A. Performance
    B. Vulnerabilities
    C. Availability
    D. Capacity

Automation and Orchestration

3. Which of the following would be used in orchestration to execute actions to automatically perform a workflow?
    A. Simulator
    B. Workplan
    C. Runbook
    D. Scheduled Task

4. Which of the following is a scripting language?
    A. Cobol
    B. C++
    C. Java
    D. PowerShell

Change and Configuration Management

5. Which of the following are objectives of change management? (Choose all that apply.)
- A. Maximize business value.
- B. Ensure that all proposed changes are both evaluated and recorded.
- C. Identify configuration items (CIs).
- D. Optimize overall business risk.

6. Which of the following are objectives of configuration management? (Choose all that apply.)
- A. Protect the integrity of CIs.
- B. Evaluate performance of all CIs.
- C. Maintain information about the state of all CIs.
- D. Maintain an accurate and complete CMS.

7. Dieter is a systems administrator in an enterprise IT organization. The servers he is responsible for have recently been the target of a malicious exploit, and the vendor has released a patch to protect against this threat. If Dieter would like to deploy this patch to his servers right away without waiting for the weekly change approval board meeting, what should he request to be convened?
- A. ECAB
- B. Maintenance window
- C. Service improvement opportunity
- D. CAB

A
SELF TEST ANSWERS

Testing Techniques

1. ☑ **B.** Testing network latency measures the amount of time between a networked device's request for data and the network's response. Testing network latency helps an administrator determine when a network is not performing at an optimal level.

☒ **A, C,** and **D** are incorrect. Network bandwidth is the measure of throughput and is impacted by latency. Application availability is something that needs to be measured to determine the uptime for the application. Load balancing allows you to distribute HTTP requests across multiple servers.

2. ☑ **B** is correct. Vulnerabilities are discovered in vulnerability management, which is not a function of baselining. Organizations may track the number of vulnerabilities and remediation of those vulnerabilities, but as a business metric, not a baseline. A baseline is used to better understand normal performance so that anomalies can be identified.

☒ **A, C,** and **D** are incorrect. Baselines commonly include performance, availability, and capacity metrics to gain an understanding on how the system normally operates.

Automation and Orchestration

3. ☑ **C.** A runbook is a workflow automation that can be used in orchestration tools.

    ☒ **A, B,** and **D** are incorrect. A workflow simulator would not actually execute the actions as the question requires, it would only test execution. A workplan is a document describing the work that goes into a project. It is not used to execute actions in a workflow. A scheduled task may be used to run an action but this does not have the level of intelligence required in orchestration nor does it have the visualization features that orchestration has.

4. ☑ **D.** PowerShell is a scripting language for Windows.

    ☒ **A, B,** and **C** are incorrect. Cobol is a mature programming language primarily used on mainframe and legacy ERP systems. C++ is an object-oriented programming language, and Java, not to be confused with JavaScript, is a platform-independent programming language.

Change and Configuration Management

5. ☑ **A, B,** and **D** are correct. Maximizing business value, ensuring that all changes are evaluated and recorded, and optimizing business risk are all objectives of change management.

    ☒ **C** is incorrect. Identification of configuration items is an objective of the configuration management process.

6. ☑ **A, C,** and **D** are correct. The objectives of configuration management are identifying CIs, controlling CIs, protecting the integrity of CIs, maintaining an accurate and complete CMS, and providing accurate configuration information when needed.

    ☒ **B** is incorrect. Evaluation of the performance of specific CIs is the responsibility of service operations, not configuration management.

7. ☑ **A.** Dieter would want to convene an emergency change advisory board (ECAB). The ECAB follows the same procedures that a CAB follows in the evaluation of a change; it is just a subset of the stakeholders that would usually convene for the review. Because of the urgency for implementation, convening a smaller group assists in expediting the process.

    ☒ **B, C,** and **D** are incorrect. A maintenance window is an agreed upon, predefined time period during which service interruptions are least impactful to the business. The requested change may or may not take place during that time frame based on the urgency of the issue. Service improvement opportunities are suggested changes that are logged in the service improvement register to be evaluated and implemented during the next iteration of the life cycle. Life cycle iterations do not happen quickly enough for an emergency change to be considered even as a short-term service improvement item. CAB is close to the right answer, but based on the urgency of this request, Dieter likely could not wait for the next scheduled CAB meeting to take place before he needed to take action. The risk of waiting would be greater than the risk of deploying before the CAB convenes.

Chapter 14

Troubleshooting

Service and maintenance availability must be a priority when choosing a cloud provider. Having the ability to test and troubleshoot the cloud environment is a critical step in providing the service availability an organization requires. This chapter introduces you to troubleshooting tools, discusses documentation and its importance to company and cloud operations, and presents a troubleshooting methodology with various sample scenarios and issues that you might face in your career and on the CompTIA Cloud+ exam.

CERTIFICATION OBJECTIVE 14.01

Troubleshooting Tools

An organization needs to be able to troubleshoot the cloud environment when there are issues or connectivity problems. A variety of tools are available to troubleshoot the cloud environment. Understanding how to use those tools makes it easier for a company to maintain its service level agreements. This section explains the common usage of those tools.

There are many tools to choose from when troubleshooting a cloud environment. Sometimes a single tool is all that is required to troubleshoot the issue; other times a combination of tools might be needed. Knowing when to use a particular tool makes the troubleshooting process easier and faster. As with anything, the more you use a particular troubleshooting tool, the more familiar you become with the tool and its capabilities and limitations.

Connectivity Tools

Connectivity tools are used to verify if devices can talk to one another on a network. These include ping, traceroute, and nslookup. Ping verifies that a node is talking on the network, traceroute displays the connections between source and destination, and nslookup performs DNS queries to resolve names to IP addresses.

Ping

One of the most common and previously most utilized troubleshooting tools is the ping utility. Ping is used to troubleshoot the lack of reachability of a host on an IP network. Ping sends an Internet Control Message Protocol (ICMP) echo request packet to a specified IP address or host and waits for an ICMP reply.

Ping can also be used to measure the round-trip time for messages sent from the originating workstation to the destination and to record packet loss. Ping generates a summary of the information it has gathered, including packets sent, packets received and lost, and the amount of time taken to receive the responses. Starting with Microsoft Windows XP Service Pack 2, Windows Firewall was enabled by default and blocks ICMP traffic and ping requests. Figure 14-1 shows an example of the output received when you use the ping utility to ping comptia.org.

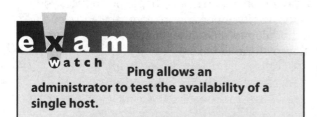

Ping allows an administrator to test the availability of a single host.

```
Microsoft Windows [Version 10.0.15063]
(c) 2017 Microsoft Corporation. All rights reserved.

C:\Users\Vanderburg>ping comptia.org

Pinging comptia.org [198.134.5.6] with 32 bytes of data:
Reply from 198.134.5.6: bytes=32 time=35ms TTL=49
Reply from 198.134.5.6: bytes=32 time=35ms TTL=49
Reply from 198.134.5.6: bytes=32 time=34ms TTL=49
Reply from 198.134.5.6: bytes=32 time=40ms TTL=49

Ping statistics for 198.134.5.6:
    Packets: Sent = 4, Received = 4, Lost = 0 (0% loss),
Approximate round trip times in milli-seconds:
    Minimum = 34ms, Maximum = 40ms, Average = 36ms
```

Traceroute

Traceroute is a troubleshooting tool that is used to determine the path that an IP packet has to take to reach a destination. Unlike the ping utility, traceroute displays the path and measures the transit delays of packets across the network to reach a target host.

The command in Microsoft Windows is written as tracert. Issuing the traceroute command followed by an FQDN or IP address will print the list of hops from source to destination. Some switches that can be used with traceroute include the following:

- **–d**   Disables hostname resolution
- **–h**   Specifies the maximum number of hops to trace
- **–j**   Specifies an alternate source address, so traceroute executes from that node instead of the one from which you are issuing commands
- **–w**   Specifies the timeout to use for each reply

Traceroute sends packets with gradually increasing time-to-live (TTL) values, starting with a TTL value of 1. The first router receives the packet, decreases the TTL value, and drops the packet because it now has a value of zero. The router then sends an ICMP "time exceeded" message back to the source, and the next set of packets is given a TTL value of 2, which means the first router forwards the packets and the second router drops them and replies with its own ICMP "time exceeded" message. Traceroute then uses the returned ICMP "time exceeded" messages with the source IP address of the expired intermediate device to create a list of routers until the destination device is reached and returns an ICMP echo reply.

Most modern operating systems support some form of the traceroute tool: as mentioned, on a Microsoft Windows operating system it is named tracert; Linux has a version named trace; on Internet protocol version 6 (IPv6), the tool is called traceroute6. Figure 14-2 displays an example of the tracert command being used to trace the path to comptia.org.

Nslookup and Dig

Another tool that can be used to troubleshoot network connection issues is the nslookup command. With nslookup, it is possible to obtain domain name or IP address mappings for a specified DNS record. Nslookup uses the computer's local DNS server to perform the queries.

FIGURE 14-2   Screenshot of data using the tracert command

```
C:\Users\Vanderburg>tracert comptia.org

Tracing route to comptia.org [198.134.5.6]
over a maximum of 30 hops:

  1    10 ms    13 ms     6 ms  box.local [192.168.1.21]
  2    18 ms    17 ms    63 ms  192.168.1.1
  3    35 ms    19 ms    24 ms  142.254.157.249
  4    22 ms    37 ms    31 ms  24.164.114.229
  5    16 ms    16 ms    16 ms  be23.bathoh0601r.midwest.rr.com [24.33.103.94]
  6    19 ms    23 ms    30 ms  be12.pltsohae01r.midwest.rr.com [65.29.1.89]
  7    34 ms    28 ms    43 ms  be25.clmkohpe01r.midwest.rr.com [65.29.1.28]
  8    48 ms    46 ms    42 ms  107.14.17.252
  9    43 ms    41 ms    49 ms  bu-ether11.chcgildt87w-bcr00.tbone.rr.com [66.109.6.20]
 10    73 ms    35 ms    82 ms  0.ae1.pr1.chi10.tbone.rr.com [107.14.17.194]
 11    44 ms    52 ms    49 ms  ix-ae-27-0.tcore2.CT8-Chicago.as6453.net [64.86.79.97]
 12    36 ms    36 ms    36 ms  if-ae-22-2.tcore1.CT8-Chicago.as6453.net [64.86.79.2]
 13    46 ms    75 ms    36 ms  p5-1.ir1.chicago2-il.us.xo.net [206.111.2.33]
 14    34 ms    37 ms    35 ms  vb2001.rar3.chicago-il.us.xo.net [207.88.13.130]
 15    41 ms    33 ms    39 ms  216.156.16.199.ptr.us.xo.net [216.156.16.199]
 16    53 ms    43 ms    80 ms  216.55.11.62
 17    47 ms    48 ms    42 ms  198.134.5.6

Trace complete.
```

Using the nslookup command requires at least one valid DNS server, which can be verified by using the ipconfig /all command.

The domain information groper (dig) command can also be used to query DNS name servers and can operate in interactive command-line mode or be used in batch query mode on Linux-based systems. The host utility can also be used to perform DNS lookups. Figure 14-3 shows an example of the output using nslookup to query comptia.org.

Configuration Tools

Configuration tools are used to modify the configuration of network settings such as the IP address, DHCP, DNS, gateway, or routing settings. Three important configuration tools you should know are ifconfig, ipconfig, and route.

Ifconfig

Ifconfig is a Linux command used to configure the TCP/IP network interface from the command line, which allows for setting the interface's IP address and netmask or even disabling the interface. Ifconfig displays the current TCP/IP network configuration settings for a network interface.

FIGURE 14-3

Screenshot
of nslookup
addresses

```
C:\Users\Vanderburg>nslookup comptia.org
Server:  box.local
Address:  192.168.1.21

Non-authoritative answer:
Name:    comptia.org
Address:  198.134.5.6
```

FIGURE 14-4 Screenshot of interfaces using ipconfig

```
eric@Neptune:~$ ifconfig
enp2s0: flags=4099<UP,BROADCAST,MULTICAST>  mtu 1500
        ether 10:c3:7b:1a:c5:2f  txqueuelen 1000  (Ethernet)
        RX packets 0  bytes 0 (0.0 B)
        RX errors 0  dropped 0  overruns 0  frame 0
        TX packets 0  bytes 0 (0.0 B)
        TX errors 0  dropped 0 overruns 0  carrier 0  collisions 0

lo: flags=73<UP,LOOPBACK,RUNNING>  mtu 65536
        inet 127.0.0.1  netmask 255.0.0.0
        inet6 ::1  prefixlen 128  scopeid 0x10<host>
        loop  txqueuelen 1000  (Local Loopback)
        RX packets 210  bytes 15568 (15.5 KB)
        RX errors 0  dropped 0  overruns 0  frame 0
        TX packets 210  bytes 15568 (15.5 KB)
        TX errors 0  dropped 0 overruns 0  carrier 0  collisions 0

wlp3s0: flags=4163<UP,BROADCAST,RUNNING,MULTICAST>  mtu 1500
        inet 192.168.1.199  netmask 255.255.255.0  broadcast 192.168.1.255
        inet6 fe80::adf1:d21b:7b0f:c02f  prefixlen 64  scopeid 0x20<link>
        ether 80:86:f2:90:32:bf  txqueuelen 1000  (Ethernet)
        RX packets 145168  bytes 215239452 (215.2 MB)
        RX errors 0  dropped 0  overruns 0  frame 0
        TX packets 24143  bytes 2361712 (2.3 MB)
        TX errors 0  dropped 0 overruns 0  carrier 0  collisions 0
```

Figure 14-4 shows the ifconfig command standard output, which contains information on the network interfaces on the system. The system this command was executed on has an Ethernet adapter called enp2s0 and a wireless adapter called wlp3s0. The item labeled "lo" is the loopback address. The loopback address is used to test networking functions and does not rely on physical hardware.

exam watch

Ifconfig lacks some command-line switches that ipconfig has that allow you to perform more advanced tasks, like clearing the DNS cache and obtaining a new IP address from DHCP, rather than just displaying TCP/IP configuration information.

Ipconfig

Ipconfig is a Microsoft Windows command used to configure a network interface from the command line. Ipconfig can display the network interface configuration, release or renew IP version 4 and 6 addresses from DHCP, flush the cache of DNS queries, display DNS queries, register a DHCP address in DNS, and display class IDs for IP versions 4 and 6. Figure 14-5 shows the command-line switch options available with the ipconfig command.

FIGURE 14-5 Screenshot of ipconfig options

```
C:\Users\Vanderburg>ipconfig /?

USAGE:
    ipconfig [/allcompartments] [/? | /all |
                                 /renew [adapter] | /release [adapter] |
                                 /renew6 [adapter] | /release6 [adapter] |
                                 /flushdns | /displaydns | /registerdns |
                                 /showclassid adapter |
                                 /setclassid adapter [classid] |
                                 /showclassid6 adapter |
                                 /setclassid6 adapter [classid] ]

where
    adapter             Connection name
                        (wildcard characters * and ? allowed, see examples)

    Options:
       /?               Display this help message
       /all             Display full configuration information.
       /release         Release the IPv4 address for the specified adapter.
       /release6        Release the IPv6 address for the specified adapter.
       /renew           Renew the IPv4 address for the specified adapter.
       /renew6          Renew the IPv6 address for the specified adapter.
       /flushdns        Purges the DNS Resolver cache.
       /registerdns     Refreshes all DHCP leases and re-registers DNS names
       /displaydns      Display the contents of the DNS Resolver Cache.
       /showclassid     Displays all the dhcp class IDs allowed for adapter.
       /setclassid      Modifies the dhcp class id.
       /showclassid6    Displays all the IPv6 DHCP class IDs allowed for adapter.
       /setclassid6     Modifies the IPv6 DHCP class id.

The default is to display only the IP address, subnet mask and
default gateway for each adapter bound to TCP/IP.

For Release and Renew, if no adapter name is specified, then the IP address
leases for all adapters bound to TCP/IP will be released or renewed.

For Setclassid and Setclassid6, if no ClassId is specified, then the ClassId is removed.

Examples:
    > ipconfig                     ... Show information
    > ipconfig /all                ... Show detailed information
    > ipconfig /renew              ... renew all adapters
    > ipconfig /renew EL*          ... renew any connection that has its
                                       name starting with EL
    > ipconfig /release *Con*      ... release all matching connections,
                                       eg. "Wired Ethernet Connection 1" or
                                           "Wired Ethernet Connection 2"
    > ipconfig /allcompartments    ... Show information about all
                                       compartments
    > ipconfig /allcompartments /all ... Show detailed information about all
                                       compartments
```

Route

The route command can be used to view and manipulate the TCP/IP routing tables of Windows operating systems. The routes displayed show how to get from one network to another. A computer connects to another over a series of devices, and each step from source to destination is called a hop. The route command can display the routing tables so that you can troubleshoot connectivity issues between devices or configure routing on a device that is serving that function.

Modification of a route requires modifying a routing table. A routing table is a data table stored on a system that connects two networks together. It is used to determine the destination of network packets it is responsible for routing. A routing table is a database that is stored in memory. It contains information about the network topology that is located adjacent to the router hosting the routing table.

When using earlier versions of Linux, the route command and the ifconfig command can be used together to connect a computer to a network and define the routes between the networks; later versions of Linux have replaced the ifconfig and route commands with the iproute2 command, which adds functionality such as traffic shaping. Figure 14-6 shows the route command using the print switch to display the current IP versions 4 and 6 routing tables.

FIGURE 14-6   Screenshot of the route command displaying current routing tables

```
C:\Users\Vanderburg>route print
===========================================================================
Interface List
 10...50 e5 49 c5 cd 4e ......Realtek PCIe GBE Family Controller
  1...........................Software Loopback Interface 1
===========================================================================

IPv4 Route Table
===========================================================================
Active Routes:
Network Destination        Netmask          Gateway       Interface  Metric
          0.0.0.0          0.0.0.0      192.168.1.21    192.168.1.162     25
        127.0.0.0        255.0.0.0         On-link         127.0.0.1    331
        127.0.0.1  255.255.255.255         On-link         127.0.0.1    331
  127.255.255.255  255.255.255.255         On-link         127.0.0.1    331
      192.168.1.0    255.255.255.0         On-link     192.168.1.162    281
    192.168.1.162  255.255.255.255         On-link     192.168.1.162    281
    192.168.1.255  255.255.255.255         On-link     192.168.1.162    281
        224.0.0.0        240.0.0.0         On-link         127.0.0.1    331
        224.0.0.0        240.0.0.0         On-link     192.168.1.162    281
  255.255.255.255  255.255.255.255         On-link         127.0.0.1    331
  255.255.255.255  255.255.255.255         On-link     192.168.1.162    281
===========================================================================
Persistent Routes:
  Network Address          Netmask  Gateway Address  Metric
          0.0.0.0          0.0.0.0      192.168.1.1  Default
===========================================================================

IPv6 Route Table
===========================================================================
Active Routes:
 If Metric Network Destination      Gateway
  1    331 ::1/128                  On-link
 10    281 fe80::/64                On-link
 10    281 fe80::44e2:6bf1:10bb:f30d/128
                                    On-link
  1    331 ff00::/8                 On-link
 10    281 ff00::/8                 On-link
===========================================================================
Persistent Routes:
  None
```

Query Tools

Query tools are used to view the status of network services. The two commands you should be familiar with are netstat and arp. Netstat displays network connections, routing tables, and network protocol statistics. Arp displays the MAC addresses that a computer or network devices know about.

Netstat

If you want to display all active network connections, routing tables, and network protocol statistics, you can use the netstat command. Available in most operating systems, the netstat command can be used to detect problems with the network and determine how much network traffic there is. It can also display protocol and Ethernet statistics and all the currently active TCP/IP network connections. Figure 14-7 shows the options available with the netstat command.

FIGURE 14-7   Screenshot of active connections using netstat

```
C:\Users\Vanderburg>netstat /?

Displays protocol statistics and current TCP/IP network connections.

NETSTAT [-a] [-b] [-e] [-f] [-n] [-o] [-p proto] [-r] [-s] [-x] [-t] [interval]

  -a            Displays all connections and listening ports.
  -b            Displays the executable involved in creating each connection or
                listening port. In some cases well-known executables host
                multiple independent components, and in these cases the
                sequence of components involved in creating the connection
                or listening port is displayed. In this case the executable
                name is in [] at the bottom, on top is the component it called,
                and so forth until TCP/IP was reached. Note that this option
                can be time-consuming and will fail unless you have sufficient
                permissions.
  -e            Displays Ethernet statistics. This may be combined with the -s
                option.
  -f            Displays Fully Qualified Domain Names (FQDN) for foreign
                addresses.
  -n            Displays addresses and port numbers in numerical form.
  -o            Displays the owning process ID associated with each connection.
  -p proto      Shows connections for the protocol specified by proto; proto
                may be any of: TCP, UDP, TCPv6, or UDPv6.  If used with the -s
                option to display per-protocol statistics, proto may be any of:
                IP, IPv6, ICMP, ICMPv6, TCP, TCPv6, UDP, or UDPv6.
  -q            Displays all connections, listening ports, and bound
                nonlistening TCP ports. Bound nonlistening ports may or may not
                be associated with an active connection.
  -r            Displays the routing table.
  -s            Displays per-protocol statistics.  By default, statistics are
                shown for IP, IPv6, ICMP, ICMPv6, TCP, TCPv6, UDP, and UDPv6;
                the -p option may be used to specify a subset of the default.
  -t            Displays the current connection offload state.
  -x            Displays NetworkDirect connections, listeners, and shared
                endpoints.
  -y            Displays the TCP connection template for all connections.
                Cannot be combined with the other options.
  interval      Redisplays selected statistics, pausing interval seconds
                between each display.  Press CTRL+C to stop redisplaying
                statistics.  If omitted, netstat will print the current
                configuration information once.
```

Recently while troubleshooting a network connection, we were having issues determining what DNS mapping an IP address had. We used the nslookup tool and entered the IP address that we were trying to map to a DNS name; nslookup returned the result of the DNS registration for the particular IP address.

Arp Command

Another helpful troubleshooting tool is the arp command. The arp command uses the Address Resolution Protocol (ARP) to resolve an IP address to either a physical address or a media access control (MAC) address. The arp command makes it possible to display the current ARP entries or the ARP table and to add a static entry. Figure 14-8 uses the arp –a command to view the ARP cache of a computer.

Remote Administration Tools

Remote administration tools allow connectivity to systems or network devices. The two tools you should know about for troubleshooting are used to connect to network devices such as switches and routers. They include Telnet and Secure Shell (SSH).

FIGURE 14-8

Screenshot of the ARP cache showing both the Internet address and the physical address

```
C:\Users\Vanderburg>arp -a

Interface: 192.168.1.162 --- 0xa
  Internet Address      Physical Address      Type
  192.168.1.1           14-cc-20-ec-2d-8e     dynamic
  192.168.1.9           00-08-9b-cf-d0-3e     dynamic
  192.168.1.10          00-08-9b-c7-64-03     dynamic
  192.168.1.11          00-08-9b-d2-56-b6     dynamic
  192.168.1.21          e8-44-7e-00-74-f4     dynamic
  192.168.1.100         b8-e9-37-af-e1-dc     dynamic
  192.168.1.104         b8-3e-59-48-39-6d     dynamic
  192.168.1.113         00-0e-58-11-c0-ca     dynamic
  192.168.1.117         d8-d4-3c-f9-56-76     dynamic
  192.168.1.168         00-6b-9e-4f-0c-77     dynamic
  192.168.1.172         a4-77-33-f5-5d-56     dynamic
  192.168.1.185         f0-79-59-2b-b1-8d     dynamic
  192.168.1.199         80-86-f2-90-32-bf     dynamic
  192.168.1.209         d0-bf-9c-b4-10-8d     dynamic
  192.168.1.233         6c-3b-e5-01-51-41     dynamic
  192.168.1.234         f0-1d-bc-3d-7f-80     dynamic
  192.168.1.255         ff-ff-ff-ff-ff-ff     static
  224.0.0.2             01-00-5e-00-00-02     static
  224.0.0.22            01-00-5e-00-00-16     static
  224.0.0.251           01-00-5e-00-00-fb     static
  224.0.0.252           01-00-5e-00-00-fc     static
  224.0.1.60            01-00-5e-00-01-3c     static
  239.255.188.44        01-00-5e-7f-bc-2c     static
  239.255.255.250       01-00-5e-7f-ff-fa     static
  255.255.255.255       ff-ff-ff-ff-ff-ff     static
```

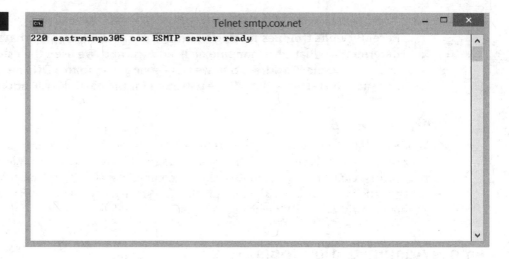

FIGURE 14-9

Screenshot of a
Telnet session

Telnet

If a user wants to connect their computer to another computer or server running the
Telnet service over the network, they can enter commands via the Telnet program, and
the commands are executed as if they were being entered directly on the server console.
Telnet enables the user to control a server
and communicate with other servers over the
network.

A valid username and password are required
to activate a Telnet session; nonetheless,
Telnet has security risks when it is used over
any network because credentials and data are
exchanged in plaintext. Figure 14-9 shows an
example of a Telnet session established with a
remote server.

e**x**a**m**
ⓦatch **Telnet and SSH both allow
an administrator to connect to a server
remotely, the primary difference being that
SSH offers security mechanisms to protect
against malicious intent.**

SSH

SSH is another protocol that enables the user to securely control a server and communicate
with other servers over the network. Secure Shell and its most recent version Secure Shell
version 2 (SSHv2) have become a more popular option for providing a secure remote
command-line interface than Telnet because they encrypt credentials and data.

Figure 14-10 shows an example of a SSH session established with a remote server
192.168.254.254. In this screenshot, a connection has been established and the remote
server is asking for a username to log in. After a username is provided, the system will
ask for a password.

FIGURE 14-10

Screenshot of a
SSH session

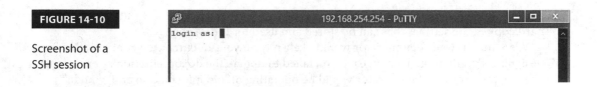

CERTIFICATION OBJECTIVE 14.02

Documentation and Analysis

Being able to use the proper tools is a good start when troubleshooting cloud computing issues. Correctly creating and maintaining the correct documentation makes the troubleshooting process quicker and easier. It is important for the cloud administrator to document every aspect of the cloud environment, including its setup and configuration and which applications are running on which host computer or virtual machine. Also, the cloud administrator should assign responsibility for each application and its server platform to a specific support person who can respond quickly if an issue should arise that impacts the application.

When issues come up, cloud professionals need to know where to look to find the data they need to solve the problem. The primary place they look is in log files. Operating systems, services, and applications create log files that track certain events as they occur on the computer. Log files can store a variety of information, including device changes, device driver loading and unloading, system changes, events, and much more.

Documentation

Documentation needs to be clear and easy to understand for anyone who may need to use it and should be regularly reviewed to ensure that it is up to date and accurate. Documenting the person responsible for creating and maintaining the application and where it is hosted is a good process that saves valuable time when troubleshooting any potential issues with the cloud environment.

In addition to documenting the person responsible for the application and hosting computer, an organization also needs to record device configurations. This provides a quick and easy way to recover a device in the case of failure. By utilizing a document to swap a faulty device and mimic its configuration quickly, the company can immediately replace the failed device.

When documenting device configuration, it is imperative that the document is updated every time a significant change is made to that device. Otherwise, coworkers, auditors, or other employees might operate off out-of-date information. For example, let's say you are working on a firewall that has been in place and running for the last three years. After making the required changes, you then update or re-create the documentation so that there is a current document listing all the device settings and configurations for that firewall.

This makes it easier to manage the device if there are problems later on, and it gives you a hard copy of the settings that can be stored and used for future changes.

Also, the firewall administrator would likely rely on your documented configuration to design new configuration changes. If you failed to update the documentation after making change, the firewall administrator would be operating off old information and wouldn't factor in the changes that you made to the configuration.

Configuration management tools are available that can automatically log changes to rule sets. These, along with orchestration tools and runbooks, can be used to update documentation programmatically following an approved change. See more on orchestration and automation in Chapter 13.

Log Files

Logs files are extremely important in troubleshooting problems. Operating systems, services, and applications create log files that track certain events as they occur on the computer. Log files can store a variety of information, including device changes, device drivers, system changes, events, and much more.

EXAM AT WORK

A Real-World Look at Documentation

We were recently tasked with creating documentation for an application that was going to be monitored in a distributed application diagram within Microsoft SharePoint. To have a satisfactory diagram to display inside of Microsoft SharePoint for the entire organization to view, we needed to collect as much information as possible. The group wanted to monitor the application from end to end, so we needed to know which server the application used for the web server, which server it used for the database server, which network devices and switches the servers connected to, the location of the end users who used the application, and so on.

The information-gathering process took us from the developer who created the application to the database administrator who could explain the back-end infrastructure to the server administrator and then the network administrator and so on. As you can see, to truly document and monitor an application, you need to talk to everyone who is involved in keeping that application operational.

From our documentation, the organization now has a clear picture of exactly what systems are involved with keeping that application operational and functioning at peak performance. It makes it easier to troubleshoot and monitor the application and set performance metrics. It also allows for a true diagram of the application with true alerting and reporting of any disruptions. As new administrators join the organization, they can use the documentation to understand better how the application and the environment work together and which systems support each other.

Log files allow for closer examination of events that have occurred on the system over a more extended period. Some logs keep information for months at a time, allowing a cloud administrator to go back and see when an issue started and if any issues seem to coincide with a software installation or a hardware configuration change.

Figure 14-11 shows the event viewer application for a Microsoft Windows system. The event viewer application in this screenshot is displaying the application log and an error is highlighted for the Microsoft Photos application that failed due to a problem with a .NET module.

There are a variety of software applications that can be used to gather the system logs from a group of machines and send those records to a central administration console, making it possible for the administrator to view the logs of multiple servers from a single console.

FIGURE 14-11   Screenshot of an error in the application event log

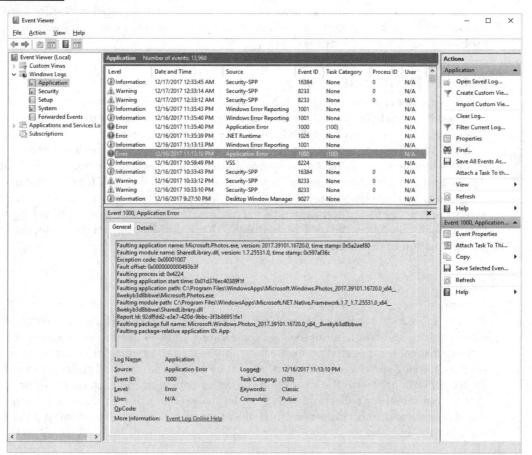

Logs can take up much space on servers, but you will want to keep logs around for a long time in case they are needed to investigate a problem or a security issue. Logs are set by default to grow to a specific size and then roll over. Rolling over overwrites the oldest log entries with new ones. This can cause considerable problems when you need to research what has been happening to a server because rollover can cause valuable log data to be overwritten.

For this reason, you might want to archive logs to a cloud logging and archiving service such as Logentries, OpenStack, Sumo Logic, syslog-ng, Amazon S3, Amazon CloudWatch, or Papertrail. These services will allow you to free up space on your cloud servers, while still retaining access to the log files when needed. Some of these services also allow for event correlation, or they can tie into event correlation services.

Event correlation can combine authentication requests from domain controllers, incoming packets from perimeter devices, and data requests from application servers to gain a more complete picture of what is going on. Software exists to automate much of the process. Such software, called security information and event management (SIEM), archives logs and reviews the logs in real time against correlation rules to identify possible threats or problems. See Chapter 10 for a review on SIEM.

Network Device and IoT Logs

Log files are not restricted to servers. Network devices, even IoT devices, have log files that can contain useful information in troubleshooting issues. These devices usually have a smaller set of logs. These logs may have settings for how much data is logged.

If the standard log settings do not seem to provide enough information when troubleshooting an issue, you can enable verbose logging. Verbose logging records more detailed information than standard logging but is recommended only for troubleshooting a particular problem since it tends to fill up the limited space on network and IoT devices. To conserve space and prevent essential events from being overwritten, verbose logging should be disabled after the issue is resolved so that it does not impact the performance of the application or the computer.

Syslog

Network devices can generate events in different formats, and they often have very little space to store logs. Most devices only have space for system and configuration data. This means that if you want to store the logs somewhere, you will need to use a syslog. The syslog protocol is supported by a wide range of devices and can log different types of events. A syslog server receives messages sent by various devices and collects those. Each device is configured with the location of the syslog collector, and each sends his or her logs to that server for collection. syslog can be analyzed in place, or it can be archived to a cloud logging and archiving service, just like other logs. For more information on syslog, see Chapter 7.

CERTIFICATION OBJECTIVE 14.03

Troubleshooting Methodology

CompTIA has established a troubleshooting methodology consisting of six steps:

Step 1: Identify the problem.

Determine when the problem first occurred and what has changed since then. Determining the first occurrence is typically accomplished by interviewing the user. Identify the scope of the problem, including which machines and network devices, subnets, sites, or domains are affected. Identifying the scope may involve interviewing others in the department or company. Before moving to further steps, ensure that a backup is taken of the system so that you can revert back if changes make the problem worse as you are troubleshooting.

Since both these steps require asking the user or others questions, it is important to be courteous and respectful. Show the user that you are concerned about the problem by actively listening to what they have to say. All too often, IT professionals want to run off as soon as a problem is mentioned so that they can begin fixing it. However, in the rush to fix the problem, they may not truly understand the problem and give the user the impression that their problem is not important.

A critical step in identifying the problem is to ask the user to demonstrate what is not working for them. If they say the Internet is not working on their cloud virtual desktop, ask them to demonstrate. They may show you that a certain site does not come up, but when you ask them to go to another site, it loads properly. In this way, both you and the user are able to better understand the scope of the problem and the user might be able to do more while you troubleshoot.

Step 2: Establish a theory of probable causes.

The information gathered in Step 1 should help in generating possible causes. Ask yourself what is common between devices that are experiencing the issue. Do they share a common connection or resource? Be sure to question the obvious (the simple things). Many times problems can be solved by something rather simple such as plugging in an Ethernet cable, verifying that users are typing a URL or UNC correctly, or verifying that target systems are turned on. Don't spend your time working out potential complex solutions until you have eliminated the simple solutions.

Documentation was mentioned earlier in this chapter and it comes in very handy when troubleshooting issues. Be sure to review documentation on how systems should be configured. You may need to review vendor documentation as well, so know where to find this documentation. Make sure you identify the product version number that the user is running so that you can refer to the correct vendor document.

Step 3: Test the theory to determine the cause.

At this point, you will likely have multiple theories on what might be the problem. Only one of those theories will be correct so you will need to test the theories to identify which one it is. Start by testing the simplest theories before thinking through the complex ones.

As mentioned in the previous step, most issues are caused by simple things, and simple things are easier to test. Ensure that the system you use for testing is similar enough to the one that is experiencing issues and ensure that you can replicate the issue on the test system before attempting a fix. Some IT professionals have worked hard to deploy a solution to a system that was not experiencing the issue and they then falsely believe they fixed the issue when they later test.

If you need to have the user test some things, be sure to ask politely. Phrase your request in such a way as to not cause the user to think that you are blaming them for the problem, even if you believe it is a user error. If you are incorrect and it is not a user error, you will look foolish and the user might be offended.

Step 4: Establish a plan of action to resolve the problem and implement the solution.

Document the steps that you want to take to resolve the problem. Ensure that you can demonstrate that your tests confirmed a non-working condition and then a working condition following implementation of the proposed actions. Review the plan with others and ensure that change controls are followed. The change management process was discussed in Chapter 13. Lastly, after approval has been given to implement the change, perform the outlined steps to fix the problem.

Step 5: Verify full system functionality and, if applicable, implement preventative measures.

Check with all users who were experiencing the issue to ensure that they are no longer experiencing the issue. Also check with others around them to ensure that you have not created other issues by implementing the fix. Lastly, implement restrictions or additional controls to prevent the problem from occurring in the future. This could involve retraining the user or placing technical controls on the system to prevent such actions from taking place again. In some cases, permissions may need to be changed or system configurations updated. System changes should follow the same change control process as the troubleshooting change did.

Step 6: Document findings, actions, and outcomes.

This last step is important to ensure that you or others at your company do not continue to solve the same problems from scratch over and over. If you are anything like us, you will need to write down what you did so that you can remember it again later. IT professionals lead busy lives, and there never seems to be time to document. However, if you do not document, you will find that you spend time performing the same research when you could have simply consulted your documentation.

The CompTIA troubleshooting steps provided here will be demonstrated in the scenarios that follow to help you understand better how the troubleshooting methodology is applied to real-world problems.

In the course of your career, you will run into a wide variety of issues that you will need to troubleshoot. No book could be comprehensive enough to cover all of them, so we have selected a few issues that you are likely to see. The issues are also ones that you are likely to see on the CompTIA Cloud+ exam.

Deployment Issues

Application deployment issues are relatively commonplace. Most applications will be deployed without issue, but you will deploy so many apps that deployment issues will be something that you see quite often.

Incompatible or Missing Dependencies

One problem you might see is incompatible or missing dependencies. When deploying a web application, ensure that programming libraries are installed first. Windows applications written in a .NET programming language such as C# will require a certain version of .NET on the machine. Other applications may require PHP or Java to be installed. Read through deployment documentation carefully to ensure that you meet all the requirements. Of course, you will also need Internet Information Services (IIS) and any other operating system roles and features. Ensure that all this is in place before application installation.

The Java Runtime Environment (JRE) can be particularly troublesome when running multiple Java-based applications on the same machine because they might not all support the same version. For example, three applications are installed on the server, and you upgrade the first one. You read through the documentation before upgrading and find that you need to update the Java version first. The Java upgrade completes successfully, and then you deploy the new version of the application. Testing confirms that the new app works fine, but a short time later, users report that the other two applications are no longer working. Upon troubleshooting, you find that they do not support the new version of Java that was deployed.

The most straightforward fix to this issue is to deploy dedicated virtual machines for each application. You can also use application containers to host each application so that dependencies can be handled individually for each container. Containers are more lightweight, quicker to deploy (less disk space since OS is generally not in the container), and start up much more quickly than virtual machines.

Now that you understand the potential problem, let's try a scenario: You have been asked to set up a new website for your company. You purchase a hosted cloud solution and create a host record in your company's hosted DNS server to point to the IP address of the hosted cloud server. You test the URL and see the default setup page. You then use the cloud marketplace to install some website applications and themes. However, when you navigate to your website, you now receive the following error message:

```
Warning: Creating default object from empty value in customizer.php
```

Step 1: Identify the problem. New applications and themes were installed since the site last came up correctly, so the error is most likely related to the new software and themes.

Step 2: Establish a theory of probable causes.　You research the error online and see issues relating to missing PHP files. You theorize that PHP is installed incorrectly or that the PHP dependency is missing.

Step 3: Test the theory to determine the cause.　To test these theories, you can reinstall PHP on the server or install it if it is missing. You first identify the required level of PHP from the software that you installed earlier. Then you log onto the cloud server and check the PHP version. You find that PHP is not installed so it seems like installing the required PHP version will solve the problem.

Step 4: Establish a plan of action to resolve the problem and implement the solution.　You log into the cloud management portal and go to the marketplace. After locating the PHP version required by the software, you review the release notes for it to determine if it is compatible with your other software and system. You find that your cloud vendor maintains a database of compatible applications and software and it has already queried your systems and noted that this version of PHP is compatible with your cloud installation.

You place a change request to install PHP and include relevant documentation on why the software is needed. Once the change request is approved, you proceed to install the software from the marketplace and then verify that the software installs correctly.

Note that because this is a new installation, no users are accessing the site. If this were a production site, installation of a major dependency like PHP would take the site down, so you would need to perform the install in a downtime.

Step 5: Verify full system functionality and, if applicable, implement preventative measures.　You open a web browser and navigate to the company website URL and verify that you can access the site. The installation of the PHP dependency solved the problem. Additionally, you find that you can enable the system to automatically install dependencies in the future so that you can avoid such a problem. You create another change request to enable this feature and wait for approval. Once approval is provided, you enable the feature.

Step 6: Document findings, actions, and outcomes.　You update both change request tickets to indicate that the work was completed successfully and that no other changes were required. Additionally, you send a memo to the other team members noting the issue and what was done to resolve it and also that dependencies will be installed automatically moving forward.

Incorrect Configuration

Computer programs need to be configured perfectly for them to run. There is really no margin for error. An extra character in a UNC path or a mistyped password is all that is required for the program to crash and burn. It is important to double-check all configuration values to ensure that they are correct. If you run into issues, go back to the configuration and recheck it, maybe with another person who can offer some objectivity. Compare configuration values to software documentation and ensure that the required services on each server supporting the system are running.

Let's look at this in a scenario and consider how the CompTIA troubleshooting methodology would help in solving a configuration issue: Your company is consolidating servers from two cloud environments into one for easier manageability. The transition team is responsible for moving the servers and the shares. The transition team successfully moves the servers to the new location and consolidates the shares onto a single server. A web application retrieves files from one of the shares, but users of the site report that they can no longer access files within the system. You are part of the troubleshooting team and you are assigned the trouble ticket.

Step 1: Identify the problem.   The problem is that users cannot access files in the application. You send a message to the user base informing them of the problem and that you are actively working to resolve it.

Step 2: Establish a theory of probable causes.   A number of changes were made when the servers were moved over from one cloud to another. The servers were exported into files and then imported into the new system. Each server was tested, and they worked following the migration. You check the testing notes and verify that the website was working correctly following the migration. The shares were consolidated after that. However, you do not see testing validation following the share consolidation. It is possible that the application is pointing to a share that no longer exists.

Step 3: Test the theory to determine the cause.   You log into the server hosting the application and review the configuration. The configuration for the files points to a UNC path. You attempt to contact the UNC path but receive an error. You then message the transition team asking them if the UNC referenced in the application still exists or if it changed. They send you a message stating that the UNC path has changed and they provide you with the new path.

Step 4: Establish a plan of action to resolve the problem and implement the solution.   You plan to change the application configuration to point to the new path. You put in a change request to modify the application configuration, and the change request is approved. You then adjust the application settings, replacing the old UNC path with the new one.

Step 5: Verify full system functionality and, if applicable, implement preventative measures.   You log into the site and verify that files are accessible through the application. You then reach out to several users and request they test as well. Each user reports that they can access the files successfully. Finally, you message the users and let them know that the issue has been resolved.

Step 6: Document findings, actions, and outcomes. You update the change request ticket to indicate that the work was completed successfully and that no other changes were required. Additionally, you send a memo to the transition team members noting the issue and what was done to resolve it. Management then creates a checklist for application transitions that includes a line item for updating the UNC path in the application if the backend share path changes.

Integration Issues with Different Cloud Platforms

Cloud applications typically do not reside on their own. They are often integrated with other cloud systems with APIs. A vendor will create an API for its application and then release documentation so that developers and integrators know how to utilize that API. For example, Office 365, a cloud-based productivity suite that includes an e-mail application, has an API for importing and exporting contacts. Salesforce, a cloud-based customer relationship management (CRM) application, could integrate with Office 365 through that API so that contacts could be updated based on interactions in the CRM tool. However, APIs must be implemented correctly, or the integration will not work.

Let's try the CompTIA troubleshooting methodology with a scenario: You receive an e-mail from Microsoft informing you of a new API that works with Salesforce. You log into Salesforce and configure Salesforce to talk to Office 365. You educate users on the new integration and that contacts created in Salesforce will be added to Office 365 and that tasks in Salesforce will be synchronized with Office 365 tasks. However, user report that contacts are not being updated and that tasks are not being created. You also find when opening your tasks that there are hundreds of new tasks that should belong to other users.

For this scenario, consider the troubleshooting methodology and walk through it on your own. Think through each step. You may need to make some assumptions as you move through the process since this is a sample scenario.

Step 1: Identify the problem.

Step 2: Establish a theory of probable causes.

Step 3: Test the theory to determine the cause.

Step 4: Establish a plan of action to resolve the problem and implement the solution.

Step 5: Verify full system functionality and, if applicable, implement preventative measures.

Step 6: Document findings, actions, and outcomes.

Template Misconfiguration

When an organization is migrating its environment to the cloud, it requires a standardized installation policy or profile for its virtual servers. The virtual machines need to have a very similar base installation of the operating system, so all the devices have the same security patches, service packs, and base applications installed.

Virtual machine templates provide a streamlined approach to deploying a fully configured base server image or even an entirely configured application server. Virtual machine templates help decrease the installation and configuration costs when deploying virtual machines and lower ongoing maintenance costs, allowing for faster deploy times and lower operational costs. However, incorrectly configuring templates can result in a large number of computers that all have the same flaw.

Now that you understand the potential problems, let's try a scenario: Karen is creating virtual machine templates for common server roles including a web server with network load balancing (NLB), a database server, an application server, and a terminal server. Each server will be running Windows Server 2016 Standard. She installs the operating system on a virtual machine, assigns the machine a license key, and then installs updates to the device in offline mode.

Karen applies the standard security configuration to the machine, including locking down the local administrator account, adding local certificates to the trusted store, and configuring default firewall rules for remote administration. She then shuts down the virtual machine and makes three copies of it using built-in tools in her cloud portal. She renames the machines and starts each up.

She then installs the server roles for web services and NLB on the web server, SQL Server 2016 on the database server along with Microsoft Message Queuing (MSMQ), SharePoint on the application server, and Remote Desktop Session Host services on the terminal server. She applies application updates to each machine and then saves the virtual hard disks to be used as a template.

A month later, Karen is asked to set up an environment consisting of a database server and a web server. She uses the built-in tools in her cloud portal to make copies of her database and web server templates. She gives the new machines new names and starts them up. She then assigns IP addresses to them. Both are joined to the company domain under their assigned names. However, server administrators report that the servers are receiving a large number of authentication errors.

Step 1: Identify the problem.   The servers are receiving a large number of authentication errors.

Step 2: Establish a theory of probable causes.   Karen theorizes that the authentication errors could be caused by incorrect licensing on the machines or by duplicate security identifiers.

Step 3: Test the theory to determine the cause.   Karen issues unique license keys to both machines and activates them. However, the authentication errors still continue. She then clones another web server and runs Sysprep on it. She adds it to the domain and observes its behavior. The new machine does not exhibit the authentication errors.

Step 4: Establish a plan of action to resolve the problem and implement the solution.   Karen proposes to remove faulty machines from the domain, run Sysprep on the defective machines to regenerate their security identifiers, and then add them back in. She puts change requests in for each activity and waits for approval. Upon receiving authorization, Karen implements the proposed changes.

Step 5: Verify full system functionality and, if applicable, implement preventative measures.   Server administrators confirm that the authentication errors have ceased after the changes were made.

Step 6: Document findings, actions, and outcomes.   Karen updates the change management requests and creates a process document outlining how to create templates with the Sysprep step included.

System Clock Differences

Networked computer systems rely on time synchronization in order to communicate. When computers have different times, some may not be able to authenticate to network resources, they may not trust one another, or they may reject data sent to them. Administrators can ensure that system clocks are kept in sync on virtual machines by installing hypervisor guest tools and then enabling time synchronization between host and guest. Virtual, physical, and cloud servers can synchronize time by configuring them to point to an external Network Time Protocol (NTP) server. Each computer will set its time to the time specified by the NTP server. The servers will poll the NTP server periodically to verify that their clocks are still in sync and avoid time synchronization issues.

Using the CompTIA troubleshooting methodology, let's consider a scenario: Eddie is a cloud administrator managing over 40 servers in a hosted cloud. His monitoring system frequently sends out alerts that servers are unavailable. He restarts the machines and the problem goes away, but the problem comes back a few days later. He scripts reboots for each of the servers but realizes that this is a short-term fix at best.

Step 1: Identify the problem.   Servers lose connectivity periodically.

Step 2: Establish a theory of probable causes.   Eddie theorizes that there could be connectivity issues on the cloud backend. There also could be an issue with the template that each of the machines was produced from. Lastly, the machines could be losing time synchronization.

Step 3: Test the theory to determine the cause.   Eddie creates a support ticket with the cloud provider and provides the necessary details. The cloud provider runs several tests and reports no issues. Eddie creates another machine from the template and finds that it also exhibits the same problems. However, he is not sure where the problem might lie in the template. Lastly, he configures a scheduled job to run three times a day that sends him the system time for each of the servers.

As he reviews the output from the scheduled job, it becomes clear that the domain controller is getting out of sync with most of the network every few hours. Upon analyzing the configuration of the servers that go out of sync and the others, he finds that some are configured to obtain their time from the cloud provider NTP server while others are set to obtain their time from a different server.

Step 4: Establish a plan of action to resolve the problem and implement the solution.　Eddie proposes to set all servers to the same time server. He creates a change request documenting the proposed change and receives approval to move forward with the change during a scheduled downtime. He makes the change.

Step 5: Verify full system functionality and, if applicable, implement preventative measures.　Eddie monitors the output from the scheduled task and confirms that each server remains in sync.

Step 6: Document findings, actions, and outcomes.　Eddie documents the NTP server settings on a standard setup configuration document. He mentions the issue in a standup IT meeting the following Friday, and the document is circulated around and placed on the company intranet for reference.

Capacity Issues

Capacity issues can be found with compute, storage, networking, and licensing. Considerable attention needs to be paid to the design of compute, storage, and networking systems. The design phase must ensure that all service levels are understood and that the capacity to fulfill them is incorporated into its configurations. Once those configurations have been adequately designed and documented, operations can establish a baseline, as discussed in Chapter 7. This baseline is a measuring stick against which capacity can be monitored to understand both the current demand and trend for future needs.

Capacity issues can result in system or application slowdowns or complete unavailability of systems. Alerts should be configured on devices to inform cloud administrators when capacity reaches thresholds (often 80 percent or so). Define thresholds low enough that you will be able to correct the capacity issue before available capacity is fully consumed.

Compute

Appropriately distributing compute resources is an integral part of managing a cloud environment. Planning for future growth and the ability to adjust compute resources on demand is key to avoiding compute capacity issues. One potential capacity issue is overconsumption by customers. Because compute resources are limited, cloud providers must protect them and make certain that their customers only have access to the amount that they are contracted to provide. Two methods that are used to deliver no more than the contracted amount of resources are quotas and limits.

Now that you understand the potential problem, try a scenario: Tim manages the cloud infrastructure for hundreds of cloud consumers. He notices that some of the consumers are utilizing far more resources than they should be allocated.

For this scenario, consider the troubleshooting methodology and walk through it on your own. Think through each step. You may need to make some assumptions as you move through the process since this is a sample scenario.

Step 1: Identify the problem.

Step 2: Establish a theory of probable causes.

Step 3: Test the theory to determine the cause.

Step 4: Establish a plan of action to resolve the problem and implement the solution.

Step 5: Verify full system functionality and, if applicable, implement preventative measures.

Step 6: Document findings, actions, and outcomes.

For more information on resource allocation and performance best practices, see Chapter 8.

Storage

Companies are producing data at a rate never seen before. Keeping up with data growth can be quite a challenge. It is best to set thresholds and alerts on storage volumes so that when they reach a threshold (often 80 percent or so), you can proactively expand the storage. Set more aggressive thresholds and alerts on physical storage because physical storage cannot be extended as easily on the fly. Physical storage expansion requires the purchase of additional hardware, approval and other red tape associated with the purchase, shipping time, and installation. You want to make sure that you have enough of a buffer so that you do not run out of space while additional storage is on order.

Let's demonstrate the CompTIA troubleshooting methodology with a scenario: Sharon, a cloud administrator, receives reports that users are experiencing sluggish performance and slow response times when accessing the company ERP systems that reside in their hybrid cloud.

Step 1: Identify the problem.   Sharon identifies the problem as unacceptable application performance.

Step 2: Establish a theory of probable causes.   Sharon collects metrics while users experience the issues. She then compares the metrics to the baseline to see if performance is within normal tolerances. The anomalies not only confirm that there is a problem, they tell where the problem might lie. The baseline comparison indicates that disk input/output operations per second (IOPS) are well below the baseline for several LUNs.

Step 3: Test the theory to determine the cause.   Sharon isolates the LUNs that are outside of their normal IOPS range. Each of the LUNs was created from the same RAID group, and an analysis of the disk IOPS shows that a RAID group is rebuilding, causing the performance issues.

Step 4: Establish a plan of action to resolve the problem and implement the solution.   Sharon discusses the risks and performance hit the rebuild is causing, and her manager agrees that the rebuild can be paused for the two hours that remain in the work day and that they should resume at 5:00 P.M. Sharon pauses the rebuild.

Step 5: Verify full system functionality and, if applicable, implement preventative measures.   Sharon confirms that application performance has returned to normal. At 5:00 P.M., she resumes the rebuild and performance drops for the next few hours until the rebuild completes.

Step 6: Document findings, actions, and outcomes.   Sharon documents the experience in the company's knowledge management system.

Networking

Each device that is attached to the network is capable of generating traffic. A single user used to have only one or two devices attached to the network, but now many users have a desktop, laptop, multiple tablets, phones, and other devices that may connect through wired or wireless connections. Many of these devices connect to cloud services and request data from them. Some cloud services may be used to keep such systems in sync. The rapid growth of devices and increasing use of cloud services can result in contention for valuable network resources.

Now that you understand some potential network contention problems, let's try a scenario: You work in the operations center of the company. Metrics show that nodes on a particular network segment are consuming a high amount of network bandwidth. You also receive alerts for a high number of network collisions on the segment, and the network switch for the segment is showing spanning tree errors.

For this scenario, consider the troubleshooting methodology and walk through it on your own. Think through each step. You may need to make some assumptions as you move through the process since this is a sample scenario.

Step 1: Identify the problem.

Step 2: Establish a theory of probable causes.

Step 3: Test the theory to determine the cause.

Step 4: Establish a plan of action to resolve the problem and implement the solution.

Step 5: Verify full system functionality and, if applicable, implement preventative measures.

Step 6: Document findings, actions, and outcomes.

Licensing

Purchased software and cloud services operate based on a license. The license grants specific uses of the software for a period. Software typically checks for compliance with licensing and may revoke access to service when the software vendor or cloud provider deems that compliance has not been met. Additionally, groups such as BSA | The Software Alliance (www.bsa.org) can perform license investigations and assess fines for companies that are not in compliance, so companies need to ensure that they are adhering to license requirements.

Software licenses may be per user of the software, or they could be based on the physical or virtual resources that are allocated to the software. For example, some products are licensed based on the number of CPU cores or vCPUs. It is important to know how many CPU cores you are licensed for when assigning resources so that you do not violate your license or cause a program to fail activation checks.

Let's demonstrate the CompTIA troubleshooting methodology with a scenario: Your organization has a self-service portal where administrators can create new virtual machines based off virtual machine templates. The portal has been very popular, but now over 500 virtual machines have been deployed to the environment and the machines deployed over the last 30 days are unable to activate Windows.

For this scenario, consider the troubleshooting methodology and walk through it on your own. Think through each step. You may need to make some assumptions as you move through the process since this is a sample scenario. We have provided Step 1 for you.

Step 1: Identify the problem.

Systems are unable to activate and the organization may have exceeded available licenses. The company has 10 hypervisors in a cluster and 10 Server 2016 data center edition licenses as well as 100 Server 2016 standard edition licenses. An assessment of the virtual machines shows that there are 200 CentOS Linux servers and 312 Server 2016 Standard edition servers.

Step 2: Establish a theory of probable causes.

Step 3: Test the theory to determine the cause.

Step 4: Establish a plan of action to resolve the problem and implement the solution.

Step 5: Verify full system functionality and, if applicable, implement preventative measures.

Step 6: Document findings, actions, and outcomes.

API Request Limits

In order to guard against abuse or malicious use of application programming interfaces (APIs), companies set request limits, usually per IP address or subnet. This limits the ability of a single client from utilizing too much of the service. Some misuse of API calls might be an attempt to scrape resources, input malformed content to trigger buffer overflows, or disrupt API availability.

Let's look at this in a scenario and consider how the CompTIA troubleshooting methodology would help in solving a configuration issue: You work for a consulting company as a developer on the DevOps team. Senior leadership have expressed concerns that some consultants may not be billing out all their time. They assume that this is just due to forgetfulness, since many do not enter their time each day, but wait till the weekend to enter most of it. You have developed an application that tracks e-mail usage against calendar entries and time entries to confirm that employees are not forgetting to put in billable time. The application ties into several APIs designed by the e-mail and time entry software companies. Your application works fine in testing. However, when you deploy it to production, the application works for about 30 minutes and then it ceases functioning. You need to figure out why the application ceases functioning and correct it.

For this scenario, consider the troubleshooting methodology and walk through it on your own. Think through each step. You may need to make some assumptions as you move through the process since this is a sample scenario.

Step 1: Identify the problem.

Step 2: Establish a theory of probable causes.

Step 3: Test the theory to determine the cause.

Step 4: Establish a plan of action to resolve the problem and implement the solution.

Step 5: Verify full system functionality and, if applicable, implement preventative measures.

Step 6: Document findings, actions, and outcomes.

Connectivity Issues

Connectivity issues can create a broad range of problems since most systems do not operate in isolation. There is a myriad of interdependencies on the modern issues of network and connectivity can be a digital monkey wrench that breaks a plethora of systems. The first indicator that there is a connectivity problem will be the scope of the issue. Because everything is connected, connectivity issues usually impact a large number of devices. Ensure that affected devices have an IP address using the ipconfig (Windows) or ifconfig (Linux) command described earlier in this chapter. If they do not have an IP address, it could be a problem with DHCP or with DHCP forwarders or cloud-based virtual network IP address ranges, firewall ACLs, and routing tables.

For example, the DHCP scope could be full so the administrator might need to expand the scope or reduce the lease interval so that computers do not keep their addresses for as much time. A user may reside in a different subnet from the DHCP server and no forwarder exists on the subnet to direct DHCP requests to the DHCP server. The connection may be on a different cloud-based virtual network IP address range from the servers it wishes to contact, and there are no rules defined to allow traffic between these ranges. There could be firewall ACLs that need to be defined to allow traffic between two nodes that are not communicating. Lastly, the default gateway or VPN concentrator, if the issue is with a VPN connection, may not have the correct information on the destination network in its routing table.

When identifying the problem, determine the scope by using the ping command described earlier in this chapter. Ping devices on the network starting with your default gateway. If the default gateway pings, try another hop closer to the Internet or to where others are experiencing issues. Try to connect to other devices that report problems as well. If the default gateway will not ping, attempt to ping something else on the same network. If neither will ping, it is likely an issue with the switch that connects both devices. If you can ping the other machine but not the gateway, it might be a problem with the gateway.

VLAN or VXLAN Misconfiguration

VLANs and VXLANs were discussed back in Chapter 4. Both the VLAN and VXLAN partition a network to create logical separation between subnetworks. Connectivity problems can appear when VLANs or VXLANs are configured incorrectly. For example, machines must be on the same VLAN or have inter-VLAN routing configured for the two machines to be able to communicate. It is common to configure virtual networks with specific VLANs or to add VLAN tagging to virtual networks. Incorrectly setting these values could allow machines to talk to machines they are not supposed to talk to, and they would be unable to talk to others. Subnets are usually assigned per VLAN, so if the IP address is configured manually for one subnet on the machine and it is placed on the wrong VLAN, it will not be able to communicate with any of its neighbors.

Let's demonstrate the CompTIA troubleshooting methodology with a scenario: Geoff configures three VLANs named VLAN1, VLAN2, and VLAN3. He has four servers that are running on a virtual network, and he plans on cloning those servers several times and then assigning the servers to each of the VLANs for use. He performs the clones and then assigns the machines to the appropriate VLANs, but finds that they are unable to communicate with one another.

Step 1: Identify the problem.   The cloned servers cannot communicate with each other.

Step 2: Establish a theory of probable causes.   Geoff determines that the VLANs could be misconfigured, the tagging could be incorrectly set, the virtual switches could be misconfigured, or the IP addresses could be incorrectly assigned.

Step 3: Test the theory to determine the cause.   Geoff tries to ping a single server called VM-DC1 from each of the other machines. None of the computers can communicate with the server. Geoff then creates a testing strategy where he will rotate VLANs and test. He explains the strategy to his manager and receives approval to proceed. Geoff then rotates the VLAN that is assigned to VM_DC1 and tries the tests again. He is unable to connect to the machine on any of the three VLANs. Geoff then removes VLAN tagging from the virtual switch configuration on VM_DC1 and receives an IP address conflict on the main VM_DC1 computer. Geoff suddenly realizes that the IP addresses are hard-coded into each of the machines and that they do not correspond to their assigned VLAN.

Step 4: Establish a plan of action to resolve the problem and implement the solution.   Geoff documents IP addresses to assign to each of the machines in each VLAN. He then creates a change request to modify the IP addresses for each of the machines and explains why the change needs to be made. Once approval is given, Geoff modifies the IP addresses on each machine as planned.

Step 5: Verify full system functionality and, if applicable, implement preventative measures.   Geoff verifies that each machine can talk to other machines on the same VLAN and that computers cannot talk to those on other VLANs.

Step 6: Document findings, actions, and outcomes.   Geoff notifies his manager that the machines are now functioning. He also updates the change control ticket to note that the change corrected the issue.

Incorrect Routing and Misconfigured Proxies

Internetwork traffic, traffic that moves from one network to another, requires routers to direct the traffic to the next leg of its journey toward its destination. Routers do this because they have an understanding of where different networks reside and the possible paths to reach those networks. Incorrect routing can result in a loss of connectivity between one or more devices. In some cases, a proxy will be used to manage communications between nodes on behalf of one or more members.

Let's now consider a routing/proxy issue and how it can be resolved using the CompTIA troubleshooting methodology: Pam is responsible for the network infrastructure, but her company recently moved many of the company servers to Amazon Web Services (AWS). A consultant configured VLANs and routing, but cloud administrators report that machines cannot communicate with devices on the Internet. Pam is asked to troubleshoot AWS routing for the VLANs. Pam confirms that devices can communicate with other devices on the same VLAN and that devices cannot communicate with the Internet.

Step 1: Identify the problem.   Traffic from VLANs is not being routed externally to the Internet.

Step 2: Establish a theory of probable causes.   Pam considers the possible causes and comes up with several theories. The problem could be that routing is not configured for the VLANs. It might also be possible that the default route was removed. Pam also theorizes that access lists could be preventing inside traffic from exiting the network.

Step 3: Test the theory to determine the cause.   Pam uses the traceroute command from one of the machines exhibiting the problem to test the path from that machine to google.com, as shown in this example:

```
C:\Users\Pam>tracert google.com
Unable to resolve target system name google.com.
```

Pam issues the nslookup command on google.com to see if she can resolve the name to an IP address. She receives a non-authoritative answer with an IP address, shown here:

```
C:\Users\Pam>nslookup google.com
Server:   box.local
Address:  192.168.1.21
Non-authoritative answer:
Name:     google.com
Addresses:  2607:f8b0:4009:812::200e
            172.217.6.110
```

She then issues the traceroute command again with the IP address instead of the name. The traceroute command shows a hop to the local proxy called box.local and then a connection to the default gateway 192.168.1.1, but the connection times out:

```
C:\Users\Pam>tracert 172.217.6.110
Tracing route to ord37s03-in-f110.1e100.net [172.217.6.110]
over a maximum of 30 hops:
  1      3 ms      3 ms      3 ms  box.local [192.168.1.21]
  2      3 ms      4 ms      3 ms  192.168.1.1
  3       *         *         *        Request timed out.
```

Pam disables the proxy to test whether that is the issue and runs tracert again, but the request times out immediately after hitting the default gateway. Pam then logs into the AWS Virtual Private Cloud (VPC) console and observes the Route Tables page. She finds that the main route table was modified to include routes between the subnets, but the route to the virtual private gateway was replaced when these changes were made.

Step 4: Establish a plan of action to resolve the problem and implement the solution.   Pam believes the problem lies with the missing route to the virtual private gateway, so she submits a change request to add this route.

Step 5: Verify full system functionality and, if applicable, implement preventative measures. Pam's change request is approved, so she makes the change and then issues a traceroute along with the –d switch to skip resolving hostnames so that the trace will run faster. She issues the command from the same machine she was using to test and receives this output:

```
C:\Users\Pam>tracert -d 172.217.6.110
Tracing route to 172.217.6.110 over a maximum of 30 hops
  1     11 ms      7 ms     11 ms   192.168.1.21
  2      4 ms      3 ms      3 ms   192.168.1.1
  3     12 ms     12 ms     15 ms   142.254.157.249
  4     85 ms     45 ms     21 ms   24.164.114.225
  5     16 ms     11 ms     18 ms   24.33.103.92
  6     21 ms     22 ms     20 ms   65.29.1.97
  7     20 ms     14 ms     15 ms   65.29.1.32
  8     48 ms     42 ms     44 ms   66.109.6.70
  9     42 ms     47 ms     47 ms   66.109.6.30
 10     42 ms     42 ms     45 ms   107.14.17.202
 11     45 ms     40 ms     39 ms   216.6.87.149
 12     42 ms     47 ms     43 ms   72.14.198.28
 13     43 ms     43 ms     43 ms   108.170.246.81
 14     45 ms     47 ms     47 ms   216.239.50.93
 15     36 ms     42 ms     34 ms   209.85.253.248
 16     36 ms     47 ms     38 ms   209.85.241.122
 17     35 ms     40 ms     40 ms   108.170.238.91
 18     34 ms     34 ms     35 ms   172.217.6.110
Trace complete.
```

Step 6: Document findings, actions, and outcomes. Pam notifies her manager that the machines are now functional. She then updates the change control ticket to note that the change corrected the issue. See Chapter 4 for more information on routing.

QoS Issues

Quality of service (QoS) is a set of technologies that can identify the type of data in data packets and divide those packets into specific traffic classes that can be prioritized according to defined service levels. QoS was introduced back in Chapter 8, and QoS technologies enable administrators to meet their service requirements for a workload or an application by measuring network bandwidth, detecting changing network conditions, and prioritizing the network traffic accordingly. QoS can be targeted at a network interface, toward a given server's or router's performance, or regarding specific applications. Incorrectly configured QoS can result in performance degradation for certain services and, consequently, irate users.

Let's demonstrate how the CompTIA troubleshooting methodology can help resolve QoS issues: Marco is a cloud administrator for Big Top Training, a company that produces fireworks safety videos that are streamed by subscribers from the company's cloud. Marco has been reading about QoS, and he thinks it can significantly improve performance on the cloud network. He discusses it with his boss and receives approval to test QoS settings in a lab environment that is set up on another cloud segment. He configures QoS priorities and tests several types of content, including streaming video, data transfers, active directory replication, and DNS resolution. He shows the results of his tests to Dominick, his manager, and they agree to roll the changes out to the rest of the network. A couple of weeks later, the backup administrator, Teresa, mentions that some backup jobs have been failing because they cannot complete in their scheduled time window and are terminated. She suggests that QoS might be the problem because the timeouts started happening the day after the QoS changes were put in place. Dominick tells Marco to look into the problem.

Step 1: Identify the problem.   Marco identifies the problem as backups are unable to complete in scheduled time windows.

Step 2: Establish a theory of probable causes.   Marco theorizes that the backup issues could be caused by a lack of a backup profile since the lab environment he worked in did not have any backups scheduled for it.

Step 3: Test the theory to determine the cause.   Marco walks Dominick through his theory. Dominick suggests that he collect baseline data on traffic from the production network and then use that to build additional QoS rules. Marco collects the data for the baseline and then reviews the data with Teresa and Dominick.

Step 4: Establish a plan of action to resolve the problem and implement the solution.   Marco, Teresa, and Dominick find that backup traffic communicates over a port that does not have a QoS rule, as Marco theorized. They also identify five other services that have no QoS rules defined, so they map out priorities for those items as well. The planned changes are put into the change management system, and Dominick schedules a downtime in the evening for the changes to be made. Dominick informs stakeholders of the downtime, and Marco implements the new QoS rules during the planned downtime.

Step 5: Verify full system functionality and, if applicable, implement preventative measures.   Marco notifies Teresa when the work has been completed and Teresa manually executes the failing backup jobs to confirm that they do run within the normal time allotted. Marco and Teresa inform Dominick that the jobs now work and the downtime is concluded.

Step 6: Document findings, actions, and outcomes.   Marco creates a QoS document outlining each of the priorities and the traffic that fits into each priority. He also schedules a time to collect a more intensive baseline to confirm that all critical services have been accounted for.

For more information on baselines, see Chapter 7, and for more information on QoS, see Chapter 8.

Latency

Network latency, when it is excessive, can create bottlenecks that prevent data from using the maximum capacity of the network bandwidth, resulting in slower cloud application performance. Latency metrics are essential for ensuring responsive services and applications and in avoiding performance or availability problems.

Let's consider a scenario: You recently configured synchronous replication of a key ERP database to another site 2000 miles away. However, the ERP system is now running extremely slow. Performance metrics on the servers that make up the ERP system show plenty of capacity and very low utilization of system resources. Management is upset and demands a resolution ASAP.

For this scenario, consider the troubleshooting methodology and walk through it on your own. Think through each step. You may need to make some assumptions as you move through the process since this is a sample scenario.

> Step 1: Identify the problem.
>
> Step 2: Establish a theory of probable causes.
>
> Step 3: Test the theory to determine the cause.
>
> Step 4: Establish a plan of action to resolve the problem and implement the solution.
>
> Step 5: Verify full system functionality and, if applicable, implement preventative measures.
>
> Step 6: Document findings, actions, and outcomes.

See Chapter 4 for more information on latency.

Misconfigured MTU/MSS

The maximum transmission unit (MTU) is the largest packet or frame that can be sent over the network. Frames operate at the data link layer, while packets operate at the network layer. Segments also have a maximum size. Segments operate at the transport layer, and their maximum size is specified as the maximum segment size (MSS). MTU and MSS are typically measured in bytes.

Higher-level protocols may create packets larger than a particular link supports, so the TCP divides the packets into several pieces in a process known as fragmentation. Each fragment is given an ID so that the fragments can be pieced back together in the correct order. However, not all applications support fragmentation. When this routinely happens, the solution is to adjust the MSS so that packets are not fragmented. MSS is adjusted because it operates at a higher layer than the frames and packets, so the data that is provided to the lower-level protocols ends up an appropriate size and does not need to be fragmented.

Let's look at this in a scenario and use the CompTIA troubleshooting methodology to resolve the situation: You configure a new VPN for your company using L2TP over IPSec. However, performance over the VPN is much slower than expected. You run a packet capture on the data over the network link using the tcpdump tool. You capture packets less than 64 bytes with the tcpdump < 64 command and then you capture packets greater than 60,000 bytes (the max packet size is 65,535 bytes) with the tcpdump > 60000 command.

For this scenario, consider the troubleshooting methodology and walk through it on your own. Think through each step. You may need to make some assumptions as you move through the process since this is a sample scenario.

Step 1: Identify the problem.

Step 2: Establish a theory of probable causes.

Step 3: Test the theory to determine the cause.

Step 4: Establish a plan of action to resolve the problem and implement the solution.

Step 5: Verify full system functionality and, if applicable, implement preventative measures.

Step 6: Document findings, actions, and outcomes.

Automation/Orchestration Issues

Automation and orchestration can be incredibly complex. The advantage of automation and orchestration over manual processes is that automation performs the task the exact same way every time. Unfortunately, things do not stay the same and processes will need to be updated from time to time. When automation or orchestration changes, evaluate the process and run a change management report to identify all changes made recently to the resources the automation depends on. Usually, something has changed in the environment that is not reflected in the automation workflow.

Some other issues that can arise in automation and orchestration include server name changes, domain changes, and incompatibility with automation tools.

Batch Job Scheduling Issues

Batch jobs often can encounter scheduling issues as data volumes grow, utilization increases, or as new jobs are added. These issues can be avoided through proper capacity planning and forecasting.

Now that you understand the potential problems, let us try a scenario to see how the CompTIA troubleshooting methodology can help: John is working for a small company that heavily uses cloud services. He has been working for the company for about a month after the previous IT administrator left. The previous administrator automated a number of tasks. John has been receiving an email each morning stating that space has been added to several virtual machines based on their usage. However, this morning, he received a message that stated the job has failed. When he checked the orchestration, no error trapping was present.

For this scenario, consider the troubleshooting methodology and walk through it on your own. Think through each step. You may need to make some assumptions as you move through the process since this is a sample scenario. We have provided Step 1 for you.

> Step 1: Identify the problem.
>
> John investigates the hypervisor cluster that the virtual machines reside on and finds that the virtual disks have been expanded using a large pool on a shared storage device. The logs on the device show expansions corresponding to the emails he has been receiving. He also finds alerts in the logs showing that the storage pool is full. John finds that the machines that were expanded each have 25 percent free space. He also finds that there is an additional 2.3TB available on the SAN that hosts the shared storage.
>
> Step 2: Establish a theory of probable causes.
>
> Step 3: Test the theory to determine the cause.
>
> Step 4: Establish a plan of action to resolve the problem and implement the solution.
>
> Step 5: Verify full system functionality and, if applicable, implement preventative measures.
>
> Step 6: Document findings, actions, and outcomes.

Security Issues

Security issues can cause significant problems for system availability and data confidentiality or integrity. Some security issues you should be aware of are as follows:

- **Federations, domain trusts, and single sign-on**   Federations, domain trusts, and single sign-on (SSO) each are technologies that extend authentication and authorization functions across multiple, interdependent systems.
- **External attacks**   External attacks can be minimized using firewalls, intrusion detection systems, hardening, and other concepts discussed in Chapters 10 and 11.

- **Internal attacks**   Separation of duties and least privilege (discussed in Chapter 11) can help reduce the likelihood of internal attacks.

- **Privilege escalation**   System vulnerabilities, incorrectly configured roles, or software bugs can result in situations where malicious code or an attacker can escalate their privileges to gain access to resources that they are unauthorized to access.

- **External role change**   Role change policies should extend out to procedures and practices employed to change authorizations for users to match changes in job roles for employees.

- **Incorrect hardening settings**   Hardening, discussed in Chapter 11, reduces the risk to devices.

- **Weak or obsolete security technologies**   Security technologies age quickly. Those technologies that are out of support may not receive vendor patches and will be unsafe to use in protection of corporate assets.

- **Insufficient security controls and processes**   Insufficient security controls, such as antivirus and firewalls, and processes can increase the likelihood of successful attacks.

This section explores three security topics in more detail along with scenarios that utilize CompTIA's troubleshooting methodology. These topics include authorization and authentication issues, malware, and certificate issues. Authorization and authentication issues include scenarios such as systems that are deployed without proper service accounts, account lockouts, employees who change positions, and changes made to permissions on a system that affects authorized user access. Malware is also a problem that is frequently encountered. Malware impact can range from low, such as malware that slows a machine, to high-risk malware that results in a data breach. Lastly, certificates are used to secure communication between devices and verify the identity of communication partners. When certificates or the systems around them fail, communication failures are sure to follow, and this can affect business operations significantly.

Authorization and Authentication Issues

Authorization governs which resources a user or service account can access and what the user or service can do with that resource.

Authentication issues can be as simple as users locking their accounts by entering their credentials incorrectly several times consecutively. The user's account will need to be unlocked before they can access network resources. If many users report permission problems, check services like DNS and Active Directory, or LDAP on Linux servers, to verify that they are functioning. Problems with these services can prevent users from authenticating to domain services. Service accounts can also cause issues. Service accounts are created for very specific uses, and their permissions are usually very granularly defined. However, as needs change, so must the permissions change.

Let's demonstrate the CompTIA troubleshooting methodology with a scenario: A service account is used to log into a database server. It issues queries to three databases. The service can add data to the tables of one database, but cannot modify the table structure. This account works fine for operating the application, but upgrading the application results in an error stating that tables could not be updated.

Step 1: Identify the problem.   The application upgrade fails when updating tables.

Step 2: Establish a theory of probable causes.   You theorize that this could be due to a permissions issue with the person running the upgrade or with the service account. You run a trace on the database as the application is upgraded and you identify the account that is being used to perform the upgrade and the queries that fail. The queries are related to adding new fields.

Step 3: Test the theory to determine the cause.   You review the permissions for the account and find that it does not have permission to modify the table structure, and adding new fields is a change to the structure.

Step 4: Establish a plan of action to resolve the problem and implement the solution.   You recommend that an account with permission to modify the table structure should be used to install the application. Management agrees, and you put in a service ticket to have an account created with the appropriate permissions and roles. Once the account is created, you provide the credentials to the application team.

Step 5: Verify full system functionality and, if applicable, implement preventative measures.   The application team reports that the application installs correctly with the new credentials. You confirm that the application upgrade is complete and then submit a ticket to have the account disabled until the application team needs it again.

Step 6: Document findings, actions, and outcomes.   You document the account that needs to be used for application updates and the process that must be followed to enable the account.

Malware

Another security issue you might face is the presence of malware. Malware infects machines through infected media that is plugged into a computer or other device, through website downloads or drive-by malware that executes from infected websites, or malicious ads known as malvertising. Malware is also distributed through e-mail, instant messages, and social networking sites.

Computers infected with malware might run slowly or encounter regular problems. Ransomware, a particularly troublesome form of malware, encrypts data on the user's machine and on network drives the machine has access to.

Let's demonstrate the CompTIA troubleshooting methodology with a scenario: Aimee, a cloud security engineer, receives reports that user files are being encrypted on the network.

Step 1: Identify the problem.   Files are being encrypted on the company NAS. Access logs from the NAS around the time of the encryption show connections from a computer called LAB1014. LAB1014 has a number of encrypted files on its local drive. No other users report encrypted files on their machines, and a spot check by another administrator confirms no encrypted files on a sample of other machines.

Step 2: Establish a theory of probable causes.   This could be due to a rogue script or ransomware running on LAB1014.

Step 3: Test the theory to determine the cause.   Both theories have the same response. LAB1014 needs to be quarantined immediately so that the problem does not spread and continue. If it is the cause of a rogue script, the activity will cease after LAB1014 is quarantined. If it is the result of ransomware, the LAB1014 will continue encrypting files on its local drive, but uninfected machines on the network and the NAS will continue operating normally.

Step 4: Establish a plan of action to resolve the problem and implement the solution.   The first step is to isolate LAB1014 from the network so that it cannot infect any other machines. Next, check other computers, starting with devices that were connected to the infected machine, LAB1014, such as file servers or departmental servers and surrounding workstations. Isolate all machines that have malware on them.

Next, make a forensic copy of LAB1014 in case an investigation is required. Once the forensic image is verified, you can begin the process of identifying the malware through virus scanning and removing the malware using virus scanning tools or specific malware removal tools. It is best to do a scan of the LAB1014 with installed antivirus tools and with bootable media that can scan the machine from outside the context of the installed operating system. Sometimes malware tricks the operating system into thinking parts of its code are legitimate. It might even tell the operating system that its files do not exist.

Virus scanning tools installed on the operating system rely on the operating system to provide them with accurate information, but this is not always the case. Bootable antivirus tools work independently from the operating system, so they do not suffer from these potential limitations.

Step 5: Verify full system functionality and, if applicable, implement preventative measures.   Verify that the ransomware has been removed from LAB1014 and any other machines that may have been identified as containing ransomware in the course of troubleshooting and that new machines are not being infected. Next, restore data to the machines where data was encrypted.

Step 6: Document findings, actions, and outcomes.   Create a report of the impact and actions taken.

Certificate Issues

Certificates are used to encrypt and decrypt data, as well as to digitally sign and verify the integrity of data. Each certificate contains a unique, mathematically related public and private key pair. During the standard process of authentication to a website, a client is presented with a certificate from a website. It then verifies that the certificate is in its trusted root store, thus trusting the certificate was signed by a trusted certificate authority. Afterward, the client verifies that the certificate is coming from the correct web server.

When the certificate is issued, it has an expiration date; certificates must be renewed before the expiration date. Otherwise, they are not usable. Expired certificates or certificates that are misconfigured can make sites unavailable or available with errors for end users.

Misconfigured certificates include sites that have a different name from their certificate, such as a site with the URL www.example.com configured with a certificate for example.com. The missing "www" in the certificate name would result in certificate errors for site visitors.

Consider a scenario with a certificate issue and how the CompTIA troubleshooting methodology could be applied to resolve the issue: Users report that the company website is showing security errors and customers are afraid to go to the website. Some customers on Twitter are saying that the company site has been hacked.

Step 1: Identify the problem.   You open the site and see that the site is displaying a certificate error.

Step 2: Establish a theory of probable causes.   The certificate either is expired or has been revoked.

Step 3: Test the theory to determine the cause.   View the certificate on the web server to see if it is expired. If it is not expired, check the certificate revocation list (CRL) to see if it has been revoked. In this case, the certificate expired.

Step 4: Establish a plan of action to resolve the problem and implement the solution.   Discuss renewal of the certificate and receive approval to perform the renewal and a purchase order to purchase the certificate renewal. Complete the renewal of the server certificate.

Step 5: Verify full system functionality and, if applicable, implement preventative measures.   Log onto the site to confirm that certificate errors are no longer displayed.

Step 6: Document findings, actions, and outcomes.   Identify all certificates in use at the company and when they expire. Discuss which ones are still required and establish a process to review certificates needed at least annually. Next, create a schedule with alerts so that certificates are renewed before they expire. Share the schedule with management so that they can budget for the certificate renewal cost.

CERTIFICATION SUMMARY

This chapter introduced you to troubleshooting tools, described documentation and its importance to company and cloud operations, and explained CompTIA's troubleshooting methodology. Troubleshooting tools can be used to help identify issues, validate troubleshooting theories, and refine theories. Some tools include ping, traceroute, nslookup, ifconfig, ipconfig, route, netstat, arp, Telnet, and SSH. Understanding which tools are best suited to troubleshoot different issues as they arise with a cloud deployment model saves an administrator time and helps maintain service level agreements set forth by the organization.

Documentation is another important concept for cloud and systems administrators. Documentation needs to be clear and easy to understand for anyone who may need to use it and should be regularly reviewed to ensure that it is up to date and accurate. Documenting the person responsible for creating and maintaining the application and where it is hosted is a good process that saves valuable time when troubleshooting any potential issues with the cloud environment.

Lastly, the CompTIA troubleshooting methodology provides an effective means for evaluating problems, identifying potential solutions, testing those solutions, and putting them into practice. The methodology is broken down into six steps as follows: Step 1: Identify the problem. Step 2: Establish a theory of probable causes. Step 3: Test the theory to determine the cause. Step 4: Establish a plan of action to resolve the problem and implement the solution. Step 5: Verify full system functionality and, if applicable, implement preventative measures. Step 6: Document findings, actions, and outcomes.

KEY TERMS

Use the following list to review the key terms discussed in this chapter. The definitions also can be found in the glossary.

Address Resolution Protocol (ARP)   Protocol used to resolve IP addresses to media access control (MAC) addresses.

arp command   A command prompt tool that resolves an IP address to either a physical address or a MAC address.

compute resources   The resources that are required for the delivery of virtual machines: disk, processor, memory, and networking.

domain information groper (dig)   Command-line tool for querying DNS servers operating in both interactive mode and batch query mode.

hop count   The total number of devices a packet passes through to reach its intended network target.

ifconfig   Interface configuration utility to configure and query TCP/IP network interface settings from a Unix or Linux command line.

Internet Control Message Protocol (ICMP)   A protocol that is part of the Internet Protocol suite used primarily for diagnostic purposes.

ipconfig   Command-line tool to display and configure TCP/IP network settings and troubleshoot DHCP and DNS settings.

limit   A floor or ceiling on the amount of resources that can be utilized for a given entity.

load balancing   Networking solution that distributes incoming traffic among multiple resources.

maximum segment size (MSS)   The largest segment that can be sent over the network.

maximum transmission unit (MTU)   The largest packet or frame that can be sent over the network.

netstat   Command-line tool that displays network statistics, including current connections and routing tables.

network latency   Any delays typically incurred during the processing of any network data.

nslookup   Command-line tool used to query DNS mappings for resource records.

ping   Command-line utility used to test the reachability of a destination host on an IP network.

quality of service (QoS)   A set of technologies that provides the ability to manage network traffic and prioritize workloads to accommodate defined service levels as part of a cost-effective solution.

quota   The total amount of resources that can be utilized for a system.

route command   A command prompt tool that can be used to view and manipulate the TCP/IP routing tables of Windows operating systems.

Secure Shell (SSH)   A protocol used to secure logins, file transfers, and port forwarding.

Telnet   A terminal emulation program for TCP/IP networks that connects the user's computer to another computer on the network.

time-to-live (TTL)   The length of time that a router or caching name server stores a record.

traceroute   Linux command-line utility to record the route and measure the delay of packets across an IP network.

tracert   Microsoft Windows command-line utility that tracks a packet from your computer to a destination host and displays how many hops the packet takes to reach the destination host.

troubleshooting   Techniques that aim to solve a problem that has been realized.

TWO-MINUTE DRILL

Troubleshooting Tools

❑ The ping command is used to troubleshoot the reachability of a host over a network.

❑ The traceroute (or tracert) command can be used to determine the path that an IP packet has to take to reach a destination. In order to query a DNS server to obtain domain name or IP address mappings for a specific DNS record, either the nslookup or dig command-line tools can be used.

❑ Ipconfig and ifconfig are command-line utilities that can be used to display the TCP/IP configuration settings of the network interface.

❑ The route command can be used to view and modify routing tables.

❑ The netstat command allows for the display of all active network connections, routing tables, and network protocol statistics.

❑ The arp command resolves an IP address to either a physical address or a MAC address.

❑ Telnet and SSH allow for execution of commands on a remote server.

Documentation and Analysis

❑ It is important for the cloud administrator to document every aspect of the cloud environment, including its setup and configuration and which applications are running on which host computer or virtual machine.

❑ Documentation needs to be clear and easy to understand for anyone who may need to use it and should be regularly reviewed to ensure that it is up to date and accurate.

❑ When issues come up, cloud professionals need to know where to look to find the data they need to solve the problem. The primary place they look is in log files.

❑ Operating systems, services, and applications create log files that track certain events as they occur on the computer. Log files can store a variety of information, including device changes, device drivers, system changes, events, and much more.

Troubleshooting Methodology

❑ CompTIA has established a troubleshooting methodology consisting of six steps:
Step 1: Identify the problem.
Step 2: Establish a theory of probable causes.
Step 3: Test the theory to determine the cause.
Step 4: Establish a plan of action to resolve the problem and implement the solution.
Step 5: Verify full system functionality and, if applicable, implement preventative measures.
Step 6: Document findings, actions, and outcomes.

SELF TEST

The following questions will help you measure your understanding of the material presented in this chapter. As indicated, some questions may have more than one correct answer, so be sure to read all the answer choices carefully.

Troubleshooting Tools

1. Which of the following command-line tools allows for the display of all active network connections and network protocol statistics?
   A. Netstat
   B. Ping
   C. Traceroute
   D. Ipconfig and ifconfig

2. You need to verify the TCP/IP configuration settings of a network adapter on a virtual machine running Microsoft Windows. Which of the following tools should you use?
   A. Ping
   B. ARP
   C. Tracert
   D. Ipconfig

3. Which of the following tools can be used to verify if a host is available on the network?
   A. Ping
   B. ARP
   C. Ipconfig
   D. Ipconfig and ifconfig

4. Which tool allows you to query DNS to obtain domain name or IP address mappings for a specified DNS record?
   A. Ping
   B. Ipconfig
   C. Nslookup
   D. Route

5. You need a way to remotely execute commands against a server that is located on the internal network. Which tool can be used to accomplish this objective?
   A. Ping
   B. Dig
   C. Traceroute
   D. Telnet

6. You need to modify a routing table and create a static route. Which command-line tool can you use to accomplish this task?
   A. Ping
   B. Traceroute
   C. Route
   D. Host

Documentation and Analysis

7. Users are complaining that an application is taking longer than normal to load. You need to troubleshoot why the application is experiencing startup issues. You want to gather detailed information while the application is loading. What should you enable?
   A. System logs
   B. Verbose logging
   C. Telnet
   D. ARP

8. How often should documentation be updated?
   A. Annually.
   B. Quarterly.
   C. It depends on how many people are working on the project.
   D. Whenever significant changes are made.

9. Fred manages around 50 cloud servers in Amazon Web Services. Each cloud server is thin provisioned and Fred pays for the amount of space his servers consume. He finds that the logs on the servers are rolling over and that each server has only about six days of logs. He would like to retain 18 months of logs. What should Fred do to retain the logs while conserving space on local hard disks?
   A. Compress the log files.
   B. Request that the cloud provider deduplicate his cloud data.
   C. Purchase and configure a cloud log archiving service.
   D. Log into the server every five days and copy the log files to his desktop.

Troubleshooting Methodology

10. Which is not the name of a step in the CompTIA troubleshooting methodology?

    A. Seek approval for the requested change.

    B. Identify the problem.

    C. Document findings, actions, and outcomes.

    D. Verify full system functionality.

11. Which step in the CompTIA troubleshooting methodology implements the solution?

    A. Step 1

    B. Step 2

    C. Step 3

    D. Step 4

    E. Step 5

    F. Step 6

SELF TEST ANSWERS

Troubleshooting Tools

1. ☑ **A.** The netstat command can be used to display protocol statistics and all of the currently active TCP/IP network connections, along with Ethernet statistics.

    ☒ **B, C,** and **D** are incorrect. The ping utility is used to troubleshoot the reachability of a host on an IP network. Traceroute is a network troubleshooting tool that is used to determine the path that an IP packet has to take to reach a destination. Ipconfig (Windows) and ifconfig (Linux and Unix) are used to configure the TCP/IP network interface from the command line.

2. ☑ **D.** Ipconfig is a Microsoft Windows command that displays the current TCP/IP network configuration settings for a network interface.

    ☒ **A, B,** and **C** are incorrect. The ping utility is used to troubleshoot the reachability of a host on an IP network. ARP resolves an IP address to a physical address or MAC address. Tracert is a Microsoft Windows network troubleshooting tool that is used to determine the path that an IP packet has to take to reach a destination.

3. ☑ **A.** The ping utility is used to troubleshoot the reachability of a host on an IP network. Ping sends an ICMP echo request packet to a specified IP address or host and waits for an ICMP reply.
☒ **B, C,** and **D** are incorrect. ARP resolves an IP address to a physical address or MAC address. Ipconfig and ifconfig display the current TCP/IP network configuration settings for a network interface.

4. ☑ **C.** Using the nslookup command, it is possible to query the Domain Name System to obtain domain name or IP address mappings for a specified DNS record.
☒ **A, B,** and **D** are incorrect. The ping utility is used to troubleshoot the reachability of a host on an IP network. The ipconfig command displays the current TCP/IP network configuration settings for a network interface. The route command can view and manipulate the TCP/IP routing tables of operating systems.

5. ☑ **D.** Telnet allows you to connect to another computer and enter commands via the Telnet program. The commands will be executed as if you were entering them directly on the server console.
☒ **A, B,** and **C** are incorrect. The ping utility is used to troubleshoot the reachability of a host on an IP network. The dig command can be used to query domain name servers and can operate in interactive command-line mode or batch query mode. Traceroute is a network troubleshooting tool that is used to determine the path that an IP packet has to take to reach a destination.

6. ☑ **C.** You can use the route command to view and manipulate the TCP/IP routing tables and create static routes.
☒ **A, B,** and **D** are incorrect. The ping utility is used to troubleshoot the reachability of a host on an IP network. Traceroute is a network troubleshooting tool that is used to determine the path that an IP packet has to take to reach a destination. The host utility can be used to perform DNS lookups.

Documentation and Analysis

7. ☑ **B.** Verbose logging records more detailed information than standard logging and is recommended to troubleshoot a specific problem.
☒ **A, C,** and **D** are incorrect. System log files can store a variety of information, including device changes, device drivers, system changes, and events, but would not provide detailed information on a particular application. ARP resolves an IP address to a physical address or MAC address. Telnet allows a user to connect to another computer and enter commands, and the commands are executed as if they were entered directly on the server console.

8. ☑ **D.** Each time a significant change is made, the documentation should be updated to reflect the change. Otherwise, coworkers, auditors, or other employees might operate off out-of-date information.
☒ **A, B,** and **C** are incorrect. Updating documentation annually or quarterly might do very little if nothing has changed in that interval. It is not the interval that matters, but the changes that are made to the device. Answer **C** also does not address what has changed. The number of people on a project does not matter. Even if there is a single person responsible for the system, it should still be documented.

9. ☑ **C.** A cloud log archiving service would allow Fred to retain the logs on the archiving service while freeing up space on the local disks. The log archival space would likely be cheaper than the production space, and log archiving services offer additional analytical and searching tools to make reviewing the logs easier.

    ☒ **A, B,** and **D** are incorrect. Folder compression would do little to extend the length of time the logs could be retained for. Fred wants to keep 18 months of logs, and compression might be able to get him a few more days. Deduplication of cloud data would operate off the entire drive. This could save space overall, but it does not specifically address the issue of log sizes. The logs would benefit slightly as well as the rest of the system, but not enough to be able to store logs long-term on primary storage. **D** is incorrect because is it not practical for Fred to perform a manual process every five days. Fred will likely forget some days and the copies will be harder to search and subject to data loss on his desktop.

Troubleshooting Methodology

10. ☑ **D.** Change requests were discussed in the previous chapter, and it important to seek approval for changes before making them. However, this is not the name of a step in the CompTIA troubleshooting methodology.

    ☒ **A, B,** and **C** are incorrect. Each of these is a step in the CompTIA troubleshooting methodology. The steps are as follows: Step 1: Identify the problem. Step 2: Establish a theory of probable causes. Step 3: Test the theory to determine the cause. Step 4: Establish a plan of action to resolve the problem and implement the solution. Step 5: Verify full system functionality and, if applicable, implement preventative measures. Step 6: Document findings, actions, and outcomes.

11. ☑ **D.** Step 4 implements the solution.

    ☒ **A, B, C, E,** and **F** are incorrect. Only Step 4 implements the solution. The other steps either lead up to the solution or validate and document following the solution. The steps in the CompTIA troubleshooting methodology are as follows: Step 1: Identify the problem. Step 2: Establish a theory of probable causes. Step 3: Test the theory to determine the cause. Step 4: Establish a plan of action to resolve the problem and implement the solution. Step 5: Verify full system functionality and, if applicable, implement preventative measures. Step 6: Document findings, actions, and outcomes.

Appendix

About the Digital Content

This book comes complete with Total Tester customizable practice exam software containing 200 practice exam questions. The software is provided on the CD-ROM that accompanies the print book and is also available for download. The Total Tester software can be installed on any Windows Vista/7/8/10 computer and must be installed to access the Total Tester practice exams. Please see the "Total Tester Online" section at the end of this appendix for more information about accessing an online version of the Total Tester that does not require installation.

Installing and Running the Total Tester

The software requires Windows Vista or later and 30MB of hard disk space for full installation, in addition to a current or prior major release of Chrome, Firefox, Internet Explorer, or Safari. To run, the screen resolution must be set to 1024×768 or higher.

From the main screen of the CD-ROM menu, you may install the Total Tester by clicking the Total Tester Practice Exams button. This will begin the installation process and place an icon on your desktop and in your Start menu. To run the Total Tester, navigate to Start | (All) Programs | Total Seminars, or double-click the icon on your desktop.

If you are unable to access the software from the CD-ROM, you can download the Total Tester from the link below after following the directions for free online registration:

http://www.totalsem.com/1260116603d

To uninstall the Total Tester software, go to Start | Control Panel | Programs And Features, and then select the Total Tester program. Select Remove, and Windows will completely uninstall the software.

About the Total Tester

The Total Tester provides you with a simulation of the CompTIA Cloud+ CV0-002 exam. Exams can be taken in Practice Mode, Exam Mode, or Custom Mode. Practice Mode provides an assistance window with hints, references to the book, explanations of the correct and incorrect answers, and the option to check your answer as you take the test. Exam Mode provides a simulation of the actual exam. The number of questions, the types of questions, and the time allowed are intended to be an accurate representation of the exam environment. Custom Mode allows you to create custom exams from selected domains or chapters, and you can further customize the number of questions and time allowed.

To take a test, launch the program and select Cloud+ SG2 from the Installed Question Packs list. You can then select Practice Mode, Exam Mode, or Custom Mode. All exams provide an overall grade and a grade broken down by domain.

Total Tester Online

Total Tester Online, a streamed online version of the Total Tester software, will be available shortly after the publication of this book.

Single User License Terms and Conditions

Online access to the digital content included with this book is governed by the McGraw-Hill Education License Agreement outlined next. By using this digital content you agree to the terms of that license.

Access   To register and activate your Total Seminars Training Hub account, simply follow these easy steps.

1. Go to **hub.totalsem.com/mheclaim**.
2. To Register and create a new Training Hub account, enter your e-mail address, name, and password. No further information (such as credit card number) is required to create an account.
3. If you already have a Total Seminars Training Hub account, select "Log in" and enter your e-mail and password.
4. Enter your Product Key: `szmr-33kn-3zss`
5. Click to accept the user license terms.
6. Click "Register and Claim" to create your account. You will be taken to the Training Hub and have access to the content for this book.

Duration of License   Access to your online content through the Total Seminars Training Hub will expire one year from the date the publisher declares the book out of print.

Your purchase of this McGraw-Hill Education product, including its access code, through a retail store is subject to the refund policy of that store.

The Content is a copyrighted work of McGraw-Hill Education and McGraw-Hill Education reserves all rights in and to the Content. The Work is © 2018 by McGraw-Hill Education, LLC.

Restrictions on Transfer   The user is receiving only a limited right to use the Content for user's own internal and personal use, dependent on purchase and continued ownership of this book. The user may not reproduce, forward, modify, create derivative works based upon, transmit, distribute, disseminate, sell, publish, or sublicense the Content or in any way commingle the Content with other third-party content, without McGraw-Hill Education's consent.

Limited Warranty   The McGraw-Hill Education Content is provided on an "as is" basis. Neither McGraw-Hill Education nor its licensors make any guarantees or warranties of any kind, either express or implied, including, but not limited to, implied warranties of merchantability or fitness for a particular purpose or use as to any McGraw-Hill Education Content or the information therein or any warranties as to the accuracy, completeness, currentness, or results to be obtained from, accessing or using the McGraw-Hill Education content, or any material referenced in such content or any information entered into licensee's product by users or other persons and/or any material available on or that can be accessed through the licensee's product (including via any hyperlink or otherwise) or as to non-infringement of third-party rights. Any warranties of any kind, whether express or implied, are disclaimed. Any material or data obtained through use of the McGraw-Hill Education content is at your own discretion and risk and user understands that it will be solely responsible for any resulting damage to its computer system or loss of data.

Neither McGraw-Hill Education nor its licensors shall be liable to any subscriber or to any user or anyone else for any inaccuracy, delay, interruption in service, error or omission, regardless of cause, or for any damage resulting therefrom.

In no event will McGraw-Hill Education or its licensors be liable for any indirect, special or consequential damages, including but not limited to, lost time, lost money, lost profits or good will, whether in contract, tort, strict liability or otherwise, and whether or not such damages are foreseen or unforeseen with respect to any use of the McGraw-Hill Education content.

Technical Support

For questions regarding the Total Tester software or operation of the CD-ROM included with the print book, visit **www.totalsem.com** or e-mail **support@totalsem.com**.

For questions regarding book content, e-mail **hep_customer-service@mheducation.com**. For customers outside the United States, e-mail **international_cs@mheducation.com**.

Glossary

access control entry (ACE)   A record that specifies the access rights of an individual principal or entity. An ACL is composed of one or more ACEs.

access control list (ACL)   A register that tracks permitted actions. An ACL for a server might contain the access rights of entities such as users, services, computers, or administrative accounts and whether those rights are permitted or denied, whereas an ACL for a firewall might contain the source address, port, and destination address for authorized communications and deny permissions for all others. ACLs are composed of a set of ACEs.

Address Resolution Protocol (ARP)   Protocol used to resolve IP addresses to media access control (MAC) addresses.

Advanced Encryption Standard (AES)   An algorithm used to encrypt and decrypt data. Principally, AES uses a 128-bit block and variable key sizes of 128, 192, and 256 bits. It performs 10 to 14 rounds of encryption depending on the key size used.

Advanced Technology Attachment (ATA)   A disk drive implementation that integrates the drive and the controller.

alternate site   A facility in which an application can run if the primary site is unavailable. Alternate sites vary in how much effort and expense is required to make them functional for the application.

antimalware software   A piece of software that looks at actions on a system to identify malicious activity.

antivirus software   A piece of software that scans files resident on a machine and processes in memory and analyzes them for known malware signatures or anomalous behavioral patterns.

Anything as a Service (XaaS)   A cloud model that delivers IT as a service through a combination of cloud computing models and works with a combination of SaaS, IaaS, PaaS, CaaS, DBaaS, or BPaaS.

application life cycle   A process whereby applications are specified, developed, tested, deployed, and maintained.

application performance monitor (APM)   A system that tracks performance metrics for systems to identify potential issues. Systems can be as simple as those that ping a resource periodically to transactional monitoring systems that simulate behavior. Some APM systems utilize agents running on the systems that make up a service to monitor performance metrics and health metrics for key services.

application programming interface (API)   A structure that exposes functions of an application to other programs.

approval process   Set of activities that presents all relevant information to stakeholders and allows an informed decision to be made about a request for change.

arp command   A command prompt tool that resolves an IP address to either a physical address or a MAC address.

asset accountability   The documented assignment of a configuration item (CI) to a human resource.

asymmetric encryption   Encryption mechanism that uses two different keys to encrypt and decrypt data.

asynchronous replication   The process of copying data between replica sets where applications are notified of successful writes when the data has been written to the local replica set. Other replicas are made consistent at the earliest convenience.

authentication, authorization, and accounting (AAA)   The set of processes that determines who a claimant is and what they are allowed to do. These processes also log activity for later auditing.

automation   The programmatic execution of a workflow that was formerly performed manually.

backout plan   Action plan that allows a change to be reverted to its previous baseline state.

backup target   The destination for a backup job.

bandwidth   A measurement of available or consumed data communication resources on a network.

bare metal restore (BMR)   A process whereby the operating system, applications, and all data are restored to new hardware without the need for any other prerequisite software installations on the hardware.

baseline   A set of metrics collected over time to understand normal data and network behavior patterns.

Basic Input/Output System (BIOS)   Built-in software that allows the computer to boot without an operating system and controls the code required to manage the keyboard, display, disk drives, and some other functions.

bit-for-bit backup   A backup that captures the entire hard drive bit by bit.

block cipher   A method of converting plaintext to ciphertext in bulk as opposed to one data bit at a time, either using a fixed secret key or by generating keys from each encrypted block.

block-level backup   A backup that captures only changed blocks of data as opposed to the entire file.

Border Gateway Protocol (BGP)   A protocol used to direct packets across an internetwork. BGP makes routing decisions based on rule sets and network policies.

bus   The communication system used to transfer data between the components inside of a computer motherboard, processor, or network device. It gets its name from the concept of a bus line where the bus stops and allows people to get off and board. It is a communication system that is attached at many points along the bus line.

business continuity plan (BCP)   A documented set of procedures and information about the organization that is collected and maintained so that the organization can continue operations in the event of an incident.

business impact analysis (BIA)   The analysis and documentation resulting from a review of the organization's systems and risks losing the potential impact of a disaster or incident.

Business Process as a Service (BPaaS)   Any business process that is delivered as a service by utilizing a cloud solution.

caching   Process of transparently storing data at a quicker response location so that any future requests for that data can be accessed faster than through the slower medium.

canonical name (CNAME)   A DNS record that specifies an alternate name for a resource. For example, a CNAME record testing for the comptia.org domain pointing to www would allow for users to enter the URL www.comptia.org or testing.comptia.org to go to the same site.

capacity management   A process to ensure that the capacity of IT services and the IT infrastructure can meet agreed size and performance-related requirements in a cost-effective and timely manner.

central processing unit (CPU)   Hardware device responsible for executing all of the instructions from the operating system and software running within it.

certificate authority (CA)   Entity that issues digital certificates and makes its public keys available to the intended audience to provide proof of its authenticity.

certificate revocation list (CRL)   A list managed by a certificate authority (CA) and often published to a public source that describes each certificate that the CA has removed from service so that users and computers know if they should no longer trust a certificate.

certificate services   The infrastructure required to manage the exchange of keys and validation of certificates.

change advisory board (CAB)　The body of stakeholders that provides input to the change manager about requests for change.

change management　The process of making changes to the cloud environment from its design phase to its operations phase in the least impactful way possible.

change monitoring　The process of watching the production environment for any unplanned configuration changes.

chargeback　An accounting strategy that attempts to decentralize the costs of IT services and apply them directly to the teams or divisions that utilize those services.

ciphertext　Data that has been encrypted using a mathematical algorithm.

client integration implementation service (CIIS)　Software that has defined workflows for multiple cloud services. Users of CIIS can select from pre-made workflows after connecting their cloud accounts and the CIIS will implement the workflow for them by utilizing the underlying APIs of the cloud services. CIIS can usually be implemented on a scheduled basis. If this then that (IFTTT) is an example of a CIIS.

cloud access security broker (CASB)　A cloud service that operates as the gateway between external users and other cloud systems. The CASB screens incoming traffic for malicious content and anomalous behavior and prevents that traffic from being delivered to the cloud systems it services.

cloud bursting　Concept of running an application on the organization's internal computing resources or private cloud and "bursting" that application into a public cloud on demand when the organization runs out of resources on its internal private cloud.

cloud management platform (CMP)　A collection of technologies such as self-service portals, cloud integration, workflow, and sometimes orchestration that are used to incorporate private, public, and hybrid cloud systems into an enterprise ecosystem.

cloud service provider (CSP)　A company that provides cloud services to users or companies on a subscription basis.

cloud systems administrator (CSA)　The person responsible for cloud services from the cloud consumer company side of the equation. CSAs provision user accounts, add or remove services, configure integration between cloud providers, and perform other administration- and management-related tasks.

code repository   A system that organizes code branches to keep code consistent even when multiple teams are working on the same areas in parallel. Developers can publish code changes to the repository, can synchronize their local copy of the code with the repository, or can revert to previously published versions.

cold site   An alternative site that includes only network connectivity. It is the least expensive alternative site option but takes the longest to ramp up. *See also* alternate site, hot site, *and* warm site.

co-location (COLO)   A facility owned and operated by a third party that houses technology assets such as servers, storage, backup systems, and networking equipment.

command-line interface (CLI)   An interface that is text-based.

Communications as a Service (CaaS)   Allows a cloud consumer to utilize enterprise-level voice over IP (VoIP), virtual private networks (VPNs), private branch exchange (PBX), and unified communications using a cloud model.

community cloud   A cloud model where the infrastructure is shared between several organizations from a specific group with common computing needs and objectives.

compression   Reduction in the size of data being sent across a network or data at rest.

compute resources   The resources that are required for the delivery of virtual machines: disk, processor, memory, and networking.

configuration control   The ability to maintain updated, accurate documentation of all configuration items.

configuration item (CI)   An asset or document that falls within the scope of the configuration management system.

configuration management (CM)   The process that ensures all assets and configuration items (CIs) required to deliver IT services are adequately controlled, and that accurate and reliable information about them is available when and where it is needed, including details of how the assets have been configured and the relationships between assets.

configuration management database (CMDB)   The database used to store configuration records throughout their life cycle. Each database stores attributes of configuration items and relationships with other configuration items.

configuration management system (CMS)   A system that stores configuration records throughout their life cycle. The configuration management system maintains one or more CMDBs.

configuration standardization   Documented baseline configuration for similar configuration items (CIs).

console port   Allows an administrator to use a cable to connect to a hypervisor host computer or virtual machine directly.

content addressable storage (CAS)   A storage system that indexes data contents and allows for retrieval based on the content of data rather than its filename or other metadata.

content management system (CMS)   A system, typically web-based, that allows for document uploading, viewing, and downloading, while tracking changes and metadata of documents and allowing for complex searching, among other things.

contingency planning   Establishing alternate practices, sites, and resources that can be used in an emergency.

continuity of operations plan (COOP)   A documented set of procedures and information about the organization that is collected and maintained so that the organization can continue operations in the event of an incident. COOP is a term primarily used in government operations or in federal compliance documentation.

continuous development (CD)   A process that creates a pipeline of tasks leading toward deployment of regular software releases. DevOps teams make regular iterative changes to the code rather than working on a large portion of the program for a long period of time. This decreases the time from the introduction of new code to the deployment of that code in production. Continuous development is also known as continuous delivery.

continuous integration (CI)   A software development process where elements of the coding and testing processes are automated and developers make regular iterative changes to the code.

converged network adapter (CNA)   A computer expansion card that can be used as a host bus adapter or a network interface card.

CPU wait time   The delay that results when the CPU cannot perform computations because it is waiting for I/O operations.

customer relationship management (CRM) The process of managing interactions with potential, former, and existing customers. CRM software enables better control and tracking of these interactions.

dashboard A visual panel showing a series of metrics on specific areas.

data BLOB (binary large object) A collection of binary data stored as a single, discrete entity in a database management system.

data classification Practice of sorting data into discrete categories that help define the access levels and type of protection required for that set of data.

data encryption Algorithmic scheme that secures data by scrambling it into a code that is not readable by unauthorized resources.

Data Encryption Standard (DES) An algorithm used to encrypt and decrypt data. Principally, DES is a symmetric key algorithm that uses block sizes of 64 bits and 16 rounds of encryption.

data integrity Assurance that data is accurate and that the same data remains unchanged in between storage and retrieval or between network sender and receiver.

Database as a Service (DBaaS) A cloud model that delivers database operations as a service to multiple cloud consumers over the Internet.

database management system (DBMS) A system that houses databases, allowing for connectivity to those databases and management of the databases through queries, scheduled stored procedures, and other functions.

dedicated compute environment Environment where a single tenant owns or leases equipment.

demilitarized zone (DMZ) An isolated network segment that has specific security rules on it DMZs are created to segment traffic based on security rules.

differential backup A backup system that backs up all files that have changed since the last full backup and requires the last differential and the last full backup to perform a restore.

digital rights management (DRM)   A set of technologies that enforces specific usage limitations on data, such as preventing a document from being printed or e-mailed, or photos from being downloaded from a phone app. DRM is typically associated with consumer applications, while a similar technology, information rights management (IRM), is associated with enterprise systems.

digital signature   Mathematical hash of a dataset that is encrypted by the private key and used to validate that dataset with the related public key.

direct attached storage (DAS)   Storage system that is directly attached to a server or workstation and cannot be used as shared storage at the block level because it is directly connected to a single machine.

disaster recovery plan (DRP)   Documented set of procedures that defines how an organization can recover and protect specific IT systems in the event of a disaster.

discretionary access control (DAC)   Security mechanism in which the power to grant or deny permissions to resources lies with the data owner.

distributed denial of service (DDoS)   An attack that targets a single system simultaneously from multiple compromised systems.

distributed file system (DFS)   A method of organizing shared folders such that the original share UNC path is obscured and shares from multiple servers can be organized into a single hierarchy. DFS also allows for replication between shares.

distributed services architecture (DSA)   A method of organizing services so that they can exchange data with one another without the use of a centralized management function.

documentation   Written copy of a procedure, policy, or configuration.

domain information groper (dig)   Command-line tool for querying DNS servers operating in both interactive mode and batch query mode.

Domain Name System (DNS)   A service that provides name resolution for devices by converting a name to its associated IP address. Also known as Domain Name Service.

downtime   Any time when the system is unavailable. Downtime can be reduced through various levels of redundancy.

dual inline memory module (DIMM)   A form of computer system memory stick that has been used since the Intel Pentium processor to organize integrated circuits of computer memory.

Dynamic Host Configuration Protocol (DHCP)   Network protocol that automatically assigns IP addresses from a predefined range of numbers, called a scope, to computers on a network.

edge sites   Data centers closer to the customer.

elasticity   Allows an organization to dynamically provision and deprovision processing, memory, and storage resources to meet the demands of the network as needed.

elliptic curve cryptography (ECC)   A cryptographic function that allows for smaller keys to be used to provide the same security as those with larger keys through the use of finite field algebraic structure of elliptic curves.

emergency change advisory board (ECAB)   The body of stakeholders that provides input to the change manager about requests for change in the case of an emergency when there may not be time to assemble the full CAB.

Encapsulating Security Protocol (ESP)   A cryptographic function used by IPSec to encrypt tunneled data using PKI certificates or asymmetric keys.

encrypting file system (EFS)   A user-based feature of the NTFS file system that provides file-level encryption.

extended file system (EXT)   First file system created specifically for Linux where the metadata and file structure is based on the UNIX file system.

extranet   Extension of an intranet, with the difference being an extranet allows access to the network from outside the organization.

failback   The process of restoring operations to the primary system after a failover.

failover   The process of switching to a redundant system upon failure of the primary system.

failover cluster   Multiple systems configured to operate together to offer a set of services.

fault tolerance A feature of computer system design that increases reliability by adding redundant hardware components so that the system can continue to function in the event of a single component failure.

federation Use of single sign-on (SSO) through a central identity provider to authorize users or devices to many different protected network resources, such as file servers, websites, and database applications.

Fibre Channel (FC) A technology used to transmit data between computers at data rates of up to 10 Gbps.

Fibre Channel over Ethernet (FCoE) A fibre channel transport protocol that enables the transport of Fibre Channel traffic over Ethernet networks by encapsulating Fibre Channel frames over Ethernet networks.

Fibre Channel over IP (FCIP) A network protocol that takes Fibre Channel frames and encapsulates them within the IP protocol.

Fibre Channel Protocol (FCP) Transport protocol that transports SCSI commands over a Fibre Channel network.

file allocation table (FAT) Legacy file system used in Microsoft operating systems and is still used today by a variety of removable media.

file integrity monitoring (FIM) A computer system process that reviews data in applications of the computer operating system and compares data values with known good values to identify if data has been altered.

File Transfer Protocol (FTP) Network protocol that allows for access to and the transfer of files over the Internet.

fingerprinting A process that determines the operating system and software running on a device.

firewall A piece of software or hardware that screens traffic traversing a network link. When the firewall screens traffic for the local links in a host, it is known as a host-based firewall.

firmware Set of instructions that is programmed into a specific hardware device that instructs the hardware device how to communicate with the computer system.

follow the sun (FTS)   A method where multiple shifts work on a system according to their time zone to provide 24/7 service.

footprinting   The process of enumerating the computers or network devices on a target network.

FTP over SSL (FTPS)   An extension of FTP that uses Secure Sockets Layer (SSL) or Transport Layer Security (TLS) to secure the transfer of files over FTP.

full backup   A backup that contains a complete copy of all files selected in the backup job. A full backup does not require any other backups for a restore operation.

Generic Routing Encapsulation (GRE)   A lightweight, flexible tunneling protocol that works over IP but does not encrypt data.

globally unique identifier (GUID)   A value that uniquely represents an entity within a directory system.

graphical user interface (GUI)   A method of providing instructions to a computer systems by presenting the user with pictures and/or text that can be selected. The information displayed on a GUI changes based on program operation so that users are kept aware and options for sending commands are context aware. For example, once a disk is mounted, the GUI would display options to allow the user to perform commands that required mounting as a prerequisite.

guest tools   Software additions that are added to a virtual machine after the operating system has been installed to improve the interaction between the virtual machine and the virtualization host.

GUID Partition Table (GPT)   A system that replaces the Master Boot Record (MBR) and organizes the data on disks.

Hadoop   An open-source distributed clustered system that can be deployed in modules for scalability and flexibility. Hadoop is the framework on which many other systems can be built.

Hadoop distributed file system (HDFS)   The storage for a Hadoop cluster that divides data blocks across members of the Hadoop cluster for resiliency.

hard disk drive (HDD)   A storage device that uses rapidly rotating aluminum or nonmagnetic disks, referred to as platters, that are coated with a magnetic material (ferrous oxide) that stores bits of information grouped into sectors, which in turn allows an individual block of data to be stored or retrieved in any order rather than only being accessible sequentially, as in the case of data that exists on a tape.

hardening   Ensuring that a system or network is configured in such a way that reduces the risk of attack from either internal or external sources.

hardware-assisted virtualization   Enables efficient full virtualization used to simulate a complete hardware environment or a virtual machine.

hierarchical storage management (HSM)   Allows for automatically moving data between four different tiers of storage.

high availability (HA)   Systems that are available almost 100 percent of the time.

hop count   The total number of devices a packet passes through to reach its intended network target.

horizontal scaling   A scalability methodology whereby more nodes are added to a configuration instead of increasing the resources for any one node. Horizontal scaling is also known as scaling out.

host bus adapter (HBA)   A network card that allows a device to communicate directly with a storage area network (SAN) or a SAN switch.

host-based intrusion detection system (HIDS)   A system that analyzes activity on a host where a HIDS agent is installed for behavior patterns and notifies if patterns match those associated with malicious activity such as hacking or malware.

host-based intrusion prevention system (HIPS)   A system that analyzes activity on a host where a HIPS agent is installed for behavior patterns and takes action if patterns match those associated with malicious activity such as hacking or malware.

hot site   An alternative site that is a duplicate of the original site, with complete hardware and backups. It is the most expensive alternative site option but takes the least amount of time to become fully operational. *See also* alternate site, cold site, *and* warm site.

hotfix   A small patch that addresses a specific issue .

hybrid cloud   A cloud model that utilizes both private and public clouds to perform distinct functions within the same organization.

Hypertext Transfer Protocol (HTTP)   Protocol used to distribute HTML files, text, images, sound, videos, multimedia files, and other information over the Internet.

Hypertext Transfer Protocol Secure (HTTPS)   An extension of HTTP that provides secure communication over the Internet using Secure Sockets Layer (SSL) or Transport Layer Security (TLS).

hyperthreading   A technology that creates two logical CPU cores for each physical CPU core that supports hyperthreading.

hypervisor   A piece of software that creates and manages the virtual infrastructure, including virtual switch (vSwitch), virtual CPU (vCPU), virtual memory, virtual disks, and virtual machines.

I/O throttling   Defined limits utilized specifically for disk resources assigned to virtual machines to ensure they are not performance or availability constrained when working in an environment that has more demand than availability of disk resources.

identity and access management (IAM)   The policies, procedures, and technologies required to control access privileges, roles, and rights of users across a heterogeneous enterprise.

ifconfig   Interface configuration utility to configure and query TCP/IP network interface settings from a Unix or Linux command line

incremental backup   A backup system that backs up the files that have changed since the last full or incremental backup and requires all incremental backups to perform a restore.

information rights management (IRM)   A set of technologies that enforces specific usage limitations on data, such as preventing a document from being printed or e-mailed, or scanned photos from being downloaded in a web application. IRM is typically associated with enterprise systems, while a similar technology, digital rights management (DRM), is associated with consumer applications.

Information Technology Infrastructure Library (ITIL)   A framework for implementing life cycle management.

Infrastructure as a Service (IaaS)   A cloud model where the cloud consumer outsources responsibility for its underlying technology framework to an external cloud provider, which owns the equipment such as storage, servers, and connectivity domains.

initiator qualified name (IQN)   The iSCSI address given to an initiator. Initiators reside on clients in an iSCSI network and initiators connect to targets such as storage resources over the iSCSI network. IQNs use the following naming convention: iqn.yyyy-mm.naming-authority:unique name

input/output operations per second (IOPS)   A common disk performance measurement of how much data is provided over a period of time.

instructions per cycle (IPC)   A measurement of the number of commands that can be executed per clock cycle.

Integrated Drive Electronics (IDE)   Combines the controller and the hard drive, allowing the manufacturer to use proprietary communication and storage methods without any compatibility risks as it allows the drive to connect directly to the motherboard.

Intelligent Platform Management Interface (IPMI)   Used for out-of-band management of a computer, allowing an administrator to manage a system remotely without an operating system.

Interior Gateway Routing Protocol (IGRP)   A Cisco routing protocol used to direct packets across an internetwork. IGRP can use a number of metrics to determine the ideal route, including reliability, delay, load, and bandwidth.

Internet   A global system of interconnected computer networks that are not controlled by a single organization or country.

Internet Control Message Protocol (ICMP)   A protocol that is part of the Internet protocol suite and is used primarily for diagnostic purposes.

Internet Fibre Channel Protocol (iFCP)   A protocol for transmitting FC data between two iFCP gateways so that the FC data can traverse a non-FC network.

Internet Protocol Security (IPSec)   A tunneling protocol that secures IP traffic using Encapsulating Security Protocol (ESP) to encrypt the data that is tunneled over it using PKI certificates or asymmetric keys and offers authentication through the Authentication Header (AH) protocol.

Internet service provider (ISP)   A company that provides connectivity to the Internet to consumers and companies.

Internet Small Computer System Interface (iSCSI)   The communication protocol that leverages standard IP packets to transmit typical SCSI commands across an IP network; it then translates them back to standard SCSI commands, which enables servers to access remote disks as if they were locally attached.

Internet Storage Name Service (iSNS)   A system that maintains a database of information on the devices that are part of an iSCSI or FC network. Devices on the network can query the iSNS server to identify resources and connect to them.

intersite replication   Replication that occurs between systems at the different sites.

intranet   A private network that is configured and controlled by a single organization and is only accessible to users who are internal to that organization.

intrasite replication   Replication that occurs between systems at the same site.

intrusion detection and prevention (IDP)   A system that analyzes activity for behavior patterns and notifies or takes action if patterns match those associated with malicious activity such as hacking or malware.

intrusion detection system (IDS)   A piece of software or hardware that evaluates data and activity on a device or network link for signs of malicious behavior and alerts or logs such activity.

intrusion prevention system (IPS)   A piece of software or hardware that is evaluates data and activity on a device or network link for signs of malicious behavior and blocks, restricts, alerts, or logs such activity.

ipconfig   Windows command-line tool to display and configure TCP/IP network settings and troubleshoot DHCP and DNS settings.

JavaScript Object Notation (JSON)   An open standard for a structured data that is used in Internet communications.

Jumbo Frames   Large frames that are used for large data transfers to lessen the burden on processors.

just a bunch of disks (JBOD)   Two or more hard drives that have not been configured as part of a RAID set. These disks can be used to form a larger volume, but RAID techniques such as mirroring, striping, and parity are not used. Instead, JBOD uses techniques such as concatenation or spill and fill to place data on disks in the JBOD array.

kernel-based virtual machine (KVM)   An open-source hypervisor that creates and manages the virtual infrastructure, including virtual switch (vSwitch), virtual CPU (vCPU), virtual memory, virtual disks, and virtual machines. Please note that this use of KVM is different from keyboard video mouse.

key management system (KMS)   A system that can issue, validate, distribute, and revoke cryptographic keys. Cloud KMSs include such systems as AWS KMS, Microsoft Azure Key Vault, and Oracle Key Manager.

key performance indicator (KPI)   A measurement of some activity. KPIs can be established for human processes or for computer functions. A KPI is also known as a metric.

Keyboard Video Mouse (KVM)   Technology that allows for the keyboard and mouse input to be sent to a machine and for the monitor output to be displayed to the user. KVM devices can use the same keyboard, mouse, and monitor with multiple machines without having to connect and disconnect the devices. Please note that this use of KVM is different from kernel-based virtual machine.

latency   The delay in time calculated from the time a service request is made until that request is fulfilled. Typically used to describe network and hard drive speeds.

Layer 2 Tunneling Protocol (L2TP)   A tunneling protocol that does not offer encryption on its own, but when combined with IPSec offers a high level of encryption at the cost of additional CPU overhead to encapsulate data twice.

least privilege   Principle that states employees should be granted only the minimum permissions necessary to do their job.

life cycle management   The process or processes put in place by an organization to assist in the management, coordination, control, delivery, and support of its configuration items from the requirements stage to retirement.

Lightweight Directory Access Protocol (LDAP)   A protocol used to exchange information on systems, users, roles, applications, and services in a network. LDAP is an open protocol.

limit   A floor or ceiling on the amount of resources that can be utilized for a given entity.

load balancing   A means of distributing workloads across multiple computers to optimize resources and throughput and to prevent a single device from being overwhelmed.

load testing   Testing that evaluates a system when the system is artificially forced to execute operations consistent with user activities at different levels of utilization.

local area network (LAN)   Network topology that spans a relatively small area, such as an office building, and allows people within that area to share files, devices, printers, and applications.

logical unit number (LUN)   Unique identifier used to identify a logical unit or collection of hard disks in a storage device.

LUN masking   Makes a LUN available to some hosts and unavailable to others.

mail exchanger (MX)   A DNS record that stores information on the mail server for the domain, if one exists.

main distribution facility (MDF)   The location where PBX equipment is stored.

maintenance mode   A process on a clustered virtualization host that will migrate all the virtual machines to another host in a cluster and prepare the host for maintenance. Many maintenance tasks cannot be performed unless the host is first in maintenance mode.

maintenance window   An agreed-upon, predefined period during which service interruptions are least impactful to the business. This could fall at any time and depends on the patterns of business activity for that particular entity.

managed service provider (MSP)   A company that provides technology services on a subscription basis.

mandatory access control (MAC)   Security mechanism in which access is mandated by the operating system or application and not by data owners.

Master Boot Record (MBR)   A boot sector residing at the first part of a drive that describes where files are located on the disk.

maximum segment size (MSS)   The largest segment that can be sent over the network.

maximum transmission unit (MTU)   The largest packet or frame that can be sent over the network.

mean time between failures (MTBF)   The average length of time a hardware component will function before failing, usually measured in hours. This differs from MTTF in that units can be repaired.

mean time to failure (MTTF)   The average time a hardware component will function before failing, usually measured in hours. This differs from MTBF in that units cannot be repaired.

mean time to repair (MTTR)   The average length of time it takes to repair a hardware component.

memory ballooning   A process whereby virtual machines give up some of their memory for another virtual machine on the host.

memory burst   The maximum amount of memory a virtual machine can allocate from the host.

mesh   Network topology where every node is interconnected to every other node in the network.

metadata   Data about data, used to describe particular attributes of data, including how the data is formatted.

metadata performance   A measure of how quickly files and directories can be created, removed, or checked on a disk resource.

metering   Ability of a cloud platform to track the use of its IT resources and is geared primarily toward measuring usage by cloud consumers.

metric   A measurement of some activity. Metrics can be established for human processes or for computer functions. A metric is also known as a KPI.

metropolitan area network (MAN)   Network topology connecting multiple LANs together to span a large area, such as a city or a large campus.

Microsoft Operations Framework (MOF)   A Microsoft framework for implementing life cycle management that is based on ITIL.

mirror site   A duplicate website used to provide improved performance and to reduce network traffic.

multifactor authentication (MFA)   Authentication of resources using proof from more than one of the three authentication categories: something you know, something you have, something you do, someplace you are, and something you are.

Multipath Input/Output (MPIO)   Technology that allows for more than one path to be used for communication between nodes and storage devices.

multipathing   The practice of defining and controlling redundant physical paths to I/O devices and/or storage resources.

Multiprotocol Label Switching (MPLS)   A wide area network (WAN) protocol that uses short labels instead of network addresses to make routing lookups quicker.

multitenancy   An architecture providing a single instance of an application to serve multiple clients or tenants.

N_Port ID Virtualization (NPIV)   Allows multiple host computers to share a single physical Fibre Channel port identification or N_Port.

netstat   Command-line tool that displays network statistics, including current connections and routing tables.

network access control (NAC)   An endpoint security technology that prevents system access unless certain conditions such as configuration settings, patch levels, or antivirus definitions are met. Conditions are defined by a policy.

network address translation (NAT)   A service that consolidates the addresses needed for each internal device to a single valid public IP address, allowing all of the organization's employees to access the Internet with the use of a single public IP address.

network assessment   Objective review of an organization's network infrastructure regarding functionality and security capabilities used to establish a baseline for future audits.

network attached storage (NAS)   Provides file-level data storage to a network over TCP/IP.

network audit   Objective periodic review of an organization's network infrastructure against an established baseline.

network file system (NFS)   A system for organizing data that can be shared with other users on a computer network.

network function virtualization (NFV)   The virtualization of network services such as load balancers, firewalls, routers, and layer 3 switches.

Network Information Service (NIS)   A computer system that manages critical infrastructure networks such as telephone service, utility services, and 911 service, to name a few.

network interface card (NIC)   An adapter that connects a node to a network. Physical transmission media is attached to the NIC to enable communication. NICs can be assigned an IP address, default gateway, and subnet mask.

network isolation   Allows for a section of the network to be isolated from another section so that multiple identical copies of the environment are executed at the same time.

network latency   Any delays typically incurred during the processing of any network data.

network operations center (NOC)   A place where management and monitoring personnel keep an eye on critical systems using a wide variety of management and monitoring tools.

network shares   Storage resources that are made available across a network and appear as if they are a resource on the local machine.

Network Time Protocol (NTP)   A method for keeping system clocks synchronized with a source clock.

network-based intrusion detection system (NIDS)   A system that analyzes activity on a network egress point such as a firewall for behavior patterns and notifies if patterns match those associated with malicious activity such as hacking or malware.

network-based intrusion prevention system (NIPS)   A system that analyzes activity on a network egress point such as a firewall for behavior patterns and takes action if patterns match those associated with malicious activity such as hacking or malware.

new technology file system (NTFS)   A proprietary file system developed by Microsoft to support the Windows operating systems that includes support for access control lists and file system journaling.

nslookup   A command-line tool used to query DNS mappings for resource records.

NT LAN Manager (NTLM)   A Microsoft networking protocol that uses challenge-response for authentication in some Windows operating systems.

object ID (OID)   A unique identifier used to name an object.

offline migration   A process that migrates a physical server to a virtual machine by taking the source computer offline so that it is not available during the migration process.

on-demand/just-in-time self-service   A system that gives cloud consumers access to cloud services through an online portal allowing them to acquire computing resources automatically and on-demand without human interaction from the cloud provider.

online migration   A process that migrates a physical server to a virtual machine while the source computer remains available during the migration process.

Open Database Connectivity (ODBC)   A standard method for communicating with database management systems.

open shortest path first (OSPF)   A protocol used to direct packets across an internetwork. The OSPF routing protocol uses link state routing to determine the best path to the destination.

Open Virtual Appliance (OVA)   An open standard for a virtual appliance that can be used in a variety of hypervisors from different vendors.

Open Virtualization Format (OVF)   An open standard for a virtual hard disk that can be used in a variety of hypervisors from different vendors.

open-source hypervisor   Hypervisor software provided at no cost and delivers the same ability to run multiple guest virtual machines on a single host.

open-source software   Software provided at no cost that is community developed and supported. Open-source code is available to everyone and changes to the code are uploaded to repositories on the Internet and subject to peer review.

operating system (OS)   Software that interfaces with underlying physical or virtual hardware and provides a platform for other software to run.

operational level agreement (OLA)   A document that describes the expectations of internal units so that service level agreements can be met.

orchestration   The management and optimization of automation workflows.

orphaned resource   A child object or resource from deleted or moved objects that remains on a system.

out-of-band management   Allows for remote management and monitoring of a computer system without the need for an operating system.

overcommitment   Assigning more resources to virtual machines than are available to the physical host.

overcommitment ratio   The number of vCPUs allocated for each physical CPU expressed as a ratio such as 3:1, meaning three vCPUs for one physical CPU.

overprovisioning   The process of creating multiple volumes using thin provisioning with a total maximum size that exceeds available storage.

patch   A software package that modifies existing software.

patch management   The strategy employed to deploy patches.

pay-as-you-grow   A concept in cloud computing where an organization pays for cloud resources as it needs those resources.

penetration testing   Process of evaluating network security with a simulated attack on the network from both external and internal attackers.

performance baseline   Performance chart displaying current normal performance of the environment used to compare against future gathered performance metrics.

personal health information (PHI)   Data that represents the identity of a patient, such as name, phone number, address, e-mail address, Social Security number, and date of birth. The PHI term is mostly used in the context of HIPAA compliance.

personally identifiable information (PII)   Data that represents the identity of a person, such as name, phone number, address, e-mail address, Social Security number, and date of birth. The PII term is mostly used in the context of privacy compliance.

physical to physical (P2P)   A transfer of the data and applications from one physical server to another physical server.

physical to virtual (P2V)   Process of migrating a physical server's operating system, applications, and data from the physical server to a newly created guest virtual machine on a virtualization host.

ping   Command-line utility used to test the reachability of a destination host on an IP network.

ping flood   An attack that sends a massive number of ICMP packets to overwhelm a system with more traffic than it can handle.

Ping of Death (PoD)   An attack that sends malformed ICMP packets with the intent of crashing systems that cannot process them and consequently shut down.

plaintext   Unencrypted data.

Platform as a Service (PaaS)   A cloud model that provides the infrastructure to create applications and host them with a cloud provider.

point in time   A discrete reference to a particular moment.

Point-to-Point Tunneling Protocol (PPTP)   A tunneling protocol that uses GRE and Point-to-Point Protocol (PPP) to transport data using a variety of now outdated protocols. Primarily used with older Microsoft Windows VPN connections.

policies   Rule sets by which users and administrators must abide.

port   Application-specific endpoint to a logical connection.

port address translation (PAT)   A system that maps external connections to internal connections by mapping an external address and port to an internal IP address so that an organization can purchase and expose only one IP address while allowing many devices to communicate behind it.

port scanning   A process that queries each TCP/UDP port on a system to see if it is capable of receiving data.

pre-shared key (PSK)   A piece of data that only communication partners know that is used along with a cryptographic algorithm to encrypt communications.

private branch exchange (PBX)   The switching system equipment that resides on premises in a building to provide telephone communication services.

private cloud   A cloud that is owned by a single organization and enables central access to IT resources from a variety of locations, departments, and staff.

private cloud space (PCS)   Cloud-based storage that exists within a company's own internal systems, but can be made available to other departments and units within the company.

private key   One of two keys used for asymmetric encryption, available only to the intended data user and is used for data decryption and creating digital signatures.

procedures   Prescribed methodologies by which activities are carried out in the IT environment according to defined policies.

proprietary   Software that is developed and licensed under an exclusive legal right of the copyright holder.

proxy automatic configuration (PAC)   A system that automatically configures devices to use a proxy server if one is required for a web connection. Also known as proxy auto-config.

public cloud   A pool of computing resources and services delivered over the Internet by a cloud provider to cloud consumers such as end users, IT departments, or business groups.

public key   One of two keys used for asymmetric encryption, available to anyone and is used for data encryption and digital signature validation.

public key infrastructure (PKI)   Hierarchy of trusted security certificates issued to users or computing devices.

quality assurance (QA)   Techniques and processes designed to identify defects or mistakes.

quality of service (QoS)   A set of technologies that provides the ability to manage network traffic and prioritize workloads to accommodate defined service levels as part of a cost-effective solution.

quota   The total amount of resources that can be utilized for a system.

read operation   Operation in which a resource requests data from a disk resource.

recovery point objective (RPO)   The maximum amount of data might be lost due to a disaster. Restore operations essentially bring files back to a point in time. The point in time is when the last backup was taken, if that backup is available. Any data written after that backup or "point" would be lost so the RPO defines how much data can be lost.

recovery time objective (RTO)   The maximum amount of time a system can be down after a failure or disaster. The RTO is concerned with how much time will elapse while backups are identified, loaded, restored, and verified. Data to be restored will not be available until these steps have been completed.

redundant array of independent disks (RAID)   A storage technology that combines multiple hard disk drives into a single logical unit so that the data can be distributed across the hard disk drives for both improved performance and increased security fault tolerance according to their various RAID levels.

redundant system   A system that is used as a backup to the primary system in case of failure.

Remote Desktop Protocol (RDP)   Provides remote display and input capabilities over a computer network.

remote hypervisor access   The ability to manage a hypervisor from another computer across a network.

remote shell (RSH)   Command-line program that executes shell commands across a network in an unsecured manner.

remote transactional monitoring   A system that simulates user activity to identify how long it takes to perform each task.

replica A mirrored copy of data created between two redundant hardware devices kept in sync with the primary copy.

replication Copying data between two systems so that any changes to the data are made on each node in the replica set.

request for change (RFC) A formal request to make a modification that can be submitted by anyone who is involved with or has a stake in that particular item or service.

reservation A mechanism that ensures a lower limit is enforced for the amount of resources guaranteed to an entity.

resilience The capability of a system to continue servicing the organization during a disruption. It is accomplished primarily through redundancy.

resilient file system (ReFS) A proprietary file system developed by Microsoft to support the Windows operating systems that includes support for file integrity monitoring, data wiping, and additional disk health measurements.

resource pool Partition of compute resources from a single host or a cluster of hosts. *See also* resource pooling.

resource pooling Allows compute resources from a resource pool to be combined to serve multiple consumers by using a multitenant model.

ring Network topology where each node is connected to another, forming a circle or a ring.

Rivest Cipher 4 (RC4) An algorithm used to encrypt and decrypt data. Principally, RC4 is a block cipher that uses symmetric keys up to 128 bits in length for encryption.

Rivest Cipher 5 (RC5) An algorithm used to encrypt and decrypt data. Principally, RC5 is a block cipher that uses symmetric keys for encryption. RC5 replaces RC4 and supports a cipher strength of up to 2048 bits.

role-based access control (RBAC) Security mechanism in which all access is granted through predefined collections of permissions, called roles, instead of implicitly assigning access to users or resources individually.

route command   A command prompt tool that can be used to view and manipulate the TCP/IP routing tables of Windows operating systems.

router   Device that connects multiple networks together and allows a network to communicate with the outside world.

Routing Information Protocol (RIP)   A protocol used to direct packets across an internetwork. The RIP routing protocol uses hop count to determine the best route to a network.

routing table   Data table stored on a router that is used by the router to determine the best path to a remote network destination of network packets it is responsible for routing.

runbook   Workflow automation that can be used in orchestration tools.

scalability   Ability of a system or network to manage a growing workload in a proficient manner or its ability to be expanded to accommodate the workload growth.

scavenging   The process of removing DNS entries for hosts that no longer respond on that address.

Secure File Transfer Protocol (SFTP)   Provides secure access to files, file transfers, file editing, and file management over the Internet using Secure Shell (SSH).

Secure Hash Algorithm (SHA)   A cryptographic function that can be used to compute a unique value for a piece of data. This value can be recomputed at a later point to evaluate its integrity.

Secure Shell (SSH)   A cryptographic protocol that creates an encrypted channel to access remote servers, configure network equipment, secure logins, transfer files, and perform port forwarding.

Secure Sockets Layer (SSL)   A cryptographic algorithm that allows for secure communications such as web browsing, FTP, VPN, instant messaging, and VoIP. *See also* Transport Layer Security (TLS).

Security Assertions Markup Language (SAML)   A method for sending and receiving authorization and authentication data between devices.

security information and event management (SIEM) A system that collects, correlates, and analyzes event logs. SIEM is also known as security incident event manager.

self-encrypting drive (SED) A hard drive equipped with internal electronics that encrypt content prior to storing it on the media and then decrypt the content when requested to return it down the data interface.

separation of duties A process that divides the responsibilities required to perform a sensitive task among two or more people so that one person, acting alone, cannot compromise the system.

Serial ATA (SATA) An interface used to connect host bus adapters to mass storage devices.

Serial Attached SCSI (SAS) A data transfer technology that was designed to replace SCSI and to transfer data to and from storage devices.

Server Message Block (SMB) Network protocol used to provide shared access to files and printers.

server upgrades and patches Updates to the software running on servers that can either provide fixes for known errors or add functionality.

service level agreement (SLA) A contract or agreement between a client and a service provider such as a cloud provider on the level of availability that will be maintained and damages awarded if the SLA is violated.

Session Control Protocol (SCP) A protocol that manages multiple connections over TCP. SCP operates at layer 4 of the OSI model.

Session Initiation Protocol (SIP) A protocol used for instant messaging, VoIP, and video sessions.

shared compute environment Environment where multiple tenants share resources from a cloud vendor or hosting provider.

shared resources Allows a cloud provider to provide compute resources as a centralized resource and distribute those resources on an as-needed basis to the cloud consumer.

Short Message Service (SMS) A messaging service that allows an alert to be sent to a mobile device.

showback   Tracking of IT services so that management can see the value of IT services in relation to their costs.

Simple Mail Transfer Protocol (SMTP)   Protocol used to send e-mail over the Internet.

Simple Network Management Protocol (SNMP)   Commonly supported protocol on devices such as routers, switches, printers, and servers and can be used to monitor those devices for issues.

single sign-on (SSO)   Authentication process in which the resource requesting access can enter one set of credentials and use those credentials to access multiple applications or datasets, even if they have separate authorization mechanisms.

Small Computer System Interface (SCSI)   A set of standard electronic interfaces accredited by the American National Standards Institute (ANSI) for connecting and transferring data between computers and storage devices.

snapshot   A method of capturing the state of a virtual machine or disk volume at a specific point in time.

Software as a Service (SaaS)   A cloud model that allows a cloud consumer the ability to use on-demand software applications delivered by the cloud provider via the Internet.

Software Defined Networking (SDN)   A set of technologies that are designed to improve the scalability and flexibility of virtualized and cloud environments by allowing for network changes to be made to the infrastructure in response to changing network conditions.

software development life cycle (SDLC)   The process applications go through whereby they are created, maintained, and upgraded.

solid state drive (SSD)   A high-performance storage device that contains no moving parts.

spoofing   The modification of data such as the source IP address to obfuscate the original source.

star   Network topology where each node is connected to a central hub or switch and the nodes communicate by sending data through the central hub.

storage area network (SAN)   Storage device that resides on its own network and provides block-level access to computers that are attached to it.

storage migration   Process of transferring data between storage devices, allowing data from a virtual machine to be migrated to a new location and across storage arrays while maintaining continuous availability and service to the virtual machine.

storage virtualization   Groups multiple network storage devices into a single storage unit that can be managed from a central console and presented to a virtual machine or host computer as a single storage unit.

stream cipher   A method of converting plaintext to ciphertext one bit at a time.

stress testing   A form of load testing that evaluates a system under peak loads to determine its max data or user handling capabilities.

subnetting   Creates subnetworks through the logical subdivision of IP network addresses.

supernetting   Combines multiple IP networks into one larger network, resulting in smaller routing tables.

switch   Network device that connects multiple devices together on the same network or LAN.

symmetric encryption   Encryption mechanism that uses a single key to both encrypt and decrypt data.

synchronous replication   A form of replication that writes data to the local store and then immediately replicates it to the replica set or sets. The application is not informed that the data has been written until all replica sets have acknowledged receipt and storage of the data.

syslog   Provides a mechanism for a network device to send event messages to a logging server or a syslog server.

syslog server   Computer used as a centralized repository for syslog messages.

system logs   Files that store a variety of information about system events, including device changes, device drivers, and system changes.

systems life cycle management   The process or processes put in place by an organization to assist in the management, coordination, control, delivery, and support of its systems from the requirements stage to retirement.

tape   A storage medium that can be used to save data to by using digital recordings on magnetic tape to store the data.

task-based access control (TBAC)   Security mechanism in which users have no access to resources by default and are only provided access when they perform a task requiring it. Access is not retained after the task is complete.

technical training device (TTD)   A simulation system used for training individuals on a particular piece of software.

Telnet   A terminal emulation program for TCP/IP networks that connects the user's computer to another computer on the network.

Temporal Key Integrity Protocol (TKIP)   A protocol specified in IEEE 802.11i that enhances the WEP/RC4 encryption in wireless networks.

testing   A proactive measure to ensure consistent performance and operations of information systems.

thick provisioning   Allocates the entire size of the logical drive upon creation.

thin provisioning   Allows a virtual disk or disk volume to allocate and commit storage space on demand and use only the space it currently requires.

threshold   Used to set the amount of resources that can be consumed before an alert is generated.

throughput   The amount of data that can be realized between two network resources.

time-to-live (TTL)   The length of time that a router or caching name server stores a record.

tokenization   Replaces sensitive data with identifiers called tokens. De-tokenization returns the value associated with the token ID.

total cost of ownership (TCO)   A method of determining more fully how much something will cost. TCO factors in the direct, indirect, opportunity, and long-term costs. Also known as total cost of operations.

traceroute   Linux command-line utility to record the route and measure the delay of packets across an IP network.

tracert   Microsoft Windows command-line utility that tracks a packet from your computer to a destination host and displays how many hops the packet takes to reach the destination host.

Transmission Control Protocol (TCP)   A protocol that provides reliable transport of network data through error checking. TCP uses ports that are associated with certain services and other ports that can be dynamically allocated to running processes and services. TCP is most often combined with IP.

transparent page sharing   A technology that deduplicates hypervisor memory allocated to virtual machines.

Transport Layer Security (TLS)   A cryptographic algorithm that allows for secure communications such as web browsing, FTP, VPN, instant messaging, and VoIP. TLS is the successor to SSL.

tree   Network topology containing multiple star networks that are connected through a linear bus backbone.

trending   The pattern of measurements over the course of multiple time periods.

troubleshooting   Techniques that aim to solve a problem that has been realized.

trusted platform module (TPM)   A microprocessor that is dedicated to performing cryptographic functions. TPMs are integrated into supporting systems and include features such as generation of cryptographic keys, random number generation, encryption, and decryption.

tunnel endpoint   Node that forms encapsulation, de-encapsulation, encryption, and decryption of data in the tunnel. Tunnel endpoints transmit encapsulated data that will traverse the intermediary network.

tunneling   The use of encapsulation and encryption to create a secure connection between devices so that intermediary devices cannot read the traffic and so that devices communicating over the tunnel are connected as if on a local network.

tunneling protocol   A network protocol that enables tunneling between devices or sites.

type 1 hypervisor   Hypervisor that is created and deployed on a bare metal installation.

type 2 hypervisor   Hypervisor loaded on top of an already existing operating system installation.

ubiquitous access   Allows a cloud service to be widely accessible via a web browser from anywhere, allowing for the same level of access from either home or work.

uninterruptable power supply (UPS)   A unit equipped with one or more batteries that provides power and line conditioning to connected devices.

Universal Datagram Protocol (UDP)   A protocol that provides transport of network at layer 4 of the OSI model. Unlike TCP, UDP does not provide error checking to improve speed, but relies upon other protocols in the stack to perform this function. UDP uses ports that are associated with certain services and other ports that can be dynamically allocated to running processes and services.

universal target adapter (UTA)   A proprietary network adapter from NetApp that is extremely versatile due to its use of transceivers. UTA has ports for one or more Ethernet or Fibre transceivers and can support Ethernet transceivers up to 10Gb and Fibre transceivers at native Fibre Channel speeds.

Unix file system (UFS)   Primary file system for Unix and Unix-based operating systems that uses a hierarchical file system structure where the highest level of the directory is called the root (/, pronounced, "slash") and all other directories span from that root.

uptime   A metric showing the amount of time a system is available for use vs the time it is not available. Uptime is usually expressed as a percentage.

USB drive   An external plug-and-play storage device that is plugged into a computer's USB port and is recognized by the computer as a removable drive and assigned a drive letter.

user acceptance testing (UAT)   The phase in software testing where real users try the software and perform tasks they would normally perform on the main system and inform developers of bugs that they encounter.

vertical scaling   A scalability methodology whereby resources such as additional memory, vCPUs, or faster disks are added to a single node, thereby making that node capable of handling more of a load within itself. Vertical scaling is also known as scaling up.

virtual allocation table (VAT)   Methods such as nested page tables or shadow page tables for mapping virtual machine memory to that of the host.

virtual appliance   Fully built and functional virtual machine that is purchased or downloaded from a vendor to perform a specific task.

virtual CPU (vCPU)   Used on a guest virtual machine and is similar to a physical CPU.

virtual data center   Provides compute resources, network infrastructure, external storage, backups, and security similar to a physical data center.

virtual desktop infrastructure (VDI)   A method of virtualizing workstation operating systems in a centralized location whereby end users connect to their virtual desktops remotely.

virtual disk   Emulates a physical disk drive to a virtual machine.

virtual extensible local area network (VXLAN)   Partitions a physical network to create separate segments for multitenant cloud environments.

virtual hard disk (VHD)   A virtual disk format used by Microsoft hypervisors. Current VHD files have the .vhdx extension. VHDs created on older Hyper-V systems may have the .vhd extension.

virtual local area network (VLAN)   Partitions a physical network to create separate, independent broadcast domains that are part of the same physical network.

virtual machine   A system that provides the functionality of a full computer by abstracting a portion of the available system resources from a host machine and presenting it to the guest machine.

virtual machine cloning   Allows a virtual machine to be copied either once or multiple times for testing.

virtual machine disk (VMDK)   A virtual hard disk format used by VMware hypervisors. VMDK files have the .vhdk extension.

virtual machine file system (VMFS)   VMware's cluster file system used with VMware ESX server and vSphere created to store virtual machine disk images, including virtual machine snapshots.

virtual machine snapshotting   A method of capturing the state of a virtual machine at a specific point in time.

virtual machine template   Provides a standardized group of hardware and software settings that can be reused multiple times to create a new virtual machine that is configured with those specified settings.

virtual memory   Hard drive storage that is used to contain data that cannot fit into RAM.

Virtual Network Computing (VNC)   A technology that sends keyboard and mouse input to a remote computer and presents the screen of the remote computer to a remote session so that a user can access the machine as they would if they were in front of it over a remote connection.

virtual NIC (vNIC)   Similar to a physical NIC and can connect to a virtual switch and be assigned an IP address, default gateway, and subnet mask.

Virtual Private Cloud (VPC)   An AWS system that isolates a portion of cloud resources.

virtual private network (VPN)   A connection that extends a private network over a public network such as the Internet.

virtual random access memory (VRAM)   Hard drive storage that is used to contain data that cannot fit into RAM.

virtual routing and forwarding (VRF)   A technique where a router contains multiple routing tables at the same time, allowing for identical IP addresses to co-exist without conflict.

virtual SAN (VSAN)   A cluster of VMware hosts where the storage from each host is combined into a single data store that each host can make use of.

virtual switch (vSwitch)   Similar to a physical switch, allows network devices to be connected and is used to control how the network traffic flows between the virtual machines and the virtualization host.

virtual tape library (VTL)   Disk or cloud storage that backup devices can interface with like tape storage.

virtual to physical (V2P)   Migrates a virtual machine to a physical computer

virtual to virtual (V2V)   Migrates an operating system, applications, and data from one virtual machine to another virtual machine

virtualization host   System that hosts or contains guest virtual machines.

Voice over IP (VoIP)   Technology that allows for the IP network protocol to transmit phone calls.

VT-x   A set of instructions performing virtualization functions that is built into the CPU.

vulnerability assessment   Process used to identify and quantify any vulnerabilities in a network environment.

vulnerability remediation request (VRR)   A formal change request to an application or system to make the required changes to remediate a known vulnerability.

vulnerability scanning   The process of discovering flaws or weaknesses in systems and applications.

warm site   An alternative site that is somewhere on the continuum between a cold site and a hot site; it includes some hardware and some backups, although the backups could be a few days old. *See also* alternate site, cold site, *and* hot site.

web application firewall (WAF)   A device that screens traffic intended for web applications. WAFs understand common web application attacks such as cross-site scripting (XSS) and SQL injection and can inspect traffic at the application layer of the OSI model.

web graphical user interface (GUI)   An interface that uses point-and-click navigation and is accessible over the Web.

Web-Based Enterprise Management (WBEM)   Standardized way of accessing management information in an enterprise environment.

wide area network (WAN)   Network that covers a large geographic area and can contain multiple LANs or MANs.

Windows Management Instrumentation (WMI)   Protocol used to gather information about the installed hardware, software, and operating system of a computer.

workflow   A business process that is organized in sets of discrete tasks from the beginning to the end of the process.

world wide name (WWN)   Unique identifier used in storage technologies similar to Ethernet MAC addresses on a network card.

world wide node name (WWNN)   A unique identifier for a device on a Fibre Channel network.

world wide port name (WWPN)   A unique identifier for a port on a Fibre Channel network. A single device with a WWNN will have multiple WWPNs if it has multiple Fibre Channel adapters or adapters with multiple ports.

world wide unique identifier (WWUI)   An address that is not used by other entities on a network and can represent only one entity.

write operation   Operation in which a resource requests that new data be recorded on a disk resource.

Z file system (ZFS)   Combined file system and logical volume manager designed by Sun Microsystems that provides protection against data corruption and support for high storage capacities.

zoning   Controls access from one node to another in a storage network and enables isolation of a single server to a group of storage devices or a single storage device.

INDEX

D

I

W

Single User License Terms and Conditions

Online access to the digital content included with this book is governed by the McGraw-Hill Education License Agreement outlined next. By using this digital content you agree to the terms of that license.

Access   To register and activate your Total Seminars Training Hub account, simply follow these easy steps.

1. Go to **hub.totalsem.com/mheclaim**.
2. To Register and create a new Training Hub account, enter your email address, name, and password. No further information (such as credit card number) is required to create an account.
3. If you already have a Total Seminars Training Hub account, select "Log in" and enter your email and password.
4. Enter your Product Key: `szmr-33kn-3zss`
5. Click to accept the user license terms.
6. Click "Register and Claim" to create your account. You will be taken to the Training Hub and have access to the content for this book.

Duration of License   Access to your online content through the Total Seminars Training Hub will expire one year from the date the publisher declares the book out of print.

Your purchase of this McGraw-Hill Education product, including its access code, through a retail store is subject to the refund policy of that store.

The Content is a copyrighted work of McGraw-Hill Education and McGraw-Hill Education reserves all rights in and to the Content. The Work is © 2018 by McGraw-Hill Education, LLC.

Restrictions on Transfer   The user is receiving only a limited right to use the Content for user's own internal and personal use, dependent on purchase and continued ownership of this book. The user may not reproduce, forward, modify, create derivative works based upon, transmit, distribute, disseminate, sell, publish, or sublicense the Content or in any way commingle the Content with other third-party content, without McGraw-Hill Education's consent.

Limited Warranty   The McGraw-Hill Education Content is provided on an "as is" basis. Neither McGraw-Hill Education nor its licensors make any guarantees or warranties of any kind, either express or implied, including, but not limited to, implied warranties of merchantability or fitness for a particular purpose or use as to any McGraw-Hill Education Content or the information therein or any warranties as to the accuracy, completeness, currentness, or results to be obtained from, accessing or using the McGraw-Hill Education content, or any material referenced in such content or any information entered into licensee's product by users or other persons and/or any material available on or that can be accessed through the licensee's product (including via any hyperlink or otherwise) or as to non-infringement of third-party rights. Any warranties of any kind, whether express or implied, are disclaimed. Any material or data obtained through use of the McGraw-Hill Education content is at your own discretion and risk and user understands that it will be solely responsible for any resulting damage to its computer system or loss of data.

Neither McGraw-Hill Education nor its licensors shall be liable to any subscriber or to any user or anyone else for any inaccuracy, delay, interruption in service, error or omission, regardless of cause, or for any damage resulting therefrom.

In no event will McGraw-Hill Education or its licensors be liable for any indirect, special or consequential damages, including but not limited to, lost time, lost money, lost profits or good will, whether in contract, tort, strict liability or otherwise, and whether or not such damages are foreseen or unforeseen with respect to any use of the McGraw-Hill Education content.